BEHIND THE
RYDER CUP
THE PLAYERS' STORIES

PETER BURNS
with ED HODGE

POLARIS
PUBLISHING

First published in 2016 by
POLARIS PUBLISHING LTD
c/o Turcan Connell
Princes Exchange
1 Earl Grey Street
Edinburgh
EH3 9EE

in association with

ARENA SPORT
An imprint of Birlinn Limited
West Newington House
10 Newington Road
Edinburgh
EH9 1QS

www.polarispublishing.com
www.arenasportbooks.co.uk

HARDBACK ISBN: 9781909715318
TRADE PAPERBACK ISNB: 9781909715455
EBOOK ISBN: 9780857908858

British Library Cataloguing-in-Publication Data
A catalogue record for this book is available from the British Library

Designed and typeset by Polaris Publishing, Edinburgh

Printed and bound by arrangement with Asia Pacific Offset

CONTENTS

ACKNOWLEDGEMENTS

ACKNOWLEDGEMENTS

Scores of books have been written on the history of the Ryder Cup and of the captains and players who have played in it. Invariably these have been written from the outside looking in. This book, in contrast, looks to tell the history of the Ryder Cup in the words of the men who have been there and done it, told from within the rarefied atmosphere of the team room, locker room and inside the ropes, right in the heat of the action. Like a fantasy dinner party, it would be wonderful to be able to sit down with all the greats who have contested for that gorgeous little golden cup from across the ages and hear them reminisce about their experiences. That scenario is of course impossible – but perhaps this book is the next best thing. We hope you enjoy.

While a more complete bibliography is available at the end of this book, special thanks must be paid for extended extract permission to the Fundación Seve Ballesteros for use of material from *Seve: The Autobiography* by Seve Ballesteros; Paul Azinger and Rich Braund for use of material from *Cracking the Code: The Winning Ryder Cup Strategy, Make It Work For You*; RLR Associates Ltd and Diversion Books for use of material from *The Ryder Cup: Golf's Greatest Event* by Bob Bubka and Tom Clavin; to Atlantic Books for use of material from *Two Tribes: The Rebirth of the Ryder Cup* by Gavin Newsham; HarperCollins Publishers for use of material from *Us Against Them: An Oral History of the Ryder Cup* by Robin McMillan; Orion Books for use of material from *Faldo: In Search of Perfection* by Nick Faldo; and Icon Books for use of material from *The Ryder Cup: A History 1927-2014* by Peter Pugh, Henry Lord.

Special thanks also to David KC Wright, the PGA Historian; Steve Doughty, European Tour media official/researcher; Bob Denney, PGA Historian, The PGA of America; Alex Podlogar, Media Relations Manager, Pinehurst Resort & Country Club; Shannon J. Doody, Archivist, Film & Video Archives, USGA; Vicky Cuming at IMG; Michael McEwan at *Bunkered Magazine*; Ian Greensill; and Keith Rose.

The authors would like to thank everyone who has given their time so generously to assist in the preparation of this book. Those whom we interviewed are too many to name individually but their thoughts are included in the pages which follow.

Peter Burns and Ed Hodge, 2016

For Isla and Hector
PB

For Iona, Andrew and Kirsty
EH

GENESIS

1921
Gleneagles Hotel. Perthshire, Scotland

1926
Wentworth Golf Club. Surrey, England

June, 1921.

On the southern edge of the Scottish Highlands, set amid rolling Perthshire hills dappled by purple heather, sat the skeletal structure of the Gleneagles Hotel – a building that, after its completion in 1924, would come to be known as the 'Palace in the Glen'.

Although the hotel was still under construction on this bright summer's day, the James Braid -designed King's Course was open for play and it was here that a match was about to commence that would prove seismic in its historical significance – the first to pitch professional golfers from the United States of America against their counterparts from Great Britain.

There is an elegant synergy that this event, which was the inspiration for the Ryder Cup, took place with a half-built hotel dominating the backdrop. In the years that followed, the hotel was completed and Samuel Ryder, who was a spectator at Gleneagles, commissioned a golden trophy as the spoils of a new competition which was officially launched at Worcester Country Club, located fifty miles from Boston, in 1927. This synergy was neatly bookended when the fortieth edition of the Ryder Cup returned to its spiritual roots at Gleneagles in 2014.

There remains some dispute as to whose idea it was to stage this contest between professionals from either side of the Atlantic. With the Walker Cup having been established for amateurs (the first Walker Cup was played in 1921 at Royal Liverpool but not officially 'launched' until the following year) it was felt that a comparable event should be created for the professionals. The idea of doing so has been attributed to both Sylvanus P. Jermain, a former President of the Inverness Golf Club in Ohio (which had hosted the 1920 US Open), as well as to James Harnett, Golf Illustrated*'s circulation manager, who had launched an initiative in the magazine to raise funds to send US players to Britain for an international match (and so, in turn, increase sales of the magazine). America's great golfing showman, Walter Hagen, was one of the most high-profile supporters of* Golf Illustrated*'s initiative, but the campaign failed to hit the requisite funding target and was temporarily abandoned. The general interest in the concept had been duly noted, however, and on 15 December 1920, the US PGA agreed to subsidise the shortfall. The match was on.*

The only thing left to decide was where in the UK the match would take place. With the Open being held at St Andrews on 23–25 June 1921, the British PGA looked around for a nearby tournament that could host the contest – and discovered that there was a professional event being held at Gleneagles that more than fitted the bill. The tournament in question was sponsored by the Glasgow Herald *newspaper and held at the King's Course with a purse of 1,000 guineas. Although the course, which was opened in May 1919, was a little unrefined at the time (Bernard Darwin of* The Times *described it as 'rather ragged in appearance, the bunkers look unkempt and the greens carry more course grass than one likes to see'), the level of prize money and its proximity and timing to the Open attracted all the big names in British golf, including the illustrious figures of Harry Vardon, James Braid, John Henry Taylor (this triumvirate were widely regarded as the top three golfers in the country), Abe Mitchell, George Duncan, Ted Ray and Arthur Havers, and supported by the less well-known Josh Taylor, James Ockenden and James Sherlock. It was agreed that the international competition would be tagged onto the* Glasgow Herald *tournament and played before it on 6 June.*

After some six arduous ocean days, the American team arrived at Southampton the week before the Glasgow Herald *event and travelled north by sleeper train to Glasgow. But any hope of a relaxing stay to rest body and soul was short-lived. With the hotel still under construction, the visiting side were billeted in five waterless railway carriages moved into a siding at the station close to the village of Auchtermuchty in Fife. This meant that the players were forced to fetch and carry their own water for much of the week and commute to Gleneagles each day. It was a barely hospitable welcome and the American players were understandably unimpressed with the arrangements.*

The 'international challenge' match was contested over fifteen points, with five foursome matches in the morning and ten singles matches in the afternoon. While the home team contained the cream of British golf, the American team wasn't nearly as strong, despite its efforts being spearheaded by Walter Hagen; it was also something of a mixed bag as it included four expatriate Scotsmen in the shape of St Andrews' Jock Hutchison, the holder of the US PGA title and soon to be the 1921 Open champion, Fred McLeod of North Berwick, the 1908 US Open champion, Clarence Hackney from Carnoustie and Harry Hampton of Montrose alongside homegrown talents Emmet French, Charles Hoffner, Tom Kerrigan, George McLean, William Mehlhorn, and Wilfrid Reid.

Duncan and Mitchell were paired against Hutchison and Hagen for the opening morning foursomes match which proved to be a hugely competitive tussle and which was ultimately halved. 'It was perhaps the most attractive match of the whole day,' wrote the Glasgow Herald. *'It was such an excellent fight, with our men never once getting their heads in front, standing even two down with only five to play, and Duncan on the home green bringing off a long putt to save the hole, and with it the match.' Vardon and Ray, meanwhile, used their considerable experience to dismantle the young US pair French and Kerrigan 5&4.*

Braid and Taylor were up next against the expat Scots, McLeod and Hackney. Taylor played sublimely while Braid used his intimate knowledge of the course (as its designer) to see off the significant challenge from their opponents to also secure a valuable half.

On a glorious morning when, as The Scotsman *newspaper described it, 'the sun lit up the golden glory of the gorse', Britain pushed this 2–1 advantage into a commanding 4–1 lead by lunch as Havers (who would win the Open in 1923) and James Ockenden, thanks to his short game prowess, completed an emphatic 6&5 demolition of Wilfrid Reid and George McLean, before James Sherlock and Josh Taylor beat Charles Hoffner and Mehlhorn by a solitary hole.*

In desperate need of establishing momentum in the singles, Hagen packed his best players at the top of the draw, sending Hutchison out first before following himself. These were two games that America simply had to win, but they failed to gain the impetus they so sorely needed as Hutchison fell 2&1 to Duncan, and Hagen could only manage a half with Mitchell. Hopes were briefly kindled when French and McLeod defeated Ray and Taylor respectively, but these victories proved to little avail as Vardon saw off the gallant Kerrigan 3&1 (hitting only 64 shots over the seventeen holes played) and Braid beat Hackney 5&4. The Scotsman *reported: 'The feature of the day was the superb play of the "old guard". Braid and Vardon produced sterling golf, which nobody probably could have beaten. The golf of Vardon and Braid was astonishing for men of fifty-one.'*

Havers lost to Reid for a consolation point for the Americans, but Ockenden, Sherlock and Josh Taylor won the remaining three matches to rack up something of a rout for the home team. Nine wins, three defeats and three halved matches – Great Britain had overwhelmed America by the score of 9–3 (no half points were awarded).

'Britain has come out with flying colours from the first American professional challenge,' reported the Glasgow Herald*'s 'Special Correspondent'. 'Today over this magnificent and testing course, a team of America's best professionals met and were beaten by ten of our own men . . . throughout the day there was bright sunshine, which was tempered by a slight breeze. Under these genial conditions, the course was seen at its best [by] the large crowds that gathered to witness the play.'*

Press reports, however, were far from extensive in nature. If there was an overall lack of commercial success, it's tempered by the fact it was 1921 and these were humble, low-key origins of international rivalry. Certainly, few could have predicted the eventual acceleration to the Ryder Cup drama of the modern day, the unforgettable, edge-of-the-seat, riveting combat.

On the night of 6 June 1921, the leading golf professionals of Britain and America toasted the match. It was agreed the contest should be repeated, that there was the potential for more. A seed had been planted. Could it blossom?

The Glasgow Herald *Tournament continued for a number of years, but the Britain–US aspect was dropped. Essentially, the international match played at Gleneagles had not sufficiently caught the public's imagination. But it wasn't doomed to fail, with Hagen continuing to support the idea.*

Ironically, a seed merchant helped the pro match to flower. Enter Samuel Ryder and his younger brother, James. In St Albans, Hertfordshire, the pair had built up a successful business selling penny seed packets through the post to garden lovers. A devoted Christian and workaholic, Samuel was advised by his church minister to play golf for exercise and relaxation. He began to play relatively late in life in his early fifties and paid the local club professional in 1909 to come to his house six days a week to give him lessons. Within a year, he was off a single figure handicap, was accepted at the local club, Verulam, and within another year was elected captain. In the early

Jock Hutchison of the USA tees off in 1921, with the Gleneagles hotel still under construction in the background.

1920s, Ryder's business, the Heath & Heather Company, sponsored professional tournaments, including matches between British and American players, as a means of business promotion and to assist professionals. One was held at Verulam in 1923, attracting the leading British pros, such as Braid, the Verulam course architect, Vardon and Duncan, thanks to a first prize that was only £5 less than the winner of the Open received. Abe Mitchell, the professional at North Foreland in Kent, also competed.

Mitchell was one of the golfing greats of the era. Born in Sussex in 1887, he went on to become one of England's most famous professional golfers. An accomplished singles and doubles player, during his lifetime he partnered many notable players including the future king, Edward, Prince of Wales, and a future prime minister, Winston Churchill. He was once described by Henry Longhurst, the renowned British golf writer and commentator, as 'the finest golfer never to win the Open Championship' and could still be considered the best player never to have won a Major. Ryder and Mitchell became friends with the latter employed from 1925 as the former's personal tutor for a generous and then princely annual fee of £500 per year. Consequently, Ryder's interest and fascination in the pro game increased and he, among others, had long harboured plans to create an 'annual' match between the leading professionals of Great Britain and America, building on what had been enjoyed at Gleneagles.

Official papers from the PGA Minute Book, kept at their headquarters at the Belfry, reveal the earliest records proposing such a game came in March 1926. The minutes of a committee meeting on 29 March state: 'A letter was read from the Secretary of the St George's Hill Golf Club dated 1 March setting out the conditions of a match to be played against a team of four American Professionals selected by Walter Hagen, and asking for approval of the same, also requesting the Association to select the British team and to fix a date for playing the match. After considerable discussion the Secretary was instructed to write agreeing the terms

The 1921 British team. Standing (*left to right*): J Taylor, JH Taylor, A Mitchell, JG Sherlock, J Ockenden, H Vardon, AG Havers. Sitting (*left to right*): G Duncan, J Braid, E Ray

and conditions of the proposed match and accepting the responsibility of the selection of the team and suggesting the date June fourth and fifth.'

In April 1926, a match over thirty-six holes at St George's Hill, in Surrey, followed the next day by thirty-six holes at Wentworth was discussed. St George's Hill had held challenge matches already and it was a popular venue. The British soon sent an invitation to their American counterparts to take part in the match, but it was the nearby new East Course at Wentworth which was chosen for the two-day contest. It was to be played out before the Americans' attempted qualification at Sunningdale for the Open Championship, being staged in the north-west at Royal Lytham and St Annes. Hagen jumped at the opportunity to act as captain and put a team together, with ten players on each side rather than the initially proposed four.

Here was to be the long-awaited first 'official' match, held on 4–5 June 1926 on the East Course at Wentworth – only for the most significant British labour dispute of the twentieth century to dash hopes. Owing to the uncertainty of the situation following the General Strike in May 1926, it was unknown up to a few weeks before the event was to start how many Americans would travel. Rather than cancelling the contest, the United States team, with Ryder's input, invited other players to make up the numbers – pulling in four expatriate Brits and one Australian. They probably wondered why they bothered . . . the Anglo-American match resulted in an astonishing 13½–1½ success for the hosts. 'Under the circumstances the Wentworth Club provided the British players with gold medals to mark the inauguration of the great international match,' wrote Golf Illustrated *magazine. It caught public attention, the match was fully reported in* The Times, *but as golf was still considered a pastime exclusive to the privileged classes, it achieved little note elsewhere. As a result of the absence of a 'full' US team, the US PGA refused to sanction the contest as the first 'official' Ryder Cup match. Yet*

The 1921 American team. Standing (*left to right*): W Hagen, W Mehlhorn, C Hoffner, F McLeod, T Kerrigan, G McLean. Sitting (*left to right*): E French, J Hutchison, C Hackney, WE Reid

Ryder, now aged 68, still watched on among the galleries enthralled, particularly delighted to see Mitchell prove the star for the Brits. He teamed up with George Duncan in the foursomes for an emphatic and frankly embarrassing 9&8 win against the legendary Hagen and defending Open champion Jim Barnes, and then beat Barnes by another huge margin, 8&7, in the singles. Ryder enjoyed the obvious camaraderie between the two teams, but he was disappointed the sides did not mix socially before or after the match – a situation he sought to put right.

So it could be said the Ryder Cup, like many good ideas, then came to fruition from a relaxed conversation in a clubhouse, this one at Wentworth. As hosts, the British celebrated their win in the typical style of the day – with a pot of tea and a round of sandwiches. Here, Ryder congratulated both sides on their play and wondered why such a match was not organised more often, remarking to Duncan, Mitchell, Hagen and Emmet French: 'We must do this again.' A BBC Radio broadcast from Ryder was even more enlightening: 'I trust that the effect of this match will be to influence a cordial, friendly, and peaceful feeling throughout the whole civilised world . . . I look upon the Royal and Ancient game as being a powerful force that influences the best things in humanity.' Duncan suggested that if there were a trophy to be played for, the competition might become a regular event. Between them they sketched plans and Ryder, being the businessman he was, made immediate enquiries with the PGA. He was soon encouraged by their backing for such a tournament. Ryder commissioned a solid gold trophy, topped off with a figure of a golfer modelled on Ryder's coach and inspiration, Mitchell, from the Mappin & Webb Company in Mayfair, London. The beautiful, strikingly simple seventeen-inch high Ryder Cup, a gleaming golden chalice weighing four pounds, was made in Sheffield by the accomplished silversmith James Dixon. It cost £250, an amount split three ways: Ryder paying £100, Golf Illustrated *likewise and the Royal and Ancient Golf Club £50. Some newspaper reports claim the Ryder Cup was presented to the winning British captain, Ray, in 1926, but construction was not finished until 1927, just in time for the first official event in Massachusetts.*

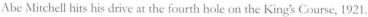

Abe Mitchell hits his drive at the fourth hole on the King's Course, 1921.

The small statue atop the cup, addressing the ball, stands as a lasting and fitting memorial to Mitchell and his contribution to the birth of the contest. 'I have done several things in my life for the benefit of my fellow men, but I am certain I have never done a happier thing than this,' Ryder stated a few years later. 'I owe golf a great deal, Sam. What you've done, putting me on top of the cup, is more distinction than I could ever earn,' beamed Mitchell. At a subsequent PGA committee meeting on 19 July 1926, attended by Ryder, he volunteered to offer his trophy for an 'annual International Match'. Minutes of the committee meeting from the Belfry archives read: 'Mr Ryder said it was a great pleasure to him to offer a Cup for competition at an International Professional Match and suggested that such a match should be under the control of the governing body, viz. the PGA. It was suggested that the International Match should be played alternately in America and in this country, the first Match for the Ryder Cup to be played in the first named country next year.' Like the Walker Cup, which became a biennial event from 1924, the match would be contested every second year. Ryder could scarcely have believed it would be a cup from which so many magical moments and memories would spawn. Any player who holds the trophy aloft can still look up to the figure of Mitchell standing atop its lid and warmly and fondly reminisce.

Jock Hutchison: Gleneagles was an absolute revelation – a delightful surprise to all American golfers.

George Duncan: I went to Wentworth as a pro in 1924 and during my stay we had the *Daily Mail* tournament, which Abe Mitchell won, and a match which I arranged between professionals of Great Britain and America in 1926, which proved to be the forerunner of the present Ryder Cup contests.

It must be stated, however, the International duel at Wentworth was not the first of its kind between the professionals from both sides of the Atlantic, because there had been a similar one at Gleneagles in the early twenties.

Nor was it, on the 'American' side, confined to purely homebred professionals, because they included such men as Jim Barnes, Tommy Armour, Joe Kirkwood, and little Cyril Walker, the Lancashire lad who had won the American Open in 1924 and fell on such hard times that he became a dishwasher in a restaurant and died destitute.

But the idea of a permanent match between the two countries, home and away, sprang from that Wentworth tussle. All the transatlantic men had come over for the Open at Royal Lytham and St Annes, and in addition to those mentioned, their team included Walter Hagen, Bill Mehlhorn, Al Watrous, Fred McLeod, Emmet French, and Joe Stein. The British team included Abe Mitchell, Aubrey Boomer, Archie Compston, George Gadd, Ted Ray, Fred Robson, Arthur Havers, Ernest Whitcombe, Bert Jolly, and myself.

It is not my intention to go into great detail, but we won 13–1, with one match halved. Bill Mehlhorn was the only winner on their side. We made a clean sweep in the five foursomes.

Charles Whitcombe: The only thing that matters in fourball golf is the score of the side and a good fourball player will think of it as such. It was this that made George Duncan and Abe Mitchell such a formidable partnership in fourball exhibition matches. They didn't care which of them won the holes as long as the side won them. On the green it was their practise to leave it to whichever of them had struck his putting form, to go for the threes, the other one playing to make sure of the par fours – irrespective of the position of the balls on the green. In such a matter, however, temperament counts for a lot. When Walter Hagen and Mac Smith were partnered together in fourball matches, Hagen practically always gave 'MacSmith' the job of putting first, regardless of the position of the balls on the green, holding himself in reserve for the special effort to secure the birdie or to save the par.

George Jacobus, president of the US PGA: Our team was hopelessly outclassed, losing every one of the five foursomes and registering in the ten singles only one win (Bill Mehlhorn beating Archie Compston by a solitary hole) and a halved match between Emmet French and Ernest Whitcombe. The total of 13½ points for Great Britain against only 1½ for the invaders might well be regarded as a repulse.

Samuel Ryder: The only condition that I attached to the trophy was that, as long as it constituted international matches against the United States, the matches should be decided by foursomes and singles. If for any unforeseen reason these international matches were discontinued, it was entirely at the discretion of the committee of the PGA to allocate it for any other competition as they thought best.

Ernest Whitcombe: The Americans come over here smartly dressed and backed by wealthy supporters, the Britisher has a poor chance compared to that.

Samuel Ryder: I will give £5 to each of the winning players, and give a party afterwards, with champagne and chicken sandwiches.

Spectators follow play on the fifteenth hole, Howe O'Hope, the King's Course, Gleneagles.

26 April 1926, newspaper announcement: Mr S. Ryder, of St Albans, has presented a trophy for annual competitions between teams of British and American professionals. The first match for the trophy is to take place at Wentworth on June 4th and 5th.

Walter Hagen: Actually, international team matches were not new when the Ryder Cup was established, but up to that time the matches were arranged by several individual pros getting together and challenging a team in the country decided upon. As early as 1913 an American pro team made up of Johnny McDermott, Mike Brady, Tom McNamara and Alex Smith played a specially arranged match at Versailles, France, against Arnaud Massy, Louis Tellier, Jean Gassiat and Pierre Lafitte. The French won that match.

World War One upset all plans for continuing the idea just then, but in 1921 another American pro team invaded Britain. During the intervening years many of the great British and Scotch golfers travelled over here to try out for our Open, but there was no concerted effort to plan and arrange a scheduled match until 1926.

That year a group of us decided on another invasion of Great Britain. I picked the team and asked Emmet French to act as captain. Homebreds on the team included French as captain, Bill Mehlhorn, Joe Stein, Al Watrous and Walter Hagen and such foreign-born pros as Jim Barnes, Tommy Armour, Cyril Walker, Joe Kirkwood and Freddie McLeod. The British were too much for us . . . we were defeated thirteen matches to one. Bill Mehlhorn, the only American to win his match, defeated Archie Compston; Emmet French halved his match; the rest of us lost. But the expedition served to point up the need for the American and British professionals to have a cup for international competition on a level with the famous Walker Cup for amateurs.

George Duncan: Arising out of the match between the professionals of Great Britain and America at Wentworth in 1926 and because of the deep interest in the Walker Cup, which was originated in 1922, the Ryder Cup series was started in 1927.

We needed a permanent match between the professionals of Great Britain and America on the home and away principle, and the idea was raised at a committee meeting of the Professional Golfers' Association. The result was that we approached Mr Sam Ryder, the famous seedsman, whose interest in golf was so great that he had a private course and appointed Abe Mitchell as his professional.

Mr Ryder's great love of golf and his benefactions to promising young players made him the man obviously to approach to donate a trophy. He gave the Ryder Cup, which, made of gold, cost £750.

Walter Hagen: So Samuel Ryder, wealthy British seed merchant, established the Ryder Cup in 1927, and the first international matches were scheduled for Worcester, Massachusetts. However, the stipulation that the United States team must be composed of American-born pros prohibited many of our fine golfers, including a number of boys who had been instrumental in getting the cup donated, from playing in the teams. The aim of every professional golfer became a berth on the PGA's Ryder Cup team and thus to represent the United States in the international matches held every two years.

ONE

1927

Worcester Country Club. Worcester, Massachusetts
(USA 9½, GB 2½)

In 1927, the editor of Golf Illustrated, *George Philpot, appealed for funding for the trip to the US in the pages of his magazine. 'I want the appeal to be successful,' he wrote, 'because it will give British pros the chance to avenge the defeats which have been administered by American pros while visiting our shores in search of Open Championship honours. I know that, given a fair chance, our fellows can and will bring back the cup from America. But they must have a fair chance, which means that adequate money must be found to finance the trip. Can the money be found? The answer rests with the British golfing public.'*

Then, in a later edition when the appeal failed, he wrote again. 'It is disappointing that the indifference or selfishness of the multitude of golfers should have been so marked that what they could have done with ease has been imposed on a small number. Of the 1,750 clubs in the British Isles whose co-operation was invited, only 216 have accorded help. It is a deplorable reflection on the attitude of the average golfer towards the game.

'We are reluctant to think that this represents the attitude of a great section of the golfing community towards a matter in which the nation's credit is at stake. When our professionals are undertaking a crusade for the sake of the prestige of British golf, an expedition in the spirit of amateurs, the people of this country might reasonably be expected to help as a duty. After all, they ought not to pursue the principle of taking everything out of the game and giving as little as possible to it. No doubt it is mainly slackness, the traditional British way of beginning slackly and muddling through, which has caused so many British clubs to allow their imaginations to slumber when it is their active assistance that is needed.'

With the match in real peril of once again failing to go ahead, Samuel Ryder and Philpot agreed to make up the shortfall. But this last-minute funding gap was not the only obstacle that beset the travelling team. Abe Mitchell was selected as the inaugural British captain, but just hours before departure he was struck down with appendicitis and had to withdraw. Ryder, also struggling with his health, was forced to stay at home, too. Ted Ray was made captain in Mitchell's place and was joined in the team by Aubrey Boomer, Archie Compston, George Duncan, George Gadd, Arthur Havers, Herbert Jolly, Fred Robson and Charles Whitcombe.

The team met at Waterloo station and travelled down to Southampton where they boarded the RMS Aquitania *and began their (somewhat rough) crossing of the Atlantic. They were met in New York by the captain of the American team, Walter Hagen and a host of dignitaries.*

Arthur Havers: The whole thing about going to America was a culture shock for most of us. When we got to New York, the entire team and officials were whisked through without bothering with customs and immigration formalities.

There was a fleet of limousines waiting for us at the dockside, and, with police outriders

Opposite: Walter Hagen holds the cup amid his victorious US teammates in 1927.

flanking us with their sirens at full blast, we sped through New York. Traffic was halted to let us through; it was a whole new world for us. Everywhere we went we were overwhelmed with the hospitality and kindness of the Americans.

Suddenly we were in a world of luxury and plenty – so different from home. It was something we never expected. Even the clubhouses were luxurious with deep-pile carpets, not like the rundown and shabby clubhouses at home, which was all most of us really knew.

The team that Hagen had under his stewardship included Leo Diegel, Al Espinosa, Johnny Farrell, Johnny Golden, Bill Mehlhorn, Gene Sarazen, Joe Turnesa and Al Watrous. On the morning of 3 June, the first Ryder Cup got underway. The format of the matches would remain the same until 1959 and consisted of four thirty-six hole foursome matches on the first day and eight thirty-six hole singles matches on the second, with a total of 12 points available to be won; all the games would be match play.

George Duncan: The first Ryder Cup contest will always be remembered as it provided us with our first experience of the bigger American ball, which duly earned me a headline for terming it 'large, light, and lousy'. It was 1.68 inches but lighter than now, and it used to get blown about like a toy balloon. Some American golfers reverted to the 1.62 British ball until more weight was put in their own.

That same contest was memorable for the fact that with Abe Mitchell taken ill at the last minute, we decided, during the train journey to join the ship at Southampton, upon a new captain – Ted Ray.

On our arrival at New York, they gave us a dinner (with the usual speeches) at the Biltmore, and in the glare of floodlights had us putting on the lawn in the early hours of the morning. Despite all the preparation, however, we were beaten by nine matches to two, with one halved. We didn't like the larger ball, but neither did our American rivals.

Something happened the night before the contest which has never been allowed to occur again. Walter Hagen outwitted us. He came round to our hotel and asked Ted Ray for the foursome pairings and order of play of our team. With a new adventure and an exciting pre-match atmosphere, Ted unsuspectingly handed them over. Walter went off and placed his own team accordingly.

We lost the foursomes by three matches to one, and I am not too certain that by his action that night Walter Hagen did not help to create a psychological advantage which has virtually been an American asset ever since. It is very important to get off to a good start, especially in a new contest. By Walter's astuteness as much as their own good play, the Americans achieved it in that first Ryder Cup contest.

I don't blame Walter for what he did; in fact, I rather admire him. He has always been a skilful, intelligent fighter, and as captain of the American team, he was entitled to use his wits. Unfortunately, we were not clever enough for him – but he didn't get the singles pairings like the foursomes! They were exchanged at the same time – and have been ever since, with each captain trying to foresee the plan of the other.

Walter Hagen: As long as I was playing competitive golf, from 1927 when the cup was established until 1938, when I voluntarily gave up the position, I was captain of the American Ryder Cup teams. In those early years, I picked my own teams with the consent and approval of the PGA. I chose fellows whose game I considered peculiarly suited to the type played by the British we were to meet. My first team consisted of Johnny Farrell, John Golden, Joe Turnesa, Gene Sarazen, Al Watrous, Leo Diegel, Bill Mehlhorn and myself, as playing captain. We had no alternates that first year. We competed against British players Ted Ray, George Duncan, Archie Compston, Arthur Havers, Aubrey Boomer, Charles Whitcombe, Fred Robson and Hubert Jolly. We won nine matches to Great Britain's two with one match halved.

The combination of Hagen and Golden beat Ray and Robson 2&1, Farrell and Turnesa beat Duncan and Compston 8&6, and Sarazen and Watrous defeated Havers and Jolly 3&2 before Boomer and Whitcombe scored Britain's first point when they emphatically defeated Diegel and Mehlhorn 7&5.

George Philpot: We expected to win the foursomes at least. The trouble is that we couldn't putt.

Ted Ray: One of the chief reasons for our failure was the superior putting of the American team. They holed out much better than we did. The result is disappointing but it has not killed our team spirit.

Samuel Ryder (holding his hat) stands with the British Ryder Cup golf team at Waterloo Station as they set off on their trip to America.

The British team prepare to set sail on the SS *Aquitania*. *Getty Images*

Gene Sarazen: When Hagen was captain, he picked the people he liked to be on the team. He was the man in charge, and what he said went. Fortunately, he was a very good captain.

Going into the singles, the momentum remained very much with the home team as Bill Mehlhorn defeated Archie Compston one-up, Johnny Farrell comfortably saw off the challenge of Aubrey Boomer 5&4, Johnny Golden thrashed Herbert Jolly 8&7, Leo Diegel did much the same with Ted Ray in his 7&5 victory, Walter Hagen edged Arthur Havers 2&1, and Al Watrous defeated Fred Robson 3&2.

The only positives from Britain's point of view came from George Duncan's one-up victory over Joe Turnesa in the final match and Charles Whitcombe's halved match with Gene Sarazen in the middle of the order. It was a dominant display from the home team, who recorded an overall 9½–2½ victory.

George Philpot: People said that the result would have been closer had Abe Mitchell been there. But several Mitchells would have been needed to alter the result.

George Duncan: I would like to pay tribute to Charlie Whitcombe. With Aubrey

Boomer, he won his foursomes 7&5 against Leo Diegel and Bill Mehlhorn, and halved with Gene Sarazen for the singles.

For my own part in that 1927 tussle, I was four-down with nine to play against Turnesa – and just about as miserable as anyone. Then Joe introduced me to his wife, who had followed us around. From that point, the fortunes of the game altered completely, and we went to the last hole level. I was inside the American on the green by five yards or so. Joe had a twelve yard putt and missed. I sank a seven-yarder for a win!

Ted Ray: Our opponents beat us fairly and squarely and almost entirely through their astonishing work on the putting greens, up to which point the British players were equally good. We were very poor by comparison, although quite equal to the recognised two putts per green standard. I consider we can never hope to beat the Americans unless we learn to putt. This lesson should be taken to heart by British golfers.

Gene Sarazen: We were excited to be playing in the first official Ryder Cup match, but that didn't mean many people would notice or that it would amount to anything.

TWO

1929
Moortown Golf Club. Leeds, England
(GB 7, USA 5)

Unfortunately for both players and spectators, the weather leading up to the second Ryder Cup and the first to be officially played on British soil was very bad, with strong winds and pounding rain battered Moortown in Leeds. The players did their best to practise in advance of the matches, but struggled badly in the conditions.

The home team was captained by George Duncan and featured Aubrey Boomer, Archie Compston, Fred Robson and Charles Whitcombe, who had all played in the first match in America, and were joined by Percy Alliss, Stewart Burns, Henry Cotton, Ernest Whitcombe and, because he had missed the 1927 match with illness, Abe Mitchell.

Walter Hagen was again captain of the American team and he brought with him seven players who had appeared at Worcester Country Club: Leo Diegel, Al Espinosa, Johnny Farrell, Johnny Golden, Gene Sarazen, Joe Turnesa, Al Watrous, plus two newcomers in Ed Dudley and Horton Smith.

Gene Sarazen: You have to remember that the Ryder Cup was the players' idea. It came from them. Even before Sam Ryder became involved we had played two matches between the professionals of the United States and Great Britain. But in those first matches we paid our own expenses. We came over for the Open and stayed on to play the match. I think there was more spirit, more of a will to win. That's what we were there for.

George Duncan: So America won the first Ryder Cup . . . two years later I was at home in Knutsford when I received a telegram informing me that I had been appointed captain of the second British Ryder Cup team for the match at Moortown.

In that contest I was to lead Britain in her first victory in the series and introduce to the team a bright twenty-two-year-old – Henry Cotton. Into the American team that same year went Horton Smith, one year younger than Henry. They were for many years the two youngest players ever to appear in Ryder Cup contests.

When play finally got underway the rain thankfully relented and a huge crowd of 10,000 spectators came out to watch. The opening match saw Charles Whitcombe and Archie Compston take on Johnny Farrell and Joe Turnesa. The Americans led one up after eighteen holes, but the British pair brought the match back all square before pushing out to a two-hole lead. They were not able to maintain this however, and were eventually drawn back to all square, which was how the match concluded.

Diegel and Espinosa then put on something of a show as they glided comfortably to a 7&5 victory over Boomer and Duncan before Britain punched back with a 2&1 victory for Mitchell and Robson over Sarazen and Dudley. The Americans ended the day in the ascendancy, however, when Golden and Hagen defeated Ernest Whitcombe and Henry Cotton two-up.

Going into the singles, Duncan knew that his team would need to play some outstanding golf to overturn the deficit and claim the cup for the first time – and the two players he selected at the top of the order did just that. First Charles Whitcombe demolished Johnny Farrell 8&6 and then Duncan himself led the way with a hugely impressive 10&8 victory over his rival captain, Walter Hagen. These results buoyed the home team enormously for while Leo Diegel defeated Abe Mitchell 8&6, Horton Smith defeated Fred Robson 4&2, and Al Espinosa secured a half against Ernest Whitcombe, Archie Compston defeated Gene Sarazen 6&4, Aubrey Boomer beat Joe Turnesa 4&3 and Henry Cotton saw off Al Watrous 4&3 for an overall score of 7–5 in the home team's favour.

Gene Sarazen: The major chunks of colour in the Ryder series were provided by Hagen, the perennial captain of the American side. Walter fancied himself as a gifted manoeuvrer of personnel, and for the most part he was. He achieved excellent results year after year in the foursomes by pairing golfers who got along well personally; it generally followed that they dovetailed harmoniously in hitting alternate shots. Hagen's strategy in arranging his singles line-up was a little less successful. In 1929 at Moortown, I remember how Walter walked into his hotel room for a chat with his charges the night before the singles. He was all smiles. He had just held a confab with George Duncan, the British captain. 'Duncan wanted to know, boys,' Walter chortled as he rubbed his palms together, 'if I could arrange for our captain to play their captain if he let me know what number their captain was playing. I said I thought it could be arranged. Well, boys, there's a point for our team.'

George Duncan: It was cold and there was snow before the contest started. Walter Hagen and I exchanged our team pairings simultaneously. I paired Abe Mitchell with

The media welcome the US Ryder Cup team on the roof of the Savoy Hotel, London.

Fred Robson and they proved to be our only winning couple in the foursomes, though Charlie Whitcombe and Archie Compston halved with Johnny Farrell and Joe Turnesa.

Down 2–1 in the foursomes, with one halved, was not a happy prospect, but for the one and only time in the history of the first eight contests, we turned deficit into victory in the singles.

After the foursomes, Hagen came to me and said there had been some talk that the two captains should play together. The sentiment was all right to me, and so was the match, because with all due respect, I never feared Walter in singles combat. I told him my place in the order – the rest was not disclosed until each captain had handed to the other the sealed list of his own placings.

That day in Moortown it seemed Hagen could do no right, while I could do no wrong. Whenever he got off the line, I produced something which gave him no chance of recovery, and beat him by 10&8. When the match finished at the twenty-eighth, the demonstration by a huge crowd was terrific. Flags were waved, hats were thrown in the air, and for a few moments delirium reigned.

Again it is necessary to pay tribute to Charlie Whitcombe, however; he had gone out in the top singles just ahead of me and set about Johnny Farrell to some purpose. He was up, I was up, and the heartening effect of both those things probably spurred on the rest of the team – at least all the team with the exception of Abe Mitchell and Fred Robson, who each found Leo Diegel and young Horton Smith in great form.

The contest was won by six matches to four, with two halved. Greatest thing of all, was

Hagen, Ryder and Duncan at the official launch dinner, 1929. *Getty Images*

that although we were down in the foursomes, we never lost heart. We stuck to our men.

Leo Diegel: I have certainly never played better golf than I did against Abe Mitchell in the Ryder Cup singles at Moortown. My driver never failed me and my iron shots and putting simply couldn't go wrong.

George Jacobus, president of the US PGA: In 1929 the British reversed matters at home, but this contest at Moortown was close, two points or the result of a single match, won or lost, deciding matters. It was in this contest that George Duncan annihilated Walter Hagen by the ghastly margin of 10&8 in thirty-six holes.

Walter Hagen: The galleries witnessed some of the greatest golf ever played in that Ryder Cup. I feel strongly that the best team won and the result was all for the good of the game.

Many people felt that I should have played Horton Smith in the foursomes, but I think I disposed of the men at my command to the best possible advantage. It was disappointing to lose the cup, but I was convinced that we would win it back two years later.

Henry Cotton: Walter Hagen was another of my heroes. I keep using the word hero, but he was the fellow who made me think, 'That's what I want to do. I want to be like "The Haig". I want to have silk shirts with monograms, and two-toned shoes, beautifully made suits and gold cufflinks.' What an impression he made, arriving at golf clubs in Rolls Royces which he rented, of course, when in Britain. That really was something in those days, right after the First World War.

I got to know Hagen in America. I went over as a young pro in November 1928 to play in the winter tour with the best pros of the USA. When in California the pros used to have their headquarters in the Hollywood Plaza, Los Angeles, which was a new hotel at that time. Two dollars fifty a night for room and bathroom – and the dollar was then five to the pound! I remember still as if it happened yesterday how, after one particular tournament, Walter's manager Bob Harlow paid the bill for Hagen and himself out of a suitcase full of dollar bills which he dumped on the cashier's counter. The cash represented the proceeds from exhibition matches played on the route from Detroit (Hagen's home town) to California. Bob collected the money at the 'gate' – but somehow never found time to count it. The bills weren't even in bundles and he went through the suitcase like a ferret, looking for twenty and fifty dollar bills, leaving the smaller ones in the bottom of the case like confetti. Then off they went to the next venue, never really worried whether he would finish well or otherwise in the tournament. I recall one tournament at which he won a prize and a law officer stepped out of the crowd to say, 'I'll take that cheque.' It was for owed alimony. Hagen just roared with laughter. He lived well and he is supposed to be the first golf pro to make a million and spend it, and in those days a million dollars was a real fortune.

Hagen won our Open in 1922 (I was only fifteen at the time,) in 1924, 1928 and in 1929 when I actually played with him, on the final day that year at Muirfield. We had already become very good friends, despite our age difference of fifteen years, and that year he went on to play in Paris with the Ryder Cup team in a triangular sort of match, British and French pros competing. Britain had won the Ryder Cup match at Moortown Golf Club, the second of the series, and it was a great thrill for me, for when I won my match, playing number seven in the singles, the Ryder Cup was ours.

Hagen was still making big money and spending most of it while living life to the full. One day I said to him, 'I would love to have one of your clubs.' 'What club would you like?' he answered. They were all hickory shafts then and I had fancied a number eight of today from his bag marked, then, a 'mashie niblick'. He said, 'Come and pick it up some time,' and so whilst in Paris I went to Claridges in the Champs-Élysées where he was staying, telephoned his room, and was invited to 'Come on up, Kiddo.' He had a suite of connecting rooms, something like 407 to 415, so I went to 407, knocked on the door and when there was no answer to my 'Hello?' I pushed open the door. Inside was a girl wearing a negligee. 'Mr Hagen?' I enquired. She appeared not to know who he was, but indicated that I should go to the next room. To my great embarrassment – I was a fairly innocent twenty-two-year-old chap – I then went through a whole series of rooms, one after the other, all full of half-dressed young ladies! I eventually found Walter lying on his bed with the telephone still in his hand – he hadn't put it down after speaking to me and he was fast asleep! I wasn't surprised that he was exhausted. I didn't know what to do, but there were a whole lot of clubs in one corner and obviously he had sorted some out. As he was soon to depart for America, by ship of course, I didn't want to wake him, so I helped myself to an eight-iron, left a goodbye and thank you note and went quietly away.

Walter loved playing golf; he had played baseball as a young man and had a natural gift

British captain George Duncan tees off while Walter Hagen follows the trajectory of the drive.

for hitting a ball. He played from a very wide stance with rather a lurch, which people criticised, but he knew what he was going to do with it. Of course, he used to make mistakes but I think he almost welcomed them as he enjoyed the extra challenge and showmanship of producing a great recovery.

George Duncan: I was a member of the first three British Ryder Cup teams, and the first British player to win in the singles, at Worcester, Massachusetts, in 1927. In the next contest at Moortown in 1929, when I was captain, I beat Walter Hagen 10&8 (I cannot recall that Walter ever beat me in singles match play, though he did it often enough in foursomes).

My foursomes record in the Ryder Cup is one of dismal failure – down in all three. I have never regarded myself as great in foursomes play, probably because I am so individualistic, but at the same time, I did not have my old pal, Abe Mitchell as a partner, though Archie Compston, Aubrey Boomer, and Arthur Havers were as good as I could have found anywhere.

Charles Whitcombe: The world's finest player of the long iron shots is Henry Cotton. He can put the ball within ten yards of the pin with a two-iron from distances for which most people would want to take a wooden club. He has an amazing ability to combine power with accuracy in the long iron shots.

George Duncan: In extenuating circumstances, I had to drop a man like Percy Alliss for Henry to receive the chance he so richly deserved by his early promise, and which he so eagerly seized.

I must say that Percy proved marvellous over the whole thing. He had suddenly been attacked by lumbago, and though he would play brilliantly one day in practise, he would be off his form the next. It wasn't a nice thing to leave him out, but I put the situation to him – we were all keen to wipe out that defeat two years previously.

'That's all right, George; whatever you decide is quite all right with me,' he replied. It cost him a lot to maintain that cheerfulness. Percy is one of the finest fellows one could wish to meet.

Henry Cotton: When I was quite young one of my greatest idols was Abe Mitchell – a man with a casual yet masterly swing and a totally individual dress sense. His playing outfit usually consisted of a tight-fitting tweed jacket, neat plus-fours with immaculate creases down the front, a matching cap, and beautifully polished expensive brown shoes. The very picture of sartorial elegance. He would walk onto the first tee as though dressed for a day's shooting, pick his hickory-shafted driver out of the bag, have one practise swing. Then he would take the club to the full horizontal position at the top, and with a terrific flash of the hands drive the ball up to 300 yards down the course. He would finish with the club shaft round the body at waist level. Abe did this time after time; it all seemed so simple. He tried to play with the steel shaft but could never play as well with it as with the hickory; I think he missed the torsion of the wooden shaft. If a weak spot ever appeared in his game it was usually on the greens because he was highly strung and used to get anxious, especially if kept waiting. But I dreamed one day of having hands and wrists that would enable me to do what he did with the clubhead; swish it through the ball with a piercing whistle. So I tried and tried, and practised day and night until I realised that just swinging a golf club and hitting golf balls wasn't enough. I was getting better, but too slowly. Abe had been a gardener as a young man and hard manual work had given him tremendous strong arms and hands and a tough yet supple back. I decided then that I too needed a stronger drill.

I had concentrated on playing and practising golf seriously since I was about sixteen and looking back I realised I should have done other exercises. I ought to have carried on playing football and cricket, and gone on building my body in the gym, and done more running. So I began thinking of what I could do to drive the ball further and develop a faster impact. I finally hit on the idea of swinging in long grass as a way of offering greater resistance to the clubhead. I used to go to a quiet spot on the golf course and swing away for hours in the deepest rough I could find, using the clubhead like a scythe. It took some doing, and was extremely hard work, but it worked; I began to win tournaments.

Bobby Jones: The 7–5 loss in 1929, probably in the long run, was a good thing for international competition and thereafter the American team were on edge, trying hard to recoup their lost prestige.

The two teams gather for a photograph at Moortown Golf Club, April 1929. *Getty Images*

THREE

1931

Scioto Country Club. Columbus, Ohio

(USA 9, GB 3)

Walter Hagen was named captain for the third time for the 1931 match and recalled Leo Diegel, Al Espinosa, Johnny Farrell, Gene Sarazen and Horton Smith to the side, alongside four rookies: Billy Burke, Wiffy Cox, Denny Shute and Craig Wood.

Charles Whitcombe was installed as captain for the visitors, but a row erupted over eligibility for the team. Percy Alliss, Aubrey Boomer and Henry Cotton were all expected to make the team, but the selection rules agreed to by the British and American PGAs stated that the players on each respective team not only had to be natives of their countries but also residents there at the time of selection. Alliss and Boomer were immediately ruled out of contention as Alliss was working as a club pro in Germany and Boomer was doing the same in France. Cotton's case was slightly different in that he was living in Britain at the time but planned to extend his stay in America once the Ryder Cup was over to play some tournaments before returning home at a later date. The rules explicitly prevented him from doing this, stating that all players had to return home immediately after the conclusion of the tournament; furthermore, there was a team rule that stated that any money earned by any members of the team during their stay in the US would be split equally among the rest of the players. Both these rules interfered with Cotton's plans so, regretfully, he withdrew his name from selection.

Henry Cotton: It was pointed out to me that if I enjoyed the benefit of a free passage to America, it was not fair of me to use that benefit for my personal gain by staying after the team had returned and playing as a freelance. It was this that caused me to intimate to the Professional Golfers' Association that I was quite prepared to pay my passage out and back. Here again the Association found my suggestion unacceptable.

Samuel Ryder: The cup is the sole property of the PGA and they can alter the terms in any way they think fit at the time.

Walter Hagen: When Samuel Ryder established the Ryder Cup as a trophy for international matches he stated that only homebred pros were eligible for the teams. However, before his death, he saw the injustice done to pros of long-standing residence in America, and let it be known that the original terms of the agreement could be changed. In that way foreign-born pros who had served a certain length of time in the United States or Great Britain would be eligible for their respective teams. PGA politics in America, however, prevented the change.

I always thought it an unhappy situation that fine players like Tommy Armour, Jim Barnes, Macdonald Smith, Jock Hutchison, Willie Macfarlane, Bobby Cruickshank and

Opposite: Charles Whitcombe, Alex Perry, President of the PGA, and Walter Hagen, stand with the Ryder Cup at Scioto Country Club. *Press Association*

Harry Cooper were made ineligible. Harry Cooper came to America when only five years of age; he learned his golf, and a good game too, in America, yet birth in Europe prevented him making the Ryder Cup team.

And yet there was another side of the argument; our American homebred pros had a very difficult time in those early days breaking into the top ranks of professional golf, so long dominated by England and Scotland. To me, it seemed only fair that our homebreds should make up the Ryder Cup team, particularly since having foreign-born pros declared eligible might have discredited our victories in the eyes of the British.

The players that did join Whitcombe were Archie Compston, George Duncan, Arthur Havers, Abe Mitchell, Fred Robson and Ernest Whitcombe, while he had three new recruits under his command in Bill Davies, Syd Easterbrook and Bert Hodson.

Travelling out with the team to America to play at the Scioto Country Club in Ohio, Samuel Ryder was in a bullish mood. 'I am quite sure we will win,' he said. 'British golf has taken on a new chapter of its history. They had been persuaded by all sorts of Jeremiahs that they were inferior to the Americans, but they are not.'

Samuel Ryder: I admire the American community immensely, and I know how much they have done for humanity; especially I know how much they have done for golf. The great lesson they have taught us, not only in golf, but in ordinary affairs, is that whatsoever the hand findeth to do, do it with thy might. Certainly, America has done this in golf, teaching us the value of science, thought, and hard work in this noble game. The great and growing friendship that exists between these two great communities will be strengthened and increased by the visit of our team. I look upon the Royal and Ancient game as being a powerful moral force that influences the best things in humanity. I trust the effect of this match will be to influence a cordial, friendly, and peaceful feeling throughout the whole civilised world. I have done several things in my life for the benefit of my fellow men, but I am certain I have never done a happier thing than this.

Charles Whitcombe: A few remarks regarding the new ball which has been adopted in America as standard for the Championship and Ryder Cup match, may be of interest. This ball is larger and lighter than our standard ball. With this ball the man who has command of all the shots and the best ball control should get the reward of his skill against the mere long hitter.

A bad shot is more likely to be punished with the lighter ball than with the standard, as spin, causing a hook or slice, has far more effect on it than on the heavier ball. The new ball may catch on in America, where the conditions of play are better than in England. It has been turned down by the authorities at St Andrews and I hope it will not be adopted here. It definitely makes the game more difficult for the average player, especially in a wind. The only points in its favour as far as this country is concerned are that in wet weather or on a heavy course, lies are better and it is easier to get the ball up, ensuring a longer carry, and in dry weather it is easier for approaching, as it is not as difficult to control as the standard ball.

I find I lose twenty to thirty yards on wooden shots, so that on a course of championship length, it often means taking a wooden club for the second shot instead of an iron, and an iron for an approach shot instead of a mashie. It is obvious, therefore, that it makes the game more difficult.

In a reflection of how the foursome matches went in 1927, the Americans pushed out into an early 3–1 lead on the Friday when Sarazen and Farrell defeated Compston and Davies 8&7, Hagen and Shute crushed Duncan and Havers 10&9 and Burke and Cox defeated Easterbrook and Ernest Whitcombe 3&2, while Mitchell and Robson secured a consolation point for Britain with a 3&1 victory over Diegel and Espinosa. It was hardly surprising that the British team would struggle for not only were they weakened by the absences of Alliss, Boomer and Cotton, but the searing 100 degree heat that the matches were played in were completely at odds with the conditions they were so used to at home.

Neither the weather nor the American momentum relented the following day as the home team cruised through the singles. Billy Burke defeated Archie Compston 7&6, which was the same scoreline that Gene Sarazen defeated Fred Robson by. Bill Davies earned a point for Britain with his 4&3 victory over Johnny Farrell, but then the American juggernaut continued sweeping up points as Wiffy Cox beat Abe Mitchell 3&1, Walter Hagen took down Charles Whitcombe 4&3 in the battle of the captains, Denny Shute trounced Bert Hodson 8&6 and Al Espinosa defeated Ernest Whitcombe 2&1 before Arthur Havers rescued a point for Britain in the last match with a 3&2 victory over Craig Wood. The cup was back in American hands, decisively so, with an overall victory of 9–3.

Gene Sarazen: It was very tense when we got together. We wanted to beat the British in the worst way. They looked upon us Americans as no more than a bunch of caddies.

I halved my singles match with Charlie Whitcombe in 1927, took a good thrashing from Archie Compston in 1929, and finally got into the win column in 1931 at Scioto, when I played Fred Robson. The match had a very bizarre turning point. Fred and I were moving along at about the same speed when, playing a short hole, he put his shot well on and I hooked mine over the green. My ball cannoned off some Coca-Cola boxes and bounded through the door and into the refreshment stand. Fred rested on the green while I walked into the stand. I found my ball nestling in a crack on the cement floor. At first I was going to pick up from my practically unplayable lie, but our match was close at this point and I didn't want to concede the hole without making some sort of stab for my half. The operator of the stand helped my caddie and me move the refrigerator out of the way. I took my niblick, and picking the ball cleanly off the cement, lofted it out through the window of the stand and onto the green ten feet from the cup. Fred three-putted carelessly from twenty-five feet, as if he were just finishing up the hole. I rolled my putt in for a three. As we walked off the green, Fred surprised me by saying, 'That was very tough luck, Gene.'

'Fred, I had a three,' I answered.

His face fell. 'You did, Gene!' he exclaimed incredulously. 'I thought you had an unplayable lie in the stand and had played a hand-mashie.'

This incident so disconcerted Fred that he never hit another good shot and lost the match 7&6.

FOUR

1933

Southport and Ainsdale Golf Club. Southport, England

(GB 6½, US 5½)

After the humiliation at Scioto, the British PGA looked back to its Ryder Cup roots and invited John Henry Taylor, who had been pivotal in the genesis match at Gleneagles in 1924, to lead the home side's efforts at Southport and Ainsdale Golf Club. Taylor, a five-time Open champion, would break the mould in another way in 1933, becoming the Ryder Cup's first non-playing captain. A staunch disciplinarian, he noted with disdain that the team that had been so badly humbled at Scioto had been physically unfit, and apportioned a considerable amount of blame for the manner of their defeat on this physical deficiency. To improve matters, he called in a favour from his military career and employed the services of Lieutenant Alick Stark, a physical fitness expert from the British Army. Even though he was in his early sixties, Taylor was so intent on setting an example to his team that he joined in with the physical exertions that Stark put the players through on Southport beach as they prepared for the matches.

Taylor's vim and vigour was also in evidence when he had selected his team. While there had been a clamour for Sam Ryder's Deed of Trust to be amended to accommodate Henry Cotton (who was now the professional at Royal Waterloo in Belgium) and Aubrey Boomer (who was still in Paris), Taylor and the British PGA held firm to the principles of the deed. The only notable change in circumstance concerned Percy Alliss, who had returned to Britain to be the pro at Temple Newsam in Leeds and was once again eligible. With Cotton and Boomer jettisoned from consideration, Taylor selected the experienced William Davies, Syd Easterbrook, Arthur Havers, Abe Mitchell, and Charles Whitcombe alongside Alliss, Arthur Lacey, Alf Padgham and Alf Perry.

Walter Hagen remained at the helm of the US effort and he augmented the tried and tested Ryder Cup heads of Burke, Diegel, Dudley, Sarazen, Shute, and Wood with the fresh faces of Olin Dutra and Paul Runyan.

This was to be the last Ryder Cup that namesake Samuel Ryder would attend before his death in 1936.

With the home team having emerged victorious in each of the Ryder Cups to date, Hagen set about trying to mischievously unsettle his opponent. One of his roles as captain was to formally exchange line-up cards with Taylor. Twice Taylor arrived at the appointed place and time for this exchange and twice Hagen stood him up. Taylor became so infuriated with Hagen that he proclaimed that if the American captain didn't show up a third time, he would cancel the match. Gleefully enjoying the angst he had caused Taylor, Hagen did show up for their third meeting, feeling confident that his strategy to unsettle was working.

The match turned out to be a classic, with over 15,000 spectators crowding the course. The foursomes set the tone with three of the matches decided on the eighteenth. The home team had stormed into a commanding lead, leading in all four matches at the turn, but an inspired comeback from Sarazen and Hagen against Alliss and Whitcombe saw them come from four

Opposite: Abe Mitchell follows the flight of his first tee shot at the short par-three first hole at Southport and Ainsdale in his singles match against Olin Dutra.

holes down to halve, while Mitchell and Havers beat Dutra and Shute 3&2; with the last two points shared, Britain won the foursomes by a point.

George Jacobus: It seems to me a very appropriate time for me, as the chief executive of the Professional Golfers' Association of America, to inform those who will follow the fortunes of our Ryder Cup Team, precisely how that team was selected. As a matter of fact an entirely new method of selection was followed in order to eliminate any partisanship. Briefly, the procedure was as follows:

There are twenty-five sections of the PGA and each section's president and executive committee submitted the names of twelve candidates for the team. When all sections had reported, the results were submitted to the national executive committee, which also cast its vote for its candidates and then selected the nine polling the greatest number of votes. The highest number of votes which any candidate could receive was 34, and four – Walter Hagen, Gene Sarazen, Olin Dutra and Densmore Shute, received this unanimous approval.

As president of the PGA I designated Walter Hagen as captain of the team. If the winner of the US Open happens to be a homebred professional, not listed among the nine members already selected, he will be named as tenth member of the team.

Personally, I consider the team truly representative of the best golfers among the Association's members. Certainly the picking of the players was conducted conscientiously and with the utmost fairness. I am confident that they will carry through to victory when they meet the British pros on June 26th and 27th, at Southport, England.

Paul Runyan: It was an experience, suddenly sailing to play for America, and Walter had picked me, which was quite an honour. I'd never been much of anywhere before, then Walter signed me up.

Walter Hagen: As well as regularly golfing with the Prince of Wales I was a regular visitor at the golfing house parties which Sir Philip Sassoon gave at his beautiful estate at Trent Park. Often, too, I took the Ryder Cup team and their wives to Sir Philip's for some practise rounds on his private course. We met numerous members of the royal family, among them King George V and his sons, who later became King Edward VIII and King George VI. Both his sons were ardent golfers.

Ryder Cup team wins zigzagged back and forth after our win in 1927, for the British took six matches to our four, with two halved at Moortown in 1929. We won again in June of 1931 at Scioto in Columbus, Ohio. At Southport in 1933, our team was composed of Billy Burke, Gene Sarazen, Ed Dudley, Olin Dutra, Craig Wood, Paul Runyan, Denny Shute and me, with Leo Diegel and Horton Smith as alternates. We had our first real chance that year to win the Ryder Cup on British soil.

Henry Cotton: JH [Taylor] never wore plus-fours: he reckoned his legs were too thick. In fact, you never see a group photo showing JH Taylor seated with his legs crossed. He just couldn't cross his legs because of his enormously thick thighs.

John Henry Taylor: To maintain anything approaching his best form, a golfer must of necessity live a clean, wholesome, and sober life. I do not advocate any special method of training, such as is the case upon the cinder path or cycle track. A man must live plainly, but well, and he must be careful of himself. If he uses up the reserve force, or abuses himself in any way, then he has cast his opportunities aside, and he drops immediately out of the game. There are no half-measures. You must do one of two things: be careful of yourself in everything, or forsake the game altogether. A man who lives a careless or a vicarious life can never succeed in golf, or hope to keep his nerves and his stamina.

George Duncan: The 1933 Ryder Cup was the most memorable and most thrilling match ever played. It also drew about 15,000 spectators, the biggest crowd ever for a Ryder Cup.

With Britain leading the foursomes for the first time by two matches to one, with one halved, the Prince of Wales, a keen golfer himself, shared the tense atmosphere of the last day. The Prince, in a light-grey suit and a soft straw hat, tried to play hide-and-seek in the crowd, but it was little use.

Before his arrival, one of the most remarkable things in this day of incident occurred. Arthur Lacey, playing the game of his life against wily Hagen, drove off the line from the sixth tee and his ball vanished over the top of the sandhills. When Lacey and Hagen – with 2,000 spectators – breasted the hill, an amazing sight met their eyes.

Marshals, waving pennants and shouting, were running about as if they had gone mad. 'Who's lifted the ball? Who's lifted the ball?' they shouted. Somebody pointed to a well-dressed man who was walking away in the direction of the sixth green. He broke into a run, and officials and crowd set out in pursuit. Realising that the odds were against him, he stopped 300 yards away and for a few moments was in danger of being mauled by the crowd.

When called upon for an explanation, he coloured to the roots of his hair and said, 'Here's the ball. I took it quite by mistake. I had no idea it was being used in the match.' He was led back to the spot where he said he found it. The ball was dropped, and Lacey resumed without penalty.

Charles Whitcombe: There is really no reason why the good golfer should not be equally good at stroke play as he is at match play events, but certain temperaments seem to be better suited to the one than the other. A player of the aggressive type, like Walter Hagen, likes to 'have a man to play against'. He likes to know what he has got to do. He tries to get past his opponent off the tee. When the other man has played his second, he tries in his turn to play his ball inside the other. When the other lays his long putt dead he tries to put his down for a win. When he finds himself three up, he goes all out to make it four up and so on. But this type of player sometimes fails in medal play because he has nothing definite to pit himself against. He does not know what score will be needed to win, and cannot pull out his best game fighting against the unknown.

Bobby Jones, the typical example of the stroke play temperament, found that, as far as he was concerned, the way to win matches was to convert them into stroke competitions and play simply for his score. 'If you keep shooting par at them,' he declared, 'they are all bound to crack sooner or later!'

It would be equally true to say that Walter Hagen won his earlier championships by converting the stroke play test in his mind into a form of match play against par. 'The Killer', as his fellow pros on the other side used to call him, was the ideal match players, but he discovered the secret of 'fighting against the figures'. If he knocked his ball off the tee into a bunker at his feet at a short hole, he still tried to put his recovery shot dead to the pin and get his three to halve with par all the same. If he was over the par figure at one hole, he hoped to win a couple of holes from par in the next three or four.

Gene Sarazen rallied the American cause on the second day when he dispatched Alf Padgham 6&4. Mitchell swung momentum back to the home team in beating Dutra 9&8 before Hagen's 2&1 win over Lacey took the scores level and the holders then pushed out into the lead for the first time when Wood beat Davies 4&3. Percy Alliss had been one up against Runyan at lunch, but the American worked his way back into the match to make it all square at the fifteenth. Alliss held his nerve to push back in front on the sixteenth; Runyan, however, buckled under the mounting pressure and hit his ball out of bounds on the seventeenth to hand Alliss a 2&1 victory. The match between Charles Whitcombe and Horton Smith also went to the seventeenth, this time the American edging matters to win 2&1. This meant that with the score tied at 5½ each, the match between Easterbrook and Shute would decide the destination of the Ryder Cup for the next two years.

Both players reached the eighteenth green in three and as the crowd jostled for position, Walter Hagen watched on from the clubhouse, where he had been in conversation with the Prince of Wales and felt unable to extricate himself to offer support to his player. It might have made all the difference if he had. Easterbrook stroked the ball to the edge of the cup and then tapped in for five; with the fate of the Ryder Cup on his shoulders, Shute overshot the hole by four feet and then missed his putt to halve, handing victory to the home team.

Gene Sarazen: The night before the singles in 1933, Walter took me aside for a chat. Playing as partners earlier that day in the foursomes, we had rallied from four-down to halve our match with Percy Alliss and Charlie Whitcombe. I thought Walter would be feeling pretty good after that, but it soon became obvious that he had something on his mind that he was trying to get around to delicately.

'I've seen you play a lot better golf, Gene, than you did today,' Walter said as he pursed his lips. 'I don't think you're hitting your shots too well.'

'You know I don't like playing alternate shots,' I sparred. 'I don't like the wait between shots. Also, you put me in several regions of the course that I'm not used to playing.'

'Then you don't want to step out tomorrow?' Hagen said, getting to the point.

'I certainly do not. I honestly think I am playing just as well, if not better, than most of the fellows on the team. You're the captain, though.'

'OK, Gene,' Walter said with a little flip of his hand, and our conference broke up.

I was not at all surprised when I learned that Hagen had placed me in the number-one position for the singles. He was figuring, I knew, that since I was going to drop my point anyhow, I might as well lose to the British number one and give the rest of our batting order the advantage of the percentages. My tête-à-tête with Hagen gave me just the stimulus I needed for my best concentration. I defeated Alf Padgham 6&4.

Walter Hagen: Denny Shute was our last man out on the course, and I was in the clubhouse with my host, the Prince of Wales. We stood at the big front window facing out on the eighteenth green. A wide path had been cleared for the Prince so that we might have a comfortable and unobstructed view from the clubhouse to see each man finish. I was having a fine time . . . laughing and talking with the Prince . . . when Denny came onto the eighteenth green. If he made the putt in one, we would win the cup; if he got it down in two we would keep it; if he took three, we would lose it to Great Britain. Of course, Denny, not knowing how some of our players before him had finished, did not know this. In fact, if Sarazen and I had done better than to tie our match with Percy Alliss and Charles Whitcombe, Denny would not have had to worry.

I was wondering if I shouldn't be down there putting him wise to how things stood. If I were at the green I could whisper in his ear, tell him to play safe, not to take three putts. I wondered if I were perhaps sacrificing the Ryder Cup for the pleasure of being with my friend, the Prince. I knew it would be discourteous to walk out on the future King of England just to whisper in Denny's ear and tell him how to putt.

George Duncan: With the Americans winning four of the eight singles matches, the countries were level when Syd Easterbrook and Denny Shute came to the last green square. Neither player could afford to make a mistake.

By this time, there was a solid mass of spectators. The hole, with the wind in the position it was, was no more than a drive and a comparatively simple pitch, but both men were bunkered from the tee, and neither reached the green in two.

Both were on in three, with Easterbrook to putt first. He laid his ball dead. Shute had two putts from twelve yards to save the match. He failed to make it, and the hole was won and lost by five strokes to six. The crowd was almost too amazed to cheer, and perhaps sympathetic with the American, for whom it had been one of the greatest disasters of his golfing life.

Walter Hagen: Denny played it bold and much too strong. His ball rimmed the hole and went three feet past. He missed coming back and three-putted for a six. There was a terrific silence . . . and then the gallery around the green broke loose from the restraining line the bobbies had formed, and surged forward to congratulate the winning British team. Enclosed in the clubhouse as we were, the Prince and I heard none of the din and the cheering. We could only take in the action – it all happened in a matter of seconds – and then he and I were on our way to the platform where the Ryder Cup would be awarded to the British team – taking it from us 6–5 with one match halved.

Some of our fellows were quite upset by Denny's failure to play it safe and keep the cup in our possession. Fortunately, I was able to persuade them to say nothing to Denny about the loss, and two weeks later he and Craig Wood came through for a tie for first place in the British Open at St Andrews. Denny beat Craig in the play-off and became British Open champion for the first time in his career.

Accepting the trophy from the Prince of Wales, JH Taylor said he was 'the proudest man in all the Commonwealth.' The Prince of Wales, in turn, announced, 'In giving this Cup, I am naturally impartial. But, of course, we over here are very pleased to have won.'

Amid the wild celebrations, British golf enthusiasts would not have envisaged that this hair-raising 6½ to 5½ victory would be their country's last Ryder Cup triumph for twenty-four years.

FIVE

1935

Ridgewood Country Club. Ridgewood, New Jersey

(USA 9, GB 3)

Travelling to Ridgewood Country Club in New Jersey, the British team felt genuine confidence that they could finally claim a Ryder Cup triumph on American shores – so much so, in fact, that the PGA took out an insurance policy for the cup's return journey to Britain.

Bolstered by the win at Southport, British confidence was further reinforced by the presence of the three Whitcombe brothers – Charles, Ernest and Reg – appearing for the first time together in the team, and also by the prospect of playing in more clement conditions than in previous sojourns to the United States as the contest had been moved to September to escape the worst of the summer heat.

Charles Whitcombe was named as team captain and alongside his brothers and Open Champion Alf Perry, his team consisted of experienced campaigners Percy Alliss and Alf Padgham, and debutants Dick Burton, Jack Busson, Bill Cox and Ted Jarman.

George Duncan: The fifth Ryder Cup contest at Ridgewood, New Jersey, was noteworthy for the fact that the three Whitcombe brothers all played.

Commander RCT Roe, PGA Secretary: I feel no team could go to America with a greater opportunity of success than Whitcombe and the boys.

Despite the optimism of Roe, on the eve of their departure, Bernard Darwin wrote, rather unsettlingly, in The Times *that despite his approval of the team selection and that it was a 'good, strong, young side', he could not believe that they could win.*

As well as considering the history of the contest – that had yet to see the visiting team emerge victorious – Darwin was well aware of the calibre of the American team. Walter Hagen had once again been named captain of the US team (in what was to be his last appearance as a Ryder Cup player) and he had selected the experienced heads of Dutra, Runyan, Sarazen, Smith and Wood alongside fresh blood in Ky Laffoon, US Open champion Sam Parks, Henry Picard, and Johnny Revolta.

The British team sailed from Southampton to Quebec aboard the Empress of Australia *and then travelled directly to New York for five days of practise before the match began.*

Despite the hype that this was one of the strongest British teams to arrive in America, it was the home team that burst out of the blocks on the opening day, rampaging into a dominant early lead in one of the most one-sided foursome matches since the tournament had begun. The only point that Britain earned was through Charles and Ernest Whitcombe, who claimed victory over Dutra and Laffoon by a single hole. Meanwhile Sarazen and Hagen beat Perry and Busson 7&6, Picard and Revolta beat Padgham and Alliss 6&5, and Runyan and Smith beat Cox and Jarman 9&8.

Opposite: The Whitcombe brothers: Reg, Ernest and Charles, who played together in the 1935
~~Ryder Cup. Charles was British captain~~

Walter Hagen: I picked Gene Sarazen as my playing partner in the Ryder Cup matches in 1933 at Southport where we broke even with Percy Alliss and Charles Whitcombe; and again in 1935 at George Jacobus's home club, the Ridgewood Country Club in New Jersey, when we won 7&6 over Perry and JJ Busson. We were tough on each other as competitors, Gene and I, but good friends when we took on the other boys. That friendship stemmed from the fact, I believe, that we shared the same sense of humour and he enjoyed a practical joke as much as I, and he wasn't above pulling one on me when he could, nor I on him.

Henry Cotton: Percy Alliss was such a great player in his time, he could have won everything. In fact, at one period in his life I thought he was the greatest and most consistent hitter of a golf ball I had ever seen. He could play for a month, rarely missing a fairway, and never failing to hit a green. He'd find the green with a wood, an iron, anything you like, but there were other players who seemed to get the ball in the hole in fewer strokes. At times, however, he was unbeatable. At Wannsee Golf Club in Berlin, before the war, three pro teams from Britain, America and the Continent went to play a seventy-two-hole medal event on this beautiful forest course where he was pro, and he won by the length of a street!

Percy held the club beautifully, played it cleanly, hardly taking a divot, to 'throw' the ball at the flag with beautiful control.

Percy Alliss: As soon as I could walk with safety I used to borrow balls from my father and clubs from my elder brothers, and spend every evening hitting about in a rough field. As often as not the balls were soon lost, but I would go on swishing at anything and everything I could see – tufts of grass, leaves, matchsticks – until I was absolutely tired out. Later on I was allowed to caddie at the local links, and so had the chance of watching all manner of styles and peculiarities of swinging the club; these were imitated in the evening on my patch of rough, with or without a ball, and the result was entertainment as profitable as it was enjoyable. I am convinced that any success I had was in very large measure due to the countless number of times I swung the club in perpetual practise from my youth up.

If any proof were needed of the benefits of thorough practise, it could be found across the Atlantic. In 1914 America was behind England in talent, and now she would seem to have overtaken us. Such splendid golfers as Bobby Jones, Hagen, Farrell and Diegel – to name but a few – have acquired their skill by constant and thorough practise. The American treatment of the game is definitely more scientific than our own, being founded on hard thinking and painstaking care. To bear out this statement I will say that the golf emigrants, Jim Barnes, Jock Hutchison, Macdonald and Alex Smith, Tommy Armour, Bobby Cruickshank and Cyril Walker, would not have become such great players had they stayed at home; five of these have won the highest honours in America.

The British professionals who have crossed the Atlantic at various times have made American golf, and American golf has made them; their employers were not slow to pick their brains, giving in return the advantages of training planned with forethought and deliberation. Writers on the game are often obsessed with the bugbear of 'temperament', pointing to Walter Hagen as an example of the ideal golf temperament as against Abe

Mitchell. Hagen himself would be the first to admit Mitchell's greatness, and yet the latter cannot win the British Open Championship. There can be no doubt that temperament does count; Hagen has confidence in himself, born of hours and hours of practise, and any of us who wish to win the big events must acquire the same frame of mind in the same way.

Johnny Revolta: I often hang around the practise tee before a tournament and watch the other professionals swing. Each of them does something different. I can imitate every well-known golfing star. If I wanted, I could change my own game and grip and swing exactly as they do. But aping other players wouldn't be right for my game.

Charles Whitcombe: The American 'homebreds' like Gene Sarazen will tell you that the 'grooved swing' comes from baseball. Every American boy, when he takes up the national game, learns to cultivate a flat one-piece swing that keeps the bat travelling in one place of movement throughout the stroke. Later on they brought the same theory to the links. It is a partial reversion to the flatter, more scythe-like swing of the old Scottish school, the swing that in this country was superseded by the more upright swing of Harry Vardon. It may be quite true that the Americans slipped more easily into this type of swing because it fitted in with the habits they had learned in baseball, but I have no doubt that it was Macdonald Smith and the other Scottish-American professionals who served the model for it.

The first example, and perhaps the best example, of a perfectly grooved swing that I ever saw was JH Taylor, and JH Taylor was the model whom we three Whitcombes tried to copy in our own style of play. I am not saying that any of us are ourselves ideal examples of the grooved swing, but it is a grooved swing that we have been trying all our lives to imitate.

Johnny Revolta: Some reporters and professionals called me the 'Iron Master'. Some have even called me the greatest iron player on the links. I don't know about that, but I do know that dropping them into the cup from off the green can make you a good golfer.

Charles Whitcombe: My brother Reg is especially good at short holes. If you want to see how to judge short holes, watch my brother Reg playing a mashie shot at a one-shot hole. The mashie, as they say, is Reg's club. He will get home with a mashie, where I, for instance would need to take a No.4. He is especially good because even when he puts a little bit extra [force] into it, he still plays it just the same way. Most players, especially long-handicap players, when they try to get extra distance with any club, tend to let their body swing too soon and draw the shot round to the left, but Reg can go all out and still pitch the ball right up to the pin. And that is the secret of good approach play.

Reg Whitcombe: The whole stroke must be smooth. Any suggestion of a stab or jab will bring failure. Any form of descending blow will cause the ball to rise with backspin, and that is the one thing you are striving to avoid. Properly executed it is one of the most artistic shots in the game and gives great satisfaction.

Johnny Revolta: Henry Picard, a truly great player, was my partner in the 1935 and 1937 Ryder Cups. We knew simply that the player who wins the hole wins for his team. And

Horton Smith putts on the eighteenth green during his singles match against WJ Cox.

the team that wins the most holes in the match is the victor. We won in 1935 against Alf Padgham and Percy Alliss when Henry dropped a twenty-five-foot putt over the worst possible area of the green, it sloped and slanted in every direction, but he had played it perfectly and it had just enough legs to drop in the cup. We won 6&5.

Byron Nelson: Just like always, Hagen was impressive because he was a showman. He played with Gene Sarazen against Alf Perry and Jack Busson. He would have a real tough shot, and he would walk up and just play it. But when he had a shot that looked fairly tough, though it was easy, why he'd move around and look at it a bit and make people think it was a real hard one. Of course, then he'd do the shot that folks thought was almost impossible, and the crowd loved it.

Johnny Revolta: A good professional competitor never hears the gallery. He is concentrating on his shot and he is oblivious to everything else. If you can learn to keep cool under pressure by thinking only about your own game, the other fellow will be buying the drinks at the nineteenth hole.

The two captains sat out of play in the singles the following day, with Whitcombe making the call on the grounds that he believed it to be unfair on the other members of the team if all three Whitcombe siblings played together. Not that it would have made much difference if he had opted to play. By mid-afternoon it was all over, with the first four matches going to the Americans as Gene Sarazen defeated Busson 3&2, Runyan defeated Burton 5&3, Revolta defeated Reg Whitcombe 2&1, and Dutra defeated Padgham 4&2. Percy Alliss briefly stemmed the tide against Wood to claim Britain's lone win of the day, before Bill Cox and Horton Smith halved, Picard defeated Ernest Whitcombe 3&2, and Perry and Parks halved for an overall victory of 9–3.

With the level of expectation that had surrounded the British team, the result was a disaster. Bernard Darwin called it 'yet another American tragedy' and the general lament at the quality of the British play was echoed by the press corps around the world.

Basking in the glory of such a dominant display as the British set sail from New York upon the Aquitania, Walter Hagen reflected on his playing record in the Ryder Cup, which stood at a hugely impressive 7–1–1.

Byron Nelson: I was the assistant pro at Ridgewood in 1935 and seeing these great players turning out for the US, I made up my mind then and there that I wanted to be on a Ryder Cup team. I was just a young whippersnapper then, and it was a lot to think I'd be good enough to make a Ryder Cup team, but I vowed I would.

SIX

1937
Southport and Ainsdale Golf Club. Southport, England
(USA 8, GB 4)

While a visiting team had yet to record a victory in the Ryder Cup, the US team of 1937 travelled to England with the same fanfare that surrounded the 1935 British team before their departure. While Charles Whitcombe's charges had fallen well short of the pre-match expectation, there was a different feel to the '37 US team's prospects. Walter Hagen was making his final appearance as captain and there was a steely focus to the holders' defence of the cup – even if there had been a serious rift in the team before they had even left America.

Gene Sarazen had, with some justification after a glorious career, believed that he was in line to be captain in 1937. When the US PGA turned once again to Hagen, Sarazen was so incensed that he swore that he would never again play in a Ryder Cup. In an acidic statement he castigated George Jacobus, the president of the PGA, who had chosen Hagen for the sixth consecutive match, saying: 'The failure of George Jacobus to name me captain of the team is an insult and a wound that will never heal. I think everyone will agree my record stacks up favourably with that of every other pro, past or present. I won every worthwhile championship, and I guess I did my share on every Ryder Cup team we ever had. But, no, Jacobus didn't see fit to let me achieve my last and profoundest ambition.'

It was an unfortunate incident that cast a shadow over the build-up – although not as long as that cast by the death of Samuel Ryder, on 2 January 1936. Buried with his beloved mashie club, the founder of professional golf's premier team contest went to his grave in the knowledge that his simple idea had become a proud legacy which was assured for future generations.

With the return to Southport and the unerring record of the home team in the matches, and with Henry Cotton returned to the team after an eight-year absence (during which time he had won the Open, in 1934 – as he would again in 1937), the British players and press were in buoyant mood – despite the disaster at Ridgewood two years earlier. Charles Whitcombe returned for another tilt at the captaincy and he brought with him the experienced Alliss, Burton, Perry, Cox and Padgham, hoping that they had learned enough salutory lessons from Ridgewood to ensure a home victory. Arthur Lacey also returned to the side having last appeared in 1933, while Sam King and Dai Rees made their debuts.

With Hagen acting as a non-playing captain, one of the most significant achievements he and the US PGA managed was in persuading Sarazen out of his sulk to join the team alongside his old muckers from Ridgewood, Picard and Revolta, and from the previous visit to Southport in 1933, Ed Dudley and Denny Shute. The rookies who joined the team included Ralph Guldahl and Tony Manero and two players who would become household names around the world – Byron Nelson and Sam Snead. For Hagen's last roll for the Ryder Cup, with a team like that at his disposal, the American captain's dice were loaded.

Opposite: Byron Nelson tees off at Southport.

Johnny Revolta: There are going to be times that every golfer's game will go bad. Back in 1936, a young professional was about to give up the game. He had gone through set after set of clubs, discarding them, chopping and filing at them, always seeking the right clubs, each time it cost money, something he didn't have in great amounts.

Finally his wife spoke up.

'Why don't you quit kidding yourself,' she said. 'It can't be entirely the clubs. The trouble must be you.'

That, the young pro finally admitted to himself, was it. He had been looking for the perfect set of clubs instead of perfecting his game. He began studying his own swing and that of others. Gradually he developed the swing and sound game which today has made him famous. His name – Byron Nelson.

Byron Nelson: I was just a young whippersnapper then, and it was a lot to think I'd be good enough to make a Ryder Cup team, but fortunately my game was starting to gel at that time. The main thing was, I won the Masters in 1937, and that put me in the team. Made me feel like I'd really arrived.

The 1937 British Ryder Cup team. Back row, left to right: Commander RCT Roe (PGA Secretary), Bill Cox, Alf Padgham, Henry Cotton, Alf Perry, Dick Burton. Front row, left to right: Arthur Lacey, Sam King, Charles Whitcombe (Captain), Dai Rees and Percy Alliss

Walter Hagen: During my years as captain of the Ryder Cup teams, I insisted that our fellows be fittingly uniformed. Various manufacturers offered knickers and coats free for our use, but I turned them down. Instead I ordered, and paid for, beautifully tailored marine-blue jackets and pale grey trousers from the Alfred Nelson Company in New York. I obtained permission from the army to use an official government eagle badge embossed with crossed golf sticks and the insignia 'Ryder Cup Team' for the pockets. Although I consistently picked my teams for their game and not their beauty, I must admit we stacked up pretty well in the Beau Brummel department, too, when we showed up for the Ryder Cup.

Sam Snead: I almost didn't make it onto the team in 1937. I was one of the last players named, because some people felt I might not be able to handle the pressure . . . Well, I did handle the pressure in Ryder Cup play.

The writers named me 'Slammin' Sam' and my career started with the Oakland Open, you could say. Three weeks later I won the Bing Crosby Open at Rancho Santa Fe in a cloudburst of rain. From there on I was hard to beat, finishing my first year on tour with $10,243 in winnings and third place in the PGA standings and landing a place on the Ryder Cup team as a freshman. The headlines called me 'an overnight miracle' and 'Daniel Boone with a driver'. With all that applause, I tried not to miss the important point: most strong young kids – about ninety-nine per cent – fade out of the PGA circuit fast. One of the main reasons I stuck was learning right at the start to avoid the error which the pros call 'thinking yourself out of action'. You've got to stay focused all the time when you play but not over-think things.

Some of the US players, who later became fine friends of mine, gave me the hey rube treatment on the boat ride to England. One of them went around imitating my way of talking: 'Why, this heah golf is easy as pie. All yuh gotta do is whip out a drive, then take an arn (iron) and hit it on that flat li'l hill up thar (green) and then give it two more whops and you gets yo'self a pah.'

When I fell seasick, the boys said the cure was to eat celery stalks and hard rolls and no other food and then do two hours of dancing every night in the ship's ballroom.

I tried it, groggy as I was, barely able to roll out of my bunk and pull on my pants, and darn if it didn't work. When that gag failed, they introduced me to one of the passengers as 'Sam Snead, who's been a prizefighter down in Virginia and would like to challenge you.'

'That right?' asked the man.

I admitted that at one time I'd done a little ringwork in the hometown. He thumped my chest. 'I'll try to work you in, pally,' he said.

The big laugh, of course, came when I found the man was Tommy Farr, the British Empire champion, who was about to fight Joe Louis for the world title.

Byron Nelson: It wasn't too long after the Masters that I learned I had been chosen for the Ryder Cup team. Boy howdy, was I excited. I'd never even been outside the United States before. I didn't think it was possible that the dream I'd had just two years before at Ridgewood could be coming true already. The US PGA picked the team then, and they didn't keep any long-term, detailed records like they do now. They didn't pick anyone who wasn't playing well, naturally. But of course, if you won a Major, that did have some effect on their decision, and so I was selected.

There were a couple of us on our team who'd never played in a Ryder Cup before – myself and Snead. So we were inexperienced to some degree, and we also knew that the Americans had never beaten the British on their own soil before. But Walter Hagen would be our captain – that really was a thrill.

When we arrived in England, we were met by the British contingent – the Royal and Ancient representatives. Our accommodations were comfortable but not luxurious, adequate for the team and their wives, six of whom went along.

As the foursomes commenced, Cotton led his team out alongside Padgham against Dudley and Nelson, hoping to establish some momentum. But it was not to be as the home pair fell to a 4&2 defeat. Guldahl and Manero pushed the American advantage in the second match, winning 2&1 against Cox and Lacey. Whitcombe and Rees managed to stem the tide by halving with Sarazen and Shute before Alliss and Burton clawed back some ground winning 2&1 against Picard and Revolta.

Dai Rees: I became a Ryder Cup player at the early age of twenty-four in 1937. The two days of the match represented a personal triumph for me, for I obtained one-and-a-half points from my two games and had the exciting experience of being chaired to the clubhouse.

The foursomes were played first and my partner was Charles Whitcombe, a great player and a wonderful man to play alongside in a contest of that kind. Naturally I was very nervous when we set out against Densmore Shute and Gene Sarazen, both of whom had won the Open Championship, but whenever I played a shot not quite up to standard Charles Whitcombe was ready to give quiet words of advice and encouragement.

As a result of his staunch support we halved our foursome, but our team finished the series one point down, and there was a big landslide in the singles on the following day, Britain having only two winners. One of them was Henry Cotton, who beat Tony Manero, and the other was myself, for I took the scalp of the renowned Byron Nelson.

I often look back on that match and still regard it as one of the best performances of my career. The weather was terrible, but I can honestly say I played very few bad shots in the two rounds. To halve a foursome and beat Byron Nelson 3&1, represented a Ryder Cup debut which for most young golfers would remain just a dream.

Sam Snead: To be able to scramble from trouble is the key to winning golf. A lot of what I picked up as a green kid came from watching masters of the sand irons, such as Henry Cotton of England, Ralph Guldahl, Jimmy Demaret, Walter Hagen, Denny Shute, and Johnny Revolta. In June of 1937, as the rookie member of the Ryder Cup team, which challenged the British at Southport, England, I was given a swell chance to study not only Cotton and Alf Padgham, the stars of the opposition, but teammates like Shute, Revolta, and Gene Sarazen. It was Sarazen who invented the sand wedge in 1931, which revolutionised trap play.

As it worked out, it seemed I'd never get to see the stars try for a tough recovery. After winning my Ryder Cup match from Dick Burton of England, I followed the big boys around. Whenever traps were ahead, I hustled down to get a ringside view.

Sarazen was playing Percy Alliss, and on the fifteenth hole he overshot the green. The ball started for a deep bunker but caromed into the lap of a woman sitting on the grass.

'Oh, what'll I do?' she said.

'Get rid of it,' said her husband.

So she gave her skirt a fling and tossed the ball onto the green, twenty feet from the cup. The officials didn't see it. It wasn't my business, so I said nothing. Sarazen knew nothing about it. He putted out, winning the hole that decided the match in his favour, one-up.

Byron Nelson: There's nothing as exciting in golf as playing for your country. In the first matches, we played a Scotch foursome, alternating shots. One player would drive on the odd holes, the other on the evens. Hagen had paired Ed Dudley and me against Henry Cotton and Alf Padgham, the reigning British Open champion. Hagen came to me before the match and said, 'Byron, you've got a lot of steam, a lot of get-up-and-go. And Dudley needs someone to push him. So I'm going to put you two together. You can get him fired up.'

We were unknowns in England, so the headline in the paper the next morning said, HAGEN FEEDS LAMBS TO THE BUTCHER. Well, we did get steamed up over that. I drove against Cotton all day, and on the par threes, I put my ball inside his every time, and we ended up winning the match. The next day, the headline read THE LAMBS BIT THE BUTCHER. It was a great thrill to win, especially against a player like Cotton.

Whitcombe knew that with the match so finely balanced that the British had to go out hard and push for an early lead in the singles. He sent out Padgham, the 1936 Open champion, at the head against Guldahl, but things didn't go according to plan as Padgham fell 8&7. Fortunately, the contest was kept alive by Sam King halving with Denny Shute, Rees and Cotton defeating Nelson and Manero 3&1 and 5&3 respectively, taking the score to 4–4.

But for the home team, this was as good as it was going to get, as the US stormed into the history books.

Byron Nelson: The weather for the matches was fine except for the last day, when it turned terrible. Cold, windy, drizzly. And pros weren't as welcome at these clubs as they are now. We were just barely allowed in the locker room, and our wives weren't allowed in the clubhouse at all. There they were, standing outside, freezing, all six of them huddled together, trying to stay out of the wind, when the mayor's wife saw them. She had enough compassion to invite them all into the clubhouse, and because she was the mayor's wife, no one could say no to her. Then she served them some two-hundred-year-old port, and they warmed up quickly after that. They said later they'd never tasted anything as good as that port in all their lives.

Gene Sarazen: My farewell singles match with Percy Alliss in 1937 at Southport contained several dramatic overtones. I jumped off to an early lead, but the prodigious iron-player overhauled me and began to build up a commanding margin in the afternoon. With nine to go, Percy was three up. Hagen, our non-playing captain, gave me a strong fight talk on the twenty-eighth tee. The outcome of the entire Ryder Cup match, he urged me excitedly in his high-pitched voice, might depend on whether or not I saved my point. I took the next three holes in a row to draw back to even. Percy and I halved the thirty-first and the thirty-second in pars.

Percy Alliss: When two players are going round together, they are bound to influence each other's form to some degree, the more highly strung of the two being naturally more susceptible to the effects of the other's play. There is no doubt whatever that if the mind is allowed to dwell upon the slowness or the speed of a partner's swing there is bound to be a reaction in one's own case. Under such circumstances it is safest to avoid all danger of infection and to ignore the other man completely. Look somewhere else, and take no notice of the other ball, you are not able to turn it into a bunker or guide it into safety by following it with your eyes. If you are busy yourself with your own game and keep your opponent's swing right out of your mind for three or four holes, he should trouble you no further however often or however closely you may watch him; the dangerous period is the earliest stage of a round, before you have safely got the feel of your own swing.

Gene Sarazen: The break came on the thirty-third. I had the honour on this short hole, about 185 yards long, whipped by a wind from off the right. I attempted to play down the right-hand side but I hurried my timing and hooked my iron shot badly. It was running like a rabbit over the green, heading for serious trouble, when it struck a woman spectator and rebounded onto the green twenty feet from the hole. Alliss then played a beautiful long iron five feet inside my ball, but when I holed my putt for a two and Percy missed his, he had lost a hole he had thoroughly deserved to win, and at a very crucial juncture.

Percy Alliss: The unexpected loss of a hole has a far-reaching effect on the whole game. A player's calmness and temper are disturbed by losing a point that he knows he should have won, and it is difficult to make up again the smallest loss of confidence. Like any other vice, slackness in golf is far easier to acquire than to be rid of.

Gene Sarazen: Percy stood one down, and the holes were running out fast. We halved the thirty-fourth. On the long thirty-fifth I drove down the middle. Percy, striving for distance, pulled his drive into a trap. He had to play an explosion, and was barely past my drive in two. My second shot, a full brassie, finished hole-high just off the green. Alliss played a strong brassie on his third, thirty-five feet from the cup. I put my chip, my third, a foot from the cup – not only that, but I laid Percy the deadest stymie imaginable. I was absolutely certain, and so was Hagen, that this was the match, 2&1. Percy could never get by my ball and he had to in order to sink his putt and halve the hole and to keep the match alive. And then I had the dubious privilege of watching the greatest competitive putt I have ever seen. Percy stroked his ball so that it just grazed mine, and as it died a ball's width to the left of the cup it veered just a fraction of an inch to the right, and with that minute twist caught a tiny bit of the rim of the cup and toppled in.

So we went to the thirty-sixth, a 340-yard par four, Alliss one down and fighting desperately for a birdie. After I had played a safety tee shot with my spoon, Percy splashed away with his driver and smote a long, arching shot far over the traps I had purposely played short of. I had a five-iron to the green and came through with a very good shot, twelve feet above the cup. Percy stayed right in the fight, dropping a neat little pitch seven feet past the hole. My try for a three, down the skiddy surface, stopped a foot above the cup. It laid Percy a partial stymie. He made a brave attempt to duplicate his impossible putt on the thirty-fifth. He slid the ball safely past mine by a hair's breadth, but this time his ball just failed to contact the rim as it shivered on the lip. It was a cruel way for Percy to have to lose after so courageous a performance.

Percy Alliss: In such a delicate stroke, steadiness of hand counts for much. Nervousness is the most general and the most charitable explanation of shakiness in this respect. It is an unfortunate and seemingly unfair handicap that one player should be more afflicted with nerves than another, and his weakness is naturally accentuated when he sets himself to play what is often the deciding stroke of the hole. Nervousness has every encouragement in green play: the shot is frequently a critical one, there is an atmosphere of expectancy and criticism which is felt too easily, and the necessity for almost complete muscular relaxation forbids any bracing of the system.

Sam Snead: Then along came Shute. He overran the green into a drainage ditch. This was a shot I wanted to see. And then another English doll in a big hat scooped up the ball and tossed it into the clear.

'Madam, you simply can't do that,' said a bystander.

'Oh, but it was in such a horrible place,' she whinnied.

Shute got his par, which enabled him to halve his match with Sam King and split points.

Snead defeated Burton 5&4, Dudley beat Perry 2&1, and Picard rounded things off by dispatching Lacey 2&1 to claim the first victory by a US Ryder Cup team on British soil.

Sam Snead: Our team took home the Ryder Cup by a score of 8–4. With women like that around, I wondered how England ever had been able to rule the roost all over the world at one time.

On one of the early holes, forgetting to take one of the most common precautions, I hit a fairway wood after glancing at the ball.

'Beg your pardon,' said my opponent, 'but you've just played my ball.'

The loss-of-hole penalty tempted me to throw my brassie, but I held back when I remembered what temper can do to you. Hanging on, I won my Ryder Cup singles match, 5&4.

Walter Hagen: At the eighteenth tee I had been standing by Gene Sarazen's bag as he came up to drive off. I suggested that he use a spoon and play safe for a safe four to ensure our win. And following his successful play, I had accompanied the Prince of Wales into the clubhouse for a hoot and to make a few notes on some cards to make certain I'd remember all I intended to say in the speech.

On the terrace in front of the clubhouse, a table and loudspeaker had been set up. The Prince, Charles Whitcombe, captain of the 1937 British team, and I took our places. I placed my cards on the table, convenient for me to push off one at a time for easy reading. Some 15,000 enthusiastic British spectators jammed the terrace, cheering and applauding loudly. The Prince stepped forward, presented me with the trophy and congratulated us on our victory. I accepted the cup and placed it on the table just as a swift gust of wind sliced around the loudspeaker and away went my cards.

The huge crowd waited in respectful silence for me to speak. I fumbled vainly in my mind for some memory of those notes. Then, 'I'm very proud and happy,' I said, 'to be the captain of the first American tea . . .' I hesitated a moment, then tossed caution to the duffers. 'I'm proud and happy to be the captain of the first American team to win on home soil.'

The crowd maintained a stunned silence, then a few giggled nervously. Finally a cockney voice called out from the back of the gallery, 'I say, High-gen, 'tis foreign soil, ye mean. Eh, old chappie?'

The gallery roared with appreciation of his correction. I'd blasted my way out of the rough too many times to let this slip throw me. I raised my hand to ask for silence, then grinned at them.

'Aye,' I said. 'And you'll forgive me, I'm sure, for feeling so much at home over here.'

Dai Rees putting on the 18th green at Southport during his singles victory over Byron Nelson.

There was a roar of applause and my ordeal was over. But I'm sure that was the fastest recovery shot I ever made.

Denny Shute: After we had won the Ryder Cup, Walter Hagen organised a bus to take us up to Scotland for the Open Championship. We left no pub un-stoned on that ride.

Walter Hagen: 1937 was the last year I captained the team . . . and the first time we won in the British Isles. The competition had run rather consistently since its inception in 1927. We won when the matches were played in the United States. Britain won when we played in the Isles. The fact that we'd finally scored a win on British soil was actually more important than the win itself.

Throughout these great matches such a wonderful spirit of competition and sportsmanship had existed; Fred Corcoran and I realised that the acceptance speech I would make when the Prince of Wales presented the cup to me at Southport would have to be one of extreme tact. I realised I must emphasise this first victory on foreign soil, and that I must make the British people feel our deep appreciation for their kindness and hospitality.

Dai Rees: That, as it happened, was the last Ryder Cup match before the war, and the series was not resumed until just ten years later, when we played at Portland, Oregon.

Lord Wardington presents the Ryder Cup to Walter Hagen.

SEVEN

1947
Portland Golf Club. Portland, Oregon
(USA 11, GB 1)

The 1939 Ryder Cup was due to be held at Ponte Vedra Country Club in Jacksonville, Florida, but due to the outbreak of the Second World War in September that year, the event was cancelled; The Times *carried the following notice on 5 September 1939: 'The PGA announce that the Ryder Cup match for this year has been cancelled by the state of war prevailing in this country. The PGA of the United States is being informed.'*

With the matches suspended for the duration of the conflict, a series of challenge competitions were played instead, primarily in America. In 1941, the US PGA selected a Ryder Cup team despite knowing that it couldn't compete in the event. This side included Walter Hagen as a non-playing captain (who had also been selected in the same role for the cancelled 1939 event), Jimmy Demaret, Vic Ghezzi, Ben Hogan, Lloyd Mangrum, Harold McSpaden, Byron Nelson, Gene Sarazen, Horton Smith, and Craig Wood.

When peace was declared in 1945, it took another two years to fully resurrect the Ryder Cup. While the majority of the elite golfers in the US had managed to maintain their careers throughout the course of the war, the same could not be said of their British counterparts. Many golf courses had been shut and with large swathes of professionals placed on active service there had effectively been no competitive tournaments held between 1940 and 1945. Indeed, it wasn't until 1946 that the first Open Championship was held, at St Andrews, since Dick Burton had won there in 1939. With rationing of food, clothing and petrol alongside other post-war privations still a prevalent part of life in the UK, the British team's preparations were gravely handicapped in comparison to their American cousins. But it didn't matter. It was the spirit of the competition that was of most importance and, after so many dark years, it was a wonderful tonic for all concerned to see the Ryder Cup back in action.

However, with British golf in such disarray, there was the significant obstacle of funding to overcome in order for the British PGA to send its team overseas to America. Furthermore, the US PGA was also struggling to muster the necessary funds to host the event. For several months, it looked as if the Ryder Cup might have to be cancelled once again – which could well have spelled the end of its existence. Fortunately, Fred Corcoran, the executive director of the US PGA, was able to woo the millionaire Robert Hudson into bankrolling the matches. A successful self-made man, Hudson, like Samuel Ryder, was a golf obsessive. He had already sponsored events around his hometown of Portland, Oregon, including the Portland Open in 1944 and 1945. During the 1946 PGA Championship – which he sponsored and which was won by Ben Hogan – Hudson heard about the financial difficulty surrounding the planned resurrection of the Ryder Cup. Over the following months he met with Corcoran several times and was ultimately persuaded to underwrite the seventh staging of the event, on the proviso that it was played in Oregon.

Opposite: Britain's Fred Daly.

The British team had only three players returning from the defeat at Southport in 1937 – Henry Cotton, Dai Rees and Sam King. The fresh blood in the team came in the form of the Open champion Fred Daly, Jimmy Adams, Max Faulkner, Eric Green, Reg Horne, Arthur Lees and Charlie Ward.

Ben Hogan captained a strong American team made up of Herman Barron, Jimmy Demaret, EJ Harrison, Herman Keiser, Lloyd Mangrum, Byron Nelson, Ed Oliver, Sam Snead and Lew Worsham.

Hudson did not hold back with his generosity. The British team travelled by first-class accommodation aboard the Queen Mary, *he held welcome parties for them at the Waldorf Astoria in New York and transported them to Oregon aboard a luxury train. The only thing that he could not account for was the weather, as the worst rain storms in sixty-five years battered the course in Portland, with over an inch of rain falling the night before the match began. But this took nothing away from the event, nor did the scoreline as the US thumped the visitors, very nearly securing the only whitewash in the history of the Ryder Cup. Fortunately for British pride, Sam King won the very last game of the contest 4&3 against Herman Keiser, securing the only point for Britain in an 11–1 drubbing. The score was humiliating, but after the deprivations and the horrors of the war, it was insignificant. The Ryder Cup was back.*

Henry Cotton: I was due to captain the team in 1939, but when the matches had to be cancelled because of the war, I sent a telegram to the US PGA which said, 'When we have settled our differences and peace reigns, we will see that our team comes across to remove the Ryder Cup from your safekeeping.' Who would have thought then that it would be another eight years before we would contest the Ryder Cup again?

Byron Nelson: The team for 1939 was already chosen, then it seemed like we'd done that for nothing because any moment the whole world was going to war. But there were a lot of people interested in the Ryder Cup, not just the pros but people interested in golf and its future. OK, if we couldn't play the English fellows, let's figure out a way to play among ourselves.

Jimmy Demaret: While the war was still in full flow there were no Ryder Cup matches with the British, but we played some exhibition matches over the next few years at home until the Ryder Cup could resume properly again. In those war years, we would have a Ryder Cup team play an invitational 'challengers' team in a series of charity matches. Gene Sarazen had been left out of the 1939 team and hadn't been one of Walter Hagen's captain's picks. He overheard Hagen talking about what a great team the '39 guys were and Gene decided to challenge him with a team of his own – for which I was selected. We played the first of these in 1940 at Oakland Hills and the Ryder Cup team won 7–5, although I was paired with Ben Hogan in the fourball and won. In 1941, Gene managed to get Bobby Jones out of retirement to play in the match at Detroit Golf Club, and there was a big upset because we won 8½ to 6½; again Hogan and I were paired together and won. We played again in 1942 and this time the Ryder Cup team beat the challengers 10–5 at Oakland Hills; I had swapped sides for that one and was on the victorious Ryder Cup team.

I suggested to the PGA that we play the 1943 match at my home course of Plum

Hollow. Walter Hagen had been left out of the Ryder Cup team that year so he captained the challengers, and I was again on the Ryder Cup team. We had over 10,000 people come out to watch the final day; we won 8½–3½, and raised a lot of money for the Red Cross.

During the war, those modified Ryder Cup matches were the crown jewel of professional golf in the US. The Majors had been cancelled for the duration of the war, so they were the big events. And from our point of view, it kept us playing in a competitive environment. That advantage told significantly when things resumed with the British in 1947.

Max Faulkner: We didn't forget about the Ryder Cup in Britain at all, but there was so much else going on with the war that it became a low priority. Even when the war ended, we weren't sure if the competition would be on again.

We had heard that the chaps in America had carried on playing a Ryder Cup competition of sorts, but apart from that there was very little competitive golf happening. But as I say, we had far too much else going on to think much about that. The issue of the survival of the Ryder Cup was not a priority.

Gene Sarazen: It didn't look good for the future of the Ryder Cup. Once the war was over, there was some room for hope, but who knew what would happen, what kind of shape everyone was in. There was very little to be sure about.

Dai Rees: Before the 1947 match there were for me and many other British golfers several years of war effort of one kind or another. No one, of course, was untouched by the war. Many were shattered by its impact, and I must rank myself and mine among the fortunate ones, but in those September days of 1939 it did seem to me, way down in the middle of Surrey, that war could not have come at a more inconvenient time.

British golf had by no means recovered from the ravages of war and we were scarcely prepared, in playing strength or financial resources, for sending a team to America so soon. But we did our best, helped by the generosity and kindness of Mr Bob Hudson, a citizen of Portland, who had done so much for professional golf on both sides of the Atlantic.

Max Faulkner: What Robert Hudson did was marvellous. He did everything he could and would not accept a penny back, nothing more than a thank you. We wouldn't be talking here about the Ryder Cup today if it wasn't for him.

Byron Nelson: I felt sorry for the British players because they hadn't been able to play golf or do anything since fighting the war over there. But they were very nice and everyone treated them well and they had a good time.

Dai Rees: It was a memorable trip, thanks mainly to Mr Hudson, but from a playing point of view a disappointing one. We were soundly whacked as we had expected to be, the only British player to avert defeat being Sam King, who beat Herman Keiser.

George Duncan: The contest in 1947 took place at Portland, Oregon, in which the unassuming Sam King proved Britain's solitary victor. Awful conditions of rain and mud handicapped the British team more than the American – conditions in which I thought we should have been more 'at home'.

Before that match, Henry Cotton, captain of the British team, was invited to inspect the Americans' clubs, did so, was not satisfied with some of them, and in consequence, 'rough spots' had to be filed or sandpapered off the faces.

Similarly at Ganton in 1949, clubs belonging to three British players did not pass the scrutiny of US non-playing captain, Ben Hogan, and one of them was not approved until the morning of the first day.

Don't blame either Cotton or Hogan for what they had a right to insist upon. Blame the fact that there is no definite ruling laid down for club inspection. There is an erroneous notion that visitors' clubs should not be inspected – neither the British team in Portland nor the American team at Ganton were asked to do so by the respective 'home' captains – but I think that all the clubs should go in for official scrutiny. Everyone would welcome it.

Henry Cotton: 1947 was the year we got thrashed; not too surprising as we travelled to America by ship and then travelled almost five days by train, 3,000 miles across the American continent. We played with the British-made large ball, which was not a very good one at that time, and on a course we never really saw, as it was practically under water, and after being there seven days we still had not practised properly. Robert Hudson, who was the host for both teams, asked if we would please play the match. It was costing him many thousands of dollars a day and the weather forecast was endless rain. We agreed and got badly beaten. I did enquire, as I kept up my friendship with Bob, 'When did the rain finally stop?' It was thirty days later, so we did Bob a good turn. He remained a friend of the British Ryder Cup players that year, and many other home players, right up until his death, which came at a period when he had lost his fortune.

Gene Sarazen: I think that when Snead, Nelson and Hogan came into the Ryder Cup, that team became too strong for the British. Look at what those three have done, and they were at their prime. How could any team match up against them?

Bobby Jones: I was always tense before I went out. I couldn't have done anything if I hadn't been. The days I didn't feel anything, I didn't score. Nelson is of the same temperament. Hogan, Hagen, Sarazen, I don't think they feel anything. They aren't built that way.

Doug Ford: I think Snead's the greatest player who ever lived. But then you talk to Snead, and he'll tell you how great Byron Nelson was. And I thought Hogan might have been a better player than Nelson. But Snead still, to me, could hit the best shots, and he could hit all the shots.

Henry Cotton: Sam Snead, that great swinger of the club (perhaps the greatest ever) has the most remarkable arms and hands. He has double-jointed wrists, which helps him tremendously, and is so strong that he used to do one-handed press-ups as if he weighed five stone rather than thirteen.

Ken Venturi: You can always argue who was the greatest player, but Byron Nelson was the finest gentleman the game has ever known.

Bobby Jones: I played some pretty good golf from time to time, but I never played anything like Byron.

Sam Snead: Ben Hogan may have been the greatest golfer of my generation. Nobody was as dedicated to golf as he was. He threw everything else aside. We might have been buddies in another life, but it just so happened that we both came into our prime at exactly the same time. It was fated that we'd become the two great rivals of American golf.

Byron was a very gentle man, but he had a streak of steel. He was a very tough competitor but very fair. When he was playing well, he kept pretty much to himself, but when he got off his game, he became very talkative.

Byron Nelson: Sam was like a cat. His coordination and his movements were so athletic, so different from most players'. When I was playing with Sam, he would surprise you with the things he could do. We would walk off a tee, and if there was a bench there, he'd hop over it just like a rabbit.

From left to right: Jimmy Adams and Max Faulkner shelter from the rain alongside Ben Hogan and Jimmy Demaret before their foursome match.

Jimmy Adams putts during the foursomes.

Sam Snead: Golf is two games, played in two ways and in two places. The first game is played by hitting your ball through the air. The second is played by rolling your ball on the ground. Some people have the nerve and the ability to roll it on the ground. It doesn't take any strength to speak of, but it takes mind, concentration, and muscle control.

Max Faulkner: I am a great believer in studying the swings of my fellow professionals, particularly those of the leading Americans. Sam Snead certainly repays detailed analysis. Few men drive with such controlled power. The distances he gets are phenomenal, yet there is a surprising absence of outward force of straining. He gets his power from the developed back muscles which he brings into use by an emphasised full backward turn. He winds up with a fluency that only Bobby Jones could rival. At impact he uses his body and arms as he lashes the club through the ball.

Sam Snead: Nothing ever stays the same in golf. Just when you think you've got it all figured out, the game jumps up and reminds you that you haven't begun to figure it out at all.

Gene Sarazen: Ben Hogan is the most merciless player of all the modern golfers. His temperament may derive from the rough, anguished years of his childhood or the hostility he sensed he encountered as a young and overdetermined circuit chaser. Whatever the reason, he is the type of golfer you would describe as perpetually hungry.

Bobby Jones: Hogan is the hardest worker I've ever seen, not only in golf but in any other sport.

Ben Hogan: Well, I think anyone can do anything he wants to do if he wants to study or work hard enough. I really believe that. And relating to golf, I think, if you study and work hard enough, you can do almost anything you want to do with a golf ball in the air.

Byron Nelson: I remember one funny thing about that Ryder Cup. Herman Barron and I were playing in our alternate-shot match. I was the captain of our twosome, and we were one up going to the seventeenth, a par three. I put my tee shot eight feet from the pin, and the British were fifteen feet away. Herman was a wonderful putter and I had complete confidence in him, so when we walked on the green, I got this idea in my head that I would give the other guys their putt, which I did. Barron looked at me like I was completely crazy, and said as much to me. But I just said, 'Herman, I have no doubt at all that you'll make this putt.' Which of course he did, and we ended up winning the match nicely.

Dai Rees: I partnered Sam King in the foursomes against Herman Barron and my old rival Byron Nelson, and we lost 2&1 after a real battle. In the singles I lost 3&1 to Jimmy Demaret. Considering I had played so little I was not displeased with my form, and felt that with more competitive play I should soon be at my best again. I'm sure all the other chaps in the team felt that way, so we looked forward to the return match in 1949.

Dai Rees is all smiles with Jimmy Demaret despite suffering a heavy defeat at the American's hands.

EIGHT

1949

Ganton Golf Club. Scarborough, England

(USA 7, GB 5)

After the long years of the war, there was great excitement in Britain at the prospect of the Ryder Cup matches returning to those shores twelve years since the last instalment there. And although British golf was still in a crippled state, there was a sense that matters would 'return to normal' and that the home team would once again start to dominate each encounter.

The hopes of the British fans would have been spurred by the absence among the American playing ranks of one of the finest golfers in the history of the game. On 2 February 1949, just hours after finishing second in the Phoenix Open, Ben Hogan and his wife Valerie were involved in a horrific road accident. Both were incredibly lucky to be alive after the car was ploughed into by a Greyhound coach, but Hogan suffered terrible injuries. In a remarkable show of resilience and power of recovery, Hogan was back playing again (albeit in excruciating pain) just eleven months later.

In the interim, he agreed to maintain his position as captain of the 1949 American Ryder Cup team, albeit in a non-playing capacity. His presence not only delighted golf fans who celebrated his remarkable recovery, but it also steeled his team.

Hogan and his players arrived in Southampton after a six-day voyage, focused on retaining the cup at Ganton Golf Club in Scarborough. Despite the absence of Hogan and two other top US players (Byron Nelson had retired from serious competition and US Open winner Cary Middlecoff was not a PGA member and was therefore ineligible for selection), the American team remained ominously potent. Four players returned from the 1947 instalment – Demaret, Harrison, Mangrum and Snead – and debuts were handed to Stewart (Skip) Alexander, Bob Hamilton, Chick Harbert, Clayton Heafner and Johnny Palmer.

The British team was once again captained by Charles Whitcombe, and featured seven players who had been thrashed at Portland – Adams, Daly, Faulkner, King, Lees, Rees and Ward – alongside Ken Bousfield and the 1939 Open champion, Dick Burton.

Despite the goodwill shown towards Hogan and the general excitement at seeing the American team in action, a media storm was created upon their arrival at Southampton. The great benefactor of 1947, Robert Hudson, had once again expressed his generosity by supplying the team with a rich supply of meat, aware that such luxuries were in short supply in rationed Britain. But the British press did not take kindly to seeing the vast quantities of steak, rib-eye beef, ham and bacon that were unloaded from the Queen Elizabeth. *Hogan tried to appease the furore by saying, 'We aren't going to eat all those steaks ourselves . . . we want to do something and give your British golfers some,' but his appeal fell on deaf ears and the US team had to endure some difficult days as the story made headlines around the country.*

On the eve of competition, Hogan raised further controversy when he demanded an inspection of the British players' clubs (although, in fairness, Henry Cotton had demanded a

Opposite: Arthur Lees tees off during his singles match against Jimmy Demaret.

similar inspection of the US team's clubs in 1947). Having gone through every single club he complained about the grooves on several of them. The British team met with Royal and Ancient Rules of Golf Committee member Bernard Darwin that evening, and Darwin said the clubs should be repaired down to meet the requisite standards. The Ganton Golf Club pro, Jock Ballantine, spent the evening filing away the prohibited grooves.

The following day, despite the hullabaloo about their clubs and the adjustments made to them, the British team raced out of the traps in the foursomes.

Jimmy Adams and Max Faulkner defeated EJ Harrison and Johnny Palmer 2&1 at the thirty-fifth hole, before Ken Bousfield and Fred Daly defeated Skip Alexander and Bob Hamilton 4&2. Demaret and Heafner pulled back a point for the US against King and Ward, winning 4&3, but then Burton and Lees saw off the formidable challenge of Mangrum and Snead by one hole to put Britain 3–1 going into the singles.

George Duncan: Expenses have risen tremendously since the first match was staged, and the cost of sending a team across the Atlantic for a two-day engagement is £5,000 or more, despite the fact that the country staging the match acts as hosts as soon as the visiting team reaches its shores. The Ganton contest of 1949 cost £8,000 to put on.

These international duels are appreciated by the golfing public, and especially by the British, despite the lamentable record of our golfers. We've got to breed and coach a new, tough young school who will match their American counterparts in skill, spirit, and cunning. And no one will like it more than the Americans themselves.

It is perhaps opportune for a change in the conditions of the Ryder Cup matches. At first it was decided that any professional resident in either country could compete for the side of his adoption as so many Scots had emigrated to the States. However, it was considered unfair to Britain and altered to allow only those born and resident in the respective countries to compete.

With the rapid development of the game in America, their bigger population, and the better opportunity they have for playing all-the-year-round golf in big competitions, it is surely sensible to suggest that Britain should be allowed to include in her team any outstanding professionals of the Commonwealth.

Such recognition of good Commonwealth golfers would not only help to improve the standard at home, but act as a tonic for any good Canadians and New Zealanders, of whom we hear so little in the golf world.

Just pause a moment to study the figures. In the first eight Ryder Cup contests from 1927 to 1949, with a ten years' gap owing to the Second World War, Britain won ten foursomes matches and eighteen singles against America's nineteen and forty-one respectively, with a total of eight halved. Making it still more specific, over the same period America won 275 holes – 96 in the foursomes and 179 in the singles – against Britain's 104 – 26 in the foursomes and 78 in the singles.

Dai Rees: In 1949 the Ryder Cup was at Ganton, near Scarborough, where the officials had got everything in wonderful order. But to this day I cannot understand why they watered the fairways so much. It was crazy and made things easy for the Americans, who, after losing the foursomes 1–3, turned on the heat on the second day and won six of the eight singles. Jimmy Adams beat Johnny Palmer 2&1, and I had a field day beating Bob Hamilton 6&4. Immediately my match was over I ran from one game to another, trying to give our men some moral support, but it was to no avail, and America kept the cup. The United States team was captained by the great Ben Hogan, just recovering from the accident in which he nearly lost his life.

Jimmy Demaret: After a terrible – and that's the only word for it – automobile accident in 1949, Ben Hogan pulled together a broken and pain-racked body, learned to walk and move about again, hit another million balls off the practise tee, gradually to regain his strength and skill, and started a second, even greater, golfing career. They have had to pull out all the stops and run down a long list of adjectives to describe this one – stirring . . . unbelievable . . . great . . . magnificent. The newspaper boys called it everything they could think of and in bold type.

I remember going to see him in hospital after the crash. I had beaten him in a play-off that day at the Phoenix Open and he and Val were driving home when they hit some heavy fog. A Greyhound bus coming the opposite way tried to overtake a truck and it ploughed head on into the Hogans' Cadillac. Ben only survived because he flung his body sideways at the last moment to try to protect Val. The steering wheel of Ben's car whistled straight back and buried itself in the seat. If Hogan had stayed behind the wheel and had not tried to protect his wife, he would have been impaled on the steering apparatus and undoubtedly killed.

They thought he was dead at first, but he rallied and they got him to hospital. For two days he couldn't be moved. On the third day in the hospital, Friday, they took X-rays and encased his body in a plaster cast from his chest to his knees and another on his ankle. He was in this condition when I arrived on Monday, after driving over from Tucson. All the way to his room I was trying to think what to say to him. You know, one of those sunny 'get well' remarks, but the words weren't forming. When I walked into his room, I just gave him a natural greeting, natural for us anyway.

'Ben, you old son of a bitch. Just because I beat you in a play-off, you didn't have to get so mad that you tried to run a bus off the road.'

The little man got a kick out of it. He gave me a weak laugh and then he said, 'Aw, I'll beat this thing.' A little later he said it again. 'I'll be back there playing real soon.' But the doctors made no secret of their opinion that he might not even be able to walk properly again and he would never play golf again. It made it difficult to look at Ben and say 'Sure, you'll be out there in another play-off with me before you know it.'

Ben planned his recovery with scientific detachment. He was going to handle the situation 'just like a round of golf. I'm going to play it one shot at a time.'

In August I stopped in to see Ben and told him the professionals wanted him to be the non-playing captain of the Ryder Cup team which was to meet England's [sic] best in September overseas. Ben came along and turned himself into the toughest captain I've ever heard of. 'Hey, Hawk!' I used to shout at him, 'We training for golf or for the Army?'

Ben carried his practise mania a little too far, for my tastes. For me, a foreign trip is always a business and pleasure combination. I planned to play a little golf, relax, and see what makes Piccadilly Circus go around.

Lloyd Mangrum and Sam
Snead.

But when we got to Ganton, where the match was to be held, the old Hogan practise bug had bitten. The man began to lay down practise rules the like of which I had never heard in twenty years of golf. He scheduled exact practise times and special competitive practise rounds – all of them early in the morning – and even decided the number of hours we were supposed to sleep every night.

The first day when I showed up for practise at about one in the afternoon, pretty early for me, I found Ben walking around the tee and spluttering. 'Aren't you going to give this routine a try, or what?' he said to me right off. 'You were supposed to play eighteen holes at ten o'clock. Come on now, Jimmy, let's get going.'

'Aw, Ben,' I told him. 'I'm still operating on Texas time. It's only six o'clock in Houston right now and that's plenty early for me to be playing golf.'

We kept up a running argument about practise and sleeping hours the whole time we were in England. I'd say the debate ended in a draw: I practised twice as much as usual but half as much as Ben wanted me to.

Max Faulkner: I remember that year the Americans brought their own steaks to have for dinner. They brought a steak for each of us on the team, too – but didn't give them to us until the last night, when the match was over.

George Duncan: In 1949 it appeared that at last we had a winning hand when we gained our biggest lead ever in the foursomes by three matches to one – thanks to Fred Daly and Ken Bousfield (playing in his first Ryder Cup), Jimmy Adams and Max Faulkner, and Dick Burton and Arthur Lees. But Ben Hogan called his boys together and gave them battle orders for the singles on the day. And did those fellows respond! They won six of the eight singles for a final 7–5 triumph.

The British team played some grand stuff to finish with an aggregate of thirty-four under-fours for the 257 holes played in the singles but it was not good enough. The Americans finished in fifty-six under-fours. Fred Daly was eight under-fours for 33 holes and Sam King six under, and yet each was beaten – Daly by Lloyd Mangrum (twelve-under) and King by Chick Harbert (ten-under).

Lloyd Mangrum: I patterned my swing after Sam Snead's, my short shorts after Johnny Revolta's, and my putting after Horton Smith's. In my own mind I was copying their style, but actually I was undoubtedly adapting all of these to my own version.

The US comeback in the singles began with Harrison's 8&7 victory over Faulkner, but all that good work was undone when Adams defeated Palmer 2&1 in the next match. Snead played beautifully to secure a 6&5 victory over Ward, only for Rees to reply in kind with his 6&4 win over Hamilton. Momentum was very much with the home team, but the US staged an incredible comeback, one of the finest in sport by that date, by storming down the home straight, winning the final four singles matches (Heafner defeating Burton 3&2, Harbert defeating King 4&3, Demaret defeating Lees 7&6, and Mangrum defeating Daly 4&3) to win the Ryder Cup 7–5.

George Duncan: 'Our team played their hearts out,' commented Hogan afterwards.

'They are a team of robots,' said British non-playing captain, Charlie Whitcombe, 'but I would still like to thank my boys for doing all I asked of them.'

In that 'furnace', two British players stood out – little Dai Rees and burly Jimmy Adams. Like Mangrum, Rees finished in twelve under-fours for thirty-two holes to beat Bob Hamilton, and Adams was five-under for thirty-five holes in vanquishing Johnny Palmer, who had been runner-up to Sam Snead in the US match play championship.

The case of Rees provided an object lesson for British golf. He was 'sore' at being left out of the foursomes and went out with grim purpose in the singles. The following week, he won the match play championship at Walton Heath for the third time in his career. We could do with a little more of that 'needle' spirit.

Jimmy Demaret: All Ben [Hogan] was able to do in England was to watch and force his team to get in a little practise time. But when he came back to Fort Worth, he picked up those golf sticks again and started practising. He dragged himself out on to the Colonial Country Club and started to hit golf balls. At first, he must have been a pathetic figure. He could move his legs very little. He hit the ball from a still position with his arms. His caddie that first day remarked that 'he looked all right when he putted and chipped, but when he tried to hit some wood shots I couldn't believe this was Ben Hogan. A little kid could have hit a longer ball.'

But by January 1950, only a year after the accident, Ben Hogan was up and ready. We played together at the Los Angeles Open and it was the first golf I'd seen Ben shoot since I beat him in the Phoenix play-off a year before. Yet it seemed as if he hadn't been away from golf for more than eight hours. He walked over that course and absolutely wrecked par, coming home with a 68. His woods were perhaps not as long as before, but plenty long enough. His irons were operating like Detroit-made machines and his putter was behaving nicely. Ben Hogan was once again the man to beat.

NINE

1951

Pinehurst Country Club. Pinehurst, North Carolina
(USA 9½, GB 2½)

With the US team having enjoyed such resounding success in the previous two Ryder Cups, there was little need to change the core of players who had established the winning formula. So it was that stalwarts returned to the fold for the ninth edition of the matches in the form of Jimmy Demaret, Ben Hogan, Lloyd Mangrum and Sam Snead (who captained the team), recent additions from 1947 in Skip Alexander, EJ Harrison, Clayton Heafner and Ed Oliver, and two extremely promising rookies in Jack Burke Jnr and Henry Ransom.

In the intervening years, Hogan had returned to playing again, despite enduring considerable physical pain, to complete one of the most moving and inspirational comeback stories in the history of sport. The man who barely escaped with his life and was then told that it was unlikely that he would even walk properly again, was back to his imperious best, claiming victories in the 1948 PGA Championship and US Open, the 1950 US Open, and the 1951 Masters and US Open. As a symbolic totem for the American Ryder Cup team, Hogan had it all.

Alexander's appearance in the team was as remarkable as Hogan's. On 24 September, 1950, he was the lone survivor of a plane crash that left him with over seventy per cent of his body badly burned. He endured seventeen operations, one of which fused his fingers so that he could hold a golf club. It was an astonishing achievement for him to return to golf at all, let alone scale the heights to the elite level again.

The British team that year was captained by Arthur Lacey (in a non-playing capacity) and also included two rookies in John Panton and Harry Weetman, while the rest of the squad returned from the endeavours of 1947 and 1949 looking to atone for their recent losses: Adams, Bousfield, Daly, Faulkner (recently crowned Open champion), Lees, Rees and Ward.

Just as in Portland in 1947, the weather at Pinehurst was atrocious, which suited the American team who proved to be longer hitters than their British counterparts. In the opening day's foursomes, the home team raced into an early lead, with only the partnership of Lees and Ward able to salvage anything for the visitors in their 2&1 victory over Oliver and Ransom. The rest of the matches went to the US with Burke and Heafner defeating Faulkner and Rees 5&3, Mangrum and Snead defeating Adams and Panton 5&4, and Demaret and Hogan defeating Bousfield and Daly 5&4.

Jack Burke Jnr: Whatever else is going on in the world, the real institutions never change. There can be wars, depressions, social troubles, or bad economies, but the Ryder Cup stands as a constant symbol of competition, sportsmanship and camaraderie. It has tremendous value because of that, and the players should always keep that in mind. They're playing for something that is honourable, that has stood the test of time and is worthy of their respect and best efforts.

Opposite: Max Faulkner and Harry Weetman.

The players, the rookies especially, as I was in 1951, have to look past the hoopla that goes with the Ryder Cup. It is not an exhibition. It's a serious professional competition, and you'd better bring your A game. If you aren't prepared, your game will not hold up because this is pressure like you've never known it.

Fred Daly: I have many memories of Pinehurst, one of which is the tremendous interest the caddies took in their master's game. I remember I was playing with Ken Bousfield, and after Ken had hit a very fine shot, the caddie remarked: 'Suh, that's the kinda shot I likes to walk after.'

I was greatly impressed with the young American caddies generally. They are very knowledgeable and many of them were good golfers. In Britain I think that the race of professional caddies is dying out. There are few real caddies nowadays and the increasing popularity of caddie-cars means that in years to come the number of genuine caddies will grow less. In America the caddie is still an institution.

Jack Burke Jnr: As a player, I never felt I had the mental freedom of intellect to incorporate the fine points of team play. I felt it was useful to consider beforehand who would hit first in foursomes, but once a team match started I was too focused on trying to hit the shots to worry about strategy, there's just too much stress that thinking clearly becomes difficult. You want to manage yourself as best you can, use your instincts, and just play golf.

My strategy was simple: I wanted to try to beat the other team on my own ball, I never wanted to be dependent on my partner. If he made a birdie, I considered that a bonus. I knew that if I played really well, any contribution at all from my partner would be enough to carry us to a win.

My partner in the 1951 Ryder Cup foursome matches was Clayton Heafner. Clayton was a terrific player, a long hitter, and a fabulous shotmaker. But he wasn't a good putter, and when he played with people who could putt, he carried a type of resentment about it.

On the third hole of our match against Max Faulkner and Dai Rees, Clayton put his approach shot onto the fringe about fifteen feet from the hole. It was my turn to play, and after looking the shot over carefully, I chose to putt instead of chip. I ran the putt into the hole for a win, and looked up at Clayton for a sign of approval. That is not what he gave me. He strode towards me, frowning.

'You knew you were going to make that putt,' he said accusingly. I was stunned.

'Hey man, I'm on your side,' I answered. Clayton just walked to the next tee and left me standing there, shaking my head.

The singles were dominated just as brutally by the US, with Britain only managing to claim half a point from the Daly-Heafner match and a single point from their only victory of the day when Lees defeated Oliver 2&1. The rest was one-way traffic with Burke Jnr defeating Jimmy Adams 4&3, Demaret defeating Rees two-up, Mangrum defeating Weetman 6&5, Hogan defeating Ward 3&2, Alexander defeating Panton 8&7, and Snead defeating Faulkner 4&3 to return a final score of 9½-2½.

Harry Weetman: It was a great experience which I shall not forget, that visit to Pinehurst.

They just could not do enough for us, and I truly believe the Americans themselves were hoping we would do well. We were not very successful, I am afraid, but there is one thing I would say: we were soundly beaten, and I for one have no excuses to offer. There is no doubt about it, the American professionals are wonderful golfers, and playing under conditions they are accustomed to they give nothing away.

I would not say they are unbeatable, but, on the other hand, nobody can say they are easy meat. They have so many players to choose from and the tournament circuit over there is so tough that only the very best golfers can survive. To survive they must reach the highest possible degree of proficiency, and to do that they practise until their hands hurt. We do not practise nearly enough in Britain.

Dai Rees: Jimmy Demaret was just astounding when I played him in the singles. He hit eleven greenside bunkers but still beat me. On the seventeenth he holed from the greenside bunker to win two-up. After I had congratulated Jimmy on his bunker play he made a typically American generous gesture, handed me his sand iron and said, 'Keep it, Dai, as a gift. The one you've got has too sharp an edge and you'll never have any finesse with it.' I took the club to Britain and had it copied for my own set so that, although I lost the match, I came away with a profit.

Jack Burke Jnr: Many people don't know how unbelievably bright Jimmy Demaret was. He had a mind like a Swiss watch, a tremendous mind. He became a pilot, and he could handle boats with big engines. He had a great memory. I don't think people know how complicated he was. He socialised a lot and many people thought that he could have won more if he had concentrated on playing more than socialising, but whatever way you look at it, he was a very, very fine golfer.

Sam Snead: I think Jimmy would have won more had he tended to business, but that's just the way he was. But his Ryder Cup record was second to none. From 1947 to 1951 he had a perfect record of six wins and no losses.

Ben Hogan: Jimmy was the most underrated golfer in history. This man played shots I haven't even dreamed of. I learned them. But it was Jimmy who showed them to me first.

Jack Burke Jnr: Jimmy had a simple move. He knew where the face of the club was at all times. The club broke the same way every time. He didn't really have to practise. Ben [Hogan] copied Jimmy's game. Jimmy was a left-to-right player, and Hogan didn't carve a career for himself until he started moving the ball left to right.

Jimmy Demaret: 1951 was the last time that Hogan and I played in the Ryder Cup. After recovering from his car crash in 1949, Hogan was still battling with leg pain and didn't feel he could continue with match play – thirty-six holes were just too much for him. As for me, I was happy to retire after three Ryder Cups with a record of never losing a match.

Harry Weetman: Jimmy Demaret in particular is a great character, particularly at a party when he does his singing act as good as anybody I have ever heard on the stage. On the course Jimmy has a very fine line in multi-coloured clothes that make Max Faulkner seem quite sombre in comparison!

Jack Burke Jnr: The Ryder Cup to me has always been almost holy. During my heyday in the 1950s, it really was the focal point of my whole year. As a player I used it as my chief frame of reference. Week in and week out, all I tried to do was play well enough to make the team. If I accomplished that, I knew I was playing pretty darned well.

Dai Rees: The United States had a wonderful team, with players like Snead, Demaret, Ben Hogan, Mangrum and Jack Burke Jnr. Over the two days only two of the matches reached the eighteenth hole. They really were a special group of players. And none more remarkable than Skip Alexander.

Skip Alexander: I was on a flight from Kansas City to Louisville on 24 September, 1950. Halfway through the flight the reserve fuel tank failed and the plane began to go down. Since we were near the Evansville airport, we banked in to land and almost made it, crashing on the edge of the field. The next thing I remember was trying to force my way out of the cabin door and meeting a wall of flames. I quickly shut the door and opened it again, running out of the wreck on my broken left ankle. I guess I got about fifty yards before I collapsed and the fuel tank exploded.

I spent five months in hospital and had seventeen different surgeries.

People thought my career was over, but I had 726 points secured towards qualification for the '51 Ryder Cup team. I was determined that I would make it.

My hands were all burned and skin-grafted. The extensors and other parts of the fingers were contracted so tightly that I didn't have any openings. The doctors opened them up. They took a knuckle out and fused the remaining two knuckles together so they would fit a golf club.

Fourteen months after the crash, I was in the team.

I didn't play in the Friday foursomes and we then took a break on the Saturday because there was a big football game on. The organisers said, 'In North Carolina when Carolina plays Tennessee in a football game on Saturday, nobody watches golf.' So they took the day off and we all went to the football game.

It was cold and (Dutch) Harrison got sick before the singles on Sunday, and Sam Snead came to me and said, 'Can you play?' I told him, 'Yes, I can play.'

I don't know whether it was mind games or whether he just thought he would sacrifice a point, but Sam put me up against John Panton, Britain's best player.

I was all bandaged up; my hands were bleeding. John Panton was a Vardon Trophy winner, Order of Merit winner, leading money winner and everything. I'd never walked thirty-six holes before that let alone played thirty-six, and it was a thirty-six-hole match. So I took off, and every time I played a hole, I wondered if I could play the next. But it worked out all right. I beat him 8&7, which, I heard, was the biggest margin that anybody had won by. I three-putted number ten though, in that afternoon round, or I might have won 9&8. I remember wondering if that was the beginning of the end and I wouldn't win another hole. As it turned out, it was. But what a match to win.

Arthur Lacey: I don't want to make any excuses as the US were a fine, winning team. But our boys did not play from the bunkers well nor were their short approaches as accurate as the Americans. They also couldn't get accustomed to the Bermuda grass or playing with the larger ball with the same expertness. But that sounds like sour grapes. We were well beaten. There can be no arguing with a 9½–2½ scoreline.

Harry Weetman: Courses on the other side of the Atlantic [in America] do differ from ours in two essentials. First, they have great wide open spaces that encourage big hitting from the tees, and, secondly, the greens are very heavily bunkered and have very narrow entrances.

The fact there is plenty of room for placing tee shots is to my mind the reason why so many of the Americans are so long from the tee, and the great tightness of the greens is the reason why the Americans are so accurate near the green.

To elaborate on this a little further, let us take the average par five hole in Britain. In favourable conditions long hitters can get on in two because the entrances to the green in the main are fairly wide. In America getting on in two at long holes is out of the question because your ball will almost invariably be trapped in the sand. That means it is the shot to green that really counts, and if you are going to pick up a shot and be down in four then the pitch has got to be near the hole. That is target golf, and because the Americans are confronted with that kind of shot regularly they take great pains to be expert at it. And because the American courses are so heavily bunkered near the greens, and these bunkers trap so many shots, it follows that our American friends are very good at getting out of bunkers. I have seen a lot of good golfers playing out of bunkers, but I think Mr Willie Turnesa is the best I ever saw at it.

You hear from time to time people saying the Americans beat us because they are better putters than we are. I do not think they are at all. Where the Americans score in putting is that they are better readers of the greens. Greens on American courses have a decided nap to them. This is due, I believe, to the texture of the grass, but anyway there is a nap, and you have got to consider your putts in the light of whether you are playing with the nap or against it. This the Americans have brought to a fine art and they have come to pay so much attention to this aspect of the game that they can read greens perfectly.

Some of the stars on the other side of the Atlantic coast are not getting any younger and certainly not getting any better. At the moment it looks as if they could also be doing with some youngsters. But the dratted thing is they will find them when they need them most and so keep on making the Ryder Cup match hard to win, particularly when the contest is over there.

I think they will always be a tough nut to crack in their own country because when our boys go over there they take so long to get acclimatised to the weather and to get familiar with conditions generally. As I said, they are not unbeatable – nobody is – but if we are going to be their masters and beat them in their own den with any success, then we shall have to raise our standard of golf, there is no doubt about it. But, anyway, long may we have healthy competition with our American friends. It is good for the players and it is good for golf generally.

TEN

1953

Wentworth Golf Club. Wentworth, England

(USA 6½, GB 5½)

Twenty-seven years since it had hosted one of the genesis matches, the Ryder Cup returned to Wentworth. Even though it had been twenty years since Britain had last held the cup, and had failed to even put up much of a challenge in an era of outright American dominance, the tenth Ryder Cup was, to the surprise of many, the most hotly contested since 1933.

Public interest in the Ryder Cup was now so great on both sides of the Atlantic that the contest had developed beyond the comfortable joie de vivre that so defined the early instalments, when taking part had been what mattered most. Now, with widespread glory to the triumphant, ignominy to the vanquished, it was all about winning.

It was therefore to the dismay of many in America when Ben Hogan, still at the very top of his game, declared himself unavailable for selection. Despite winning the Masters, the Open and the US Open that year, he did not feel that he had the stamina to play the required thirty-six holes a day as he continued his rehabilitation from his car accident.

With Hogan absent, the US team, captained by Lloyd Mangrum, may have lacked the stardust of previous years, but it was predictably strong nevertheless. Returning to the team were Jack Burke Jnr, Ed Oliver, and Sam Snead, who were joined by five rookies – Walter Burkemo, Dave Douglas, Fred Haas Jnr, Ted Kroll, Cary Middlecoff and Jim Turnesa.

The British team was captained by Henry Cotton and had an even balance of youth and experience, with Jimmy Adams, Fred Daly, Max Faulkner, John Panton, Dai Rees and Harry Weetman joined by debutants Peter Alliss (Percy's son), Harry Bradshaw, Eric Brown and Bernard Hunt.

Peter Alliss: It was very exciting to follow in father's footsteps, of course. He could have played, should have played maybe, if the rules had been different, two or three more times, but you had to be resident in the UK to be eligible for the team then and in 1931 he was a pro in Germany. 1933 was the last time we had won, so it was twenty years on, at Wentworth, which I was very fond of, and it had happy memories from my father. And the Ryder Cup was of great importance. It's interesting when people today sort of make out as if nobody was interested in it back then. We had about 6–8,000 people at Wentworth, and the Ryder Cup was only over two days then. It always looked very busy. It was very exciting. Henry Cotton was the captain; rationing was still on; we stayed at the Dormy House at Sunningdale, which is now an old folks' sort of home right opposite Sunningdale clubhouse. Henry Cotton knew a butcher so we had a few steaks, which was a great excitement. We actually had steak and a glass of red wine. I was only in my early twenties, it was a whole new world for me. It was very exciting.

Opposite: Sir Leonard Lyle, Baron Lyle of Westbourne (left) presents the Ryder Cup to American captain Lloyd Mangrum at Wentworth, 3 October 1953.

Eric Brown: It's been said that I hate Americans, but that is a gross exaggeration. What I do admit to is having had a fierce determination to beat Americans on the golf course – aye, even to show them no mercy when I had the chance. After all, British golfers had suffered thrashing after thrashing from our opposite numbers in the States. Part of our trouble, I'm sure, was that we treated the Americans as super-golfers; some of us were defeated before we had even started. There was nothing like showing an American that you thought you were just as good as he was, and in each of the Ryder Cup matches in which I played I made it my business to do just that – by word and by deed.

My introduction to the British Ryder Cup team is one I'll never forget. We weren't altogether a happy party for the 1953 match at Wentworth. In the days before the event we were ordered not to be in the company of wife or sweetheart, and driving a car was forbidden. Henry Cotton, our captain, was the man who issued the instructions, and some of us got the impression we were being treated like children.

Peter Alliss: It was very ordinary behind the scenes in those days. The ladies gave over their quarters in the clubhouse at Wentworth for the teams. There was a masseur there; well he was there for about fifty years at Wentworth. It was very low key compared to today. Then, of course, there was really no television, so it was all done in newsprint and newspaper people were there. It just had a two-minute or so piece on the news in the cinemas that week. It was very different.

The foursomes started ominously for the British and it looked at first as if the contest was set for another foregone conclusion early in the piece as the Americans raced into a 3–0 lead. Douglas and Oliver beat Weetman and Alliss 2&1, Mangrum and Snead beat Brown and Panton 8&7, and Kroll and Burke beat Adams and Hunt 7&5 before Daly and Bradshaw salvaged a point for the British by beating Burkemo and Middlecoff one-up.

Peter Alliss: I played alongside Harry Weetman against Dave Douglas and Ed Oliver in the opening match. I was nervous, but I thought Harry was more so; he was a much more established player than me. He didn't play very well and we only lost 2&1. I was quite pleased with the way I played, but he appeared to be much more nervous than I thought he would be. We were very much in the doldrums at half-time, 3–1 down, but then we came back a bit. I remember there was fog, early morning mist, so play was delayed for about an hour-and-a-half. Do you know, we got round in under three hours? It's a bit of a joke now. We were round with the spectators on the fairways, and we still got round in three hours. By today's standards, they wouldn't believe you.

Eric Brown: John Panton and I were teamed up in the second match against Lloyd Mangrum and Sam Snead, who at that time were probably the greatest match play couple in the world. This was Snead's fifth Ryder Cup match – he had played in the singles in 1937 at Southport and Ainsdale – and Mangrum's fourth. And they had been mates in the foursomes in the previous three matches. They had beaten Fred Daly and Charlie Ward 6&5 at Portland, Oregon, in 1947; lost by one hole to Dick Burton and Arthur Lees at Ganton in 1949; and beaten Panton and Jimmy Adams 5&4 at Pinehurst, North

Sam Snead and Max Faulkner practice before the competition at Wentworth.

Carolina, in 1951.

They proceeded to thrash Panton and yours truly even more severely – by 8&7.

They started 4, 2, 4, 3; won three of the first four holes; and, out in 34, were four up. My driving was erratic, and when I got it straightened out John lost his touch on the greens. At the 551-yard seventeenth Mangrum really had us spread-eagled, for he hit a three-wood to five feet from the pin, and Snead holed the putt for the eagle three. The Americans were eight up there, and that was their lead at the end of the round, for which they took 67 against our mediocre 76.

Though John and I were much steadier in the afternoon, ours was a hopeless task. Mangrum and Snead went out in 35 and when the match finished two holes later they were seven under-fours.

America won the first three foursomes – Daly and Harry Bradshaw took the last match by one hole – and Cotton was most displeased! He gave Harry Weetman and Peter Alliss some stick for their defeat and was almost as cross with Adams and Bernard Hunt. Much to our surprise, Panton and Brown got off lightly.

Harry Bradshaw: I remember being delighted to be paired with Fred Daly in my first Ryder Cup. And we were the only ones to win the foursomes which, of course, were thirty-six-hole matches in those days. I always thought Fred was a fantastic player and I'm proud of our unbeaten record, even in exhibitions against some of the greats from around the world.

He had a wonderful temperament. Whatever was happening in a match, he would just go along, whistling to himself. And if I put him on the green, he would take out the putter and the whistling would get even louder. I called him Fred but he sometimes called me Harry or Brad, I suppose depending on his mood.

In the match against Walter Burkemo and Cary Middlecoff we were three up at lunchtime after a morning round of 70. But things changed when the Americans won the thirtieth and thirty-first and we were eventually taken to the final hole, one up; that was where I hit a bad drive into the semi-rough down the left, but Fred hit some two-wood, right up the fairway.

25,000 people were there, hanging out of the beech trees on the right of the green. And the branches cracking under the weight. 'Look out! Look out!' they were shouting as fellows fell to the ground. I had this shot of maybe sixty, maybe seventy yards and as I walked up to it, my knees were knocking, looking at this crowd. I'd never seen anything like it in my life.

I said to Fred, 'I don't know whether to play a nine or a ten up there.'

'Just play what you like,' said Fred, throwing his hands up. And the mere fact of him doing that, gave me a lot of confidence. Whereas most fellows would say, 'Now leave this close and I'll hole the putt,' it didn't matter to Fred what club I played.

Anyway, I knocked it in to six feet and Fred holed the putt for a birdie. Burkemo and Middlecoff had missed the green on the right and nearly holed a chip for an eagle. Then, when it was over, there was a mad rush for Fred, and I've often said it to him since that but only for the police being there, they'd have knocked him into the hole after the ball.

Henry Cotton: I always thought of Harry Bradshaw's putting slogan of 'hitting and harking' as one of the best I ever heard. The genial Irishman was certainly a perfect example of not taking the eyes, or the head, from over the spot where the ball is until it arrives at the hole or is heard to rattle in the cup. On his best days, he was a superb putter.

At 3–1 down, things looked as bleak as ever for the home team, but they got off to a fine start in the singles when Fred Daly defeated Ted Kroll 9&7. Dai Rees battled hard with Jack Burke Jnr, but ultimately fell apart on the seventeenth when he three-putted to hand the match to the American. Eric Brown and Harry Weetman, however, managed to keep the British challenge alive when they secured two huge points by beating Lloyd Mangrum and Sam Snead two-up and one-up respectively, to take the score to 4–4.

Eric Brown: When we got to the course the next morning for the singles the newspaper bills were telling the world in their brief, bold way of Cotton's dissatisfaction with the team's display. Though John and I had more or less been spared the lash wielded by the captain, Henry had got my dander up.

'As for you,' he said, 'I've put you high up in the order for the singles, and all I want from you is one point.'

I was there to win if I could, and, just as disappointed as Henry was at our defeat in the foursomes and a bit browned off with the whole set-up, I retaliated with: 'You'll bloody well get your point!'

I wondered then and I've wondered since if Cotton had decided to use the psychology of a football manager in provoking players into trying even harder by being critical of them. Maybe Cotton thought I needed extra incentive, especially in view of the class of my opponent in the singles. Of one thing there wasn't a shadow of a doubt – I would need to play all I knew to justify my reply to the captain. For I was to meet Mangrum, conqueror in the singles in the three previous Ryder Cup matches of Max Faulkner, Daly, and Weetman. And, apart from the fact that I had on the previous day seen evidence of Mangrum's magnificent stroke-making, I knew full well what a fine temperament as well as ability he had.

They don't come any tougher than Lloyd Eugene Mangrum, the yellow-skinned Texan from Trenton, who won $192,000 between 1947 and 1958 and who shot an average round of 70.5 in 104 tournaments in 1951.

Guts? Any doubts about this man's make-up were dispelled when he finished the Second World War with three Purple Hearts pinned on his chest. He was a fighter, all right, as the American circuit and the golf world found in no uncertain manner when Uncle Sam handed him his demob papers.

And this was the man, the American Ryder Cup captain, who was to be my first Ryder Cup victim.

Cotton's order had turned out to be a tall one. I don't suppose Mangrum gave a thought one way or the other to the newcomer Brown, unless it was that what he had done in the foursomes to Brown he could do again in the singles. Brown, for his part, reckoned that if he were to beat an American it might as well be one of the best.

It came down to the thirty-sixth hole and he putted out for five. I had two putts from under six yards to win the match. Mangrum looked at me, at my ball, and then again at me, and said: 'Do you think you can get down in two from there?' A little puzzled, but not unduly disturbed, I replied: 'I'm quite sure I can.' Some of the spectators were eager listeners to this exchange of words, which continued with Mangrum saying: 'Well, let's just see you hit one, anyway.'

I putted cautiously to within a foot of the hole, and naturally expected Mangrum to concede the putt and come over and shake hands. But there was no move from Lloyd; his face was inscrutable. 'All right,' I said to myself, 'I'll play it your way.' I addressed the ball and, still looking down, said loudly enough for his and some of the spectators to hear: 'You must be expecting me to drop down dead,' and holed the putt. The victory was the greatest of my golfing career to that point.

I would like to say how sorry I felt for Peter Alliss and Bernard Hunt that last day. They, like myself and Harry Bradshaw, were new to the occasion, but Alliss at twenty-two and Hunt at twenty-three were the 'babies' of the side. In the end it was those two youngsters who had the heavy burden of responsibility; on them depended the winning or losing of the entire match.

Middlecoff pushed the US back into the lead when he beat Faulkner 3&1 and with Bradshaw defeating Haas 3&2 the spotlight fell on the last two matches out on the course, between Alliss and Turnesa and Hunt and Douglas.

One up on the eighteenth, Turnesa sliced his drive into the trees while Alliss was able to guide his safely down the fairway. Advantage was very much with the young Englishman, but the pressure told and as both men fluffed their lines badly to double-bogey and halve the hole, the point went to America.

All eyes were now on Hunt and Douglas, with Hunt needing to win in order to draw the overall score 6–6. Arriving at the eighteenth one up, Hunt just needed to halve the hole to secure the precious point for Britain. His initial drive was good, but his second shot sliced into the trees. He recovered from this to reach the green and he needed to two-putt for the win. Having sent his first putt from the back of the green to within four feet the pressure was at boiling point. It proved too much. Hunt missed, the match was halved and the cup was on its way back to America once more.

Bernard Hunt: I made a bit of pig's ear of it all in the foursomes. Then I played pretty well for much of the singles, but I went and mucked up eighteen to halve the match. I don't really know why I was involved in so many halves during my Ryder Cup career. It's just the way it turned out.

Peter Alliss: The team had been beaten so badly over in America in 1951 that there was a cry for new blood and Bernard Hunt and myself were selected to play. I was the youngest ever to have played, and my father and I were the first father-son combination.

I was paired against Jim Turnesa in the singles, who had just won the PGA Championship. I gave a very good account of myself, though, and was one up after fifteen. I hit a good drive on the sixteenth, but I ultimately took a five and he won the hole to make it all square.

I must have got nervous or something, I don't know. I finished 6, 7, 6 I think. And he finished nearly as badly as me, but he won two holes to beat me one-up. Then dear old Bernard came up and three-putted the last, so he only got a half. And if I'd done my bit and Bernard hadn't three-putted we'd have won, which would have been a huge boost to British golf at the time – but it wasn't to be.

I made an awful bodge of it. I've had to live my whole life with the guilt of messing up that chip from the moss.

You look back now on those tiny variables – if only I had managed to get that half point and if Bernard Hunt hadn't three-putted against Dave Douglas then we'd have won the Ryder Cup. We should have won. It still aches to this day.

Ken Brown: It stayed with Peter forever, missing that putt.

Peter Alliss: The papers had a field day. They ripped into us like nobody's business. Bernard recovered from that quicker than I did. I bore those wounds for . . . oh, several years. I kept meeting people who would say, 'Ah, I saw you, I saw you make a mess of it there.' Well, I reckon there must have been about 38,000 people around that last green for the number of people who said they were there and saw me make a mess of it. But it was an experience.

I took it very personally – I think because of my father and his influence in the world of golf; he was big stuff in the world of golf, the old man. And I thought I had let him down. It was a poor time.

Eric Brown: I thought the criticism of Alliss and Hunt was severe and unfair. Had they had a year or two more of experience, or had happened to play higher up in the order and been spared the extra responsibility, I'm sure, the other circumstances being the same, they would have succeeded.

Dai Rees: The 1953 match at Wentworth is fresh in the memory as another occasion, like that at Ganton, when we had dreams of victory rudely shattered. We lost in the end by one small point, and in fact by one putt. Peter Alliss and Bernard Hunt each had a chance on the last green. It would be uncharitable to call them short putts. No putt is a short one in such a crisis. But they were eminently holeable putts, and if both had gone down we would have won the cup. But both were missed. Alliss lost his match with Jim Turnesa instead of halving it. Hunt halved with Dave Douglas instead of beating him, and that was that.

I must say I had done little to help the cause. I was not played in the foursomes and in the singles I ran up against Jackie Burke in one of his best moods, and was beaten 2&1.

Henry Cotton: I was so proud to be captain in 1953. The boys worked very hard before the matches, playing thirty-six holes a day, getting ready for the match. At lunchtime between rounds we had a good meal; meat was still rationed, but people very kindly sent us steaks. We each had a glass of wine with every meal, because I thought that it was a good builder-up of nerves and strength. But the result was that they all passed out after lunch – which must have been very good for their nerves in the end anyway, and thirty-six holes in a day was just a walk. We lost by only one point, so near and yet so far. I think they all enjoyed their week and the routine, which was tough, tough enough to make Fred Daly exclaim, 'I'm walking me legs off – almost down to my knees!'

Lloyd Mangrum: My nerves were so shredded that I remember saying, 'I'll never, ever captain an American team again because of the 9,000 deaths I suffered in the last hour.'

Bernard Hunt: I missed the following Ryder Cup in 1955, which was Henry Cotton's fault. He told me that I would never be consistently good with that 'awful' swing. I didn't think it was too bad, then I saw it on Movietone News at the cinema. I must confess it didn't look good. Until then I imagined it was just like Ben Hogan's. Anyway, I took Cotton's advice and tried to sort it out but struggled and eventually reverted to my old swing, which was short and flattish.

The one whose swing I most admired is not terribly well known. His name is Ted Kroll. He was a bit like Mark O'Meara in that he had only a shortish swing, but he rifled it all the time. I thought his swing was great and I liked the man. He was a New Yorker and seemed so relaxed.

In my day, there were five or six in our team of twelve who were as good as the Americans. But the rest weren't. The problem was that we weren't deep enough. I think that we did as well as we did because we played as a team. Today it's a lot tighter. I would say the Americans could probably pick three teams whereas we could probably pick two.

ELEVEN

1955

Thunderbird Ranch and Country Club. Palm Springs, California
(USA 8, GB 4)

In an effort to redress the Ryder Cup balance, which had been heavily tilted in favour of the Americans, the British PGA altered their qualifying criteria. A list of tournaments, which included the Open, was drawn up in which players could earn qualifying points depending on where they finished. The top seven players were then automatic selections for the team and they were joined by three players chosen by the PGA committee.

Under this new selection format, the British team for the 1955 encounter at the Thunderbird Ranch and Country Club in Palm Springs was made up of debutants Christy O'Connor, John Fallon, John Jacobs and Syd Scott, and old hands Ken Bousfield, Harry Bradshaw, Eric Brown, Arthur Lees and Harry Weetman, while Dai Rees, appearing in his sixth Ryder Cup, was the playing captain. Peter Alliss and Bernard Hunt were unlucky to miss out and would have to wait until 1957 before they could attempt to redeem themselves from the pain of Wentworth.

The home team was captained by Chick Harbert and featured debutants Jerry Barber, Tommy Bolt, Doug Ford, Marty Furgol and Chandler Harper, while Jack Burke Jnr, Ted Kroll, Cary Middlecoff and Sam Snead returned.

Despite the new qualifying system designed to ensure the players in the best form and consistency were selected, the British effort was hit by a serious setback when the PGA Match play Champion, Ken Bousfield, picked up a stomach bug during the practise week and failed to make a single appearance in the matches.

Dai Rees: Our experience at Wentworth had convinced all concerned that British professional golf was recovering from the wastage of the war years, and we approached the next trip to the United States with a certain amount of confidence, not in our ability to win (because that is a very difficult task in America) but in our capacity for giving the Americans a very close run.

I was already assured of a place on the points table and looking forward to another trip across the Atlantic, when my pleasure was immeasurably increased by the fact that the other members of the team chose me as their captain.

In the past, captains had been appointed by the PGA selectors, and the new departure was calculated to ensure the solidarity of the side. I am quite sure that if a choice had fallen on any other member of the team that year he would have had the whole team behind him. But the choice fell on me, and no prouder golfer than I had ever set foot in the United States.

The match was played at Palm Springs, California, on the Thunderbird Ranch course, and although I knew the odds were against us, as they always were in America, I saw no reason why we should not do well enough to give us the utmost confidence for the match

Opposite: 1955 US captain Chick Harbert (*left*) stands with the cup alongside sponsor Robert Hudson (*middle*) and British captain Dai Rees (*right*).

in Great Britain two years later. So we went into battle full of determination, with the result that we gave our rivals the closest match they had yet experienced on their side of the water.

Christy O'Connor: I was first selected to play on the team in 1955, and the general feeling among the players travelling to America was that 'we are on our way to be slaughtered, but in the circumstances, let's do the best we can'. And that was the feeling for many years. I am not totally condemning the captains of the time, but I believe they should have been more strong-willed, and in control of our team. They should have been telling our players: 'Let's go out and win', rather than what became the catchphrase: 'Let's go out and put up a good show'.

Jack Burke Jnr: In 1955, the American players had quite a different view of the Ryder Cup. We didn't know the British players very well because none of us played in Europe at all except for the British Open occasionally. Likewise, the British rarely travelled to America – there wasn't enough money on our tour to justify the trip. All we knew was they were coming over to try to take the Ryder Cup away from us. And we were damned if we were going to let that happen. I think patriotism ran a little higher in those days. People didn't just stand during the national anthem, they actually put their hands over their hearts. It was a source of American pride.

Man, did we get up for it. We never thought of it as a 'war' as the press and players later built it up to be. That would have been crazy, because guys like Lloyd Mangrum and Ted Kroll had been shot up in World War II and knew what real war was like. But we did view

The 1955 US Ryder Cup team.

it as though something were at stake, and we weren't going to allow ourselves to lose. All of our players were close to begin with because we travelled together and stayed together. But when the American flag went up, we were brothers in arms.

The British players, I think, were attuned to that. Our nation was so much bigger than theirs and they were still recovering financially from World War II. We had more resources and better players. Maybe the biggest factor was that they didn't have the whole continent of Europe to choose from, just Great Britain [and Ireland]. It was hard for them to look across at Sam Snead, Ben Hogan, and Cary Middlecoff and not feel distress, especially when they knew our guys meant business. We knew the Brits were a little intimidated and we took advantage of it. We beat them badly most of the time.

I want to emphasise that the best fourball partner in history was Ted Kroll. On his own Ted was slightly better than ordinary, but as a partner I'd take him over Ben Hogan, Sam Snead, or anybody else. Ted was shot three times in World War II, and when he was your teammate, he fought like he was sharing a foxhole with you. His game was transformed. He never missed a fairway or a green and very rarely made a bogey. He never complained when you played poorly; he saw it as his mission to carry you. He was outstanding under pressure. He'd won those Purple Hearts and a four-foot putt didn't faze a guy with those experiences behind him. I won some Ryder Cup matches with Ted and a ton of money in practise rounds on tour. In fact, I don't think we ever lost. Some players are better suited for team competition than individual play. Ted was like that.

In the face of this setback – and the searing desert heat at Thunderbird – the British pairing of John Fallon and John Jacobs made a magnificent start in a match of high quality against Jerry Barber and Chandler Harper, with Fallon holing on the thirty-sixth green from three feet after a wonderful chip from Jacobs to secure the opening point for the visitors.

Ford and Kroll took the score level when they saw off the challenge of Brown and Scott 5&4, before Bolt and Burke made a powerful late surge to defeat Lees and Weetman one up. After another very finely fought battle Bradshaw and Rees lost 3&2 to Middlecoff and Snead, to give the USA a 3–1 lead.

The singles were as equally well contested, but with much the same outcome, with the American players just edging their rivals to record a comfortable looking victory in the history books which, in reality, was anything but. John Jacobs once again played superbly to defeat Cary Middlecoff one up after thirty-six holes, Lees beat Furgol 3&2 and Brown defeated Barber by the same scoreline to notch three points for the British, but those were the only returns. Bolt defeated O'Connor 4&2, Harbert defeated Scott 3&2, Snead saw off Rees 3&1, Burke beat Bradshaw 3&2 and Ford defeated Weetman 3&2 for an 8–4 victory.

John Jacobs: I played Cary Middlecoff in the singles. Cary was the top dog at that time. He won the Masters in 1955 and was US Open champion in '56, but I birdied the first three holes. I was totally relaxed even though Cary was such a great player and everybody had written me off. I thought, 'I know I can get round here in 70 twice today, so he'll have to play well to beat me.' We had a wonderful, wonderful game, and I shot a 65 in the afternoon to win.

I was one up on the eighteenth. We were both on the back of the green in two, and the

Sam Snead tees off at Thunderbird Ranch in 1955.

flag was right down at the front. He hit a wonderful putt first, and I gave it to him for a four. Then I putted down and left a putt to tie the hole and win the match that was about five feet downhill with a hell of a swing on it. The whole world thought I was going to miss, but I knew I was going to hole it. I was standing there, and all I was thinking was, 'I must remember to take my cap off when the day ends.' You see, I never wore a cap in those days, but I did in that desert heat. I give you my word, that's exactly what I was thinking. And it went straight in.

Then Cary shook hands with me and said, 'John, well played. I want you to know you've beaten me on one of my best days.' He was an absolute gentleman – and a much better player than I was. We eventually became great friends.

Eric Brown: My second Ryder Cup match, on the course of the Thunderbird Ranch and Country Club at Palm Springs, California, was to be as unsuccessful at the halfway stage, from a personal point of view, as the first had been. Syd Scott and I lost the first three holes of our foursomes against Doug Ford and Ted Kroll, the two demon putters of the American team, and weren't in the hunt. The margin of our defeat was 5&4.

Ford in particular went crazy on the greens. I am supposed to be no slouch at the putting business, but I have rarely if ever seen such consistently good holing out from all ranges as Ford's on that day.

Again the United States led 3–1 in the foursomes; another Scot, Johnny Fallon, had done what I couldn't do – form a successful partnership. The slim, sedate Johnny had joined John Jacobs in beating Chandler Harper and Jerry Barber, the latter of whom was to be my opponent in the singles.

This was definitely the match I wanted – for me it was a 'blood' match, one which I hadn't expected would come as soon as the Ryder Cup of 1955. I had had some of Barber and it was a portion I hadn't digested very well. Indeed, after we had crossed swords the previous year at the 1954 Canada Cup match in Montreal, he had got my goat in a way Mangrum had failed to do at Wentworth.

A pipe band played on the first fairway before the start, but neither Barber nor I was in the mood for pleasantry. There were only the barest necessities of greeting on either side, and I don't suppose we exchanged more than a dozen or so words throughout the day.

It was a real tussle for much of the match but I led after the morning round and at the short thirteenth in the afternoon I scored my second two of the round and went three up with only five holes to play, and no one as determined as I was that day could have lost then.

Barber was beaten 3&2, but he was only one of three losers in the singles – John Jacobs and Arthur Lees were the other British winners – and the United States retained the trophy by eight matches to four.

Dai Rees: The margin of their victory was 8–4, and of our eight defeats one was suffered on the home green, one at the thirty-fifth hole and five at the thirty-fourth. The biggest occurred only four holes from home, so I think I was justified in saying to the press on our arrival at Southampton that we were sure we had the beating of the Americans on a British course.

Jack Burke Jnr: The main problem for the British players, as I saw it, was that they didn't compete with the best and get better. We played each other [on the US Tour], best against the best, and then every two years we kicked butt in the Ryder Cup. It's as simple as that.

TWELVE

1957

Lindrick Golf Club. Yorkshire, England
(GB 7½, USA 4½)

The twelfth Ryder Cup, held at Lindrick Golf Club in Rotherham, England, would prove to be an oasis in the desert for British golf in the transatlantic competition.

Captained by Dai Rees, the home team was full of experience, with only Peter Mills making his debut. After the agonisingly close contest at Wentworth in 1953, the core of that team returned in the shape of Peter Alliss, Harry Bradshaw, Eric Brown, Max Faulkner, Bernard Hunt and Harry Weetman, and reinforced by the presence of Ken Bousfield and Christy O'Connor who had both been selected for Thunderbird (although Bousfield hadn't played).

The Americans, as ever, were formidable. Even if they lacked some true stardust among their ranks, the team captained by the routable Jack Burke Jnr contained three players who had won Majors that year – Doug Ford, Lionel Hebert and Dick Mayer – and a very solid selection in the rest of the line-up in Tommy Bolt, Ed Furgol, Dow Finsterwald, Fred Hawkins, Ted Kroll and Art Wall.

Dai Rees: There is no doubt in my mind, looking back, that the victory which came our way at Lindrick in 1957 was forged two years earlier on the flat mountain-ranged expanse of Thunderbird Ranch, where millionaire golfers lived in luxury and went around the course in mechanical buggies.

There were no buggies at Lindrick, but we took Jackie Burke and his men for a ride in October 1957 all the same.

Max Faulkner: We players got the course ready, and we made it very English. We didn't water the greens for three days before the Ryder Cup, and we left the grass around the green an inch and a half long. In those days the Americans didn't know how to play a shot from there.

Dai Rees: Before the match I was most anxious about press reactions to our chances, for my experience of these matches, and in particular of those played in America, had shown me how much influence golf writers have in these matters.

So on the morning of the last practise day I asked for a press conference at some unearthly hour before I went on to the course. The golf-writing boys turned up in force, and after I had said my piece they were kind enough to assure me of their support and express their confidence in our chances. My object was very simple and straightforward.

'Give us a break,' I asked, 'and do not write up those Americans as invincible until they have shown themselves to be so.'

I said a few other things which were listened to with attention, and the evening papers

Opposite: Home team captain Dai Rees holds aloft the Ryder Cup at Lindrick after a rare British victory.

of that day and the morning papers the next day carried just the right kind of sober, objective summing-up of our chances for which I had hoped. There were no vainglorious boasts about what we would do to the Americans, but on the other hand there were no gloomy forecasts of what the Americans would do to us.

Max Faulkner: It was first class all the way for the Americans. By the 1950s the US were putting on the course all full-time players, part of a regular tour, and they always had the best in transportation and accommodations. Some of our fellows had two or three jobs and tried to win the occasional tourney. It was a bit irritating, but we so enjoyed the competition.

I remember on practise day I was playing the sixth hole with Dai Rees and Ken Bousfield, and Jack Burke was backed up in this grass, and he had one stab at it. He grabbed the club too tightly and the ball just jumped in the air and went a foot forward. He did it again, and it jumped a foot forward. Then he picked the ball up and walked away. We saw before official play started that we had an advantage.

Jack Burke Jnr: I sometimes wish the captains of the individual teams were still required to play. I was a playing captain in 1957 and I thought it did a lot for the team, for me, and for the media. When the captain plays, there is more speculation about the pairings, the messages from the captain to the team carry a lot of weight, and the captain is forced to be very involved. He has to play a lot leading up to the competition and is therefore in closer touch with the players. It gives him more insight into his picks as captain.

Dow Finsterwald: Lindrick in 1957 was my first trip to Britain. The opening ceremonies, you know, 'God Save the Queen' and 'The Star-Spangled Banner,' made a very favourable impression. But I was very nervous.

They had pretty good galleries there, which I attribute a lot to the fact that at that point there weren't many US players going to the British Open. It was the one chance that British golf fans had to see the so-called top players in the US.

Peter Alliss: It would be very easy to drool with sentimentality over the Ryder Cup but at the end of the day, it is simply two teams trying to knock seven bells out of each other in the nicest possible way.

The visitors got off to very fine start in the foursome matches and their performance appeared to add grist to the mill for those who had predicted that, despite overcast and damp conditions, Lindrick would give an unfair advantage to the American players as it was very similar in design and condition to courses found in the US. Ford and Finsterwald duly led the way with a 2&1 victory over Alliss and Hunt, before Bousfield and Rees were able to claim a point back for the British in their 3&2 victory over Hawkins and Wall.

Peter Alliss: I played with Bernard Hunt in the foursomes. Thirty-six-hole matches then, remember, and it was still only two days. We lost 2&1 to Ford and Finsterwald, so we weren't heavily beaten.

The score did not stay level for long as Bolt and Mayer crushed Brown and O'Connor 7&5, and Burke and Kroll beat Faulkner and Weetman 4&3.

Eric Brown: Henry Cotton said after the 1955 match that he couldn't visualise a British team winning in America but that we had every chance of doing so in Britain. But when the Lindrick match of 1957 loomed up Britain were again the non-favourites. Not since 1933 at Southport and Ainsdale had America been beaten, and the team captained by Jackie Burke were considered certain by all but a few of us to prolong our agony when they won the foursomes at Lindrick by 3–1: the margin they had gained on both of my previous encounters with them in the Ryder Cup. For the third time I was in a losing couple, for Dick Mayer, the American champion, and Tommy Bolt whacked Christy O'Connor and me by 7&5.

I had taken as many opportunities as I could of studying the American team in practise and I had not been over-impressed. Indeed, though I was in a very small minority, I thought we had a good chance of beating them. So did Dai Rees, our captain, who at a press conference before the match expressed that opinion.

And even after the hiding Mayer and Bolt gave O'Connor and myself, and despite the fact that we were down 3–1, I still felt the Americans could be defeated.

There is no doubt at all, however, that Mayer and Bolt played supremely well in the foursome against O'Connor and me. The wayward long game of both Christy and myself helped them a lot, of course. It wasn't until the tenth hole in the morning that either of us put his tee shot on the fairway. Strangely enough we were still only one down after fourteen holes – Bolt put his approach in a bunker at the fourteenth – but O'Connor failed with a very short putt at the fifteenth and I hooked my approach at the sixteenth, so we lost both holes. Mayer and Bolt retained that three-hole lead at the end of the first round, for which their score was 67 – the best performance of any pair in the morning's play. We had scored 71.

My best drive of the match helped us to make a winning birdie three at the first hole of the afternoon, but our opponents won the twenty-first and twenty-second and thereafter didn't make one mistake. They were no fewer than eleven under-fours when the match ended; in the thirty holes they had eleven threes and a two. That was extraordinary golf.

Going into the singles, the US only needed to win three points in order to retain the cup for a further two years and as a stiff wind dried out the course and the PGA issued an order that the greens should be cut as short as possible to make them play quickly, it seemed that the result was all but a foregone conclusion. Which made the spectacle that unfurled all the more remarkable.

Dai Rees: After the foursomes I did not feel like having another press conference. We were 1–3 down and the newspaper boys just had to write that it looked like another American victory.

But most of them were still kind, and the only one to stick out his neck good and proper was a daily paper representative (not a regular golf writer) who announced in print that if Britain won the match he would be happy to be buried under two tons of compost.

Eric Brown: Before the singles there was a row over the team selection which blew up between Rees and Harry Weetman, who along with Max Faulkner was dropped for the second day. America's captain, Jackie Burke, left himself out of their team and by doing so created the impression that he at least thought the Ryder Cup was already theirs. He did play after all, however, for Ted Kroll was indisposed and with permission he was withdrawn. Incidentally, only Burke and Kroll had previously played Ryder Cup golf in Britain.

All in all, only super-optimists such as myself fancied that Britain could still win the singles by such a margin as would neutralise America's lead in the foursomes. Perhaps the fact that our own newspapers didn't give us the slightest chance of making up the leeway inspired us to surprise the Yanks – and the golfing world. Some of the writers wrote us off so superciliously that I for one was determined to make them eat their words. And how well we succeeded in making them do that.

Eric Brown was sent out at the top of the order to face Tommy Bolt in what became a real battle of wills – and indeed fury – between the two. The crowds were soon whipped into a frenzy as the two firebrand players aggravated one another around the course, wildly cheering anything Brown did well and being equally vociferous whenever Bolt's game went askew. At the end of the encounter, which the Scotsman won 4&3, Bolt exclaimed to Brown that, 'You may have won, but I didn't enjoy that one bit.' To which Brown retorted sharply, 'After the whipping I gave you, I wouldn't have enjoyed it either.'

Peter Alliss: Eric Brown led the singles, playing Tommy 'Thunder' Bolt. What a match they had.

Jimmy Demaret, one of the American players who happened to be there as a spectator was heard to say (when the starter was getting anxious that Brown and Bolt had not appeared on the first tee) that he had seen them but thirty minutes before at thirty paces on the practise ground throwing clubs at each other. Well I admit it was a bit of a fiery match, with Brown coming through as the victor.

Eric Brown: I had the privilege of starting the victory march with a 5&4 win over Bolt, the American champion of the previous year, which was particularly to the crowd's liking. There was one small fly in the ointment: some of the spectators were guilty of describing the British team as English, just as some television and radio commentators are wont to speak of England when they should say Britain. This sort of thing annoys more than myself; it seems to me a combination of ignorance and insolence. Apparently, however, Brown of Scotland, Rees of Wales, and Bradshaw and O'Connor of Ireland – half of the singles team – were Englishmen, for that day at least at Lindrick.

Anyway, I had watched Bolt play in the Labbatts tournament in Canada and had been present on three occasions of his club-throwing, for which he had become notorious in the States and which had cost him more than a few dollars as punishment. Indeed, I well remember him at the fourth hole in that Labbatts tournament, first of all hurling his driver from the tee after he had hooked into trees and then throwing another club, which actually broke, after an unsuccessful attempt to get out onto the fairway. Mind you, club-throwing, so long as it isn't in the direction of anybody, does no one but the thrower any

Eric Brown escapes a bunker at the eighteenth during the foursomes as
Christy O'Connor looks on.

harm. And even that's a matter of opinion. As a matter of fact, it lets off steam. I have
thrown a few in my day, so I know.

Tommy was the most pleasant fellow on that first day of the Lindrick match. I would
suggest at this point that possibly the ease with which he and Mayer beat Christy and
me had something to do with that. I myself, like most people, generally contrive to look
happier when I am in front than when I am behind. If anyone tries to make a case that a
golfer or a player of any game of sport should be pleased while he is being beaten I give
him the horse laugh.

But Bolt didn't get much cause for joviality on the second day, for yours truly played
very much to his own liking and satisfaction. During the first eighteen holes, Bolt made
some light mutterings about the crowd being all for me. I wondered what he expected
them to be, though I didn't mention that to him, and just as I had found in 1955 in the
States, many of the spectators were free with their praise for the shots of the visitor as well
as the home player.

The spectators at Lindrick could surely be excused for showing their enthusiasm for
a British fightback; in addition, the British victory, which now seemed possible, as good
news of nearly all our players spread through the crowd, was something of a phenomenon.
Yet I recall the great spontaneous cheer the crowd gave Bolt when he holed his chip shot
from behind the fifth green in the afternoon.

But you cannot prevent a golf crowd spotting your idiosyncrasies or your momentary
indiscretions, and by the turn in the afternoon they had quite clearly noted Bolt's
increasing tendency to grumble about unfavourable lies and bad luck. Probably, too, they
had read or heard of his outbursts in his own country. Once or twice I reminded too-
exuberant spectators to keep quiet and still when the American was lining up for a shot,

but at the ninth, after his second shot had rolled through the green and down a slope into rough, and he suggested to me in no jocular fashion that if it had been my ball someone would have kicked it into a good lie, I told him to stop moaning.

Tommy Bolt: Eric Brown and I were both temperamental, and the people might have applauded one of Eric's shots and not applauded mine, or something like that. You know how spectators are sometimes. But I lost control of my emotions and I tossed a couple of clubs around. Stuck 'em in the ground or they bounced up in the air, and you can't play when you do that. That's all there is to it. I was four down by lunchtime and I couldn't get my concentration back – and golf is a game of concentration.

Eric Brown: The crowd were gloating now over the discomfiture of one who, they had made up their minds, couldn't take it. But no one could have expected him to make such a mess of the fifteenth as he did. First he hooked his drive into the rough, then he made a furious uncontrolled slash which left him still forty yards short of the 351-yard hole, proceeded to pitch far too strongly, and then overran the hole with his long putt by more than three yards. I lay quite close to the hole in two, and he strode up to my ball and by way of conceding the hole and match he swiped the ball right off the green. His way of congratulating me was to say that I had beaten him but that he hadn't enjoyed a single minute of the match. At least that's a printable version of the words he used. What I gave back in reply also cannot be repeated here.

Tommy's tantrums didn't end on the course; I heard two of his teammates, Ed Furgol and Doug Ford, reprimand him in the clubhouse for his manner of accepting defeat.

Tommy Bolt: The crowd cheered when I missed a putt and sat on their hands when I hit a good shot. I got so angry about it that I broke my putter over my knee shortly after completing my match. I told Ed Furgol about my annoyance and he said, 'Pipe down – you were well and truly licked.'

Ben Hogan: If we could have screwed another head on Tommy Bolt's shoulders, he would have been the greatest golfer that ever lived.

With the battle lines now well and truly drawn between the two teams, Mills secured another point for the British with his 5&3 victory over Burke.

Jack Burke Jnr: My lone loss as a player came during that 1957 debacle. I had a 6–0 record heading into the matches and stretched that to 7–0 when Ted Kroll and I beat Max Faulkner and Harry Weetman unmercifully in the first-day foursomes. The Ryder Cup only lasted two days back then, and there were foursomes and singles matches only, no fourballs.

At dinner after the first day, we led 3–1 and I was feeling pretty good about things. I liked our chances in the singles matches so much I had a glass of wine. There were only eight singles matches played in those days, and I wasn't going to play.

The next morning I found out I was playing. My partner the day before, Ted Kroll, had come down with – no kidding – a chafed rear end. It happened a lot in those days, maybe because the pants we wore were so course. In any case, Ted's buttocks were so sore he couldn't play. I can only imagine how the media these days would handle a chafed ass.

Dai Rees objected to Ted withdrawing from his match. He made me go get a doctor to confirm that Ted indeed had a chafed butt and couldn't play. That hacked me off. I'd beaten Rees in the singles at Wentworth in 1953 and again at Pinehurst in 1951 with my foursome partner, Clayton Heafner. I thought it was small of him not taking me at my word on Ted's condition. After the doctor confirmed the sorry condition of Ted's rear end, I took off my overcoat and walked to the first tee.

I felt confident filling in for Ted. My game was in good shape. Somebody asked who I was playing. 'His name is Peter Mills,' I said. 'I've never heard of him.'

'I have,' somebody said. 'He has a reputation for being a very shaky putter.' That was music to my ears. Well, Mr Mills proceeded to birdie three of the first seven holes. On the other holes, he left every approach putt four feet short then made the tough putts for par. I couldn't get it going, and Peter Mills killed me, 5&3. We lost six of the eight singles matches, winning only one and tying another. And we lost the Ryder Cup. It was the last time I felt overconfident about the Ryder Cup.

Harry Bradshaw: Dai Rees and Ken Bousfield were the only ones to win the foursomes on the opening day. And Tommy Bolt and Dick Mayer, the reigning US Open champion, beat Eric Brown and Christy O'Connor 7&5. Christy asked me after the foursomes who I was playing in the singles. And when I told him I was playing an American chap called Mayer, he covered his face and said, 'Oh Brad, I feel sorry for you.' But my reaction was, 'I'll knock in putt for putt with him.'

Well, I won the first and second and I also won the third where I holed a great bunker shot. Going to the fourth tee, Mayer said to me, 'You're a great trap player, Harry.' And I replied that I generally holed four or five in a round, as a rule. And he says, 'I hope you don't do it this morning.' I was giving him the old one and two, you know.

He was a helluva nice fellow. Of course, we finished all square after I had three-putted the ninth, morning and afternoon. Only for that, I would have had him. I always took the wrong borrow on that green.

Peter Alliss: The young Peter Mills was given the task of playing at number two and he took on their captain Jack Burke and gave him a good trouncing, 5&3.

Peter Alliss battled manfully in his match against Hawkins, but fell to a 2&1 defeat which, for a period, suggested that the US might be back on the march – but that result proved simply to be a stumbling block in an otherwise stunning comeback from the home team. Score after score tumbled in as the tide turned the way of the British; Bousfield beat Herbert 4&3, Rees beat Furgol 7&6, Hunt beat Ford 6&5, and O'Connor beat Finsterwald 7&6. The only respite appeared in the match between Bradshaw and Mayer, which was halved, to leave the final score at 7½–4½ and hand a rare victory to Great Britain.

Harry Bradshaw: After Christy and Eric Brown had lost the foursomes by 7&5 to Tommy Bolt and Dick Mayer, who was the reigning US Open champion, Christy said to me, 'Brad, I feel sorry for you, facing Mayer in the singles – he had 67 against us!' But I assured him I would knock in putt for putt – and I managed to halve the match with him.

Peter Alliss: We were down after the foursomes, 3–1, then we came roaring back. It was a great victory. Oh, there were people everywhere, it was very exciting. But the disappointing thing for me, I was having a great battle, and I was one-down with about four to play, and then Dai Rees, or someone, came rushing out and said, 'It's all over, don't worry, we've won, we've won, we've won, you don't have to win.' I wanted to play right to the end, try hard, and it deflated me a bit, and I lost 2&1 to Fred Hawkins. I didn't contribute any points at all. So my celebrations that night were a little bit muted. It's rather like being in a cricket match and you score only three runs and you win the Test match handsomely because two or three others scored a hundred. You were in the team, but you didn't contribute much. So I was always very conscious of that. I enjoyed Lindrick, the old grand hotel in Sheffield. Sir Stuart Goodwin who paid for the whole thing, he kept the Ryder Cup going that year really. It was very nice to be part of it.

Eric Brown: The huge crowds who swarmed over Lindrick were overjoyed; I've never seen so many delighted folk on a golf course.

Harry Moffitt, President of the US PGA: Several of the team came to me and said how the crowd had been very fair. They had applauded their good shots as well as those of their opponents . . . The result will prove to be a wonderful boost to the competition and the Ryder Cup will go on for years and years.

Dow Finsterwald: In fairness to the home team, when a guy misses a putt they could be applauding the fact that the British team had won a hole. It wasn't maybe the missing of a putt and may have been misinterpreted by some of us.

Peter Alliss: The crowd were getting excited, and were very much behind us. It got a little bit partisan, but nothing compared to today. It was a great victory, a lot of celebrations that night that when on and on and on and on, the happier we got the more miserable the Americans got! It's a dim memory, but it's relatively bright still in my mind.

Dai Rees: Between the foursomes and singles they brush-harrowed the rough at the backs of the greens so that, if a ball slipped through, it was going to be difficult to play. And indeed the Americans did have difficulty. It wasn't jiggery-pokery. It was there for all to see.

The singles were magnificent – we turned a 1–3 defeat in the foursomes into a glorious victory, I felt the happiest man in the world and the most fortunate captain. For not only did I have seven colleagues playing on the course with me and solidity behind me from the start, but I also had the invaluable services of dear old Max Faulkner as a self-appointed cheerleader and whipper-in.

Max Faulkner: I didn't play all that well and wasn't selected for the singles, but I didn't mind too much. I think a part of me knew that was my last Ryder Cup, and all I cared about was winning, whoever I played. If I couldn't do it with a club in my hands, there were other ways, so I made sure I was as big a support for the other players as I could be.

It was a highlight for me to finally win. We were rather like heroes for a while. It was a great, great cap on my career.

Dai Rees: Max took more out of himself on that great day by rushing between matches reporting on progress and radiating encouragement than he would have done by playing. I think his enthusiasm alone was worth a point to our side.

Eric Brown: Max was never far away with a word of encouragement. He traversed the course, repeatedly keeping an eye on every British player and telling us all what the state of the matches were. He was a tremendous source of inspiration. When victory was assured Max was more delighted than the rest of us and jumped around like a dog with nine tails. I don't think any of the British team that day will forget the wonderful contribution made by Max towards our victory.

Jack Burke Jnr: It was the one team I was associated with that lost. We went down 7½–4½ and it hurt that I was a playing captain. The British were fantastic in the singles matches, pure magic. It was a big upset.

Peter Alliss: There were tremendous celebrations. Nothing was as big then as it is today, but everybody got drunk at the dinner, and old journalists, old people, were jumping up and saying a few words and singing and dancing. The American team was like a funeral parlour. The glum faces were just unbelievable. We hadn't won since 1933, and the American team looked on in disbelief that they could have lost to this ragtag outfit.

Harry Bradshaw: We drank champagne until five o'clock in the morning. We went mad. It was the first time the Americans had been beaten since 1933.

Jack Burke Jnr: Being the captain of a losing team is pitiful. There's all kinds of reasons, none of 'em happy ones. Hurts like hell, but you got to suck it up and hope you get another shot. I did, in 1973, and thanks to fellows like Nicklaus and Trevino, I was able to make the most of it.

Dai Rees: We did not hold the newspaper man to his promise to be buried under the compost. We could afford to be magnanimous, for did we not win six of the eight singles, halve another, and win back the cup by 7½ matches to 4½?

Were we proud? We had that golf cup on many top tables during the succeeding winter, and I had to be forgiven for repeating myself, so often was I called upon to reply to the toast of 'The Ryder Cup team'. I took tremendous delight and pride at each dinner when some or all of my chaps were present in getting them onto their feet to receive their share of the applause.

For they were a grand bunch of fellows, and I knew how much they had tried.

THIRTEEN

1959

Eldorado Country Club. Palm Desert, California
(USA 8½, GB 3½)

If the win at Lindrick had suggested that there might be a prospective sea change in the US dominance, the omens of ill fortune for the British cast their shadow once more as the team travelled to the Eldorado Country Club in Palm Desert.

The British PGA had decided that instead of flying to the US, the team would benefit from some bonding time together to build on the momentum gained in 1957. The theory went that by the time they arrived on US shores after a luxurious journey aboard the Queen Elizabeth *they would be in the best possible frame of mind for a successful tilt at winning away from home for the first time. But the best laid plans . . . The crossing of the Atlantic was a torrid one with terrible weather and many of the players suffered from seasickness. But this was a mild discomfort compared with what was to come. After travelling by train across the country, the team had to take a flight from Los Angeles to Palm Springs. As the plane crossed the San Jacinto Mountains it ran into a storm which rocked the plane violently before it suddenly dropped 4,000 feet without warning. The pilots were thankfully able to regain control and so prevent a tragedy, but the passengers all suffered horrifically from the shock. To make matters worse, Bernard Hunt had given up his seat to one of the air stewards so was not strapped in when the plane went into its free fall. He was battered against the ceiling of the cabin and sustained significant damage to his shoulder.*

To compound matters, the pilots were told that Palm Springs airport was closed because of the storm and they had to fly back to Los Angeles. Following the trauma of the experience, it was no surprise that the team shunned the offer of another flight once the storm had passed and instead opted to travel to Palm Desert by Greyhound bus.

Peter Alliss: We were the last team to go to America by sea, we went on the old *Queen Elizabeth*. November, it was very rough, very, very rough. We landed in New York and then we went down south, we played a couple of matches first outside Washington, and then we went across to Los Angeles. Then we got on the plane; it was only about a hundred miles to Palm Springs. The weather was atrocious, the plane dropped about 4,000 feet going through it. The pilot had to come back, as the conditions were so wild. There was a sandstorm in Palm Springs, so we had to go back and hire a bus. What a journey!

Eric Brown: The last stage of our trip from Britain was a flight from Los Angeles of an estimated forty minutes' duration – at least that was the schedule. We boarded the plane around 7:00 pm in pitch black darkness and settled down comfortably and happily. After half an hour's flying there were several little bumps and then there was a series of much more severe jolts in rapid succession. We took this discomfiture as a sign that we were over the mountains in the Palm Desert area and weren't unduly alarmed. But the bumping got worse, and the fact that our stewardess was the first to make a grab for the paper bag didn't help us. Dai Rees was the next to 'lose face'.

Peter Alliss: We took off, and the pilot said it was likely to be a bit rough – and it was. It was horrendous! We plunged about four thousand feet. Lots of people were sick, and the smell was bloody awful. Frank Pennink, the writer, and former English amateur champion, was looking out the window at the electrical storm, amazed by the patterns of lightning. When we dropped – there were no bins, just open storage trays – coats and cameras and other things were stuck to the roof by the sheer force. And then suddenly – bang! It was as if we'd hit the top of a mountain, and all this stuff dropped down on top of everybody. The pilot came on and said, 'I'm very sorry but we can't go any farther, we have to go back again.' Eventually we landed back in Los Angeles. The pilot came out. He'd bashed his head and was bleeding all over the place. I think a stewardess may have broken an ankle.

Eric Brown: Another bang-bump-bang of terrific jolts dislodged coats and hats, brief-cases, light travelling bags, pillows and blankets from the racks. As lightning flashed vividly and dangerously close, the plane suddenly dropped . . . down, down, down. Utensils from the kitchen burst through the doorway and samples of various foods came flying in, newspapers and magazines shot from the racks to the roof and stuck there. Then just as suddenly we began to fly in an approximately horizontal direction again, and the shocks of the bumping gradually became less severe.

There were some really stricken folk around us, including Doug Ford, one of our Ryder Cup opponents. Through came the pilot at this stage to apologise for the weather, of which he had had no warning when we took off at Los Angeles. It would be impossible, he said, to land at our destination because of sandstorms – the airport couldn't be seen for the billowing, sweeping sand – and we were on our way back to Los Angeles.

Doug Ford: I missed my plane to Palm Springs from Los Angeles, so I bummed a ride with the British team, which had a charter plane. It's a forty-five minute flight, and somewhere we ran into the Santa Ana winds, which were a lot more severe than the pilot had been told. The plane dropped 700 feet in just a few seconds and 4,000 feet overall before the pilots regained control. Books and magazines were glued to the ceiling of that plane. It was terrifying, and when the plane somehow got on the ground – we were back in Los Angeles, not in Palm Springs – every person on that plane was soaked in sweat. My grey suit was black. For several Ryder Cups after that, there was a reunion dinner. I was the only American member of The Long Drop Club.

Christy O'Connor: We formed a special club after that – the Jolly Lucky Long Drop Club, 5.30 p.m. October 25th 1959, Los Angeles to Palm Springs, Almost! On that day each year, at the precise time, each of the team members must raise a glass and toast each other.

Eric Brown: We must have circled the airport there half a dozen times before we touched down. We had been ninety minutes in the air, and I for one have never been so glad to be on terra firma. Most of us bent down after we had left the plane and thankfully placed our hands on the tarmac.

Peter Alliss: There was a fellow called Lou Freedman who was a [PGA] vice president. When he got off the plane, Ron Heager of the *Daily Express* said to him, 'Lou, I nearly shit myself up there,' and Lou said, 'I've got news for you. I did.' And he rushed off. Oh, Christ, what a mess.

The next day Ron says, 'Congratulations, for the first time golf leads the *Daily Express*.'

The front page of the *Daily Express* recording the terrifying plunge over the mountains.

As preparations go for a major international sporting event, the whole experience had been far from ideal for Dai Rees's side. The Welshman, playing in his eighth Ryder Cup, had a fine team at his disposal, despite the disruptions they suffered before arriving in Palm Desert. The team was full of experienced campaigners in Peter Alliss, Ken Bousfield, Eric Brown, Bernard Hunt, Peter Mills, Christy O'Connor and Harry Weetman, with Norman Drew and Dave Thomas making their debuts. The Americans, captained by Sam Snead (also, like his counterpart Rees, making his eighth appearance), had four rookies in their ranks in Julius Boros, Jay Hebert, Bob Rosburg and Mike Souchak, while Jack Burke Jnr, Dow Finsterwald, Doug Ford, Cary Middlecoff and Art Wall all returned.

Following the success at Lindrick, the score after the foursome matches was as evenly poised as many had predicted it might be. Rosburg and Souchak beat Hunt and Brown 5&4 and Boros and Finsterwald beat Rees and Bousfield by two holes before O'Connor and Alliss claimed Britain's first point by beating Wall and Ford 3&2, and Weetman and Thomas halved with Snead and Middlecoff.

Mike Souchak: They put Bobby Rosburg and me in the first match. I was so nervous when they played 'God Save the Queen' and 'The Star-Spangled Banner.' We decided that he would drive on the odd holes and I would drive on the even holes, because of the setup of the par-threes. I was a little longer than Bob, and I could handle the par-three holes with a shorter iron club.

Anyhow, he got the privilege of teeing off at number one, a par-five in the middle of an orange and grapefruit grove. It had a very narrow fairway and trees on either side. I told Bobby, 'Look, I don't care how far you hit it. Just keep it between the trees.' When he got up to tee his ball, he couldn't keep the ball on the tee, he was so nervous. The ball fell off two or three times. He finally had to put the ball on the tee with both hands! And I'm standing there just grinning because I was so happy it wasn't me up there on the tee, because I would have been doing the same thing. Anyhow, he hit a low slice, about two hundred yards. It wasn't very long but it was effective, right in the middle of the fairway. And then I took a three-wood and just killed it, put it right in front of the green. He pitched it on the green about three feet from the hole. The British team had made a five, and I got over the putt for a four, and I jerked that three-footer so badly. Bobby says, 'I'm glad you're so nervous, too.' And after that, we played beautifully and beat them pretty badly [5&4].

Peter Alliss: Christy O'Connor and I were paired up for the first time that year. We got on very well. He was a wonderful partner. We just hit it off. I always say that nobody else would play with us! He could be a bit tricky when he had had a couple of shandies, and everybody thought I was a bit aloof. So we teamed up wonderfully. Christy could argue with a lot of people, but we never had a cross word. In the very first match Christy O'Connor and I played, I missed the first green and said, 'I'm sorry.' He just stopped and said, 'Listen, I know you're trying to do the very best you can, so if we're going to play well together we don't want any more apologising.' And that's how we played. He used to encourage me and I used to encourage him, and he played the most wonderful shots. I thought he was crazy at times. I mean downhill, wind left to right, out of bounds on the right, small green. And we were one up or two up and two to play or something. And he'd say, 'They're in trouble. I think I'll just cut a driver in there.' He had no fear.

It seemed that destiny had decided we were a partnership for the long haul. They didn't have player-power in those days, so there was no question of the two of us informing the captain that we'd like to play together – you were told what to do and you simply got on with it, despite being terrified of coming up against such American legends as Sam Snead.

Anyway, who would have thought of pairing chalk and cheese? Because that's what we were. Though we've broken bread together, Christy and I have never dined in each other's homes, we've never done anything that might prompt people to suggest, 'Oh, they'd make a great partnership; they're like blood brothers.'

Chalk and bloody cheese. In those days, Christy was what you might describe as a little bit rebellious, a bit of a smoking gun, and I suppose, in a quiet English way, I could have been considered a sort of wayward catapult. Anyway, fate threw us together and I know I always did my very, very best for Christy and, God knows, he did his very best for me.

I just had the most amazing confidence in him. Neither of us were good putters, yet we holed putts when it mattered. We gave confidence to each other to the extent that we became a very solid partnership. All the while, a wonderful golfing friendship developed over the years.

I would have been among those who considered Christy to be in the genius class as a striker of the ball, despite relaxing his right hand fingers at the top of his backswing. He had all the shots except one – the putt.

He won numerous tournaments with a flicky putting stroke. God knows how many more he would have won had he had the putting skills of even a modest player of today. Anyway, I had been doing some good things myself, when the Americans recognised what a wonderful player Christy was. So we were respected and feared for a variety of reasons.

Dave Marr [1956 US PGA champion] once said to me that the Americans all wanted to get at me first, because they thought I was a toffee-nosed, if quite an elegant player. A bit snobby, having served my apprenticeships in Ryder Cups going back to 1953 at Wentworth, while my father [Percy] was in the winning team at Southport and Ainsdale, 20 years previously. And, of course, Christy and I were both part of the wonderful 1957 victory at Lindrick.

It didn't matter to us whether it was foursomes or fourballs, though I suspect we were better at foursomes. Better than the record books would suggest. I know I concentrated more on foursomes, you know the thing, if it was my tee shot I had to get Christy on the fairway, or if it was an approach iron, I had to get him on the green. And I gave similar care to putting. I concentrated on getting him closer than four feet from the hole, if I could.

Eric Brown: My partner in 1959 was Bernard Hunt, and I am bound to say that I think that Bob Rosburg and Mike Souchak, who beat us by 5&4, weren't too hard on us. They may have been somewhat sorry for Bernard, who had developed a cold and a hacking cough. It's fair to assume that the germ attacked him when his power of resistance was low as a result of the dreadful experience on the plane.

My partner had to get medical attention in the clubhouse at the end of the morning's play, at which stage we were ingloriously six holes down. Rosburg, who was runner-up in

The British team enjoy the feeling of arriving in America with the cup in their possession.

the United States Open Championship and winner of the American PGA title that year, and Souchak were out in 34 to our 36 and were one up, and Bernard and I were still only a hole down after eleven holes. But then came a landslide, and the Americans won five of the next seven holes.

Even had Bernard been in better fettle I don't think we would have beaten this pair, who were almost autonomous that day. But Britain should without doubt have halved the foursomes. Harry Weetman and Dave Thomas were one up with one to play and even then Dave had missed a putt of four feet at the thirty-fifth which would have enabled them to beat Dr Cary Middlecoff and Sam Snead by 2&1 and have given us a 2–2 score in the foursomes.

At the last hole Middlecoff hooked his drive, whereas Thomas hit his a long way and right down the centre of the fairway. Snead knew that it was all or nothing with his second, and he had to go for the green from an awkward position. But he cut his shot and landed in one of the water hazards. Weetman and Thomas looked stonewall certainties to win the match.

We expected Harry to play his second shot just short of the green – safe, to avoid the water – but he went for the green, didn't hit the ball quite in the middle, and plopped into the water. So Thomas as well as Middlecoff had to lift and drop. Thomas chipped to three yards from the hole and Middlecoff just landed inside him, but Weetman missed his putt and Snead holed for the Americans.

I am all for taking a chance when the reward is sufficiently worthwhile, but Harry had practically nothing to gain and almost everything to lose by playing his second shot as he did.

Harry Weetman: I didn't play safe, I never do – it's not my game. I just didn't hit the right shot.

However, for all that the British team had still been very much in contention after the first day, they were comprehensively blown away in the singles – in the final reckoning at any rate, even if the matches themselves were often closer than the story the scoreboard told. Eric Brown was the only British player able to return a point for his team and while his teammates battled valiantly, none more so than captain Rees who just failed to halve with Finsterwald on the final green, the Americans reclaimed the cup with a comprehensive 8½–3½ victory.

This edition of the Ryder Cup, the thirteenth, was the last time a visiting British Ryder Cup team (despite the horrors of the aborted flight to Palm Springs) made a journey by sea. And it marked the last time the matches were contested over thirty-six holes of foursomes and singles. These changes, however, would do little to change the tide of results.

Eric Brown: Long before I finished my singles with Middlecoff the issue had been decided in America's favour, for the doctor and I were in the last match and his colleagues had long since made sure of the points they needed for victory.

I was the only British winner in the singles – Norman Drew and Peter Alliss halved their games – and the American margin of victory was 7–2 with three halved [to give a final score of 8½–3½].

A shot from the foursomes at Eldorado Country Club.

Britain's surprising victory at Lindrick ended a run of seven consecutive wins for America and proved that for all their advantages the Americans are not invincible either as individuals or as a team. It had, in my opinion, an even more important effect – it reduced to the merest whisper the outcry that the match in its form should be discontinued and that Britain should have the aid of South Africans, Australians, New Zealanders etc, and be only part of a composite team against the United States. I am not one who would like to see the conditions changed and Britain lose her identity. Indeed, I am strongly opposed to the idea of introducing players from overseas to the British side and making it one of the Empire or Commonwealth.

It is true that the ever-increasing popularity of golf in the United States, a vast country compared with Britain and with many times the population, and the great professional tournament circuits, in which many of their players are able to reach a degree of tournament toughness that only few of ours can attain, give the Americans an advantage over us. It has been said with justification that the United States can pick two or even three teams of Ryder Cup class to our one.

But I am sure that it will be a sorry day for British golf if we agree to lose our identity and enlist the assistance of golfers from other countries in order to try to make a more level Ryder Cup match with the Americans. It is up to us to try of our own accord to keep the match going as it is – so far as personnel is concerned, that is to say. It befits British professionals, therefore, to become more dedicated to their task.

FOURTEEN

1961

Royal Lytham and St Annes. St Annes, England
(USA 14½, GB 9½)

With the changes to the format of the Ryder Cup now in place, the fourteenth instalment of the international challenge matches had quite a different look to its predecessors. The first day's play would consist of eight foursome matches of eighteen holes each, and the second day's singles would be divided into two sets of eight, one played in the morning and one in the afternoon, making a total of 24 points now up for grabs instead of just 12.

The matches were played once again at Lytham and the home team, captained by Dai Rees in his final appearance, was little changed to that which had travelled to Eldorado Country Club two years previously. The only alterations saw Eric Brown, Norman Drew and Dave Thomas replaced by rookies Tom Haliburton, Ralph Moffitt, and Neil Coles, who would go on to have a long and distinguished Ryder Cup career.

The American team was captained by Jerry Barber (after Sam Snead was snubbed by the US PGA for taking part in an unauthorised tournament) and featured some outstanding rookies in Billy Casper, Bill Collins, Gene Littler and, most notably, Arnold Palmer, fresh from his maiden win at the Open Championship earlier that year. The veterans were Art Wall, Mike Souchak, Doug Ford and Dow Finsterwald.

Billy Casper: We gathered as a team in Washington, DC, and flew together to England, where we were met by the Lord Mayor of London in an elaborate welcoming ceremony. It was more pomp and circumstance than I'd ever seen. The British made it feel like a really big deal and the tone was set. The Ryder Cup never stopped being special for me after that.

The next morning we boarded the train in London. As captain, Jerry Barber was carrying the Ryder Cup with him, since America had won it in 1959. When he boarded the train he stowed the cup in an overhead bin, then he and Palmer got in a gin game and forgot all about it. When we got off the train in Lytham and St Annes the president of the PGA was there to meet us.

He looked around and asked Jerry, 'Where's the Ryder Cup?'

'Oh, it's in the overhead,' Jerry answered, only then realising we weren't still on the train and the Ryder Cup was.

The bobbies met the train in Blackpool, retrieved the cup and sent it back to us. But the British had the Ryder Cup there for a few hours. We managed to lose it before the matches even began.

Arnold Palmer: Even though my relationship with the Ryder Cup developed into one that I came to cherish, my earliest experiences of the competition were not of a happy nature.

Opposite: Jerry Barber is hoisted high by members of his team in 1961.

It was deeply frustrating to me that I won the 1958 Masters, and nine other tournaments prior to that, but that I was denied the opportunity to collect Ryder Cup points for my play. The PGA's rules stipulated that I had not been a member of the tour for long enough to have earned the privilege to play in the Ryder Cup.

Whatever hard feelings I privately nursed about being ineligible for the Ryder Cup of 1959, they vanished in 1961. The American squad and our wives walked onto the hushed grounds at Royal Lytham and St Annes for the opening ceremonies of the competition. I remember standing with my teammates near the first tee and feeling a lump rise in my throat and tears fill my eyes as the brass band played the 'The Star-Spangled Banner' followed by 'God Save the Queen'.

Peter Alliss: The new format was more exciting for the spectators. They were seeing more games, more matches, more people playing. I remember big crowds at Lytham.

Neil Coles: The PGA gave us a special uniform with a jacket to wear off the course, four golf shirts and one blue pullover to play in and the plastic golf bag with head covers. But my pullover was too small and I asked for a bigger one. The PGA people said they didn't have one even after I told them it felt restrictive when I swung and I couldn't play in it. They said I just had to wear it. I went into the Pringle tent in the golf village and asked if they had a bigger blue pullover. They said they didn't have one, but they had a cardigan. I said: 'That'll do.' So I played the entire tournament in that, with no badge on it. You can see it in the photos.

The night before play began, Dai Rees had told us all that the key to winning the Ryder Cup, in his eyes, was to get a good start in the foursomes. We should get going quickly and make sure that we won the early holes. The next morning I stood on the tee and Mike Souchak hit this one-iron that just went straight as an arrow to about a foot. 'Welcome to the Ryder Cup!'

Even under the new format, which many felt might aid the British effort, the home team were unable to replicate the form they had displayed at Lindrick four years previously. They lost both the morning and afternoon foursomes 3–1 to take a 6–2 deficit into the Saturday singles sessions.

Mike Souchak: We [Souchak and Bill Collins] were one up in that match on the eighteenth green, which at Lytham backs right up to the clubhouse. My partner drove, I put him on the green, and he put it up about fifteen, sixteen inches short of the hole. They'd made their four, and Neil came up to me and said, 'Mike, under any other circumstances I'd give it to you, but it's the match and it's right here at the clubhouse.' I said, 'Neil, don't worry about it. I'd do the same thing.' So I went over and got ready to putt.

People were hanging out of the windows on the second floor of the clubhouse, which was right over the top of us and, on my backswing, this lady, who must have been half drunk, hollered at the top of her voice, 'Miss it!' Well, fortunately the ball went in the hole and I just told her, 'Sorry, lady, not today.' She was half in the bag, I'm sure, and it was only lunchtime! I think she ran and hid.

Arnold Palmer: The highlight of my week came when Billy Casper and I teamed up in

Dai Rees tees off, watched by Ken Bousfield, during their foursome match against Arnold Palmer and Billy Casper.

the foursomes to defeat Dai Rees and Ken Bousfield, 2&1. Counting my singles win over Tom Haliburton, a lovely gentleman, I departed Lytham with three-and-a-half points and contributed to my team's winning total of 14½.

Billy Casper: The first time Arnold Palmer and I got to know each other on a close level was when we became Ryder Cup teammates in 1961. We played together in both the morning and afternoon and our first opponents were Ken Bousfield and Dai Rees. Arnold and I went one up on the par-five seventh hole and the match stayed that way all the way to the seventeenth. Arnold was driving the odd-numbered holes. Seventeen is a short par five with a narrow driving area. I said, 'Arnold, just take that one-iron and hit it in the fairway and I'll knock it on the green.' He stared at me, threw down his cigarette, gripped his driver, let it rip, and missed the fairway by maybe six inches. I hit an iron six feet from the hole and he holed the putt and we won, 2&1.

That afternoon Palmer and I teamed up again, this time against John Panton and Bernard Hunt. We won 5&4.

Neil Coles: On the Friday afternoon, against Barber and Dow Finsterwald, Tom Haliburton and I again lost ground at the start and were three down with five played, but recovered to be only one down at the seventeenth. Barber, with his unusual style which always seemed chancy to me, cut his drive into the bushes at the eighteenth and I was down the middle. Finsterwald hit the American ball straight into the bushes in front of him but he happened to clear everything and finished pin high about thirty yards from the hole. Tom hooked to the left of the green and Barber's pitch, by no means a good one, finished five yards short of the hole.

Then came one of the worst moments I've experienced in big golf. I had a slightly downhill lie and a little rise between ball and green. I had to plop the ball over the rise and stop it so that it would run down near enough to the hole to make sure of a four. With all those people watching and Finsterwald standing there, as likely as not to hole his long putt for the match, I had to be sure. How I did it, I don't know, but that shot came off just right and the ball ended up a foot from the hole. It would be nice to record a happy ending, but the cold-blooded truth was that Finsterwald did hole his putt and Tom and I were once more beaten by a hole. We had lost but that shot left a glow in my heart which returns whenever I think about it.

The morning singles session followed much of the pattern of the previous day as Ford beat Weetman, Souchak beat Moffitt, Casper beat Bousfield, and Finsterwald beat O'Connor; Peter Alliss did marvellously to halve with Arnold Palmer, as did Neil Coles with Gene Littler, while the captain and Bernard Hunt both claimed a point for the British in their victories over Hebert and Barber respectively.

Arnold Palmer: Another powerful memory from that weekend on the Lancashire coast involves Peter Alliss, who I played in the morning singles. Peter was an elegant and accomplished player. As most of the British players did, he shaped his shots for control purposes, from left to right in a controlled fade. I greatly admired the way Peter played the game, with such precision and accuracy, which was almost nothing like my style. It says something about the man's quiet tenacity that I had to work my tail off simply to halve with him. Cordially shaking hands at the match's conclusion, I think both of us knew we'd been in a dogfight – and would probably be in a few more before things were over.

Peter Alliss: I faced Palmer in the singles because nobody else wanted to play him! I mean they all came with reputations, much bigger than our reputations. All our team were nervous of playing him, and I was nervous, but I was probably so nervous I concentrated more. I didn't want to be beaten 8&6. So he hit the fairway, I hit the fairway, he hit the green, I hit the green, and so on and so on. That's the way I still think a lot of people should play today. If you hit the fairway, hit the green and don't three putt you are a success, a huge success, not just a success. That's what I did.

We were all square on eighteen and I hit into the left rough and couldn't reach the green. He hit a good drive. I was forty yards short of the green in two and he was about twenty feet away in two. I'm like, 'Jesus, he's going to beat me.' And I looked at the clubhouse and saw my father sitting in the window, looking out. I chipped it up close then Arnold putted up. He missed. His putt was about the same distance as mine. And he picked my coin up. He gave me my putt. And so I'm looking at him and I thought, I've had a good result today and you've had a good result – because he was Jesus then, he was the Almighty – and I said, 'Pick it up, Arnold, we'll call it a half.' And I was disappointed to hear him say when he was talking to the press how badly he had played. And I thought, 'Well, that's not very generous,' – because I'd actually played him off the course!

People said afterwards that I did well to halve the match with him – but he got a half with me! He holed from off the green three times. He holed a bunker shot, a chip shot and a pitch shot.

Neil Coles: In my first Ryder Cup match I'd had four eighteen-hole finishes and emerged with one-and-a-half points out of four. I had also had a good look at all the Americans in practise and made a lot of mental notes. I was rather fascinated by Jerry Barber, who apart from being a very human and loveable person was a living example of how it was possible to score well at golf without being an orthodox striker. I did not see how he could be really effective in a wind with that kind of high, cut drive, but there was no question about his toughness and determination, and he was a real wizard at the short game.

Going into the afternoon singles, the British needed to win every match in order to reclaim the cup. As expected, the task was beyond them – even if they gave it a stirring effort, with Alliss beating Collins, Rees beating Ford, Bousfield beating Barber, Coles beating Finsterwald and O'Connor and Littler halving.

Peter Alliss: In the afternoon, I beat Bill Collins 3&2. By that time, there was a change of format, twenty-four points up for grabs.

Over the years they've tried to make it, and they have, into much more of a spectacle for spectators. Although the matches were close, a lot of them very tight, the US kept winning all the time. Of course, there was this feeling, rather like the old tennis Wightman Cup, the British women against the Americans – they beat us all the time so they packed it up. The same thing wasn't far away from happening with the Ryder Cup, because they kept winning all the time.

But thanks to Wall's defeat of Weetman, Souchak's of Hunt and Palmer's of Haliburton the score ended 14½–9½, and the cup returned across the Atlantic once more. In the wake of the defeat, Henry Cotton spoke with deep despondence about the gap in class between the sides. 'I repeat what I have often said,' he announced morosely. 'Despite the advantages we have in playing our own small-sized golf ball on these short visits to play in international encounters, we again were outclassed. We know, and have known all along, since the game of golf got underway in the twenties, that good players were in great numbers in America, and with the sun throughout the year, practise facilities and huge rewards, we were up against an insoluble problem. The present top players, by no means poor performers, are leagues outside the tough American ones.'

Peter Alliss: The matches were much closer than the scores suggest. They weren't all 6&5s and 8&6s and that sort of thing, as many people thought or imagined or even pretended that's how it was. The matches I had with Casper were special and, still whenever I saw him, he said, 'I'm one or two-up on you in holes.'

Arnold Palmer: I loved the Ryder Cup because it simply wasn't about playing for money – it was about playing for something grander and more personal.

It doesn't matter how many Open championships or titles that you may have won. When you stand on the tee at the Ryder Cup match and play for your country, your stomach rumbles like a kid turning up for his first tournament.

FIFTEEN

1963

East Lake Country Club. Atlanta, Georgia.
(USA 23, GB 9)

In 1963 the format of the tournament changed once again. Fourball matches were introduced for the first time and, in order to accommodate them, the tournament was extended to three days. The first day's play would consist of two sets of foursomes, the second would see two sets of fourballs played, and then two sets of singles would be contested on the third. Every match would consist of eighteen holes and the number of points that were available was now 32.

The fifteenth Ryder Cup was held at East Lake in Atlanta and the home team was captained by Arnold Palmer, who was the dominant force in the game with three Masters titles, two Open Championship titles and the US Open crown already to his name. As well as veterans Julius Boros, Billy Casper, Dow Finsterwald and Gene Littler, Palmer was joined by rookies Bob Goalby, Tony Lema, Billy Maxwell, Johnny Pott and Dave Ragan.

Britain, meanwhile, felt that they had been disadvantaged in 1961 by having a playing captain in Dai Rees, so opted instead for the non-playing John Fallon. It was to make scant difference to the outcome. Peter Alliss, Neil Coles, Tom Haliburton, Bernard Hunt, Christy O'Connor, Dave Thomas and Harry Weetman joined forces with rookies Brian Huggett, Geoffrey Hunt and George Will.

Arnold Palmer: When I had the opportunity to be the playing captain, I suppose my ambitions and desires then were strongly in favour of a playing captain. As time and the years slipped by, I found it intriguing to be a non-playing captain. I suppose that, if I had my druthers, I would have chosen to be a playing captain.

Ryder Cup participation came to mean an awful lot to me. At East Lake in Atlanta, I narrowly defeated Dow Finsterwald in a close team vote for captain. I was honoured to be chosen to head the American squad. Actually, I became the last playing captain in the matches. This time I lost a close singles match to Alliss, who, for a man whose Rolls-Royce bears the licence plate '3 PUTT', certainly made his share of fine strokes. On the other side of the coin, though, I won four other matches against two defeats and contributed four points to our team's winning total in a lopsided romp, 23–9. Peter was one of their few bright spots – and don't believe it when he says he can't putt.

Peter Alliss: Atlanta was an interesting city then. Coca-Cola was there, a mighty big company then, although not as big as today. It was a very exciting, small city, good golf course, East Lake, which fell into disrepute. They have resurrected it now and it hosts the Tour Championship. It was the home of Bobby Jones – he had played a lot of golf there, so there was a lot of history. Well, I had a good Ryder Cup at East Lake, so I came away happy, but the rest of the team, they were totally overwhelmed.

Opposite: The British team board a BOAC aircraft at London Airport, en route to Atlanta.
Getty Images

Brian Huggett: Making the Ryder Cup was the next best thing to winning the Open. It wasn't the same for the Americans. They won quite easily and it wasn't a great competition back then. I always felt that if it all went really well, we could have won. But looking back, we had no bloody chance. We only had half a team that thought like me, that we could win. There were some players who got the blazer and thought that they could walk around and live off that for the rest of their lives. They didn't care enough if we won or lost. I was naïve to think we could win, especially away from home.

The Americans tried to make you feel inferior. And we were. They loved to give us a whacking. They were very tough about the matches in those days. They never took it easy.

Before a single ball had been struck in anger, Palmer declared of his side that, 'This team would beat the rest of the world combined.' It would prove accurately portentous – even though Palmer and Pott lost the opening foursomes 3&2 to Huggett and Will, and Boros and Lema and Littler and Finsterwald halved with Coles and Hunt and Thomas and Weetman respectively. The US claimed a point in the morning via Casper and Ragan's one-up victory over Alliss and O'Connor, but then upped the ante considerably in the afternoon to deliver on their captain's promise, sweeping the afternoon foursomes 4–0.

Johnny Pott: I was paired with Arnold the very first match and he made me run out and hit the first ball because he was doing some other stuff. I wasn't quite ready for that.

Neil Coles: I am always inspired by a good golf course, but Atlanta did not inspire me. Perhaps I had expected too much. At any rate I was disappointed. The course was too much like our parkland courses, and very artificial. Even the lake in the middle looked contrived, although it made a useful hazard at two of the better holes.

The Ryder Cup match was a three-day affair for the first time, two series of eighteen-hole fourball matches being added to the traditional foursomes and singles. When the Americans talk of a foursome they mean a fourball match, and what we regard as a foursome they call a 'Scotch foursome'. All very confusing. The foursomes were played first at Atlanta and I partnered Bernard Hunt and, later, his brother Geoffrey, on the team for the first time. I think it was a mistake to make Bernard and me change partners between rounds, especially in foursomes. A midday switch is bound to be unsettling and in this particular case the effect was accentuated. Bernard and I had halved our match with Tony Lema and Julius Boros and felt pretty good about it. We would have lunch together, we thought, and then set about whoever we were to play in the afternoon.

Then Johnny Fallon comes up and says, 'You boys played so well this morning, I'm going to split you up this afternoon – Neil to play with Geoff Hunt and Bernard with Tom Haliburton.' We couldn't believe our ears. We just sat and gaped. Naturally Geoffrey and I didn't win in the afternoon. Neither did Bernard.

Billy Casper: Arnold Palmer was our captain in 1963, and on the first day he paired rookies with seasoned players and we lost big. So we met after we'd finished playing and I said, 'Arnie, we need to pair strength with strength, so you and I play.' We played in the afternoon and won and that started the comeback.

Arnold Palmer gives a team talk before play gets underway in the foursomes.

My first partner, Dave Ragan, was so tight you couldn't have driven a tenpenny nail up his ass with a hammer, but that's just the way the Ryder Cup is. I mean, when they play the music at the opening ceremonies you can hardly breathe.

Johnny Pott: We had ten players, and eight played in each of the matches, but Arnold couldn't keep up with who was playing and, with all those rookies on the team, he didn't know what he had. I wasn't, like I say, at the top of my game. [Brian] Huggett dusted me off in the singles, and I didn't know Brian Huggett, other than that he was a little Welshman who beat my brains out.

Anyhow, I was choking and I told Arnold, 'I'm just not playing good. I'm swinging too quick.' I think that that was the honest thing to do, since Arnold couldn't see me playing. This was probably the reason that they started having non-playing captains.

Brian Huggett: You don't forget your first Ryder Cup match. George Will and I were playing Johnny Pott and Arnold Palmer. On the first hole, George hit the first tee shot and split the fairway. And then I knocked a six-iron onto the green. That was us away really. We were very nervous, but we had nothing to lose because we were playing against the King. I mean, everybody watched Arnold, and when he hit the ball in those days, the ground kind of shuddered. So it was a great thing for us. We were the underdogs, but we won 3&2, and when we won there was applause from about twelve, fifteen people. They

Arnold Palmer and Peter Alliss pose for photographers before their morning singles match.

were all the officials from the Great Britain and Ireland Ryder Cup committee. It was amazing. Hardly anybody else clapped!

In those days, seventy-five per cent of all the crowd at the event always watched the Palmer match. On the whole, the crowds were pretty good in America, they were very friendly, but not when you beat Arnold.

Christy O'Connor: I partnered Neil Coles to a one-hole win over Bob Goalby and Dave Ragan in the Saturday morning fourballs. We were both having lunch when the American team enquired about our pairings sheet for the afternoon matches. Nobody could find our captain. Apparently he went shopping while we were playing the morning matches, and must have got caught up in the traffic.

Arnold Palmer and Don Finsterwald were named at number one for the Americans in the afternoon and were anxious to get on with the match, but had no opposition. I told Neil that we would pair up again and go into battle. But he was totally drained and did not want to play. He had been involved in both morning and afternoon foursomes the day before, and was certain to be selected to play in both sets of singles the next day. But I convinced him to play and we went out and put up a great show, though going down 3&2.

The next day proved equally as grim for the British as the Americans took the fourballs 6–2, with Coles and O'Connor the only pairing to win a full point for the British against the rookies Goalby and Ragan.

Neil Coles: On the second day I was with Christy O'Connor morning and afternoon. First we beat Bob Goalby and Dave Ragan on the last green. Then we ran up against Arnie Palmer in his best mood. He and Bill Collins had a better-ball score of twenty-nine for the first nine holes and Christy and I couldn't do much about that. Palmer himself was out in thirty and he got round in sixty-seven. This was magnificent scoring and we thought we'd done well to take Arnie and Collins to the sixteenth. Then came the singles. I must say I prefer this to any other form of match. At Lytham I scored one-and-a-half points out of two in the singles, and at Atlanta I got half-a-point, which was about right proportionately.

My halved match was with Billy Casper and I putted extremely well, particularly when it mattered most. That match was an object lesson to me in the value of good putting. I hadn't played the long game at all well, but I knocked in so many putts you'd have thought I had been brought up in America.

With a 12–4 scoreline in their favour going into the third day, the Americans kept their foot down in the singles, winning ten matches and conceding only four full points (plus two halved matches) for a final 23–9 margin of victory, the second-largest in Ryder Cup history.

Peter Alliss: I had a good singles record at East Lake. I beat Arnold Palmer on his own ground, and then I halved with Tony Lema. I was driving badly in the Palmer match, for some reason hitting small slices. I drove with a three-wood, just to try and keep it in the fairway, and I was fifty yards behind Arnold every time. But I played my irons well and putted soundly, and found myself one up with two to play. I hit my little squirty three-wood off the seventeenth, then played a six-iron to ten feet. Arnold played his approach to three feet away, and I holed my putt. So now he's got to hole his for a half, which he made, and then we halved the last hole, and I won. That was a very good day's work.

SIXTEEN

1965

Royal Birkdale Golf Club. Southport, England

(USA 19½, GB 12½)

With Royal Birkdale hosting the Ryder Cup for the first time, there were a number of changes in the air surrounding the event. The British PGA, struggling to finance the full running costs of the Ryder Cup, received a generous donation of £11,000 from businessman, British PGA Vice President and Royal Birkdale member, Brian Park, who in turn also added some of his marketing nous to bring both value and prestige to the event.

For the first time in the UK there was a tented village constructed for spectators and a media centre for journalists, trade exhibition and expanded souvenir programmes, and scorekeepers carrying individual match results on boards around the course, providing the first modern touches to the event and establishing a new standard for subsequent instalments.

Peter Alliss: There was a man called Binnie Clark, a Scotsman, who worked for Gallaher's, the giant tobacco company. Binnie was a member of the Kingswood Golf Club next to Walton Heath and he was a very go-ahead fella, he was the sort of PR man for Gallaher's. He was responsible for introducing tented villages and where spectators could buy things. It was the start of big things. It was somewhere you could leave your left luggage, you could leave your coat and umbrella. It was all very nice. A few little shops came along and they were selling hamburgers, sandwiches, toffees, coffees, things like that. You see what it has grown into today, but they had those sorts of facilities at Birkdale. It was a great success.

The Americans, led by Byron Nelson, recalled Julius Boros, Billy Casper, Tony Lema, Gene Littler, Arnold Palmer and Johnny Pott to the team, while handing debuts to Tommy Jacobs, Don January, Dave Marr and Ken Venturi. The most notable absence from the team was Jack Nicklaus who, despite having won his fourth Major title as a professional at the Masters in April (to add to his US Open victory in 1962, his PGA Championship crown in 1963 and his maiden Masters triumph in 1963), the US PGA's eligibility rules, which required a minimum five-year PGA Tour membership before points could be counted for team qualification, barred his inclusion – indeed, he would not be selected for the team until 1969. Fortune seemed to be against them when Johnny Pott ruptured a muscle in his lower back during practise and was sidelined from proceedings. Furthermore, 1964 US Open champion Ken Venturi had surgery for circulatory problems in his hands earlier in the year and was still to regain his best form.

The home team, meanwhile, was captained by Harry Weetman and retained the experienced heads of Peter Alliss, Neil Coles, Bernard Hunt, Christy O'Connor, Dave Thomas and George Will, who were joined by rookies Peter Butler, Jimmy Hitchcock, Jimmy Martin and Lionel Platts.

Opposite: Peter Alliss celebrates as Christy O'Connor sinks a putt. *Getty Images*

Byron Nelson: It wasn't very long after winning the US Open in 1964 that Ken Venturi began to have trouble with his hands. A golfer's hands are pretty important, and Kenny's hands got so bad that he finally had to have them both operated on in June of 1965. I was concerned about what this might mean to Kenny's career in golf, and my concern became considerably stronger when Kenny was selected to be on our Ryder Cup team. The rest of the team included Julius Boros, Billy Casper, Tommy Jacobs, Don January, Tony Lema, Gene Littler, Dave Marr, Arnold Palmer, and Johnny Pott. It was a good team, I felt, and I had just begun to wonder who the captain would be when I got a call from Warren Cantrell, president of the PGA, who happened to be from Amarillo, Texas. Warren said, 'Byron, I talked to the players on the team and asked if they would like you as captain, and they said, "Absolutely!"' There wasn't one dissenting vote, which made me feel very happy and very honoured.

Warren's call took me right back to the days of the 1935 Ryder Cup at Ridgewood when I was assistant pro. While I knew then that I wanted to be on the team one day, I never dreamed about being captain. This wasn't even on my list of goals when I was on the tour. It was certainly one of the greatest honours in my career, but I wanted it to be more than an honour – I wanted it to be a victory. The Americans had held sway for quite a while, but I knew the British players were getting stronger and were looking forward to the chance to trim our sails. In those days, the captain had nothing to say about the selection of the team – it was all done on the basis of points earned by winning or playing well in various events over the two-year period between the matches. When my captaincy was announced, it was only three months before the matches, so I didn't really have much time to work with the team.

The Great Britain team pose for the press. *Getty Images*

Because of the lack of time, right away I began thinking about what I could do to help the team before we went over to England. Our opponents were still using the smaller British ball and we would have to use it too, so I got some for the team to practice with when we all met in New York before flying to England. I made arrangements with the good folks at Winged Foot, and as soon as the team arrived, we went out there to practice. They were amazed at how differently that British ball behaved. Because it was smaller, you didn't get as much ball on the face of the club, so it didn't have as much backspin and it wouldn't fly as high as the American ball. Also, the heavier, wetter air they would encounter in England would affect the ball even more. I'd always felt that was why the British played more pitch-and-run shots than we did, because the small ball lent itself to that type of shot more.

I already had Venturi's hands on my mind, and then during the practise round that afternoon, Johnny Pott got a stitch in his right side that was hurting quite a little bit. But we had a doctor examine him who decided it was only a pulled muscle and shouldn't be a problem. That relieved me considerably, because Venturi had only recently gotten back to playing and was just now at the point where he could play without gloves, so he was somewhat of an unknown quantity.

We had a good flight over on BOAC and landed in London, then boarded a smaller plane which took us to Southport, near the Royal Birkdale course. When we'd recovered from the trip and began practising, it soon became apparent that Johnny Pott's side wasn't any better. As it turned out, he never so much as hit a ball. That cut me to nine players, and I knew Venturi's hands wouldn't allow him to play every match, so I had to figure very carefully how I would use him and the rest of my team.

Despite our situation with Pott and Venturi, when there was a press conference that afternoon, I was not about to let the British know my concerns. The British captain, Harry Weetman, had his say first. By now, we had become the underdogs in the British press, so Harry announced that the British definitely had the stronger team and would win the match. Then it was my turn. I got up, looked at him and said, 'Harry, we didn't come 3,000 miles to lose.'

It's very awe-inspiring to represent your country in the Ryder Cup, and I'll never forget the feeling of pride and excitement as I raised our country's flag at the start of the matches. The Prime Minister, Harold Wilson, was there and welcomed us, Harry Weetman and Warren Cantrell made some remarks, and the match was on.

After the routing in Atlanta, there was a wonderful (and very welcome) balance to the Thursday foursomes, which ended 4–4.

Peter Alliss: Christy O'Connor and I were reinstated to the team at Royal Birkdale in 1965, and I must confess, even if I do say it myself, we were in cracking form. In our opening foursomes we beat Ken Venturi and Don January by 5&4 and in the afternoon we beat Billy Casper and Gene Littler by 2&1.

The following morning, in the fourballs, we were defeated 6&4 by Arnold Palmer and Dave Marr. That was a very unusual occurrence for Christy and me and by way of proving it, we went on to beat the same pair on the eighteenth in the afternoon. I tell you, over the years O'Connor and I had the ability to surprise the best that America could throw at us. My best and worst moments in golf occurred during the Ryder Cup. The worst was in 1953, the eighteenth at Wentworth, when I took four to get down. Best was in the final hole of the 1965 Ryder Cup. It was Alliss and O'Connor against Palmer and Marr – I hit a four-wood to within ten feet.

George Will: Heavy rain made the course heavy and slow and the last six holes were par fives, so it wasn't possible to reach the green in two.

I noted that the Americans played their shot with their wedges much more stiff-wristed than our team. This produced the low flight, the quick check and then roll. Perhaps one reason why the Americans excel at this shot is that they invariably play on well-watered greens, whereas we play on a different type of course each week – sometimes fast-running and sometimes soft. Birkdale was in really magnificent condition but the rain prior to the match had made it ideal from the American point of view.

Dave Marr: I had a terrible start on the first morning. Arnold Palmer and I were playing Dave Thomas and George Will. I noticed Arnold's hand shaking as he teed up at the first hole. That scared me half to death and my golf thereafter certainly didn't help Arnold.

At the start I was nervous, and by the third hole I was downright embarrassed. Some of the places I put him in weren't even on the golf course.

Byron Nelson: Most of the matches were very exciting and quite close, except for Davey Marr and Arnold Palmer's showing in the morning foursomes on the first day. It was Dave's first time to play in the Ryder Cup and he was very nervous. I watched him and he hardly got the ball off the ground the first seven holes. Obviously, even Arnold couldn't overcome that and they lost to Dave Thomas and George Will, 6&5. However, I'd noticed that Dave finally settled down and was playing real well at the end, so I got an idea. Since this was the second match that morning, I figured Harry would move Thomas and Will to the first match that afternoon, so I did the same thing with Dave and Arnold. When I announced at lunch that Palmer and Marr would be playing Thomas and Will again, Arnold and Dave didn't even finish their food, they jumped up from the table and charged off to the practise tee. My guess was right, because in the afternoon they shot 30 on the front nine – a remarkable score at Royal Birkdale, where par is 73 – and they turned the tables completely, winning 6&5. We were all pretty happy about that, and I think it was the most exciting match of the whole tournament. There are things a captain has to do, sometimes challenge or rile your players.

Dave Marr: I asked Arnold once whether he ever prayed during a tournament, and he told me, 'No; all I ever ask is that I'm healthy when I get there. I'll take care of the rest.'

Byron Nelson: If I had to stake the family jewels on a single eight-foot putt, I'd want Palmer to putt it for me. He exerts so much physical and mental force, it's almost as though he commands the ball to obey him.

Fans watch the action on the sixth green at Royal Birkdale. *Getty Images*

Arnold Palmer: When I take a shot that seems bold, it never occurs to me that I might miss it. And when I do, I'm surprised as hell. I can't believe it.

You've got to learn to live with trouble, and you've got to learn how to get out of it. It's a little like bleeding. Your first objective is to get it stopped. Then you try to heal it. You tell yourself there's nothing here you haven't faced before; and if you've done it once, you can do it again.

I don't look on it as a gamble, really. I just look on it as a harder shot. Why hit a conservative shot? When you miss it, you're in just as much trouble as when you miss a bold one.

Trouble is bad to get into but fun to get out of. If you're in trouble, eighty per cent of the time there's a way out. If you can see the ball, you can probably hit it; and if you can hit it, you can move it; and if you can move it, you might be able to knock it into the hole. At least, it's fun to try.

I suppose there's a place to play it safe. But as far as I'm concerned, it's not on the golf course.

Dave Marr: I liked playing in front of Arnold's Army, as his huge band of supporters were known. He was the biggest thing in golf for a long, long time. It was wild at times. When Arnold teed up his ball, they cheered. And if I'd walked on water, they wouldn't have noticed. But I enjoyed the excitement of all those people, and I think the Army was good for golf.

Arnold Palmer: This might sound corny, but I tried to look the whole gallery in the eye.

Maybe it was a selfish thing on my part, but I liked seeing the happiness my golf seemed to give them.

The Friday fourballs held some trepidation for the home fans after the trouncing their team had received in that format in 1963, which had effectively sealed the result for the US. While the Americans once again emerged with their noses in front at Birkdale, it wasn't by anywhere near as decisive a margin, this time concluding 5–3 to give the Americans a 9–7 lead going into the singles.

Byron Nelson: Though Tony was playing well and Arnold and Davey had come back, at the end of the first day we were tied at four points apiece. Kenny had not played well in his first two matches, so I had him rest during the morning of the second day. That was when we played the alternate shot format properly known as fourball. In the morning we won two matches, lost one, and halved one, so we were needing to do better in the afternoon. For the last match of the afternoon I decided to pair Ken with Tony because they were good friends; they were both from San Francisco, and I knew they enjoyed playing together. They went up against Hunt and Coles and came to the last hole, a par five, deadlocked. It was Kenny's turn and he hit a good drive, then Tony pulled the second shot and the ball ended up left and short of the green, back of a small shallow bunker. I was standing back of the green and knew we needed a point badly. The British players left their second shot short but on the right side, with only a simple chip to the green. Prime Minister Wilson was standing next to me and he said, 'I say, sir, it appears as though we have the advantage.' I answered, 'Yes, Mr. Prime Minister, it appears that way, but of all

Arnold Palmer drives from the tee, watched by his partner Dave Marr during their match with George Will and Dave Thomas. *Getty Images*

the people on my team, I'd rather have Venturi playing this shot than anyone else.' Then Kenny gripped down on the club, used a little short firm motion, and chipped close to the hole. The British chipped short and missed their putt and we won, one-up. At the end of the second day we had taken the lead, 9–7, and went on to win decisively.

It was only on the final day that the US team showed its real class, mastering the difficult and persistent wind to push out into a commanding lead in the morning session, with Palmer, Boros, Lema, Marr and Jacobs all winning, while January halved with Will; Hunt and Alliss returned the only two full points for the British with their victories over Littler and Casper respectively.

The afternoon session followed much the same pattern with Alliss, Coles and Platts claiming points for the British, but every other match going the way of the visitors. It was a spectacular display from the Americans to dominate in such a fashion in tricky conditions, to seal a final – and decisive – victory.

Arnold Palmer: We retained the cup, 19½–12½. Another rout by the Yanks.

Byron Nelson: It was a very emotional moment when the matches were over. The bugle corps played 'Taps' as Harry Weetman and I lowered our country's flags, and everyone had tears in their eyes. We had a beautiful flight home and we were a very happy group, believe me. The PGA officials had a celebration party for us when we arrived, and it was an occasion I will always remember, for a very good reason.

All through the matches, I had wanted so much to do a good job and help our team win that I moved around more those three days than for any other tournament in my life. I tried hard to see at least part of every match and was very visible at all times. The team must have appreciated that, because unbeknownst to me they got together and had a duplicate made of the actual Ryder Cup trophy and presented it to me when we arrived back in New York. It's a beautiful piece, and of all the trophies I've won, that is one of my most prized possessions.

Peter Alliss: If you look at a lot of the results, it was 2&1, 3&2. When they were thirty-six-hole matches, if you lost by that margin, that meant it was a very close affair. Although we were losing, we still had hope. I thought we always had five or six good players. We were always two or three players short really, in those days, we didn't have any strength in depth, whereas they did. We lived in hope 'we can do this, we can do it if everyone plays their best and we get a bit of good luck, we can win.' But it wasn't to be.

SEVENTEEN

1967

Champions Golf Club. Houston, Texas

(USA 23½, GB 8½)

There has seldom been a more memorable quote in the history of the Ryder Cup than that uttered by US team captain, Ben Hogan, during the opening ceremony of the seventeenth Ryder Cup, held at Champions Golf Club in Houston, Texas, in 1967. After a long and interminable introduction to his team and their achievements by visiting captain Dai Rees, Hogan stood, introduced each of his players by name only and then, with his team now standing, simply said, 'Ladies and gentlemen, the United States Ryder Cup Team – the finest golfers in the world,' before returning to his seat. The audience broke into a wild applause as the British team contemplated the challenge that awaited them. And what a challenge it would prove to be.

The team that Hogan introduced in such glorious fashion was made up of Julius Boros, Billy Casper, Gene Littler, Arnold Palmer and Johnny Pott, with rookie places handed to Gay Brewer, Gardner Dickinson, Al Geiberger, Bobby Nichols and Doug Sanders.

Their opposition from across the pond had well-known faces among the ranks in Peter Alliss, Neil Coles, Brian Huggett, Bernard Hunt, Christy O'Connor, Dave Thomas and George Will, and new faces in Hugh Boyle, Malcolm Gregson and, most notably, the young firecracker, Tony Jacklin.

Johnny Pott: We were having a Ryder Cup team meeting during the Colonial tournament in preparation for that year's Ryder Cup match to be played at Champions in Houston. The ten-man team had already been determined, and this was only the second time that a non-playing captain would be elected for the team. The last playing captain we had was on the '63 team and that was Arnold Palmer. The thought was to honour past PGA champions by making them captain of the Ryder Cup.

The first non-playing captain was Byron Nelson, when the match was being played at Royal Birkdale. Ben Hogan was playing in the Colonial that year, and we felt that if there was ever an opportunity to have Hogan be the non-playing captain, it would be at Champions because he was such good friends with Jimmy Demaret and Jackie Burke. I don't know exactly how I was chosen to be the one to ask him if he would be the captain, but I guess I was unanimously elected to do that – which probably meant that I was the last man on the team or something like that.

Hogan was not playing much when I came out as a rookie, except for just an occasional tournament. Like so many of the other golfers, I was in awe of Ben Hogan. I never really knew what to call him. I certainly wasn't familiar enough to call him Ben, and I didn't want to call him Mr Hogan, because I thought that might make him think I was being a smarty. So I'd call him something like, 'Hey, Mr Ben Hogan,' or whatever.

Anyhow, I went out from the meeting to find him, and I found him in the locker room.

Opposite: Billy Casper watches the progress of his putt as his ball rolls towards the hole.

I approached him and I probably said, 'Mr Ben Hogan, I'm Johnny Pott.' I didn't know if he had any idea who I was, even though just a couple of years earlier at Colonial I had tied with Arnold Palmer, and Arnold beat me in an eighteen-hole play-off on Monday. I said, 'I'm a member of the current Ryder Cup team and the team would like for you to be our captain at the matches at Houston in September.' And he says, 'Uh. Champions, huh? September, huh? I'll let you know tomorrow.' And I said, 'Well, I really would appreciate a positive answer because it would just be an honour for you to be our captain.' I went back up to the meeting with the PGA and the rest of the players and relayed the story to them. They said, 'We'll just have to wait to find out tomorrow.'

It worked out at the Colonial tournament that I had opposite tee times with Mr Hogan. At Colonial, you walk out of the locker room through the pro shop to get to the first tee or the practise tee or whatever. Next day I was going out of the locker room and he's coming in, and as we passed he said, 'I'll do it.' A man of very few words. He never broke his stride as he looked me in the eye. That was all I heard from him, so I reported that to the PGA and the rest of the players that Ben said he would love to do it.

Ken Venturi: Hogan was not a teacher. Byron Nelson could teach; he could volunteer it. With Hogan, you had to ask him, 'What do you feel like when you are doing this?' 'What do you have in your mind when you're going to play this shot?' He would say, 'Well, I'd do this…' and he could never say, 'Ken you ought to be doing this, this, and this.' You had to pick his brain, and not many people could get into his brain because he wouldn't tell you. And so he would say, 'This is what you do.' If you played with Hogan and the pin was on the right-hand side next to a creek, and you swooped it over the creek and knocked it within two feet of the hole, Hogan would say, 'Get yourself another game, boy, you don't know how to play. You've got to come in left to right.' With Hogan, you had to be able to shape your shots the right way.

Hogan had one secret. He said, 'Muscles do not have memories. I tell my muscles what to do.' He could visualise everything that he was doing in his golf swing. He could create an image in his mind of what he wanted to do to make the swing do what he had to do – whether it be a long draw, high draw, a high fade, a knockdown, a feather shot. He had all these finishes and all these swings that he created himself to create the shot that he had visualised in his mind.

Arnold Palmer: My troubled relationship with Ben Hogan began when my pal Dow Finsterwald arranged for us to team up and play with Hogan and Jackie Burke in a practise round before the 1958 Masters. I had a bone-wearying midnight drive across South Carolina and I went out on the course that morning and played abysmally. A little while afterward, as we were changing in the club locker room, I heard Ben Hogan remark to Jackie, 'Tell me something, Jackie. How the hell did Palmer get an invitation to the Masters?'

That really stung me. I'll never know if Hogan knew I overheard the comment. But he certainly was aware that I was nearby and could have overheard it. I knew he was probably the most precise shotmaker who ever played the game and no particular fan of my style of play, having once said of my game, 'Palmer's swing might work for him, but no one else should try it.' In any event, the question burned me up and set my mind on showing

Arnold Palmer arrives at the course by his private plane.

him why the hell I'd been invited to the Masters. To go on to win it that year was quite something.

Johnny Pott: Hogan was a totally different captain than Byron Nelson had been. Byron wrote us a letter every week and kept us informed and all that. Byron was very outgoing and kept us abreast of everything that was happening. And maybe that had been because we were going to England for the 1965 matches. But we really never did hear much from Hogan, except we knew from our correspondence from the PGA that he definitely was going to be there.

We were told to arrive in Houston on the Monday of Ryder Cup week. There were ten players on the team, and we were told to be there on Monday for a practise round. Normally, what we would do was play two fivesomes. Well, we were getting ready to play about ten o'clock and Arnold Palmer hadn't arrived. Hogan goes around to everyone and asks, 'Where is Arnold Palmer?' Somebody said, 'Well, he's not here yet. We haven't seen him.' Hogan says, 'I'm gonna wait a little while. I really want us all to play in two fivesomes, and I'd like to see how you guys are playing.' About a half hour later, Arnold buzzed us at Champions in his jet. He flew by about five hundred feet above the ground, made some funny turns and all that kind of stuff. Hogan looks up and says, 'Oh, there's Arnold Palmer, huh?' There's an airport in the vicinity of Champions where Arnold landed, and I think Arnie got a citation from the FAA for buzzing the golf course. But that's another story.

Arnold shows up and he walks out on the practise tee hitching his pants, and you know how Arnold is, and he says, 'Hey, Ben, what ball are we playing?' Hogan says, 'Well, Mr Palmer, when you make the team, I'll let you know.' He was pretty hot at Arnold for not being there with the rest of us.

Peter Alliss: That was the first time we saw Arnold Palmer in his jet plane. He zoomed over the course and got a telling off from Ben Hogan for behaving badly. 'What the hell do you think you're doing, flying over the course?' He had got Henry Longhurst and Pat Ward-Thomas, two journalists, up with him, giving them a ride around in his new jet. It was revolutionary, his new plane. It was all very exciting. I remember Arnold's plane had gone zooming round and suddenly there was a little bi-plane that came across, obviously a flying club plane, and somebody said, 'That's the caddies arriving!' It was quite funny.

Hogan couldn't believe Arnold had pulled that stunt. We couldn't believe that a golfer had his own plane!

Arnold Palmer: I loved it, that was my thing – I loved flying my plane.

Jack Burke Jnr: Palmer went to Hogan and said, 'Are we gonna play the little ball or the big ball?' – because we had an option in those days to play the English ball or the American ball. And Hogan said, 'Fella, I'll tell you when I tell you if you've made the team.' Palmer never did like that.

Arnold Palmer: The thing I remember about Hogan was that he never called me by my name. It was always, 'Hey, fella!' He was pretty standoffish. He wasn't a real friendly guy. His friends were Burke and Demaret and as far as I knew those were his best buddies. Demaret always kidded with him and talked to him a lot, wasn't intimidated by him.

Ben Hogan: If Jimmy Demaret had concentrated on golf as much as laughing and making people laugh, he might have won more tournaments. Of course, I wouldn't have liked him as much.

Peter Alliss: We played at the Champions Club in Houston, which was owned by Jack Burke Jnr and Jimmy Demaret. Everyone thought they had gone mad. It was about ten miles outside Houston and they had got options on about 1,000 acres or more, swamp land, and they built this golf course and put all their money in it. The powers that be thought Jimmy and Jack had gone crazy; they had put all their money into the project and it would never do any good. Of course, now, with the growth of Houston, it's almost in the middle of the city. Then they made millions out of the development of housing round the golf course, one thing or another, a fantastic success. But the course was new when we played the Ryder Cup matches then, it was almost a PR exercise, not only for the US PGA, but for Burke and Demaret, who were very well-respected pros.

Jack Burke Jnr: In 1967 Demaret and I were told by the PGA that we would be working as hosts for the Ryder Cup that year. We had to organise a dinner downtown, and it was the first time we had given a dinner for Ryder Cup matches. Barry Goldwater was a senator and we got him to come down and speak; it was a great dinner. Hogan told us to get ten caddies ready; and Billy Casper told our superintendent that he wanted to have his own caddie and I had to go down and say, 'Billy, we were told to get ten caddies and we have one for you and you're gonna have to use him.' And he wasn't very happy about that.

He also gave me a message that he needed some buffalo meat, and he needed a pillow that kept him from sneezing, so I had to organise all these things for him.

Peter Alliss: Hogan was serious as ever. Doug Sanders and I were friendly, and we played a few practise holes together. Hogan tore into him afterwards. 'What in hell are you doing?' he said to Doug. Fraternizing with the opposition you know.

Doug Sanders: Hogan was a great champion and great motivator, and I was proud to play for him and my country. He'd stop you that week, take a puff of his cigarette, stare into your eyes and say, 'You will win today won't you?' He'd put pressure on you, and we responded. He didn't care if you carried only a driver and putter, as long as you won. He lived his life for one thing – to win.

Johnny Pott: In the team meeting, the first thing Hogan said to the guys was, 'You know, I never was comfortable playing in anybody else's clothes.' And, of course, on the Ryder Cup we had these uniforms and everybody was supposed to dress like a team. 'You fellows can wear whatever you want. And [Doug] Sanders, if you want to come out here dressed like a peacock, you just go right ahead and make yourself comfortable. But let me tell you one thing. I don't want my name on that trophy as the losing captain.'

He was a hard man to address. He addressed you. At one meeting with us he said, 'Boys, let me tell you something. You don't have to be a rocket scientist to do this job. I'm going to pair straight hitters with straight hitters and crooked hitters with crooked hitters so you won't find yourselves in unfamiliar places.' Hell, Bobby Nichols and I were paired, and we'd learned to play out of the woods. We won every point.

Billy Casper: Every two years playing in the Ryder Cup was the highlight of my career. I felt very fortunate to have played on eight consecutive teams. At the time that I made the team, you had to earn the points, there was no picking of players on the team, so you really had to earn what you got.

Peter Alliss: At the opening ceremony, Dai Rees introduced our team: here is so and so, who has won the Welsh Open, and won the Croydon Alliance and the Musselburgh Pro-Am or something. Then, suddenly, Hogan just turned, gestured, and they all stood up and he said, 'Ladies and gentleman, the finest players in the world.' That was it. He didn't say any of their names. It was a brilliant bit of PR, and we were very down.

Malcolm Gregson: He just flicked his hand, and they all got up quickly and then sat down again. Take that! The whole place went berserk.

Peter Alliss: It felt like we were ten down before we had even started.

Malcolm Gregson: You look back now and it really was something else. Hogan said they were the best players in the world – and that's exactly what they were.

Johnny Pott: Hogan as a captain? Magnificent. *Magnificent.*

Peter Alliss: Hogan was a hell of a figure. He gave you an inferiority complex just by being there.

Jack Burke Jnr: We had an elaborate pre-match dinner at Champions, one of the nicest I've ever seen. But very few Texans knew or cared much about the Ryder Cup. It was a much bigger deal when we played in England. We played the same weekend as the big Texas-Arkansas football game, so while we had had big crowds at the Houston Open in the spring, we struggled for numbers for the Ryder Cup. There weren't many people at all; we basically left the gates open on Saturday. But bringing the Ryder Cup to Champions was something that needed to be done for golf in Texas.

The home team roared out of the traps in the foursomes, winning 5½–2½. Huggett and Will halved with Casper and Boros in the morning and Jacklin and Thomas won both their sessions (against Sanders and Brewer in the morning and Littler and Geiberger in the afternoon), but everything else went the way of the US.

Johnny Pott: Champions had a first hole on the Cypress Creek course that was a par-four dogleg left – kind of down and to the left. You know how festive the Ryder Cup is. Well, it was a foggy morning and on the green the marine band started playing all those songs, like 'The Star Spangled Banner' and 'God Save the Queen', and marching up that fairway in the fog. Somebody said, 'God, Ben, who's going to hit the first ball?' He says, 'No doubt about it: Gene [Littler] is first. He don't give a crap about nothing.'

Jack Burke Jnr: I'll never forget a moment at the 1967 Ryder Cup. Billy Casper was going off in the first match on the first day. The band from the University of Houston played the national anthem, and the American flag went up. At that moment, Billy, one of the truly great players of all time and a guy who never melted under any kind of pressure, turned to me. His face was white; he looked scared to death.
    'Wh . . . wh . . . what do I do now?' Billy asked me.
    'Get up there and hit that squiggly little slice of yours right down the middle,' I answered.
    That sort of snapped Billy to attention and he hit a fine drive.

Billy Casper: My commitment has always been towards taking the emotion out of my game. I have always tried to stay calm and cool under any pressure and my focus has purely been in concentration. Ben Hogan was one who had incredible concentration on the course and didn't get too excited one way or the other. This has been my style as well trying to meet every shot good or bad with an even keel and not get too bothered by it. Hogan used to say, 'Golf is thirty per cent physical and seven hundred per cent mental'.
    Hogan put Julius Boros and me off first because both of us were very quick players and he wanted us to get out there and get up so that the other players could see it and it would sort of rub off on them. He wanted to set the tone. Hogan wanted to win all the matches. He didn't want to lose a point.

Malcolm Gregson: On the first day I played in the afternoon with Hugh Boyle against Gardner Dickinson and Palmer. Arnold was on his game. Gardner Dickinson lined up every putt and Arnold holed everything. He was just fantastic.

Tony Jacklin: In those days, I was full of confidence, so I revelled in the whole thing. I played with Dave Thomas as my foursomes partner for both sessions on the first day. Dave was a terrible chipper. The par threes at Champions are long with difficult carries, and all are even-numbered holes followed by par fives, so he hit on the threes, and I chipped if he missed the green. I chipped on the fives, too. And as long as my drives were on the fairway on the par-fives – which were all odd numbers [five, nine, and thirteen] – he'd never have to chip. And that's the way it worked. We had a hell of a record, two wins in the foursomes and a half in the Saturday afternoon fourball.

I was twenty-three, just finding my sea legs. I had won a couple of tour events in the UK that summer and just got my tour card over in the States. I got thrown into the deep end to learn.

Peter Alliss: When we went back to America in 1967 to play the matches at the Champions Club, Christy and I were once more put together on the Friday morning and afternoon foursomes and were perhaps rather unlucky to lose both by a narrow margin [both 2&1], but still we persevered. Christy was one of the finest strikers of the ball that I have ever seen. The only chink in his armour was that he was an inconsistent putter. He never had a method that looked secure – although he did have periods when he putted the eyeballs out of everybody.

It was Christy's cavalier approach to life that intrigued me. He was always good for a bit of conversation and a jar, or three.

I'm very proud of the fact that he and I were partners. Although we didn't win every game we played together in Ryder Cup and international events, I could not have wished for a better partner, or a more considerate one.

He was, although only a few years older than I, by far the senior partner and he encouraged me and did everything he possibly could to set my mind at rest. We pulled each other along. We were very good for each other, and I just wish we could do it all over again, because it was enormous fun.

The fourballs on the second day really showed the difference in class between the two teams as the US won seven matches outright, with the only blight (if it can be called that) on their record being the halved match between Littler and Geiberger with the resolute Jacklin and Thomas.

Julius Boros: I was playing with Arnold Palmer against George Will and Hugh Boyle in the Saturday afternoon fourball, and at the halfway point we were down by four. So I turned to Arnold and I said, 'I've heard about these famous charges of yours. Let me see you get out of this one with one of 'em.' Arnie was so used to challenging himself, he was surprised when he was challenged by someone else. So he said, 'You follow me.' I did, and I'm a son of a gun if he didn't pull that damn match out the bag. We won one-up.

Arnold Palmer: Julius Boros and I were getting trounced early in the fourball matches against Hugh Boyle and George Will when I glanced up and saw Jackie Burke looking on. Jackie was the host professional at Champions and a long-time friend who loved to pull my chain whenever he could. 'Well, Palmer,' he drawled slyly as we walked off the green where Julius and I had gone three down. 'Looks like you two have gotten yourselves into a real mess.'

I glanced at him as if I had no idea what he was talking about. 'What do you mean, Jackie?'

He grimaced. 'I mean, I don't think even you will be able to get your team out of this one.'

'Jackie,' I replied, 'I'm sorry you don't have any faith in us.'

'Sorry. Not this time,' he said.

'Well, if that's the case,' I proposed thoughtfully, 'you wouldn't care to put a little something on it, would you?'

Now the old rascal smiled. 'I tell you what. If you somehow get out of this mess and win this match, I'll make you a clock.'

'A clock?' I asked.

'Not just any clock,' he added. 'A beautiful handmade clock.' So a clock it was. On the very next hole, Julius and I started a charge and went on to secure a come-from-behind one-up victory. That momentum propelled us through the rest of the weekend. I won five matches, gave the Brits a joyride in my airplane that brought the wrath of the FAA down on my head and scored five points, contributing to one of the largest American margins of victory in the history of the Ryder Cup. That handmade clock, incidentally, which has the twelve letters of my name where the numbers usually are, sits on a shelf in my office workshop. That's a place very special to me – the place I really love to go and work on clubs and be alone with my thoughts. So it's only fitting the clock is there, reminding me of a wonderful moment in my playing career and how much fun it was to take that clock out of Jackie Burke's hands.

Going into the singles, the US held a 13–3 advantage. Over the course of the two sessions they once again demonstrated their outstanding abilities to finish the third day's play 10½–5½. The final overall score of 23½–8½ was the largest margin of victory ever posted in Ryder Cup history.

Ben Hogan's words at the opening ceremony had been more than apt.

Doug Sanders: Hogan made it very clear to the entire team that he didn't want to be associated with failure. Standing there, tapping the ash off a cigarette and with those cold, grey eyes boring into me, he said, 'Doug, you will win today, won't you?' I took it as an order. There wasn't a mention of country allegiance: I was playing for Hogan.

Tony Jacklin: I was up against Arnold Palmer in the morning singles. I'd played with Arnold in the Masters that year, and beat him in the first round. But it was always difficult playing Arnold in America, because of the following he got. You're still made to feel in some respects that you're there to make the numbers up. That's just the way it was. But I didn't play particularly well [lost 3&2], and I certainly didn't play well against Dickinson in the afternoon [same score]. I just didn't get it together, but you can only do what you can do. It was fun.

Gardner Dickinson: I was so pleased when I was paired with Jacklin in the afternoon. We didn't get on well. He despised Bob Goalby and me, and I do take pride in that. When Jacklin first came to the USA, he acted as if he were the great-grandson of George Washington instead of a guest, and, for the most part, he seemed to think he was doing our tour a favour when he played in it . . . and nobody shed any tears when he went back home. When I beat him in the singles that year it was one of the highlights of my career.

Ben Hogan: Several of the matches could have gone either way. A few short putts here and there and it might have been a different story. We had a very strong team, but even so I think the final score board flattered us a little at 23½ points to only 8½. But as a captain, I was very happy with that result; winning was what I liked to do.

Peter Alliss.

EIGHTEEN

1969

Royal Birkdale Golf Club. Southport, England
(USA 16, GB 16)

The Ryder Cup returned to Royal Birkdale in 1969 for its eighteenth edition. And just as the British team had responded so gloriously to the crushing defeat they had suffered at Thunderbird in 1955 by storming to victory in 1957 at Lindrick, so too did they muster a most magnificent response in 1969 to the humiliation that had been dished out by the Americans at Champions two years previously.

It was the closest contest to date in the history of the competition, with seventeen of the thirty-two matches going to the last hole.

The teams were now made up of twelve players instead of ten and the composition of both were vastly different in terms of Ryder Cup experience. Sam Snead captained a US side that had only two returning players in Billy Casper and Gene Littler. After serving his five years on the US PGA tour, Jack Nicklaus was at last eligible for selection (by this time he had three Masters titles to his name, two US Open titles, and one win each at the Open Championship and the US PGA). He was joined by fellow rookies Tommy Aaron, Miller Barber, Frank Beard, Dale Douglass, Ray Floyd, Dave Hill, Dan Sikes, Ken Still and Lee Trevino.

Britain was captained by Eric Brown, whose team consisted of Peter Alliss, Peter Butler, Neil Coles, Brian Huggett, Bernard Hunt, Tony Jacklin, Christy O'Connor and rookies Brian Barnes, Maurice Bembridge, Alex Caygill, Bernard Gallacher and Peter Townsend. Jacklin had impressed on his Ryder Cup debut at Champions, claiming a very respectable two-and-a-half points amid the routing of his teammates, and came into the 1969 edition in tremendous form after becoming the first Briton in eighteen years to claim the Open Championship crown. Of all the intriguing match-ups between the teams there was little doubt that the one that generated the most interest was the potential head-to-head between Jacklin and Nicklaus.

Bernard Gallacher: Being selected in 1969 was the proudest moment in my career at that stage. Obviously you want to win the Open Championship and things like that, but as a kid practising at Bathgate Golf Club, you want to be in the team playing the Americans. You aspire to be in that side, you practice in order to achieve that aim. And when I got picked by Eric Brown, I'd been having a good year, it was my second year as a pro, and I couldn't believe it when I got the phone call saying that I'd been picked and I was in the team. 'You're playing at Royal Birkdale in four weeks' time.'

It was so one-sided until 1969, but in '69 we really thought we had a good chance of winning. British golf was on a high – Tony Jacklin had just won the British Open, and we felt we had a good balance of young players and experienced players like Peter Alliss, Christy O'Connor, Neil Coles, Peter Butler, and then other young players were coming through like myself, Brian Barnes, Peter Townsend, Maurice Bembridge and of course we were led by Jacklin. Our chests were really puffed out because we knew we had the best player in the world on our side in Jacklin and a very good captain in Eric Brown who was very inspirational.

Brian Huggett: Eric didn't like the Americans at all, maybe because they'd hammered us so many times when he played. All the team knew how he felt and, for some, it got them to try extra hard. He had more of our guys believing that they could win. Eric was strong compared to captains before him. 'We're going to beat this lot,' he said in the locker room, so he was a bold one and he'd say bold things to you. 'Give them a whacking,' he'd say and he'd use pretty strong words to back that up. Maybe we hadn't had enough of that before.

Peter Alliss: I liked Eric. He could be difficult, Eric, he could be very fiery. Well, he went a bit over the top. He told us not to go looking for the Americans' ball in the rough and all that sort of thing, but he was trying to get the players geed up a bit which was only right and proper, I suppose. Eric was Eric. He was a very determined player. I didn't see him all that often, because he always lived up in Scotland. I enjoyed spending time with him, he had a cockiness about him, some would say was typically Scottish. He was a bit abrasive, liked a dram and a cigarette, and didn't suffer fools. Somebody said to him, may have been one of the members, 'Brown, Brown'. And he whipped round and said 'it's Mr or Eric to you'. I thought, 'Oh, crikey'. I wasn't used to that sort of thing. Everyone called everyone by their surnames where I was, so it didn't sort of matter, but it mattered very much to Eric.

Bernard Gallacher: Our team in 1969 was very optimistic that we could win. The main reason for the optimism was that Tony Jacklin had won the British Open that year, and British and Irish golf was really on a bit of a high. I was having a particularly good season, the second as a professional. Eric Brown was our captain, a very optimistic captain, a fiery Scot. Eric had a great Ryder Cup record [4–0–0 in singles], and he just made us firmly believe that we were going to win. And that's really what captains do.

Neil Coles: Eric was that kind of character. He said to us 'just go and kill them'. He was very confrontational and generated a lot of the heat.

Brian Barnes: I found him embarrassing. He hated the Yanks and it was win at all costs for him, but I was brought up in public school, to be a good loser and a good winner. Eric tried to get in my face and he just buggered me up completely.

Brian Huggett: I mean I wanted to beat the Americans, but I didn't hate them. There was some needle in this match, but I didn't hate them. I definitely wanted 100 per cent to beat them, but they're nice people, very hospitable. Hate is not the right word for me, but that's the way Eric Brown felt about them and he told us so in very strong words. He said we could win and he had a strong team and maybe if they were a fraction off, yes, we thought maybe we could do it.

Tony Jacklin: By 1969 I was Open champion and had been playing the American tour fulltime. All I remember was that there was a lot of bravado at the British end of things. But nobody other than myself had really done much to justify thinking that we might win. It's as simple as that. On the American tour the purses were so much bigger than ours, and everything about it was managed better. It was a better all-round thing. But when the Ryder Cup came round, no one liked to believe that.

Lee Trevino: There's nothing quite like playing in the British Isles. Golf is in the air there. You breathe it, like smelling home cooking. It makes you hungry. You want to play.

I liked Birkdale. It was a seaside course with some sand dunes, and you had to hit your driver very straight there. If you kept the ball low, letting those sand dunes shelter it, the wind wouldn't affect your shots. It had five par-fives, and I could reach all of them, which was something unusual for me.

Brian Barnes: In all honesty, we felt we were struggling. I didn't play in one Ryder Cup where we had twelve fellows out there to play against the Americans. Instead we had six or seven fellows and the rest were second-raters. So the six or seven had to play all six matches, where the American boys had the opportunity to rest and were fresh and raring to go when it came to the afternoon matches on Sunday. It's a matter of depth.

The morning foursomes couldn't have got off to a better start for the home team as they won three and halved one of the four matches. The US struck back in the afternoon to claim three points to end the first day 4½–3½ in Britain's favour.

Neil Coles: Tony Jacklin and I defeating Jack Nicklaus and Dan Sikes in the Friday morning fourball was probably my favourite Ryder Cup memory. The match was all square on the seventeenth tee. I was first away with the second shot and got up on the par-five seventeenth in two. All the three other members of the group missed the green, having failed to get there in two. I two-putted from a long distance to a back left pin to go one up. Tony made four at the last for us to win the match.

Jack Nicklaus: Because of US PGA restrictions when I turned pro, it wasn't until 1969 that I became eligible to play in my first Ryder Cup, at Royal Birkdale in England in the fall of that year. Because the US captain, Sam Snead, wanted me to be in good shape to anchor the final day's two series of singles matches, he gave me only one foursome and one fourball match the first two days of the event. Even so, playing thirty-six holes on the last day, I became seriously tired on a golf course for the first time in my life. Part of that could be ascribed to pressure.

Miller Barber: Ryder Cup pressure is something. In 1969 I was at the peak of my game and was paired in the alternate-shot matches with Ray Floyd on the first morning. We talked strategy and decided that Ray would play first on the odd-numbered holes, and I'd play the even-numbered holes, where most of the par threes fell. Well, they play the national anthem and Ray is crying. I'm crying, too, but now the song ends and it's time to play. Ray says, 'I can't hit it.' I said, 'Ray, you've got to hit first, otherwise it'll foul up our whole strategy.' He says, 'I don't care, I can't hit it. Well, Ray missed the green on every par three that day and we lost, 3&2.

Frank Beard: I look at the meetings today that they have and all the strategies. We had a meeting the day we got there, when Sam Snead asked us to write down who we did and didn't want to play with. That was the last meeting we had. He put some pairings up and that was the end of the story. He was a nice man; don't get me wrong. But there were no pep talks.

I played with Billy Casper in both the foursomes on the first day and in the afternoon fourball on the second, but he would not have been my choice. I didn't write his name down. He was just older, and more established, and I had friends, like Kenny Still and Dale Douglass and a few of those guys that I would have preferred to play with, who were more of the same generation. In the '60s there were no better golfers than Billy Casper. I do remember that Billy and I played alternate shot, and I put him up under a tree somewhere and I thought, 'Oh my God, I can't believe I just did this to Billy Casper.' But he was very good about it. He went up, played it out, and we went on.

I remember a shot Christy O'Connor hit, on the very first hole on the first morning. He'd driven it in the rough, and I looked at his lie, and thought, 'He's in deep trouble now.' And he went in there with some kind of wood, had a very abrupt pickup on the backswing, and the ball flew straight out and right onto the green. I mean, it had to be in the two-hundred-yard range. I couldn't have gotten a seven-iron in on it, but he did it with the wrist, the abruptness of the angle of attack, and obviously had some experience. I'll never forget that shot.

I have other very specific memories of 1969. First, it was a great honour to play. I welled up with tears when the 'The Star-Spangled Banner' played. I didn't know that I would, but it was a great feeling. But it was also bittersweet because I was not used to anything that resembled team play. I'd never played team sports, and I didn't like it at all. I did not enjoy it. I shouldn't say it was too much pressure; it was just a different kind. I much preferred having a six-foot putt for my own well-being or loss, but to have teammates, and to have it mean something for the team, I did not look forward to that. And I don't mean just the alternate-shot matches with teammates. Even in the singles matches, it was still for the team. I found it very, very difficult. Beforehand I was looking forward to it, but it was just an overwhelming feeling of 'Whoa, man, this is a whole different pressure I'm not used to having.' It was not a fun feeling.

When we'd miss a putt, the gallery would clap and cheer, and that was also totally new. I don't think we expected anybody to be pulling for us, but if you hit a good shot, they would politely recognise it and clap or something, but if you missed a putt or hooked the ball into the gorse or something, they were very, very vocal about it. With Tony Jacklin in particular it was much more of a raucous crowd. They were loud. It was a very antagonistic atmosphere.

Lee Trevino: Miller Barber and I played Tony Jacklin and Neil Coles in the Friday afternoon fourball and when we came to eighteen it was almost dark and we were feeling a lot of pressure. These points were important because the teams were tied. When I got to the tee and I looked for my bag and Willie [Aitchison, my caddie] wasn't there. The next

The crowds hemmed the greens all around Birkdale.

thing I knew here comes a guy carrying my bag and I've never seen him before. 'Where's Willie?' I ask.

'He was talking to someone coming up the hill,' this stranger said, 'and he slipped down and broke his ankle.' Now that's got to be a first in the history of golf!

While I was still trying to figure that out, I missed an eight-foot putt to keep us from winning outright. Hell, the British should have given Willie a team blazer!

The even pattern of play was repeated in much the same way on day two. The British claimed two-and-a-half points in the morning foursomes, the US claimed three in the afternoon. With the matches so finely poised, it is of little surprise that tempers began to fray between the players on each side. This came to a head in the afternoon foursomes match between Brian Huggett and Bernard Gallacher and Dave Hill and Ken Still. Coming to the seventh green, Hill was the only player to make it on in two. As he was the furthest away he putted to within two feet and then tapped in; Still, who had made it to the green in three, realised that he couldn't improve on his partner's score, so picked up his marker and then waited for the British pair to putt. It was then that Gallacher pointed out that Hill had putted out of turn for his tap-in and appealed to the referee that the hole should be forfeited. The referee had little choice but to adhere to the rules, which backed up Gallacher's claim, and award the hole to the British. Still was absolutely incensed by the decision – and by what he felt to be Gallacher's petty gamesmanship. After a furious remonstration he was forced to accept the decision and he angrily picked up Gallacher's marker to concede the hole. The discontent fired the Americans' ire to positive effect, however, and they went on to claim the match, winning on the seventeenth green for a 2&1 victory.

Peter Alliss: It was one of the situations like the Solheim Cup [in 2015], where there was a ball on the edge of the hole and it was picked up. It was that sort of situation but it cooled down by the time they got to the eighteenth.

The final two matches of the day were halved between Bembridge/Hunt and Aaron/Floyd, and Jacklin/Coles and Trevino/Barber to take the score to 8–8.

Peter Townsend: After seven holes in the afternoon of the second day, my legs just turned to jelly: I had nothing on which to base my swing. After all, if you include time spent on the practise ground, I and others were out there for the best part of eleven hours on fourball day.

Frank Beard: I couldn't believe the intensity of my teammates, the screaming and hollering.

With the score tied at 8–8 going into the final day, the British won five of the eight morning singles matches before the US roared back into contention by winning four of the first six afternoon matches to even the score once more.

Peter Alliss: I was top of the order in the Saturday morning singles, playing Trevino. I played very well actually, but I was putting badly then. I retired that year aged thirty-eight, which looking back was far too young. I played him off the course, but, oh, I must have missed six putts of under four or five feet, and he beat me 2&1 over eighteen holes. I was doing television at that time and I said to Eric, the captain, 'Look, I don't think I'm much use to you, I'm putting so badly,' so I did the television in the afternoon and they played on without me. I was hitting the ball beautifully, but my putting had gone. My international career finished at the end of 1969 and I played in the Open up to 1974, but that was virtually the only tournaments I played in, and I finished altogether in 1974.

Brian Barnes: The Sunday singles in 1969 were split into morning and afternoon sessions and both Neil Coles and I were sent out twice without much warning. I'd just lost my morning match when Eric told me I was lead-off man in the afternoon. I literally had ten minutes to get a bite to eat and I was off again.

Neil Coles: Eric originally said he wouldn't play me twice on the last day, but then he changed his mind. In the afternoon, I played Dan Sikes and was out in forty-two, yet I was only two down. There were people like Bernard Hunt who were as fresh as a daisy, but didn't play at all in the singles. Anyone could've beaten Sikes that day.

Bernard Gallacher: I was a little disappointed when I was dropped by Eric Brown for the morning singles. Eric told me that he wanted me to be fresh for a big challenge in the afternoon. What a challenge it proved to be. I found myself up against the 1968 US Open champion, Lee Trevino, whom Maurice Bembridge and I had beaten in the first series of foursomes. The exuberant Trevino had beaten the stylish Peter Alliss in the morning singles but in the afternoon I surprised some people, but not myself, by beating the much more experienced American 4&3.

Billy Casper: Bernard Gallacher was a good player. A bulldog. I loved to play against those guys.

When Peter Butler beat Dale Douglass, the score was dead even at 15–15, with two matches still to conclude – me against Brian Huggett and Jack Nicklaus against Tony Jacklin.

Huggett and I went shot-for-shot for the entire eighteen holes and he secured a tie with a clutch five-foot putt on the final green. Just as the ovation for his putt was dying down at eighteen a roar went up from seventeen. Assuming Jacklin had won the cup, Huggett was so overwhelmed with joy he grabbed me in an embrace. I was hugging Huggett.

What he didn't know is that the roar was because Jacklin had holed a long putt to get back even with Nicklaus. They came to the final hole with still nothing decided and the Ryder Cup on the line.

Tony Jacklin: I didn't know I was going to play Jack Nicklaus in the afternoon singles until lunchtime. I had beaten him 4&3 in the morning. He wasn't at his best, and I was bloody determined, at the top of my game.

In those days the captains usually put the strongish men out at the end. Obviously Snead thought Jack was his anchorman and Eric went to me because I was unbeaten. I'd lost sixteen to a par, to go one-down, and then on seventeen [a par-five] I hit a two-iron second shot, but pushed it. It hit a bank at the side of the green and came down onto the green, but a long way from the hole.

Jack hit a much better drive than I did and a wonderful second shot to about fifteen, twenty feet. I then holed this bloody putt from here to eternity and got back to level.

Eighteen was plain and short, and they played it as a par-four. Three-woods off the tee for position, both of us. We were walking off the tee, me ahead, when Jack hollered after me. I waited for him and when he caught up, he said, 'How are you feeling? Are you nervous?' And I said, 'I'm bloody petrified.' And he said, 'Well I just thought I'd ask because if it's any consolation I feel just like you.' Which was kind of nice, putting it all in perspective. You know, it was an unenviable position to be in. It all depended on us.

I then hit an eight-iron, a good shot, right in line with the pin, and it ran to the back of the green, about thirty feet away. Then Jack hit a super shot, to about fifteen feet. I putted up to about twenty inches to two feet, and marked it.

Jack took a good run at his, because he had it for the match, and he ran it about four and a half feet by. He holed that and, as he picked his ball out of the hole, he picked my marker up. He conceded the putt and we halved our match and the overall match.

Jack Nicklaus: Tony Jacklin, still on top of the world from his British Open win a couple of months previously, had defeated me in the last of the morning singles to give the British a two-point lead with eight more singles to play. To try and ease the tension as we followed our drives down the eighteenth fairway, I asked Tony if he was nervous. 'Bloody petrified,' he told me, and we laughed, and I admitted to him that I was also feeling the squeeze.

We both hit good second shots, Tony to about thirty feet from the cup, and me to within half that distance. Tony then left his putt a couple of feet short, after which I knocked mine about five feet too far. After I had holed the comeback putt and was picking my ball out of the hole, I also picked up Tony's marker, conceding the putt. As I handed it to him, I said, 'I don't think you would have missed that putt, but under the circumstances I would never give you the opportunity.' The reason, of course, was that I believed good sportsmanship should be as much a part of the Ryder Cup as great competition. With the match thus ending in a tie for the first time in its forty-two-year history, we walked happily off the green arm-in-arm. But it had been a draining experience for both of us.

Tony Jacklin: The length of the putt has varied after all these years. It's been reported as long as four feet. But my recollection is twenty inches. Of course, I could have missed it; there are no guarantees in golf, especially in the crucible of the Ryder Cup, but I believe I would have made it. But Jack saw the big picture – two months before I had become the first British player in eighteen years to win the British Open – so there was very much a pro-British fervour at the Ryder Cup in England that year. Jack saw that that putt on the last hole in 1969 meant a heck of a lot more to the Ryder Cup than who won or lost that particular match. It was a great moment.

Nicklaus's gesture was one of the finest acts of sportsmanship witnessed not simply in golf but in any sporting arena. Their halved match resulted in the first draw in the Ryder Cup, 16–16, and with the rules stating that in the event of such a result, the trophy was retained by the holders.

Jack Nicklaus: Today, they consider my decision 'memorable', but at the same time, I simply considered it the right thing to do in a competition founded on sportsmanship.

It was a great honour to make the team and to represent my country, but frankly, by the time the matches rolled around in September, I was nearly golfed out. The Major-championship season was over, and I was already in the process of recharging for next year. I think a lot of my teammates felt the same way.

I've read where players say that the Ryder Cup is the most pressure they've ever felt. That wasn't the case for me. Part of my preparation for my best golf was the intentional pressure I placed on myself, and often I couldn't get in that mindset in a Ryder Cup. I admit that my 1969 match with Tony Jacklin was a little nerve-wracking, but it was still about goodwill, and I was comfortable picking up Tony's coin on the final hole.

Tony Jacklin: I was a pretty fierce competitor, and I remember standing on the green before Jack conceded the putt, thinking, 'Now, whatever else happens, get ready. You're going to have to make this putt.' Mentally I knew it wasn't over for me, so it came as a shock, a surprise anyway, when Jack picked the marker up.

There's no way I would have missed the two-footer Jack Nicklaus gave me for a tie in the 1969 Ryder Cup. But you'd better believe I sent him a thank you note when it was over.

Lee Trevino: The whole place went mad, absolutely crazy when Jack gave that putt to Tony Jacklin, but I loved it. You see, the British team had tied for the first time in Ryder

Cup history, and while it wasn't a win, it was a big, big thrill for the home fans. So it might seem that Jack was giving something away, but in what the Ryder Cup is supposed to represent, I loved what he did and the reaction.

Bernard Gallacher: I don't think Sam Snead was pleased, and some of the more hard-nosed Americans weren't pleased. But it was the right thing to do. In my opinion, it is one of the great moments in sport. A gesture that defined the man: a great champion and a true gentleman.

Frank Beard: Snead didn't like it. I don't think any of us cared for it. We had the cup and the tie meant we kept it, but nobody was thinking about that. We wanted to win.

Sam Snead: We went over there to win, not be good ol' boys.

Peter Alliss: Just for a moment, Snead wanted to win, not halve. But it was rather like Tiger Woods. Tiger did the same thing when we won at Medinah in 2012. Woods gave a putt on the last hole of about four foot for Francesco Molinari which was, in fact, quite important [for a win or a tied match[, but he didn't care.

Brian Huggett: Some of the bad feeling remained with the players afterward. But of course they were probably a jealous lot as well. 'Oh, Jack's going to get all the plaudits for being such a sportsman and this, that, and the other.' I'm sure Jack wasn't thinking about that at all. I think he was looking at the game overall.

Miller Barber: Jack has said that he conceded the putt purely out of sportsmanship, but I was on the team, and none of us players believed that. See, Sam Snead sat Jack down in the morning the first day and in the afternoon the second day because he didn't want Jack to get worn out. Jack wanted to play and was upset about being benched. Most of us believe Jack conceded the putt at least in part to get back at Sam. And it worked, because behind the scenes Sam was furious that Jack didn't make Jacklin hole that two-footer.

Frank Beard: Was it the right decision by Nicklaus? Well, why do you play? You play to win, don't you? It would be interesting to see what Tony would have done in the same situation. I wouldn't have given him the putt. But we'll never know if he'd have made it. It's tough. Everything's on your shoulders. But if Tony had holed the putt it would have been a bigger thing for him. It would have been a great boost for him. But then it was a great boost for Nicklaus.

I agree with what Jack did now, but it took me a long time. Jack Nicklaus was always lightyears ahead of us when it came to maturity and thinking. And, in some way, he had figured out that for the good of golf, and for the good of European golf, for the good of the Ryder Cup, a tie was best.

NINETEEN

1971
Old Warson Country Club. St. Louis, Missouri
(USA 18½, GB 13½)

After the draw at Royal Birkdale, the British team, captained by Eric Brown, travelled with confidence to St Louis, Missouri, for the nineteenth Ryder Cup at Old Warson Country Club. Brown's team contained nine players who had appeared at Birkdale – Brian Barnes, Maurice Bembridge, Peter Butler, Neil Coles, Bernard Gallacher, Brian Huggett, Tony Jacklin, Christy O'Connor and Peter Townsend – while Harry Bannerman, John Garner and Peter Oosterhuis made their debuts.

The home team, meanwhile, was captained by Jay Hebert and featured six players from Birkdale – Miller Barber, Frank Beard, Billy Casper, Gene Littler, Jack Nicklaus and Lee Trevino – while also seeing the return of Gardner Dickinson and Arnold Palmer from the 1967 team. Dave Stockton, who would later captain the team, made his debut, as did Charles Coody, Mason Rudolph and JC Snead. Trevino was selected despite only recently undergoing an appendectomy; the only other concern for the team emerged when Billy Casper broke a toe while groping in the dark to find his hotel bathroom. Ridiculously, Tom Weiskopf missed out playing in the 1971 Ryder Cup because his membership to the US PGA hadn't been forwarded to national headquarters.

The temperatures during the practise days was an oppressive – for the visitors at least – 90°F, but on the first day there was a complete change in the weather as the course was hit by such a downpour that the opening ceremony, and subsequently play, had to be delayed by an hour and a quarter. These conditions appeared to hearten the British players as they pushed out into an early 3–1 lead during the morning foursomes. The Americans fought back in the afternoon to secure two wins and a halved match to Britain's solitary victory, to end the first day 4½–3½ in the visitors' favour, their best ever start in America.

Harry Bannerman: We flew to St Louis via Ottawa on British Caledonian and it was economy all the way. To the consternation of our captain, there was a chauffeur-driven, air-conditioned limousine waiting at the airport for one of our players – Tony Jacklin. I was left sweating like a pig trying to load my gear onto the bus laid on for the rest of us. Then we had to unload it all when we got to the hotel. Not exactly the welcome we were expecting. Nor, needless to say, was it anything like the treatment players get at modern Ryder Cups.

The gear we got was hardly luxurious. I do recall being handed an envelope containing $500. But most of that went to my caddie. And there were other out-of-pocket expenses. I'm sure I made a financial loss on the week.

Brian Barnes: As a team we were very much the poor relations. We'd walk onto the first tee with our plastic golf bags, Aertex shirts, two-ply wool sweaters and two golf balls and the Americans would be there with beautiful leather bags, cashmere sweaters and trousers that actually fitted. But there was never any sense of them looking down on us for all that. I'd go into the American dressing room at the end of the day and Lee Trevino and I would go out to dinner together.

Peter Oosterhuis: The first time I played in the Ryder Cup was in 1971 at Old Warson in St Louis. I was twenty-three and the whole thing was pretty low-key. Concorde was nowhere to be seen! And the matches got less attention than they do now. While there were always plenty of golf fans watching, there wasn't much going on off the course, in terms of the media. There was nothing like the hype we have nowadays.

Harry Bannerman: It was an experience, not least of which was being left out of the line-up on the first morning. There were thirty-two points to play for then, two sets of fourballs and foursomes on the first two days and then eight singles games morning and afternoon on day three.

What's wrong nowadays with all twelve players playing foursomes on day one, kicking off at mid-morning to save people getting buses at 4:00 am? On the second day, you have all twelve players playing fourballs? Then twelve singles on the third day. So thirty-six points available in total? John Garner, a British team member in 1971 and 1973, played one match out of twelve. That is nonsense. Players work so hard to make the team, then don't play. It's just totally daft.

Eric Brown was much maligned by the media. Yes, he was abrasive, but he had a heart of gold, generous to a fault. Maybe at the height of his prowess he suffered with an inferiority complex/chip on his shoulder. Tony Jacklin reaped the benefits of Eric's mistakes in subsequent years and that should be noted.

Eric did everything his own way. For example, he never asked any of us who we wanted to play with, or who we didn't want to play with. I remember Peter Oosterhuis pleading with him to keep Bernard Gallacher and I together after we won on the first day. But he broke us up and we never played together again. I never did get to know why.

I learned a lot about Bernard in that match, though. As we walked off the first tee, he turned and loudly said, 'Harry, if we cannae beat these two fat guys we need to chuck it'. He wanted them to hear him and he wanted me to believe we could win.

At the short third, I put our tee shot in a bunker and Bernard splashed out to maybe five feet. As the Americans were lining up their putt, he walked up to me and, nose-to-nose, told me to start thinking about holing my putt for the half. 'Casper won't hole this one,' he said.

After Billy lipped out, I did hole mine. A bit nervously, but it went in. I ran after Bernard to give him the ball for the next tee shot. At first, he just stared at me. Then he spoke. 'I hope you're not looking for praise,' he said. That told me so much about how competitive Bernard was.

Dave Stockton: We had an extremely strong team, but in the morning foursomes I was paired with Jack Nicklaus, and we lost to Tony Jacklin and Brian Huggett. That was a

Neil Coles watches his putt as it heads towards the cup.

lousy pairing because in alternate shot you can't play two people who have completely different games. Nicklaus and I in a better ball would be awesome, because he can be aggressive, and I'm going to do what I have to do. In fact, they sat me out in the afternoon and put JC Snead with Nicklaus, and they did fine [they beat Maurice Bembridge and Peter Butler].

But I was mad when I was sat down for the entire second day. It was like they were saying, 'If Nicklaus can get beat, then it must have been Stockton's fault.' But it was the pairing that caused us to get beat.

Peter Oosterhuis: On the first day I was paired in the foursomes with Peter Townsend against Arnold Palmer and Gardner Dickinson. On the first hole Peter put me on the green but a long way from the hole. I walked up to the hole and, while I was studying the line, checking around the cup, a butterfly flew out of the hole, which some people seemed to think was an omen. Then I made this monster putt on the first green – a good way to start a Ryder Cup career.

But Arnold was playing brilliantly – and a bit too well for us. They won two-up, and then we lost to them again in the afternoon. Arnold was a real force, and we couldn't quite handle him.

The momentum could not be continued the following morning, however, as the US roared back into contention with a clean sheet in the morning fourball to take the lead 7½–4½. One of the major talking points from this session had occurred in the match between Palmer and Dickinson and Gallacher and Oosterhuis. Having watched Palmer smash a spectacular tee shot on the 7th, Gallacher's caddie asked the American what club he had played. The match referee overheard the question and Palmer's reply that he had used a five-iron; when the pairs tied the hole for par, the referee took the players aside and informed them that he was awarding the hole to the US because Gallacher's caddie had violated Rule 9a, which prevented the giving and taking of such advice. Palmer tried to persuade the referee to change his decision, but he held firm – and in doing so increased the Americans' advantage to two-up.

Bernard Gallacher: In the Friday morning fourballs, Peter Oosterhuis and I were playing Dickinson and Arnold Palmer. At the short seventh hole, a 207-yard hole where the green was elevated and the tee shot blind, Palmer played and received a tremendous ovation for what we reckoned was a five-iron shot that finished pin high. As I stepped onto the tee to play my shot with a three-iron, my caddie, an American, casually asked Palmer's caddie what Arnold had hit. The question, while illegal, had no bearing on the club I was using. I heard neither the question nor the answer. I was busy lining up my shot and subsequently hit my ball inside Palmer's. The hole was halved in three but Dickinson then claimed it, because we had broken Rule 9 which states that a player or his caddie cannot ask advice from the opposition or their caddies. In this case, my caddie had asked Palmer's caddie a question. The referee had no option but to give it to them although Palmer tried to reverse the ruling. The Americans went on to win by 5&4.

Peter Oosterhuis: Do you know something funny? On the first green, in my first match, I leaned forward to look at the hole and a butterfly flew out. Peter Townsend, Arnold Palmer and Gardner Dickinson all missed it, but I saw it. And then I managed to sink my putt from right across the green.

We just didn't have the depth in Britain. Our top handful of players, Brian Barnes, Bernard Gallacher, Tony Jacklin, could compete, but our last few players really couldn't be expected to beat the last few Americans.

Harry Bannerman: I played a lot of bridge with Peter Townsend that week. We couldn't hit balls because there was no range. It was just awful really. Not that it seemed to make much difference. On the second afternoon, Peter and I covered the opening nine holes in 29 shots against Arnold and Jack and were only one up.

We were all square playing the last. I made a par four. Peter had a long putt for a birdie. Arnold was in his pocket. And Jack was maybe thirty-five feet away in two shots. After Peter missed, we were standing watching Jack. 'You don't think he's going to hole this do you?' he said to me. But I thought he would. And halfway there, I knew I was right. When the ball fell in, Jack jumped at least a foot into the air. And there was a huge roar. It was very exciting. We had maybe 10,000 people watching. Lorna Townsend and my wife, Hazel, were side by side at the green and Jack noticed them both in tears after our defeat and he took them one in each arm and took them up to the clubhouse. Now that tells you a lot about Jack Nicklaus. Then, of course, we had to go to the press room and I was interviewed. 'You seem to be in a state of shock, Harry?' said the questioner, wanting a reply. I said, 'Well, we were out in twenty-nine, which wasn't bad, but we still got beaten. So I've now learned at first hand why these two guys have dominated the sport'.

Arnold Palmer: That was the first time Jack and I teamed up in what would be several Ryder Cup collaborations, defeating Peter Townsend and Harry Bannerman one-up in a closely contested fourball match on the afternoon of the second day. Gardner Dickinson and I proved even more formidable as a team that year, however, winning three of our team matches to give me a record of four wins against one loss and one tie.

By the end of day two, the US had overturned a one point deficit and were now leading 10–6 going into the singles. It was not all plain sailing for them, however, as reports filtered through the next morning that Billy Casper had broken his toe in the night during his fumble to find the bathroom, so would have to sit out the singles. It was a blow to the home team but even with Casper's absence, the British had a daunting mountain to climb if they were to win the cup – of the sixteen points that were available, they had to claim ten-and-a-half.

Arnie's Army watch their hero in action. *Getty Images*

Harry Bannerman: One of the real highlights of the week though was playing Arnold Palmer in the morning singles and halving the match with him. Arnold was always my hero, to play him was a pleasure. He birdied three of the first four holes and was two up. But I got it back to square by the turn. I was playing great and hit a lot of really good iron shots. On the last tee I was one up, at which point a member of the PGA appeared from the crowd. He was a bit excited and told me: 'Harry, you're a star!'

That was nice but not quite what I needed to hear at that moment. I hooked my drive into the rough. Now, am I looking for an excuse? Not really. But hearing what he said didn't help.

I gave Arnie a run for his money. It's a long time ago. It was a high and low moment, if you know what I mean. Being in his company was fantastic, absolutely. Let's get it straight, I didn't get a square match with Arnie. He got a square match with me. After all, I was one up with one to play. As I hit one imperial iron shot after another, I remember my caddie saying, 'Boss Harry, let's take Mr Palmer out and he ain't going to like it.'

Eventually I had a five-foot putt to win and I missed. That was disappointing. Arnold was a wee bit past his peak, but not much. It would have been a great scalp.

It was a fine match, but I remember my great Arnie story was at the 1971 World Disney Open, Magnolia Course, Orlando. After the Ryder Cup, I went back to play a few tournaments in the States. I had a 140 (four under) thirty-six-hole total and as was my wont that day, I headed to the range for a hit. Arnie was on 141 or 142 and was moving back with his 'army' to the first tee after practising. I was maybe ten to fifteen paces to Arnie's right when he noticed me and spoke to me. He said, 'Harry, you keep it going today, you play well.' I replied, 'Thanks, Arnie.' Mayhem ensued. I never saw the range. People came after me. All I heard was, 'Why did Arnie speak to you? Who are you? What's your name? What are you doing here? How did you get in the tournament? Blah blah blah. Could you sign this autograph?' I spent the practise ground time signing autographs. And it was just because Arnold Palmer spoke to me. There was the measure of the man in a nutshell.

The morning session was very finely balanced, the US winning three to Britain's two and with three matches halved.

Lee Trevino and Brian Huggett were the first men off the tee in the afternoon. As the rest of the order followed out behind them, the British led in six of the eight singles matches at one stage with only Trevino holding a comfortable lead for the US, finally winning 7&6 to put the home team within one point of winning the cup.

JC Snead was out next against Tony Jacklin and was one up with two to play, only for Jacklin to roll in a stunning sixty-five-foot putt on the seventeenth for birdie to bring the match back all square.

They both made it to the eighteenth green in three, but Snead had chipped to within eight feet, while Jacklin left himself with another long putt; the Englishman couldn't repeat his trick on the seventeenth and missed and had to watch Sam Snead's nephew knock the ball in for his fourth victory in three days.

While the result was now confirmed, there were still six matches out on the course. Dave Stockton and Jack Nicklaus secured a further two points for the US against Peter Townsend and

Neil Coles respectively, but the British won the other four, with Brian Barnes defeating Miller Barber 2&1, Bernard Gallacher defeating Charles Coody 2&1, Peter Oosterhuis defeating Arnold Palmer 3&2 and Harry Bannerman seeing off Gardner Dickinson 2&1 to record their best result – albeit still in defeat – on American soil.

Peter Oosterhuis: The pairings for the final singles matches in the afternoon were made over lunch. [British captain] Dai Rees told me, 'You're playing Arnold Palmer.' It was really great seeing Dai, this wonderful enthusiast of the game, enjoy telling me that I was playing Arnold because he knew I wanted a chance to play Arnold. But after a couple of holes I could tell that Arnold wasn't the force he'd been two days previously. He'd played in all the matches and wasn't playing quite as well.

I was two or three up with maybe six to play and it started raining. The result of the matches had already been decided and Arnold asked if I wanted to walk in. So I asked him if he was conceding. There was a big grin on his face; he was just having fun with an inexperienced rookie. Needless to say, we played on.

Harry Bannerman: Back in '71 there was definitely an inferiority complex in maybe two-thirds of the team. And Jacklin got a bollocking for separating himself from the rest of us. I think he learned from that when he was captain himself. Anyway, how much we thought about winning varied from individual to individual. I am one who relishes a good battle, though. I was up for it.

Brian Barnes: We felt a change in the air by the turn of the 1970s because there was a group of us were coming of age who were committed to giving the Yanks a very serious run and turning things around. Of course, this didn't happen overnight, and it took more than the British and Irish could do. But we were determined to give as good as we got and we weren't afraid at all.

TWENTY

1973
Muirfield, East Lothian, Scotland
(USA 19, GB&I 13)

The twentieth Ryder Cup, held at Muirfield in East Lothian, was the first time that the Ryder Cup had been officially staged in Scotland, fifty-two years since the genesis match at Gleneagles. 1973 was also notable for attracting the first significant commercial sponsorship for the Ryder Cup in Britain. It came from Sun Alliance, whose golf-obsessed chairman, Lord Aldington, regarded his company's backing (£375,000 for the next three matches) as a matter of duty for the survival of the contest rather than as a marketing strategy.

The home team was captained by Bernard Hunt who handed debuts to Clive Clark and Eddie Polland before calling on an experienced field in Brian Barnes, Maurice Bembridge, Peter Butler, Neil Coles, Bernard Gallacher, John Garner, Brian Huggett, Tony Jacklin, Christy O'Connor and Peter Oosterhuis.

The American team, captained by Jack Burke Jnr, was sprinkled with stardust in Jack Nicklaus, Arnold Palmer and Lee Trevino, who were ably backed up by Tommy Aaron, Gay Brewer, Billy Casper, Dave Hill, JC Snead, and rookies Homero Blancas, Lou Graham, Chi Chi Rodriguez and Tom Weiskopf.

Colin Snape (Executive Director of the PGA): Muirfield in '73 was a big moment in many ways because it was the first time that 'Ireland' became part of the title of our team. There had been Irish players on the team for years by that stage, of course – like Christy O'Connor Snr and Harry Bradshaw, for example – but until then it had always been known as the 'British' team with the Union Jack on show and the British anthem being sung at the opening ceremonies. So it was very important that it was recognised that the team was more than that and from then on until Europe came into things, we were known as Great Britain and Ireland.

Brian Barnes: As you can appreciate, 1973 was completely different from the way the Ryder Cup is run now. It was hard enough when we stood up on the tee in our era, because you were as nervous as a kitten. It didn't matter how many people were around, you were playing for your country which was a great honour. I tended to play the first tee shot in the doubles and every captain who put myself and Bernard Gallacher together [they were also a pairing in '75, '77 and '79] always made sure we were the first game out. I guess it was felt we had a good chance of winning our match, which might have then given the other guys a little bit of heart. So I can remember, to this day, standing there on the first tee being quite convinced I was going to miss the ball. Fortunately, I never did.

It was a dominant period for America. In all honesty, throughout the whole of my time, the six consecutive Ryder Cups that I played in, you could virtually guarantee there were only six players that could really play against the Americans and the rest were also-rans. So we finished up with six of us virtually having to play all the matches.

Jack Nicklaus: For me, and I think a lot of other golfers who've been fortunate enough to participate in them, international team contests are the most enjoyable events in golf. If the game has one drawback, it is its individuality, its self-concernedness – its selfishness, to be blunt about the matter. Playing for a team, and particularly for your country in someone else's country, really brings a group of players together.

Tony Jacklin: It's a wonderful course, Muirfield, but Christ it's hard. The first hole is one of the scariest opening holes in golf.

The home side started brilliantly, building a 5½–2½ lead from Thursday's opening foursomes and fourballs. Gallacher and Barnes won both their matches (against Trevino and Casper, and Aaron and Brewer), while Bembridge and Huggett enjoyed a memorable win against Nicklaus and Palmer in the afternoon fourball after Bembridge and Polland had been crushed by the pair in the morning foursomes.

Tony Jacklin: I played with Oosterhuis against Weiskopf and Casper and we were miles under par after nine holes. It was unbelievable golf. On the tenth hole, Billy Casper said to me, 'I hope you're enjoying this.' I said, 'I bloody well am – very much. Thank you.' He was furious, but we weren't gloating. We were just doing our best, and everything was going our way.

Bernard Gallacher: Being in Scotland at Muirfield, we were very optimistic going into it, we thought we could do well. We got off to a very good start and I was playing great with Brian. The Americans were a good side, but over eighteen holes you've always got a chance to win, we always felt that.

Brian Barnes: Why Bernard Hunt put Bernard Gallacher and I together, whether it was because it was two Scots, I don't know. Maybe he realised that the two of us together were completely different, chalk and cheese as far as characters were concerned. Of course, Bernie was a wonderful short game player and I was rubbish, yet he wasn't the greatest driver of a golf ball and that was the best department of my game. Our games complemented each other.

The two best areas in the UK that we always got good crowds were Ireland and Scotland; it was always far, far better than England. Many of the British tournaments were in England and they were easy to get to so people got a bit blasé. There was only the Scottish Open and the Irish Open. The Scots are always very knowledgeable about the game and being the first Ryder Cup in Scotland, just being down the road from Edinburgh it was obviously a very knowledgeable crowd. But I can't honestly remember the atmosphere being any different to any of the others. Other than being invited in 2002, the only Ryder Cup I've been to in modern times was Tony's last one in Britain

[1989]. I couldn't believe the atmosphere. The atmosphere between the teams was always very, very good. You became a fraternity really, you became good friends.

The euphoria in the home side's team room was dampened overnight when Gallacher contracted food poisoning. Peter Butler was summoned to replace Gallacher and team up with Barnes and the substitute responded in spectacular fashion by becoming the first player to record a hole-in-one in Ryder Cup history at the par-three sixteenth (although it was not enough to prevent Nicklaus and Weiskopf from ultimately claiming a one-up victory).

Bernard Gallacher: We weren't celebrating or anything after the first day; we had done well on the opening day and felt OK about it. We just had a little meal [in a local hotel] and I ate something that obviously affected me. I woke up in the middle of the night feeling unwell; sick, dizzy, hot and cold. I was in pain all night. I ate a piece of fish, but it was nothing exotic – it was on the table d'hôte. Some commentators said, 'Oh well, if he goes off and eats oysters, scallops and all that sort of thing', but I didn't. It was on table d'hôte, we were all eating off table d'hôte, off the set menu. It was just one of those things, nobody else got sick, I got sick. It was an unexplained thing.

At the time, I was on good form and dropping out was a bad omen. Brian, I think, was upset more than anybody because we had such a good relationship going, we were going so strong, and I think that upset him more than me. We got off to a very good start and then I went downhill, like the team. It was just circumstantial really.

Peter Butler was always on the team but hadn't been practising with Brian. Bernard Hunt, probably quite rightly, didn't want to upset or shake around the team much. I fell out and he simply put Peter into my slot. But it doesn't always work like that when you don't know the person who is coming in, don't know their game. Brian got sort of shuffled to playing with someone that he wasn't really used to playing with. It was just a difficult situation for everybody.

Brian Barnes: It was a real shame that Bernard suffered food poisoning after the Thursday games. We got to the situation where I was paired with Peter Butler on the Friday morning and we were just beaten by Nicklaus and Weiskopf. As you can appreciate, it's completely different from the way the Ryder Cup is run now. The opening ceremony was prior to the first round. I remember we were staying at the hotel, it was dark, and we had to get down for breakfast. It was about 6:00 am and there was not a sound, everyone was still half asleep.

The Friday morning foursomes were shared two apiece, but the Americans pulled back the arrears when they won three of the afternoon fourballs and halved the fourth to bring the score to 8–8.

Tom Weiskopf: I partnered up with Jack Nicklaus on the second day. We were one or two up on the two Brits we were playing [Clark and Polland] when Jack and I both knocked the ball close. He's about ten feet away and I'm within five or six feet, with my ball on his line. I went forward to mark my ball when Jack said, 'Pick it up.'

'What?' I asked.

'Rack your cue,' said Jack. 'I'm gonna sink mine.'

The Great Britain & Ireland Ryder Cup team of 1973,
captained by Bernard Hunt (*far right*).

So I picked it up and stood back and Jack drills it home. He loved things like that – he loved to dominate the game and it put the wind up the Brits.

Even with Gallacher restored to the side for the singles, the home team continued to struggle against the tide of American momentum, with Jacklin recording the only full point for the British in the morning singles (when he beat Aaron 3&1), while Bembridge and Oosterhuis tied their matches against Nicklaus and Trevino.

Brian Barnes: It was such a dominant period for the Americans. The Ryder Cup when Bernie [Gallacher] and I were playing, virtually all six I played in, the Americans were just unbelievably good. The only one I played in when Europe were involved was the first one in 1979. The rest of the time it was purely Great Britain & Ireland. We just didn't have the strength in depth to have any chance of beating the Americans. The only time we did, in actual fact, was the first one myself and Bernie played in back in 1969, when we tied. Anything could have happened there, but it really was a foregone conclusion anytime we went out and played. It was probably the strongest team the Americans had produced in 1973 up until that time and the second strongest to the one they brought over in 1981, which was probably the strongest team ever.

Lee Trevino: You don't know who you'll play in the singles until the names are drawn each day, and Peter Oosterhuis was giving us a difficult time. Nobody could beat him. So I sounded off at a team meeting. 'I wish I could draw him. I can beat him.'

Well, the next thing I knew I had drawn Oosterhuis. Unfortunately, I couldn't stop talking. I was so confident that I told my teammates that if I didn't beat him I would kiss each of them in a most unlikely place.

Damn, talk about pressure! The next day I had Oosterhuis one down coming into the seventeenth, but I three-putted to square the match. I missed the eighteenth green and he didn't, so then I really had a problem. He two-putted, so that meant I had to chip up and make the putt or I'd lose the match.

This was the last match of the day. It was dark and I had the most difficult eight-foot putt I've ever seen in my life. I didn't look at the hole because I couldn't see it anyway. I just put my putter down in front of the ball, hit it, and it went dead into the cup. I didn't lose, but I didn't beat him either.

Peter Oosterhuis: Lee Trevino was interesting to play against in the morning singles. He was chatting away on the first tee as he always did. I was used to him doing that, so that was no big deal. I ignored him. Then I birdied the first two holes and was two up. So he stopped talking. On we went and I three-putted the fourteenth green to go back to all square. Whereupon he started talking again!

In his book, he says he let me off the hook in that match. But I know I let him off the hook! He drove into a bunker on the seventeenth and had to chip out. I was on the fairway and hit my second shot into sand and had to chip out myself.

I think halving the match was a fair result for us both.

Bernard Gallacher: Trevino apparently said before he played Oosty, 'If I don't beat that Peter Oosterhuis, I'll kiss the asses of every member of my team.' And they went on to halve the match. When Trevino got back to the locker room he found Nicklaus, Palmer,

Arnold Palmer lines up a putt. *Getty Images*

Brewer and Hill all waiting for him with their trousers down. The great thing about Trevino was that he could take a joke as well as make them.

The afternoon saw the Americans' dominance continue as they secured five-and-a-half out of a possible eight points to return a final score of 19–13 to comfortably retain the Ryder Cup for a further two years.

Brian Barnes: The Americans had guys like Nicklaus, Palmer and Trevino. They were winning Majors left, right and centre. They also looked larger than life, especially when they were wearing their cashmere sweaters, the trousers that fitted and had their beautiful leather bags. We, the poor relations, had nothing that fitted and it was a canvas golf bag. We were two down on the first tee nine times out of ten. That was true of the Ryder Cup. The person that got things going there was Tony [Jacklin], who insisted on first-class travel and first-class equipment, to look as though we were not the poor relations. He got the ball rolling and then Bernie [Gallacher] took it over from there.

Christy O'Connor: While I was happy that I had done my bit for the team in the 1969 series, I was especially pleased that I bowed out of the Ryder Cup as the most honoured player in fairly commendable fashion. I was at the ripe old age of forty-nine years, eight months and thirty days, just short of Ted Ray's 1927 'oldest competitor' record of fifty years, two months and five days!

In practise for my swansong 1973 appearance, I had produced a ten under par 61 around the honourable Muirfield links where I covered the back nine holes in twenty-nine shots.

Bernard Hunt was our captain and on the third day, with the match tied at seven points each, he might well have found reason to rest this old man! Instead, he kept faith in his old buddy and I reckon I did as much as I could to vindicate his confidence in me. In the morning singles, I was around in seventy-one shots which was the best figure produced by the home team. But I lost by one hole to JC Snead.

Then, for what proved to be my farewell Ryder Cup appearance in the afternoon I was pitted against Tom Weiskopf, reigning Open champion. One down with four to play, I mustered a birdie at the fifteenth hole to square and at the last hole I somehow found the strength to concoct quite a good bunker shot to within four feet of the hole and to slot it for a half. I was more relieved than the appreciative crowd, who gave me such a heart-warming ovation, had realised. That was my eleventh bunker shot of the day and I was pleased I had gone out on a high note, although sad that we lost the match by 19–13.

Bernard Hunt: Christy asked to be stood down for the singles so a younger player could have a shot and he retired to the bar. Obviously I knew Christy very well and knew that he could, if necessary, play stunning golf with a few drinks under his belt. But I also knew that if the alcohol started to run out, he could struggle. My plan was simple. I pulled aside a couple of his pals, one of them a priest, and said, 'Whatever happens, keep him topped up'. We made sure there was a tot available on every tee. By the time Christy came down to play, he was clearly, shall we say, happy.

Weiskopf couldn't believe it. 'Has he been drinking?' he asked.

'Yes,' I said. 'And if we can keep him that way, you don't stand a chance.'

They ended up having a great match which they halved in the end. I knew Christy had it in him.

Peter Oosterhuis: In my last singles match I beat Arnold Palmer. It was a cold, damp day, and Arnold's great big gnarled, workmanlike hands that controlled the club were just too cold. It didn't look as if he could play the way he wanted to.

Arnold Palmer: Muirfield happened to be the setting of my poorest performance in Ryder Cup competition. Jack and I beat Maurice Bembridge and Eddie Polland, 6&5, in the first foursomes match, but turned right around and dropped the fourball to Bembridge and Brian Huggett, 3&1. For the first time, I failed to win a singles match and my losses outnumbered my wins, 3–2.

Jack Burke Jnr: I think the thing that welded the team together was that we got beat so bad on the first day. That pulled them together.

Bernard Gallacher: We lost pretty heavily in the end. Although I played well against Weiskopf on the final day to only lose at the seventeenth, I ran out of steam really against Brewer [lost 6&5]. It was my third Ryder Cup and it was a big disappointment, a big disappointment for everybody.

As it turned out, it was a good American team in 1973. It was a sort of nail in the coffin for a British and Irish side, put it that way.

Christy O'Connor: I look back on the Ryder Cup with fond memories, though saddened by the fact that they never made me captain. It was not something that bothered me much down the years, though since my last appearance the point has been raised frequently by those who ponder why I was never asked to lead the team. Yes, it would have been nice. I certainly could not have made more of a cock-up of it than some of them.

Was it that they felt I was not up to making speeches? If so, then it was a pretty lame excuse. Surely there would have been enough PGA officials hanging on to have satisfied that end. I have always let the golf clubs do the talking for me and if the powers of oration are adjudged to be a deciding factor in picking a Ryder Cup captain, then I rest my case!

TWENTY-ONE

1975

Laurel Valley Golf Club. Ligonier, Pennsylvania
(USA 21, GB&I 11)

The twenty-first Ryder Cup was held at Laurel Valley Golf Club in Ligonier, Pennsylvania. For the US captain Arnold Palmer, it was as close a home match as it was possible to be – as his house stood just a few miles from the course.

The course at Laurel Valley was long which was seen as being advantageous to the US team, having many long-hitters. It wasn't the only advantage they enjoyed as their settled team was full of experience in Billy Casper, Al Geiberger, Lou Graham, Gene Littler, Jack Nicklaus, JC Snead, Lee Trevino and Tom Weiskopf, and their three rookies were Hale Irwin, Johnny Miller and Bob Murphy, while Raymond Floyd returned to the side after a six-year absence.

Great Britain and Ireland were captained by Bernard Hunt, who could call on Brian Barnes, Maurice Bembridge, Bernard Gallacher, Brian Huggett, Tony Jacklin and Peter Oosterhuis while there were debuts for Eamonn Darcy, Tommy Horton, Guy Hunt, Christy O'Connor Jnr (the nephew of Christy O'Connor Snr), John O'Leary and Norman Wood. While Huggett's experience was undoubted (this was his sixth Ryder Cup), there was no doubt that he was feeling the effects of age, and Tony Jacklin was also no longer the player he had once been.

Colin Snape (Executive Director of the PGA): On another note, I remember that women weren't allowed in the clubhouse at Laurel Valley, and that included the wives of players. On the first night we always had a team meeting with the respective teams, just to go through the rules and all the rest of it. I'll never forget Jack Nicklaus coming in all steely-eyed and saying, 'Never mind the rules and all that crap, Arnold. If my wife is not sitting down to have lunch with me tomorrow, I'm going home.' There was a deathly silence. Such consternation. So a compromise was effected whereby the wives of the players – and only the wives of the players – were allowed in the clubhouse between twelve and two to consume lunch with their husbands. As Murphy's Law would have it, there was a rain-out when play started, so by the time Jack got in it was twenty minutes to two. So Barbara was allowed to have the soup before she was ejected with everybody else.

Norman Wood: When I was playing as a lad in Scotland, every time I practised and hit shots, you always said, 'this is the last hole of the Open, you've got this five-iron to knock it onto the green'. You were talking to yourself like that on the practise range, pretending a shot was to win the Open or to play in the Ryder Cup. It always went through my mind when I was young. You think you are the greatest player of the lot, as you are going round your home course in 65s or 66s all the time. You think you can go away and play tournaments and shoot those numbers. But you go away and different courses are longer,

Opposite: Brian Barnes, pipe in mouth, escapes from a bunker at Laurel Valley. *Getty Images*

tighter and the pressure is on, and you end up shooting 75s and 76s. I really wanted to get on the American Tour at one time, but it was just impossible. Being a Ryder Cup player, I didn't even get invited to the Masters at that time, it was so hard to get into America. It was a hard school to get into.

But making the Ryder Cup that year was just wonderful, although it was different then to the way it is now. You can't even compare it to when I played in it. OK, the crowds were quite good out in America, but nothing like what it is now. I mean, it's massive. It must be one of the biggest sporting events in the world now. You can't explain it. The atmosphere was amazing at Gleneagles in 2014, the crowds, the cheering, it was just great. I noticed it at the Belfry as well, in 2002. Even now, it's much, much bigger than that, since 2002. It's fantastic. But I loved my time as well. Different to today, but still wonderful.

Christy O'Connor Jnr: After a hugely successful season I made it into the side fairly comfortably by finishing seventh on the European Order of Merit. I remember going over to England for my Ryder Cup fitting and I will never forget the day my gear arrived.

En route to the States from Heathrow we took part in the World Open which was played at Pinehurst's No.2 course. It was a fantastic set-up and we mingled with the American team. This was a wonderful introduction for us and it helped us to relax ahead of the cup, although there were warning signs everywhere for the challenge ahead because the Americans all played wonderfully and Jack Nicklaus walked away with the title. We realised then, if we hadn't already, that they would be formidable opposition, although I don't think any of us dreamed quite how formidable they would prove to be.

Norman Wood: They had Nicklaus, Trevino, Miller, Irwin, Floyd, Casper, Weiskopf, Littler, and Palmer was the captain. They had a lot of good players. At that time, it was always the same. We had about four really strong good players, five maybe, and the rest were not as good as the Americans. They had ten players out of twelve, I would say, who were top, top players. We had Jacklin, Oosterhuis, Barnes and Gallacher, they were our top players. But the rest, guys like myself, John O'Leary, Guy Hunt, we weren't really in the same class as them. But on the day, you never know . . .

Tony Jacklin: For a dozen years or so I had been playing mostly in the States, and was constantly aware of how much higher the standards were over there. I am not talking about players' skills, but about the running of tournaments, the excellence of events week after week. The conditioning of the courses was far superior; they felt it important to get the greens as good as they could be. All the facilities were first class, the locker rooms, practise grounds, food in the clubhouse, all were absolutely as good as they could make them.

I particularly remember 1975 at Arnold Palmer's home club, Laurel Valley. We were all given Stylo plastic shoes, and one of my soles came completely off during my singles against Ray Floyd. Meanwhile, there they were, travelling by Concorde, looking a million dollars, wives to match and the best of everything laid on. In those days we really were second-class citizens and like lambs to the slaughter.

Arnold Palmer: With my Ryder Cup career clearly waning, I pulled just about every string available for the Ryder Cup to come to Laurel Valley in 1975. Perhaps someone high up in the organisation thought of it as a suitable reward for my decision a decade before not to bolt from the organisation when temptation was so strong. Whatever their reasons, I was very pleased that the cup was coming to my place in Pennsylvania for what would clearly be my fare-thee-well to Ryder Cup participation.

I'd hoped to play my way onto the team, but it wasn't meant to be. Everyone knew that my selection as team captain was a very symbolic and sentimental choice. My record as a player in the event spoke for itself in that regard.

At that point in time, no American had a better win-loss record in Ryder Cup competition than me, but it was obvious that my better days on tour were behind me – as my mediocre tournament record from that year indicates. I was deeply honoured to be selected captain, and what a team I had that year – golf's equivalent of the Dream Team, and maybe the best Ryder Cup squad ever: Nicklaus; Littler; Trevino; Miller; Weiskopf; Floyd; Casper; Irwin; Geiberger; Dave Hill; JC Snead; Lou Graham; Bob Murphy.

I suppose the outcome was a foregone conclusion.

Hale Irwin: Arnie had that steely mindset of a winner and was a no-nonsense kind of guy when it came to his captaincy. He brought us all together and just said, 'We're here to win. And as far as I'm concerned, I don't want them winning even a single point.'

Norman Wood: Bernard Hunt was a great captain. Arnold Palmer was his opposite captain, so he always faced a challenge. Bernard did well. He had a nice manner and I think everyone wanted to play their best for him. He was a good Ryder Cup player as well, playing in eight matches.

But right from the off I felt like we were up against it. I think most of us did. Being realistic, even though we had the 'let's get them' attitude, deep down, I think we knew. Coming up against the likes of Nicklaus, Trevino and all the really top players, you knew you had to play to your best, and sometimes your best wasn't even good enough, that was the thing. Jacklin and Oosterhuis, you always felt like they could take on anybody and beat them. We really had to get them to win their matches, and Barnes and Gallacher too, hoping that we would sneak in the odd win as well.

The Friday morning foursomes got underway and it was as daunting a start as any for the visiting team in a Ryder Cup as the Americans blew their opponents out of the water. Nicklaus and Weiskopf set the tone in the first match, defeating Barnes and Gallacher 5&4 before Littler and Irwin combined to beat Wood and Bembridge 4&3. Geiberger and Miller then defeated Jacklin and Oosterhuis 3&1 before Trevino and Snead saw off Horton and O'Leary 2&1.

The afternoon was better for Great Britain and Ireland, but only just. Oosterhuis and Jacklin played well to defeat Casper and Floyd 2&1 to register the first blue point on the board and Barnes and Gallacher managed to secure a half against Nicklaus and Murphy, but the US continued to build their score with a 3&2 win for Weiskopf and Graham over Darcy and O'Connor and a 2&1 victory for Trevino and Irwin over Horton and O'Leary.

Christy O'Connor Jnr: There were three Irishmen in the team that year: me, Eamonn Darcy and John O'Leary. Today, European captains often pair the Irish players together as an essential part of team selections. Bernard Hunt saw fit to do exactly the same thing in 1975. He left me out of the first day's morning foursomes but pencilled me in for the afternoon fourballs with Eamonn Darcy.

Eamonn and I faced a daunting task against Tom Weiskopf and Lou Graham. Graham may not be universally known to golf fans but he won the US Open and finished second and third in it as well.

Weiskopf was a giant. He stood 6'3" and was perhaps the best golfer in the world at the time. He won the British Open but he also had an amazing dozen or so top ten finishes and was runner-up on half a dozen occasions in Majors.

Darcy and I started with fire in our bellies. Eamonn birdied the first and second holes. I birdied the third and we both birdied the fourth. But Weiskopf was unbelievable – we were one down after four holes!

Something like that really knocks the stuffing out of you. We were deflated after all our opening efforts. It went on like this right to the end. Eamonn and I knocked sparks off our clubs and played brilliantly, but lost 3&2.

At the end of the first day's play we had put a bit of respectability on the scoreline but we trailed by 6½–1½ overnight. In what is traditionally our strongest format, we failed.

If there was any sense of a real contest emerging between the sides, it was swiftly dispelled on the second day as Great Britain and Ireland only managed to secure a further two points out of a possible eight, with all the American wins confirmed by the time they reached the sixteenth green. The day ended 6–2 in favour of the United States, who led 12½–3½ overall.

Christy O'Connor Jnr: The next morning trumpeted a similar story, as the Americans won the morning matches 3–1 and so stretched their lead to 9½–2½. There was still hope but it was not looking too healthy. Tony Jacklin and Brian Barnes won their match in the afternoon [3&2 against Trevino and Murphy] to give us another point and renewed hope but then along came Mr Weiskopf.

For the second day running I faced up to Tom who was paired on this occasion with Johnny Miller. What a combination. John O'Leary and I were faced with some task and so it proved. We were well and truly beaten 5&3. The USA won two more matches that day to leave us with what we now virtually accepted as an impossible task. Going into Sunday and the final day's singles matches, we were a whopping nine points in arrear, 12½–3½.

It looked as if the match might turn into something of an exhibition – and in many ways it did, with the Americans rampant throughout the morning session; indeed they only dropped three points when Peter Oosterhuis defeated Johnny Miller two-up, Brian Barnes beat Jack Nicklaus 4&2 and Bernard Gallacher and Lee Trevino halved alongside Tommy Horton and Hale Irwin. The US secured victory by lunchtime with Tom Weiskopf's 5&3 victory over Guy Hunt; the real story of the day, however, came from the battle between Nicklaus and Barnes. Nicklaus came into Laurel Valley Golf Club playing what he called 'the best golf of my life', having won his fifth Masters in April, his fourth PGA Championship in August and the World

Open at Pinehurst. While Barnes was without doubt a very fine golfer, the conclusion to their morning singles match was considered a foregone conclusion. It was to great surprise, therefore, that the Scotsman triumphed 4&2. This heralded a media scrum at lunchtime as the press clamoured to interview the pair. With the result decided, the captains conferred and decided that the best way to keep interest up in the afternoon session was to take advantage of this attention and pit Nicklaus and Barnes together once more.

The vistors showed admirable tenacity in the afternoon by refusing to roll over at any stage. This was typified in the afternoon singles session, which they won 4½–3½, when Peter Oosterhuis beat JC Snead 3&2 and Tommy Horton beat Lou Graham 2&1. Although Raymond Floyd defeated Tony Jacklin one-up, Al Geiberger halved with Bernard Gallacher, Hale Irwin beat John O'Leary 2&1 and Bob Murphy saw off Maurice Bembridge 2&1, the real talking point of the session came in the final two matches when Norman Wood took on Lee Trevino and Brian Barnes faced Jack Nicklaus for the second time that day.

Norman Wood: I remember Trevino hardly spoke for the first eight holes. On the eighth

green I holed a putt to go one up and between the green and the tee it was like flicking a switch. He was 'yak, yak, yak' to me and the crowd. At the tee, they were all giggling and it was then that I realised – it was gamesmanship. It made me more determined to beat him – and I managed it [2&1]. But we didn't have the overall class, as a team, to match the Americans and lost heavily.

Everybody still speaks about that win. I remember being beaten in a captain-pro challenge at Royal Guernsey. My opponent went into the club and was telling everybody he was the man that beat the man that beat Lee Trevino!

Every time somebody realises you have played at the Ryder Cup and you beat Trevino, it's mentioned. When you go out and play with somebody, they always check up on the competitor to see what you have done! So it usually crops up after two or three holes: 'I see you played against Trevino . . . ' I'm always talking about it. It was a great achievement, I was really proud of myself that day. I had my mum and dad walking round, and my

Lee Trevino. *Getty Images*

wife. It was just so nice. But even in those days, when people said the event was losing its appeal, the players were still as determined. The crowds as well, when you were hitting a shot. I remember hitting one over a lake and as soon as I hit it, the crowd shouted, 'Get in the water, get in the water!' They were so anti- the British and Irish team, and rooting for their own team. It was still passionate in those days, and it's had to be quietened down a bit in years gone by.

The match was tight all the way and by the time we reached seventeen I was still one up. I drove my tee shot straight into a bunker, and as I walked towards it I knew that if I lost the hole we'd be level going to the last where anything could happen. I managed to play a good bunker shot and got a par whilst Trevino bogeyed and handed me the win. I genuinely didn't think about beating him until I had putted out on seventeen. It was a great relief to see that putt go in.

The key to beating an American in those days was the putter. We were all pretty evenly matched off the tee and with approach shots, but it was with the putter that they were superior. We had to try and match them on the greens to have any chance. They had outplayed us over the first two days and for most of the third, so although my match against Trevino wasn't vital to the result of the cup, it was still one we both wanted to win.

Looking back now it was one of the biggest victories of my career, but I remember Trevino didn't take it too well. He just shook my hand and walked off. I saw an article by him afterwards saying how he hated playing dead matches and that he didn't care about losing to 'some unknown' when America already had the Ryder Cup won. He couldn't even remember my name.

Lee Trevino: In 1975 we played thirty-six holes a day and we were so far ahead before the last afternoon's round that some guys told Palmer they were tired and didn't want to play. I told him to put me in the first match, but before I teed off I enjoyed a lunch of six beers. I lost, 2&1 to Norman Wood, but it didn't matter. I was just out for fun.

After the first nine, we went right by the pavilion. I saw Palmer sitting on the lawn and I screamed at him. 'Hey, Arnold, give me a couple of beers!' So he grinned, grabbed the beers, ran down to the fence, and handed them to me. He was a helluva captain.

With his pride clearly dented after his morning loss, Nicklaus arrived at the first tee and said to Barnes, 'You've beaten me once, but there ain't no way you're going to beat me again.' He then backed up these words by winning the first two holes. But Barnes was obstinate, unwilling to surrender. Slowly but surely he got himself back into the match.

Arnold Palmer: In retrospect, the most interesting drama centred around the two singles matches played between Nicklaus and Brian Barnes. It's kind of funny now, but it was no laughing matter then. In their first singles match, Brian shocked everybody – and probably even himself – by upsetting Jack. During the lunch break, everyone was buzzing that I should engineer a rematch with Barnes so Jack could get his revenge. I could see that even Jack was itching for a rematch, so I pulled it off. They met again a little while later on the first tee. 'Well, Brian,' Jack said to Barnes. 'You beat me this morning. You're not going to beat me again.' I don't think anybody there would have disagreed with that assessment.

Certainly not a Ladbrokes bookie. That season Jack had already won six tournaments, including two Majors, was the Tour's leading money winner, and was en route to PGA Player of the Year honours. He was the game's presiding master, at the top of his game.

Brian Barnes: It was match play where anyone can beat anyone. On my day I can hole a few putts at the right time and win. That, of course, is what eighteen hole match play is all about. It's Russian roulette really. You go out and if you are holing a couple of putts you will beat the best in the world, and that is exactly what I did. Jack had won two Majors that year and Arnold Palmer wanted someone to give him a game. I won 4&3 in the morning. Then Jack said to Arnie: 'Give me that Barnes again.'

I'd played with Jack a fair number of times by then and I think Bernard Hunt felt that, of everyone in the team, I was the least likely to be overawed by playing him.

Hale Irwin: Of all the players I've played against in some sort of match play format, Brian was the least impressed about the player that he was playing, his record, or what he had done before. Barnesy looked upon it as just another game, and he was not impressed by a name. It was a great attitude. And if he got a bit nervous, out came the pipe.

Peter Oosterhuis: Brian Barnes. What a character. A big guy who smoked a pipe and frequently hit shots with the pipe still in his mouth. Brian hit the ball very long and straight. Other parts of his game and a fast lifestyle held him back, but he's a great example of a player who would have benefited from modern equipment. Brian in his prime would have destroyed courses the way Rory McIlroy and Dustin Johnson destroy them these days. A wonderful player.

Brian Barnes: Beating Nicklaus twice in the same day was my finest Ryder Cup moment, without a doubt. I've always admired Jack enormously, and here I was playing for my country and defeating the greatest golfer of all time twice in the same day. My God, what do you do for an encore?

I was a little surprised when we were paired up again in the afternoon. I told the press after the first morning, when asked if I would like to play Jack again, that lightning doesn't strike in the same place twice. Unbeknown to me, Jack had gone to Arnie and said he wanted to play me again, and Arnold and Bernard Hunt got together and the draw was changed for the first time ever in a Ryder Cup, due to the fact the match was effectively over. So Jack had sense enough to realise that if we wanted to keep the punters there, the only match they really wanted to see was the match between Jack and myself. That is typical of the man. If you go back to 1969, the putt that he gave Tony. Although he got a tongue lashing from Sam Snead for doing it, he realised the best thing that had happened for Britain for many, many a year was Tony winning the Open Championship in '69. If he had missed that Ryder Cup putt, that win would have gone out of the window completely. And, of course, it was thanks to him that the Ryder Cup is still going, his letter to Lord Derby to get Europe involved. It's a different ball game now. Having the opportunity to pick Seve Ballesteros, José María Olazábal et al, it was fantastic for the game, fantastic for the Ryder Cup and it's made it, of course, probably the most prestigious match of any sport,

I would probably say, including the Olympics. I think the Ryder Cup is watched by every country in the world.

So anyway, Jack and I get to the first tee and he fixes me with a glare and says, 'You beat me once, but I'll be damned if you'll beat me twice.' My knees should've been shaking, but I figured, 'What the hell, let's just play,' and wouldn't you know, I win again.

Jack's fit to be tied, but great sportsman he is, he puts his hand out. I was rather stunned, actually. Jack, as ever, was an absolute gent. Mind you, he was bloody pissed off at the end. I can still hear the thump of his golf shoes being flung into the locker.

Arnold Palmer: All that proves in my book is what splendid unpredictability match play golf provided. It's a reason I wish the PGA Championship would consider returning to its original match play format.

I loved the Ryder Cup, because it simply wasn't about playing for money. It was about playing for something far grander and more personal. I'm proud of what the Ryder Cup did for me – and for what I contributed to my teams in six Ryder Cup competitions as a player. I won twenty-two matches against eight losses, with two ties and a total of 23 points. That was a record that stood from 1973 until Nick Faldo won two more points at Valderrama Golf Club in Spain in 1997, pushing his career points total to 25. That's how it should be, for records are not meant to stand forever.

The game brings out the best in us, and the best will always bring out their games at the Ryder Cup.

For all Barnes's heroics, the final 21–11 result was another humiliation to add to the record books. The pressure was building on the British PGA to do something to reconcile matters and make the matches more competitive. But they were not yet for turning.

Bernard Gallacher: I think that was quite a low point, '75, because we lost before the last singles, the match was over. I thought we had a reasonable chance, but the course was too long for quite a few members of our team, to be honest. It was a typical, long American golf course and we just couldn't handle it.

I think if you put 1975 and 1977 together that was probably the reason that Jack Nicklaus said to Lord Derby that he felt we should become a European side. He could see America losing interest, especially if going into the last series of singles the match is over. TV cameras switch off, everybody switches off, it was like a lap of honour for the Americans. It was a bit embarrassing, to be honest, from our team's point of view.

Lee Trevino: You have to understand that when we played the Ryder Cup in the sixties and seventies, they always had five players who could compete with us but they couldn't compete with our bottom seven.

Bernard Gallacher: Playing in the States in the '70s, it felt like the Ryder Cup was on its knees. We were losing badly and it wasn't much fun. In 1975 at Laurel Valley, the Americans had already won the cup before the final round of singles matches. That was tough and people were beginning to question the validity of the Ryder Cup continuing in that format.

The Ryder Cup at this time was not a money-spinner. Compared with today there was little or no hype and with it being played in such an out-of-the-way place at Laurel Valley where the crowds were inevitably going to be small, it underlined, too, how casually the US PGA approached the match.

It was highlighted for us by Jack Nicklaus losing twice to big Brian Barnes, but the Americans won by ten points and the cup as a spectacle and a contest was again in danger of being shelved. The Americans had won all but two of the sixteen meetings since 1947 and there seemed little prospect of the match becoming more competitive.

It was mooted that Commonwealth players might be used to strengthen the British side but all that was done for 1977 was to change the format, reducing the points availability in order to dilute America's strength in depth. There were huge gaps between the games at Lytham and the format was hardly a success with the Americans who felt it was a long way to come to play for just 20 points.

And with the emergence of players like Seve Ballesteros, thoughts began to stray more forcibly towards expanding the team to include players from outside Britain and Ireland. Unless we turned things around in the next few Ryder Cups to make it more competitive, or we looked to expand our team, we knew the whole thing was in serious danger of falling apart.

TWENTY-TWO

1977
Royal Lytham and St Annes. St Annes, England
(USA 12½, GB&I 7½)

The Ryder Cup returned to Royal Lytham and St Annes in 1977. Following the humiliation at Laurel Valley, the Great Britain and Ireland team had lobbied for another format change, which reduced the number of matches by nearly a third to leave a total of just 20 total points to be contested between the teams. It made little or no difference to the result and failed to supply the invigoration the competition so sorely needed. Indeed, the dangerously waning interest in the Ryder Cup was epitomised by Tom Weiskopf's decision to declare himself unavailable for selection for the US team in favour of a hunting expedition in Alaska. 'It's the lions against the Christians,' he wanly explained. 'Lop-sided. I've done it before, let someone else have a chance to play.'

Tony Jacklin: 1977 was the year that Tom Weiskopf was selected for the American team but controversially chose to decline the invitation and go on a hunting trip instead. It sent shock waves around the golf world and we knew then that something major had to happen to keep the Ryder Cup going as a blue riband event.

Peter Oosterhuis: I remember hearing that Weiskopf said that the reason he chose to go hunting was because the Ryder Cup was more of a parade than a golf match. I know now that he hated all the public scrutiny of his career and that there was a lot of pressure on him from the media who felt that his talent merited more success than he was achieving. So maybe that whole media circus just got to him.

Tom Weiskopf: Golf was not the most important thing in my life back then. It was widely recognised that I had an ability and talent for it, but I enjoyed practise rounds more than tournaments. In competition, I put way too much pressure on myself. I put too much emphasis on perfection instead of just going out and having fun. I wish I could have taken into that environment the attitude I had in practise, but instead I turned on another switch and it short-circuited. I didn't have tremendous patience. I look back now and I thoroughly regret turning down that Ryder Cup place, but my head just wasn't in it at the time. I came to dislike the constant questioning in interviews. I was always a fairly private person and I spent a lot of time with my friends and family. I didn't like being bothered. That's why I have so much respect for Jack Nicklaus, Arnold Palmer, Tom Watson and especially Tiger Woods. To handle that kind of stuff year after year is phenomenal. I just didn't deal well with it. I kind of rebelled.

Neil Coles: That may have been his reasons for going hunting, but that wasn't revealed for

Opposite: Tom Watson and Nick Faldo. *Getty Images*

many, many years. At the time it was just taken as a sign that the Americans were losing interest in the Ryder Cup and a lot of the prestige about playing in it was fading. I think Weiskopf's actions were the final straw for Jack Nicklaus – he knew that something had to be done, something had to change in order to keep the Ryder Cup alive.

Weiskopf's sentiments, which stirred considerable consternation on both sides of the Atlantic, were nevertheless pertinent. Even with the revised format, home advantage and the emergence of a young player who would take the Ryder Cup – and the golfing world at large – by storm in years to come in the shape of Nick Faldo, Great Britain and Ireland were swept aside once again.

Home captain Brian Huggett had called upon the services of old hands Brian Barnes, Neil Coles, Eamonn Darcy, Bernard Gallacher, Tommy Horton, Tony Jacklin and Peter Oosterhuis while there were debuts for Ken Brown, Howard Clark, Peter Dawson and Mark James alongside Faldo.

In the opposite corner, Dow Finsterwald led a strong team that hardly noticed Weiskopf's absence. Raymond Floyd, Lou Graham, Dave Hill, Hale Irwin, Don January, Jack Nicklaus and Dave Stockton all returned to the fray to guide rookies Hubert Green, Jerry McGee, Ed Sneed, Lanny Wadkins and Tom Watson through their debut Ryder Cup campaign.

Colin Snape: The 1977 match was the fiftieth anniversary of the Ryder Cup, so we brought together all the surviving members of the first matches. We brought in three American players – Gene Sarazen, Johnny Farrell, and Wild Bill Mehlhorn, who came in his Stetson! It was also Queen Elizabeth's silver jubilee – her coronation had been in 1952 – so we had special plates made that commemorated both jubilees and presented them to the previous players and the 1977 teams. It was an open-air presentation by the eighteenth green, and it really was very impressive. We had the bands and the flags and all the rest of it. It was a super occasion. The match afterwards really was an anti-climax.

Tom Watson: Dow Finsterwald was our captain and he talked about what it meant to be part of the Ryder Cup, about all the great players who had taken part and how honoured he was to follow in the footsteps of all the captains who had come before him. I just stood there with shivers running down my back thinking, 'I want to do that someday.' It was my first Ryder Cup and I just loved every second of it.

Dow Finsterwald: At that point Nicklaus and Watson were one-two in the world, and Don Padgett [PGA president] said, 'Don't get those guys out there in fourballs; they may start playing against each other.' I kept that in mind, but I thought they'd make a great team playing alternate shot.

One of the things I said to them beforehand was, 'I want you guys to do whatever you do normally the night before you play. If you drink a bottle of whisky, drink a bottle of whisky. If you don't drink at all, don't drink at all. Just keep your norm. You got here by playing well and on your own schedule of what time you go to bed.' I always remember about the guy who was playing in the club championship and he normally stayed out late or did something. And the night before the championship at the club he went to bed real early but he didn't sleep. So I just wanted them to do whatever they normally did.

Mark James: Our captain for the 1977 competition, Brian Huggett, was a no-nonsense guy who told it as it was. For the first day's foursome he decided, in his wisdom, to send me out last, alongside Tommy Horton. 'On the tee, representing the United States of America, Jack Nicklaus and Tom Watson.' What a pair to face! Jack and Tom were pretty much at their peak; Tommy and I were facing the two best players in the world, who a few months earlier had gone head to head at the Open at Turnberry in one of the most memorable shoot-outs in the sport's history. Nicklaus was such a good player that if he hit a fade it moved about four feet left to right; if he hit a wild slice it moved twelve feet in the same direction. Watson was nearly as powerful as his partner, and I had never seen anyone with chipping ability quite like his. I got the impression with Nicklaus and Watson that they knew how good they were, although not in a boastful way. But they knew that unless they had a really off day, there was no way we could play well enough to beat them.

Nick Faldo: Without a doubt the Ryder Cup is the most emotional, nerve-wracking week in golf. You are there because you have wanted to be there, and with no money at stake, it is somehow the ultimate test of your ability. There are simply no rewards for not winning; no few thousand pounds for being beaten in the first round, or having finalist in this or that world championship after your name.

Every match has been memorable. My first was in 1977 at Royal Lytham and St Anne's and I was the new kid on the block. In those days there were only three matches – a foursomes, a fourball and a single on the last day. I was paired with Peter Oosterhuis, who was just about our best player, winning the Order of Merit four years in a row. It was a great start for me, but you know you were one of the pairings that was expected to win a point or two so there was a lot of pressure. The foursomes started badly for us as a team as Bernie Gallacher and Brian Barnes lost 3&1 to Lanny Wadkins and Hale Irwin, and then Neil Coles and Peter Dawson lost by a shot to Dave Stockton and Jerry McGee. Oosty and I were up third and we were playing Raymond Floyd and Lou Graham. It was agreed that I would drive the odds, which meant I would hit the first tee shot and the first at Lytham is a short hole. On the practise ground I hit a lot of four- and five-irons, and when the moment came, I got it on the green.

So far so good, but Oosty was a bit off that day, and I found I was supporting him. We were three down after ten holes, but then Oosty got going and we won five of the next seven holes. It was a hell of a comeback and we won by 2&1 – and I had my first Ryder Cup point.

Peter Oosterhuis: My form was all over the place that year. I started out badly and I couldn't hit a fairway until the eighth hole, so the pressure was really on Nick to carry the team. And he did. He played beautifully for those seven holes. He may have been only twenty but his talent and determination were obvious already.

It was a tough first day – that point that Nick and I won was the only full point our team managed, although Darcy and Tony Jacklin managed to halve with Ed Sneed and Don January. Jack Nicklaus combined superbly with Tom Watson for the final round of the day and they dismantled poor old Tommy Horton and Mark James 5&4, so we were up against it after the first day with the score already 3½–1½ to the Americans.

Tom Watson: It was a great first day and we kept that momentum going into the fourballs the next morning. I played with Hubert Green against Barnes and Horton and we were hitting some beautiful shots around the course. I think we won that one 5&4.

Just behind us Ed Sneed and Lanny Wadkins were enjoying themselves as much as we were and they beat Neil Coles and Peter Dawson by a similar score [it ended 5&3].

Peter Oosterhuis: Nick and I were out third against Nicklaus and Floyd and it was another great match, but I remember at one point Floyd missed a putt and someone in the crowd cheered. It was nothing like we sometimes see these days, but Jack was moved to comment, walking down the next hole. 'You know,' he said, 'I love playing golf in Great Britain, but not in the Ryder Cup.' He had a point. Lots of players were feeling the same way. It isn't complicated for the spectators: clap when someone hits a good shot, shut up when they don't.

Nick Faldo: Yeah, for a young kid from Welwyn Garden City who had only started playing the game of golf six years before that, it was quite something. It was more than a dream start to my Ryder Cup career, especially beating Nicklaus, who was my idol. I was long in those days. I had one of the early graphite drivers – it looked like a stick of liquorice – and I was hitting it way past Jack. I could feel his eyes boring into the back of my head, and I'm thinking, 'Don't look back . . .' But I loved it. It was the first time I'd played when my stomach churned all day. That was the effect of the Ryder Cup.

At the eleventh, a huge hole back into the breeze, I was the only one on in two and that put us a couple ahead, and on we went to win 3&1.

Eamonn Darcy: Unfortunately that point that Nick and Oosty got was as good as we got that day. Dave Hill and Dave Stockton absolutely brutalized Tony Jacklin and me 5&3. It was pretty dispiriting. And then Mark James and Ken Brown had a good tussle with Hale Irwin and Lou Graham, but they ended up losing by a shot. So we ended up losing the session 4–1, taking the overall score to 7½ to 2½.

While the scoreboard was making grim reading for British and Irish fans, the lead was not insurmountable – as long as the home team stuck together and went out with the ambition to play the best golf they were capable of. The odds were against them, of course, but it was still mathematically possible. But the odds stacked against them rose even higher when there was a major fallout between Tony Jacklin and captain Brian Huggett .

Mark James: I remember little of Jacklin in the Ryder Cup team of 1977, but I was impressed by the way Brian Huggett dealt with that episode. There was less golf played in that match: one series of foursomes on the first day, another of fourballs on the second and just ten singles on the last. In one of the first two days there was a match still left out on the course and, quite rightly, everybody who was finished was expected to go along and support. I think Jacklin was in the clubhouse having tea and scones; he certainly wasn't out there with the rest of us, and Huggett fell out with him over that. As a result, he left Jacklin out of the last day's singles. It was a brave move to make, but there was no bullshit with Huggett. He had not approved of what one of his team had done, and he was determined to do something about it.

Tony Jacklin: I got left out because I told Huggett what I bloody thought of him. Basically Brian went through an acute personality change as soon as we got to the golf course. He set himself apart from the players, sat and ate only with his wife in the evenings; and we asked him to join us on a couple of occasions. He'd taken this thing on, but he wasn't creating much team spirit. Then after Eamonn Darcy and I were beaten in one of the early matches we went back out on the course to support the match that was behind us. Huggett came up to us and said, 'Why aren't you out practising?' Bloody cheeky bastard, telling grown fellows who are out there giving it our best shot that that wasn't good enough. I've never been one to think that practise can create instant success anyway, and if I thought I needed to practice for the afternoon I would have been practising. I was old enough to know what my own game was.

So I just took him to the other side of the fairway and told him in no uncertain terms to mind his own goddamn business. So he dropped me from the singles.

Colin Snape: In terms of trying to appeal to the crowd and get the blood pumping and atmosphere ramped up, the decision to leave out Tony Jacklin from the singles was a disaster. The crowds wanted to see their hero in action – and he was nowhere to be seen, and it wasn't even as if he was injured so it was an unfortunate twist of fate. Huggett just decided to drop him because they fell out.

Tony Jacklin: I didn't actually speak to Brian for a few years after that. I didn't agree with the decision at the time and I've never been able to get my head round it in the years since. He was stubborn on the course when he played – and he retained that quality when he was captain, which was disastrous.

Dow Finsterwald is surrounded by the victorious United States team. Standing (*from left to right*), Hubert Green, Raymond Floyd, Dave Stockton, Lanny Wadkins, Tom Watson, Hale Irwin, Jerry McGee, Jack Nicklaus, Ed Sneed, Don January, Lou Graham and Dave Hill. *Getty Images*

With Jacklin absent from the singles line-up, Huggett needed the top of his order to start with a bang. Unfortunately, they couldn't manage it and the US extended their lead further as Lanny Wadkins beat Howard Clark 4&3 and Lou Graham saw off Neil Coles 5&3. Peter Dawson fought back for an equally emphatic 5&4 victory over Don January, and Brian Barnes kept up the fight with a one-up victory over Hale Irwin. Dave Hill then enjoyed a comprehensive 5&4 victory over Tommy Horton before all eyes turned to Jack Nicklaus's battle with Bernard Gallacher.

Bernard Gallacher: I was up against Jack Nicklaus in the singles. Jack had a terrible start – three bogeys in a row and I was three up out of nowhere. I then birdied the fourth and was four up. But Jack being Jack kept at it and clawed the score back and by the time we got to the seventeenth we were all square. I had a monster putt, an eighty-footer, and I was just trying to get it near the hole – and the bloody thing went in! So I was one up going to eighteen and I managed to keep my nerves and we halved the hole to give me the victory. It was a magic moment.

Hubert Green struck back for the US in the seventh match out against Eamonn Darcy, winning one-up before Raymond Floyd defeated Mark James 2&1.

Nick Faldo: I drew Tom Watson in the second last match out. Tom was Open champion at the time, having just won that fantastic contest against Nicklaus at Turnberry. After beating Nicklaus the previous day, some people thought the outcome was fixed. Neither of us played well, but I hung on to win at the last.

Though the teams split the singles, 5–5, the US had won another Ryder Cup, this time by a margin of 12½–7½. Although it was a comprehensive victory, there were some impressive performances from the home team, most notably from Nick Faldo who, despite suffering from glandular fever, won all three of his matches. The highlight for the home side was notable wins for the partnership of Peter Oosterhuis and Faldo in their victory over Raymond Floyd and Lou Graham in the foursomes and then Jack Nicklaus and Floyd in fourballs. Faldo then triumphed over Tom Watson for a flawless start to his Ryder Cup career.

Of much more significance than the result of the matches, however, was the meeting held during the matches between officials from the US PGA and the PGA of Great Britain to discuss the introduction of players from Continental Europe into the competition. Jack Nicklaus took it upon himself to meet with Lord Derby, the president of the British PGA, and his American counterpart, Henry Poe, to lend his support to the notion that the qualification criteria for the Great Britain and Ireland team should include players from the European Tournament Players' Division (the forerunner to the European Tour). 'The Americans are quite happy to treat this match as a goodwill gesture, a get-together, a bit of fun,' said Nicklaus at the time. 'But here in Britain it's treated differently. The people here seem to want a serious, knock-em-down match. If that's what's wanted, there has to be a stronger opposition. Something has to be done to make it more of a match for the Americans.' It took some deliberation but shortly after the 1977 Ryder Cup was concluded, the original Deed of Trust struck between Samuel Ryder and the PGA of Great Britain was amended to allow for the expansion, and a new era of Ryder Cup history was born.

Jack Nicklaus: When I'm asked what my favourite Ryder Cup moment is, it's funny but I don't think of something that happened on the course. Making it more inclusive is my best Ryder Cup memory.

Bernard Gallacher: Jack was always ahead of his time, always had his ear close to the ground. He wanted the Ryder Cup to continue, but it wasn't going to continue if we were going to be beaten all the time. But he had a vision on how to fix it.

Jack Nicklaus: The US had won eighteen of the first twenty-two Ryder Cup matches, mostly by lopsided margins. By the time of the 1977 contest it had become clear to me that the imbalance inherent in pitting a nation that then possessed about fifteen million golfers against two countries, Britain and Ireland, with barely a million between them was turning the match into a non-event, at least as far as the American public was concerned, and also to some extent for its top players.

I had enjoyed a friendly relationship with Lord Derby, the long-time president of the British PGA, for many years. During the 1977 match, I asked him if we could talk, as a result of which we sat down together one evening at the Clifton Arms Hotel, where both of the teams were staying.

'John,' I told his lordship, 'please don't think me presumptuous, but I want to be honest about this. The American players love to get onto the Ryder Cup team, because there is no greater honour in sport than representing one's country. But the matches just aren't competitive enough.' Also, I told him I thought the British and Irish players must be frustrated too, if only by the futility of the results. We talked for a while, then he asked me how I thought we could fix things. I told him the best way I could think of would be to match the USA against a team from the entire European Tour, which by then had brought all the countries of the Continent together with Great Britain and Ireland.

A proud traditionalist, his lordship seemed initially shocked at the idea but eventually he told me he thought there was some merit in the idea and asked me to write him a letter formalising my case that he could put before his fellow PGA officers. I did so, with a copy to Don Padgett, then the president of our PGA. The crux of my argument could be summed up in a sentence: 'It is vital to widen the selection procedures if the Ryder Cup is to enjoy its past prestige.'

Dow Finsterwald: When I heard they were considering the change, I said I didn't think the Europeans should be included. Regardless of the number of matches the US had won, winning wasn't what the matches were about. They were about the game of golf, about sportsmanship, and there was enough tradition and history that they were going to be successful regardless. I also said, 'I don't give a damn if they include the rest of the world; we're still going to beat them.'

Hale Irwin: The move was to get Seve Ballesteros on the team more than anything else, and I think that was a good move. It added a great dimension to the Ryder Cup.

TWENTY-THREE

1979

The Greenbrier, White Sulpher Springs, West Virginia
(USA 17, EUR 11)

The Ryder Cup, played at the Greenbrier, West Virginia in 1979, was a landmark for the competition with players from Continental Europe considered for selection for the first time.

Other significant changes saw the format change the total number of points available to twenty-eight, with eight foursomes, eight fourballs, and twelve singles matches, as well as the introduction of the 'envelope' – a process whereby each captain placed the name of a player from their team in a sealed envelope; should a player from the opposition team withdraw during the matches due to injury or illness, the player named in the envelope would then have to sit out the rest of the competition to balance the sides at eleven players each (and a half point would be awarded to both sides). Furthermore, as well as the newly formed European Ryder Cup team containing two Spaniards in Seve Ballesteros and Antonio Garrido, Lee Elder became the first black player to represent the US.

Billy Casper led the home team and as well as handing a debut place to Elder, also inducted Andy Bean, Tom Kite, John Mahaffey, Gil Morgan, Larry Nelson and Fuzzy Zoeller into the US Ryder Cup family. Alongside these debutants were the returning Hubert Green, Hale Irwin, Lee Trevino and Lanny Wadkins. Jack Nicklaus failed to make the team for the first time since becoming eligible in 1969, while Tom Watson was initially selected by Casper, but withdrew the day before the matches began so that he could attend the birth of his first child. His place on the team was taken by the rookie Mark Hayes.

John Jacobs was named captain of the visiting team and selected Michael King, Sandy Lyle and Des Smyth alongside the Spanish newcomers, and recalled Brian Barnes, Ken Brown, Nick Faldo, Bernard Gallacher, Tony Jacklin, Mark James and Peter Oosterhuis to the team.

Sandy Lyle: John Jacobs was a good man at the job. I had done a bit of work with him before, so it was always nice to have somebody who knows your swing, just to sort of point you in the right direction. As a leader, I think he was very understanding as he listened to what you had to say and I think everybody gelled well together. Putting a team together, who plays with who, is difficult, and he had new players with the Continentals coming in. It was a little different, I know most of them spoke English anyway, but it made the team a lot stronger. You could see a difference straight away. As a captain, he did a pretty good job really. I don't think he was quite as thorough as the modern ones are now, like going to the sports psychologists and more research going into it, as any kind of team manager would do. At the time, it was the best of the best that we had.

Des Smyth: Making the team fulfilled a lifetime ambition for me, because ever since I started playing golf, certainly professionally but even before that, the Ryder Cup always captivated me, as it has done for millions of people around the world. I was hooked early on in the game, and the Ryder Cup in particular because we had a number of famous Irish and Northern Irish Ryder Cup players like Harry Bradshaw, Fred Daly and guys that I would have known better like Christy O'Connor Snr. It always had a magic atmosphere for me, so when I got on tour it was one of my burning ambitions to be a Ryder Cup player. I got selected in 1979, because it was my breakthrough year. I had been a bit of an average player for a few years, trying to get into the top sixty in those days, otherwise you pre-qualified for events. Yeah, it was a big thrill to get on the team. It was also the first time we had any guys from the Continent then. It was a good decision; I think it was an easy decision to make, it made sense. Seve and Antonio Garrido were the first two. I knew Seve very well. I was a few years older than him so I remember him coming on tour as a young man, as a late teenager. I had heard all the talk about him, how good how he was, and it didn't take him very long to show just how good he was.

Seve Ballesteros: My Ryder Cup debut was in 1979, when it was decided to create a more competitive team by bringing in players from Continental Europe. I don't think I felt anything special in my first match, but I was clearly receptive to its hitherto unknown charms.

Nick Faldo: The first time the Europeans took part in the cup was in 1979, but the appearance of Seve Ballesteros and Antonio Garrido in the team was far outweighed by the match being played on a totally typical American course. The Greenbrier is in West Virginia, and it was hot and humid. The greens were faster than anything we had played on, and those well-documented collars of rough around each green were an examination we just weren't prepared for. Those were the days before a lot of us went and camped on the American circuit, so it took a lot of faith to believe we could win. I'm sure a lot of people felt if we couldn't win it at home, we didn't stand a chance away.

Sandy Lyle: The European Tour was involved that year, as far as the extra Continental players. That was really the starting point for me. Having the extra strength behind us, the likes of Seve, made a huge difference to our confidence. Instead of the old habit of 'we're the underdog again' we went in with a little bit more up and go, if you like. You could tell the matches would become an awful lot closer.

Des Smyth: It was a strong team. We had Faldo and four Scots in the side, they were all there, and Peter Oosterhuis. We went over there, I remember, full of confidence. I was a rookie, along with Michael King, and three others but, yeah, it was a very exciting time. You could see with the young players – Seve was young, Sandy was young, Faldo was young – that they were all emerging, talented guys. It was a daunting task, but we went to America full of hope as you always do and you could see even from the Americans' reaction to some of the young players that a change was coming in the competitive nature of the Ryder Cup. I remember Lee Trevino having played against Sandy Lyle and coming in and saying, 'God almighty, I've never seen a guy with so much talent.' They could recognise there were a lot of very strong players in our team then.

Seve Ballesteros makes his Ryder Cup debut. *Getty Images*

Hale Irwin: You had the dynamics of newer, younger American players entering the scene: Tom Kite, Fuzzy Zoeller, Jerry Pate. At the same time, the Hale Irwins were starting to assert some of their games and their personalities, and I think that made the Lee Trevinos and Jack Nicklauses, the stalwarts of the game, bear down even more. So the US team became very competitive all around. What I recall most about 1979 was that it wasn't so much the attitude of 'Were we going to win or lose?' because we knew we were going to win. It was more 'Who's going to be on the team?'

While there was obviously much excitement at the prospect of this revamped Ryder Cup – which ultimately paved the way for a complete regeneration of the competition and its development into the global sporting phenomenon that it is today – the real drama of the 1979 Ryder Cup turned out not to centre on the young Spanish pair but rather on two other junior players in the European team.

Both Ken Brown and Mark James had made their debuts in 1977 and would go on to have distinguished Ryder Cup careers as players, commentators and, in James's case, as captain in the 1999 instalment at Brookline, but their behaviour in 1979 very nearly derailed their Ryder Cup careers forever as well as damaging their team's efforts at the Greenbrier. They broke team protocol with almost pathological repetition, from turning up in their own clothes for the flight to the US, showing complete disinterest in proceedings at the opening ceremony, to missing team meetings in favour of shopping trips. James's on-course contribution lasted just one foursomes session (which he and Brown lost 3&2 to Trevino and Zoeller) before retiring injured with a back problem. Brown continued to undermine his team's efforts by largely ignoring his new partner in the afternoon fourballs, Des Smyth, which they went on to lose 7&6 to Irwin and Kite.

But it wasn't just James and Brown who played badly as the US stormed to a 5½–2½ lead after the first day.

The opening match of the morning foursomes had seen the Spanish newcomers pitched straight into battle against Wadkins and Nelson, but while their arrival signalled a new dawn in the Ryder Cup, they did little to trouble the status quo on the scoreboard as the Americans emerged 2&1 victors.

After Brown and James were defeated by Trevino and Zoeller in the second match, Bean and Elder took on Oosterhuis and Faldo and also notched a win for the home side, triumphing 2&1, before Gallacher and Barnes combined to get the new European team's first points with a 2&1 win over Irwin and Mahaffey.

Following Brown and Smyth's demolition at the hands of Irwin and Kite, the second of the afternoon foursomes saw Ballesteros and Garrido finally bring something to the party when they defeated Zoeller and Green 3&2, before Lyle and Jacklin played well to halve the third match with Trevino and Morgan. The US sealed another point in the final match of the day when Wadkins and Nelson defeated Gallacher and Barnes 3&2.

Sandy Lyle: I played three times with Jacklin. As a rookie, my nerves were reasonable. For a young lad, playing with Jacklin, you could only use it as a positive. You can't feel, 'I'm so nervous playing with Tony, I don't know if I can play with him', it was a case of 'this is a great chance to win some points'. We claimed a half point against Trevino and Morgan, then beat Elder and Mahaffey 5&4 and it was wonderful to play with Tony and feed off him. I was the rookie, he had been around for quite a few years. It happens these days in Ryder Cups, we sometimes put an old hand at the game with a rookie who gel well together. Playing with Tony, I thought it was a positive rather than a negative. I enjoyed it, I really did.

The second day was a lot more productive for the visitors, however, when they won the morning foursomes 4–1 before splitting the afternoon fourballs 2–2 (with Brown stood down by Jacobs for both sessions – which would extend to a £1,000 fine and a full year's ban from international competition thereafter; James would be fined £1,500) to leave the score at 8½–7½ in the home team's favour before the singles.

Tony Jacklin: For whatever reason, in 1979 Mark James and Ken Brown acted like buffoons and did what they could to sabotage any chance the new European team had. They wouldn't wear the right stuff, wouldn't stand at attention during the flag rising, wouldn't show up for meetings. They refused to help their partners look for balls in the alternate shot format if they happened to hit it in the trees. A cameraman would come round with film rolling to take the kind of footage we'd all had taken hundreds of times in our lives, and both of them would hold magazines or napkins in front of their faces so the cameraman couldn't do his job. It was a pretty disgraceful performance, I thought, and since they are both intelligent fellows it could only be said that they acted that way based on a conscious decision to do so. It wasn't accidental.

I've always felt that John Jacobs was too soft on them. If I'd been captain that year I'd have packed them onto the next plane and said, 'Get the hell out of here, I never want to see either of you again!'

John Jacobs: I'd written to everyone and told them that the only thing I wanted from them was for them to be on time if I called a meeting and to dress as per the agreed dress code. It was not a bombastic letter. James and Brown arrived looking like tramps. Somebody – Peter Alliss, I think – wrote that I should have sent them straight home. But it's very easy to say that. Suddenly you're stuck. You're heading for America and you think, well, surely we can get them in order a bit.

Colin Snape: We got to the Greenbrier, and James literally took to his bed. He started ordering room service and stuffing himself with double cheeseburgers. It was pouring rain when the opening ceremony was held the following day, so it was held in a huge hangar that housed the resort's indoor tennis and other recreational facilities, about a mile from the Greenbrier. With twenty minutes to go, everybody was lined up, the bands and everything, but guess who's missing – James. We rang the hotel and finally got through to his room. 'No, I'm not bothering to come,' said James.

By now Brian Barnes is furious, so I said, 'Come on, we'll go and fetch him.' Barnes and I got a golf buggy and rode to the hotel in the pouring rain. We knew what room he was in, and we hammered on the door. 'No, I'm not coming!' James replied. That was when Barnes literally went through the door!

John Jacobs: The flag raising was being televised, and I could see the pictures on television. I'm introducing my team to the great American public, and I'm going down the line, but I can see on television these two, James and Brown, are chatting away, and when the national anthems were being played and the flags were going up, they were still just chatting. It was absolutely abhorrent.

When I introduced them, they sort of just raised off their seats a bit. It was pathetic. And at a big dinner we had, they wouldn't let photographers take pictures of them. They kept putting their hands in front of their faces.

(*From left to right*) John Jacobs, Brian Barnes, Bernard Gallacher and their caddies. *Getty Images*

Mark James: On the list of misdemeanours we accumulated we were late for a team meeting and for the opening ceremony, then we were accused of yawning and fidgeting during the national anthem. There was a definite feeling that we were being frowned upon, and we were less than enamoured with the way we were being treated.

Hale Irwin: Ken Brown played like he didn't care.

Mark James: Ken and I were paired against Fuzzy Zoeller and Lee Trevino, and I was sure I would be alright despite carrying a bit of a back injury. But I was wrong. We lost and I was in absolute agony and could not play again; it was a nightmare because I was desperate to get out there and play. I do not know if any of the others felt I had had enough and just did not want to play, but that certainly was not the case.

John Jacobs: What was so annoying was that they were two of our strongest players. Both had been playing and practising well. On the first day they lost a close foursomes match, and Mark reckoned he'd pulled a muscle. We'll never know whether he had or not, but he couldn't play in the afternoon. I put Ken with Des Smyth. Ken hit a couple of bad shots early on and didn't try a lick for the rest of the round.

Des Smyth: Ken and Mark James were hauled over the coals for bad behaviour. They didn't behave properly. They're terrific guys today and they're great Ryder Cup supporters. But they were young and I would think our captain was a little too soft on them. It wouldn't be tolerated today. They weren't good team players. But they subsequently became such. And probably have regrets. They were very lucky they weren't sent home.

Hale Irwin: I was paired with Tom Kite to play against Ken Brown and Des Smyth in the afternoon. It was then that we realised how big a problem the European team had because Brown and Smyth hardly spoke to each other during the whole round. They didn't play well at all and, if I'm honest, it didn't look like they even cared all that much. It looked like they just wanted to get the round over and done with as quickly as possible. Tom and I pasted them.

Des Smyth: In the match against Hale and Tom, they played well and we didn't play well. It was my first Ryder Cup match, I was very nervous, I can't deny it. You give it your best shot and if you don't produce the golf, you get turned over fairly quickly. It is a hard thing to do to get points in the Ryder Cup. No, we didn't do so well; I was disappointed with my performance, I must say.

John Jacobs: I took them to task on the Friday evening. I said that it had been a mistake to play Ken in the afternoon because he was acting like a child and I apologised to Des Smyth for pairing him with Ken for his first Ryder Cup match.

Mark was injured out at that stage and I couldn't pair Ken with anyone after the way he had played, so I had to just play the other guys over and over again, which put a real strain on them. They did magnificently well on the Saturday, but they just ran out of steam.

Fuzzy Zoeller and Lee Trevino shake hands with
Mark James and Ken Brown after their match.

Tony Jacklin: You can't operate a team with members acting like that. We had ten other guys trying their hearts out, men who cared, and who managed to act like grown-ups. Then there were those two buffoons undermining every one of us.

Nick Faldo: After our good debut two years before, Peter Oosterhuis and I were paired up again, and this time we won two of our three games.

With no disrespect to the Spanish, I think it took them a match or two to come to terms with the whole concept of the Ryder Cup. Representing a team and playing foursomes and fourball matches was foreign to them, and the whole history of the event was a bit of a closed book.

Seve Ballesteros: Antonio Garrido and I played the fourball games against Larry Nelson and Lanny Wadkins. We lost both matches because our adversaries played wonderfully well. We also lost one of our foursome matches, but we won the other, rescuing a point for Europe at the expense of Hubert Green and Fuzzy Zoeller, the Masters champion at the time. Nelson won his singles match against me.

I remember on the afternoon of the first day, Antonio and I were playing against Fuzzy Zoeller and Hubert Green in the second foursomes. There was a bit of an incident on the sixteenth green, where we won the match. Antonio conceded a putt to Hubert and he threw the ball back to him with his putter. I guess Hubert was upset because he was losing. Whatever, he started to say something and Antonio got upset and it was a very difficult situation. I had to stand in between them. At that moment I could see that the Ryder Cup was important. Even though we didn't play for money, we played for pride. That's when I started finding out how tough it was.

Hale Irwin: By the second day we had a fairly good lead, and it was a matter of how soon into that third day were we going to win. At that stage the American teams were still flying high with a great deal of confidence. We had a very strong team, and the European side, other than Seve and maybe one or two others, hadn't really contributed to the extent that they would in later years.

Larry Nelson: I didn't take up golf until I had come back from serving as an infantryman in Vietnam. I was twenty-one when I started playing. I was a squadron leader in Vietnam and so the teamwork and camaraderie aspect of the Ryder Cup came very naturally to me. That also put the pressure of sport into perspective. After being in the army I was always just happy to see the sun rise in the morning.

I always enjoyed the Ryder Cup and I did well in 1979, winning all five of my matches. It was almost like playing the eighteenth hole of a Major on every hole and that helped my concentration I guess. Because I didn't go to college, match play was new to me, but my military background helped.

I kept getting drawn against Seve, who was about the world's best at that time. Some were intimidated by him but it wasn't a problem, I was not even intimidated by Jack Nicklaus. I heard things like Seve might try and psyche me out or put me off but there was no animosity. We actually became quite close after.

I played him four times over the three days and won each time, which I was pretty proud of as a rookie.

Tony Jacklin: There have been few players in the history of the game with charisma and talent in equally massive doses. Seve was one of them. Not that he played perfectly that week. I think he was a bit nervous, and it showed at times. He was barely out of his teens, after all; I think he'd turned twenty in the spring. He had a losing record, but it was just a tune-up for him, a prologue to his Ryder Cup heroics in the decade and a half that followed.

Ken Brown: We in Britain loved Seve so much that we can forget the impact he had across the whole of Europe, giving so many non-golf people an interest in the game. In a way he was our Arnold Palmer, who glamorised the game in America in the 1960s. But it does Seve Ballesteros a disservice to compare him to anybody. He was unique. He was Seve. Say no more.

Bernard Gallacher looked as if he was heading up a continued European revival when he won the opening singles match 3&2 against Lanny Wadkins, but the Americans smashed any hopes of a maiden win for the new team by taking the next five – Nelson winning 3&2 against Ballesteros, Kite winning one-up against Jacklin, Hayes winning one-up against Garrido, Bean winning 4&3 against King and Mahaffey winning one-up against Barnes. Nick Faldo responded for Europe by beating Lee Elder 3&2 before, surprisingly after the week he'd had, Ken Brown defeated Fuzzy Zoeller one-up. Lee Trevino triumphed in the final match 2&1 against Sandy Lyle to take the overall aggregate to 17–11 in the USA's favour, securing the cup for the Americans for the tenth time since their defeat at Lindrick.

Nick Faldo: I again got a point in the singles, though Lee Elder wasn't quite the scalp Tom Watson had been. Brian Barnes and Bernard Gallacher had a good match and overall we seemed to give them a better run than we had at Lytham a couple of years earlier.

Colin Snape: We had the victory dinner, which is quite an occasion, a time to say thank you to sponsors, the host club, and everything. Traditionally one passes around menu cards to get the players' autographs. Brown and James both wrote childish comments. I can't remember the exact words, but they were mildly offensive and viewed with extreme displeasure.

Mark James: Oceans of water have flowed under the bridge since then. Some incidents that reportedly happened have gone into folklore but have no basis in truth. Neither Ken nor I can remember the incident in which Brian Barnes was said to have asked us to step outside – it's hardly something that would slip our memories. My relationship with the press wasn't too good for a number of years – that was because so many things were said that were blatantly untrue. Ken and I were indelibly labelled rebels, bad guys, whatever, and it was a title neither of us felt we deserved.

I got a mammoth fine afterwards which soured things for me to a certain extent, but I did not get into any more trouble in the next two years as the maturing process started to kick in… I gradually started to clean up my act and generally tried to behave a lot better. I learned that sometimes it can be better to back away from confrontation.

John Jacobs and I got on fine and two years later he gave me a Ryder Cup wild card, so he could not have held any grudges.

Billy Casper: I didn't get a strong sense of the opposition being that much changed by the inclusion of the European players, but we never took them for granted, and I especially wasn't going to as captain. The overall score wasn't that close, but many matches went down to the wire. As it turned out, the scales were soon to tip the other way.

The US team celebrate their victory. *Getty Images*

TWENTY-FOUR

1981

Walton Heath Golf Club. Surrey, England

(USA 18½, EUR 9½)

In 1977, the PGA relocated their head office from the Oval cricket ground in London to the Belfry in the West Midlands, signing a ninety-nine-year lease and with it plans for an overhaul of the course and its environs. The plans for the Belfry were impressive – two new courses, a sports complex and a hotel. But by the time the 1981 Ryder Cup hove into view, the Brabazon Course, which had been completed just four years earlier, was still bedding in and was considered unfit for tournament play. The event was moved to Walton Heath and although the Surrey heathland course was a vast improvement on the condition of the Belfry, the weather across the British Isles that September week was terrible, turning the course into a bog. Heaven knows how the Belfry would have stood up had the matches been played there.

Of much higher standard was Dave Marr's US team of 1981, which is considered by many as one of the finest, if not the finest, group of US players ever assembled for the Ryder Cup – even better than Ben Hogan's all-stars of 1967. Ben Crenshaw, Raymond Floyd, Hale Irwin, Tom Kite, Bruce Lietzke, Johnny Miller, Larry Nelson, Jack Nicklaus, Jerry Pate, Bill Rogers, Lee Trevino and Tom Watson were the line-up. There was strength everywhere, with nine of the team already Major winners; by the time they retired only Bruce Lietzke had failed to join the pantheon with a Major title.

Des Smyth: I think the only player who wasn't a Major winner on that team was Bruce Lietzke. And Bruce was the star performer on their Tour for a long time. At Walton Heath, all the big US names were there.

The Europeans, meanwhile, although much more callow (and without a Major title amongst them, yet) could not be discounted; their line-up contained significant quality, with many of the team set to carve their names in Ryder Cup history over the coming years. There were two Spanish rookies in José María Cañizares and Manuel Piñero and the first German to play in the Ryder Cup in Bernhard Langer. They were joined by Irishmen Eamonn Darcy and Des Smyth, Scotsmen Bernard Gallacher, Sandy Lyle and Sam Torrance and Englishmen Howard Clark, Nick Faldo, Mark James and Peter Oosterhuis.

The most notable omissions were those of Seve Ballesteros and Tony Jacklin. Ballesteros was the leading European player, having claimed the Open in 1979 and then made history in 1980 by becoming the first player from outside the USA to win the Masters, and was seen as nothing but a dead cert for the team. But a row erupted between him and the European Tour over appearance fees. As he had been playing a number of exhibition tournaments he did not have the requisite qualifying points to make the team automatically; European captain John Jacobs tried to persuade him to play in the two tournaments before selection that would gain

Opposite: Tom Watson and Jack Nicklaus. *Getty Images*

him the required number of points, but Ballesteros refused and missed out on selection as Jacobs did not name him as one of his captain's picks. Similarly Jacklin was also snubbed by Jacobs, who selected Mark James in preference. Jacklin was so incensed that he availed himself of any future involvement, in any capacity, with the Ryder Cup again.

With such an apparent disparity between the teams it was rather inevitable that the atrocious weather that hit Walton Heath was greeted warmly by the home fans who hoped it might act as a potential leveller.

Nick Faldo: The Americans brought over just about the best team ever. Nicklaus and Watson at that time seemed to be carving up every Major between them; Trevino was a superb match player, and Bill Rogers had won the Open at Sandwich. There was also Johnny Miller, who was capable of the most wonderful streaks of golf, and Ray Floyd and Larry Nelson. Nelson had only just scraped into the side by winning the US PGA, but prior to that his record in previous matches was nine wins from nine games – quite a last-minute addition.

Hale Irwin: That was the best team I was ever on. The strength throughout the line-up was very, very good, physically and mentally. And the captain, Dave Marr, was a great stabilising influence. He had the task of taking twelve distinctly strong personalities and coalescing them into something that was manageable, and that's the hardest thing for a captain. Your players are living together for a week and playing golf in a format that they've never played before. Outside the Ryder Cup, you don't spend seven hours with these guys in a week, but now you're spending every moment with them. Dave was probably one of the best captains I was ever under.

Tom Watson: We went into the Ryder Cup with the idea that it was a foregone conclusion – that we were going to win. That's not to be bigheaded about it. It was just a matter of fact. It was a one-sided competition for the most part.

Bernard Gallacher: We knew it was going to be a difficult week. John Jacobs was a great captain but we had a problem with Seve; Seve was the number one player in the world and he should have been in that side – but he was in dispute with the European Tour and John wasn't able to pick him. So we went into the match minus the best player in the world.

I felt very sorry for John Jacobs but it was also a very, very difficult time for Seve and a very difficult time for the European Tour.

Nick Faldo: We, of course, had shot ourselves in the foot by not having Seve playing. He had won the 1979 Open Championshop and the 1980 Masters and felt he was entitled to appearance money in Europe for sacrificing the lucrative pastures of America to support his home tour. The authorities were trying to stamp out appearance money at that point and the result was a stand-off. He hardly played an event in Europe, and being so at odds with everyone, he didn't get picked in the end. So we didn't actually go into the match as favourites.

Tony Jacklin: The decision about Seve was sheer insanity. He was royally pissed off and threw his hands up and walked away – completely understandable. The man deserved better and was treated awfully. I was pissed off about the way I was treated. So in 1981 we both walked off, ignored Walton Heath, and went about our own business.

Seve Ballesteros: It is regrettable that the Tour didn't put forward its best possible team. I felt so bad and so let down at the time that I decided never to play in the Ryder Cup again.

 If being a rebel means not accepting authoritarian decisions, then I'm certainly one. I have always defended the interests of the Tour and its players, facing up to problems and never hiding behind others. Consequently, I haven't always behaved like a politically correct person.

Bernhard Langer: I made my debut in the opening foursomes round on the Friday, playing alongside Manuel Piñero against Larry Nelson and Lee Trevino. I was shaking, really nervous. I think it is the same with ninety-five per cent of players making their debuts. It is not easy for a player to turn up and play his best golf in the first round of the Ryder Cup.

 Foursomes is the most difficult form of golf. You only hit a shot about every ten minutes and it is hard to keep your rhythm going. You might not get to putt for three or four holes or to hit a driver for a few holes. In fourballs, if I mess up it doesn't matter as long as my partner delivers the goods. But in foursomes every shot counts and it all adds up to the most severe pressure I can think of in golf.

 The problem in 1981 was that most of us didn't feel we stood a chance before we even got started. We'd been losing for twenty-five years in a row, they had a very strong team and our whole attitude was totally different to theirs. Nowadays the European players have a much more positive approach and they'll go in with an attitude of winning, not 'how much are we going to lose by'. I remember when we were trying to lose by only five points instead of ten.

Johnny Miller: The Ryder Cup is such a pressure zone that it picks out any flaws you might have in your game. If you are a bad putter, you will not make a putt. If you have a tendency to chili-dip wedges, you'll be chili-dipping them all over the place for sure. Whatever your weakness, it will come up in spades during the Ryder Cup.

 The number one source of pressure and choking is that you don't want to let your teammates down. It's the only time of year when you care more about others than yourself.

Ben Crenshaw: It took me several rounds to figure out the course at Walton Heath. I'd never played a heathland course, because usually when I'd gone over to Britain it was to the British Open and links courses. But I loved it. You had to keep the ball in play, and if you were off the fairway the rough and gorse was very tough. But it was a wonderful, wonderful experience. I knew about the history of the Ryder Cup and had read all about it, but Dave Marr kept saying to me, 'You don't know what it's like until you've played in it.'

Trevino and Nelson got the first red points on the board in the opening match when they beat Langer and Piñero one-up, but Europe fought back superbly in the difficult conditions as Lyle and James defeated Rogers and Lietzke 2&1 and then Gallacher and Smyth dispatched Irwin and Floyd 3&2.

Des Smyth: That match was at Walton Heath and I played my way onto the team. I was kind of developing myself as a player and I moved into the ranks where people were almost expecting you to make the team. I played better in that Ryder Cup. I had a couple of good wins. I was very happy to beat Hale Irwin to get a wee bit of revenge for 1979; I played with Bernard Gallacher, and we beat Irwin and Raymond Floyd 3&2 which was a pretty big feather, because they were pretty tough guys.

The dream team of Watson and Nicklaus then routed Oosterhuis and Faldo 4&3 to ensure that honours were even at lunchtime. While that could have been a momentum changer, Europe bounced back to perform admirably in the afternoon. Torrance and Clark halved their fourball with Kite and Miller before Lyle and James beat Crenshaw and Pate 3&2, and Smyth and Cañizares beat Rogers and Lietzke 6&5. Irwin and Floyd then fought back as Watson and Nicklaus had done in the fourth match of the session by beating Gallacher and Darcy 2&1. Considering all the doomsayers writing off Europe so comprehensively before the matches had begun, it was an impressive 4½ to 3½ point lead that Europe finished the day with.

Sam Torrance: Like Bernhard, that was my first Ryder Cup as well – and it was against the strongest team the United States ever assembled. I made my first outing in the afternoon fourball with Howard Clark, who was to become my best and favourite Ryder Cup partner over the years. We still call each other 'partner' when meeting or telephoning each other. We were supposed to assume the role of cannon fodder to the American duo of Johnny Miller and Tom Kite. We had other ideas. I remember eagling the fourteenth to square the match. And I had a twelve-foot birdie putt on the final green to gain an unexpected point. I cried in frustration as the ball horseshoed out. That miss broke my heart.

Nick Faldo: John Jacobs tried to keep the Oosterhuis/Faldo partnership going that had done so well in '79 – but without success. We were paired in the morning fourball against Tom Watson and Jack Nicklaus, but I didn't play very well, and Oosty was right off his game, so we were split after lunch and tried with different partners. But it was all to no avail; neither of us got points in either foursome or fourball. My one consolation was to salvage a point in the singles.

Frankly, I don't think it would have mattered what we did against such a team. They would have beaten any side we ever put into the field and probably most of theirs as well.

Crowds swarmed the course on day two to see if the Europeans could maintain their momentum and power their way to a shock victory; but the Americans were not prepared to belie their superiority and swiftly set about sweeping aside any European pretentions by winning seven of the eight points available.

Sam Torrance: On the Saturday, my partnership with Howard Clark surprisingly broken up, I teamed up with Nick Faldo. We were thrashed 7&5 by Lee Trevino and Jerry Pate.

It was an extraordinary performance. Pate never hit a shot without Trevino telling him exactly what to do. Pate followed the instructions to the letter every time. As Trevino quipped, 'Jerry has everything… from the neck down. With my brains and his swing we were unbeatable. I told him what clubs to play and even gave him the line of the putts.'

That victory for Trevino and Pate set the ball rolling for the US. Nelson and Kite then battled past James and Lyle for a one-hole victory before Langer and Piñero stepped up to try and stem the flow.

Bernhard Langer: Manuel Piñero and I beat Ray Floyd and Hale Irwin in the fourballs, but then Nicklaus and Watson came in and did more damage to our hopes by beating Cañizares and Smyth 3&2. They were just unbelievable as a pairing, Nicklaus and Watson – which I learned to my expense in the afternoon when Manuel and I played them in the foursomes and lost 3&2. But it was a great experience and in those two days I had come face-to-face with some of the greatest players of that era. I learned an awful lot from it all.

Sam Torrance: The Americans were just unstoppable in the afternoon foursomes. Peter Oosterhuis and I went out first against Trevino and Pate and they beat us 2&1. Then Nicklaus and Watson picked up their point as expected against Langer and Piñero 3&2; Floyd and Rogers then beat Sandy Lyle and Mark James 3&2; and then Kite and Nelson saw off Bernie Gallacher and Des Smyth 3&2. I mean what an afternoon: 2&1, 3&2, 3&2, 3&2, bang, bang, bang, bang – America firmly in the driving seat.

Des Smyth: It was an incredible match against Nicklaus and Watson, playing with José María Cañizares. We also beat Bruce Lietzke and Bill Rogers in a match, 6&5, and then we drew Jack and Tom, yeah that was fairly daunting. We played quite well but, I mean, they were just almost invincible at that time.

The victorious team with the cup.

With a 10½–5½ lead, the visitors kept their foot on Europe's throat in the Sunday singles, and won the four points they required for victory in the first five matches. They finished the day with a record 18½–9½ score, a crushing victory – although one that did something of a disservice to the European team, who were much more competitive than the final ledger suggests.

Sam Torrance: Through my connection with John Letters golf clubs I'd got to know Lee Trevino and we became good friends. So of course I get drawn to play him in the singles and on the Saturday night I bump into him at the hotel and he says, 'Hey Sammy, I'm gonna beat the moustache off you tomorrow.' I couldn't really argue because I thought he was going to as well.

The next morning with it being at Walton Heath I've got my own car there so I offered Lee a lift to the course. 'Yeah, sure Sammy, let's go.' So we get in the car and as we got to the end of the road instead of turning right towards the club I turned left. And he's like, 'Hey Sammy, where are you going?' So I say, 'Lee, to hell with you. We're going to London – half a point each!' Which was quite funny at the time but he beat me 5&3 and I had to shave my moustache off that night, which I'll never live down.

Lee Trevino: That was the kind of fun we had in those days. I loved it – the rivalry but also the friendships that developed. For some guys, like Sammy and me, it was like playing a brother at sport when you're a child; but, as with the Ryder Cup, you never want to lose to your brother – in fact, you probably want to beat them more than anyone else.

Bernhard Langer: I halved my singles match with Bruce Lietzke. Overall the Americans played extremely well. In the singles for example, Sandy Lyle was something like nine-under, but lost to Tom Kite, who was about eleven-under.

Sandy Lyle: In my match in the singles, I unfortunately played against Kite. We had an unbelievable amount of birdies and eagles between the pair of us, something like seventeen birdies and two eagles. I was six or seven-under after ten holes and all square! I ended up losing 3&2. My score would have won any match that day, but unfortunately I got drawn out against Kite. That was the standard of golf that was getting played at Walton Heath.

Des Smyth: I was playing against Ben Crenshaw and I remember opening with a birdie and thinking, 'Right, I'm going to get stuck into this.' Then he had eight threes on the next ten holes . . . I was a good player. I was never at that level. I never won Majors. I wasn't a world star. I tried hard to get to that level and never made it.

Peter Oosterhuis: I played six straight Ryder Cups [1971 to 1981], and every time it was like walking into a dark room. We lost every one of them.

Bernard Gallacher: Oh God it was tough. I was out third and managed to get a half point against Bill Rogers, but it was only delaying the inevitable at that stage. Larry Nelson beat Mark James and then Ben Crenshaw did a bit of a job on Des Smyth, beating him 6&4 and they had all the points they needed. Bernhard Langer managed to get a half against

Bruce Lietzke and Manuel Piñero, Nick Faldo and Howard Clark all had great wins [against Jerry Pate, Johnny Miller and Tom Watson respectively] but overall it was a bit of a hammering – which had, unfortunately, been predicted from the outset.

But you look back and you can see seeds being planted even though the score was very one-sided. Many of the matches felt close and we were beginning to develop that identity of being a united European team. You have to remember that it was all still very new for us and we had to bed into the idea that we were a European team not just a British and Irish one. No one will have expected us to improve the way we did over the coming years, but within the team we felt like 1981 was a bit of a marker in the sand for how the team was going to progress.

Larry Nelson: Looking back, I remember feeling happy with my performance and felt that I had done well that year; but what really stays in my mind about that Ryder Cup was being in the locker room afterwards and looking around at my teammates. We had won and I felt so proud to be part of that team and proud that I had done my part in a great team win. For a professional golfer, that's such a unique thing to experience – being part of a team. But I loved it. I think every guy on that team loved it. And that's what means the most about the Ryder Cup.

John Jacobs: I was very proud of my players. Considering the quality of the team that they faced, not one of them was intimidated. But in order to beat a team like that American one, every one of our players had to be in the form of their life and the reality was that they were not all able to produce their best. But there was no shame in losing to a team as magnificent as that American one.

Des Smyth: It was a heavy defeat, but they were a very formidable team. The simple fact was they were better than us. We were getting stronger, our top players were improving and you could say our top three players were world class players. But maybe the rest of us were good players, but not good enough.

Bernhard Langer: The US had not lost a Ryder Cup since 1957 and they had a very strong team that year. It was a mountain for us to climb. 18½ to 9½ points; that's a heavy defeat, there's no hiding from that. But I think that if one match pushed us into being a European side it was the one-sided nature of that contest. Going forward we felt that we were developing as a team and we knew where the bar had been set. We weren't afraid of the challenge – we felt that we were more than good enough to take it on and were all looking forward to 1983.

TWENTY-FIVE

1983

PGA National Golf Club. Palm Beach Gardens, Florida
(USA 14½, EUR 13½)

After the fallout over their selection for the 1981 Ryder Cup, it would have taken a brave pundit to predict that the next European challenge – which would take place on the Champion Course at the PGA National Golf Club in Palm Beach Gardens, Florida – would be spearheaded by Tony Jacklin in the captaincy role and feature Seve Ballesteros back in the team. But that was exactly what happened, although it took some diplomatic negotiation to achieve.

In May 1983, while Jacklin was hitting some practise balls on the range at Moortown Golf Club, European Tour Director Ken Schofield and Secretary of the British PGA Colin Snape approached Jacklin with the offer of the captaincy. Jacklin was due to commentate for the BBC on a tournament that day at Moortown and asked for time to think about the proposal. The following day he went back to Schofield and Snape and accepted the position – on the condition that certain criteria were met. Jacklin had for years berated the standard of care for the British and Irish and then the European teams in the Ryder Cup. Throughout his playing career, just as previous generations had done before, he had watched with envy as the Americans travelled to Britain in first class, stayed in the best hotels and had the finest playing kit available. The standards that Walter Hagen had first set during his captaincy in the very first years of the Ryder Cup had never been adopted by the opposition and Jacklin was one of many who felt that such treatment gave the Americans an advantage every time they played the Ryder Cup. If Jacklin was to accept the captaincy, no expense could be spared for the team. They would travel by Concorde, stay in the best accommodation and have the finest clothing. Schofield acquiesced.

Bernard Gallacher: I was on the selection committee and voted for Tony Jacklin. He stood head and shoulders above everybody else in terms of being a Ryder Cup captain, just from his record [seven appearances, thirteen wins, fourteen losses, and eight ties], the US Open champion and British Open champion. So it was an easy decision, more or less unanimous.

Tony Jacklin: I wasn't picked in '81 and – to add insult to injury – they asked me to go along as an official. Naturally I told them to stick it in their, er, ear. I was in thirteenth place in the table and they picked Mark James, who two years previously had been levied the biggest fine in PGA history for his behaviour in the 1979 Ryder Cup at the Greenbrier. I don't forget these things. At a time when he was arguably the best player in the world, Seve was left out, too, as he was involved in a row over appearance money. So if I was teed off, he was even more so.

Ken Schofield approached me with Colin Snape while I was hitting balls up at Moortown. I was shocked, to tell you the truth, and told them I couldn't answer their question on the spot and that I'd see them the next day. I thought about it that night. My first instinct was to tell them to stuff it but I could see there was an opportunity to make the changes that I knew needed to be made. I knew how organised things were in America and how disorganised things were here. I always felt that we were second-class citizens. How can you compete on the same level if you are treated poorly? We were flying in the back of the plane, not knowing who was paying for the bloody dry cleaning, not being able to take caddies with us – everything was about what we couldn't do. The attitude of the PGA was that it's always been done this way so why did it need changing. So the next day I told them, 'Here's what I want.' Concorde, cashmere, caddies, first-class accommodations, three captain's picks, and such and such – Ken said they'd have to think about it. Then he came back and said yes; I asked for more, they kept saying yes. Clearly, the attitude had changed and everyone over here was tired of losing; we were just not going to take it anymore.

Having achieved this landmark change in how the European team was prepared for the matches, Jacklin set about righting another wrong. If his team were to stand any chance of making history by winning for the first time in America, he needed Seve Ballesteros back in the fold.

He met the Spaniard for breakfast at the Prince of Wales Hotel in Southport during the Open Championship, explained about the improvements he had demanded and did all he could to persuade Europe's best player that the Ryder Cup was a tournament he had to be involved in. Ballesteros listened, considered Jacklin's pitch, and then asked for some time to discuss the matters with his family – particularly his brothers, whom he always turned to for advice. Jacklin had to wait for two weeks for an answer, but when it came he was over the moon. Seve was in; the challenge was on.

Tony Jacklin: I went to Lord Derby and said, 'What about Seve?' He replied, 'Since you're the captain, he's your problem now.' I tracked Seve down and I said that if we were ever going to have parity or better in the Ryder Cup, we had to have the best of the best, world-class players, on board all at the same time – Seve, Nick Faldo, Ian Woosnam, Bernhard Langer, and the rest of that core group. If we weren't going to do that, then why bother? Let's win.

He vented for about an hour, on this, that and the other, and I said, 'I understand all that but it is going to be different now because I have got the reins and I think with your talents and abilities and with me on the inside organising we can make a difference. Look, if we can turn this around you will get treated like a real hero, as you should be.'

Seve Ballesteros: I rang Tony Jacklin a few days later and told him he could count on me. He was grateful and pleased, because he was convinced we could win now. Tony paired me with Paul Way, who was making his debut, and commented: 'Seve, you are the hero of our team, you've just won the Masters, you are the best and the one with most experience. There's no one better to play with this new lad, right?' I was surprised by Tony's decision but I went along with it, because he was our captain and I was prepared to play with whichever player he suggested.

Ken Schofield: We agreed by shaking hands that we would put all that behind us and go forward together. And from the moment Tony Jacklin most successfully got Seve to commit to playing again in 1983, Seve became synonymous with the Ryder Cup.

Ken Brown: When Tony Jacklin became captain in 1983, he and Seve were a team within a team. They had this intense chemistry. Somehow Tony talked Seve into playing for the cause and Seve gave everything. He was so helpful to the youngsters and I remember him giving some of us a lesson on how to play out of the rough at PGA National. It was four inch Bermuda rough, the like of which most of us had never seen. He spent half an hour showing us the shots he played but it was hopeless – like Ronnie O'Sullivan showing you how to play snooker left-handed. It's just not going to happen. But he was prepared to give his time and help the team.

Seve Ballesteros: I'd go to the first tee, clap my opponent on the back, wish him a good game. I'd look into his eyes and I'd think, 'I will bury you.'

When you finish, no matter what your score, you always think you could have done better, that you lost a shot here, a shot there. But when I played, there were many times I had the feeling that I could really dominate the ball on every shot I faced on the golf course. That was the best thing of all.

I had that feeling often, over a chip, a pitch, anything. It is the greatest thing a golfer can feel. It's hard to explain, but it's the feeling that I can see the shot, feel the shot, and that I can make it happen. That's something that is really very special.

There's no money in the world that can pay for it. It's a tremendous feeling. From the start, from a very early age, I played the game because I loved it. I never played because I wanted to become professional, make a lot of money, have a big house and drive a Ferrari. It was all because I enjoyed doing it.

Alongside Seve, Jacklin selected a strong team in Ken Brown, José María Cañizares, Nick Faldo, Bernard Gallacher, Bernhard Langer, Sandy Lyle and Sam Torrance and handed debut spots to Gordon Brand, Brian Waites, Paul Way and Ian Woosnam.

Bernard Gallacher: In 1983 I think we all felt America had quite a strong team at West Palm Beach. In the past, I always felt the Americans had the best players in the world and certainly the best player in the world by a long way in Jack Nicklaus. But now in our locker room we had the best player in the world in Seve and it made all the difference.

Nick Faldo: By 1983 it had become obvious that Europe at last had some players who could expect to beat any American they came up against. Certainly half the side went over believing we could win, whether it was in America or at home. Those who believed, played well and won their matches, but some I feel were still in awe of the Americans and didn't play their best.

Tony Jacklin: When they asked me to be captain I very nearly declined. But then I spent the night thinking about it and I thought about how important the future of the European Tour was, how good it could be, and I didn't want to end my days in dispute with them and certainly not do anything that would drag them down.

So I gave a lot of thought to all the things I felt should happen if our team was to go into the matches at least on a level footing. It wasn't that difficult. You looked at how they travelled, flying Concorde, and that would be how we should go. We should be properly dressed, plenty of shirts and trousers, good quality materials and suppliers. Of course you should have your own caddie and it should not cost you to have him there.

The team room was something I instigated. For me, it was absolutely vital to have a room at the club or hotel where the team could get together and away from all the people who are invariably around. Only there could a good team spirit be created and nurtured. In my day, playing under Eric Brown or Bernard Hunt, team get-togethers used to take place in some corner of the locker room; a quick huddle there, hope nobody was listening, and we all went our separate ways, some to eat on their own, or with a chum, others to hit a few shots; the absolute opposite of creating camaraderie and a sense of unity and purpose.

A day or so after I had been asked to be the next captain, I put all these issues on the table to Ken [Schofield, executive director of the European Tour] and Colin [Snape, executive director of the PGA]. All the way through they kept saying, 'OK,' and when I got through nothing had been refused. Frankly, if they had said no to any of the big issues, then I would have just walked away, and with a clear conscience.

Bernard Gallacher: Tony had been a player when we weren't going first class, but we couldn't afford to at that time. When he said that he wanted the players to go first class, the Tour, now the Volvo European Tour, could afford to accede to his request. And that really was the turning point in the success of the Ryder Cup, when the European side could afford to be on equal terms with the Americans in terms of preparation.

Peter Oosterhuis: You always felt that the Americans put much more money into everything they did, whether it was the uniforms or the travel or whatever. Tony made a good point. In some ways we felt we were second-class citizens, and Tony was determined to change that. And, of course, he was in the best position to do it, having won a Major in America and having made a real statement at the highest level of the game. And it worked. From that year on, things turned around.

Nick Faldo: Tony Jacklin was a big factor. His attributes and demands for everything to be first class are well known, but he was a captain very much of the generation of his players, and his record meant that no one questioned his right to be calling the shots. Above all, it was his enthusiasm that was infectious. At the end of each day it would be us calming him down. He would rave on about this shot or that, the way this match had turned our way or how we were so unlucky not to have won that, so that we would have to sit him in a corner with a large whisky and tell him to settle down.

He certainly got the whole team pulling for him, and that's one way of building great team spirit. If I had to sum up his best qualities for the job, I would say it was his ability to pull together a dozen players who, apart from this one week every two years, were fiercely independent competitive individuals. He turned us into a group of players who forgot about themselves and thought only of what the team might achieve.

Jack Nicklaus had been named as captain for the Americans and he led a typically strong team, which included Ben Crenshaw, Ray Floyd, Tom Kite, Lanny Wadkins and Fuzzy Zoeller, rookies Bob Gilder, Jay Haas, Gil Morgan, Calvin Peete, Craig Stadler and Curtis Strange, and spearheaded by five-time Open Champion Tom Watson. It was an impressive line-up even though it did not contain the reigning US Open and US PGA champions, Larry Nelson and Hal Sutton, who had not, incongruously, met the US PGA's qualification criteria.

Sam Torrance: Before the matches started, the European team were invited to the West Palm Yacht Club, a short drive from our team hotel. I noticed Fuzzy Zoeller giving directions to someone and, like in a film, ordered our driver to 'follow that car'. Ian Woosnam just giggled and, like me, paid no attention to where we were going.

Fifteen minutes later we arrived at a magnificent property to see Calvin Peete emerge from the car in front. We thought nothing of it. We made it to the door before the Americans and I rang the bell.

Jack Nicklaus, looking somewhat bemused it has to be said, answered the door. 'Is this the yacht club?' I asked rather limply.

'No, this is my home,' the great man replied. 'But come in.'

Nicklaus poured us a drink and pointed out of the window to the yacht club on the other side of the lake. We had gatecrashed an American team meeting!

Tony Jacklin: In 1983, I had no particular view as to how we might shape up against the Americans. I hadn't quite got the team I wanted because of the selection process, but with Seve on board once again, I felt we had the nucleus of a good team with some really good players coming through. Sandy Lyle was winning regularly, and often posting very low scores; Nick Faldo was clearly of a different class to much that had gone before in Europe; and Bernhard Langer could be among the very best if he could sort out his putting problems. Ian Woosnam, who had by then won a couple of tournaments and was a wonderful striker of the ball, looked to be a cut above the rest as well.

Craig Stadler: I had an absolute blast that week. I didn't really know what to expect, but I just had a great time and I played pretty well. We had a bunch of rookies that year, but we still had an experienced core. It was a good mix.

The press wrote that there was more pressure on us as Europe looked stronger going into the 1980s. But as far as we were concerned, we didn't feel any more pressure. We always thought we should win and had a great chance to win. All the pressure, if you can call it pressure, has really been created by the press over the years, especially now. It is a huge, huge week now. Back then, it was a big deal, but I bet on Sunday we didn't have 3,000 people out there. I'm just guessing, though. I don't remember there being huge crowds, but you might go back in the archives and there were 12,000 there. There were probably five or six writers, *Golf World*, you had USGA guys there, PGA guys there, obviously. Maybe one writer would come over from the UK with the team or something. That is kinda what it was.

It was still kind of nerve-wracking at times, you don't want to get beat, that's the last thing in the world you want to do – who you are playing, or the whole match. You had to pay attention to what you were doing, but at the same time I had a lot of fun, I really enjoyed it.

It's incredible how much the Ryder Cup has changed over the years. It's the equipment, shafts and balls, and everything else. It's just unbelievable. I love it. It's my favourite. I don't watch much golf on TV, but I absolutely watch the Ryder Cup. The thing that has amazed me over the last ten years, not only is there the global respect and admiration for it, and everybody is just getting into the whole week of things, but for me it's amazing the pressure that I think the press has put on everybody, more than anything. The pressure they are under . . . but all the putts these guys make. I mean the last five Ryder Cups, you turn on and nobody hardly misses. It's just boom, boom, boom, twenty-footers, thirty-footers, just one after another, especially at Medinah. It was unbelievable. Nobody missed a putt for like three straight hours. The quality of golf, for what is on the line in the Ryder Cup now, I think is exceptional. You get the rare, rare day when somebody plays badly. In a better ball, you are going to have to go out and shoot seven or eight under to win. If you don't . . . goodbye. The depth is just incredible with these players now on the tours, and it shows. I think it's the greatest event in golf, I really do. I think it's awesome. It's great entertainment.

The US started strongly in the opening morning foursomes when Watson and Crenshaw crushed Gallacher and Lyle 5&4, but Faldo and Langer fought back in the second match to defeat Wadkins and Stadler 4&2; Kite and Peete then defeated Ballesteros and Way 2&1 before Cañizares and Torrance squared matters with a 4&3 victory over Floyd and Gilder.

Sandy Lyle: I played with Gallacher on the first day. But Gallacher and Lyle weren't at their best that day. We lost 5&4 to Watson and Crenshaw. We never really gelled very well in that match. My golf really wasn't up to standard for that week. I was disappointed with the way I played.

Nick Faldo: Jacklin had an instinct of who would play well together. His pairing of Ballesteros and Paul Way was an inspiration, giving Seve a paternal role in nursing a young first-timer that brought the best out of both. He saw that Bernhard Langer and I would get on and do a competent job and we won three points out of four.

Sandy Lyle: Tony Jacklin was becoming a driving force, very much so. He was in the early stages really of doing more homework, talking to players individually, finding out how you felt about the course, how you saw the match panning out, what characters he had. I think, as Azinger did when Faldo was captain in 2008, he put his team into sort of pods, and I think that was the early stages of that, who gets on well together, the pod system or whatever you want to call it. I think it helps if you play with somebody in a Ryder Cup, or in anything, that you get on well with. I get on with Woosie, with most players really, but Woosie is a player that I've played with for many, many years and against him, and we got on well together. That's what it's all about, being comfortable with that player, working well together, gelling well together. You take the hits, take the good times and you get on with it. That's all for the better. I think Jacklin worked that way. He would speak to me individually, say 'how do you feel, I've got these players lined up for you'. He was working the team, not just as a front man, doing what he thinks, he was talking to all the players. I think that was a good way of rising the team up into working as best as we could at that time.

Paul Way: It's a long, long week and there's a hell of a lot of pressure. You're up at six o'clock and then there's dinners in the evening and all sorts of other functions to attend. Then, if you're playing thirty-six holes a day as well, as I did, it can be really tiring; I was knackered and I was a young twenty-year-old.

We were only given one shirt a day to play in, but it was so humid there that after the morning round that shirt was bloody wringing wet so we had to nip into the pro shop and buy some new ones. It was still all about money and there wasn't very much of it knocking around then.

Sam Torrance: Woosie and I were on the putting green before playing Crenshaw and Calvin Peete in the first day's fourballs; Woosie was a bit jumpy because it was his first Ryder Cup. Of course, it was my second Ryder Cup, so I'm Mr. Experience. And I said, 'Come on, Woos, for chrissake, let's go and kill 'em.' So we got on the first tee and I hit it straight right – lost ball. Woosie hit a perfect one-iron, then a wedge to three feet, made birdie. After that I played the best round of golf I've ever played in the Ryder Cup. I made birdies on six of the last twelve holes. But Crenshaw and Peete played really well, too. We ended up all square. It was a great match.

Tony Jacklin: Paul Way was a young kid, still young enough to think he was going to be better than Ballesteros. He was a cocky little bugger and wasn't intimidated by being put with Seve.

But the interesting part was Seve. On the second day Ángel Gallardo [former player, at that time an official] came up to me and said, 'I think you'd better talk to Seve.' So I took Seve to one side, and I could see there was something he wanted to get off his chest. I said, 'Seve, do we have a problem?'

He said, 'Well, you know, this boy Paul Way, I feel like I have to hold his hand all the time. I'm, you know, telling him which club to hit. I feel like his father.' I said, 'You are his father, Seve. You are. In here.' And I pointed to Seve's head. 'That's exactly why you're bloody well paired together.' I said, 'Is that a problem?'

And Seve looked at me. It was like the penny dropped. He said, 'No, for me, it is no problem.'

Paul Way: After three games I thought I'd probably get the chance to sit out the afternoon on Saturday and take a breather, but Jacklin said, 'No, you're going out with Seve again and you're playing Tom Watson and Bob Gilder.' Watson was my hero but we went five up after six holes and won quite comfortably.

Tony Jacklin: Seve wasn't easy to partner, as great a player as he was. Even his own teammates were intimidated by him because of his persona. He had a lot of charisma, he was a strong character. But his partnership with Paul Way was very strong and the main reason was because Paul was not intimated by Seve.

Paul Way: I wasn't really intimidated. I was young so I was full of confidence and I hadn't really experienced anything like it before so I knew no better. Getting paired with Seve was incredible. He was the reigning Masters champion at the time and the best player in the world.

The Europeans edged the afternoon fourballs 2½–1½ to finish the first day 4½–3½ ahead. The score on the second day was then reversed with the USA finishing with 4½ points to Europe's 3½ to tie the score at 8–8 going into the singles.

Jack Nicklaus: As a captain, after we select our teams each day and hand in the piece of paper, all that's left is to go on course and act important. You have to leave it up to the players, there's very little more you can do – and that can sometimes be a horrible situation to find yourself in. It was the first tournament I'd ever been to when I wasn't playing and couldn't do anything about what was happening. It was the damndest thing I'd ever been involved in.

Craig Stadler: Jack as captain was fantastic. He had no assistant captains, any of that stuff, didn't have a whole lot of people and not a whole lot of press. Jack was driving this cart that had a makeshift kind of cabin on the back of it – and it was just him. He was running all over the golf course. It was hot and humid and he had extra shirts in there, towels if you needed them, Cokes, water, whatever you needed. It was like he was on a mission and I thought it was just awesome.

I got paired both times with Lanny Wadkins in the foursomes and fourballs. Lanny had a shot from the fairway on eighteen on Saturday, stuck it about six inches to win against Waites and Brown one-up. It's nice to look back on; it's a long time ago now.

Bernhard Langer: That was the first year that I thought we could win the Ryder Cup. We went into the final day 8–8. I won my single against Gil Morgan but in the end we lost by the narrowest margin, 14½ to 13½. In fact, it all came down to the last match when Bernard Gallacher lost to Tom Watson on the seventeenth. And of course, when it is as close as that, there are always one or two matches that could have gone either way and made the difference.

Curtis Strange: Back in 1983 we knew they were going to become a much better team with the involvement of European players, but we didn't know how good. We never anticipated just how good Seve, Sandy Lyle, Ian Woosnam, Bernhard Langer, and Nick Faldo were going to be, and how long they would lead that team. That nucleus lasted for a long, long time. Sure, there were always a couple of new guys, but that was the nucleus that really made the Ryder Cup what it is today.

Lanny Wadkins: I was playing against José María Cañizares and it was one of those matches where I felt like I should have been winning the whole day but Cañizares was pulling his magic and holing shots from everywhere. The two holes that come to mind were the first hole where he drove it into the woods, chipped out and hit it on the green to fifty feet and holed it for par, while I drove it down the middle, hit it to six feet and missed a birdie putt and we tied the hole. Then I was one-down going to the sixteenth and hit a two-iron about twelve feet past the hole and he puts it to the edge of the lake and splashes it out thirty feet from the hole on the green and I miss a twelve-footer. He holes his and we tie again. It seemed like there was a bunch of holes like that during the day.

The deadlock continued with the teams still tied after the first ten singles matches. There were a number of hugely impressive performances during these matches, but the brightest moment was provided in the very first between Zoeller and Ballesteros. After driving into rough on the eighteenth, the Spaniard chipped into a bunker, some 240 yards from the green. Taking his three-wood he hit an extraordinary shot to the edge of the green, which Nicklaus afterwards declared to be the greatest shot he had ever seen. Seve then chipped and putted for par to halve the match with Zoeller.

Seve Ballesteros: I went out to play the first game on the Sunday against Fuzzy Zoeller. Tony came to see me when there were still seven holes to go and, as I held a three-hole lead, he went off sure my point was already in the bag. But Fuzzy won four holes on the trot and I had to win the sixteenth to tie level.

When Tony came back I was level on my second shot, from the bunker of the eighteenth fairway. I looked a certain loser, as my drive had left me so badly placed it seemed I couldn't get out of the bunker even if I used a sand wedge. I looked at Jacklin at that exact instant and from his expression I imagined he must be thinking, 'That blasted Spaniard was all set to win and now we're going to lose his point.' He looked so angry and disappointed, I pledged to myself that I wouldn't fail him.

Even with the game going my way I would never normally have attempted the stroke I eventually made. The ball had lodged in an elevated position, making it easier to lift, but also more difficult to gauge the distance it had to carry. The wind was blowing from left to right and I had no choice but to aim out of the left side of the bunker and to really dig the ball out, making sure it shot up straight away to avoid any slope. In normal circumstances I'd have chosen a five-iron, but as it was match play and the last hole I took a big risk and

Seve Ballesteros watches a wondrous three-wood bunker shot sail towards the green. *Getty Images*

opted for a three-wood. The ball flew some 225 metres to the edge of the green. From there I chipped and putted for a five to tie with Fuzzy.

Jack Nicklaus, captain of the American team, was rubbing his hands when he saw I was in the sand, but later he came over and said, 'Seve, that's the best stroke I've seen in my lifetime.'

Ben Crenshaw: That was one of the greatest, most amazing shots any of us had ever seen. Seve had hit it in a fairway bunker on the par-five eighteenth in his singles match that he halved with Fuzzy Zoeller, and when he got down in there he was in a position where you would take a five-iron or even a seven-iron just to get it out. But here comes this three-wood. I remember watching it on television. I don't remember exactly who I was with, but I remember we all went, 'What?' And then Seve took this big cut at the ball, and up it popped and ended up on the green. And none of us could believe what we'd just seen. Absolutely amazing.

Bernhard Langer: The bunker shot that Seve played at the eighteenth when he was up against Fuzzy Zoeller was the greatest shot I ever experienced. He hit a three-wood from the sand and it flew 240 yards to the edge of the green.

Nick Faldo: The bunker had a steep lip, and those were the days of the old Toney Penna three-wood, which had about twelve degrees of loft, and he just whistled it up there, over water, and it barely missed the back left corner of the green, about twenty-five feet from the hole. That was an unbelievable shot. Classic Seve.

Bernard Gallacher: That was one of the great pressure shots. A chip and putt later, Seve had secured a half against a shell-shocked Fuzzy Zoeller.

Nick Faldo: The Americans knew that there at last was a side that could beat them. I think that was the first time they ever really questioned whether they were the better team. For a time that final afternoon it looked very much like we would do it. You make a big effort to keep what's happening around you out of your mind, but even ignoring the scoreboards, you can't avoid the feeling of how it's going – and it was going alright.

The turning point must have been Seve not winning, having been three up with seven to play against Fuzzy Zoeller. Seve was such a mercurial player he might have felt the job was done, particularly against a player who wasn't a hundred per cent fit. What we didn't know was how great a shot he had to play from a fairway bunker at the last to get a half.

Craig Stadler: It is kinda of my claim to fame that I beat Woosie in both my singles matches in the Ryder Cup, in 1983 and 1985. I beat him on the sixteenth on the Sunday in 1983, which helped us get close to the line to clinch it, which was kinda cool. We were almost there. I think I was two up going to sixteen and I hit a really nice shot in there, about fifteen feet and two-putted. That was cool.

With two matches eventually left out on the course, it appeared that the match might be heading for a draw: Tom Watson was in control against Bernard Gallacher and José María Cañizares was leading Lanny Wadkins. Coming to the eighteenth, all Wadkins needed was a half to retain the Ryder Cup for his team. After each player had shot twice, Cañizares hit his third shot short and wide of the green. Wadkins, ignoring a lightning storm that filled the skies behind him and the huge weight of expectation on his shoulders, lofted a wonderful pitch to within fifteen feet of the hole. Cañizares could do nothing to win the hole. Afterwards, Jack Nicklaus bent down and kissed the divot left by Wadkins' pitch. Tom Watson, meanwhile, held on to his two-shot advantage over Gallacher to give the US a final winning score of 14½–13½. It had been a nail-biting finale and one that would inspire the Europeans for the return fixture in 1985.

José María Cañizares: In the last match with Lanny Wadkins, I was three up with seven to play, and was playing good golf. On the eighteenth hole, a par-five with water on the right of the green, I was one up and hit a very good drive, and a very good second shot. Nobody had come out to watch me, but suddenly everybody comes out. 'Win the match, and we win the Ryder Cup.' Seve asked me, 'Why didn't you hit the green?' I said, 'I have 105 yards or 110 yards left, and that pin position is in a very, very difficult place, in the left corner.' I have an easy pitching wedge. And then Seve said, 'You are one-up, you go to the green, you make par.' And that hurt my confidence, and changed my game. Then I hit a sand wedge a little short, in the big grass. Wadkins hit a very good shot [a wedge shot stiff] and made a birdie, just like that. And that evened the match. That is for me very, very angry. Maybe it was my fault that we did not win, because maybe I lost my concentration. I was very angry.

Lanny Wadkins: We came to the eighteenth and we all knew what the situation was. I had been one down at the seventeenth but holed to keep things alive. The only other match on the course was Tom Watson playing Bernard Gallacher and at that point Tom was two up with two to play and if Watson was two up he didn't lose matches. We weren't concerned about Tom – the one that made the difference was mine.

The whole team were standing by the eighteenth green and pretty anxious as you can imagine. It was a tough shot I had because the pin was on a back ledge and it was too close to carry up there and spin with a fifty-six-degree wedge. A shot that everybody hit at that time was a driving sand wedge where you skipped it back there and I played it perfectly. That was the most pressure I have ever felt over a shot, but feeling pressure means you are where you want to be. That's when it's fun. That's when it means something. And it never means quite as much as it does at the Ryder Cup.

The whole team got pretty excited after that and I remember Jack Nicklaus kissed the divot I had made in celebration.

José María Cañizares: I remember Jack Nicklaus kissing the ground. Jack Nicklaus is happy. Everybody is very happy. The American team is very happy. I'm very, very disappointed. It's a very rough time for me.

Sam Torrance: It came right down to the wire. Bernard's shot over the green when playing

Tom Kite chips onto the green. *Getty Images*

[Tom] Watson was the best shot he'd hit in his life, but it was half a club too much and he lost the hole. Then Cañizares lost the last. Right up until those two matches we looked like we were going to win it. Maybe it was just too much for us, but we knew we'd come back much stronger because we realised, 'Jesus, we should have beaten them.'

Tony Jacklin: We went very close that day and frankly were unlucky to lose. Deep down we all felt it was a match we'd let get away. Look at the photographs taken afterwards, and there we all are with glum faces. We were so close, then Lanny Wadkins hit that stunning shot on the last hole, and I can remember Jack Nicklaus kissing the divot afterwards as if it was yesterday.

Perhaps in the end we hadn't really believed enough it was possible. But the great thing was we had shown ourselves that this match really was winnable with the players we had; it was definitely a springboard for the next match at the Belfry. As Seve said at the end, 'This wasn't a loss, this was a win, just to have got so close.'

Tom Watson: That year, that was the awakening for the European team. They certainly had the ability that week to beat us, it was a very close match and it could have gone one way or the other on that last day, no question.

Seve Ballesteros: Tony Jacklin's greatest achievement was to ensure all the players respected him as captain. He called on his firm, elegant manner and experience as a winner of two Grand Slam tournaments. Tony knew what he was talking about and what he wanted. He was a born captain and knew how to lead. He made me feel at ease, confident and able to summon up all my golfing skills and he got the others to overcome difficult times and believe in their potential.

Nick Faldo: It was Seve who picked us up from the disappointment of losing so narrowly and said, 'This we must celebrate, this was a great victory for us. Now we know we can beat them and will do so next time.'

Ken Brown: At the end, when it had been so close but we had lost again, Seve was just as disappointed as everyone. But he said we had achieved something great and that next time we would win. There wasn't a person in that locker room who didn't leave that night believing that, if we got on the team in two years' time at the Belfry, we would win.

Jack Nicklaus: I had never been as nervous on a golf course in my life as I was during the final hours of that memorable battle along with every member of our team, I was aware that the standards of European professional golf had been rising steadily for years. Until that 1983 encounter, though, I don't think anyone in the US fully appreciated how good our friends across the pond had become. For me, and I'm sure for a lot of others, that event marked the burial of any notion that Europe's best golfers were less than world class.

José María Cañizares: Coming so close was the extra bit of motivation we needed. We realised we could take it to the next level and win. For so long the Ryder Cup was dominated, it was almost viewed as a lost cause. And then, when we knocked on the door, we realised the goal was in reach. It especially helped the young and lesser-known players in that actually slaying the giant, if you will, meant immediate global recognition. We all felt that if we came so close this time, we could win next time.

Bernhard Langer: As a team, we were excited. We felt that we had got a lot closer than most people expected. We had all but beaten them on their own territory. That confidence carried forward and we thought we would have a great chance at the Belfry in 1985.

TWENTY-SIX

1985

The Belfry. Sutton Coldfield, England
(EUR 16½, USA 11½)

The twenty-sixth Ryder Cup was staged at the Brabazon Course at the Belfry for the first time. Tony Jacklin was at the helm of the European challenge, while the Americans were led by the great Lee Trevino. For the first time in decades there was a genuine sense of expectation that the home team might produce something special thanks to a growing acceptance that the balance of power in the world of golf was shifting across the Atlantic; even Jack Nicklaus picked Europe as his favourites to lift the trophy. You could see why. Not only were they playing at home, but it was clear that the team felt that they had momentum coming out of their narrow loss in 1983; furthermore, Jacklin had three Major championship winners in his side, all of them playing at the very top of their game. Seve Ballesteros had, by this stage, four Majors to his name, while Bernhard Langer had claimed the Masters in the spring and Sandy Lyle had then won the Open in the summer. These three were backed up José María Cañizares, Howard Clark, Manuel Piñero, Sam Torrance, Paul Way and Ian Woosnam. Jacklin's wild cards weren't too shabby either – Ken Brown, Nick Faldo and José Rivero (although there was some controversy over the selction of Rivero over the more experienced figure of Christy O'Connor Jnr).

Tony Jacklin: The American captain was Lee Trevino, and I was just glad he and I weren't going to have to play one another. There was no telling what he might have done to me.

There were certainly hard decisions to make before play began, the hardest by far being my decision to pick José Rivero instead of Christy O'Connor Jnr. Christy was so hurt it was years before he spoke to me again. They were so close on the money list, but Rivero had won a tournament at the Belfry that year. I can put my hand on my heart and tell you there was not an ounce of personal bias in the decision either way, but Christy took it hard and took it personally. I picked who I thought would be best for the team, plain and simple.

Christy O'Connor Jnr: So am I happy all these years later with Tony Jacklin's version of events? Tony maintains that he was not influenced by Seve in the choice of Spain's José Rivero over me. My answer is an overwhelming no. I should have been picked ahead of Rivero. The whole of Ireland knew it.

Trevino's team might have lacked the mighty figureheads that were so synonymous with American Ryder Cup teams of the past, but the general strength of the team was good and contained a number of players who would go on to have illustrious Ryder Cup careers: Raymond Floyd, Hubert Green, Tom Kite, Calvin Peete, Craig Stadler, Curtis Strange, Hal Sutton, Lanny Wadkins and Fuzzy Zoeller alongside rookies Andy North, Mark O'Meara and Peter Jacobsen.

Opposite: Sam Torrance celebrates as he holes his match-winning putt. *Getty Images*

Lanny Wadkins: We went out with a pretty good team in '85. I wouldn't say it was as good as some of the other ones we had but it was a good team with a lot of youngsters.

However, while many pundits felt confident that Europe had a very strong chance of victory, these expectations were somewhat tempered by the layout of the course, which was felt to favour the Americans' style of play as it contained features seen regularly on the US Tour courses. The Brabazon was bedecked with thick rough, narrow fairways and water hazards on eight of its holes. After the first few practise rounds, Trevino added grist to the sceptics' mill when he joyfully announced, 'My guys love this course!'

Jacklin calmly retorted that his guys rather liked it, too.

Tony Jacklin: I worked with Brian Cash, chief executive of the Belfry, for the best part of eight months setting up an atmosphere which guaranteed we had our own rooms to eat together, relax together and above all, offered complete privacy; almost a family atmosphere you might say.

There wasn't a great deal to do to the course, but I made sure there would be none of that fluffy long grass close to the greens that was the staple diet for the Americans; I had all the areas round the greens shaved so you could chip, something they don't get to do very often. Then I made sure the speed of the greens was right for our side, so quite a bit slower than they were used to.

Nick Faldo: The last win had been in 1957 and only the halved match in 1969 had interrupted a string of American victories. That close-run affair the time before had given us an appetite for the match when we came to the Belfry for the first time in 1985.

Most of us turned up that year convinced we were going to win. Bernhard Langer had won the Masters in April and Sandy Lyle the Open in July. The Belfry was a course we all knew well – there was a tournament there every year – and even though they said it was American in style, it played like an inland British course with hard, bouncy fairways and slow greens. The main thing was that we arrived as a team and stayed that way. We got together regularly and discussed pairings, the way the course was playing and had all our meals together. That was important because there was so much of a hullabaloo now surrounding the match that you almost had to build an imaginary wall around the team to keep the pressure and the media hype at bay.

Tony Jacklin: I was committed to winning the Ryder Cup. It was what I wanted more than anything else in the world. There had been anticipation that week in '85 but we weren't as much concerned with what other people were thinking. We were just all closer as a team, all in touch with each other. It was two years that had gone by so quickly. When we arrived at the Belfry it was like no time had passed. We just hit the ground running.

Howard Clark: Sam Torrance was inspirational that week. He did so much to really rouse the players, I suppose, into battle mode.

Tony Jacklin: We were pretty confident. Home side, home crowd, home course preparation. I took the rough down around the greens a bit to help our guys, because it's the home captain's prerogative to have the course set up the way he wants. Didn't have the greens too quick because I didn't want to play into their hands.

Curtis Strange: The weather was kind of crappy, and it was a tough week. I have nothing derogatory to say about Lee Trevino as captain; he was fine. And you have to remember that captains back then didn't do as much as they do now. Dow Finsterwald told me after a dinner in Dallas, 'The only thing I told my guys was to do what you normally do. If you're used to drinking a fifth of liquor, drink a fifth of liquor. Don't change because of the Ryder Cup.' So captains didn't do as much. They dressed you up and said, 'Go get 'em, boys.' They paired you together properly, and that was it.

Oh, we had meetings every night, but you didn't have all these meetings with all that inspirational bullshit that you have now. All we had was our hotel room and a room to go eat. No ping-pong tables, no physios.

Nick Faldo: I think it probably shook the Americans when they arrived, even the closely fought match in 1983 hadn't really woken the American public up to the excitement of the contest. They weren't prepared for the great buzz they found when they turned up two years later. It was noticeable that they didn't behave like a team: they ate in twos and threes, then maybe disappeared to the movies. It was as though they still hadn't realised they were going to have to work really hard to keep the cup.

In that way I don't think Trevino was a good captain. He is a great character and a fine player, but the psychological intricacies of captaincy weren't for him. I remember hearing he allowed arguments to develop about who would play with whom, and when and how the team should practise foursomes.

Hal Sutton. *Getty Images*

Curtis Strange: 1985 was the first time I'd ever played in front of fans that weren't rooting for you real hard. Know what I'm saying? They were rooting like hell for their own team and didn't give a rat's ass about you. So that was an eye-opener. I was fine with it, but it was troubling to some of the players on the team.

Craig Stadler: From my own perspective, I never really had an issue being a rookie, but some guys struggled a bit with the new experience. I couldn't care less when I was a rookie in '83, I just wanted to make the team. The first morning in the 1985 foursomes, I was paired with Hal Sutton; at the second hole, I drove it down the middle. The green is a little raised with a big bunker on the right. Hal had a five-iron and he pushed it, buried it inside the lip of the bunker. To the left of this, about a hundred people started applauding and screaming. He just looked at me and said, 'What are they doing?' I said, 'They are clapping for you.' He said, 'Did they see where I hit it?' I said, 'Yeah.' He was like, 'Why would they do that?' I said, 'Dude, get used to it, it's going to happen again, and again and again and again'. It just threw him. He was just devastated. But I loved it when the crowd did that. I thought, 'Really? Oh, OK, it's on!' But he had issues with it.

Sam Torrance: The Ryder Cup is as intense as it gets. When you're playing a Major and you three-putt on the last hole to miss out on a play-off, you come off the green devastated; but if you lose your match in the Ryder Cup you've got to go back into the team room and the other players are sitting there – and there's nothing worse than having to go in there having lost. And there's nothing better than to go in their having won. And it's great to play with your peers as well. Sitting in the same room as Faldo and Ballesteros, it was so special; and it was a great thing too, because you can ask them stuff that in tournament golf you can't do. You know, you couldn't go up to Seve and say, 'Can you help me with my chipping?' In tournament golf there's no way you would ask that and no way they would help you – but in the Ryder Cup they'll go down to the range with you, spend an hour with you working on your shots, doing everything to help you get better.

Paul Way: Looking back, I was definitely a lot more nervous in 1985 than I was in 1983 because I knew what to expect. I was suffering from tonsillitis and the pressure was getting to me, I think. I'd won the PGA at Wentworth that year and I was pretty much the first person to qualify for the team but I came down with tonsillitis in the build-up and the pressure started to get to me – the enormity of the Ryder Cup, the history, the sense that we might create some history by winning it for the first time in almost three decades – all these doubts started getting into my head. Psychologically, the Ryder Cup is as tough as it gets.

Sandy Lyle: I don't really think my role within the team changed that much, even though I was Open champion and it was my fourth Ryder Cup. I might have moved up the rankings of expectations, in your own mind and probably the team's as well. We had four or five players, Seve, Faldo, myself, Woosie, that were all big names in golf. In Ryder Cups, you need to have your top dogs playing well. I presume I was seen as one of the top dogs, so there was a little bit of added pressure, that you were expected to put points on the board. Seve was always a good front runner, he got out there and got some points. I think generally he pulled the whole team along really nicely. If you compare it to cricket, and your main batsman gets out in the first hour of play, you are thinking, 'Oh gosh.' You needed to put points on the board and that's what we did, we got points out there, although it was tight overall. The other players did remarkably well.

Sam Torrance: I loved the Belfry from day one. It was a very demanding course where you couldn't get away with anything. Howard Clark, the best partner I ever had in the Ryder Cup, drove the tenth nearly every day in 1985. They used a forward tee, so it was just a three-wood, and wasn't that tough. But the atmosphere was just electric. The crowd really went bananas if you brought a wood out on the tee.

Peter Jacobsen: It was quite a gamble. It was a narrow little green with a water hazard in front of it. The back nine was really good, too. Seventeen was a reachable five, eighteen was a very difficult driving hole, a dogleg left around the water, which turned out to be the downfall of three or four of the American players. I don't think the Belfry being an inland course helped the Americans. Americans can win on links courses, too, and besides, the players are so good now and have been for years that they can adapt very quickly.

The opening match in the foursomes laid down a marker for the rest of the tournament. Jacklin paired the Spaniards Ballesteros and Piñero against O'Meara and Strange and the Europeans roared into a four-hole lead. The Americans dug in and managed to stay in touch at the turn, and then came the tenth. A plaque beside the tee was commemorated to Seve, who had been the first professional to drive the green, back in 1978. With a reputation to uphold, Seve stepped up to the tee and ripped his drive, which soared through the English skies and landed on the green. The crowd erupted. The pair holed out and re-established a three-hole lead, which the Americans were unable to overturn. When the seventeenth was halved, the Spaniards had the match 2&1 and the first blue point was on the board.

Lanny Wadkins: I was partnered with Mark O'Meara for the fourball against Seve and Manuel Piñero. The whole grandstand just booed us. It was Mark's first Ryder Cup and he was shocked. But I was like, 'Man, don't you love this? Let's go!' I loved stuff like that.

It was a brilliant start for Europe – but it did not last as America thundered back in the next three matches as Peete and Kite beat Langer and Faldo 3&2, Wadkins and Floyd beat Lyle and Brown 4&3 and Stadler and Sutton beat Clark and Torrance 3&2.

Nick Faldo: We got a nasty shock the first morning. Seve and Manuel Piñero won the top match, but the other three went comprehensively to the United States. Jacklin had, I think quite understandably after 1983, looked to put Bernhard Langer and me back in harness again. We had done so well two years before that he hoped we could rekindle the memories. But it wasn't to be.

Jacklin knew he had to take evasive action before the Americans extended their lead much more. Brown, Faldo and Lyle were switched out in favour of Cañizares, Way and Woosnam, and clear instructions were given that the afternoon fourballs could not go the way of the foursomes. The tactical changes worked brilliantly. Way and Woosnam beat Zoeller and Green one-up, Ballesteros and Piñero beat North and Jacobsen 2&1, while Langer and Cañizares halved with Stadler and Sutton; Floyd and Wadkins held on to beat Torrance and Clark one-up to make the score 4½–3½ to the Americans at the end of the day.

Tony Jacklin: That opening morning was definitely a reality check but I still thought it would prove a small blip. As for the two Spaniards, I hadn't been thinking of them as partners. I thought Seve could shepherd José Rivero, as he had Way two years earlier. But Rivero just looked overawed in practise, so I asked Manuel.

Manuel Piñero: I thought I was going to play with Bernhard Langer or José María Cañizares until Tony pulled me to one side. I'd played with Seve many times and I felt comfortable. He was the ultimate team player. I remember walking over the bridge on the eighteenth after one victory and letting him go first because the people loved him but no, he waited for me and held my arm in the air. That meant a lot to me.

When it was all over, he said to me, 'You know, you're going to have a real problem with me. We won the World Cup together, we won the Ryder Cup together and people will think you won it all because of me. But you finished ahead of me in the World Cup and you won more points than me at this Ryder Cup.' That was Seve. It was a real honour to stand alongside him.

Tony Jacklin: In 1985, Nick Faldo was going through a divorce. When the Ryder Cup got underway, he didn't look comfortable and lost his morning foursomes match. I took him aside after that and said, 'Nick, I've got a job to do. Do I send you out this afternoon, or do I sit you down?' Nick told me, very quietly, 'Sit me down.' It took enormous courage and humility for Nick to put himself aside. Now there is a team player. It took a big man, a real man, to say something like that, and Nick is a man. That's what you call commitment and humility.

Nick Faldo: At a major you go out and do your own thing, and if you play great, fine, and if you make a mess of it, that's that. The hardest thing about a Ryder Cup is, if you're playing well, you can't wait to get out there. You and your partner can't wait to go out and to take everybody on. But if you're playing poorly, and you know it, and you're fighting your swing, then you've still got to make something happen with a game you're not confident with. And that's brutal, because you don't want to let your teammates down.

Paul Way: I was thrilled when I found out I was playing with Woosie. Seve in 1983 and now another great player. It was a great match. We were three up at one stage against Fuzzy Zoeller and Hubert Green but they came back at us. At the last I hit a fantastic four-iron and managed to sink a twelve-foot birdie putt to win. It was a brilliant feeling. The crowd went wild.

Ian Woosnam: I think Tony wanted us to prove a point after what had happened in the morning and I suppose we did that. I was slightly older than Paul and probably a bit steadier but Paul came in at the right time. That birdie at the last was something special.

On the Saturday morning, Torrance and Clark got off to a strong start for Europe when they defeated Kite and North 2&1 in the opening fourball. Way and Woosnam followed this lead and demolished Green and Zoeller 4&3 before O'Meara and Wadkins took a big scalp for the Americans by beating Ballesteros and Piñero 3&2. Langer and Lyle and Stadler and Strange battled each other to a dead heat to halve the final match of the session (after an incredible final two holes from the Europeans to claw back a two-hole advantage held by Stadler and Strange, which included an eagle on the seventeenth from Lyle and a horrible tap-in miss from Stadler on the eighteenth) and tie the overall scores at six points each.

Bernhard Langer: In 1985 I played all five rounds, and had four different partners. My record was two wins, a defeat and two halves. I played very well that week, especially

Craig Stadler contemplates his missed putt.

in the singles where I beat Hal Sutton, 5&4. I ended in quite spectacular fashion by knocking it stiff on the fourteenth.

That week there was a good illustration of the special character of match play golf. In the fourballs, Sandy Lyle and I were one down on the eighteenth green to Craig Stadler and Curtis Strange. All Craig had to do was hole a two-foot putt. In all honesty, it was really a 'gimme'. Sandy and I were thinking, 'Let's give it to him and then we can go.' But then we said, 'We know we have lost but let him putt it.' Incredibly, he missed it – it lipped out – and we halved the match. That just proved that ridiculous things can happen and it is never over until it is over.

Sandy Lyle: To this day, I've got a great relationship with Bernhard, very much so. He was a whole different type of player to compare to. I know Bernhard is renowned for his attention to detail, regimental, but he gives 110 per cent and that's all you can ask for. He was good to have on board. We got a halved match against Stadler and Strange, but we should have probably won it. The sixteenth could have been a turning point, but we lost it and went two down with two to go. I made a great eagle on the seventeenth which sort of kept us going, and then we had the short putt missed by Craig Stadler at the eighteenth. That was probably kind of a turning point, going into the afternoon. That half point was huge. At the time, you are thinking, 'Oh, I only got a half point,' but looking at it later on it was a really good turning point, for the momentum of the Ryder Cup.

Nick Faldo: Craig Stadler missed a tiny putt on the eighteenth on the second morning, which really shook the Americans. It was probably the first time in the entire history of the matches that an American had so obviously buckled under pressure.

Sandy Lyle: We didn't think we were getting anything from the match when Craig stood over his short putt. It was the sort we would have conceded if it had been for a halved match but we had to see it in as it was for a win. Was he in shock when he missed? How would you know – he always looked a bit grumpy anyway, didn't he?

Craig Stadler: It was a good week. I had never been to the Belfry before and loved it. I've mentioned it to him before, but about two or three years later there was an article in *Golf Digest* or something on the Ryder Cup and they interviewed Curtis. I love Curtis, I'm very good friends with him. He made a comment that it was looking to be a pretty good week and I basically lost the Ryder Cup for him. I missed the putt on Saturday morning on eighteen in the fourballs, playing with Curtis.

You look back at the whole thing. We got up on eighteen and the wind was into us; I hit a really nice drive. Curtis snap-hooked it into the water. Langer and Lyle were both on the fairway, so I was kinda on my own. I hit a one-iron about thirty feet past the hole. It was a little slick, I rolled it about four feet by and then I 360'd that one and missed it. There was another whole set of foursomes matches to come. It was a half point, which was a huge half point, as you don't want to lose ever. I think Curtis was a little harsh, but I just kind of laughed and thought, 'If that is the way you feel, it's the way you feel'. I played every session that year. I won the week before, won over in Crans-sur-Sierre. Lee Trevino said, 'You just won, you are playing every day.' I said, 'Whatever you want me to do.'

Curtis Strange: I don't remember where I was on the hole. All I remember is that Craig had a two-foot putt, maybe three feet, to win the match. I was standing right there on top of him, helping him read it, although there wasn't anything to read. He just missed it, and we halved. At that moment, you don't say anything. You certainly don't say, 'That's all right.' He might slap you upside the head, because it's not all right. You shake hands and go about your business. Recoup in a hurry, because you have to play more golf in a few minutes. But it gave them such momentum. Half a point can mean a great deal, and it just changed the course of the matches. I don't mean anything against Craig, but that's just the way it worked.

Sam Torrance: I was in our team room watching it. There was such a roar when that happened, it was unbelievable.

Tony Jacklin: I'm convinced Stadler missing that putt was the turning point. Our team seemed to take it as meaning the Americans weren't supermen after all, that they were as susceptible to pressure as we were – in other words, human. It's a cruel game. It was an example of what pressure can do. In all my years I don't think I ever saw anything that changed a Ryder Cup quite like that putt.

Curtis Strange: Every one of us has missed a putt of that length, more than once. But you do it in the Ryder Cup, and it stays with you forever.

Tony Jacklin: We took that and ran with it. As a team we knew that was a sign, a chink in the armour, a weakness, and you have got to pounce on it.

Ray Floyd: There are little movements during the play that can change everything. A half point loss or win, a stroke instead of getting a half, you win one and they get nothing, it's huge.

Seve Ballesteros: The Americans were agitated because they weren't used to being in this situation and they complained that the spectators had applauded Stadler's miss. This is common in the Ryder Cup, but I think the spectators weren't applauding that player's miss as such; they were cheering because things were going well for their team. The reaction of the Belfry crowds was actually quite understandable – they hadn't had anything to cheer about in the Ryder Cup since 1957, the year I was born.

We were told about Stadler's miss while having lunch and we realised at once that it was a huge psychological blow for the Americans, as well as a huge boost to our morale.

Although the scores were even, the momentum shift towards the European team was palpable and after lunch they kept their foot to the floor to win three out of the four foursome matches to establish a 9–7 lead going into the Sunday singles.

Bernhard Langer celebrates after sinking a putt during the Saturday afternoon foursomes against Lanny Wadkins and Raymond Floyd. *Getty Images*

Nick Faldo: The two Spanish pairings rushed off immediately after lunch and notched huge victories in the second series of foursomes.

Andy North: The whole tone of the entire '85 Ryder Cup was that the European team made some remarkable shots. Chipping in from off the greens and the kind of stuff you have to do to win. Piñero made one in that first match, I believe, from thirty or forty yards off the green to win the sixteenth hole. It was a tough loss, but at that time Seve was at his best, and it seemed that no matter what Spaniard he played with, he seemed to get that Spaniard to play the best he could possibly play.

Nick Faldo: Langer and Ken Brown got a point at the end, and suddenly we had a two-point lead going into the final day.

Ahead of the singles, the two captains approached their order selection quite differently; Trevino split his best players between the top of the order and the tail, while Jacklin grouped his best players in the middle. You could see the thinking from both camps. Trevino needed to get points back on the board and look to build momentum for his team, with strength at the end to finish the job. Jacklin, meanwhile, took the gamble that if he could gain anything from the first few matches then they were a welcome bonus and his middle order could secure the cup if things went according to plan.

Tony Jacklin: I shocked Nicklaus in 1983 when I flipped the whole line-up. Historically, the strongest player has always gone out last. But I thought, 'What the hell's the good of the strength at the end if we've already lost?' In West Palm Beach, Joe Black, the US PGA president, was there when we opened the envelope with the line-ups. He said, 'What have you done?' Well, I started with Seve and propped the low end up with Cañizares, who ended up halving with Lanny Wadkins.

That strategy of tipping it upside down came out of bouncing stuff off Seve. Not off everybody, but off Seve, because if I went to two players I'd get two opinions and that would complicate it. In 1985, I thought we should put the strength in the middle, Seve said, 'I agree with you.' I went and sat at a table on my own, and wrote Piñero, Woosnam, boom-boom-boom, boom-boom-boom, then gave it to Seve. 'That's what I've come up with.' And he said, 'That's fine.' I started off with Piñero, then Woosnam, Way, then Seve, then Sandy Lyle, who was British Open champion at the time, then Langer, who was Masters champion, Sam Torrance . . .

You wouldn't believe the power and strength of mind that Seve brought to our team. When I saw a player who maybe I felt needed a little bit of encouragement or whatever, Seve was always there. I remember David Gilford walking in a bit disheartened one night, I think in 1991, and I said to Seve, 'Just go and sit next to him. Tell him how well you think he played.' In those days just a word from him was enough. He was formidable, just formidable.

Sam Torrance: At the team meeting the night before the singles, Manuel Piñero stood up and said, 'I want Wadkins. Work out where Wadkins is going to be and let me play him.' Now you have to bear in mind that no one wanted Wadkins, he was as tough as they come. But Manuel had this fire about it, so we looked at their order and figured they would put Wadkins out first, so we put Manuel there. Manuel was a tenacious player, a great match player. When the draw came out half an hour later we saw Wadkins at the top of the order. Manuel jumped about four feet in the air, fists pumping. It was fantastic.

Manuel Piñero: The only match Seve and I had lost was to Wadkins. That was why I wanted to play him. And it went like a dream.

Nobody gave the European players much hope in the first few rounds, but Piñero confounded these expectations right off the bat by rising to the challenge and defeating Wadkins 3&1.

Stadler clawed back a point for the US by beating Woosnam before Way edged Europe's nose further in front when he dispatched Floyd two-up. Ballesteros and Kite finished all square for a half point each and just minutes later Lyle completed a 3&2 victory over Jacobsen and Langer finished off a 5&4 thrashing of Sutton. Europe needed just one point from the remaining six matches to win the cup.

Craig Stadler: We had four rookies that year, North, Sutton, Jacobsen and O'Meara. A lot of things happened that week. I remember a comment Peter Jacobsen made on the Sunday. I'm thinking he was probably like five down after eight in the singles, then he won nine, ten, eleven and twelve. He was playing Sandy Lyle. He got up on the thirteenth tee and hit it right down the middle and Sandy drove it out of bounds left. Lee was sitting in the cart over to the left and Peter walked over and said, 'Lee man, I've won the last four. I'm coming back.' I don't know what exactly Lee said but it was something like to the tune of, 'I don't care about that, just play golf.' I honestly think Peter was devastated by that.

Peter Jacobsen: I played Sandy Lyle in the singles. I thought he was just a masterful player, and a wonderful guy. His length off the tee was Tiger-like, Nicklaus-like; he hit the ball a long way back then. He hit his one-iron 250 yards off the tee.

He was two up on sixteen, hit it in a very tough spot on the green. I thought I was going to get one back as I had maybe a ten- or twelve-footer for birdie, but he holed a putt from off the fringe to win.

Nick Faldo: In the singles, Piñero was the inspiration. He asked for, and got, Lanny Wadkins and saw him off 3&1. Wadkins and Floyd had been put in at the top to try to get the two missing points back early on. The plan misfired as Paul Way beat Floyd as well.

Seve only halved his singles again, this time against Tom Kite. But on this occasion he came back from three down to get something out of a match that had looked well lost.

Paul Way: I took lots of major scalps in my Ryder Cup career – Floyd, Watson, Zoeller – and they weren't too happy about it. But everybody struggled that day because the wind was up. I shot maybe a 73 or 74, but that was still good enough to beat Ray Floyd. Over eighteen holes, anyone can beat anyone. I was never as good a player as Ray Floyd or Curtis Strange but over eighteen holes you've always got a chance.

Sandy Lyle: I didn't have a great Ryder Cup record to that point and you feel you have a responsibility as a Major winner. I was desperate to win to help the team, because we were conscious how important it was to get off to a good start, so to go out and beat Peter Jacobsen 3&2 and get a good early point on the board for the team was amazing. After that you go out and support the rest of the team on the course and that is a nerve-wracking time where you're just waiting to see if the rest of the guys can come through to make history.

Peter Jacobsen: After I lost to Sandy Lyle, I went to watch Seve play. Seve was the most inspirational player that I ever played with and I loved watching him play. It didn't matter if I was competing with him or against him, whether it was in a Major or just on the PGA Tour, I just loved watching the man play.

Ballesteros played well against Tom Kite but did not dominate the American as he might have hoped. But with their match halved, another crucial half point had been added to the European total. At almost the same time as Ballesteros and Kite were shaking hands, Lyle sewed up his win over Jacobsen and Langer finished his 5&4 thrashing of Hal Sutton with a flourish. It looked as if the honour of holing the winning putt would come down to either Sam Torrance, who was playing Andy North, or Howard Clark, who was playing Mark O'Meara a hole behind.

Howard Clark: Should it have been me who holed the winning putt? In many ways it would have put a dampener on it if such a historic moment had been decided on the seventeenth green. I've seen the video many times and how fitting it was that it came down to the eighteenth, and to Sam. It was the start of the legend of him and the Ryder Cup.

Andy North: That was a horrible day. You looked up at the scoreboard and we had a whole bunch of guys who couldn't get a grasp on any matches where we could get some momentum. My match was a pretty good example. I got off to a really good start and got way up on Sam Torrance. Then he made some birdies on the back nine and before you knew it we came to the last hole even. I knew we were in big trouble at that point.

Sam Torrance: I never won a Major so this was, by far, my best moment as a player. I'd dreamed about winning the Ryder Cup and I wasn't scared of the challenge, I was ready to embrace it. I'd come back from three down after nine to be all square on the eighteenth and I absolutely nailed my drive. But I'd pulled it a bit and I was worried it wouldn't carry the water. When I heard this great roar from the crowd it was such a relief. Then Andy skied his drive and it fell into the water and I knew that was it. I only had a nine-iron for my second shot and I'd back myself against anyone in those circumstances.

I'm not being blasé about it, but the eighteenth green was the easy bit. On seventeen I'd hit an eight-foot putt to get from one down to all square to give me the chance to win the point, the last which Europe needed – so that was the hardest putt I ever had to hit in my life. I holed it, went to the last tee and actually tried to hand my driver over to my captain Tony Jacklin and let him hit it for me. But he said, 'Go on son, you can do it.' And I hit the drive of my life, enormous.

When Andy North's drive went straight up in the air I knew it was in the water. He couldn't get on the green. That's when I knew. 'I've got this.' I was actually crying coming over the bridge over the water. All the American wives were sitting there and there were tears streaming down my face. I just couldn't control it. And the roars along the fairway from the bridge to the green gave me goose bumps like I've never felt before.

Andy North: I knew I needed to win the hole, and I popped the drive up just enough that it didn't carry over the water. From that point, it was over. Sam played a good shot and put it up on the green, and you know that was the point that decided the cup.

Sam Torrance: North pulled his approach shot left, to about forty feet. I was about twenty-five feet away. So if he holed for a five, I had to two-putt for the match. I was praying he didn't hole it. I did not want to have to two-putt. So he misses. And then he did a really classy thing. He could have conceded, but he didn't. He let me have my moment.

The greens weren't as slick in those days. The putt had probably a six-to eight-inch break, and I had to hit it maybe a foot right, dead weight, which means it's going to swing more. Three feet short of the hole I knew it was in, or not going more than a little past. Then it fell in, and I've never felt as strong, as good, on a golf course in all my life. I gave the ball to some kid. The memory's better than the ball. Without doubt, my best golf moment. By a million miles.

Tony Jacklin: I was around the green everywhere that a match was won. That was the oddest thing because you had to be there to congratulate or commiserate if it was required. But I was certainly there when Sam won, and I can see it now, I can see him stroking the putt, I can see the arms going up, and I can see him crying. He was so emotional. But he was riding an incredible wave of emotion and destiny.

Our first win in twenty-eight years. What a moment.

Curtis Strange: The '85 match was over before I finished. God, it's a terrible thing, isn't it? I was on the fifteenth green. You can just about see the eighteenth green from there, but I could hear the roaring and the singing.

Seve Ballesteros: This was the starting point for a new era for the Ryder Cup and for European golf. It was at that instant, when I saw the euphoria of the spectators and my colleagues' display of emotion, that I understood the real meaning of the Ryder Cup.

The European team's victory wasn't only historic because it ended the unchallenged domination of the USA, but also because it resulted in a huge leap in quality in the Ryder Cup itself. Our victory meant that it was now the biggest event on the international calendar.

Lee Trevino: Looking back, I feel satisfied that I did everything I possibly could. I teamed my guys the best I could. But I couldn't play for them . . . They criticised me afterwards, but I wasn't the one who lost the matches.

I'll tell you what hurt my players more than anything. This is the one thing I preached to them every time I got them in that room. I said, 'Don't pay any attention to the gallery.' I played in six Ryder Cups and the galleries can really get to you, especially when you're away from home. When you miss a putt, it sounds like you made an eagle. The galleries laugh and applaud like you ain't never seen before. It makes the hair up on your neck stand up – and not in a good way. In '85 I think it's safe to say that my players weren't able to handle the galleries.

Craig Stadler: Without trying to be negative, I really don't think Lee embraced the whole thing of being captain. He wasn't keen on having a big part in making the pairings. We were sitting there, making the pairings, and he would look at us and say, 'Play with who you want to play with,' which is the way he is. 'Just play well, whatever you do, I don't care who you play with.' We rarely saw him on the course, he was out there somewhere, I don't know where. I love Lee to death, he is a very, very dear friend of mine, and I don't mean to be bad-mouthing him, I'm not. He agreed to be captain, but I think, he'll tell you, it probably wasn't his cup of tea.

It went from one extreme to another, with Jack at us each day in 1983, 'What do you need? What can I do for you?' to get a captain two years later who was there and supportive, but fairly non-existent as far as having any input on who played with each other, how you were playing, what was going on – it was a big swing in approach. Lee just kind of watched it, hung around and had a good time, but didn't give a whole lot of input. I think that's what he wanted. He probably decided he had the players, they were good players, so what could he do for them? I think that is the attitude he took, which is pretty much how he works.

Peter Jacobsen: Losing the Ryder Cup did not bother me as much as the behaviour of the galleries. All that cheering when we missed shots. I've never known anything like it before and especially not from a British crowd. You expected so much more from them.

Sam Torrance: When the crowd is against you I find that it can work in your favour because it really fires you up. I remember Trevino saying, 'The only way to shut the crowd up is with birdies. And we didn't make enough birdies.' I'm with him on that – you need to use the crowd as a motivator, whether they're with you or against you.

Tony Jacklin: I was bawling like a baby aftewards. A few years earlier the cup had been on death watch for lack of competition, now we had a serious event – and it's just grown and grown since then. I wish I could say it was extra special, as a captain, to beat Lee Trevino, but that wasn't really part of it. It was about more than me as an individual, or any of us as individuals. It was about representing where we were from. It was about Europe, and we were the champions. It was euphoria. It was beautiful. It was freshly made history and it will never be forgotten.

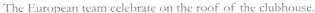

The European team celebrate on the roof of the clubhouse.

Seve Ballesteros: Winning the Ryder Cup felt like winning another British Open. Seeing the crowds and how it affected people, it was just tremendous.

Ian Woosnam: It was great drinking the champagne left over by captain Dai Rees from the last success in 1957. My abiding memory from the celebrations afterwards was standing on the Belfry roof, looking out at thousands of people and seeing a friend. All those people and I could see a mate. I remember lowering a bottle to him.

Craig Stadler: It could have gone either way. But, again, for me, it was a great week. You want to win, but even if you don't, I just basked in it, loved the format, loved the competition it is and always have. I didn't find it hard watching the European team celebrate. When you get down to the end, they are all friends. They're not your friend when you are playing against them, but once you get done you can go and have a beer with them and have a good time.

Tony Jacklin: It was Bernhard Langer who brought it home to me what we'd achieved. He pointed out the last time we'd won was the year he was born, and he was 28 at the time.

Manuel Piñero: It was the moment the European Tour took off. Our top players went from strength to strength and became almost unbeatable.

Nick Faldo: I didn't do my bit that year, which is tough to look back on now. I was coming to the end of my swing change, things hadn't quite clicked yet, but Tony gave me a chance as a wild card. I just didn't perform, and when the guys were celebrating at the end, I couldn't. I didn't feel like part of the team.

Paul Way: My abiding memory of the celebrations was being in the leisure centre and we chucked Faldo into the swimming pool. He'd lost two matches out of two. Then we all jumped in.

Sandy Lyle: The champagne was flowing straight away. It was really, really nice to be on the other side, to be winning for a change, after so many years had gone by of frustration. I suppose America is almost going through the same thing now themselves, thinking, 'How do we beat this European team?' Quite a few times they have been dusted. I had to go off for another tournament the following day so I was leaving fairly early in the morning to set off for my next event. I think a lot of them were still going on until all hours and the swimming pool got a bashing, and stuff like that. So it was a bit wild, but expected really. Years and years of frustration, to all of a sudden being on the other side of it. It was a wonderful thing to see, and also to be at the Belfry at the time, the crowds got on our side, and the crowds were huge as well. Yeah, it was something that I'll never forget.

Sam Torrance: It's a wonderful thing when you see the guys from that team. You don't have to say anything. You just look at each other. The respect, the joy – it's there. It'll always be there.

Later that night we went down to the spa where there was a pool and pretty much everyone went in – fully clothed. We just had a ball. I went to bed at 5:00 or 6:00 am. The next morning I met up with John O'Leary, one of my best mates on tour, and we brunched over five or six bottles of champagne. A driver then took me down the M1 and I stopped at a friend's house near Woburn, and we had another night of celebration. The next morning I was up and off to Spain for the next tour event, back to the day job, and of course you then see all of your friends on tour, and that's probably the best part, going over it all again and again with your mates. At about 4:00 am in a nightclub on the Wednesday I can remember telling the boys, 'That's it – I have to go.' It was virtually four days of celebrations. I made the cut, too, in Spain, which was impressive.

TWENTY-SEVEN

1987

Muirfield Village Golf Club. Dublin, Ohio
(EUR 15, USA 13)

1987 marked sixty years since Ted Ray had led the first British team across the water to America for the inaugural Ryder Cup. Half a dozen decades later, Tony Jacklin's class of '89 boarded Concorde to fly to Muirfield Village and 'the course that Jack built.'

Shortly after his triumph at Muirfield in Scotland in the 1966 Open Championship, Nicklaus purchased a plot of land near his home in Columbus, Ohio, and set to work creating Muirfield Village. A beautiful yet devilishly difficult course, it was coined by some as 'the Augusta of the North'. The US PGA then appointed its creator as the US captain tasked with regaining the cup.

Jack Nicklaus: Muirfield Village had been nicknamed the 'Augusta of the North', which was great. I had set out to build not only an outstanding golf course for every level of player, but a magnificent course for watching a tournament. I thought the Masters was a great thing for golf and that I wanted to do the same thing in Columbus.

Howard Clark: Jack made us very welcome as he and all the Americans always did. As a European player in those days we didn't get invites to play in tournaments unless we had won a Major or we were top of the Order of Merit – it was highly unlikely that you were going to get invited to Muirfield Village let alone any other tournament for that matter.

Tony Jacklin: The overall impression I can still so easily recall from the 1987 cup was that it was just done right. Everything was perfect. The course was great. The accommodations were great. Our hosts, Barbara and Jack Nicklaus, were unfailingly gracious and generous while also being competitive in exactly the best way.

Sandy Lyle: I'm not sure if I agree with Tony entirely about that, to be honest. Yes, the hospitality was amazing, but there was nothing laid out for us on that Muirfield course, everything was done to help the American side – if it was faster greens, or it was fairways narrower, it was all done. That, to me, is what made the challenge all the greater.

Both teams were very strong but for different reasons. The four best players in the world were European – Seve Ballesteros, Nick Faldo, Bernhard Langer and Sandy Lyle – but only six of the team were ranked in the world top forty, while all twelve of the US team were there.

The build-up was fierce, with the Americans desperate to reclaim the initiative after the Belfry. 'We've got the best tour in the world and the best players,' stated Payne Stewart, clearly employing psychological gamesmanship, while the fiery Lanny Wadkins remarked more bluntly,

'I get sick and tired of reading all that stuff about Ballesteros and Langer being the best. If they're the best, why haven't they won in America in two years?'

Jacklin, leading the team for the third time, welcomed back nine players from the side that had triumphed at the Belfry, with Ken Brown, Howard Clark, José Rivero, Sam Torrance and Ian Woosnam joining forces with veteran Eamonn Darcy and rookies Gordon Brand Jnr and José María Olazábal.

Nicklaus, meanwhile, only retained the services of Tom Kite, Curtis Strange, Hal Sutton and Lanny Wadkins from 1985 and handed debuts to Mark Calcavecchia, Larry Mize, Dan Pohl, Scott Simpson and Payne Stewart, while recalling experienced hands Andy Bean, Ben Crenshaw and Larry Nelson.

Sandy Jones: I was Jacklin's assistant that week and it was fascinating to see how the players acted behind the scenes. With Bernhard Langer, everything was perfect in that Germanic sort of way. At Muirfield, we had a message on one of the practise days that there was a threat of rain and I was sent back to all the players' rooms to get sweaters. Langer's room was laid out perfectly; here was Monday, here was Tuesday, here was Wednesday – it was perfection. I remember then going into Sam Torrance's room and there was stuff everywhere. I shouldn't pick on Sam, but you can imagine the situation, there was a shoe here, a shoe there . . .

Sam Torrance: 1985 was the best performance of any of our team matches, but 1987 was the one that made the Ryder Cup. We had a team that was just magnificent.

Tony Jacklin: I remember we landed in America as champions, brimming with confidence. It was a marvellous year to be captain, because we had great returning strength and experience from the previous Ryder Cup, but we had new blood, too. What a roster I had! Seve, Faldo, Langer, Woosnam, Sandy Lyle, the new face of José María Olazábal. All of them true greats who would end up with multiple Majors on their résumes. I remember being asked by the press what I thought was going to happen that week.

'Oh, we'll win,' I said, simple as that. I meant it. It wasn't a boast. It wasn't a challenge. I wasn't trying to anger the Americans or motivate my own team. It was just what I thought, what I felt. Question. Answer. Next?

Howard Clark: We had great confidence and natural partnerships. Woosnam and Faldo, Lyle and Langer, were just fantastic players. There was a very strong top half of the team, with another team, if you like, that could back the top half up.

Gordon Brand Jnr: When we got together we realised what a strong lead to the team we had in those six guys up front; and I think the rest of us were just trying to gain some points. And that was the case as the week went on – the six best players we had played some fantastic golf and we backed them up a bit.

Seve saw that the team was capable of winning, and the belief that he had in the team had a huge influence on our confidence. And anyone who saw Seve play, he played with a great deal of passion and that integrated into the team very well.

Sam Torrance: It couldn't have looked worse for us, playing against a team captained by Jack Nicklaus on a course designed by him. But we had some pairings that week that were just phenomenal: Langer and Lyle; Seve and Ollie; Faldo and Woosie. These guys were unbeatable and they played golf that had just not been seen before from Europeans. It was just amazing.

Tony Jacklin: I felt it was essential to set up a family atmosphere off the course, involving the wives and girlfriends in the hope that this relaxed attitude would stretch out onto the course. I had never felt that at any of the cup matches I played in, starting in 1967 at Houston. We had meetings, were told to keep practising and to stay on the course and encourage other members of the side if and when we got beaten or won. I made no such demands; the team were all professionals and it would have been an insult to their intelligence to suggest that. If a team really is operating as a unit the players will do things automatically and do not need to be reminded or cajoled. We were a proper unit and in this respect the two or three days before the match were so important. I insisted, for instance, that everyone attended the evening meal. We had a twenty-five-place table set up in the basement of my villa and no one was excused even if they felt tired. I stressed it was essential that we did that for team morale and no one argued.

On the eve of the matches, the captains traded positive outpourings for their respective teams. Nicklaus confidently predicted that the cup would soon be returned to American hands, citing the lessons learned at the Belfry as proof that his men would not be taken unawares by a talented European outfit. 'Our guys know that they can be beaten,' he said. 'But the European side winning the last time is more of an advantage to us.'

Jacklin, meanwhile, claimed that the confidence gained from 1985 was the spur needed to alter the course of history. 'We all believe we can win on American soil for the first time. I have been coming to America for twenty years and this is the first time I am really confident of winning.'

The sky was overcast and the air chilly as Nicklaus sent his top pairing of Curtis Strange and Tom Kite out for the opening Friday morning foursome with Sam Torrance and Howard Clark.

It was a good move from Nicklaus as his players shot into an early lead, quickly dispelling the magic that surrounded Torrance from his Belfry heroics. Kite and Strange were three up after five and although the European pair settled into things thereafter, the best they could do was to match their opposition as they halved the next ten holes. When Torrance put a six iron shot for the green into a bunker the Americans held out for par and in so doing secured a 4&2 victory.

Tom Kite: Sam and Howard didn't play to their capabilities while we just had a nice solid round. When we were two up after two it was just a case of making steady pars.

Nicklaus had the start he wanted and his players continued to deliver, shooting into an early lead in every one of the matches on the course. Hal Sutton and Dan Pohl secured America's second point with a 2&1 victory over Ken Brown and Bernhard Langer before the pendulum began to swing back the other way.

Ben Crenshaw and Lanny Wadkins. *Getty Images*

Tony Jacklin: We expected the galleries to be noisy and I had prepared the team mentally for the expected partisanship of the Americans, increased by the US PGA's decision to give their supporters flags to wave and Jack Nicklaus's plea for them to be more vocal. But in the end the fans were very fair. There was no talking while a player was over a shot and there was as much applause for us as for their own team. Mind you, we had a loyal group of up-front supporters ourselves and that did no harm.

Bernhard Langer: We were confident that we could go one better and beat the Americans on their home soil. Again I played all five matches. I really liked Muirfield Village, which reminded me a lot of Augusta. In the first-day foursomes, I played with Ken Brown and lost.

After the first two hours of play on the first morning, the USA were three up in the top match, three up in the second, four up in the third and two up in the fourth. It was hardly the start we had planned.

Nick Faldo had lost all his matches in 1985 at the Belfry but he had remodelled his swing under David Leadbetter and won the 1987 Open Championship. He was expecting to be paired with Langer, but Jacklin had other ideas and instead teamed him with Welshman Ian Woosnam against Lanny Wadkins and reigning Masters champion Larry Mize.

Woosnam and Faldo turned out to be an inspired pairing. The 5'4½" Woosnam may have appeared diminutive to onlookers but he was one of the longest hitters in the game and this power was deftly complemented by Faldo's precision.

Things were not going well for the Europeans early on. Not only had they lost the first two matches, across the board they were struggling. They needed a flash of inspiration from somewhere – and it came from Faldo. As they arrived on the tenth he smashed a three-iron second to three feet and Woosnam holed to bring the score back to three down. Wadkins began to get edgy. He hit a bunker on the short twelfth and clattered into a stream on the fourteenth. Faldo and Woosnam were now only one down.

Nick Faldo: I stood on the thirteenth tee and I knew we could still do it. The pressure was suddenly on them.

At the fifteenth Mize drove into the trees, while Faldo found the fairway and Woosnam then rifled a spectacular one-iron 250 yards into the wind, from an uphill lie, passing over a deep depression in front of the green and landed the ball fifteen feet from the hole, pin high. They two-putted for birdie and the match was all square.

Nick Faldo: Woosie's iron approach on sixteen? That was a great shot.

At seventeen, and clearly rattled, Mize drove far right behind some trees that left Wadkins with a 200-yard shot with a forty-yard fade from the rough. He hit it short of the green and into even deeper rough, from where Mize tipped it into a bunker. There were no such problems for Faldo and Woosnam who were now, incredibly, ahead. Both pairings shot par on the eighteenth and Europe had secured a point that had looked well beyond them at the turn.

Tony Jacklin: Ian and Nick's comeback from four down at the turn on the first morning was just the boost we needed.

The final match that morning was between Larry Nelson and Payne Stewart and Seve Ballesteros and José María Olazábal. This was an intriguing battle on a number of fronts. Seve, the darling of the Ryder Cup, was back in action once more, this time helping the precociously talented twenty-one-year-old Olazábal, with whom he would go on to forge a long and successful partnership. Across from them they faced the flamboyant and popular Stewart, who would go on to win two US Opens and a US PGA Championship, and Nelson, who had just won the US PGA and also held a remarkable Ryder Cup record of played nine, won nine, including four victories over Ballesteros.

Bernard Gallacher: Seve was so dominant that the big problem was getting somebody to fit with him because Seve made his own team nervous. It worked with Manuel Piñero, it worked with Paul Way, but the real combination was Seve and Olazábal. You just can't put these superstars with just anybody because some of the lesser players get a bit jumpy and a bit nervous and don't play their own game playing with such a good player.

José María Olazábal: Seve gave me a call when I was fifteen years old and asked me to play in a match, a charity match, against him at his home club in Pedrena. And I said, 'Yes,' without knowing the implications of that answer in my future career. Something really special happened that day. I don't know what it was, but it was truly special. A few years later, I played in my first Ryder Cup at Muirfield Village, I was a twenty-one year old boy, and the captain, I guess, didn't know what to do with me. Seve approached Tony and said: 'Tony, I will play with Ollie.' And the rest is history.

The relationship has so many memories of moments that are unique to us from the Ryder Cup. In a way, he was like a big brother to me. He was always helpful and he gave me a lot of belief. Seve was incredible the way he played golf – the way he visualised shots, how he imagined them, how he escaped from unbelievable situations. And he was so strong. He never gave up. Absolutely never gave up. Seeing that from him, perhaps the best player of his time, that was a great confirmation of what you had to do to get to the top.

Seve Ballesteros: José and I knew each other very well and we came from the same background, and I think that helped.

José María Olazábal: I will never forget that little walk from the putting green to the first tee. I was shaking like a leaf. The crowds were huge. Very loud. So I kept my head down, and Seve approached me as we were walking on the first tee. He looked at me and said, 'José María, you play your game, I'll take care of the rest.' And he did. He was a great figure, I think not just for myself but for the whole European squad, not just that year but every year that he played in that team. He was a special man.

Nick Faldo: To have those two going out and leading us in that era was absolutely fantastic.

Stewart showed no debutant nerves as he rolled in an eight-foot putt to birdie and win the first and they pushed into a two-hole lead after five. But the initiative turned Europe's way before the turn as the Americans bogeyed the sixth and Ballesteros sank a twenty-five foot putt at the eighth. The Americans then three-putted the ninth and it was all square. The US pair pushed out in front at the eleventh but were soon reeled back in again; the key moment in this match came on the fifteenth when Seve sent a majestic chip to within three feet of the pin and his partner holed out to give Europe a one-hole advantage they didn't relinquish. 'That's about the best I've ever seen Seve play,' said Nelson afterwards. 'He did not miss a shot and his birdie at fifteen came after about as good a chip as I've seen. You could see a little bit of the youth in José María, but Seve more than made up for it. I missed a couple of easy putts that really hurt us, but when you get beat one-up by such a great player, you are disappointed, but not depressed.'

Tony Jacklin: The psychological shift thanks to those two points we won in the morning was huge. Both physically and mentally it would have been very tough to come back from a four-nil beating in the opening session, which looked a very real possibility at one stage, and the energy we got from their comebacks was huge. It gave us all a big lift at lunch and then sent us out in the afternoon with momentum.

While pleased with the salvage job his team had managed in the morning, Jacklin was ruthless with his afternoon selection. Howard Clark was dropped for debutant Gordon Brand Jnr and just before he handed in his envelope with his selected pairings, Jacklin opened it and crossed out Torrance's name, replacing him with José Rivero. 'All I'm interested in are points and the best way I think we will get them,' said Jacklin.

Jack Nicklaus also mixed things up. Having taken the surprise decision to omit Ben Crenshaw from the morning session, he was called up to partner US Open winner Scott Simpson against Brand and Rivero.

The Americans won the first hole after a nervous start from their opponents but thereafter it was all Europe. They were two up after five holes and when Simpson looked to have sewn up the seventh with a birdie four, Brand sunk a thirty-footer for the half, a trick that he repeated at the ninth to give Europe a three-hole lead and the Americans were unable to hunt them down, eventually losing 3&2.

Gordon Brand Jnr: Both Crenshaw and Simpson were Major champions, but I think it was irrelevant who you played, because everybody was a big name in the American side. You don't think about it, it's just another game of golf. Whoever stands on the tee, I just wanted to beat them. If you start thinking, he has one Major or he has been there and I haven't, then you would never take the club back. You play really hard to get into the Ryder Cup and you've got to make the most of it while you are there, not get awe-inspired. It was great to be part of the sides and to also get some points.

Andy Bean and rookie Mark Calcavecchia were sent out second by Nicklaus to face Sandy Lyle and Bernhard Langer. The Europeans went into an early two-hole lead after three, but the Americans produced some scintillating golf to win the seventh, eighth and ninth to lead by a hole at the turn. When Calcavecchia sank a ten-footer at the thirteenth the US were two up. But the Europeans were not considered two of the world's best for nothing. Langer pulled back a half point on the fourteenth with a ten-foot putt, and Lyle saved a half on the sixteenth with a twenty-five footer. They needed to win the final two holes to win the match – which they duly did, by scoring pars on each while the Americans imploded to take the overall score to 4–2 to Europe.

Hal Sutton and Dan Pohl were then sent out to take down the new super partnership of Woosnam and Faldo, but they were unable to match the class of the European pairing, despite giving it a hell of an effort. The match hinged on the eleventh and a stroke of luck. Woosnam smashed long for the green on the 538-yard par five but his shot drifted into the trees – where it hit a branch and rebounded to land twelve feet from the pin, which was sunk for an eagle which put Europe one up. Faldo extended the lead to two on the twelfth and although the Americans, Sutton in particular, refused to buckle, it was all over on the seventeenth green as Europe triumphed 2&1.

The final fourball of the day saw Curtis Strange and Tom Kite take on Seve Ballesteros and José María Olazábal.

On the first hole, a par four, Ballesteros was short of the green, while Olazábal was about four feet away in three. Seve asked his partner to putt out so that he could have a free chip, but Strange objected, claiming that Olazábal would be standing on the line of his putt and might leave spike marks. 'OK, no problem,' said Seve and chipped the ball forty feet and into the hole for birdie.

Curtis Strange: We had a rules meeting the night before, when it was made clear players should mark if they were going to be on an opponent's through-line [the line a missed putt might travel beyond the hole]. On the first hole, Ollie putts up to three feet or so, but he's on my through-line. Seve is away, just off the green. He wants José to putt. I point out that he'll be standing on my through-line. Seve asks if that will bother me. I tell him it will. So he shrugs, walks over to his ball and chips in to win the hole. Incredible. I almost wanted to applaud.

The Europeans extended their lead at the sixth when Seve rolled in a sixteen-footer. Kite looked to have halved the seventh with a ten-foot putt only to see Olazábal steal it with a twelve-foot putt for birdie. The Americans then found themselves four down on the tenth when Seve hit the target from forty-five feet and although they clawed back two holes by birdying the eleventh and twelfth, it was all over at the seventeenth. The Spaniards' 2&1 win secured Europe's first ever whitewash in any series in the Ryder Cup's sixty-year history.

The next day Nicklaus sent out his number one pairing of Strange and Kite against Rivero and Brand Jnr in an effort to redress the balance. It didn't bode well for the Americans when Brand Jnr holed from forty-five feet to birdie and win the first, but it proved to be something of an anomaly as Strange and Kite dominated much of the rest of the match to win 3&1.

Gordon Brand Jnr: The decision to pair me with José Rivero was a complete mystery to me at the time. You would have thought that in preparation – in practise rounds – that you would possibly be playing with someone you had been friends with or whose game you knew, or even, quite simply, someone who could speak your language. Sometimes captains just see a pairing and think they'll match. José and I weren't boom-boom hitters, we were very much steady Eddies, so he may well have actually looked at that. It would have been different if I had been playing with Sam Torrance or Howard Clark who were people I had gone out for dinner with or played World Cups with, so I would have had some knowledge of them, but even to this day I don't know why I was paired with Rivero.

But we got a result. I think at the time you are not really aware of what's happening. It sounds a bit blasé but I just looked at it as another game of golf. Maybe that was a good thing.

The second match that morning saw Hal Sutton and Larry Mize take on Nick Faldo and Ian Woosnam. Each pairing won three of the first six holes and they then halved the next two. Europe pushed into a one-hole lead when Sutton's approach landed in the greenside bunker and gave Mize a devilishly difficult lie, from which he could not escape and they were forced to concede. Woosnam then claimed the tenth with a lovely thirteen-foot putt before the Americans won the eleventh. The next six holes were halved and it came down to the eighteenth to decide it. Sutton and Mize showed tremendous grit to par the hole while the Europeans bogeyed and the match was halved.

The third match pitched Lanny Wadkins and Larry Nelson against Sandy Lyle and Bernhard Langer. The Scotsman got the European pairing underway in sound fashion when his right foot putt at the first for birdie put them one up. It set the scene for some outstanding golf between the four players as they traded birdies, and spectacular shots, around the course. When Langer chipped in from deep rough at the tenth he collapsed onto his back to rapturous applause; his partner, meanwhile, was on fire, birdying twelve and fourteen and then sending a three-iron approach shot on the fifteenth 232 yards to twenty feet of the pin, which he then sank for an eagle.

Seve Ballesteros: Sandy is the greatest God-given talent in history. If everyone in the world was playing their best, Sandy would win. And I'd come second.

Sandy Lyle and Bernhard Langer. *Getty Images*

Bernhard Langer: Sandy and I played some of the best golf I have ever seen in my life. We both played well and combined brilliantly. I could hardly believe some of the shots Sandy played. He could hit the ball almost straight up in the air with a two-iron and carry it 240 yards.

In the second-day fourballs against Larry Nelson and Lanny Wadkins, we came down the eighteenth one up. All four drives hit the fairway but mine was the longest. Larry Nelson played first and hit the green. Sandy also put his ball on the green and inside Nelson. Wadkins, a great player under pressure, had come off two birdies. His shot produced a great roar from the gallery so, without being able to see it, I knew it was close. I had 150 yards and it looked as though we needed a three for victory. I struck an eight iron well. It was on line, landed on the green and stopped next to the pin, inside Lanny's ball – a gimme. The atmosphere was electrifying and there was incredible noise.

Sandy Lyle: I loved playing with Bernhard, he was an incredible partner to have. I'll give you an insight into what he was like, how meticulous he can be. In one of the practise rounds, we were at the ninth or tenth and we were querying a certain yardage. I had 179 yards or something and Bernhard was looking at his notes. He looked at me, with a very straight face, and said, 'Is that the greenside of the sprinkler, or the tee side of the sprinkler?' It must have been an eight-inch sprinkler. I'm going, 'Is he serious?' He still kept a straight face, stayed serious, and my caddie and I looked at each other and we thought, 'He is serious!' Yardages down to the last half-foot! But that's Bernhard, he doesn't leave a stone unturned. We had some good scalps that week. In the Saturday morning foursomes, we were against Wadkins and Nelson, who were a very, very strong duo together and had not lost a Ryder Cup match in many, many years. They were a couple of old dogs, hard, hard to beat, and we beat them in the morning. It was funny as the draw came out and we got them in the afternoon as well, in the better ball. It went right down to the wire on the last hole. The last nine holes were unbelievable. Five birdies and an eagle and still they kept coming back. To this day, if you talk to Lanny about that particular match, he is not bitter about it, he just still shakes his head in disbelief. 'Do you realise I played those last five holes in five-under and we lost ground?' That was how strong a pairing we were, Bernhard just kept going. He didn't back off. There was no sign of Bernhard backing off, never; even if he was three or four-down, he still put the same routine in, the same time, the same concentration. As a partner, it was really good to have. He would hole the odd chip shot, the odd big putt, it was all good stuff. He gave 110 per cent. For me, he was the best partner I've ever had, by far.

The final match that morning pitched Ballesteros and Olazábal into action against Crenshaw and Stewart. The Spaniards had been a wonderful pairing throughout the first day's play, with Ballesteros in a guiding role as he and the twenty-one-year-old navigated the course. It was on the eighteenth hole of that Saturday session, however, that Olazábal really came into his own. He drove well off the tee but Seve bunkered the second shot. Olazábal then pulled off a marvellous escape to leave the ball five feet from the hole. Crenshaw and Stewart were also making life difficult for themselves and the Spaniards had to get down in two to win the match. Seve blasted his putt and it rolled almost as far to the other side of the hole. Olazábal then had to hole out for the point. He coolly slotted it and was enveloped in a bear hug by his partner.

Ken Brown: We shared houses in those days – I was with Ollie and Tony Jacklin. It was one of the turning points in Ollie's career. He was twenty-one, a bit nervous and playing with his good friend Seve, the man he so admired. It was a tremendous responsibility – we all know how much Seve liked to win. But Ollie holed one putt that week, after Seve had knocked it five feet past when they needed to get down in two, and you thought, 'This chap is young but he's got heart and nerve and is a tigerish competitor'.

Seve Ballesteros: I remember asking him for help to read the putt and he said, 'Be careful, the green is fast, very fast.' And I hit it and it went four, five feet past the hole. And I turned to him and said, 'That's really fast, isn't it!'

So then José had a putt to win the hole and he sank it, so we held on to win the match.

José María Olazábal: Which was just as well, otherwise he would have hanged himself for missing that putt!

Ben Crenshaw: That was a marvellous pairing, and you could see Seve teaching José as they went around the course, telling him what to do and when. And the great thing was the way José not only understood but responded as well.

Going into the afternoon fourballs, Europe held an 8½–3½ lead. It was a crucial session; Europe needed to hold or extend their lead, the Americans needed to claw their way back into proceedings. It might have been cagey, edgy stuff; as it was, both sides went out on the offensive and played some towering golf.

Kite and Strange opened against Faldo and Woosnam. They were America's top pairing yet after five holes they were five down. On one of the world's hardest courses, the European pair were relentless, scoring seven birdies between them on the opening seven holes, to the Americans' two birdies on the sixth and seventh. They went six up at the tenth with another birdie and although Kite and Strange birdied the eleventh and twelfth, Faldo and Woosnam held on for a 5&4 victory.

Bean and Stewart were paired against Darcy and Brand Jnr in the second fourball and they played wonderfully to dispatch the European pair 3&2 before Sutton and Mize finally broke the previously imperious combination of Ballesteros and Olazábal to win 2&1 and hand the initiative back to the home team.

Sandy Lyle and Bernhard Langer were up against Larry Nelson and Lanny Wadkins in the final match of the day. This match also contained some extraordinary golf from both pairs and while the Europeans hung on to win with a nine-under par score, it took until the eighteenth green to secure the point for their team.

Lyle looked to have settled things on the fifteenth when he belted a huge drive, a stunning iron to the green and then slotted home his putt for eagle to give Europe a three-hole lead.

Jack Nicklaus had designed the par fives so that the eleventh green would be extremely difficult to reach in two, while three other holes – the fifth, seventh and fifteenth – were unreachable in less than three, yet their distance didn't seem to faze Lyle in the slightest. 'He plays all my par fives with a driver and a three iron,' said Nicklaus, watching on. 'And all my par fours with a one-iron. You're not supposed to be able to do that. In fact, it's not allowed.'

But for all Lyle's extraordinary ball striking, the Americans fought back and very nearly sealed a half point. First Wadkins hit his sixteenth tee shot to five feet of the pin to win the hole, then landed an amazing shot onto the seventeenth green and slotted his putt to take him and Nelson to one down. The crowd were roaring. All four players hit wonderful solid drives on the eighteenth and then pitched up to the green, but it was Langer, playing last, who stole the show by landing his ball just inches from the hole. The Americans sportingly picked up his ball without hesitation.

Nick Faldo: Again we started poorly on the first morning and were down in all four foursomes matches by the turn. Fortunately Woosie and I got our game back under control and beat Wadkins and Mize on the last green, and Seve and Olazábal did the same against Larry Nelson and Payne Stewart. Two-all at lunch felt like a considerable victory.

That afternoon we did what no British or European team had done before: we won all four matches – a whitewash. It was an unbelievable experience, greatly enhanced by the support of the small band of European fans. There were only some 2,000 of them, but it seemed more like 20,000. They were outnumbered five to one, but by sheer volume it seemed the other way around.

Woosie and I were playing Dan Pohl and Hal Sutton, who got quite cross and kept muttering, 'Is nobody supporting us?' I held Woosie back, so that when we walked onto the green second and waved to the crowd they just erupted.

That round and all the next day everyone played fantastic golf. Woosie and I, it seemed, just took turns in getting birdies, and it was much the same story in other matches and by the time the singles came around we had a huge five-point lead. It should have been plenty, but it nearly wasn't enough, rather like going into the final round of a championship four or five shots ahead, it is very difficult to go further ahead. You inevitably become a bit defensive and the opposition, with nothing to lose, go for everything and narrow the gap.

Tony Jacklin: I never thought I would live to see the day when I would see golf played like that. Muirfield Village was one of the toughest courses in the world. It was pure unadulterated inspiration on the part of both teams. It was fantastic.

Jack Nicklaus: They played beautifully. They beat our rear ends.

It was extraordinary that Strange and Kite finished five under par and yet lost, as did Nelson and Wadkins, who shot an eight-under-par 64.

Tony Jacklin: Bernhard Langer's second shot to the last, the last shot of that day's play, was just incredible. And it was a hugely important point for us because it ensured we went into the final series of singles with a five-point lead . . . and I always knew we would need that.

Nicklaus knew how difficult it would be to overcome the five-point deficit, but he also knew that American players always produced their best during the singles. But there was little room for error; Europe needed just three-and-a-half to retain the cup, four to win it outright.
It was David versus Goliath at the top of the order as Ian Woosnam took on Andy Bean, the American standing a foot taller and five stone heavier than the Welshman and famed as a one-time boxer and former alligator wrestler. But defying all expectations, Woosnam out-drove Bean on every hole. 'Shoot he's strong,' said Bean afterwards. 'It hurts when a little bitty fellow out-drives you.' In the end, however, it was Goliath who conquered David, with Bean's superior play on the short holes the decisive factor in edging ahead one up, which he held to the game's conclusion on the eighteenth green, and lit a fire for Jack Nicklaus' ambitions for his team to stage a mighty comeback.
In order to arrest this resurgence, the pressure was placed on the shoulders of Howard Clark, who was playing Dan Pohl in the second match out. This would prove to be another close encounter with neither player ever able to establish more than a one-hole lead. Pohl pushed ahead at the second green but it would be for the only time that day. He bogeyed the fourth to allow Clark to draw level and then did so again at the fifth to see the Yorkshireman take a one up lead. But just as Clark looked to have stolen a march on his opponent, he was reeled back in. They arrived at the eighteenth all square.

Howard Clark: We had a real battle out there and although I edged ahead a few times, he always managed to get back level. I bogeyed the twelfth and the sixteenth to make it all square just when I thought I was getting the upper hand. By the time we got to the eighteenth the blood was really pumping. I hit a big drive and it went 310 yards and almost ended up in the water. I then got a bit of a lucky break because there were TV cables lying near my ball so I got a free drop and in doing so I got an improved lie. I then hit a really good approach that flew to fourteen feet or so of the hole, while Pohl ended up in a bunker. He conceded soon afterwards and we had another point on the board.

Dan Pohl: It was like drawing teeth out there. I'm just sorry that such a close game had to end in such a fashion.

The third match of the day followed the pattern of its predecessor as Larry Mize and Sam Torrance traded blows over eighteen holes with one never able to break free from the clutches of the other. Mize parred the seventeenth to Torrance's bogey, handing the rookie American a one-hole lead. Whether Mize could handle the pressure of the moment would decide the match. His drive landed close to a hazard and there followed several minutes of deliberation as officials tried to decide whether he should take a penalty or a free drop. In the end, to Mize's chagrin, they decided on the latter. He then sent his subsequent shot into the greenside bunker. Although he was able to chip out and then sink a downhill putt for bogey, Torrance was left with two putts to halve the match.

Sam Torrance: Ryder Cup, Muirfield Village, 1987. The most terrifying putt I've ever stood over. Last hole, one down against Larry Mize and he hooks it into a hazard and I'm down the middle. I had to wait twenty minutes for a ruling and he actually got a drop in the hazard because of line of sight, which I couldn't believe but it's true. But he still had to drop it in the hazard. He just hacked it out and I hit a five-iron to twelve feet short of the pin – as good a shot as I've ever hit under pressure. He ended up forty to fifty feet behind the hole in four, and I'm twelve feet away in two and he holed it, which meant I had to two-putt this twelve-footer up the last green. My hands were shaking more than they ever have and it was within a year of that that I stopped using a short putter. My hands just shook like a leaf and how I got it stone dead I don't know but that was the most terrified I've ever been over a putt.

Europe now only needed two points to retain the cup, two-and-a-half to win it outright.

With the way that Faldo had played on the previous two days when paired with Woosnam, it might have seemed like a foregone conclusion that the next point would be Europe's, but Mark Calcavecchia, having the best season of his career, had other ideas. Like the preceding matches, it was close throughout, but the turning point came on the fourteenth when Calcavecchia edged ahead and then kept a grip on his advantage as they halved the remaining four holes to keep Nicklaus' hopes alive.

The fire in the American resurgence was burning brightly when the fifth singles match was concluded as Payne Stewart emerged victorious over the Spanish rookie, José María Olazábal, who had been enjoying a remarkable debut Ryder Cup before meeting his match in Stewart, who did just enough to edge another thrilling encounter.

Just as Faldo had been expected to win his match against Calcavecchia, so too was Ben Crenshaw expected to do the business against Irishman Eamonn Darcy. The European was playing his eleventh Ryder Cup match, but had the unfortunate record of never having won one. His prospects weren't looking like improving when Crenshaw sank a forty-foot putt on the first to an explosion of applause from the crowd.

Eamonn Darcy: I remember walking to the first tee for my singles with Ben Crenshaw and there was this big fat guy in the gallery, he was frothing at the mouth and screaming,

'Kill him, Ben, kill him. No prisoners today.' I thought to myself, 'Here we go.' It was going to be that kind of day.

Darcy got into his stride at the fourth, however, winning it with a birdie and then claiming the next three holes for a three-hole lead at the turn. Crenshaw then roared back, winning the twelfth, thirteenth, fourteenth and sixteenth to go one up, but he surrendered the initiative at the seventeenth when he took two shots to exit a bunker and Darcy held his nerve to win the hole.

Nick Faldo: All those who had played so well over the two days suddenly ran out of inspiration. The final push to victory became a struggle against the tide. Sam Torrance and Howard Clark, who hadn't played since the first morning, were the only Europeans in the first seven matches to add to the overnight total. Howard beat Dan Pohl and Sam halved with Larry Mize. Of the rest, only Seve looked to be in control of his match with Curtis Strange.

Eamonn Darcy had been a couple up on Ben Crenshaw, but came to the seventeenth one down. Crenshaw made a mess of seventeen and then drove into the ditch at eighteen. Darcy had an awful downhill putt to win. If he had missed on that green, there was no way the ball would have stopped, and he would have been further away than before.

Ben Crenshaw: Oh gosh, Muirfield Village . . . Eamonn Darcy and I have had so many chuckles over that match. It was one of the most remarkable things that's ever happened to me in golf. Though I had hit my approach shot on the sixth very wide of the target, I was so angry at myself for three-putting that I snapped my club. As I walked off the green I just . . . you know, there were times when I hit my implements much harder, but on this occasion it just happened to snap. I had to putt with my one-iron or sand wedge for the rest of the match.

I'll never forget it. A couple of holes later, we went to a par three and I walked up the steps to the tee, only to be confronted by Jack, who enquired, 'How's it going?' And I said quietly, almost under my breath, 'Not so good.' 'What do you mean?' said Jack. And I somehow managed to tell him, 'I broke my putter back there on . . .'

Before I could finish my sentence, Jack said, 'You did what?'

'I broke my putter, back on the number six.'

'Well, the way things are going for us,' he said, 'I might be tempted to break a few clubs myself.'

Eamonn Darcy: I wasn't aware that Ben had broken his putter. I thought he was putting with his one-iron because the greens were so quick and he had missed a couple on the front nine.

All square on the eighteenth, Crenshaw had a disastrous drive that saw his tee shot land in the water. After his penalty drop he hit his third into a bunker. He escaped and then rolled a ten-foot putt home. Darcy stood over his putt, pin high but only four feet away.

Eamonn Darcy: I was nervous playing the bunker shot at eighteen, but my hands were rock steady. I kept telling myself I could get the ball close to the pin. Mind you, that was the toughest putt I ever faced.

All I could think was, 'Don't fucking miss . . .'

It was the hardest putt I ever stood over. It was all downhill and oh, so fast. I thought I could hole it, but if I didn't, I didn't think I would be able to get the one back; there would be just nothing to stop it. There was a little break from the left and I just kissed it, and in it went.

Tony Jacklin: When old Darce sank that putt . . . well, what can you say? It was a dream come true for us – a victory that we felt could change the entire course of world golf. I could not have been happier for anyone than I was for Eamonn Darcy at Muirfield Village. I cannot tell you what courage it took for him to hole that putt and what it means to all of us.

Ben Crenshaw: Eamonn played so well that day. And he killed me off at the end by making a beautiful birdie at seventeen. Then he got what he needed on eighteen, getting up and down from the greenside bunker for a winning par after I had driven into the water. Eamonn deserved it. He made a beautiful putt coming down the hill. But I'll always remember the match for the way the Europeans, Ian Woosnam, Sandy Lyle, all of them, handled the course so beautifully. They played as if they'd known it all their lives.

Scott Simpson was in action against José Rivero and while neither man particularly sparkled, it was the American who played the steadier golf and was deserving of his 2&1 win.

All eyes turned to the tussle going on between Larry Nelson and Bernhard Langer. Nelson was one up at the turn and then moved further ahead when he won the tenth and eleventh. Langer showed his appetite for the challenge, however, and counter-punched by winning the next three holes to go all square on the fifteenth.

They halved the sixteenth and seventeenth to take the match to the eighteenth where it was apparent that all Europe needed at that stage was a half point to retain the cup. Even though Tom Kite was in the process of defeating Sandy Lyle 3&2, Ballesteros, playing behind, was dormie two against Curtis Strange and was guaranteed at least half a point (he would win 2&1).

Both men drove well and then hit two spectacular approach shots to the green. Nelson's ball finished two feet from the hole, Langer's less than that. The German glanced at the American and after a brief pause Nelson bent and picked up both balls. Nelson's gesture was appropriate for the moment and in picking up Langer's ball, the Ryder Cup was won by Europe for the first time on American soil.

Bernhard Langer: It is funny how the draw can keep throwing two players together, and that week I played against Larry Nelson three times. My singles match with him was very tight. It seesawed back and forth, but there was never much in it. We came to the eighteenth, level. We each had a putt of two-and-a-half feet and we just looked at each other and said, 'Good, good?' shook hands and walked off. Larry and I are friends and I think we both felt, 'I don't want to miss this putt but equally I don't really want you to miss yours.' While I did not realise it at the time, that half point took us to fourteen points and meant that, even if we had not yet won, we could not lose.

It is all part of the mystique of the Ryder Cup. Even in the most competitive situation imaginable you don't want your opponent – who may well be a friend – to lose a match by missing a putt and having to live with that for the rest of his career. I always wanted to beat them fair and square and not in controversial circumstances.

Larry Nelson: Bernhard and I had played seventeen really good holes – back and forth, back and forth. On the last green we had the same length of putt, a couple of feet, and we just kind of looked at each other and said, 'Good, good?' It was not like they were four-footers. Jack Nicklaus said something to me later about how I should have made Bernhard putt it, but I replied, 'Jack, I remember you giving Jacklin a putt on the last hole in 1969. I thought we were out here to have a good time.' I don't think there was any comment.

Tony Jacklin: I've never known or experienced such pressure. I was glad I wasn't playing, to be honest. I doubt I could have coped as well as my team did, swapping birdies and eagles with the Americans and in the end breaking their hearts. The standard of golf throughout was incredibly high – Muirfield Village is not an easy course – but we tamed it hitting longer tee shots, crisper irons than the opposition and putting well, not least down the closing stretch. Eight of the twelve games on the tense last day came to the eighteenth and we never lost the hole once. That used to be what we expected from the Americans. We didn't win all of those eight games, but the points we lost were not lost on the last.

Eamonn Darcy: The honour of holing the winning putt went to Seve, bless him, but he always said that it was my putt that really secured the famous victory.

   The pressure was immense and not just because the Ryder Cup was on the line. I had been four up against Crenshaw, who was playing with a broken putter. I would have been crucified if I had let the American off the hook.

Seve Ballesteros: I confronted Curtis Strange again in the singles. It was a charged, tense

Seve Ballesteros and Tony Jacklin celebrate Europe's win. *Getty Images*

atmosphere. At the tenth, Strange hit his third stroke out of turn and I had to ask the umpires to warn him, although I didn't ask for the redress within my rights. After two more holes he'd reduced my lead from two holes to one. I looked at the scoreboard and realised I couldn't afford any loss of concentration: the way things were going my game was crucial. We had to forget any idea that the lead we'd built up over the first two days would give us a comfortable victory. That was wishful thinking.

At the seventeenth I learned that Langer and Nelson were level at the last hole. As I was two up with two holes to play, if Bernhard drew his game – something I knew might happen – I only had to beat Curtis for Europe to triumph. My second shot was an eight-iron which left the ball in the centre of the green, a good seven metres from the pin. Strange could only make a par and my putt left the ball half a metre from the hole. I had the game in the bag. In the meantime Langer had tied with Nelson in very strange circumstances. Each man conceded a putt for the draw. The agreement benefited us more than it did them, since it was in the Americans' interest to play to the last shot to win the point.

Curtis Strange: My singles match decided it. I knew I was playing Seve when the draw came out Saturday night. That was fine, because I was playing really well [Strange would win the US Open in each of the next two years]. But he chipped in on me on the first hole for the second time in that cup! And you know what he did this time? We were right beside each other, both in a greenside bunker, and he questioned who was away. He started his stuff on the first hole! He knew damn well that he was away, and he knew also that he wanted to go first, but he was just screwing around. And then he made it. So I was one down after one.

José María Olazábal dances on the eighteenth green. *Getty Images*

I didn't play well, and Seve played okay. I got way down, three-down I think, and came back – and if I'd have made any putts at all, I could have really gotten back into the match. I was two down on seventeen, and we were getting beaten pretty well, so at this point it was a matter of time. I think I lost 2&1, and it just so happened that this was the match that decided the points.

Seve Ballesteros: For my part, I holed my putt and immediately discovered that that shot had given us fourteen-and-a-half points. My putt at the eighteenth to win the Open in 1984 is undoubtedly the happiest stroke I've hit in my whole career, but this shot to win the Ryder Cup on the Americans' home soil isn't far behind. The great pleasure I derived from winning the Ryder Cup again was complemented by my pleasure of defeating Strange, then considered by the Americans to be the best player in the world. A few moments after my ball went in the hole, Tony Jacklin, Nick Faldo and I hugged each other on the edge of the green. The three of us cried. We were so excited!

Jack Nicklaus: I have always had wonderful respect for Seve's ability, how he played the game, and the flair he brought to the sport. It was his creativity, his imagination and his desire to compete that made him so popular not only in Europe but throughout American galleries too. He was a great entertainer. No matter the golf that particular day, you always knew you were going to be entertained. Seve's enthusiasm was just unmatched by anybody I think that ever played the game. Seve was, without argument, a terrific player – his record speaks for itself – but more important was his influence on the game especially throughout Europe.

Through the years, his involvement with the Ryder Cup, as both a player and captain, served to further elevate the stature of the matches. He was probably the most passionate Ryder Cup player we've ever had. I think his teammates always rallied around him and that passion of his. He was Europe's emotional and spiritual leader, the heart and soul of their team. The Ryder Cup was something that was very, very special to Seve and Seve was very special to us.

Seve Ballesteros: In 1987 all the stars in the team were on best form. Nick Faldo was the reigning Open Champion and Sandy Lyle, Bernhard Langer, José María Olazábal, Ian Woosnam and I were playing our best golf; our other teammates were at the height of their powers too. As usually happens, it was the latter – Eamonn Darcy, Howard Clark, Sam Torrance and Gordon Brand Jnr – who gained the vital points, when it seemed that all the effort we'd put in on the first two days had been for nothing. That was a true testament to the team we had – everyone played a part.

Nick Faldo: Finally we had done something no British or European team had done in the Ryder Cup before – we had won in America. All wins are special in their way, and certainly I will take my victories in the Majors, each and every one of them to the grave. But for sheer euphoria, that win in America was the best.

Jack Nicklaus: The eighteenth was the difference. That's where I would have expected to win. But our guys weren't quite as tough as the Europeans. The problem was really with the American golf system. Because it was so difficult to win, our guys rarely got in position to contend down the stretch. Instead of being aggressive, they developed a percentage type of style. On the European Tour, there was less competition, which put players in contention more often and made them better, more aggressive finishers.

Captaining a US team to its first loss at home has to be my Ryder Cup low. Looking back, though, I'm glad I was in that position, because I wouldn't have wanted anyone else to go through all the criticism and anger and second-guessing that came after that match.

When Ballesteros concluded his match on the seventeenth he punched the air repeatedly while Jacklin wept with his team and Olazábal danced on the green. History had been made.

Gordon Brand Jnr: I remember Olazábal started dancing on the green after we won. Some people thought he should rein it in a bit, but Jack came on the green and said, 'Don't worry lads, don't worry about the green. I'm going to dig it up on Monday.'

Curtis Strange: The dancing was OK. I never took offence to any of that type of stuff after play. They were celebrating. They had all the right in the world to be excited. All you can do is shake their hands and applaud them, because they came over to America and beat us. It was a hell of a win.

Bernard Gallacher: What wonderful imagery. The thing about that moment, though, is that José María would probably have done the dance, win or lose. He was so full of the joys of life.

Payne Stewart: Muirfield was not nice. And Jack Nicklaus let us know about it when we finished. We had a little meeting before the dinner we had to go to that night, and Jack just wore us out. He told us, 'You guys just don't know how to win. How many matches were we leading going into eighteen and didn't win them? Look at you, Payne Stewart. You make all this money on tour, but how many tournaments have you won? Why don't you win more?' He said, 'You guys need to learn how to win or you're going to continue getting beaten in this thing.' There wasn't any sugarcoating it. I'll tell you, that speech was good for me.

Jack Nicklaus: Early on, our team had difficulty winning the tight matches. I got after them in our team meeting, saying, 'Guys, we have got to find a way to win the eighteenth hole.' In retrospect, I might have been too hard on them. I added to the pressure and made them tighter. We won the eighteenth hole in only one match, and we lost the Ryder Cup on American soil for the first time. Reflecting on that time helped me to refine my philosophy about Ryder Cup captaincy.

Tony Jacklin: Winning in 1985 was enormous, then it was exceeded. There's nothing like the first time for anything, and in 1987 we won for the first time on American soil, and nothing can top that. It was the sweetest moment of all.

TWENTY-EIGHT

1989
The Belfry. Sutton Coldfield, England
(USA 14, EUR 14)

After the historic events at Muirfield Village, there was an air of feverish anticipation among European golf fans as the Ryder Cup returned to the Belfry in 1989, and an equally determined approach from the Americans to re-establish their traditional dominance.

The two captains approached the matches with contrasting experience on their CVs. This was Tony Jacklin's fourth and final outing at the helm of the European mission and he had a winning mindset and momentum in the team. Raymond Floyd, meanwhile, was new to the captaincy but as a player he had competed on six different Ryder Cup teams. Although Floyd's personal record wasn't particularly impressive, he was a man on a mission to restore both American pride but also to wrest the cup back to what many felt was its rightful home on the other side of the Atlantic. He was bullish in his approach, announcing his team at the opening ceremony as Ben Hogan had done back in the 60s as 'the best twelve golfers in the world.' It was a remark viewed rather scathingly, particularly by Jacklin who responded afterwards that, 'I suppose that this means Seve is the thirteenth best player on earth, does it?'

Sam Torrance: That was a bit of a faux pas. We just loved it. Carry on, say what you like. It worked for us, not against us.

It was hyperbole from Floyd, but he was looking to instil confidence in his players, and his team, it couldn't be denied, was full of quality. The rules surrounding selection of the US team had been altered slightly that year, allowing the captain one pick, which would be extended to two if the US PGA champion had already qualified for the team. When Payne Stewart duly won the championship while riding high in the official money list, Floyd was able to pick Tom Watson and Lanny Wadkins to join his team alongside Stewart, Paul Azinger, Mark Calcavecchia, Tom Kite, Mark O'Meara, Curtis Strange, and rookies Chip Beck, Fred Couples, Ken Green and Mark McCumber.

Tony Jacklin: I suppose my reason for wanting to take on the captaincy again, even if it was only partly conscious at the time, was, 'What's left to do? If we won, which I fully expected us to, it would be three in a row, and if we lost, then that was likely to be a signal some new blood was needed anyway. Probably with that partly in mind, I was determined we were going to make it one to remember.

I knew that playing at home would give us a big advantage and I knew a loud home support would give us a big advantage. But I also knew that Floyd would whip his players up for the match, that he would be calling on them to re-establish American dominance; but most of all I knew that they would come into the matches with nothing to lose and everything to gain – and that's a dangerous opposition to come up against.

Curtis Strange: Floyd was a great captain, but he was intense. His eyes were like lasers, when he switched them on he only had to give you that slow burn and bits of you started to melt very quickly.

Jacklin's European team, meanwhile, was top class and packed with Ryder Cup experience with only one rookie in twenty-five-year-old Ronan Rafferty. The rest of the team consisted of Seve Ballesteros, Gordon Brand Jnr, José María Cañizares, Howard Clark, Nick Faldo, Mark James, Bernhard Langer, Christy O'Connor Jnr, José María Olazábal, Sam Torrance and Ian Woosnam. Jacklin had originally selected Sandy Lyle in the team but the Scotsman withdrew his availability because his confidence was shot after an indifferent year on the course and he didn't want to let down his teammates. In his stead, Jacklin called up O'Connor, a player with whom he didn't have the best of relations, the two having fallen out after Jacklin overlooked O'Connor for the 1985 and 1987 Ryder Cups.

Raymond Floyd: From our point of view, we were pretty happy to see Sandy Lyle not in the team. We all thought that, no matter how he was playing, Sandy would have brought something to the European team. But, as it turned out, Christy O'Connor Jnr wasn't a bad replacement.

Christy O'Connor Jnr: Tony and I had an awkward relationship for a few years before that when I didn't make the team in '85 or '87. It was suggested in '89 that he had put me in the team to clear his conscience. Anybody who says that doesn't know Tony Jacklin. We had our differences but he was a great captain and he put the team before any personal feelings he may have had with me.

Sandy Lyle made himself unavailable because he had lost confidence in his game, so Tony picked me in his place. Some things that were said and written suggested I wouldn't come up to scratch, but I felt that was complete rubbish. I felt I was worthy of a place and that I was in on merit. It annoyed me that some people had the nerve to question Tony's decision. I knew there were those that wanted Sandy on the team but Sandy made his decision and it was a very brave one.

Sandy Lyle: I had given myself a couple of later events in America to see if I could sort of turn my golf around. I was really, really disappointed in my golf and I just couldn't face playing so badly in front of my home crowd. So I said to Jacklin, 'Tony, this is the toughest phone call I'm ever going to make and I would like to pull myself out of a captain's choice.' But I knew in the back of my mind that Christy had been playing well all that year, very consistently, so he would be a great plus for the team.

Sam Torrance: It's hard not to feel sorry for Sandy. He's a great big lump of a lad, and just as soft and as nice as they come. You couldn't meet a nicer bloke. Yet you felt sometimes like kicking him in the arse. Put him into gear. He had so much talent. I don't know where he went wrong. I really don't. The best thing you can say about him is that he is exactly the same today as he was when he was winning Majors. Not many people would have handled the ups and the downs as well as he has.

Christy O'Connor Jnr: We all flew to the Belfry for a team meeting on the Monday morning. It was so strange to see us all together – the most famous names in European golf and there we all were sitting down together and chatting.

It was a funny situation to me. Week in and week out we were all in competition. We were trying to outdo one another and win as individuals. Now here we all were mingling as one big team, some guys who we thought did not get on were now the best of friends.

Gordon Brand Jnr: I remember waking up one morning and looking out of the hotel window and seeing the crowds. It hit you like a sledgehammer then – you realise what a big thing the Ryder Cup is. The adrenaline was fairly pumping then.

Mark James: The whole thing had just become an awful lot bigger. The players were feted a bit more, the press interest was enormous and the crowds were a lot bigger.

Tom Kite: There's no way of getting used to it. For every eight Major championships, you get one Ryder Cup.

Gordon Brand Jnr: The spectators were clapping us all the way from the locker room to the tee. You felt two up before you had even started.

There was only a light breath of air on a crisp but bright Friday morning when the match got underway. Both pairings in the opening foursomes were burdened with the responsibility of kick-starting the cup challenge for their respective teams; for the US it was Tom Kite and Curtis Strange who bore the weight of expectation, while for Europe it was Nick Faldo and Ian Woosnam.

After their successful pairing at Muirfield Village, Faldo and Woosnam looked as if they were continuing from where they had left off when they were two up after just three holes, a lead that they still held when they stood on the seventh tee. By the time they were standing on the eleventh tee, however, they were two down after a stunning comeback from the US. The Europeans dug in and by the time they were at the eighteenth the score was all square. As they arrived on the green Kite was left with a nine-foot putt which he sank to rapturous applause, followed by a dance of triumph. Woosnam had a six-footer to halve the match and the little Welshman held his nerve to sink it to deafening roars from the crowd. If this opening foursome was anything to go by, the 1989 Ryder Cup would go down to the wire.

The pattern was repeated for much of the day. The remaining morning foursomes were contested by Howard Clark and Mark James against Payne Stewart and Lanny Wadkins (the Americans edged it by a hole), Seve Ballesteros and José María Olazábal against Chip Beck and Tom Watson (halved after a storming comeback from the Americans who had been three down on the eleventh tee), and Bernhard Langer and Ronan Rafferty against Mark Calcavecchia and Ken Green (won 2&1 by the Americans), giving Floyd's team a 3–1 lunchtime lead.

Howard Clark: Though I didn't play badly I never really gelled in a foursome partnership.

Raymond Floyd and Tony Jacklin.

It was one of the most difficult if not the most difficult forms of golf to play. You can end up going four or five holes without having a putt, or go three or four holes without having a chip shot, things like that. So it's difficult to get into your stride. In Ryder Cup foursomes everybody would go back and discuss shots which became a bit tiresome and tedious. You know, we wanted to get on with it but the captains wanted us to be together to make decisions. But what decisions have you got to make? To take a driver out? But it's the next shot that is the decision and if you are waiting for the guy who has hit the drive 280 yards down the fairway then you are out of your stride.

Christy O'Connor Jnr: Tony didn't play me in the Friday foursomes and fourballs, but he played Ronan in the morning foursomes with Bernhard Langer. Their match was actually the turning point in the morning play. After the first three games we trailed the Americans 2–1 with Ronan and Bernhard the last match on the course. If they won then it would be all level going into the afternoon play. But they lost 2&1 to Mark Calcavecchia and Ken Green. Europe trailed 3–1. However, the Americans were in for quite a shock later in the day.

Raymond Floyd stuck to his pre-match assertions that every one of his players would be given a chance to play and threw in fresh pairings for the afternoon fourballs. Jacklin was more pragmatic, making only minor changes by swapping Langer and Rafferty for Gordon Brand Jnr and Sam Torrance. It would prove to be a major tactical error by Floyd to break up his morning pairings so completely.

The new European combination repaid Jacklin immediately by defeating Paul Azinger and Curtis Strange thanks to a nerveless six-foot putt on the eighteenth from Brand Jnr.

Ballesteros and Olazábal then teamed up to annihilate Tom Watson and Mark O'Meara, the 6&5 defeat the heaviest ever suffered by Watson in his Ryder Cup career, and the point secured by the Spanish duo levelled the score at 3–3.

The momentum from this continued for the Europeans as Clark and James made amends for their morning loss by defeating Fred Couples and Lanny Wadkins 3&2, and Faldo and Woosnam beat Mark Calcavecchia and Mark McCumber two up to give Europe a 5–3 lead at the end of the day.

'I wasn't terribly disappointed after the morning session because I thought we finished it unlucky to be 3–1 down,' said Jacklin that evening, 'and I can't say I was particularly surprised at what happened in the afternoon because nothing that these guys do surprises me anymore.'

Seve Ballesteros: The crowds were great but we started the tournament badly, losing in the morning, but we recovered in the afternoon. Chema [Olazábal] and I crushed Watson and Mark O'Meara 6&5. I remember that I finished them off with one of my best runs in the Ryder Cup – an eagle at the tenth followed by three birdies. When we got together at the end of the day, we all reckoned our 4–0 victory in the afternoon's fourballs had been the best possible response to the provocative declaration made by Raymond Floyd, the new USA captain. In the opening ceremony, still bleeding from the previous defeats, Floyd had said his team comprised 'the best twelve players in the world'. Jacklin reacted brilliantly and asked, 'Where does that leave Seve, thirteenth? What about Nick Faldo? And Bernhard Langer? And while we're about it, what about Greg Norman?'

With so much Ryder Cup experience in his locker, Jacklin was well versed in how to keep his team motivated, happy and focused. Breakfast, for example, was a focal point. Every player was instructed to turn up for breakfast even if they weren't involved in the morning session; the team would meet and collectively focus on the task ahead of them, the non-playing members there in support of their teammates who were going out to do battle.

Christy O'Connor Jnr: I never realised just how good a feeling it would be to be part of

Payne Stewart and Curtis Strange. *Getty Images*

that Ryder Cup. Jacklin was fabulous. Every day he made everyone feel better by what he said and how he said it. It takes a special kind of man to be able to do that at 6:30 in the morning but Jacko did it every time. Those breakfasts set the mood for the rest of the day. No matter what you were to do that day, Tony made you feel part of the whole thing. It was terribly uplifting and very exciting. Jeez, it was exciting.

Tony paired me with Ronan Rafferty on the Saturday despite pairing me with José María Cañizares in a practise session where we had beaten Seve and Olazábal. Ronan was a very talented golfer but I found it very difficult to gel with him. Generally I would be a laid-back and easy-going character. When you don't know someone particularly well it is difficult to make a judgement but I found with Ronan that I always needed to please him. That is the best way I can explain our not gelling. We went out against Mark Calcavecchia and Ken Green, and Ronan and I lost pretty badly.

Mark Calcavecchia: Ken and I played well. We made a couple of mistakes but by then we were five up and if you're going to do something wrong then that is a good time to do it. Really Ronan putted poorly, missing from five feet at the ninth and four feet at both the eleventh and twelfth. Three misses in four holes. If he had made those putts then it would have been a different game.

Ronan Rafferty: I let Christy down on the greens. It was typically poor foursomes golf. I would leave Christy five feet short and he would miss. Then he'd leave me short and I'd miss. Apart from that we combined well!

The Irish pair lost 3&2, but Nick Faldo and Ian Woosnam extended their winning Ryder Cup run as a pair to seven wins from seven matches as they saw off the challenge of Lanny Wadkins and Payne Stewart. The Americans had their own wonder pair, however, as Chip Beck and Paul Azinger played supremely to shoot six under par in a 4&3 dismantling of the Scottish duo of Gordon Brand Jnr and Sam Torrance. The two-point lead that Europe had established on Friday was in danger of being clawed back by the US. All eyes turned to the match between Tom Kite and Curtis Strange and the Spanish double act of Ballesteros and Olazábal. After seven holes the Spaniards were three up, but they then bogeyed the eighth and ninth and the match opened up once more. Par followed par until the pairings stood on the eighteenth. Olazábal escaped the greenside bunker to give Seve a tricky seven-foot putt to halve the hole and give Europe the point. Even with the fringes of the green packed with spectators, you could have heard a pin drop – or, indeed, Seve's putt, as it found its way home, and the crowd erupted in celebration.

Seve Ballesteros: We knew we had to win because that last point meant a lot, not just because it was another point but because of the boost we knew it would give the whole team psychologically. I just had to sink that putt, I just had to.

If Europe could repeat their heroics from the previous afternoon, the cup would be all but won. But Floyd and his team were not about to lie down and give up the fight.

The opening fourball was between Faldo and Woosnam and Azinger and Beck and all four played golf from the gods in one of the highest quality fourball matches in the history of the tournament. Birdie followed birdie and by the eleventh the fourball was eleven under par, with the Americans one hole ahead. There was a miniscule blip to the quality on show when the twelfth was halved with two threes, but the standard was restored when the fourteenth was halved with two birdies, before Azinger stole the show on the fifteenth with two monstrous driver shots followed by a forty-foot putt to birdie and win the hole. When the sixteenth and seventeenth were halved once more (the latter with two more birdies), it was over and one of Europe's dream teams had at last been vanquished.

Ian Woosnam: It was a good game, we all played well. They just played a bit better.

Nick Faldo: Woosie and I continued our successful partnership in 1989, until running into Chip Beck and Paul Azinger in the second series of fourballs. We didn't play too badly, but they were thirteen under par for seventeen holes. I remember one shot by Azinger. We were on the front of the fifteenth green, the par-five, in two. The approach is blocked by the bunkers that run out in front of the green from the left, and Azinger, who was a natural fader of the ball, needed to draw it about thirty yards in the air if he was to find the green. He not only did that, but put it by the pin to win with an eagle to our birdie. Sometimes a single shot can decide the match, and I think that was one of those occasions.

Tony Jacklin: Paul Azinger was a constant thorn in my side. He was the best American player in my years as captain. Match play was in his blood. The better the player Azinger went up against, the better he played. Even Seve Ballesteros, who could intimidate almost anyone, couldn't faze Paul.

Paul Azinger: Once you get on the first tee and you hit the first shot and you're walking down the fairway . . . it's just you against them, and you kind of put behind you the importance of it and the magnitude of what it means. I was just playing those two guys over there. That's the way I looked at it.

The US comeback was on and the momentum seemed well and truly with them as Kite and McCumber edged Canizares and Langer 2&1 to take the overall score to 7–7. But the Spanish pair of Ballesteros and Olazábal then came to the rescue once more when they cruised to a 4&2 victory over Calcavecchia and Green.

The final match of the day saw Clark and James in a pitched battle with Stewart and Strange. The lead swung back and forth until they were all square after sixteen holes. After the Americans both fluffed their drives into the trees on the right of the seventeenth fairway, James held his nerve to sink a birdie and claim the hole.

Raymond Floyd: Pressure will affect the greatest player in the world at times. Sometimes it has a good effect, sometimes a bad one. They were very poor shots. What more can you say?

The European pair then played a couple of exceptional approach shots on eighteen to make the green, which were mirrored by their American counterparts. The hole was halved in fours and Europe had the point that re-established their two-point lead going into the singles.

Seve Ballesteros: We had no difficulty beating Mark Calcavecchia and Ken Green in the fourballs, but the big victory for Europe that afternoon was Mark James and Howard Clark over Curtis Strange and Payne Stewart. Mark and James recovered from one down with three holes to play. Poor Curtis, the world's best player in the Americans' book, had drawn his first game and lost his next three at the final hole.

The beautiful weather that had bathed the Belfry all week continued on the Sunday as the final showdown for the cup commenced.

Ballesteros and Azinger got things underway and it looked at first that Seve might stroll away with it when he birdied two of the first four holes and took an early lead, but Azinger battled back to win four of the remaining five holes on the front nine. By fourteen they were all square, but Azinger then won the fifteen to go one up. Coming to the eighteenth, it looked as if Azinger had surrendered the initiative to Ballesteros when he sent his tee shot into the drink. But Seve followed him into the water and they ended up halving the hole in fives and, crucially, handing the first point of the day to the US.

Paul Azinger: I never set out to be controversial or anything like that. I was just passionate, like everybody else. When I played Seve, somehow I was never nervous. I was always just hyped and motivated. You know, we're both very patriotic, and occasionally we had run-ins.

Curtis Strange: Paul and Seve got a little bit of press for having some confrontations on the golf course. By the 1987 matches I'd come to realise that that's what you have to deal with when you play Seve. And so I just didn't mess with it. And that's mainly what I told Paul Azinger when he played him in 1989: 'Just don't mess with him.' But Paul is even more outspoken than I am. He wasn't any more inspirational or enthusiastic about the Ryder Cup than many players. He was just more vocal.

At that point the scoreboard showed virtually nothing but red. Kite had demolished Clark 8&7. Beck vanquished Langer 3&2 and the two-point advantage that Europe had taken into the singles had been eradicated.

Howard Clark: Mark James and myself beat Strange and Stewart on that Saturday evening but it took over six hours to play, and you know, it wiped me out for the next day for the singles – and Tom Kite went on to record the largest winning margin in Ryder Cup history over me. I wasn't so bad when I was playing with somebody, there was a bit of confidence there, there was a bit of back-up, but on my own I was very fragile.

The Americans had now won three matches, led in four, trailed in one and stood even in four. 'It looked like our side might overwhelm Europe,' said Floyd later.

José María Olazábal and Payne Stewart were going at it hammer and tongs, with the lead shifting back and forth, but with there only ever being a hole in it either way. Stewart looked to have stolen a march on his opponent when he birdied fifteen, but Olazábal pulled it back to all square with a birdie on seventeen. Stewart's tee shot on the eighteenth hit water and although he courageously decided to hit it out from beneath the waterline, he took three attempts to pitch it back into the grass. Olazábal had made no such error and with his ball safely placed on the fairway, Stewart conceded the hole and the match.

The encounter between Ronan Rafferty and Mark Calcavecchia followed a very similar script. Rafferty had endured something of a baptism of fire in his debut Ryder Cup and had so far returned zero points for his team, but he held his own against the reigning Open champion and they were all square when they stepped up to the eighteenth tee. Astonishingly, Calcavecchia became the second '89 Major winner to fail to carry his tee shot over the water that day. Rafferty, meanwhile, had mirrored Olazábal and was safely on the fairway. Calcavecchia realised the writing was on the wall and conceded the hole and the match point to Europe.

Ronan Rafferty: It was an incredible day. It was like walking up the eighteenth at the Open at every hole. I'd never experienced anything like it before.

Mark James made a better fist of things when he took on Mark O'Meara, and although O'Meara took an early lead, James was two up at the turn and kept his foot on the throttle to close out a 3&2 victory on the sixteenth green.

Tony Jacklin: Mark was exactly the sort of player you wanted on your team when it was match play and the going was tough.

Having had his credentials for making the team questioned by a number of pundits and former players in the build-up to the tournament, Christy O'Connor Jnr's confidence might have been in a fragile state as he took on Fred Couples. The Americans would have certainly hoped that that would be the case and Couples was sent out with clear instructions that he should target the Irishman for a crucial point for his team. As it transpired, however, the criticism that O'Connor had endured ultimately served to inspire him.

Christy O'Connor Jnr: Going into the singles we were 9–7 in front. Jacklin put Seve, Bernhard and Ollie out as the first three. The thinking was that if they could get off to a solid start, Europe would be almost home and hosed. However, if things didn't go to plan then he put Ian Woosnam, Nick Faldo and Sam Torrance as anchors in the last three. I was due out in the seventh match against the then world number one Fred Couples.

Amazingly Seve and Bernhard were beaten. Paul Azinger beat Ballesteros on the last hole and Chip Beck had a surprisingly comfortable 3&2 win over Langer. The sides were level again at 9–9. Olazábal steadied the ship once more by beating Payne Stewart on the final hole and we went two points clear again after Ronan Rafferty won. Ronan took out a great scalp in Mark Calcavecchia after Calc drove into water on the last hole.

Seve was wonderful with me all week, but especially before I went out for the singles. He said he was sure I would win and I could tell that he meant it. That gave me a great boost.

They were all square at the turn before Couples took a one hole lead on the tenth. O'Connor produced a stunning wedge approach on sixteen to make birdie and even the score again, which is where it remained as they reached the final hole. O'Connor hit a decent shot to the fairway which was then eclipsed by a monstrous drive from Couples that left the American an easy eight-iron shot to the green. O'Connor looked to be in trouble but he unleashed a spectacular two-iron shot that landed just four feet from the pin. It was the shot of the week.

In the face of such a dazzling piece of play, the pressure was firmly on Couples – and he was unable to deal with it. He sliced his second horribly and it landed in a bunker. After his drive, his third shot should have been a putt for birdie, but instead it was another approach shot. He landed it six feet from the hole and needed to sink his next shot for par, but he failed to do so. O'Connor was left with two shots for the match, but Couples didn't let him make either, conceding the hole instead.

Tony Jacklin: The definitive moment of the whole competition, in the end, was Christy O'Connor Jnr beating Fred Couples. Freddie's a good fellow, but I'm telling you I saw it all coming. Or at least I saw something coming. On the seventeenth green I thought I saw the slightest hiccup of tension affect Freddie's stroke. He always has this kind of shrugging loose air to him, but there was no relaxation in that stroke. I told Christy this as we walked to the next tee. 'Stay focused,' I told him. 'I don't think he's quite right. Just get it on the green. Couples will choke.' I knew a bit about Freddie and I'd seen him fold like that before. 'He just doesn't react well to pressure,' I said to Christy. 'He can't handle it.'

Christy O'Connor Jnr: I'd felt terrible at breakfast that morning. I felt the pressure it put on me was too much.

Tony Jacklin was brilliant on the final hole. He said on the eighteenth tee if I put the pressure on, Fred wouldn't be able to take it.

I was miles behind him after the tee shots, but Jacko didn't lose faith. 'Put it on the green,' he said. 'I have a feeling something will happen.'

I played the shot of my life from 235 yards to finish four foot from the hole. You could say I did put it on the green and something did happen.

Tony Jacklin: The eighteenth at the Belfry is a long brute of a par-four, with water curving in and out all down the left side. Only the longest hitters can carry it far enough to cut off a big chunk of the hole, and Christy wasn't that long. So he hit his drive, a decent enough shot, but he was left with a long approach. Freddie got up on the tee and pulled the shit out of it, but he's such a long hitter that he actually carried his ball out onto this little peninsula nobody in their right mind would ever aim at, especially under that kind of pressure. But he was dry and now he only had an eight-iron to the green. I was beside myself, because this was a key moment in the cup; my guy's got a two-iron in his hands and the other guy's got an eight-iron. But I was walking the fairway with Christy, and something inside me still wasn't convinced Freddie was steady.

Bernard Gallacher: Christy was miles behind Couples facing a shot to the eighteenth green, but then he unleashed the perfect two-iron to within a few feet of the hole to secure his win. Pure magic.

Tony Jacklin: He struck that two-iron so damn pure I wonder if he even felt the contact. It flew to the green and stopped four feet from the hole. Freddie was rattled something awful, because he hit the worst-looking eight-iron that bailed way right of the hole. The rest was history.

Christy O'Connor Jnr: I remember looking up to the sky with my arms outstretched and tears ran down my face. It was unforgettable; the greatest and most emotional moment of my professional life.

Tony Jacklin: It was a massively important point, given that, surprisingly, some of our big artillery didn't play their best that day. Christy and Freddie shook hands and that was that. We'd won it again. Through a tie, yes, but the cup was still ours.

Sandy Lyle: I cheered as loudly as any other spectator in the land when Christy edged out Fred in that thriller. I get a lump in my throat when I think about it now. It was a great memory for him, taking the chance to do it. Couples was a strong player and was really hard to beat, on any course, short or long. It was a great one-hole win for him. Christy loved the moment and it was great to see that. Unfortunately, he has passed away now, but good memories.

It was now 13–10 to Europe and they needed just one more point to retain the cup.

This was produced in the very next match when José María Cañizares and Ken Green followed much of the trend of the day by coming to the eighteenth all square.

Green made sure he avoided the errors of Stewart and Calcavecchia by landing his shot on the fairway and Canizares followed suit. They made it to the green on level terms but Green missed his second putt, leaving Canizares a four-foot putt for the match. He coolly slotted it home.

José María Cañizares: Ken Green at that time was the best putter on the American tour, so everybody thought I would lose that match. But I played very good golf, five or six under par. On the eighteenth, the pin was in the middle of the green, and that green has three tiers. My ball was on the top tier, sixty feet away, so my putt was very difficult. Ken Green hit his second shot short, on the very front of the green. I hit the first putt close. Then Ken Green putted, to maybe six feet. Ken missed his putt. My putt looked nice, left to right, and – boom! – I hit it in the hole. My point kept the cup for Europe.

Everyone was very happy, and I was very happy. I was forty-four years old, and everyone looked at me very, very nicely. Seve very happy. Tony said, 'Muy bien, muy bien.'

Europe could not now lose the cup and all eyes turned to the remaining matches to see if another half point at least could be delivered to win it outright. But Raymond Floyd's men were not about to roll over for a European victory parade.

In an extraordinary show of grit, will and tenacity, the Americans refused to buckle and all returned a point as first Tom Watson beat the hero of '85 Sam Torrance 3&1, McCumber defeated Brand Jnr one-up, Wadkins defeated Faldo one-up and Strange defeated Woosnam two-up.

Few, if any, would have predicted from the outset that Ballesteros, Faldo, Langer and

Christy O'Connor Jnr raises his hands and face to the sky in celebration. *Getty Images*

Woosnam would fail to register even a half point for Europe in the singles. Nor would they have predicted that Cañizares and O'Connor would prove to be the key men in Europe's defence of the cup.

Mark James: No one seemed to know what to do when we'd retained it. I will be careful not to slag anyone off here, but I think the players who were still out on the course were left wondering what on earth to do, whether to play or not to play, whereas someone should have gone out and said, 'Come on, we haven't won it, get stuck in, think of your Ryder Cup record, we want to win this, not halve it.'

Tony Jacklin: All my main men lost in '89. Shit, Seve got beat, Woosie got beat, Faldo got beat. I mean it was a miracle we finished up tied.

Nick Faldo: As had been the case in 1987, it was those players who didn't play very much during the first two days, or had not won many points, who managed to squeeze out the points to get us a half. I think one of the reasons for this was the different approach the two captains took in selecting the pairings and who played when.

The Americans always had a policy of trying to give every player a game on each day. With twelve players for only eight places in each series of games, they were prepared to break up successful partnerships to do it. I think this worked against them over the first two days but usually left them better prepared and fresher for the singles. This goes back to the days when they used to win the matches comfortably and were more concerned that everyone felt they had played a real part in the match.

Tony Jacklin, on the other hand, always went hell for leather to get points on the board and played his strong partnerships throughout. There's an argument that this drained the top players, particularly as some didn't do as well in the singles as they should have. In

The crowd cheers as Europe retain the Ryder Cup after
Christy O'Connor Jnr secures victory over Fred Couples.

1989, Seve, Langer, Woosie and I all failed to win on the Sunday, so we were lucky in the end to halve the match.

Tom Watson: We had basically lucked into a tie. It was one of those matches where it didn't look very good for the US team at all during those matches but we pulled it out in the end and got the tie.

Tony Jacklin: I think that a draw was good for the Ryder Cup. From a personal point of view I was obviously delighted that we held onto the cup, but I think it was also good that America were able to restore some pride after losing in '85 and '87.

Raymond Floyd: In many ways I was disappointed with the half because we felt we could have won. There were a lot of peaks and valleys out there. Early on I would have felt like a tie was a defeat. Later on I thought we had no chance at all. To come back after that and draw tickles me to death. Golf was the winner.

Howard Clark: Ray Floyd made a point in his closing ceremony speech that Europe hadn't won the match, we had tied it. When we heard that, some of the players wanted a play-off to decide the match. There was a little bit of sour grapes, with the speeches and stuff. But there were a few of us who let the team down on the last day and I wasn't the only one.

TWENTY-NINE

1991

The Ocean Course. Kiawah Island, South Carolina
(USA 14½, EUR 13½)

The 1991 Ryder Cup, held on the Ocean Course at Kiawah Island in South Carolina, set new standards for tension and high drama – but it also marked a new low in the relations between the teams and opposing fans. It came to be dubbed the 'War on the Shore'.

Dave Stockton was the man placed in charge of the home team's charge to regain the cup after an eight-year absence from the US PGA's trophy cabinet, while Bernard Gallacher had the daunting prospect of following in Tony Jacklin's hugely successful footsteps as leader of the European defence.

Bernard Gallacher: It was a proud moment to be chosen as captain for Kiawah Island in 1991, a delight. I was the professional at Wentworth so the captaincy was fitted in around other parts of my life. I dealt with the players OK because I handled staff at Wentworth, but I didn't have to market the event so much. Nowadays, the captaincy has become quite an important position in terms of doing TV, radio, press and everything else. There is a worldwide audience. It's a much bigger responsibility now.

1991 was a turning point for the Ryder Cup. And not in a good way. Suddenly, there was hostility out there . . . it was the first sign of a downturn in the matches that came to a head eight years later in Boston. It's better now, thankfully.

Dave Stockton: We had just lost six straight years, hadn't seen the cup, probably forgotten what it looked like. So there was a sense of urgency. When Nicklaus lost at Muirfield Village, it became apparent to me, and every captain after me, that if Nicklaus can lose on his own course then anybody can get beat. If you're going to be successful you're going to have to dot the 'I's and cross the 'T's of this thing.

I knew I had to get the team to bond. I did a number of things to try and ensure it wasn't just one or two individuals that were going to carry it. I worked on getting them all to a whole team concept.

I got the Tour to play shoot-outs on Tuesday at tournaments, not just the usual old practise rounds. At half a dozen events I was able to put various players together, to see how they got on, what worked and what didn't. A couple of times we even had a Ryder Cup format, a little match if you like. There were about four of us who used to meet up and talk Ryder Cup stuff; that was Paul Azinger, Payne Stewart, Lanny Wadkins and myself. We talked strategy, psychology, different things like that, and when we got to Kiawah I felt the team was ready to play, to win. It still blows me away that Lanny is one of the ones that didn't win when it was his turn in 1995, because he understood what we were about.

Opposite: Mark Calcavecchia is spurred on by his teammate, Payne Stewart, at the Ocean Course at Kiawah Island, South Carolina. *Getty Images*

Both teams had a core of experience with Stockton able to call on the services of Azinger, Chip Beck, Mark Calcavecchia, Fred Couples, Raymond Floyd, Hale Irwin, Mark O'Meara, Stewart and Lanny Wadkins while Gallacher had Seve Ballesteros, Nick Faldo, Mark James, Bernhard Langer, José María Olazábal, Sam Torrance and Ian Woosnam in his ranks. Many pundits felt, however, that America had a clear edge for not only did they have the considerable advantage of playing at home, but they also had just three rookies in their team in Wayne Levi, Steve Pate and Corey Pavin while Europe had five: Paul Broadhurst, David Feherty, David Gilford, Colin Montgomerie and Steven Richardson. Of course Europe had been to America and won in 1987, so winning away from home was clearly possible, yet the odds looked stacked against them from the outset.

Bernard Gallacher: When you become captain, it's all about being optimistic. I mean, if you don't think you're going to win, don't be captain. So think you're going to win, be optimistic, give the players a chance. And then when you get into picking foursomes and fourballs, you really need your players to give you some input. You don't want to put people on the golf course if they don't get on. At the end of the day, the players have got to enjoy your captaincy, and they have to have respect for you. It's all about respect and being optimistic.

Colin Montgomerie: Bernard Gallacher had a difficult gig because he was new to the captaincy and he had to follow on from the success of Tony Jacklin, who had won two and halved one of his four, which was remarkable. So he had a difficult job to fill Tony's shoes. He obviously took a lot of what Tony had done and put his own emphasis on it. But he came up against three things – a very good American team; playing away from home in a very hostile environment; and playing against a very tough captain in Dave Stockton, who would do anything for that win.

Following the conclusion to the first Gulf War earlier in the year, there was an intense patriotism that surrounded the event – even if many in the host nation seemed to have overlooked the fact that the European nations had been allies in the conflict rather than adversaries.

Bernhard Langer: Corey Pavin had the idea of wearing camouflage caps that had the Marines logo on it. We felt that wasn't appropriate. This was not a war. We had been allies in the Gulf War. Now they were portraying it like they were fighting us in a war. Corey was trying to honour the people fighting in the war, but it came over as if they were making it into a war when it was only a golf game.

Corey Pavin: A lot was made of us wearing the military hats, but it was largely misconstrued. It was just a show of support for our troops over in Iraq. I think a lot of people took it the wrong way; I was showing patriotism to the guys out there putting their lives on the line for our freedom. If that's wrong then so be it, but I don't think that's wrong.

Dave Stockton: The first Gulf War had just ended, so there was a lot of pride in America at the time. That certainly brought the guys together. The old forage caps might have looked a bit aggressive, but it was the symbol of pride we felt at the time.

An already febrile atmosphere was inflamed still further on the eve of the matches when a video montage was shown at the pre-tournament gala evening.

Bernhard Langer: They showed the history of the Ryder Cup, all the best players, and all they showed was Americans. No Europeans. We'd just won the two previous Ryder Cups and tied the other. That didn't go down well with us. It was like, 'What are you guys trying to do here? Make us mad?' That wasn't a good thing to do.

Dave Stockton: The dinner in Charleston on the eve of the matches was the biggest fiasco of the week as far as I was concerned, because the PGA [of America] showed a very distasteful videotape about our side, and there was nothing about the Europeans. I have no idea why they did that.

I have no idea why they called the videotape The War on the Shore either. I didn't agree with that at all.

Nick Faldo: And it didn't just stop with the video, there was loads going on. A local radio programme had this thing called 'Wake the Enemy' that week when they would call the European players' rooms in the middle of the night. But he was a bit of an idiot because he didn't realise that we were all getting up at five or six in the morning anyway to go and practise, so he'd ring up at six and it was like a morning call, it was great.

Mark James: I just turned over and went back to sleep. It's amazing to think it happened and ever since then you can't ring a player's room without going through the main switchboard.

Hale Irwin: 1991 was the first time in the US that the Ryder Cup had really been recognised as something. It was on a new course; it was being hyped; it was on television. There was a great deal of, let's say, good old southern-boy hospitality. There was a lot of that rolling out of the marshlands of South Carolina, which was good in the sense that it upped the tempo of things.

Americans tend to make assumptions that they're the best, and then when you lose it you say, 'What happened?' And I think that's what happened in the '80s. The other side had some great players, and now suddenly the cup was not around and people were starting to take notice. And now they're thinking, 'Maybe there is something here'. And that sort of came together in '91, the recognition of 'It's not here, so let's get it back. Let's go! Rah-rah! U-S-A!' That kind of stuff.

Having overcome this incident-filled start to the week, the players were ready to get on with the real business as the weekend rolled around.

Bernhard Langer: The 1991 Ryder Cup was the first time the Ryder Cup nearly got out of hand. Seve was accused of gamesmanship, and there were comments and things written that were not what the game of golf is about. While the Ryder Cup is very important to both sides, it has a great tradition of sportsmanship and fairness. It is about the best twelve golfers from Europe playing against the twelve best golfers from the United States, with a view to creating friendship between the nations, not to wage war on the shore.

Dave Stockton: Some say the crowds were over the top, but all I know is we had the best support we'd ever had. I'm proud of the role Kiawah played in the history of the competition – I think it was the start of Americans realising the Ryder Cup meant something.

Colin Montgomerie: It was very hostile. We didn't give credit to the fact that America had lost in '85 and '87 and they had tied in '89 and they didn't want to lose again – and they had a very, very tough captain in Dave Stockton. I see him on the Champions Tour as he is now a putting coach for many of the players – a very, very tough man. So they had a very hard captain; we had a new captain in Bernard Gallacher, away from home, in a very hostile environment – Desert Storm was still very much in people's minds and a lot of Americans didn't seem to understand that we were allies in that, we had been out there too. They thought they were fighting the whole world at the time – including us. That was the problem. There was very much a feeling of them-and-us between us and the crowd. Then two of the players came out in Desert Storm caps, Pavin and Pate, and you were thinking, 'Hang on a minute this isn't quite right, this is a bloody golf competition. It's mad; what are you doing?'

Tickets for the 1991 Ryder Cup had sold out in less than a week and NBC and USA Network had pledged to televise every shot over a planned twenty-one hours of live coverage (which actually extended to twenty-four hours), marking new ground in interest. But as vast swathes of home support flocked to the Ocean Course where they were pumped up by Stockton and his team into a patriotic fervour, the Europeans also had another key obstacle to concern them: the challenge of the course.

Nick Faldo: 1991 was so brutal with the 'War on the Shore' stuff. Europe had been doing well and it was time for America to get the cup back again, so it was a brutal week, a tough week on Europe, with little niggly sportsmanship going on behind the scenes. And then we came to play the golf course and it was rough and wild and rugged; it was amazing and we hadn't seen anything like it. It was so severe, we had so many waste bunkers and you could hit a ball into a hole and it could take a funny little bounce and end up no more than twenty, twenty-five feet from the hole but in thick shrub and you might not even be able to finish the hole let alone make a bogey or a double bogey. It was really severe and it was windy; it was a tough week and a few guys left there with some scars in their golfing games.

David Feherty: It was absolutely the hardest golf course that I'd ever seen. As close to unplayable, unmanageable as I've ever seen. The weather was OK – not much rain, but it blew. The golf course is built right on the ocean with the greens built up, so you have to have some kind of a high shot to hold the green, but it requires a low shot to keep out of the wind. That's a fundamental design flaw. I heard it was supposed to be like Scottish and Irish golf, but I'd been all over Scotland and Ireland and I'd seen nothing like that.

Colin Montgomerie: It was a very difficult course, but it didn't really matter. The courses in the Ryder Cup have never been the star of the show, ever. It's always been about the players. The course was difficult at Kiawah, yes, but it wasn't about the course, it was about the players and how we reacted to certain situations within that environment.

Lanny Wadkins: It wasn't a normal golf course that you would see even in the British Open that had places for galleries. It was all sand hills, so what happened was the Europeans would congregate on one dune and the American galleries on another and it ended up like a big soccer match. It was like one side of the stadium yelling at the other. And they would almost go to these sand dunes and plant their flag, plant the Euro flag or plant the American flag so it became a different spectacle than I had ever seen in golf anywhere any time. I have heard a lot of people say they didn't like that. Personally, I loved it.

I thought 1991 was great. It really kind of put the Ryder Cup totally on the map. A little antagonism is not a bad thing. If everyone is sweet and pats each other on the back all the time, what the hell good does that do? Why even play? If you don't want to beat the crap out of someone let's not go out there.

Dave Stockton: I actually think the switch to Kiawah favoured the Europeans, because it was built on a sand dune; it's a links course. It may not look like normal European courses, but you're elevated and the elements are hitting you, and it's nothing like what we normally play. Some of the guys actually visited three, four, five times to get the feel

for the course. I also extended Gallacher the opportunity to have his players come up after the Masters, even though the course wasn't really complete. None of them, to my knowledge, ever went.

Paul Azinger and Chip Beck were chosen by Stockton to lead the side out in the opening foursome against Ballesteros and Olazábal. The noise as the pairings arrived on the tee was deafening. The War on the Shore was about to commence.

Dave Stockton: I read all the stuff written later about the fans, and you'd think there were all these idiots running around, but I didn't see that. The fans on the first tee were awesome. There was one with a Union Jack flag wrapped around him, and another wrapped in the flag of Spain, and they would yell and scream after the Europeans

José María Olazábal and Seve Ballesteros were once again in wonderful form at Kiawah.

teed off. And when the Americans were announced they'd clap and yell again – which to me is what it's all about.

Tom Watson followed me as captain in 1993, and said he was going to make a gallant effort to cut down on all this stuff, but that puzzled me. I didn't agree with the 'War on the Shore' stuff, but I thought the American fans really supported us. And if there had been somebody rude, I'd have found them and thrown them out.

The Americans raced into an early lead, holding a three up advantage at the turn. The Spaniards were not about to go out without a fight. Having already demanded a questionable free-drop on the second, Ballesteros kicked up a fuss at the tenth when he complained to the match official that Azinger had been playing with the wrong ball since the seventh. The Americans were furious at what they took for gamesmanship.

Paul Azinger: There's nothing like taking on Europe's finest first thing in the morning! Seve and José had never been beaten in Ryder Cup action when they had played together. Chip and I were hoping to end that streak.

We were embroiled in a conflict over what I considered a controversial drop of the ball on the second, and we had another question over their lost ball on the fourth. It went on like that all day, one controversy after another. By the ninth hole I was livid. When José hit his drive off to the right I was right there to help spot the drop. The referee was intimidated by Seve and José, so he simply stood aside and waited to see how we would settle things. Seve and José wanted to drop the ball much farther up the fairway from where I thought the ball had gone into the water. We argued over it for a while, and finally Seve looked at me in disgust and said, 'OK, where do you want us to drop the ball?'

'You need to drop it back here,' I said as I pointed to the original position I had indicated. Reluctantly Seve dropped the ball at that spot.

On the tenth tee Seve and José accused me and Chip of hitting the wrong compression balls. I was playing a 90-compression ball and Chip was playing a 100-compression. Because a 100-compression ball is wound more tightly, it flies further. When we got to number seven, which is a par-five, Chip was going to hit my 90-compression ball in the hope that I could put our second shot with the same ball onto the green. Looking at the distance, I was a little sceptical. 'I'm not sure we can hit this green,' I said. 'If you hit your 100-compression ball, then I can lay up, and you can hit your 100 onto the green.' Chip agreed and that's what we did. Seve and José had overheard this and when we got to the tenth they called the officials to charge us with playing with the wrong balls. I was furious! I couldn't believe it was happening, especially after all the questionable stuff that had been going on already.

The officials ruled with the home pairing as the infringement had not been called up at the time on the seventh, and play continued, but in many ways Seve had achieved his goal – he had got under his opponents' skin. The European pair dug in and began to claw back the deficit, eventually drawing level at the thirteenth and then moving one up at the fifteenth. When Seve rolled in a snaking putt at the seventeenth to move two ahead, the Europeans had the match and an important point. Azinger and Beck could barely bring themselves to shake their opponents' hands.

Paul Azinger: Chip and I were so shaken by the incident on the tenth that we three-putted the next green and our game went downhill from there. It's no excuse, but they succeeded in breaking our momentum with all that stuff with the officials.

Seve Ballesteros: They were three up and we called the referee over and the referee said one thing, Chip Beck said another thing, Azinger said another thing and all of a sudden José says to me, 'OK, let's go and play, we're going to beat these guys.' And we won on the back nine, it was fantastic. That was probably the best nine holes we ever played together.

Bernard Gallacher: At the end of the day the Spaniards won. I was quite pleased about that. It was probably justice.

First blood to the Europeans. Out second were Floyd and Couples against Langer and James. Couples had a poor Ryder Cup record to date, but his forty-nine-year-old partner and former Ryder Cup captain cajoled and encouraged him around the course, praising everything he did. It seemed to work some magic over Couples and they were four up after ten. Although Langer and James won the twelfth, thirteenth and fourteenth, Floyd holed an eight-foot putt for par to win the sixteenth to keep them two up. With both sides finishing seventeen for par, the match was over and the US had their first point.

Fred Couples: That was a great match and very important for me; Raymond was a huge help to me going around. He was always like, 'Great shot! What a golf shot!' whenever I did anything good. It kept my spirits up all the way around. I had gone zero and two in '89 so it was a big moment for me to finally win a Ryder Cup match.

Raymond Floyd: That mentoring role is a subtle thing. It's mostly reassurance. There are certain things you can do in a team situation to make your partner very comfortable. There are players who can just absolutely carry another guy. Your partner can freewheel because he feels in his mind that you can handle it if it gets tense. And then he watches how you handle it and learns from that.

The third match saw Wadkins and Irwin take on the rookie pairing of Gilford and Montgomerie.

Colin Montgomerie: The second shot into the last hole of a Major, one ahead – that is the pressure you feel with every shot in the Ryder Cup. It's that much pressure.

1991 was my first Ryder Cup and, looking back, the rookie experience is a very interesting one. The worst experience I ever had on the first tee of a tournament was at the Walker Cup, the amateur Ryder Cup. I was in America in '85 at Pine Valley and I hit the first shot playing with a guy called George Macgregor, a recent captain of the R&A. I have never felt as bad ever as I did during that first shot. I managed to hit the fairway thank God. Going to the Ryder Cup six years later in 1991 felt different – it was my job then and the expectation was completely different. You were expected to perform and you expected it from yourself. Like a rugby penalty kick under the posts, it's hard because you're expected to do it. So, I didn't have the same pressure there as I did as an amateur, but expectation is still probably the hardest thing to handle in sport. It's like a Premiership football team paying a non-league team – you're expected to win, so it can actually become harder because the expectation is that much higher. So '91 as a rookie, here I was thrown into this cauldron of Faldo, Langer, Woosnam, Lyle, Seve, I mean Christ, a hell of a team. And I found myself thinking, 'What on earth am I doing in this?' You've got to get over that feeling of 'I don't belong', because you're part of the team and your points are going to count, however many you can get.

David Gilford and I were a bit of an experimental pairing, and quite a brave pairing to put together because we were both rookies. It would have been nice to have had an experienced hand to guide each of us around our first round of the Ryder Cup, but Bernard felt that we could do a job together. Unfortunately we came up against a very experienced pair in Lanny Wadkins and Hale Irwin and they did a bit of a job on us, winning 4&2.

The final match of the morning saw Stewart and Calcavecchia take on Faldo and Woosnam. Bernard Gallacher had voiced before the match that he 'could not imagine why' Dave Stockton would put Calcavecchia out in the foursomes as his play could be so erratic and the format favoured those with a steadier disposition – characterised by their European opponents. Calcavecchia dismissed this notion entirely, however, with two spectacular iron shots on the thirteenth and fourteenth to move the US pair two ahead and it was his putt on eighteen to just a couple of feet that won the match and gave the US a 3–1 lead.

The first of the afternoon fourballs saw Mark O'Meara and Lanny Wadkins take on Sam Torrance and the Northern Irish rookie David Feherty.

David Feherty: The Ryder Cup is an incredible experience. You look around at players you respect and whom you hope respect you. And you sense that they're expecting a certain level of performance from you and that you daren't let them down. And if you don't deliver, you will never be able to face them again. Yet at no stage did I want to get out of the place, to leave all the pressure behind. To walk away would be to deny everything that you are; to deny your reasons for playing the game. Your whole golfing life has been geared towards becoming a member of this exclusive club and now that you're in, there's no turning back.

No player but Seve had the ability to make my hair stand on end simply by watching him play. By that time, I had idolised him for the best part of fifteen years, since he first hit the headlines at Birkdale in 1976. I found his presence to be quite extraordinary and I can still picture him prowling around, prodding players, grabbing them by the back of the neck, hugging them. He was a very physical person; personal contact was very important to him as a means of communication. At Kiawah, he made a particular point of coming to the newcomers in the side, players like myself and David Gilford, Paul Broadhurst and Steven Richardson. He deliberately made himself feel small in our company so as to strengthen the bond between us. He bared his soul to us, telling of his own vulnerability, so that we might think of him as an equal, as just another member of the team. His motivational powers were phenomenal and as far as he was concerned, we were all in this thing together, all pulling together.

Sam Torrance: When David Feherty and I both made the team in 1991, it was pretty much taken for granted that Bernard Gallacher would put us together. We sat out the morning foursomes and emerged as the first pair in the afternoon fourballs against that golfing gunslinger Lanny Wadkins and Mark O'Meara.

To say Feherty was nervous is something of an understatement. His first putt from fifteen feet did not so much threaten the hole as run away from it as the ball rolled three feet short and four feet wide. It was basically a duff. He was so jittery that I felt I had to say something of a consoling and encouraging nature, one friend to another.

'If you don't get your act together,' I said, 'I'm leaving you, joining them and you can play all three of us, you useless bastard!'

David Feherty: In the Ryder Cup you spend most of your time trying to look invincible and trying not to show any kind of soft underbelly. I think most people do. It's about controlling the panic. You're thinking, 'Oh God, no, my head's going to fall off!' It's a strange thing. So when I hit my first putt, everything moved but my bowels. It was a fifteen-foot putt, and I left it four feet short, and five feet right. Sam just quietly walked over to me and said, 'Pull yourself together, or I'm joining them and you're playing the three of us.'

I made the next one. And then it was nice to make a couple of putts at the right moments, especially one on the last hole. It was dusk, and all four of us had played the hole as though it was completely fuckin' dark. You couldn't see the ball.

Sam Torrance: Mainly due to my partner's good play we reduced a three-hole deficit to one by the short seventeenth, which I birdied by hitting a four-iron stone dead. But O'Meara managed to match my two. That guaranteed the Americans at least a halved match. But David was faced with a ten-foot birdie putt on the final green to gain Europe

David Feherty and Sam Torrance.

a half point. For the first time in the entire day he asked me to read the line.

'Left edge,' I said positively. 'Just knock it in.'

David Feherty: I had read the greens like a Russian newspaper all day so I asked Sam to aim me. Somehow I made a controlled spasm and the ball rolled into the centre of the cup. The crowd roared; I almost fainted.

Dave Stockton: After the ruckus in the morning, Zinger and Chip played the Spaniards again in the second of the afternoon fourballs. Chip didn't play that well, and Azinger had been emotionally derailed a little bit by what happened in the morning. The Europeans won again, 2&1. Ballesteros had a knack for getting under your skin if he wanted to. He could be tough to deal with. I lucked out the next day because I got Floyd and Couples playing against him, and Ballesteros was much calmer playing against Floyd. I think he could realise that gamesmanship should not be how you win or lose the Ryder Cup. It should be by hitting fantastic shots.

Curtis Strange: To say that Seve was difficult is an understatement. To a man, every player who went up against him in the Ryder Cup had a run-in with him. His gamesmanship was irritating, and he never let up. He'd do outrageous, childish things like coughing as you got set to swing, and if you objected he'd act wounded and escalate the situation. He'd put himself into the role of victim, that's when he'd play his best. Just knowing he'd use a nasty incident to play well made me so mad that I'd play worse. There was only one Seve, and a little of him went a long way. But I'll tell you this, he could back it up. If you were 0–5 against a guy, that would hack you off, too.

Mark James: Seve was always fantastic. He could have played with my mum in the Ryder Cup and been quite happy and it wouldn't have surprised me if they had got half a point – and she doesn't even play.

The third match pitted Corey Pavin and Mark Calcavecchia against Steven Richardson and Mark James. No one would have predicted just how comprehensively the European pair would outplay their American counterparts as they virtually strolled their way to a 5&4 victory.

With Europe clearly in the ascendancy, Gallacher would have felt assured of an undefeated afternoon as he sent out Faldo and Woosnam to face Floyd and Couples. He was understandably shocked, therefore, when the star pair came back with their tails between their legs having suffered a heavy 5&3 loss.

There was a familiar feeling to the Saturday morning foursomes as America dominated once again, winning three of the four matches (two of which were annihilations). First Feherty and Torrance fell 4&2 to Irwin and Wadkins before Calcavecchia and Stewart beat James and Richardson one-up. It had been hairy for the American duo, however, as Stewart, the reigning US Open champion, hit the water on the seventeenth and then shanked his ball into the dunes lining the eighteenth fairway as he and Calcavecchia threatened to throw away the two-hole advantage they had carried onto the final two holes. The match was only saved from being halved when Richardson fluffed a four-footer on the eighteenth.

Nick Faldo and David Gilford then joined up for one of the Ryder Cup's most notable failures as a pairing as they lost 7&6 to Paul Azinger and Mark O'Meara.

Nick Faldo: After the first day Woosie, Bernhard Langer and I all said we didn't think we were performing well enough. It was decided that I was the one who should play, but the question arose, with whom? The choice lay between David Gilford and Colin Montgomerie. I didn't know Monty that well, so I asked who was playing better. David was the reply; he was hitting everything straight down the middle.

In foursomes it is even more important for partners to get on well. David and I didn't know one another that well then, and the cauldron of the Ryder Cup wasn't really the time to start. We never really gelled, and if he missed a green, I didn't chip close enough to hole and vice versa. Everything that could go wrong, did.

Bernard Gallacher: Nick and Ian didn't gel and it wasn't until later that I found out they didn't want to play together. By then they had lost two matches on the first day.

Successful partnerships occur when one player is more assertive than the other, a sort of team leader if you like. In the past, Woosnam had looked up to Faldo, who made all the decisions. Nick always made all the decisions! By 1991, Ian had won the Masters, was number one in the world and instead of working together, they competed with one another.

Nick was playing alright when he arrived, hitting the ball very well, but like most of the team found the new strain of grass on the greens, Tifdwarf, difficult to read. He couldn't hole a putt for love nor money. He let it affect the rest of his game. By now I realised what I should have known from the start. He and Woosie no longer wanted to play together. I thought to give Nick some responsibility for shepherding one of the newcomers. I still felt David Gilford was basically playing well; his game was ideal for foursomes, so I sent the pair of them out on the second morning. It was a disaster. Nick by now was so deep inside his own shell, he never made the effort to communicate with his partner, let alone help him through the rigours of a Ryder Cup. That was another bit of inspiration that went wrong!

Nick Faldo: I am castigated to this day for that one miserable match with David Gilford. To me that is baloney. We were an untried and unproven partnership thrown together by circumstances and the chemistry just was not there.

David Gilford: I am a big fan of what Nick Faldo has achieved, but he's not a wonderful man.

The only respite for Europe came in the final match when Ballesteros and Olazábal salvaged a point for their side with a 3&2 victory over Couples and Floyd.

Bernard Gallacher: Our butts had certainly been kicked in the morning foursomes, but we had clawed our way back on the first day with a good performance in the foursomes and we saw no reason why we couldn't do the same again on the second afternoon.

Woosnam and Broadhurst were chosen to try and get the European campaign back on track when they took on Azinger and Irwin. And they did just that in producing a very gritty effort to come from one-down at the turn to bring the match all square on the tenth before edging ahead at the thirteenth. When they birdied the seventeenth to win the hole they had an insurmountable 2&1 lead.

Langer and Montgomerie were out next against Pate and Pavin and the European pair were in the driving seat for much of the contest. They were all square over the first three holes before moving one ahead on the fourth and two up on the seventh. Although they were pegged back to all square at the ninth, they moved ahead again at the tenth and then extended that lead to two on the twelfth, a lead they did not relinquish.

The third match saw James and Richardson take on Levi and Wadkins. Once again the Europeans were unstoppable. They were three up after three and were only then pegged back by one hole before reasserting their three up lead on thirteen and held that advantage to the seventeenth where the US at last conceded.

The final match of the day saw the irrepressible duo of Ballesteros and Olazábal back in harness against Fred Couples and Payne Stewart.

José María Olazábal: The biggest mistake you can make is assuming you have won a hole before it is over. At Kiawah Island in 1991, Seve and I were playing Fred Couples and Payne Stewart in the final match of the Saturday fourballs. At the sixteenth hole, Seve had maybe a ten-foot putt for birdie. Fred was in the greenside bunker after three shots, and Payne was out of the hole. I turned to Seve and said, 'This is looking good for us.' He was not pleased. He looked at me and said, 'Hang on a minute; let's see what happens.' Sure enough, Fred holed his shot for a par. But Seve wasn't surprised. He was ready and prepared for that. And he holed his putt on top of Freddie. I learned a lot from him in those few minutes.

Seve kept his cool and continued to guide his friend through the turmoil of that closely-fought match. It was all square after sixteen and that's the way it remained to the final hole, where the eighteenth was also shared and the match halved.

David Feherty: We nearly swept the afternoon, winning three and halving one. Woosnam went out first with the tough northerner Paul Broadhurst, making his debut a happy one with a 2&1 win over Irwin and Azinger. In the second, Steve Pate, who'd been hurt when his limo crashed coming back from the big pre-match dinner, tried to play. I have a confession to make about this; it was my limo that caused the crash. We were on our way to Charleston in the cavalcade of limos, and I was sharing a car with Nick Faldo and one of his ex-wives, when my ex-wife asked the driver a stupid question, just as a state trooper was waving us through a red light. The driver looked over his shoulder just as the officer changed his mind, and ended up having to slam on the brakes. We heard the squealing of tyres behind, and a few seconds later the crump of a collision as Pate's limo parked itself in the trunk of the one in front, and Pate parked his ribs into a decanter of Jack Daniel's. Sorry about that, pal.

Moving right along, he was paired with Pavin – both of them wearing those ugly Desert Storm camouflage hats – and they were lucky to stay as close as they did, only losing to Langer and Montgomerie 2&1. Levi also got his first chance to play, but out of form, he was a load on Wadkins' shoulders and they lost 3&1, to James and Richardson. That left Ballesteros and Olazábal, who it seemed were tiring from the non-stop action. But these two were unbreakable. From two-down with six to play against Stewart and Couples, Ollie holed a five-footer on the last hole for a half, and he and Ballesteros virtually danced off the green, re-energising themselves, the team, and a pretty large European contingent in the crowd, which was making some noise of its own. 'Ole, Ole, Ole,' went the soccer-style chant.

Nick Faldo: Bernhard and Woosie had the morning off and came back in the afternoon to win with Monty and Paul Broadhurst, respectively, as did Mark James and Steven Richardson. That got us back to all square with the singles to come.

With Steve Pate continuing to struggle badly with his chest injury, there was great uncertainty about whether he would manage to play in the singles. He was selected (and had been drawn to play Ballesteros) but was then withdrawn. Gallacher was extremely unhappy about the situation, feeling that the move favoured the Americans. The rules stated that if Pate had not played at all in the pairs matches and then immediately been removed from the singles, Europe would have been awarded a full point. But this late withdrawal meant that both teams were awarded a half point each.

Bernard Gallacher: They had all night to look at the draw and they pulled Pate out the next day. Usually, it's a matter of courtesy to alert the opposing captain that there's a possibility that one of their players would be pulled out, but they didn't.

A couple of years later [in 1993] Sam Torrance wasn't well, and his name went in the envelope. I told US captain Tom Watson early on that there was the possibility that one of my players wouldn't play. It just gives the captain a bit more leeway to think about who he puts in the envelope. He can then prepare the player who's in the envelope and give him the reasons why.

They saw that David Gilford was playing Wayne Levi which meant that Seve would come down the draw and actually play their worst player. But I wanted Seve to play their best player because anyone could beat Wayne Levi. He was having a terrible week.

We had to put a player in the 'envelope' and had selected David Gilford, but he hadn't known that. He was distraught when he found out because he'd had a poor Ryder Cup until then, but I had actually thought that he hadn't played that badly and had just had a few breaks go against him. I was absolutely convinced he would win his singles because I had a lot of confidence in him that he would have got his Ryder Cup point there. If I'd been told that Steve Pate wasn't going to play, I would have prepared him a bit better for it. I would have said, 'David, I put your name in the envelope for this reason, that reason.' But it came out as if I didn't have any confidence in David Gilford.

After talking to him, I then asked Tony [Jacklin], 'Could you go and have a word with David? He might take it a little bit better from you.' As it turned out, he didn't.

Tony Jacklin: Bernard Gallacher, bless his heart, chose me to inform David Gilford he wouldn't be playing. When I broke the news, Gilford was absolutely gutted. I've never seen a man so broken. That's one part of the Ryder Cup I do not miss.

Corey Pavin and Steve Pate in their Desert Storm caps.

Nick Faldo: That evening Bernie Gallacher told me I would be playing top, which was fine by me. That night, though, I was the most nervous I have ever been. I had trouble getting off to sleep, and I was prancing round the room at 4:00 am with my heart going flat out.

At least I knew what I had to do in the morning. First out, you have to get the blue numbers on the board, get holes up for your side. I made a great start and won the first three holes and went on from there. In the end I was four up with four to play, and even though Floyd dragged me up the last, I was still only one or two over par. Matches were being won later in the day with 78s and 80s.

For me, it became a matter of wait and see, of watching all the others struggle in the wind on that extraordinary course.

The Ryder Cup is an amazingly long week. By the time you get there you have three practise rounds, you have gala dinners and the first three days feels like a week before you've even got to the first tee on Friday morning. I had a tough time, I wasn't playing well that week but then I was drawn with Ray Floyd on the Sunday and knew Ray was really struggling with that hard left-to-right wind, which was blowing like that on most of the holes on the course. And even though I was struggling I just thought, if I can just squeeze a point out of this then I've done my bit. And I managed to do it. But all-in-all, it was a tough week for a lot of us.

David Feherty: Before the match Seve took me aside. 'They put you out early because they think you will lose,' he said, then grabbed me by my shirt and chest hair and pulled me close. 'But I know you have this heart.' I got chills. I thought, 'Wow! He believes I can win – and so do I.'

I can only describe the Ryder Cup in the same way that women describe childbirth, which is that there's no way of adequately explaining what's involved. It's unique – a lot like what you imagined it to be, yet not like it at all. At Kiawah, I was fortunate in having had the advice of an old hand in Sam Torrance and, like everything else, there are tricks for survival. For instance, before my singles match, Sam warned me not to walk onto the tee until my opponent was formally announced to the crowd. Otherwise, I would stand petrified, just as the Christians must have felt before being thrown to the lions, while this golfing god, the reigning US Open champion [Stewart], was being introduced like some fabulous prizefighter.

Everything settled down on the first tee. I just felt like the ball was going to go where I wanted it to go. It was one great shot after another. I went three under par through twelve holes – which was unheard of! – and I was four up on the fourteenth.

But fifteen I bogeyed after a poor tee shot, and on sixteen I hit one almost into the ocean. So now I'd lost two holes in a row, and I got to seventeen, which is the hardest par-three in the galaxy, where you have to hit a long shot to a green the size of a monkey's nipple. Just the thought of trying to get the ball on the green is nauseating.

I managed to get onto the green, an absolute miracle – and then there was another miracle as Payne hit it to the left where it was basically impossible to play from. I had a putt and missed and then Payne conceded to give me a 2&1 victory. I turned around, and Bernard Gallacher was running up the tee waving his arms in the air. Jacklin was facing the other direction, covering his eyes. He had less faith in me than I had!

Playing in the third singles match, Mark Calcavecchia faced Colin Montgomerie and was five up at the turn. Although Montgomerie pulled one back at the tenth and eleventh, Calcavecchia was eventually four up with four to play. He then triple bogeyed the fifteenth and bogeyed the sixteenth. Montgomerie then hit water on the seventeenth and Calcavecchia looked home and hosed. But he too found water with his tee shot. After both made it to the green, the American had a two-foot putt to halve the hole – and missed. With a one-hole lead, Calcavecchia was feeling the heat of his spectacular collapse. And it only got worse. Montgomerie parred and Calcavecchia bogeyed to halve the match.

After such a strong start from the Europeans, it was only a matter of time before the Americans hit back. This they duly did in match numbers four and five as Paul Azinger finally exacted some revenge on one half of the Spanish super team by defeating José María Olazábal two-up and then Corey Pavin followed his lead and defeated Steven Richardson 2&1.

Paul Azinger: When José and I teed off, we didn't say a word to each other. We were both still smarting from our opening matches. Besides, words weren't necessary in this match. This was war. It was the most incredible match I had played in the Ryder Cup. It wasn't my best golf ever, but the seesaw battle with José made it an extremely exciting day.

José was brilliant. I never felt as though I had him beaten. We tied four holes of the eighteen. I had to save par on sixteen with a huge sand wedge blast, followed by a twelve-foot putt that slammed into the hole to keep me even. I finally went one up on the seventeenth after I sank an eight-footer. When I won eighteen as well, I let out a shout that must have scared people as far away as the clubhouse!

Out next was Seve, facing off against Levi, who had made only one appearance thus far – part of a 3&1 defeat in the Saturday afternoon fourballs at the hands of James and Richardson.

Seve Ballesteros: That last day my game with Wayne Levi had a bit of everything. The second hole was perhaps the most insane. We were all square after the first, but I drove so badly off the tee I had to take a drop. I then over-hit to the left and found the bushes. A disaster. Levi, on the other hand, was in easy reach of the green, having played just two shots.

'Seve, that's the end of that,' Billy Foster my caddie remarked. 'I'd concede this hole. There's nothing to do here.'

'Hold on for a minute,' I replied. 'Let's see what he does with his third shot.'

The pin was at the back of the green and behind that water lay. Instead of taking care to pull up short, Levi went for the pin. The ball ran off the green and into the water. Instead of dropping the ball from where he'd entered the water, he did so from where he'd played his approach – only to end up in the water again. Levi was betrayed by his nerves and I won the hole.

'Funny things can happen . . .' I commented to Billy.

Ballesteros moved to two up at the third and was three up at the turn. He was in irresistible form, moving to four up at the eleventh and although Levi put up a fight to win the thirteenth and fifteenth, it wasn't nearly enough to prevent Ballesteros from securing a comfortable 3&2 victory.

The US pulled even at 12–12 with Beck's 3&1 victory over Woosnam. Paul Broadhurst nudged Europe back into the lead with a very tidy 3&1 victory over Mark O'Meara, but then the Americans went ahead 14–13 when Fred Couples beat Sam Torrance 3&2 and Lanny Wadkins defeated Mark James by the same score. Two years after weeping on the shoulder of his wife, Deborah, as Christy O'Connor Jnr had secured the winning point for Europe, Couples had found redemption at Kiawah. 'I wanted to go from being our worst player to maybe being our best,' he said – and that was exactly what he did, securing two-and-a-half points out of a possible four and then won a further point in his victory over Torrance.

It was all going to come down to the last match. The War on the Shore had lived up to its billing. Now it was going to have a fittingly dramatic conclusion: Hale Irwin versus Bernhard Langer.

Hale Irwin: Dave Stockton asked me where would I prefer playing, and I said, 'Dave, I can play front, I can play back. I'm comfortable wherever you think it would be best to put me.' So he put up the line-up and I saw I was last, and then as the two line-ups were put together, I told my wife, 'You know, I think it's going to come down to our match.'

The next day, the wind was blowing, and I felt the early holes and the finishing holes, which were playing into the wind, were going to play more into Langer's forte than they were mine. I was not hitting the ball that strongly, and Langer, he could play that low hook he hits to keep the ball down. But the middle holes were more to my way of playing. I managed quite well with the outgoing holes, then when we turned again with the wind, that's where I felt like, 'OK, now I have to make up ground.' And that's exactly what happened. I just held my own. I went through the first holes in decent shape. I got to the middle holes and when we sort of made the turn at fourteen and started going back to the finish, I had a two up lead.

You don't win three US Opens without having some ability to handle pressure. But the 1991 Ryder Cup was another animal. I wasn't playing particularly well, and I'm playing Bernhard Langer, one of the toughest players of all time. As the day went on, it got more and more intense. By the time we reached the seventeenth hole, it became difficult to breathe. I was one up but missed the green with my tee shot. As I'm walking to the green I see Seve Ballesteros talking to a teammate in Spanish. Trying to keep things light, I say, 'Hey, Seve, what did you say?' He looked at me and says, 'I said, "Too bad you didn't knock it in the water."' That didn't bother me at all. He was competitive. That was fine.

They reached the eighteenth tee and Langer hit first, driving his ball onto the fairway. Irwin tried to follow suit but hooked his shot and it fell into the crowd, about ten people deep and hit a spectator in the back – yet the ball somehow found its way into the short grass on the fringe of the fairway.

Hale Irwin: There was not a lot of rough there, just grass or sand. I do remember thinking that I might have been better off if the ball hadn't hit anyone. I was so far back I couldn't reach the green.

Irwin hit a high fade that left him with a long putt to the hole from the right of the green, while Langer hit a three-iron to land his ball on the right front of the green, which then bounced a yard off it.

Hale Irwin: Can we really describe the amount of tension in the air? I was nervous. Flat out, I was nervous. I've been nervous before but in a different kind of way. Absolutely was I nervous. Bernhard was nervous.

Langer putted from the fringe but slid his shot just past the hole and it came to rest two yards further on. Irwin followed suit and hit his thirty-yard putt firmly towards the flag, but the ball came up short by a foot and half. Langer conceded it.

Bernhard Langer: I thought he was close enough. I didn't think of not giving it to him. And I was going to make mine.

Dave Stockton: I was at the front of the green with the rest of the team. We'd walked down the fairway, so we were down below looking up at the green. I was kneeling down to let the people behind see. At that time I was just kind of depressed, for two reasons. One, I was mad that there was a chance we might not win this thing, and two, if we did win, it would be because Langer missed the putt, and that just didn't seem fair.

Hale Irwin: I did have a glimmer of hope. In my earlier practise rounds I had hit a putt from the left side of that green to the right side of the green, and I remembered telling the team in one of the team meetings that if you ever had to putt across that green, it breaks more than you think. The grain was stronger; there was something there that pulled the ball more than you anticipated. And that's what I was thinking to myself: if there is local knowledge, I hope that I have it and he doesn't. And that was exactly what happened. He said he read it to be left edge, hit it about where he wanted to – and it missed on the short side. Exactly what I had seen in earlier practise runs.

There's not a whole lot you can say. I told him no one deserves that. With all the pressure coming down I thought he handled it extremely well. I know he was bitterly disappointed, and I must say I was a little disappointed for him.

Johnny Pott: I was right behind Langer, fifteen feet from him, when he missed the final putt. He could have probably putted it fifty times and not made it twice. It was a hard putt.

Bernhard Langer: Nobody remembers that I was two down with four to go. I had to make three putts on fifteen, sixteen and seventeen to even get into that position to have a chance to win. If I'd missed any of those earlier putts, I wouldn't even have played eighteen. There's a lot more to it. Every point, every half point, counts equally, whether it's in the morning or the afternoon. My caddie Peter Coleman and I, we read the putt together. We both agreed it was breaking left to right and that I was going to putt it left edge.

I said, 'What about those two spike marks?'

'I see them too,' he said. 'They're pretty bad. They're pretty high.'

It was a sunny, windy afternoon. The greens were crusty and firm. If you hit one of those, the ball could go anywhere. So we decided not to go at the spike mark and take a different line. Putt the ball straight and firm, and hope it wouldn't break.

Hale Irwin: I couldn't breathe; I couldn't swallow.

Bernhard Langer: I made a pretty good stroke, but it did break too much and the ball went right over the side of the hole. I was obviously disappointed. I could have been the hero of that Ryder Cup, and now I was the guy who missed that putt. Seve came over and gave

The agony of missing is writ large on Bernhard Langer's face.

me a hug. Eventually he started crying, and that set me off. I just felt bad for my team, that's all.

Hale Irwin: I knew what he was going through and if it was me, I would have been devastated so I wanted to temper my enthusiasm for a later time. I didn't think it was appropriate at that time to be jovial, simply because that was a lot to ask of one man in one putt.

I would never, ever, ever wish that last hole on anyone.

Payne Stewart: I'm glad I didn't have it. I wouldn't have wished that on anybody. But I will tell you who would have liked to have been in that position: Jack Nicklaus.

Nick Faldo: We came close; really close. I remember winning that point in the singles and then David Feherty won and you look back at the footage and you watch the finish and you see Langer and Irwin coming down those last couple of holes, you watch Calcavecchia shanking it on seventeen, you can really sense the tension of the whole event. And so when you see how close it was, what could have happened, it was pretty cruel; it was one of the hardest moments in sport when Langer faced that putt. He hit a good putt and probably hit a tiny little mark and it missed and the difference between a win and a loss – when it's such a fractional miss – was just massive.

The pressure of playing in the Ryder Cup is totally different to trying to win a Major because you're playing for a team and there's no prize money, you're playing for a point. And the hardest thing is playing for other guys – you don't want to let them down. If you have a bad week on the tour you kick the bag a few times and you go home, you missed the cut or you missed winning the tournament by a shot, but with the Ryder Cup you don't want to give up a point, you're going out there to win every match, to get a point; you might get put through the wringer and if you don't pull it off or if you're just hanging on by a point and you're desperate to get into the clubhouse, you realise how important that one point might be to your team. And you can see how the momentum shifts happen in the Ryder Cup – that's the real pressure. Especially with the expectation if you're up that you're going to win, or that you're meant to win, that makes it really tough.

Bernhard Langer: Certainly for the few hours afterwards, and probably into the next day or two, I thought about that putt quite a bit. But otherwise I really have not thought about it very much.

A week later, in the final round of the German Masters, I faced a fifteen-foot putt on the last hole to get into a play-off, and my first thought was: you just missed a six-footer a week ago, and so I walked around for a moment and said to myself, 'Don't go there. Don't think about that. Let's focus on this.' I was able to make the putt, and I won the play-off.

Dave Stockton: When Bernhard won the very next week, in Europe, I was never so glad to have somebody win. I mean, what a class individual.

Ian Woosnam: We were all down, some of the lads were in tears. So I grabbed a few of the team – I remember Sam and Jesse [Mark] James came with me – and we walked to the big tent where all the European fans had gathered and sank a few beers and sang a few songs with them.

Lanny Wadkins: We wanted to win and we had been pushed to win and Stockton was kind of a fiery captain. But we had a good team, and the team played with a lot of emotion.

Paul Azinger: Our celebration was like no party I had ever attended before. Golf doesn't have the tradition, like NFL football, of dousing the coach at the end of a super performance. Instead, we simply tossed our captain, Dave Stockton, into the Atlantic Ocean, as part of our congratulations.

Colin Montgomerie: I got into the locker room afterwards and it was a scene that I'll never forget – one that kept the juices flowing for many Ryder Cups afterwards. Langer came in and he was distraught, he'd just missed his putt to lose and Seve was on the side of the green – and it meant so much to Seve, his passion for it was unbelievable – and Seve and Langer were in the corner of the team room and they were crying, embracing each other and crying openly. I remember thinking, 'This is different'.

The guy I was playing against, Mark Calcavecchia was on the beach needing oxygen because he couldn't breathe. And you're thinking, 'God, this isn't the Walker Cup, this is something else entirely.' Olazábal was in tears, he'd given his all, Woosnam wanted to hit everybody, it was awful and yet really interesting to see the passion involved and what it meant to those players because it didn't mean that much to me yet because I hadn't experienced it before. It couldn't mean that much to me. They had played in it five or six times each by then and I was a rookie coming into this, and I'm sure the other rookies in

The victorious 1991 US Ryder Cup team.

there, they couldn't get it either. I looked at that and I said to myself, 'I want to be part of this, I want more.'

Bernard Gallacher: The one thing I learned from Kiawah Island was to think more deeply about the pairings, talk more to the players about who they would like to play with, even who they wouldn't want to play with. I still had Seve and Ollie, who never imagined they wouldn't be playing together. Other than that I still had a great side, we were back at the Belfry, a tried and tested venue, where we were guaranteed great support, where everything was sure to work well.

Dave Stockton: My time on the Ryder Cup is totally different than everybody else's. Yes, I wanted to get it back. No, not at all costs, but I did want to get it back.

It would have helped if the PGA hadn't called it the 'War by the Shore,' and it would have helped if I hadn't have been a hunter. And I decided I was going to have some camouflage hats because we were just coming out of Desert Storm, and I was going to be able to use those hunting hats later on. So I mean, I understand. I appreciated Tom Watson, following me as captain in 1993, saying he was going to try to get some civility back into it and all that. That's fine. I'm all for that. That's part of the core values of this game we play. But I'll tell you what, I stirred up a hornet's nest, but I don't care, because it's good to have; we tend to get complacent. We can't sing as good as the Europeans. We've got no chance to sing as good. But as long as our clubs play better, I don't care.

I've seen Bernard Gallacher a couple of times since then but have I tried to talk to him? No, he's not a friend of mine. I'm not even sure he likes himself and I don't think it's worth my time to speak with him.

But that's not what I like to remember from Kiawah. What I like to remember was when we were going to the last dinner, the US PGA had put on two buses for the teams, the American bus and the European bus. Woosie came up to me and said, 'Stock, we can get everybody on one bus, we're only two people shy.' And with that he picks up Corey Pavin and carries him on the bus so he counts as one person. A wonderful moment and we had a great time all together on that bus. That's what I like to look back on and remember.

Dave Stockton is thrown into the surf by his team.

THIRTY

1993
The Belfry, Sutton Coldfield, England
(USA 15, EUR 13)

The thirtieth Ryder Cup returned to the Belfry in 1993. After the controversy of Kiawah, the respective Ryder Cup committees and the captains that they appointed were determined to bring things under more civilised conditions once again. The men charged with leading each side were Tom Watson for the visitors and, once again, Bernard Gallacher for the home team. Watson, an eight-time Major winner was a smart choice as he was immensely popular in the UK having won the Open in 1975, 1977, 1980, 1982 and 1983. In advance of the 1993 matches, Watson contacted Nick Faldo and discussed at length the issues that had arisen at Kiawah from the European perspective.

In advance of the US team's departure for England, Watson issued a diplomatic statement which clearly set the tone for the manner in which he hoped the matches would proceed. 'This isn't war, this is golf,' he said. 'We're going over there to try like hell to kick their butts. And they're going to try like hell to kick ours. That's as it should be. But when it's over, we should be able to go off together, lift a glass and toast one another. That's what the Ryder Cup is all about.' They were sentiments that Gallacher wholeheartedly agreed with.

Bernard Gallacher: When I was appointed Ryder Cup captain for Kiawah in 1989, a few weeks after we had drawn the match at the Belfry and retained the trophy, I always saw it as a two-match job – home and away or, in my case, the other way round. Most other people saw it that way too, assuming, of course, that everything went all right for me at Kiawah. Well, we lost, but only after one of the most tense finishes in Ryder Cup history, and the support I had from the players to continue made it easy for me to carry on. In all honesty I would have been disappointed not to have been asked to continue and been given the chance of winning back the trophy at the Belfry.

Gallacher's team had some real class amid their ranks in the experienced Seve Ballesteros, Nick Faldo, Mark James, Bernhard Langer, Colin Montgomerie, José María Olazábal, Sam Torrance and Ian Woosnam, while the rookies were Peter Baker, Joakim Haeggman, Barry Lane and Costantino Rocca. There were one or two concerns for Gallacher within that selection, however, as Langer had been out of action for around six weeks with a neck injury coming into the Ryder Cup, and Ballesteros had been in poor form that season. Indeed, Seve had failed to qualify for the team and had been one of Gallacher's captain's picks alongside rookie Haeggman and his old playing partner Olazábal.

Bernard Gallacher: I had to give Seve a captain's pick. A Ryder Cup without Seve in those days was unthinkable, especially as we knew that his partnership with Olazábal

Opposite: Davis Love III raises his arms aloft after sinking his putt on the eighteenth to defeat Costantino Rocca. *Getty Images*

would be strong and we would probably get points in the foursomes and fourballs from them, but he was struggling with his game. The biggest problem with that was that I didn't get his usual attention to the rookies, that arm around their shoulder, the advice, the on-course leadership, because he was too wrapped up in trying to fix his own game.

Watson's twelve were formidable and consisted of the tried and tested in Paul Azinger, Chip Beck, Fred Couples, Raymond Floyd, Tom Kite, Corey Pavin, Payne Stewart, Lanny Wadkins and rookies John Cook, Jim Gallagher Jnr, Lee Janzen and Davis Love III.

Unfortunately, the American captain's lofty ambitions for genial relations between the teams were somewhat undone during the pre-match gala dinner – by Watson himself.

Tom Watson: After all that had happened at Kiawah, I had wanted to avoid any controversy as captain, but I got embroiled in it at the gala dinner before the first ball had even been hit. I hadn't wanted the distraction of my players having to sign hundreds of autographs, so I made a blanket decision not to sign any. When Sam Torrance asked me to sign his menu I said no because I didn't want to make any exceptions to my rule. The fallout from that, particularly in the press, was enormous. It shook me up. I knew what the tabloids in the UK were like but some of the things that were said by people hurt. It was exactly what I didn't want to happen.

Sam Torrance: Tom insisted that he had banned signature-seekers from the team table and did not want to make any exceptions. I was furious. We were the players in the bloody event, not some random punters.

Bernard Gallacher: I just found it funny. Sam had a few beers, because that's what Sam does, and he just slipped across and Tom told him off, and Sam had his tail between his legs for a bit.

It was a storm in a teacup but showed that tensions were still high after the events at Kiawah.
After a delayed start due to fog, the first day's play got underway shortly after 10:30 am. Gallacher was determined to get off to a flying start so sent out what he considered to be his strongest pairings. If he had hoped to lay down a statement of intent, it did not go exactly to plan. The morning was by no means a disaster, with Langer and Woosnam setting a European foursome record with their 7&5 victory over Azinger and Stewart and Faldo and Montgomerie showing the potency of their partnership with a 4&3 victory over Floyd and Couples, but Wadkins and Pavin had comfortably beaten Torrance and James 4&3 in the opening match and then Kite and Love defeated the Spanish double-act of Ballesteros and Olazábal 2&1.

Tom Watson: Being captain was a great pleasure, and I had a lot of people help me out, but I think the most important thing about the Ryder Cup is the attitude of the team going in. The attitude that you're going to win and nothing can stop you is one that the captain can instil in his players. With all the responsibilities involved, I think instilling the will to win and belief in winning is the most important thing I did as captain in 1993.

Lee Janzen: From watching the Ryder Cup and talking to the other players, I was expecting a lot of commotion surrounding the 1993 match, but what happened was a lot more than I expected. And nothing prepared me for that moment during the opening ceremony when I stood with Tom Watson and the rest of the team watching the American flag being raised and hearing the national anthem. It's a moment that . . . well, you can't be more proud of representing your country.

Davis Love III: Tom Kite pulled me aside on the Thursday and said, 'Remember one thing, if they've got a sixty-foot putt, expect them to make it. If they're in an unplayable spot, figure they'll find a play. If you're sure we've won the hole, flush the thought. Things are going to happen you've never seen happen before in your entire life.

I still remember Tom Watson saying the night before those matches, 'Rookies, be ready tomorrow. This is the only event in golf that will make your legs shake.' I thought he was nuts. The next day, walking to the first tee behind Seve and José, I realised my legs were shaking.

1993 was my first Ryder Cup and I was partnered with my mentor, Tom Kite. We had decided that alternate shot, I would hit off the odd holes and he would hit off the even holes. Then we had a fog delay Friday morning, so I got to sit around and think about it for about an hour and a half. Then walking up to the first tee, I tried to convince him to hit off the first tee, because although we had agreed that I would play the odd holes, I wasn't ready for it on the first. And he had to calm me down and give me a three-iron and said, 'Just get me in the fairway and get going.'

When you walk up to that first tee in a Ryder Cup, even if you have played six of them or it's your first one, it's a nerve-wracking experience. But I'll never forget that, playing Seve and José, and with Tom Kite there beside me; it was an unbelievable moment in my career.

Colin Montgomerie: I felt more a part of the scene by my second Ryder Cup. I was coming up to be the number one in Europe by '93, very much part of the team. Bernard Gallacher gave me Nick Faldo to play with for all four of the paired sessions. And I knew I was playing with Nick about two months beforehand because I was sitting at home when twelve dozen Rextar golf balls arrived at my door with instructions that I was to learn to play with them. So I knew then I was playing with Nick because those were the balls he played with. That was a real honour to play with him. He was number one in the world at the time and to play with him under those circumstances was a big thing; and I learnt a lot from him about certain aspects of the match play game.

We talked in practise – he'd say, 'What do you think of this? Let's have a practise here, what do you think the line of this putt is?' And I would say, 'Well it's just outside of the right lip, but it depends how hard you hit it. But it's just outside the right lip at perfect pace.' So then he said, 'Well, what's perfect pace?' And I said, 'Two foot past the hole is perfect pace. That's what I'm seeing.' And he said, 'OK.' I'd go from the ball to the target, but he didn't, he putted in an action track way – every two foot is a ball and if the ball goes over that particular spot it's going to go in. So every putt for him is a straight putt – two foot at a time. But I always think that that's difficult because I feel the pace of a putt is more important than the direction. Yes, he's got the direction of the putt right every time, but in my view if the pace of the putt is wrong you can miss every putt even if it's on line. So we had that problem to get over first, which we worked out. I just said to him that if he was in trouble, if he wasn't confident then he should ask me what I thought. It was difficult though, I was very much the rookie still in many ways and he was number one in the world, but I said to him – 'I'm going to leave you with this; you're number one in the world, how the hell can I tell you what to do? But if you don't know or if you and your caddie are struggling at all, ask me and I'll give you an opinion – as long as you don't tell me what you think first. I'll tell you right lip and if that's what you thought it was after you had done all your tracking bit, then great, go for it. That'll give you the confidence to go for it. If we agree then you can commit to the shot. If I'm giving you right lip and you think it's straight or left, then we'll have a discussion about it. But you do your own thing – and I'll be delighted if you leave me to it as well, if you don't mind.'

Nick Faldo: Monty had a sound understanding of partnership play and the importance of getting along. He certainly accepted that I needed to be in charge. Most important of all, he was a great foursomes partner; he hit the ball straight and holed out well.

Colin Montgomerie: But I was very much the junior. We had a sort of lobster coloured sweater that the team wore one morning. But in all the footage and the photos, if you look back, you'll see that our jumpers were a different colour to everyone else's. We were at breakfast and he came in and told me that his jumper didn't fit. He's a big lad, 6ft

4in, you know, and he obviously found that it didn't fit him comfortably, it was too short or what have you. So he says to me, 'Monty, go down to the pro shop and buy us a couple of sweaters, will you?' This is at breakfast just before we're about to go out and play. So I say, 'Uh, OK.' And that was how the relationship worked, how the partnership worked – he told me what to do and I did it. He wasn't going down to the pro shop, I was. So I had to go down to the pro shop, buy us a couple of sweaters – and they didn't have the team sweaters for sale. The team sweaters were cashmere, these were lamb's wool and a different colour. We turned up in these kind of red sweaters and everyone else is in these lobster coloured ones and they were all like, 'What the hell are those?' But that was how it worked. He used me like that

Colin Montgomerie leans over Nick Faldo as they discuss the line of a putt – sporting their newly bought jumpers. *Getty Images*

– and it was fine, it worked well.

The afternoon fourballs saw Woosnam and Baker take on Gallagher Jnr and Jansen, Langer and Lane face Wadkins and Pavin, Faldo and Montgomerie go up against Azinger and Couples, and then Ballesteros and Olazábal play Love and Kite.

Peter Baker: After the first team meeting, I came back to my room and my wife asked me if I was OK. I said 'I thought that I was motivated and driven, but these guys . . . well, it's unbelievable.' I couldn't quite fathom what I'd seen and heard in the team room. It was so intense, incredible. It rubbed off on me and meant I wanted to prove a point. Seve and Langer were so desperate to win. They weren't derogatory about the Americans, but what they said was just rallying us. This was our chance to prove we were the best players in the world. We were fed up of being told their tour was better than ours.

The Belfry was like a home ground for me. I had a good five months where I had played really well and come from really nowhere, not even in contention for the Ryder Cup, and made the team.

What made things even better was my partnership with Ian Woosnam. We played in the afternoon fourball on the Friday against Gallagher Jnr and Janzen and won and then went out together against Couples and Azinger in the Saturday afternoon fourball. Woosie carried me the first two or three holes but then I absolutely smashed them. All Woosie kept saying was, 'Keep going, keep going!'

That was great. What wasn't so great was playing the Saturday morning foursomes. It was Barry Lane and me against Raymond Floyd and Payne Stewart. On the fifteenth hole I had to hole a six-footer to win the hole. As Floyd picked up his ball he backed away right along our line. I just stood there open-mouthed, but Barry got stuck into Floyd. 'What the fuck do you think you're doing?' Lane asked. 'Oh, did I?' Floyd said with a smirk. Great golfer, not a nice guy.

The session would conclude with Europe just ahead after Woosnam and Baker defeated Gallagher and Janzen one-up, and the Spaniards had seen off Love and Kite 4&3. Faldo and Montgomerie halved with Azinger and Couples (concluding their match on the Saturday morning after poor light had forced them to abandon that evening), while the Americans had secured a point through Wadkins and Pavin's 4&2 victory over Langer and Lane to make the overall score 4½–3½ in Europe's favour.

Europe's good form continued in the Saturday morning foursomes as Faldo and Montgomerie defeated Wadkins and Pavin 3&2, Langer and Woosnam combined to beat Couples and Azinger 2&1 and Ballesteros and Olazábal defeated Love and Kite 2&1, while the US secured a consolation point when Floyd and Stewart beat Baker and Lane 3&2.

With things looking rosy for the home team, Watson fired some rockets at lunchtime and made it clear to his charges that they had to start performing or else face humiliation. His players responded. First Cook and Beck defeated Faldo and Montgomerie two up before Pavin and Gallagher Jnr comfortably saw off James and Rocca 5&4. Woosnam and Baker struck back with an impressive 6&5 victory over Couples and Azinger before Floyd and Stewart combined to defeat Olazábal and Haeggman 2&1 to cut Europe's lead to a single point, 8½–7½.

Nick Faldo: My partnership with Colin started really well. That first morning we saw off Floyd and Couples 4&3, then in the afternoon, with Paul Azinger joining Couples in place of Floyd, we had a superb fourball match. Both sides were round in a better ball of 63 and a half was a fair result.

The game couldn't be finished because we ran out of light, all square after seventeen. The following morning it was pistols at dawn; if there is a more frightening drive than the eighteenth at the Belfry in the Ryder Cup, it is hitting the same tee shot as your first of the day. In the end I had to hole a ten-footer for a four and a half. Nerve-wracking stuff – and I think the stress of having to go through that fifteen-minute exercise on the Saturday morning took its toll later in the day. Monty and I played well enough to beat Wadkins and Pavin in the morning, but there seemed little inspiration left for the fourball in the afternoon.

Colin Montgomerie: Nick and I did OK, two-and-a-half points out of four. We should have won the last one. We played John Cook and Chip Beck and we were expected to win but they beat us on the last hole. Everyone can beat anyone on any given day and that's what that was. All credit to them, they played well.

I remember we birdied the first four holes, I birdied the first two, he birdied the second two – and we were all square! And I went, 'Shit, this is going to be a hell of a tough day!'

Nick Faldo: We went one down after neither of us could get a par at the eighth, and every hole thereafter was halved. The putts suddenly stopped dropping, and however hard we tried, nothing worked. It was all so frustrating, particularly on an afternoon when Europe lost the initiative for the first time in the match. We were never really able to get it back.

Tom Watson: Any time you beat the star, that's a very big plus from a psychological standpoint for your team. You know, one of the things that really turned our team around in '93 was the pairing of John Cook and Chip Beck beating Colin Montgomerie and Nick Faldo the last match on Saturday. That was a big turnaround. We were still behind on points but the team room on Saturday night was just like the team room probably was at Medinah for the Europeans in 2012 after Poulter birdied the last five holes on the Saturday. It just gives you a ray of hope. In '93 it was more than a ray of hope that said, 'Yeah, we can still do this'. That was the critical match of the whole week. Neither Cook nor Beck had played yet, then they bounced off the bench to take on Faldo and Montgomerie. They showed real true grit.

I chose Raymond Floyd in 1993 as one of my picks along with Lanny Wadkins and they performed admirably. In that Ryder Cup, the go-to group that I had picked was Paul Azinger and Payne Stewart. They were just shooting lights out in the practise rounds. They were making eight, nine birdies. They were the team. They were the team that was going to propel us to victory. Well, that first morning, that Friday morning, we had a fog delay and that went one hour, two hours and three hours, and I was looking over at Paul and Paul's eyes got wider and wider and wider, and you could just see the tension building and building with Paul and Payne and they went out and it was kind of a whitewash. They got beat 7&5, and basically I said, you know, I don't want to have an effect on their confidence, but I have to split up the team and do something with it. So I took Payne and put him with Raymond the next morning, and they went out and won the match. And that was a move that was discussed with Raymond and Lanny and we made that decision and it was a good move. You looked at Raymond's eyes, you never saw his eyes waver, no matter if he was shooting 80, which he rarely did, or shooting 65, his eyes had a focus that you like to see. The way he played the game, every shot counted.

Peter Baker: We were having breakfast when Seve appeared; you always sat up when he was around. He joined us and you could see there was something he wanted to tell us. 'Your opponents [Ray Floyd and Payne Stewart], they are good players,' he said. 'Floyd is a very tough man to beat. Somewhere along the line he will do something to put you off: rip his golf glove off; rattle his clubs or something.' Me and Laney looked at each other and we said: 'You mean, like you do, Seve?' – we couldn't help ourselves. 'Oh no, not like me . . . well, maybe,' Seve said.

There are certain things that you can do to impose yourself on the other guy in match play, maybe calling whose shot it is or something like that, dominating the pairings. But the niggles do go on in these matches and all the players know it. Even if the fans might not notice these little moments, they are there. You see, Seve was right.

John Cook: I can honestly say that my experience at the Ryder Cup wasn't one of my highlights. Making the team was wonderful. I enjoyed being with the guys. But I didn't play a match until Saturday afternoon. Even then there was hesitancy on Tom Watson's part to even put Chip Beck and me out. There was a chance I wasn't going to play until Sunday and then a chance I wasn't going to play at all. And I had earned my way on that team through points. I wasn't a captain's choice and I felt that I should have at least played once on Friday and again on Saturday. Fortunately we won a big match on Saturday, Chip and me, beating Faldo and Montgomerie. Maybe Tom didn't think I was playing that well, I don't know. But I don't think that should have had a bearing on my not being able to play. Like I said, I was a point-earner.

Tom Watson: It takes experience to understand the pressure and appreciate what it's like to play with the noise the Ryder Cup generates when you're out there. You miss a putt and people cheer. The beauty of it is that after the infamous 'War on the Shore' and the mentality of some of our fans at Kiawah, Bernard Gallacher and I basically just made an agreement to try to keep it down. We made a point to talk about it in front of the public and to say, 'Keep the etiquette of the game right. This isn't a soccer match. This isn't a baseball game where you yell, "Swing, swing, swing, batter."' It's not that sort of stuff. We don't do that in golf. That's what separates golf from other sports, honestly. And I think that's why it has a different set of rules of etiquette that makes it refreshing.

Lee Trevino: I remember when I used to win a match in Britain, people would cheer me. The Ryder Cup isn't like that anymore. Make a birdie now and they boo.

Bernard Gallacher: I felt we could pretty much win the whole match by the Saturday afternoon. But our momentum got stopped. Seve wouldn't play that afternoon. Seve and Olazábal had beaten Love and Kite in the morning foursomes 2&1 and I really wanted to put out a very strong team in the afternoon, even though I had promised to play everybody before the singles. But I thought we could win it, virtually, in the afternoon. I obviously wanted to play Seve and Olazábal in the afternoon, but Seve refused to play.

From my perspective, that was the week that Seve's game started to go down. I know he's not around now, and we're all sorry about that. But 1993 at the Ryder Cup, in my opinion, was the time when we had to accept that Seve was on the way down. It didn't matter what I said to him, or didn't matter what Olazábal said to him, he just point blank refused to play. He said he wasn't playing well enough and needed to practise before the singles. Coming into that match, he obviously wasn't playing great either, but having Olazábal was such an inspiration to him, they combined so well and they worked hard for each other. But he was adamant he couldn't play in the afternoon. He felt he would let Olazábal down. I remonstrated with him, but he was adamant. He was really struggling with his game, worked on it all week, and he felt he needed practise before the singles, but it didn't work. He was fiddling around with his game too much.

And I think that was the turning point in the match. The Americans suddenly said: 'Oh right, Seve doesn't want to play. Now that's interesting.' And I think our team felt, 'That's not good news.'

Colin Montgomerie: Some of the golf played that day was exceptional. Faldo and Azinger were out of this world. Ollie and Joakim Haeggman were two down with two holes to play against Ray Floyd and Payne Stewart and on the par-five seventeenth, Joakim hit his approach to about four feet from the pin. It was a great shot. Ollie then got Joakim to run up and mark his ball! He was eighty yards away, but felt he could pull off just as good a shot. And you know what? He hit it off the pin and it ended two feet from the hole. Unbelievable. That kind of play usually turns matches but Payne Stewart kept his cool and sank a fifteen-foot putt to halve the hole and that won them the match because they were already two-up.

It was the first time in twelve years that the US had won the Saturday afternoon fourball session and it set the scene for a dramatic and emotional Sunday singles.

There was some drama on Saturday evening when Sam Torrance announced that he was struggling badly with a toe problem.

Sam Torrance: I have always regarded Mark James as the strongest-minded player out there with a wonderful head on his shoulders. He deserved a far better partner than he got in the morning foursomes of the match at the Belfry in 1993 when I was injured and had to have a toenail removed that evening. I was so disappointed because he was playing great and I was simply horrible – no use to him whatsoever. When you play with a friend in the Ryder Cup you really want to be at your best.

Bernard Gallacher: Sam Torrance couldn't play after the opening day foursomes play, because he had a poisoned toe. It was the left toe as well, the one you really pivot on

The eighteenth at the Belfry. *Getty Images*

in golf, the one that you basically throw your weight onto on the downswing, and he couldn't play the rest of the week. Sam was one of our best players at that time. He finished fifth on the money list that year, had just finished second in the Lancôme Trophy, the previous tournament before the Ryder Cup. That was really quite a blow. I told Tom Watson, pulled him aside, and said Sam was unlikely to play. I said, 'You are welcome to come into the team room and have a look at his toe,' and Tom duly came along. I think Tom felt he was doing the right job as captain by seeing for himself, and I think he was. Tom's a straightforward guy. I had no trouble at all with it, and in some way, him coming to look helped me. It killed off any suspicion that I'd decided to pull Sam out because he was playing badly or whatever reason. He was injured and couldn't continue and Tom saw that for himself.

We had had an issue in 1991 because Dave Stockton pulled Steve Pate out without telling me, which altered the balance of the singles draw. It became a defining moment in the Ryder Cup, as you now can't pull somebody out, it has to be agreed on both sides that a player is injured.

Back in 1993, the doctor said Sam could play if he had a painkilling injection on the first tee, and another one on the tenth tee. I said 'I think that is just unfair, it's too important this match. I don't think we should put anybody through that.' Tom came up and had a look at the toe and said 'well fine, I'll go and pick my man [to miss out]. The reason Lanny Wadkins was picked was that he was the last captain's pick, so he volunteered to step down. He felt it was only fair because he hadn't actually won his way into the team. We paired them up and we got a half each.

Tom Watson: When we realised that Sam Torrance wasn't going to play, Lanny took me aside and said, 'Tom, I want you to put my name in the envelope.' I said, 'I'm not doing that. You're one of our best players out here.' He said, 'No, Tom, you have to put me in. I was one of your picks, I didn't qualify for the team. I'm not staying in the team over someone who earned the right to be here.' It was a hell of a thing for him to say and when I look back at '93 that is one of my favourite memories because of how much it meant for Lanny to do that for his team and for his country and how much his unselfish act contributed. He made a very difficult situation a lot easier for me and in doing that he also didn't cause any ructions in the team room. It was one of the greatest gestures I've ever seen anyone make.

I had tears in my eyes. As the players prepared to go out I said to them, 'If it gets too tough out there for you, remember what Lanny did for you.'

I think Lanny's actions had a huge bearing on the team's attitude and how they went out to play that day.

Lanny Wadkins: Tom looked at the guys and said, 'We are going to win tomorrow, and I can tell you why we are going to win because I am the luckiest son of a bitch that has ever played golf.' When he said that I looked at Raymond Floyd and he looked at me . . . We were the only two people around who were old enough to get that, to understand the things that Tom had done and we looked at each other like, 'No shit Tom, we have known that forever.'

Tom Watson decided to leave most of his big guns at the tail of the order, looking for a strong finish – although he did send out Fred Couples at the top to take on Ian Woosnam.

Colin Montgomerie: I managed to beat Lee Janzen, who was the current US Open champion at the time in the singles, but I was put at number three again as I had been in '91. You're not going to lose or win the Ryder Cup from number three, you're hidden; I managed to win both OK. I went out to follow Faldo in his singles against Azinger in '93 and it was funny, on the fourteenth hole on the par three at the Belfry, in the foursomes and the fourballs, Nick and I went 2-2-2-2, and walking off on the Saturday afternoon after our fourth two in a row, he said to me, 'Wouldn't it be good if I holed it tomorrow?' *I.* Not 'you or I holed it tomorrow.' *I.* 'Wouldn't it be great if *I* holed it tomorrow?'

I said, 'Yeah, it would be great. You'd probably win the hole!' And he bloody well did it. So he played that hole 2-2-2-2-1. And I remember thinking, 'OK, that was pretty good.' Pretty good? It was bloody incredible.

Nick Faldo: I walked onto the tee and kicked the leaves away, and I said to my caddie, 'OK Fanny [Sunesson], good time for a hole in one.' That week I was hitting the ball so well and I said, 'I'm going to hole a full shot.' Because it's match play, that's what you're trying to do. If you're standing over the ball with any club in your hand, you're thinking, 'How close can I get this?' So I actually said to Fanny, 'I know I'm going to hole one this week.' And I did.

Colin Montgomerie: Nick knew he was number one in the world and he knew everyone else knew it. That's key – not just you knowing it, but everyone else knowing it, too. It's a huge difference. It's like the New Zealand team in rugby. They're the best – they know it, and everyone else knows it. It gives you an edge. You walk differently through the clubhouse. The chest is out. You are hot, hot favourite. Just like Tiger Woods in the year 2000 when he walked on the first tee with that red shirt on and everybody just looked and him and thought, 'Shit, we're in trouble here.' That aura just cowed everybody else. That was what it was like around Nick back in those days. He was phenomenal.

Peter Baker: I was playing against Corey Pavin who had been outstanding that week. Seve took me aside over breakfast and he said, 'Peter, you have got a very, very tough game today, this guy is a tricky customer.'

But I had been playing well, too. I was aware of how Pavin had behaved at Kiawah in 1991, but he couldn't have been nicer. We were both several shots under par for our round and we were putting out of our skins. When I finally beat him by holing a twenty-footer on eighteen it was an amazing feeling, one I think you can only get in a Ryder Cup. By the end I was mentally shattered.

It had been an incredible game and the best scoring of the day. That night we had to go to dinner which was the last thing Pavin wanted to do. He was chatting away and he said, 'Do you know, you had twenty-three putts today.' After I got back home and thought about it I realised that he had had twenty-six putts; so between us we had had forty-nine putts, which was some sort of record.

Europe started strongly. Although Chip Beck had beaten Barry Lane and Ian Woosnam had halved with Fred Couples, Colin Montgomerie had defeated Lee Janzen, Peter Baker had triumphed over Corey Pavin and Joakim Haeggman had beaten John Cook. Payne Stewart then pulled back a point with a 3&2 win over Mark James.

With the big guns in the US team starting to roll out across the course, the match between Costantino Rocca and Davis Love III was reaching its denouement. Standing on the seventeenth green as Rocca lined up a twenty-five-footer for birdie, Love sidled up to his captain and murmured, 'It's about time for him to miss one and me to make one.'

Rocca took his time; perhaps took too much time. He rolled his putt beyond the hole.

Davis Love III: He was surprised it went so far. He thought he was going to have an easy tap-in. For the first time all day, he looked just a tiny bit scared.

The match was all square as they came to the eighteenth. The tension was palpable – although Love showed zero nerves as he split the fairway with his best drive of the week. Rocca, clearly feeling the weight of the moment, swiped too quickly at his and sent it far to the right.

Love was faced with a six-footer to win the hole.

Davis Love III: I almost threw up on myself. I couldn't breathe. There was no saliva in my mouth. It's one thing for me to miss a putt to lose the Masters. But to miss a putt to let down your team, that's bad.

I'll always remember that putt. That's as nervous as I've ever been in my life . . . I almost got knocked down. I was lucky to hang onto my putter.

Bernard Gallacher: Costantino had given us great hope because against the run of play he went one up with two to play. He'd hit three good shots into the seventeenth, went for the match and knocked it four foot past and then lost the last and that was that.

Tom Watson: That is the tragedy of sport. Costantino missing that putt at the seventeenth against Davis turned the match.

Costantino Rocca: The team was sorry for me. They all pat me. I miss putt because I go to look too quickly the ball go at the hole . . . The tension, the tension.

Nick Faldo: I think everybody was stretched to where he had never been before.

As the cheers rang around the green, Love walked over to Lanny Wadkins and said, 'That putt's for you.'
   That putt and that match marked a turning point as an American tide swept down the final straight. Faldo halved the final match against Paul Azinger but by then it was all over. Jim Gallagher Jnr beat Seve Ballesteros 3&2, Raymond Floyd defeated José María Olazábal two-up and Tom Kite hammered Bernhard Langer, who was till struggling with his neck injury, 5&3. The final score was 15–13 to the USA and the cup was going back across the Atlantic with them.

Raymond Floyd: Of all the matches I played, that one with Olazábal was probably the best moment for me. The Ryder Cup was on the line, you've got your most experienced players out there, and Tom had placed me in a very meaningful slot to take on one of the better players in the world. It was going to come down to whoever played best toward the end would win. I'm sure the Ryder Cup experience I had helped me not to falter at that crucial moment.
   It was a wonderful way to end the experience. The Ryder Cup is the hardest golf that you will ever play. It is a long, trying week. Intense pressure. You've got the weight of your country and your fellow Ryder Cup members and your captain and I was picked. I was a captain's pick, and here I am, put in next or third to the last slot and I'm paired against Olazábal and as it came down I beat him to win the deciding point. It was something that was very special and I played probably as well as I had played in six months and I don't know where it came from but it came at the right time.

Peter Baker: Seve was absolutely bawling his eyes out after we lost. He wasn't alone either, but his desire to win was incredible. His emotion was unbelievable.

Tom Watson: I have to say that I've never been as nervous on a golf course as I was as a captain in '93. Because golf is the game it is, an individual sport, I had asked Roy Williams [the prominent college basketball coach], 'How do you coach somebody? What do you do?' He said, 'When we go to an away game, Tom, I tell players two things. I say: The first thing I want you to do is make the crowd go silent during the game and the last thing I want you to do, I want you to watch them leave early when they are beaten.'

We got behind early in '93 and then we came back and Davis made that five-foot putt to win and Raymond followed it up at the last hole. And as we were going up the last hole following Raymond, Payne Stewart came up to me and he slapped me on the shoulder and said, 'Captain! Look at the stands up there!' He didn't have to say they were half-empty, we could feel it and we knew the momentum was with us to win.

Colin Montgomerie: It was devastating at the end to see Barry Lane three up with five to go and he lost; Chip Beck played a great finish. Costantino Rocca three-putted seventeen, so Davis Love won his game. And the US just turned it around and that was it. And you just think, 'Aw God, not again. I've played twice, lost twice, what the hell can I do to win this thing?'

Tom Watson: Yes, the Ryder Cup is a great sports event because of the rivalry between the US and European teams, and that can't help but be exciting every two years. But I think the most beautiful thing about it – and I say 'beautiful' because you don't have this too much in professional sports – is that the players are in this event for the love of their country and for the love of the game. They're not playing for any type of financial reward at all. And I think that's why the Ryder Cup is about the purest event in professional sport in the world.

Tom Watson and his team celebrate retaining the cup. *Getty Images*

THIRTY-ONE

1995

Oak Hill Country Club. Rochester, New York
(EUR 14½, USA 13½)

And so it was to Oak Hill Country Club in Rochester in upstate New York in the autumn of 1995. The course was a return to a more traditional layout than had been seen at Kiawah Island, and as such many observers (on both sides of the Atlantic) believed that it would serve the home team a considerable advantage, with no European player having secured the US PGA or the US Open for many years.

There was a controversial change to the team selection made by the European Ryder Cup Committee shortly after the defeat at the Belfry. They had decided to reduce the number of wild cards available to the captain from three to two in order to reward those who played on the European Tour rather than offering the captain the chance to pick the best team available to him. Interestingly, Gallacher himself had been part of the committee that had made the decision, and he was widely derided in the press as being a European Tour yes man. This piqued Gallacher considerably and his relationship with the press became increasingly frosty.

In the end Gallacher awarded his wild cards to Nick Faldo (who had chosen to play the '95 season in America) and José María Olazábal, only for the latter to withdraw a week later with a foot injury. He was replaced by Ian Woosnam, who joined Seve Ballesteros, Howard Clark, David Gilford, Mark James, Per-Ulrik Johansson, Bernhard Langer, Colin Montgomerie, Costantino Rocca, Sam Torrance and Philip Walton.

The team flew by Concorde from Heathrow to Greater Rochester International Airport, where they were greeted by over 5,000 locals and balmy autumn sun, and an American team that had also endured something of a bumpy start to proceedings. Lanny Wadkins had been installed as team captain and had been roundly criticised for his wildcard picks of Fred Couples and Curtis Strange. Strange in particular raised the ire of golf columnists around the country as he was out of form and had made the team ahead of Open champion John Daly and leading money winner Lee Janzen.

In terms of Ryder Cup experience, the difference between the teams was seismic. The European team counted thirteen Majors among them to the USA's six, and fifty-one Ryder Cup appearances to a mere fifteen from the Americans. This dearth of cup experience in particular was compounded by Wadkins' selection of five rookies in Brad Faxon, Tom Lehman, Jeff Maggert, Phil Mickelson and Loren Roberts (Europe's rookies were Johansson and Walton).

Colin Montgomerie: Oak Hill '95, you know, there wasn't a massive change to things. Same captain. I don't know how the captains were selected in those days but to get a third chance was a delight for Gallacher. He got backing from senior players to continue; that's how it was really. Faldo, Langer, Woosie and Seve picked the captain. And if Seve and Faldo said they wanted Gallacher as a captain, he was captain. That's how it worked.

Opposite: Unheralded rookie Philip Walton is lifted by his captain, Bernard Gallacher, after defeating Jay Haas one-up. *Getty Images*

Bernard Gallacher: I was quite happy to stand down as captain after the second defeat but there were people who thought maybe I should get another crack. It's not as if we had been heavily defeated in 1993. It's not as if the tactics were all that wrong.

Seve and Nick Faldo gave their backing publicly and then Bernhard Langer sent me a letter that said, 'We hope you don't stand down because we need someone who has the experience going to America.' That's what really clinched it for me. If people like Langer and Seve and Faldo had the confidence in my captaincy then I was very happy to do it again.

Brad Faxon: The Ryder Cup really is extraordinary. I played Monday at Oak Hill and there was no crowd; and then on Tuesday there were 40,000 people. We walked through this throng to the first tee and there was Byron Nelson and President George HW Bush. 'You shoot first, Fax,' is what Lanny Wadkins said, and I heard the announcer say, 'Brad Faxon, United States of America', but I still can't remember actually hitting that first shot.

For Friday morning's foursomes, Gallacher pitched his power pairing of Nick Faldo and the in-form Colin Montgomerie into action against Tom Lehman and Corey Pavin.

Lanny Wadkins had wanted his team to build up a head of steam and get the crowd jumping and his pairing delivered just that, sprinting into a four-hole lead.

But the European pair had undeniable pedigree and soon got into their rhythm. They roared back into the match and by the ninth they were only one-down. At the thirteenth, a long par-five named the Hill of Fame thanks to the grove of trees surrounding the green dedicated to legends of the game, Faldo produced a stunning forty-five-foot putt for birdie to make the match all square.

Alas for Europe they couldn't quite gain the ascendancy and the brilliance that Faldo had demonstrated at the thirteenth came to naught at the eighteenth as he drove his tee shot wide; once Montgomerie had chipped it back to the fairway, Faldo's second shot landed in a bunker. Lehman, meanwhile, found the green with a delightful approach iron; Pavin left him with a four-footer with his next effort, and Lehman coolly sank his putt for the point.

Tom Lehman: Corey was a great partner. He gave me the best piece of advice I've ever gotten in golf. We were on the seventeenth hole, the match was tied, and I said to him, 'I'm so nervous I can hardly swing the club.' The situation was just so new to me. And he just said, 'Tom, it's really simple. Just get committed and swing. Get committed and swing.' And so the idea was, you know, commitment. Then on the eighteenth hole I hit the best shot I've ever hit under pressure. It was a five-iron from 205 yards, crossing wind, raining sideways. I just said to myself, 'Get committed and swing.' And I hit it on the front part of the green forty feet short of the hole. We two-putted to win.

Gallacher had more luck in the second match as his unheralded pairing of Rocca and Torrance got the better of Haas and Couples. They were all square after five, but then went on a mesmeric run that saw them five ahead at the tenth. They won 3&2.

Maggert and Love added to the US tally, breaking little sweat in dispatching Clark and James 4&3 and producing some scintillating golf in the process, birdying four of the first seven holes and only dropping a single shot all morning when they bogeyed the thirteenth.

The final foursome out saw Crenshaw and Strange take on Johansson and Langer. Although

Johansson showed some nerves on the first with a poor chip to the green, he recovered his composure and dovetailed nicely with the German; they pushed into a one hole lead at the turn and went on to win the tenth and eleventh. At that stage Gallacher had to submit his pairings for the afternoon fourballs and assumed that this duo would continue their fine form in the afternoon. But no sooner had he submitted his pairings, the rain, which had been a persistent nuisance all morning, began to hammer down and his players began to struggle badly and their match slowed to a crawl. Gallacher watched with growing horror as he realised that Johansson and Langer would have hardly any time for a rest before going out again in the afternoon.

The pairings eventually came to the eighteenth all square and Langer was presented with a six-foot putt that would either hand Europe a crucial point or would see them halve the match. Shutting out the demons from his final stroke four years earlier, Langer kept his cool and nailed it.

Bernard Gallacher: I had one or two other pairings for the fourballs that afternoon, but as the time approached to put in the afternoon line-up [midday], Bernhard and Per-Ulrik were something like three or four up with just five to play. Now, when I played in the Ryder Cup and won, I just couldn't wait to get out there and do it again, so I put them together again. What a disaster.

No sooner had I put my pairings in than it started to rain and they [Langer and Johansson] started losing holes; more than an hour later they scraped home on the last green, but were soaked through, cold, and only had half an hour for a sandwich and a change of clothes. They were no match for a fresh, dry and fit Pavin and Mickelson. When I went into the team room that evening I told the team that if we lose the Ryder Cup by a point, they could blame me. It was my mistake; I got that one completely wrong.

In the afternoon session, Gallacher at last unleashed Seve and his combination with David Gilford worked better than he could possibly have hoped. Seve had been the heartbeat of the team

Curtis Strange and Sam Torrance. *Getty Images*

ever since the competition had been expanded to include Continental Europe, but by 1995 his considerable powers were on the wane; the one thing that had not dimmed, however, was his fire for the competition. He and Gilford combined brilliantly to defeat Faxon and Jacobsen 4&3.

David Gilford: Seve wanted to win so much it was infectious. To have him as a partner was very special for me. I listened to him but I still played my own game.

Seve Ballesteros: He did all the work. I just caddied for him and told him where to hit his putts.

Bernard Gallacher: 1995 was the first time that Seve started to have a real dip in his career, but it was so important for the whole team that he was there, even if he wasn't playing well. And it was just as important for the Americans to have him there. His presence alone meant so much.

Colin Montgomerie: That was the last time that Seve played in the Ryder Cup and he was beginning to lose his game by then unfortunately. Who knows if his illness had been kicking in by then?

Seve Ballesteros: I only played in three matches in 1995, and I hit three fairways the whole week, but I cleared out a lot of rough and all the branches on the golf course. I'm sure the members of Oak Hill weren't going to lose balls any more after I'd been there.

Bernard Gallacher: Seve was as honest as the day was long. He said, 'I am not the player I was and it is going to be a tough week.' And I said, 'You know that doesn't matter, Seve, I am glad you're here and the team want you here.'

Seve Ballesteros: That's the only way you can understand these things, by being realistic about them. You are born, you live and you die, and it is the same with golf: you go up, you are there for some time, and then you go down. If you look at the records of all the great champions, you see that they were only at the top for ten or twelve years. The only exception was Jack Nicklaus; he was there for what looked like a thousand years. I think my best time was from 1979 to 1991. Twelve years. It's normal.

Bernard Gallacher: I paired him with David Gilford and I was right in my thinking that he was the perfect partner for Seve because, first of all, he was a very, very straight hitter, he never missed a green, and he was not going to be put off by all the hullaballoo around him.

Lanny Wadkins: The thing about Seve, even though he wasn't playing his best, was that he always managed to have a putt that would matter. You know, he would have an eight-footer for a par to save the hole and I saw him do that on several occasions when he needed to. In that respect, he would cover Gilford so he was a very good partner. The other thing about Seve was that he never quit trying. He always thought, 'I am going to hole this next shot.' He didn't care if it was from 200 yards and behind trees, he thought,

'I am going to hole it' and that was the way he played. He never took himself out of a hole mentally and that's a great thing in a partner.

Brad Faxon: Seve was past his prime by this time. He wasn't the intimidating and swashbuckling Seve that we all watched. I think he hit three fairways the whole day. But he never let Gilford out of his sight. He talked to him the whole time. He was doing everything for him. He'd take his practise swings for him. On the long thirteenth, Peter and I both had birdie putts. Gilford was just off the green with his second shot, and Seve pointed to where on the green he should hit his ball. He hit it and it rolled round and round and round and round – and into the hole! That was the swing point there.

Peter Jacobsen: David Gilford played as well as Seve played poorly but Seve was still inspirational. Seve was literally on his shoulder the entire time, helping him, which just goes to show you how much impact a player like Ballesteros can have not only on one player but on an entire team and in the Ryder Cup's case on an entire continent. There has never been a player like Seve Ballesteros in the Ryder Cup.

But if it looked as if Europe were about to make a charge, Wadkins and his team had other ideas. In contrast to Gallacher, Wadkins only sent out Pavin, Love and Maggert again from those that had played in the morning session and the impetus from the fresh players paid huge dividends.

Maggert and Roberts went to work on Torrance and Rocca and eviscerated the European pair 6&5. Faldo and Montgomerie then teamed up once more for the third match, this time to face Couples and Love, and got off to yet another bad start, finding themselves four-down after five holes. Gallacher had assumed that this dream combination would comfortably dispatch any pairing sent out by Wadkins, but the plan was backfiring disastrously. Having lost in the morning, Faldo and Montgomerie were once again overcome, losing 3&2.

The final match of the day saw Pavin and Mickelson take on the clearly exhausted Langer and Johansson and the toils of the morning session quickly took its toll as the Europeans collapsed 6&4 under a barrage of brilliant golf from the American duo to give their team a 5–3 lead overall.

The rainclouds had thankfully cleared by the next morning and with the weather positive in its outlook, so too was Bernard Gallacher as he persevered one more time with his Faldo/Montgomerie combination as they took on Strange and Haas in the opening foursome match. Having disappointed on the Friday, the European pair roared back into form to win 4&2.

With their talismanic duo finally on song, Europe were back in the mix and the scores were soon tied at 5–5 when Torrance and Rocca made amends for their Friday afternoon performance by getting back into the groove they had carved so brilliantly the previous morning. They sizzled around the course to defeat Love and Maggert 6&5, with the highlight undoubtedly Rocca's wonderful hole-in-one at the 167-yard sixth.

Wadkins badly needed a point on the board – and he got it in the third match as Roberts and Jacobsen battled hard to beat Woosnam and Walton one-up.

The final match that morning pitched Pavin and Lehman against Langer and Gilford. Having been the dominant force the previous day when paired with Seve, Gilford once again produced a performance oozing with class as he and Langer recorded a vital 4&3 victory to tie the score at 6–6 going into lunch.

Lanny Wadkins: I was surprised by the way the Europeans nailed us 3–1 in the morning session. If I had to do things again, I don't know if I'd change my pairings much. I had good, solid guys out there. The Europeans just played exceptional golf.

Having finally justified his perseverance with the Faldo/Montgomerie combination, Gallacher felt comfortable enough to split up his big guns and filter their experience through the team with a reshuffled pack in the afternoon fourballs. Torrance and Montgomerie would go out first to face Faxon and Couples, followed by Woosnam and Rocca taking on Love and Crenshaw before Ballesteros and Gilford faced Haas and Mickelson, before Faldo and Langer went head to head with Pavin and Roberts.

But just as momentum had shifted Europe's way in the morning, so it swung back America's that afternoon. It was all relatively tight in the opening match with Faxon and Couples stealing a narrow lead at the sixth when the Scottish duo bogeyed, but after the turn the Americans ramped things up as they birdied the tenth, eleventh, twelfth and thirteenth. They would go on to record a 4&2 victory.

Sam Torrance: Monty was number one for seven years. What a feat! He struggled with the crowd; that was his problem. Tony Jacklin had the same problem. That just builds up over the years. It was very easy to say to him, 'Just relax and play your game.' But not that easy to do. If Monty could have cut the crowd out of things, he'd have won four or five Majors. But it was frustrating for him to know how good he was and what he was capable of, and then things just didn't come off. People say a lot of stuff happened to Greg Norman in Majors, but look at Monty. There was Tom Kite at Pebble Beach. Then Ernie Els at the US Open. And Steve Elkington at the PGA. But a great man to have on your side. I've got a lot of time for Monty.

Freddie Couples is a great friend of mine. When Monty and I played against him and Faxon he was great. I think we were one down. They both missed the green, but Fred chipped in. The green was in a big amphitheatre, and you have never in your life heard a roar like he got.

So we walk up to the next tee and I just sidled up beside him, leant over to his ear and said: 'Fuck you.' And he laughed, he really laughed. But he told me a little while later that he told the rest of the American team and some of the young guys couldn't believe that I'd said that to him, thinking I was serious. It wasn't, it was in jest.

Woosnam and Rocca punched back in the second match to win 3&2 against Love and Crenshaw, with Rocca in particular in irresistible form, birdying the second, eleventh and twelfth.

It would prove to be the only piece of good news for the Europeans that afternoon. With Ballesteros struggling around the course, Gilford tried his hardest to keep them in it, but he was unable to land even a single birdie; they were ultimately overwhelmed by the cool play of Haas and Mickelson, who triumphed 3&2.

The final match of the day was an epic. When the Europeans bogeyed the seventh, Pavin and Roberts went two up and it looked as if they might pull away from Faldo and Langer. But the German produced the goods at the ninth, his birdie drawing their rivals back to a one-hole lead, and then when the Americans bogeyed the tenth it was all square. Pavin edged his team in front once more with a birdie at twelve only for Faldo to repeat the trick at the thirteenth.

They were all square through the remaining holes until they came at last to the eighteenth tee. Faldo swept a wonderful approach to eighteen feet, but Pavin stole the show with an astonishing four-iron approach from a tricky stance to the edge of the green which he then chipped in to win the hole and hand his team a vital point.

Lanny Wadkins: People obviously spoke a lot about Costantino Rocca's hole-in-one, but for me the shot of the day that Saturday was Corey Pavin's approach on eighteen in that final match. That shot was as tough to position and execute as the chip itself. Somebody said his lie was pretty good, that he could probably get his shot to the green. But for me it was still a hell of a shot, unbelievable when you think about the stance and distance.

The morning defeat gave my guys a jolt. But I just said to them, 'We've had a bad morning but we're still tied, so let's go out and put some wins on the board.' And they did it.

With a 9–7 lead going into the singles, the Ryder Cup appeared to be America's to lose.

Tom Lehman: We had a two-point lead, a huge lead really, and everybody was feeling pretty confident. I was up first, and I think Lanny felt comfortable with that. They were probably going to put a strong player up first, so I took it as a compliment. But I got Ballesteros. I think that Lanny was expecting, you know, Faldo or Montgomerie or someone like that. I don't think he expected Ballesteros to be put first. Seve wasn't playing his best.

Seve and I had a good match. He showed a lot of heart in the way he hit it all over the park but managed to stay in the match for a long time. His short game was phenomenal. It was a pretty amazing performance.

Bernard Gallacher: Oak Hill was tremendous because we suddenly did well in the singles. Why we didn't do well in singles before was always beyond me because we had good players. I thought it was coincidental. But this time the players were fired up. We were disappointed we were two points behind on Saturday night.

I think Seve knew that he shouldn't have been at Oak Hill. He had qualified for the team almost a year-and-a-half beforehand, but his career was in decline by then. But I felt he should play before the singles, I always believe that players should get a game before the Sunday and he did well to get a point with David Gilford in the opening afternoon fourballs.

By the end of Saturday's play we were trailing by two points and I was preparing my team order for the singles when Seve came to my room. He said, 'Where are you playing me tomorrow?'

I said, 'You should always play number one, Seve.'

But he said, 'I can't play number one because I'm playing so bad.'

So I said, 'Well you can play number twelve then.'

'Oh no, I can't play number twelve because if it goes down to the last match I will let the team down.'

I said, 'Well, Lanny Wadkins is two points ahead and knowing him he's going to go straight for the jugular and put all his best players right in the front to the middle of the order. So that's where I want all my best players too.'

So Seve goes, 'OK, I'll go off number one.'

Out he went the next day against Tom Lehman and proceeds to put his opening shot unplayable. One down after one hole, he chipped in at the second – all square. He didn't hit one fairway between the third hole and the ninth but he was still all square at the turn. That inspired our team because the guys playing behind him looked at the board and could see he was trying his heart out and still holding his own with Lehman.

Seve hit the tenth fairway with his driver and all the American spectators standing around the tee stood up and cheered him!

Howard Clark: I got to the seventh and I had seen Seve out of the corner of my eye so I said to one of the marshals, 'How is Seve doing?' and he said, 'He's all square.' I said, 'You are kidding me, that's amazing.' He had been all over the joint, I had just seen him at the seventh and he had hit it left of the green, and it had gone miles away and yet he had halved the seventh and he was all square. I kind of thought, 'I have got to try and back him up, because if he is going to win I have got to win too.'

Colin Montgomerie: What Seve did in that singles match against Tom Lehman was extraordinary. Extraordinary. He would never hit his fairway, he would never hit a green in regulation, and yet he got to the turn and he was all square. It was ridiculous. And I speak to Tom Lehman now about it because I'm on the Champions Tour with him and he said it was the most extraordinary match he's ever been involved in. And if it wasn't someone as tough as Tom Lehman, who was about to win the Open the following year, Seve would have beaten them, he'd have broken them. 'OK, Seve, I submit. How the hell are you doing this?' Eventually Tom got him from his steady play, but Seve gave all of us a bit of a boost.

I remember I was out on the range with Faldo, I was off at seventh in the order, Faldo was just behind me and we were watching Seve's front nine on the range and I remember he was on about the fourth or fifth by the time I teed off, and I said to Faldo, 'What hole's he playing? I don't recognise it.' And Faldo didn't know either. He had hit a shot off the fifth or sixth and there was a water hazard and he had to drop it and we had no idea where the hell he was – and the next thing we knew, his ball just appeared on the green. It was magnificent.

Tom Lehman: Seve kept getting the clubface shut at the top of the backswing. As a result, the ball was liable to go anywhere – and it generally did. In the circumstances, I find it hard to believe that he took me to the fifteenth. If any other player in the world had been playing Seve's second shots, I would have beaten him 8&7.

Bernard Gallacher: There was no happy ending for Seve, going on to lose the match – but only losing 4&3 it was a remarkable achievement and the heart he showed was an inspiration for the rest of the team.

Seve's heroics, even in a losing cause, did indeed seem to inspire his teammates. Howard Clark was out second against Peter Jacobsen; the pair were all square at the turn, both having level par on the front nine. Jacobsen then pushed ahead at the tenth only for Clark to pull a rabbit from the hat on the eleventh with a hole-in-one to draw level again.

Howard Clark: It was a six-iron. Just about the sweetest shot I hit in my life.

Despite the raucous applause from the crowd, Jacobsen appeared unfazed and soon went ahead again when he won the thirteenth. But Clark wasn't finished yet. The Yorkshireman's breakthrough eventually came at the sixteenth when Jacobsen three-putted while Clark recovered from an approach into the greenside bunker to land just a foot from the hole. The final two holes were halved and Europe had their first point of the day.

Mark James was up against Jeff Maggert in the third match and the Englishman was in dominant form as he sank three birdies in the opening nine for a two-hole lead at the turn. Such was the excellence of James's play that the only two holes he lost were to birdies from Maggert, as he secured a 4&3 victory.

Mark James: The sheer relief of winning will always remain with me. It meant so much.

Fred Couples and Ian Woosnam were once again battling against one another in the singles in a repeat of their clash at the Belfry two years earlier when they had halved their match. For much of this encounter it looked as if it might be going the same way, only for Woosnam to advance into a one-hole lead with just two remaining. But at the 458-yard par four seventeenth, Couples belted a magnificent drive over 300 yards, followed it up with a 150-yard eight-iron approach and then sank a fifteen foot putt for birdie to level the score. At the eighteenth Woosnam very nearly stole the point for Europe when his twenty-foot downhill putt just rimmed the right-hand side of the cup but it failed to drop; in the light of another titanic contest, a half was probably a fair result.

Davis Love III was out against Costantino Rocca and with Europe snapping at the heels of the US, Love knew how important it was to get a red point on the board, while Rocca could draw the score at 10–10 if he could win the match. It was all square by the time they reached the eleventh, but Love then conjured up an irresistible run of birdie, birdie, par, birdie, birdie, to take a four-hole lead and which ultimately secured him a 3&2 victory.

While Colin Montgomerie was taking care of the challenge of Ben Crenshaw, which would see him win 3&1, all eyes turned to the match that had teed off just before them between David Gilford and Brad Faxon, who were now at the eighteenth. Gilford was one up and needed only to halve the hole to seal the point for Europe. Faxon, meanwhile, knew the importance of netting a half for his country. The pressure that both were under was immediately apparent from their approach shots as Gilford hit his into the left-hand grandstand while Faxon hit the greenside trap. Gilford took a relief shot and attempted to chip and run over the greenside rough, but his shot was slightly undercooked and he landed on the trim of the green. From there he sent the ball ten feet below the hole. Faxon had a six-foot putt for par, which would see him halve the match. Gilford held his nerve to sink his putt for bogey; Faxon stood over his ball and then sent it towards the cup. The gallery groaned; Faxon had missed, the hole was halved and the point was Europe's.

Brad Faxon: The day started out OK, but in the middle of the day we started losing some matches, and other matches were getting tight. David Gilford and I were having a tight match. Gilford had been playing beautiful golf.

I drove it perfectly on eighteen. Gilford drove it short, popped it up, then hit a long straight shot, over the green, which was dead. Absolutely dead. And he couldn't even get it on the green from there; he left it on the back fringe. I'd hit my second shot into a front-left greenside bunker, but I didn't have the hardest shot; unfortunately I hit my bunker shot just a little too hard. We were both lying three, but I was about seven, eight feet from the hole, and he was still off the green. He chipped his fourth shot fifteen feet past the hole, so he was still away. But he made that for a five. That was huge.

I now had a putt to win the hole and halve the match to get half a point and at the time it was a crucial half point. Because by now everything was big. The putt looked like it was going to break right-to-left, the line just outside the hole. I want to think I hit it right where I was trying to hit it, but it missed on the right edge; it hit part of the hole. And I remember being in kind of disbelief that it didn't turn and was distraught because I knew it was a big point. Frank Harmon, the golf professional at Oak Hill, told me later that he was wishing he could have come out onto the green and told me that the putt just doesn't break like it looks. Not that that made me feel any better.

Sam Torrance, meanwhile, had taken care of business against Loren Roberts. Their match was decided on the sixteenth green when Torrance sank a ten-foot putt for birdie that ultimately gave him a 2&1 victory.

Just behind Torrance and Roberts, Corey Pavin was attempting to redress the balance for the home team against Bernhard Langer and he managed it with a tidy 3&2 victory over the German.

At eighth in the order, Curtis Strange was clearly up for the challenge posed by his pairing against Nick Faldo. 'There's nobody I would rather go head-to-head with in this world than Nick,' he said beforehand, 'because I admire him as a player, his work ethic; you always want to beat one of the best in the world.'

At this stage it was a pressure cooker. Once again it all came down to the eighteenth. Having pushed into a one-hole lead at the eleventh, Strange fluffed his lines at the seventeenth when he missed a twelve-footer for bogey, while Faldo had sank his ten-footer for par. Coming to the final green, Strange slid his seven-footer past the hole. Faldo was then presented with a four-foot putt to claim the point. If the match was halved, it seemed increasingly likely that the US would retain the Ryder Cup.

Bernard Gallacher: As a captain you don't want to single out a player or two as being the significant difference, because all the players played so magnificently – but the two key moments for me came from Nick Faldo and Philip Walton. Nick had been down against Curtis Strange on the seventeenth but managed to pull it back to make it all square. The nerves were clearly affecting both of them on the eighteenth and they both played a mix of shaky and sublime shots – Curtis Strange hit a perfect drive, Nick hit a bad one; Strange played a bad three-iron shot to the right of the green, Nick hit a sublime pitch to four feet. Strange then had an eight-foot putt for the half.

Nick Faldo: I couldn't look when Curtis was putting. He just missed and so I had to sink the putt for the point. The pressure was immense. Everything was shaking; everything except my putter – and I was able to send the ball right to the middle of the hole. What a feeling.

José María Olazábal: When I played my first Ryder Cup in 1987, to be honest, I really didn't know what the Ryder Cup was all about. But it all changed that year and it got into my blood; I loved it from the first moment, playing with Seve, and that has never changed down all the years. It's something that, somehow, brings out the best in us. To be part of that group of people, players of the highest calibre, playing just for pride and honour – I don't think it gets any better than that. Through all these years, the friendship within the team, within each team I played on or captained or was vice-captain for, that is something that a lot of people don't see because they only see the play on the course, but there are moments in that locker room that bring not just every player together, but the spirit of Europe together. And that is something that you don't see in any other sport. When you see a picture of, for instance, Nick Faldo and Seve hugging each other after Nick won his singles in 1995 and both are crying . . . you know, they were rivals for many, many years, but that disappears in just one split second. A moment like that is priceless. That really tells you what the spirit of the Ryder Cup is all about.

Nick Faldo: I walked off the green and Seve was in tears. He hugged me and said, 'You are a great champion.' That was the greatest moment of my career. We'd battled so hard against one another over the years, but there we were coming together . . . that was very special.

Seve Ballesteros: It was a fantastic piece of play. Fantastic.

Curtis Strange: Everybody and everybody's brother was questioning me being on the team. But if you're rooting for the American team, why do that? When I was standing on the eighteenth green, I knew what was going to happen to me; they were going to hang me out to dry. And the only thing I said on television was, 'You can say I played badly – but just

A tearful Seve Ballesteros embraces Nick Faldo.

leave it at that.' It hurt me enough to know I let my teammates down. It hurt me enough that Lanny put his trust in me and I let him down. Nobody played well that day, but I got the brunt of the criticism. Crenshaw never won a point all week either. And seven of our guys lost that day; I wasn't the only one to lose. You get over it, but it hurt for a long time.

Colin Montgomerie: It was difficult to see the witch-hunt that went after Curtis Strange in the aftermath. He was picked by his pal Lanny Wadkins and Curtis took a hammering from the media and fans for losing to Faldo the way he did. He was picked because he had won the US Open on that course. But being a captain's pick is bloody difficult. Having said that, captain's picks are usually a strength. I looked at it when I was captain. You look at the last three that qualify against the three picks, over the years – and the last three qualifiers get about thirty per cent of the points they play for. But the picks get about seventy per cent. So the picks are usually the strength. But on that occasion, of course, it didn't happen. Curtis was a pick and he didn't win. And it was the last time he played, so it was a shame.

Curtis Strange: People want to know what happened. The media's going to write it anyway, so I always figured, at least if they get the facts right it'll be a better story. And so I faced the music. I always have said that if you think you're good enough to be good, you'd better take the bad with it. You don't think the sun's going to come up the next day, but it does.

Gallacher had placed two rookies at the bottom of the order, with Philip Walton facing off against Jay Haas at number eleven and Per-Ulrik Johansson at number twelve against Phil Mickelson.

Bernard Gallacher: I saw the players from three to eight [James, Woosnam, Rocca, Gilford, Montgomerie and Faldo] as the main part of the team. But I had a job trying to convince myself that Philip and Per-Ulrik wouldn't have too much pressure on them.

Johansson had started off well and was two up against his old university friend at the turn, only for Mickelson to turn on the magic as he birdied the tenth, eleventh and twelfth. They would make it as far as the seventeenth where the American would claim a 2&1 victory.
And so it all came down to Walton's match against Haas, playing just in front of Johansson and Mickelson. Walton had seemed to be in complete control by the time they got to the sixteenth green; his ball was a mere two feet from the hole after three, while Haas was in the greenside trap. All Walton had to do was to tap in for a 3&2 victory; but he didn't get the chance as Haas executed a stunning escape shot that hit the flag and then dropped for a winning birdie. Luck seemed to be building for the home side as Walton was once again faced with a winning putt on the seventeenth, this time from four feet, only to roll it past the cup. With Faldo having sealed the point for Europe just ahead of him, Walton knew that the winning of the Ryder Cup rested on his shoulders as he and Haas came to the eighteenth tee.
Clearly Haas knew it too as, under the mounting pressure, he pulled his drive and lanced his ball dead behind a tree. Walton didn't hit his finest drive of the day either, but its eventual lie in the light rough to the right of the fairway was eminently playable – especially when compared to Haas's. The American pulled off a decent shot, albeit after some considerable procrastination, to find the fairway and Walton had a 195-yard shot to the green; he played a

five-wood but underestimated his lie and failed to gain enough height from his shot to clear the rise to the putting surface, landing his ball in more rough.

Haas pitched onto the green and saw his ball spin back into the fringe. He would need to chip it in if he were to save par and win the hole.

Walton played his sandwedge and landed ten feet from the hole; Haas chipped from the fringe but overhit and his ball ran eight feet beyond. Walton stood over his ten-footer and rolled his ball towards the cup, coming to rest just a foot below. Haas had battled hard but he knew it was over and he duly conceded. The Europeans around the green erupted. Victory was theirs.

Bernard Gallacher: We all had to walk back and watch Philip. It was his first Ryder Cup. He had played just once before the singles. He had played with Woosnam, and he played well, but they lost. But I knew from his amateur days that he was always a good driver of the ball, and it was a driver's golf course, so I wasn't so worried about him. But the pressure fell on him. I really felt quite bad for him. I tried to keep out of his way, but at the same time as I walked up the fairway I tried to make myself noticeable as well just in case he wanted to come over and speak. But, of course, everybody knew exactly what was happening. He didn't need to be told that he needed to hang on and somehow get a point.

Philip Walton: I remember so clearly standing over that putt. I could feel the hair standing on the back of my head, and then my right leg started shaking.

Jay Haas: I still see the replays of that moment when I'm sitting at home flicking through the sports channels. And every time I just turn it off because I don't want to see it. It's not just one guy who loses the Ryder Cup but you can't help thinking it's your fault, especially if it turns out to be your match that decides it.

It was heartbreaking. We had them. We had a chance. Our matches, mine and Phil Mickelson's, were supposed to be the icing on the cake. It wasn't supposed to end like that.

Curtis Strange: I really didn't think they could win; I honestly thought we were too good. But that's what makes the Ryder Cup so exciting.

Seve Ballesteros: In the midst of all our celebrations and the Americans' misery I realised a despondent Jay Haas had been abandoned. I went over, put my arm round him and said all you can say at such time: 'Jay, it's sport . . . you've played well, but sport's just like that.'

Tom Lehman: Afterwards we were in shock – and it was not fun watching the Euros celebrate on the eighteenth. But that's all part of the Ryder Cup. It's like the Stanley Cup when people pile on the ice after it's over. The thing about sport that makes it great, I believe, is the emotion that's involved.

THIRTY-TWO

1997
Valderrama Golf Club. Sotogrande, Spain
(EUR 14½, USA 13½)

Seventy years after the first official match, the Ryder Cup was played for the first time outside the United Kingdom and the United States, travelling to the Valderrama Golf Club in Sotogrande, Spain. Having become synonymous with the European team since its creation and now that his playing career was on the wane, it was fitting that Seve Ballesteros was named as captain.

There was some controversy in the team's selection, however. Seve had requested three captain's picks but had been restricted to just two, much to his frustration. But he discovered a way to get around this when his compatriot, Miguel Ángel Martín, who had qualified for the team, suffered a wrist injury at the Scottish Open that required surgery and kept him out of action for several weeks; he returned shortly before the Ryder Cup but when Seve demanded that he should undergo a fitness test at Valderrama, some four hundred miles from his home in Madrid, Martín refused. A few hours later Seve informed him that he had been dropped from the team. It had been a fairly cack-handed piece of cloak and dagger theatre but it ultimately meant that Seve was able to jettison the services of a player that he clearly didn't rate and selected instead his three wildcard choices of Nick Faldo, Jesper Parnevik and his old friend José María Olazábal. Martín was furious, particularly as Olazábal had only just returned to fitness himself after an injury lay-off with a crippling foot problem. Lawyers were engaged and legal action was only avoided when an odd compromise was reached whereby Martín was named as the thirteenth 'unofficial' member of the team. He was issued with all the team's kit, posed for the official photos and attended the team's functions – but did not play a single shot. Those who did, however, were Thomas Bjørn, Darren Clarke, Ignacio Garrido, Per-Ulrik Johansson, Bernhard Langer, Colin Montgomerie, Costantino Rocca, Lee Westwood and Ian Woosnam.

Tom Kite had no such issues in putting the American team together. While his players had limited Ryder Cup experience (there were only fourteen appearances between them and just twenty wins, while Nick Faldo alone had twenty-one to his name), they were long on quality, believed by many to be the best team assembled by the US since 1981. Fred Couples, Tom Lehman, Davis Love III, Lee Janzen and rookies Justin Leonard and Tiger Woods were all Major champions. Alongside this sensational sextet were quality lieutenants in Brad Faxon, Jim Furyk, Scott Hoch, Jeff Maggert, Phil Mickelson and Mark O'Meara. Kite himself also had huge experience, being the veteran of seven Ryder Cups and winner of the 1992 US Open at Pebble Beach. The most talked about player in the team, however, was the young Woods. Having destroyed the field as an amateur (including winning three consecutive US Amateur Championships), he had quit his studies at Stamford to turn pro in 1996 and immediately signed multi-million dollar sponsorship contracts with both Nike and Titleist. The Masters in April 1997 was his first Major tournament as a professional and he smashed it – recording a record low total of 270 and winning by a record twelve shots to become the youngest winner

Opposite: Checking the rain clouds or praying to God? Seve Ballesteros gives the engine on his buggy a brief break as he casts his eyes skywards during play at Valderrama. *Getty Images*

of the Green Jacket in history and the first player of African-American origin to win a Major. Just a year into his pro career he was already box office and whenever the team got together the media scrum revolved almost entirely around just him.

Colin Montgomerie: The Tiger magic was evident from that first Ryder Cup. His was the first name you looked for when the draws were announced. If you were up against him in the fourballs, or the singles, it was exciting. And there was nothing to lose – there was almost an air of freedom because you were not expected to win.

Tom Kite: It was important for me to try and take some of the heat off Tiger's shoulders and make sure everyone felt part of one team, not just Tiger and eleven sidekicks. I told the entire team to have some fun with the matches. I have always believed that players play their best when they are enjoying the competition, the course, and the interaction with the fans. So as much as we could, we tried to create an enjoyable attitude towards the matches.

Seve Ballesteros: Once Spain was designated host country for the 1997 Ryder Cup, everybody took it for granted I would be team captain, however I wasn't so sure. I was keen to play. For a time I toyed with the idea of being both captain and player, two roles that Ken Schofield had told me could be combined. In the end I concluded it was impossible to be a good captain and to play golf at one's best. A Ryder Cup captain has lots of duties; they take up all his time.

The bookies made the Americans overwhelming favourites, with odds as short as 4–9 on them recapturing the cup. Their team had five players ranked in the world's top ten, nine in the top fifteen. Europe, meanwhile, had only one top ten player in Colin Montgomerie.

In advance of the Ryder Cup, Seve had worked with Jaime Ortiz-Patiño, Valderrama's owner, to tweak the course. The most notable change was at the par-five seventeenth. He added a ribbon of thick rough at 290 yards and a greenside lake. The changes to seventeen were widely derided but Ballesteros had done it with the American players in mind for as well as adding that ribbon of rough he had also narrowed the fairways on a number of holes at the same yardage – which was the distance that the long hitters in the US team, like Woods, Mickelson, Love and Couples, would be expected to land their drives. Despite the criticism he suffered for these changes, Ballesteros was sanguine. 'I designed the seventeenth hole and I know how it should be played strategically,' he said. 'When my players are playing the seventeenth, I will use my experience and I can tell them the way it should be played.'

As well as these changes, the challenge presented to the players, on both sides, was increased dramatically by the weather. A Ryder Cup in Spain had come with the expectation of clear skies, bright sun and warmth. But instead it rained. Horrendously. Storms battered the course the week before the matches and made intermittent cameos throughout.

Seve Ballesteros: The opening day of play finally arrived, and I must have been the first to jump out of bed. It was about 6:00 am on Friday morning and I peered out to see what the weather was doing. It had obviously been raining for a while and it was still pouring down. I felt incredibly frustrated.

'For God's sake! Look at that rain; we've been waiting for two years for the Ryder Cup, we've moved heaven and earth to bring it to Spain and when it's finally all about to happen, we can't get on the course!'

Brad Faxon: Valderrama is a beautiful place, but there are some strange holes. It was a course that certainly took a little bit of getting used to, things like trees in the middle of the fairways. The course was as well-conditioned a course as we could play, but I thought the seventeenth and eighteenth holes were very tricked up. The seventeenth was similar to the par-five fifteenth at Augusta National, in that anything hit short and landing on the front of the green would spin off and hit the water. Then they had redesigned the back of the green so it had, like, a ditch where, if you hit it over, your pitch back was very hard. The rough crossed the fairway where it made the long hitters have to hit three-woods off the tee. So you couldn't go at the green as easily if you hit a good drive.

Nick Faldo: Seve took the drivers out of their hands. I played with Tiger, and he only hit a driver once. Tactically, that was huge from Seve.

Seve Ballesteros: One of the things I'd decided on as team captain was the need to change the order in which the foursomes and fourballs were played. I'd put this change to the European Tour in the spring, and, much to my surprise, after I'd spoken to Tom Kite, the American captain, it got the support of the American PGA.

Quite apart from the stress and mental pressure which the competition subjects you to, the Ryder Cup is physically very draining. The changes I'd suggested were designed to save our team's physical energy – the loss of which would also drain our mental power as the encounter proceeded. I knew from the statistics that the Americans had historically failed to make full use of all twelve team members. My plan was to ring the changes more frequently than Tom Kite. The fourballs tended to wear a team down more quickly, so if we played those in the morning and the shorter foursomes in the afternoon, the players would be fresher the next morning. They'd also be less tired when it came to the singles on Sunday. Equally, playing the fourballs in the morning would give my men a bit of a cushion. The foursomes risk exposing a pairing and making it vulnerable if one player isn't playing well or seems under stress.

Tom Lehman: When it came to the golf course I felt like we were behind the eight-ball. Valderrama is a real 'local knowledge' kind of course, and the European Tour played there every year for the Volvo Masters. That was a huge advantage, but the home team should always have the advantage. It's like any other sport. If you're playing on my court or on my ballfield, I should have the advantage.

And it was a smart move by Seve to switch the format to have the fourballs in the morning and the foursomes in the afternoon. The Europeans have generally been stronger in best-ball than in alternate shot and Seve obviously wanted them to get off to a good start.

Seve Ballesteros: I gave the players a very clear message when we arrived at Valderrama: 'On the first two days there'll be eight players on the course and four in a temper because they're not playing, but you know you can't all play and that this is a team effort. I'm not worried about your individual performances because our mission here is to win fourteen and half points. If we can do that, we will all have won.'

Colin Montgomerie: Seve was always the leader, he just couldn't help himself. Here we were in Spain; losing just wasn't an option. It was Seve and the King of Spain; you felt you were part of an irresistible force.

Ignacio Garrido: Seve wasn't so much a captain as a father to us. Every time I was thinking, 'What can I do here?' he'd appear out of nowhere and tell me what to do. We put our hands on the clubs, but Seve was the one who played the shots.

Tiger Woods: Seve really was everywhere. He did a great job as a captain. And his players played really well when they needed to.

Bernard Gallacher: It was just a shame that Seve's game had gone by 1997 because I think he wanted to be a playing captain. Nevertheless he threw himself into the captaincy. He almost got too involved.

Colin Montgomerie: He was only forty-one, the youngest captain we'd ever had, and he wanted to play – which was the problem. He was a nuisance really the way he wanted to play every shot. And he was there all the time. He got a map of the underground tunnels at Valderrama, and appeared all over the place. And Tom Kite was left there saying, 'Where the hell have you just come from?' It was fantastic. It was the only captain's golf cart that I felt had to be retired because it needed a 10,000 mile service after three days. He'd just appear from these tunnels, he was everywhere, he was brilliant. But a nuisance because he wanted to play and he saw shots differently to everyone else.

Bernhard Langer, Nick Faldo and I were practising on the Thursday and we made a real hash of the seventeenth. Seve was bloody furious and made us all go back and play it again. The whole point of redesigning seventeen like he did was to flummox the Americans and give us an advantage but we were making a balls of it. He told us exactly where we had to hit and we did a better job of it, but it was a hellishly difficult hole.

Nick Faldo: Seve was off the charts when he was captain. Miguel Ángel Jiménez was his vice-captain and he came down to breakfast before the foursomes and he was looking exhausted. And I remember asking him what had happened. And he said, 'Seve came to my room at four in the morning, he said, "Ángel, we have a team to put out. We know who is first playing and we know who is last playing," and we discussed for hours who would be two and who would be three.' He drove everyone up the wall.

Bernard Gallacher: Seve hadn't decided until the last moment who would play with whom in the matches. And I could see some of the players getting a little bit tense.

This was indeed true. When he announced his morning pairings, Ballesteros hadn't told any of

US team captain Tom Kite with Mark O'Meara and Tiger Woods. *Getty Images*

his players whether they were going to be playing or not. 'I suppose they will see it on TV right now,' he said nonchalantly.

Torrential rain delayed the start of the morning fourballs by an hour-and-a-half and so it wasn't until after 10:00 am that the first match, between Olazábal and Rocca and Love and Mickelson, got underway. The US duo got off to a wonderful start as Love sank a twenty-five foot putt on the first green to win the hole, and they pushed out into a two-hole lead at the eleventh. Olazábal and Rocca had been playing steadily but unspectacularly, but they moved through the gears on the last seven holes to stage a stunning comeback to win the match and get the crowd pumping.

The second match saw veteran Faldo partner with rookie Westwood to take on Couples and Faxon. It was a close battle across the eighteen holes but Faxon was able to play the role of the redemption man – his one-up victory with Couples going some way to make amends for his missed putt at Oak Hill that had handed Europe the Ryder Cup two years previously.

Brad Faxon: I thought about 1995 at Oak Hill, the eighteenth hole. I thought, 'I can do something here to redeem myself'.

I knew it was going in before I hit it, and it was a great feeling because I hit it dead square, right in the middle. When it went in, Fred gave me a big Freddie hug, and, to tell you the truth, I was in tears.

Tom Lehman: Jim Furyk and I were paired against Jesper Parnevik and Per-Ulrik Johansson in the third group. That was a good match; it was Jim's first Ryder Cup match and he was nervous. He didn't play very well at the beginning but played much better on the back nine. But the two Euro guys really ham-and-egged it. Johansson would go birdie, birdie, double, double; but Jesper would go double, double, birdie, birdie. They were a great team. When you play well and you lose, especially when it comes down to eighteen, you can feel good about it even though you lost. Those guys did a little better, but I was proud of the way Jim and I had played.

With Europe leading 2–1, focus switched to the final group playing that session. While Montgomerie and Langer would have drawn the crowds in any case, interest in the match was ramped up to the max as the crowds jostled and the world tuned in to see Mark O'Meara play alongside Tiger Woods. O'Meara and Woods had become firm friends on the PGA Tour and lived close to one another in Florida, often practising together. Their unity was demonstrated admirably that morning as Woods eased himself into his first Ryder Cup with a steady round, while O'Meara played the mentor. Despite the pedigree of their opposition, the American duo claimed a 3&2 victory, which was sealed when O'Meara sank a delicious thirty-foot putt at the sixteenth.

Kite had promised in advance that all his players would get the chance to play and so it was that he threw the fresh legs of Scott Hoch and Lee Janzen out for the first of the afternoon foursomes to play Rocca and Olazábal. With the rush the European pair must have been feeling after their morning comeback against Love and Mickelson still buzzing through their systems, it was a gamble on Kite's behalf – but one that paid off as Hoch and Janzen dovetailed beautifully to secure a one-up victory.

Lee Janzen: There's nothing like winning your first Ryder Cup match. It's like you've really arrived as a team player. That first day at Valderrama when Scott Hoch and I won our match against Costantino Rocca and José María Olazábal was an experience I will never forget.

Out second, and clearly stung by their morning loss, Montgomerie and Langer combined once again to play O'Meara and Woods and they exacted their revenge to win 5&3.

The final two matches saw Faldo and Westwood take on Leonard and Maggert, while Parnevik and Garrido faced Lehman and Mickelson. With both matches evenly poised the weather once more intervened and, as night drew in, both matches were abandoned for the day.

The following morning the rain was still beating down and play was once again delayed, this time for two hours, before the suspended matches resumed. Who knows what might have happened had they been completed the day before, but the Europeans appeared to have taken greater sustenance from the delay than their American counterparts as Faldo and Westwood played ferociously to win 3&2 while the majestic combination of Lehman and Mickelson could only manage a half against the relatively unknown Parnevik and Garrido.

The proper Saturday schedule then got underway as Montgomerie partnered rookie Darren Clarke in the first fourball against Couples and Love.

Colin Montgomerie: I played with Darren Clarke in his first game on Saturday morning, after he had been left out on the Friday; we played against a very tough duo of Davis Love and Freddie Couples who had won the World Cup together. And we won one-up. So we did well there. I loved being in that leadership role. I felt pumped up and wanted to take on Love and Couples. I felt I was walking a bit taller. I felt I could beat them. Or at least go head-to-head with them.

We were all square going onto the seventeenth when Seve appeared out of nowhere. Darren's ball was lying quite well but the obvious play was for him to lay up and then I could go for the green. But no, Seve insisted that Darren have a go for it, which he did, and as well as he hit it, it didn't make the carry. I now had to lay up; the risk of both of us going in the pond was too great. I hit it to fifty-eight yards, the fairways still sopping wet, and there's Seve at my side telling me, 'Hit it in softly, feel it in.' In the end I had to tell him to piss off. Fortunately, I did hit a good shot and holed the putt to go one up, and a half at the last was good enough for us to win the match and take the point.

Seve had benched Ian Woosnam, Darren Clarke and Thomas Bjørn for the whole of Friday. Sitting Woosnam down, in particular, was widely discussed; but the Welshman reacted in the best way possible by going out with Bjørn and beating Leonard and Faxon 2&1.

Ian Woosnam: Maybe that's what I needed. Something to get me mad.

Faldo and Westwood were back in harness once again, this time facing O'Meara and Woods. Where it had all gone so well for the American duo the day before, it went wrong on the Saturday and the English pair played superbly to win 2&1.

With the first three sessions going Europe's way, it would go down to the wire in the fourth match between Olazábal and Garrido and Mickelson and Lehman. On the seventeenth, Mickelson hit what Lehman described as 'the single greatest shot I've ever seen' when he crunched a 239-yard two-iron out of the rough to land within six feet of the hole, only for him to subsequently slide his putt past the cup. Garrido, meanwhile, hit his approach into the steep back bunker and managed to get up and down from his lie, which no one else had managed all week. 'That was maybe the second-greatest shot I've ever seen,' said Lehman.

All square on the eighteenth, Olazábal hit into trees and embedded his ball on a bed of bark chips. He was forced to take a drop and then hit his approach into the greenside bunker. From there he escaped to within eighteen feet of the hole and then sank his putt for a half point that was greeted with an air-shuddering roar from the crowd.

At lunchtime, the scoreline stood at 8–4 in Europe's favour.

Langer and Montgomerie resumed their partnership for the first of the afternoon foursome matches, where they faced Janzen and Furyk.

Dusk was falling fast as the four players arrived at the eighteenth tee. As they played to the green, Janzen and Furyk found themselves thirty-five feet from the hole. If they could two-putt, they would win the hole and salvage a half for their team. But visibility was now very poor. The sensible thing to do would have been to call it a day and resume play the next day – especially as Montgomerie had played in every session and having to rise early the next day to finish this match before playing in the singles might well have handed a crucial advantage to his singles opponent, Scott Hoch. In a tactical blunder, they played on. Janzen sent his putt ten feet past the hole. Furyk had to roll his in for the half. He missed. The point went to Europe and Montgomerie got a full night's rest. It would prove telling.

With the light too poor for play to continue, the remaining three matches on the course (Faldo and Westwood against Hoch and Maggert; Parnevik and Garrido against Leonard and Woods; and Olazábal and Rocca against Love and Couples) were all suspended until the next morning.

As the teams disappeared off the course and back to their team rooms, they reflected on bare statistics that the Americans had failed to win a single point during the course of the entire day, the first time it has happened to any team since 1967. Europe were 9–4 ahead and looking comfortable in each of the remaining foursome matches.

Tom Lehman: What happened that Saturday? Europe just made tons of putts and we didn't make squat. That was the real difference between the teams – but what a difference it was.

Nick Faldo: At the beginning of the week Seve was great. He said, 'I don't want to put any pressure on you. I want you to relax. No pressure.'

It got to Saturday night. 'We have to win! We have to try really hard! I don't want you to hit into a bunker, I don't want you to three-putt, and don't hit into the trees on sixteen on the right! I want you to win everything!'

José María Olazábal: Seve was always the backbone of the team. That is something I will always miss.

The weather on Sunday morning was, at last, clear and dry. Faldo and Westwood had been three up on Hoch and Maggert, but the overnight rest and bright September morning obviously had an empowering effect on the Americans as they overcame the deficit to record a vital 2&1 win. It was exactly the response that Kite needed from his men. Woods and Leonard worked hard to try and do the same to Parnevik and Garrido, but they were only just unable to do it and had to settle for a half. In the final match of the resumed foursomes, Olazábal and Rocca reasserted the Europeans' advantage by crushing Love and Couples 5&4. And so it was on to the singles.

Tom Lehman: We were five points back going into the singles, and had to win nearly every match. One of the things that worked against us in the overall course of the matches was the delay caused by the big rainstorm on the first day. After that it was non-stop golf. You played, you kept on playing, it got dark and then you kept on playing, kept on playing. There was never a chance to regroup, perhaps in the middle of the day between the foursomes and the fourballs. For the team that had the momentum it was easy to keep it going, but for the team that didn't, it was hard to turn it around. Not having a chance to regroup really hurt us. It's like in a basketball game when you have one team dominating. At half-time the other team gets a break, comes back out, and they just roar back to life and turn it around. Well, we never had that half-time.

Despite the odds being heavily stacked against them (Americans needed to score 9 points to win), Kite's players came out swinging. Lehman, Mickelson, Couples, Maggert and O'Meara all won and at times played some of the most sensational golf ever witnessed in a Ryder Cup. Two key men fell, however, when Love lost to Johansson 3&2 and Rocca played wonderfully to defeat Woods 4&2.

Costantino Rocca: I started the match very strongly and after ten holes I was in the lead by four. Tiger was forcing it a little bit. At the time he was a slightly different player – the only part of his game that wasn't perfect back then was his short irons, eight-iron to wedge. That day he wasn't controlling them too well, leaving some short and flying the green with others.

Costantino Rocca and Tiger Woods do battle in the singles.
Getty Images

But he wasn't playing too badly – in fact he played well, it was just that I was playing better.

As we went round it wasn't really the time to talk with each other, but I enjoyed playing with him. Tiger was only twenty-two years old and the world was expected of him, but he handled it very well.

At the eleventh, Tiger made a birdie and I missed one. For me, the next holes – twelve and thirteen – were the most important ones of the match. All he needed was a couple of chances and he would be back in it. But we halved them both. Then at sixteen I played the most beautiful shot of my life. A one-iron, it was the sort of shot you can't try, you can't practise. It was the shot that won me the hole and sealed the victory. As I was standing on the tee, Seve had warned me, 'Whatever you do – don't miss right.' So I hit my tee shot right – straight in among some cork trees. Tiger hit his shot cleanly onto the fairway and played his next onto the right-hand side of the green.

It was a bad situation. It would have been very easy to lose sixteen, seventeen and then maybe eighteen and the game would have been halved. Seve suggested I try and chip it out or hit it into the bunker on the left side. But I don't like long bunker shots. The Ryder Cup is different – you can sometimes make special shots in match play. That day was special, so, I went for the one-iron. I played the perfect shot. After I hit it, Seve said, 'OK – that is your own shot – you definitely play that sort of shot better than me!'

Renton Laidlaw: Costantino Rocca beating Tiger Woods was a terrific scalp for Rocca [Rocca won 4&2 and later said it was the best he'd ever played]. And Fred Couples just annihilated Ian Woosnam [8&7].

With Thomas Bjørn halving with Justin Leonard, Europe only needed a point to retain the cup and a point-and-a-half to win it. Brad Faxon needed to sink a ten-footer on the deadly seventeenth to take his match with Bernhard Langer to the eighteenth but he slid it agonisingly past the hole and the crowd exploded into raptures.

Colin Montgomerie: There was a thing that Canon used to sponsor called the Canon Shot of the Year and my shot off the tee on the eighteenth in the singles won that. Scott Hoch had won the seventeenth and drove off the eighteenth first. And he hit a good shot with his driver down the left-hand side. But there was no applause. I know it was raining and it's hard to clap when you've got one hand holding an umbrella, but I remember thinking, 'There are a lot of Americans here, surely someone would have applauded.' But there was nothing. And I thought, 'He's clipped the last tree.' There were all these cork trees at Valderrama, and you know this ninety per cent air theory we talk about in golf – trees are ninety per cent air, so if you hit the ball straight at a tree there is a ninety per cent chance of it finding a gap and getting itself back out on the golf course – but that didn't apply at Valderrama with the cork trees. If your ball hit one of those it dropped down dead. So I thought, right, I really need my driver for this, but I can draw my three-wood easier, it's got more loft. So I hit my three-wood off the tee and I drew it round the corner perfectly. And I knew as soon as I hit it that it was perfect and it got a big applause. So I thought, 'Right, that's good. All square here and I need a half. I'm not allowed to lose this hole, I need a half at the very least.'

Scott hacked out of the rough and went short left of the green. And I remember thinking, 'All eyes are now on this game.' We were the only game left out on the course because although we were tenth in the order, Faldo had already lost 3&2 to Jim Furyk and Ignacio Garrido had lost 7&6 to Tom Lehman.

I hit my nine-iron in for the approach and it landed about fifteen feet left of the hole. Scott chipped up to about twelve foot just inside me.

I rolled my putt down to about an inch short of the hole and he gave it to me. My caddie, Alastair, and I then backed off to see if Scott could make this twelve-footer for a half. And then I saw Seve starting to run onto the green and people started to clap and I remember thinking, 'I know what's happening here. Seve wanted a half, we needed to get to 14½ points, that was what we got and . . . he's going to give it to him.' And he did. He shook Scott's hand and it was over. And then of course the green was mobbed and it's a shame in many ways to end like that. But it ended and there was nothing I could do. I couldn't say, 'No, no, back away, make him play it.' The captain's decision is final and that was that. It was Seve's decision and we'd won and that's all he'd wanted to do. I got a lot of emails afterwards with betting slips attached for the score to be 15–13. Hundreds. And all these people felt it was my fault for not making Scott take the putt – and so I replied to them all saying, 'Look, it wasn't my decision and I'm sorry for your bet, but you speak to the captain about this. I wanted to finish the job.'

The Ryder Cup should be played to a finish. And imagine if someone had done that to Seve! He wouldn't have appreciated it if it had happened to him.

Seve Ballesteros: There was no point forcing Hoch to putt just to see whether we could extend our margin of victory. We had won the Ryder Cup!

Tom Kite: Only when it was finally over and they had retained the cup did I think it was over. For a lot, if not most, of the last day I was convinced that the US would take the cup home. We jumped out to such a strong start the final day and every player was into the comeback. We came very close but just could not pull it off on the back nine.

Mark O'Meara: If the team plays well, the captain looks like a hero. If it plays poorly, then he gets badgered. I thought Tom Kite actually did a very good job at Valderrama, but he got blistered in the press afterwards, which was hugely unfair.

Olazábal was the first player on the victorious European team to be asked to say a few words by the captain. 'This has been very special to me,' Ollie began. 'A year ago I could not walk . . .' But he was so overcome with emotion that he couldn't say any more.

José María Olazábal: That was my most emotional moment in golf as a player. It happened just after two years of suffering with my injuries and treatment, everything was very recent. Being the Ryder Cup, being in the team with the rest of the boys, and being in Spain, it was extremely emotional.

Colin Montgomerie: It was great afterwards, great celebrations. Do you know something? Seve was the one captain that we won it just for him. Everyone won it for him. Nobody else. I've never played under anyone else that I was playing just for the captain. Not for Europe, not for myself, not for anyone else. For Seve.

THIRTY-THREE

1999

The Country Club. Brookline, Massachusetts
(USA 14½, EUR 13½)

From the Drama at Valderrama in 1997 it went to the Battle of Brookline in 1999. Not that the combatants would have envisioned the drama that would unfold in Boston before the week started.

Those with only a casual interest in golf would have seen the appointment of 'Gentle' Ben Crenshaw as the home captain as perhaps indicative of a placid contest to come – but the nickname was ironic, Crenshaw renowned for his furious intensity as a player with a fervent will to win.

Seve Ballesteros had announced his decision to quit the captaincy in the wake of Valderrama with the intention of qualifying for the team again in 1999. It was not to be, with the veteran unable to muster the points to qualify outright and with form that would have been madness to back as one of the captain's picks. The man that was selected to lead the European chase for a hat-trick of victories was the former bad boy of the team, Mark 'Jesse' James. Having disgraced himself alongside Ken Brown in 1979, James had subsequently made amends in the Ryder Cups of 1981, '89, '91, '93 and '95 and had become an important cog in Europe's efforts in the process. The team that he took to Boston was contentious to say the least. The top three players in the team were no real surprise – Colin Montgomerie, Lee Westwood and reigning Masters champion, José María Olazábal, were all world class. The controversy surrounded James' decision to dispense with the services of any other Ryder Cup veterans. Obviously, Seve's selection was out of the question, but what about the likes of Bernhard Langer, Sam Torrance, and Ian Woosnam? The omission that earned the most column inches was that of Nick Faldo. The Englishman was a Ryder Cup great, with more points earned than any other player, ever. He might not have been scaling the heights as he had once done, but his experience would surely have been invaluable – particularly in the light of the number of rookies in the team, which totalled seven: Andrew Coltart, Sergio García, Pádraig Harrington, reigning Open champion Paul Lawrie, Miguel Ángel Jiménez, Jarmo Sandelin, and Jean van de Velde.

Mark James: The Ryder Cup is a fantastic experience, no matter what, but it's the hardest part of the captaincy, the wild cards. I got shingles two or three days after the wild cards had been selected and they say stress brings that on. I think occasionally too much credence is given to experience and past performance and not enough to some up-and-coming players who may have played extremely well and deserve a spot. I had a situation where Langer was off form and whether or not to pick him. The criticism of the wild cards wasn't that great but I was happy with my choices. I don't have any regrets about it.

Colin Montgomerie: When we got to Brookline we made one major error. Mark James was brilliant as a captain, absolutely brilliant, but if he made one mistake it was that we didn't foresee that America wanted the Ryder Cup back so badly. They had never lost three in a row before and that's what they were facing. They did not want that to happen. It was similar to 1991.

We had a very young team, seven rookies and we'd never won with any more than five. That was the era that Faldo wasn't playing any more, neither was Langer, Lyle, Woosnam, Seve. I was the oldest on the team. I remember when Jiménez was selected, I thought he must be the oldest – sorry, Miguel Ángel! – but then I found out he was six months younger than me! That was the big change, the end of the era of our big five.

Mark James: The Ryder Cup captaincy was something I had neither sought nor thought about at all during my career until after the 1997 competition at Valderrama, during which I had helped Seve. After that I spoke to Sam Torrance about who was going to be the next captain. We just about came to the same conclusion: there were not that many candidates apart from the two of us. It was going to be a tricky decision because neither of us had gone after the captaincy or discussed it in any detail with anybody and I was not particularly ambitious in that area, and I think Sam considered it as something which might come to him one day, but he was not interested in chasing it either. Both of us still had our playing careers to consider.

The powers-that-be approached me, but I told them I would have to speak to Sam first. I told him I would take the captaincy as long as he was not interested, because I did not want any bad feelings with someone who had been such a close friend and colleague over the years. Sam told me to go for it because he was still very keen to play. It was only then that I said I would love to accept the invitation, even though I knew I too wanted to be in the team rather than leading it.

Sam Torrance: It was a strange experience for me because my job was totally different to anything I had come across in the Ryder Cup before. Watching as an assistant was totally different to spectating when still a member of the team. I did not feel as negative because when you are in the team and not selected for a particular series, your heart is always in your mouth, but as a vice-captain I had so much confidence in the people I was watching.

Andrew Coltart: There was obviously consternation regarding more experienced players, the likes of Faldo and Langer. Langer was probably a much more legitimate case at that time than Faldo, whose game was fading away a bit. So there was a bit of conjecture about that, but I put all that to the side and just tried to focus on myself and the game and what I needed to do to play well. I wondered what it would be like, took advice from other players around me, to try and enjoy the week. I just tried to put everything into it.

I knew the other Scots guys, Monty and Paul Lawrie, I was in a management company with Westwood and Clarke, and played an awful lot of golf with Harrington. I had also got to know Jean van de Velde and Jarmo Sandelin very well over the years. I had played with Sergio in his first professional golf event. Even though we were rookies – seven in total – we still knew everybody in the team and got on well with everybody.

Crenshaw, meanwhile, had an easy time of things when it came to selection. Harking back to the golden days of American participation in the Ryder Cup, Crenshaw's team was dazzlingly strong. World number one Tiger Woods was the stand-out name but his supporting cast were also stars: David Duval, Jim Furyk, Tom Lehman, Justin Leonard, Davis Love III, Mark O'Meara, Jeff Maggert, Phil Mickelson, Steve Pate, Payne Stewart and Hal Sutton. Not only did it contain eight players who had nearly won in Valderrama (David Duval was the only rookie), ten of the squad were ranked in the world's top twenty (to Europe's four), and they had a combined eleven Majors to their name (to Europe's three). Add in home advantage and things were looking rosy.

Bruce Lietzke [US vice-captain in 1999]: Going in, the mood of the squad was wonderful. The team had a great mixture of veterans and younger players and was a mesh of wonderful personalities. And only one or two guys appeared to be struggling with their games.

There were huge, huge crowds, even during the practise rounds, 20,000 people sitting around the practise tee.

Seve was flown out to speak to the European team during the week, in turns inspiring them with his words yet placing the pressure firmly on their shoulders to retain the cup once again. But it wasn't the only pressure applied that week. America had never lost three times in a row and Crenshaw and his team were determined not to make history by breaking that record. 'We've got the team to get the job done, but a lot more factors go into succeeding at the Ryder Cup,' said Hal Sutton during the build-up. 'I've been on two losing teams. I've been on two experienced teams and we came out losers. So we're all going to have to do a little gut check to decide how bad we want this. We better go in there focused, and we better get the job done.'

There was an uncomfortable sidebar to the tournament build-up when the thorny issue of player payment was raised. Beyond a standard allowance of $5,000 there was no other compensation or prize money available to the players for their participation in the Ryder Cup. While it was an issue that had been raised sporadically from time to time, it had a more serious edge in 1999 when there were whispers that some US players were considering boycotting the event in protest over the lack of serious payment.

A few days before the PGA Championship began, PGA CEO Jim Awtrey and the PGA Tour commissioner, Tim Finchem, met with Crenshaw and sixteen players who were in contention for the team to address the subject before it became any thornier.

The meeting did not go as smoothly as the officials might have hoped. When Crenshaw reflected on it with the press the following day he was clearly simmering with barely controlled anger. 'I want to say one thing,' he said, 'I'm personally disappointed in a couple of people at that meeting. Whether some players like it or not, there are some people who came before them that mean a hell of a lot to this game. And it burns the hell out of me to listen to some of their viewpoints.'

Over the following months there was a hiatus as the status quo was clearly not going to be resolved before the Ryder Cup got underway. When Crenshaw's team eventually arrived at the Country Club, Justin Leonard appeared as the spokesman for the players. He insisted that there was no bad blood among the team or officials and that the issue had been put to bed for the duration of the week while they all focused on winning the cup back. They were the noises that had to be made, but were the statements genuine or just a veneer that masked a deeper unrest among the team? Time would tell. The matter would finally be resolved that December with the announcement that each player would receive $200,000 from the Ryder Cup profit, with *half going to a charity of the player's choice and the other half dedicated to developing golf programmes in each player's local community.*

Ben Crenshaw: I knew the subject of payments had been discussed but no, I did not think players should be paid for playing in the Ryder Cup.

Larry Nelson: I think the players should be paid a lot. Yeah, it is an honour but sometimes that honour is not the way it used to be. You have guys making $7 million, $8 million a year. The Ryder Cup they play for free and then are made to sound greedy when they ask for some sort of compensation. It used to cost us to play in the Ryder Cup. But times change. It was not as commercialised as it is now. So yeah, I think guys should be compensated.

Mark James had no such issues among his team. Despite the large number of rookies, the bond among the players was almost immediate and they were clearly enjoying themselves during the practice rounds in the early days of the week. They looked relaxed, confident and focused on winning the cup for a record third consecutive time.

In contrast to Valderrama two years before, the weather on Friday morning at Brookline was beautiful – cold, crisp, bright. James selected Montgomerie and his compatriot Paul Lawrie to get Europe's defence underway against Crenshaw's pairing of Mickelson and Duval. Despite Lawrie's inexperience at the Ryder Cup, the Scottish duo exuded cool confidence as they went about their business. Duval holed his putt to halve the first hole and make an early statement that he and Mickelson would go toe-to-toe with their opposition; but it proved to be a false indication of how the match would unfold as the Scotsmen showed a wonderful cohesion to their play as they cruised to a 3&2 victory.

Paul Lawrie: The first shot I hit at Brookline was probably as nervous as I've ever been. I always feel a little nervous over the opening tee shot at any event but knowing so many people are watching, understanding the significance of the matches, and being a rookie, it was a thousand times more nerve-wracking than normal.

The match referee spoke to us both, announcing he was 'Scotch' to which Monty replied, 'No. That's a drink.' And then the ref thought it'd be a good idea to show us pictures of his 'Scotch' grandkids just minutes before I hit the biggest tee shot of my career . . .

Monty at his peak was incredible and I had long admired him as a golfer, so it was great to play alongside him. I learned every moment I was on the course with him and his experience was invaluable. We formed a strong partnership that week.

Mark James: We knew that at Brookline the rest of the team would look to Monty for a lead, and he would give it. No matter whom he partnered it would be a good pairing, and once you have a player like that it gives the rest confidence.

Lehman and Woods were next out of the traps against García and Parnevik and the sense of excitement around the first tee as the world number one stepped up to play was palpable. But, as he would often experience during his Ryder Cup career, Woods struggled to transfer his dominance to the team environment as the European pair won 2&1.

If the second match had failed to get the home crowds going as expected, the third would surely manage it as the US veterans Love and Stewart took on the rookies Harrington and Jiménez. But once again the match did not go according to the script and while the halved match at last got the US on the scoreboard, there was no doubt that the home team would have expected more.

This sense of disappointment was finally arrested in the final match of the morning when Sutton and Maggert notched the first full point for the US when they defeated Westwood and Clarke 3&2.

While the morning hadn't been a disaster for the US, it had been underwhelming. Disaster was to befall them that afternoon instead. The best result in the Friday fourballs was the half point that Love and Leonard secured against Montgomerie and Lawrie; everything else went Europe's way with García and Parnevik beating Furyk and Mickelson one-up, Olazábal and Jiménez beating Maggert and Sutton 2&1 and, most shockingly of all, the combination of world number one Woods and number two Duval losing one-up to Clarke and Westwood.

Mark James: As the groups progressed on the first morning there was absolutely no hint of the crowd trouble which would spoil the final day. If anything, it was the Americans who came in for a little bit of stick. When David Duval came on the first tee, somebody shouted out, 'Hey, David, play your ranking.' That was probably a by-product of the pay-for-play issue and other comments he had made about the Ryder Cup just being an exhibition match. The taunts would become even more distasteful as the Americans struggled for points early on. 'What kind of exhibition is this?' and 'How much you being paid to play like this?'

David Feherty: David Duval asked over and over and over again why there's such an obsession with what's basically an exhibition match. And I was thinking, 'After he's played in one he will understand.'

Then I saw him in his first match. He holed a putt and punched the air and I thought, 'There you go. Now you understand.' When was the last time you punched the air after a seven – and before the tournament was even over? But that's what the Ryder Cup is about. It makes you feel the best you've ever felt on the golf course, and it makes you feel the worst.

Darren Clarke: Lee and I were paired again to take on David Duval and Tiger Woods in the afternoon fourball and that was a much better result for us. It was really tight all the way through; we holed a few, they missed a few, but we made the putts at the right time and because of that we won the point and finished the day 6–2 up.

Having been installed as such clear favourites at the outset, it was almost shocking to read the scoreline of 6–2 in Europe's favour at the end of the day. Crenshaw shared the sentiment. 'We saw some outstanding golf from the Europeans,' he said that evening. 'I can't believe that we're looking at a four-point differential.'

Bruce Lietzke: At the end of the first day, we were not discouraged but just truly perplexed that we were behind 6–2. I had seen some great golf, from Colin Montgomerie as well as

Hal Sutton, who was probably the best player we had. I think Colin Montgomerie was the best player on the golf course between both teams. He truly was magical.

Having dominated proceedings on the first day, James sent out the same pairings for the Saturday morning foursomes as had played the previous morning (although in a slightly rejigged order). Having returned two-and-a-half points in the first session, his troops fared well again in delivering a further two crucial points as Clarke and Westwood beat Furyk and O'Meara 3&2 and Parnevik and García beat Stewart and Leonard 3&2, while Sutton and Maggert won a point for the US by defeating Montgomerie and Lawrie one-up, and Woods and Pate did the same in beating Jiménez and Harrington with the same score.

Mark James: It would have been madness not to go with the first-day line-up at the start of the second. There was too much risk involved in doing anything other than staying faithful to the guys who had performed so well in the previous day's foursomes. We had a healthy lead going into a rainy Saturday morning, but I was all too aware that without doing anything particularly wrong that scoreline could easily be reversed.

Lee and Darren beating Tiger Woods and David Duval had been a massive psychological boost for the team, as had winning a couple of matches on the last hole, which is always a considerable accomplishment.

Ben Crenshaw: Tiger is hard to find someone to pair with him. There's no one really with comparable skills and I don't think any captain has found the answer yet. But that week I discovered that Tiger grew up in California with Steve Pate's brother and he and Steve were already quite friendly, so I put them together the next day and they got us a point in the morning foursome against Jiménez and Harrington.

With the score sitting at 8–4 at lunchtime, James had a decision to make. Did he stick with his tried and tested combinations or throw in some rookies to give them a taste of the action before the singles? Thus far Coltart, Sandelin and van de Velde had yet to play a single competitive round. In the end James opted to keep his foot on the Americans' throats by playing his top combinations in the afternoon. While it caused some frustration among the three omitted players, the gamble paid off as the session was once again shared. Montgomerie and Lawrie defeated Pate and Woods 2&1; Mickelson and Lehman claimed a point for the US in defeating Clarke and Westwood 2&1 and the remaining two matches between Parnevik and García against Love and Duval, and Jiménez and Olazábal against Leonard and Sutton were halved. That took the score to 10–6 in Europe's favour. Surely it was all over. Europe needed just four points out of an available twelve to retain the Ryder Cup.

Mark James: The point that Paul Lawrie and Monty gained against Tiger Woods and Steve Pate in the afternoon fourball was huge in every respect. The USA had thrown a lot of good golf at us and we were in the process of trying to build a wall to stop them breaking through. Their point was a very big part of that barrier. Monty's performance all week had been enormous on and off the course.

Paul Lawrie: Colin was like a man possessed with the putter that week, I don't think he missed a putt from inside fifteen feet the first two days. I had played with Colin a lot before but I learned a lot those two days, how to handle and go about things.

Back then I was better at fourballs as I didn't drive the ball very well but now my driving is a strength. When you are a poor driver foursomes is a tough game as you are apologising a lot but I drove it well that week and he putted as he did so it didn't really matter.

We played Tiger and Steve Pate and Steve and I didn't do an awful lot. Tiger was the world number one and Colin was three. I chipped in at sixteen and came in a couple of times but basically it was Colin versus Tiger and we won 2&1.

Mark James: It was an equally brilliant performance by Ollie and Mechanico [Miguel Ángel Jiménez] to squeeze a half out of Leonard and Sutton. Miguel had produced extremely solid golf, and the two shots he hit into the eighteenth were right out of the middle of the bat. I could not have asked for more from him.

A lead going into the final day was more than we could have hoped for. There would be no over-confidence, though, no room for gloating. Our attention had to be devoted to the twelve singles matches which would decide the outcome.

At the press conference that evening, Crenshaw seemed to be fighting to hold back tears as he espoused the qualities of his 'twelve special men'. There was no doubt they were wonderful golfers and seemed to get on well with one another under the umbrella of Team USA, but they had failed as a collective when it mattered. But then, as things began to wrap up, Crenshaw paused. 'I'm going to leave y'all with one thought,' he said, index finger raised. 'I'm a big believer in fate. I have a good feeling about this.' And with that he stood and exited the room.

Crenshaw left the Country Club and headed to the team hotel in Boston, where the Europeans were also based on the floor below. He gathered his team together for a meeting. They were four points down; no team had ever come back from more than two down. But he put up his singles order in the team room, turned to his players and simply said, 'We can whitewash 'em.' Gentle Ben was once again revelling in the irony of his nickname. He would rage, rage against the dying of the light.

George W. Bush, Govenor of Texas and a close friend of Crenshaw's, was invuted to speak to the team. He spoke passionately about patriotism and read the famous letter that Colonel William Barret Travis wrote to the people of Texas during the Battle of the Alamo. 'I shall never surrender or retreat . . . Victory or Death.' There were tears shed in the team room. The Alamo had been lost, but the war to confer Texan independence from Mexico had been won just a few weeks later. Parallels could be seen by the players and they drew inspiration.

Crenshaw then asked each man to stand and talk about his experiences at the Ryder Cup and their expectations for the next day. If a player said, 'should we win tomorrow,' or, 'if we win tomorrow,' Crenshaw was on them in a flash. 'When we win tomorrow,' he would correct them. It was siege mentality time; no room for doubt, no inch was to be given. Hal Sutton perhaps summed it up best for his teammates. 'I believe there's more talent on the sixth floor than there is on the fifth,' he said. 'But we've got to play with more emotion. We've got to raise our fists, get the crowd into it.' The battle plan had been laid out.

Tom Lehman celebrates during the foursomes. *Getty Images*

Tom Lehman: Ben, Lietzke and [vice-captain Bill] Rogers had put together this line up, and they had Tiger second to last. We all said, 'Hey, if we're going to win this thing, we're gonna have to get on them early and get on them hard. Tiger needs to be nearer the top.'

Jim Furyk: Guys started offering solutions. Davis [Love] was kind of a veteran member – everyone looked to him for ideas. Hal [Sutton] was the same way.

Ben Crenshaw: It was a collective effort. Like putting a recipe together, you throw in a little of this, a little of that.

Mark O'Meara: Mickelson and Davis were really talking about strategy, what they wanted to do and what they thought would work. The rest of us just kind of sat around. I kept my mouth shut, because I'd played in only one match and got beat.

Jim Furyk: I went from being really upset to thinking maybe we had a strategy. We went up to the team room, and that's when I really started to believe, 'Hey, this could really happen.'

David Duval: Our best guess was that they were gonna go from strongest to weakest. We thought their guys who hadn't played would be in the last matches. Then we saw their line-up a while later, and that wasn't the case.

Ben Crenshaw: I just could not believe Mark James sent them out three in a row.

Bruce Lietzke: Those were like three automatic points to me – they were going against Mickelson, Love and Tiger. That put the real pressure on Lehman [against Lee Westwood] and Sutton [against Darren Clarke] in the first two matches. Those two points became critical.

Sam Torrance: The only contentious issue, although it was never one inside the team room, concerned the three players who did not appear until the Sunday, but I stood right behind Mark in what he did. No disrespect to our lads, but I didn't believe we were as strong nine through twelve as the Americans were. It gave them greater options. They could put out their twelve fairly confidently whereas on Friday and Saturday we had to put out our best team and get as many points as we could.

Jesse got us a four-point lead on Saturday night and that's the captain's job done. The singles take care of themselves.

Colin Montgomerie: If we had been told on the Concorde flight over to Boston that we would be 10–6 up going into the singles, we'd have taken it, it didn't matter who played or didn't play. Mark James was absolutely chastised for not playing three guys until the singles, but I wouldn't have worried about that myself. I'd have said, 'Get on with it lads, we're 10–6 up.' And the fortunate thing about that whole thing was that the guys that didn't play – Jean van de Velde, Jarmo Sandelin and Andrew Coltart – they took Love, Mickelson and Woods with them in the singles. Perfect. Because those American guys were probably going to win their games anyway. So they took our weakness with them and left us with nine guys to get four points. Clarke and Westwood started one and two in the singles and they would say themselves that they were not as fit then as they are now. They were carrying extra weight, they were tired and they both lost. The next three were those three rookies in a row and they lost. So that was the first five games and from 10–6 up we were suddenly 11–10 down. Game on.

The scoring from the Americans was as relentless as it was brutal. There was red everywhere on the scoreboard. When the first six matches were over, the US were leading 12–10. It was an extraordinary comeback. It was like Mohammad Ali and George Foreman played out on a Massachusetts golf course instead of a Zaire boxing ring. But could Europe pull off the rope-a-dope comeback?

Where the Europeans had played so effectively as pairings, they looked lost out on the course on their own. America had been made favourites by the bookies because their players ranked collectively higher on the world rankings where play is all about the individual. The make-up of that US team was designed to dominate singles; and dominate it they did.

Tom Lehman: To put me out first was one of the great compliments of my golf career. Ben said to me, 'You're a strong man, I know you can get the job done for us.' But we all felt we had a chance. We're four points down; we can still win. We can win eight out of twelve singles matches; we can do this.

Andrew Coltart: It was always going to be tough to play any of the Americans on the last day because they were so far behind that they had to go for everything.

Sam Torrance: We did so much work that week on the gallery. You're there for four days before the matches begin, so the galleries see a lot of you. The players would go over into the crowd, get their pictures taken, smile, laugh, get them on our side. They really were on our side. And then on Sunday the whole thing changed.

Colin Montgomerie: They talk about 1991 and the 'War on the Shore', Brookline was 'Into the Bear Pit'. My God, it really was. And in that Sunday singles it took on a whole new meaning. Those shirts that Ben Crenshaw had made had all the winning Ryder Cup teams all over them; they were hideous looking shirts but an amazing thing to rile the troops with. Every American winning team was on the shirts. And we were a very immature team by comparison, a very young team anyway, but one thing we didn't understand was the passion that America had for this Ryder Cup and how much they wanted it back.

Mark James: Ben had delved into the photo archives and pulled out pictures of winning American teams. They were then turned into a montage on which the design of the shirt was based. God they were ugly.

Ben Crenshaw: The idea for the shirts began back in 1995, when I won the Masters wearing a shirt that bore a lot of images of Bobby Jones. We got some photographs together of some previous winning US Ryder Cup teams and asked a shirt company if it was possible to put them on shirts. They said, 'Sure.' When we showed them to the players, there were some raised eyebrows. But most of them just said, 'Yup, that'll work.' But, of course, they weren't meant to be a fashion statement. They were a symbol.

Andrew Coltart: I was one of the guys left out until the singles but I still absolutely back the captain for not bowing down to egos at that time, and just picking a team on the strength of partnerships that he felt at the time were working. I go back to the fact we were four points in front going into the last day singles, and that hadn't been done before. Admittedly, what subsequently happened, and this I partly blame a) on the captain and b) on the experienced players, was that they should have known that five matches takes a hell of a lot out of you mentally and physically. They should have known that with twelve points available on the last day, as opposed to four in each doubles session morning and afternoon, that ultimately the singles are the most important day. You've got to be absolutely fighting fit and raring to go. It strikes me that has only occurred to Paul McGinley in the last few years, that he has turned to the guys and sort of said: 'What is really important is that you win your singles match on the last day, it takes more pride to do that than being helped through by a foursomes or a fourball partnership.' Being an individual sport, even though it is a team competition, there is a huge emphasis now on being fit and ready to play for that. So, partly I blame the guys that should have known better, who perhaps felt, at that stage, it wasn't the time to step aside and let a rookie in. So there are several things there I think that are worthy of being addressed.

Tom Lehman: I was nervous, being first off. So I go to the first tee and they're singing the national anthem, which loosened me up. On the right side, all the European fans were singing 'Olé,' that typical song you hear when they're getting drunk.

Lanny Wadkins: If there's ever been anything about the Europeans that irritated me it was when they come over here and, whether they win or lose, they always find something wrong with the galleries.

Mark James: It went wrong from the start when they got on a roll. You hope for a point in the afternoon when the momentum starts to shift a bit and your team holes a few putts but that never really happened. They got the momentum and fair play to them, they hung on to the momentum for pretty much the whole afternoon and that makes for a big swing.

Lehman defeated Westwood 3&2. Having waited three days to play, van de Velde was dismantled 6&5 by Love who had played three times. Sandelin fared nearly as badly, losing 4&3 to Mickelson, while Clarke lost 4&2 to Sutton. Parnevik, who had played so well with García, was whipped 5&4 by Duval. Woods showed his quality in beating the raw Coltart 3&2. Pate did a number on Jiménez, beating him 2&1 to take the score to 13–10.

When Furyk then saw off the challenge of the exciting young Spaniard García 4&3, the US had fourteen points. They needed just a half to win the cup.

But Lawrie was fighting hard for Europe and was in the process of beating Maggert 4&3 to give Europe their eleventh point and a chance in the match. Harrington was also throwing punches, refusing to lie down under the US onslaught. His match with O'Meara went to the eighteenth, but while O'Meara looked set to claim the vital half he crumbled under the pressure and bogeyed while the Irishman held his nerve to win one-up. 14–12. Knife-edge stuff.

Mark James: The momentum was turning against us and I could feel the crowd starting to turn, too. The noise levels were going up and up, especially when our players were about to hit their shots. There were repeated calls for silence, but it didn't make any difference, which was disappointing. People pointed out afterwards that the same thing had happened at Valderrama, but my response then – and now – is that two wrongs don't make a right. That's not golf; there shouldn't be noise like that when players are taking their shots.

Hal Sutton: We knew we had to set the pace and get the crowd involved. The crowd was incredible, and you could feel it every shot. You could hear the roars all over the course, so you had an idea that things were going pretty well.

Renton Laidlaw: People were shouting at the top of Monty's backswing and the stewards were doing nothing about it. Ludicrous. Instead of watching the crowds, they were watching the golf. And some were even encouraging the Americans as well.

Jesper Parnevik: I had a lot of American friends in the crowd. They were embarrassed to hear some of the heckling that happened to Monty. I can understand the Americans rooting for the Americans, but it should never get personal – not in golf, anyway.

Colin Montgomerie: I was paired with Payne Stewart and he was brilliant. I'd just holed a huge putt at three for a half, which he must have been a bit miffed about, but as we were walking to the fourth he turned to me and said, 'Look, if there are any more problems, let me know, and I'll let the referees know, and we'll deal with it.' I thought, 'What a decent man.' That was really good of him. And then the noise was up again on the fifth, and somebody shouted out during my backswing – and Payne marched over and said something to the stewards and I think they threw some people out.

Jim Furyk: The best part was going out late, eleventh off. I was on the range with that huge screen, and I kept seeing the leaderboard light up with 'US' the whole way down. I found myself leaning on my club and looking at the board more than I was hitting balls. I'm like, 'Holy shit, we're right in this.'

Paul Lawrie: I remember Mark and Sam [vice-captain Torrance] were very adamant: don't watch the board. They emphasised there was going to be bleeding early on. Just play your match. When I got on the course, I looked at the board on the third tee – you walk right toward it; you can't not look at it. I'd never seen so much red in my life.

Andrew Coltart: José María Olazábal had been one of Europe's best players over the last twenty years and we could see it was going to come down to him. He was four up with seven to play and you would never think that a character like him wouldn't push on for victory in a situation like that. So we still thought, even though the score was getting tighter all the time, 'Hold on, we'll be alright, we'll be fine'. Harrington went down the last and beat Mark O'Meara. We still thought, really, that it was going to be close but we were just going to do enough. It all changed in a very short period of time.

Olazábal had looked comfortable on the front nine against Justin Leonard, but then he hit a bad run of form and bogeyed four straight holes from eleven to fourteen. Leonard held in there and then sank a thirty-five foot putt on the fifteenth to level the match.

José María Olazábal: I opened the door a little. I missed a short putt on eleven, then I lost the next two holes.

Justin Leonard: I finally hit a couple of decent shots and made a six-footer for par on twelve. I didn't do anything stupid – I played my game and won a hole. Then I hit a good drive on thirteen and José hit a quick hook. All of a sudden, everything just flip-flopped. I was still three-down, but I felt like I was in control.

Tom Lehman: Justin made a thirty-five-foot bomb on fifteen that broke maybe three feet right to left. Just swished it.

José María Olazábal: It was a huge putt, a very long putt. That helped him believe he could win the match. He never gave up.

By the time they came to seventeen they were still all square and they both reached the green in two; Olazábal thirty feet from the hole, Leonard forty-five.

Justin Leonard: We got to seventeen all square, and I hit my best drive of the week and

Olazábal hit his left, which was no problem. I'm walking off the tee and I'm thinking, 'If I win this hole, it's over.' It was about that time I found out Mark [O'Meara] had lost eighteen. I hit a wedge in, but the harder you hit it, the more spin comes off it, and mine came racing back. Ollie hits a good shot, maybe ten feet inside of mine.

As Leonard stood over his ball there was no expectation that he could sink it; not from forty-five feet. He would play as close as he could to the hole and then wait for Olazábal to probably do the same. It would all finish on the eighteenth. He struck the ball. It tracked. It vanished.

Justin Leonard: I was trying to two-putt, trying to get it close enough so I don't have to do anything. If there's a two-foot bucket around the hole, my goal is to get it in that bucket. When it got on top of the hill and started moving, I knew it was pretty good. I thought I hit it a little too hard, but three or four feet from the hole, I said, 'Unless something goes crazy, this falls in.' It was fun having an idea it was going in before it got to the hole.

It was a wondrous shot and as Leonard roared in celebration his teammates were lost in the moment and charged the green in celebration, forgetting that Olazábal was still to play.

Ben Crenshaw: You know, had that putt of Justin's been holeable, say ten or fifteen feet, then I don't think the reaction would have been the same. But it was just so improbable, so extraordinary, and we just completely lost our minds; we all lost them – I did. Our emotions completely got the better of us. It was all so highly improbable. But you know, there was no excuse for it, and there is no question that it is a lifelong regret.

Colin Montgomerie: Payne and I were playing behind Olazábal and Leonard and it was

The American team envelop Justin Leonard on the seventeenth green.

tight. As soon as Leonard holed his putt and people ran on the green, having seen Olazábal hit his drive and his second shot onto the green, I said to Payne, 'What's going on?' They were all running onto the green 130 yards ahead of us. Payne frowned and said, 'Something isn't right.' I said, 'Olazábal can still win this, what's this all about?' We were so shocked about the invasion of the green.

Tom Lehman: We were thinking, you know, he makes this putt, we get that last half point, we win. Obviously, our thinking was misguided, because José María still had a putt to tie. So when Justin's putt went in, we went dancing across the green, and the rest is, unfortunately, history.

Curtis Strange: I don't condone what went on with the players at the seventeenth green, but I can understand the spontaneous reaction to Leonard's putt by the players.

José María Olazábal: I have to say if it would have been just the opposite, we might have reacted the same way. We're all human beings; we have our emotions. The Ryder Cup brings them to the highest level possible.

Tom Lehman: There ought to be a movie. Call it, *The 42 Seconds to Eternity*. From the time the ball went in the hole when Justin made that putt until the time the green was clear was forty-two seconds. I wanted to see how long it took. It was forty-two seconds but it's also lasted ever since. It seems that I'm never going to be allowed to forget it.

Colin Montgomerie: Lehman gets singled out because he was first on the green.

Jim Furyk: I've seen it a billion times; I haven't watched that closely to see where Tom was. But for a million dollars, I couldn't swear he was even on the seventeenth green.

Tiger Woods: I've no idea why people single Tom out about it. It wasn't like he was the only one.

Tom Lehman: Having watched the video back I know I actually was the fifth guy on the US team to react. And I know I never set foot on the green. Not that it matters. I think it stemmed from Sam Torrance laying the blame with me afterwards; but Sam and I have made peace over it, and he sent a nice note when I was made captain for 2006. So I've moved on from it.

Colin Montgomerie: So Payne and I were left standing there saying, 'Well what the hell's going on here?' And then Olazábal did miss his putt – he had a hell of an effort at it, by the way, a hell of an effort at it, up the hill, forty-footer. He missed it and then, of course, it was a victory. Payne and I were on the seventeenth fairway and we were saying, 'Well, what do we do?' We were all square. The referee with our game said we had to finish it, so that's what we were doing. By that stage everyone had piled onto the last hole, America had won and the flags were flying. I hit it onto the green in two, Payne hit it into the front bunker in two. He chipped out onto the green. I was about thirty feet away, he was about twenty feet away. Alastair my caddie was looking after the clubs in case they were stolen because people were running all over the fairway in celebration, it was just mad. There were mad, mad scenes. And Payne realised this and walked up and gave me the hole. I suppose I was favourite to win it, but you never know what is going to happen and he was a very fair man to say, 'Look, I've had enough of this, let's stop.'

Peter Jacobsen: I loved when Payne gave Monty his putt on the last hole. That just showed you the kind of person that Payne was. If Payne had been thinking about his own personal Ryder Cup record, he would have made him putt it. But he gave it to him, and that gave Colin the match. There were ugly things, like what happened on the seventeenth hole, but many good things came out as well.

Darren Clarke: Mark James was fantastic that week. Perhaps we got a bit ahead of ourselves when we went into the last day four points ahead and, yes, we did lose, but what people tend to forget is that the Americans on the final day played golf that was nothing less than stunning. That's often been overlooked. They played sensational golf and deserved to win, given how they had come back when their backs were to the wall.

Andrew Coltart: There were tears in the locker room. People were down. José María was very cut up, very cut up. Not so much about the reaction, I don't believe, just about the fact that the Ryder Cup came down to his shoulders. He was well in control of his match and he couldn't pull it off. That disappointment for him was very, very difficult to take. The class of the man, the quality of the man, he picked himself back up out of that. Other players you would never have seen again. But he was gutted, absolutely gutted. It was as if somebody had just crept in there, just pulled everything that he had inside him out and dumped it somewhere. For a short period of time, he was broken. It was horrible to see a player of that stature, of that class, being put through the mill that he was putting himself through. But he pulled himself together and came back out of it. And what a career he has had.

Bruce Lietzke: Afterwards, the team didn't quite make it to the clubhouse; they were on a balcony above the locker room spraying champagne over everyone. Tom Lehman took his shirt off and threw it to the crowd. It was on eBay the next day.

David Duval had been disparaging about the Ryder Cup in the build-up, saying it was little more than an exhibition. He was neither the first nor the last to deride the Ryder Cup in this fashion, nor was he alone in changing his tune afterwards. 'I love the Ryder Cup,' he said, emotion trilling in his voice. 'I just didn't know. The only frame of reference I had was the Presidents Cup, and now I know there is no comparison. Someone said the best analogy is having your first child. Until you have one, you don't understand what it means.'

As the sun set over Brookline and the celebrations continued among the raucous home crowd, the final scoreboard read 14½–13½. Forget the controversial finish and bask instead in the glory of such a remarkable comeback; such a remarkable match.

THIRTY-FOUR

2002

The Belfry. Sutton Coldfield, England
(EUR 15½, USA 12½)

Just a month after Brookline, the US PGA appointed Curtis Strange as the captain they believed could defend the Ryder Cup at the Belfry in 2001. Strange was a veteran of five Ryder Cups, winner of the 1988 US Open and the first player since Ben Hogan in 1951 to defend the title a year later. He was a hugely popular figure, but also a fighter who was determined to build a tight bond among his players, as Ben Crenshaw had done, in order to achieve victory in England.

In the opposite corner, Sam Torrance was announced as European captain. For many, Torrance was the obvious choice to lead the home team's effort to reclaim the trophy having served as one of Mark James's vice-captains at Brookline and played in eight consecutive teams from 1981 to 1995.

Sam Torrance: I'd enjoyed the experience as a vice-captain, but I only really decided that I wanted the main job when they asked me. You don't really want to think that you might be captain, especially when you're still playing because it's not good for your game.

Curtis Strange: The day the announcement was made that I was the 2001 US Ryder Cup captain was probably the toughest day I've ever had as a professional, because that was the day Payne Stewart died.

On 25 October 1999, Payne Stewart had been part of a group of four men travelling by private jet from Orlando to Dallas when the plane lost cabin pressure mid-flight. After travelling 1,500 miles, most of it controlled by autopilot while the pilot, co-pilot and passengers were apparently unconscious or dead, the plane ran out of fuel and crashed near Aberdeen, South Dakota. There were no survivors.

Curtis Strange: The captaincy announcement was held in the morning in PGA headquarters in Palm Beach Gardens, and afterwards PGA president Jim Awtrey said, 'We might have a problem here.' I'm thinking, 'What have I done already?' But then he told us what had happened. We stayed another day for meetings, but it was tough to focus. Everybody knew Payne was going to be Ryder Cup captain one day.

Phil Mickelson: My favourite memory of Payne was from the 1999 Ryder Cup after we won and he was standing around with a cigar in his hand and these wild flower sweatpants and we were up and partying all night. And I think that was the last time I saw him. He knew how to have a good time and knew how to celebrate. And he also was a fierce competitor.

Paul Azinger: I played with Payne on the Thursday and Friday the week he died, and on Saturday night we had a party for my mom. Payne came, and Robert Fraley who was also on the plane came; my wife and I were leaving our children to Robert and Dixie Fraley if anything ever happened to us. And Van Ardan and his wife Debbie were there, and he was on the plane too.

My wife and I took our kids to a theme park the day of the crash and my phone had been off all day. I remember driving on the interstate on the way home and I flipped it on and all these messages started coming through. So we stopped and I called my brother and he said, 'Listen, there's been a tragedy.' And then I called my dad and he told me that they were all dead. And I just fell down on the ground, everything was sucked out me. I'll never forget that.

I spoke at the funeral and had no idea at the time that it was aired in sixty countries; I had no idea that Payne Stewart was as big as he was around the world. In my mind I was doing it for the four or five thousand who were there that day. When I was asked to do the eulogy it was probably the hardest thing I'd ever done, but somehow it was also the easiest thing I've ever done.

Payne was different from everybody else because he wanted to be different. And Payne always made a difference. Always made a difference. He was a great cook, a terrific family man, he loved sports, and he loved beer. He was the life of the party. He was a guy's guy, even though he wore knickers.

Strange and Torrance knew one another well from three decades of competition on the pro circuit and both were determined that the shameful jingoism that had overtaken events at Brookline would be banished from the 2001 edition and the traditions of respect and sportsmanship would be returned to the forefront of the Ryder Cup – something that Payne Stewart would certainly have approved of.

Sam Torrance: I was lucky in that their captain was Curtis Strange. We took about three seconds to agree there wasn't going to be a repeat of Brookline.

Further, even more seismic, events were about to unfurl, however.

On September 11, just over two weeks before the Ryder Cup was to commence at the Belfry, twoAmerican Airline and two United Airline planes were hijacked by terrorists; two of these were flown into the World Trade Center in New York; the third plane was flown into the Pentagon in Washington DC, while the fourth crashed near Shanksville in the Pennsylvanian countryside before it could reach its strategic target following heroic intervention from passengers on board. 2,977 innocent victims were killed that day and in the years that followed the aftermath of the attacks proved catastrophic. 9/11, as it came to be known, shook the world.

After five days of deliberation following the tragic events in New York and Washington DC, the decision to postpone the 2001 Ryder Cup was announced in joint statements by Europe's Ryder Cup Board and the US PGA. 'The PGA of America has informed the European Ryder Cup Board that the scope of last Tuesday's tragedy is so overwhelming that it would be impossible for the United States Ryder Cup team and officials to attend the matches this month,' said Mitchell Platts, the European Tour's spokesman. 'We have been placed in a position beyond our control and therefore the matches, out of necessity, have been postponed. The invitation for the United States team and officials to attend the thirty-fourth Ryder Cup has not been withdrawn but extended. We will now start the process of rescheduling the matches for 2002.'

Eamonn Darcy: The intensity surrounding the Ryder Cup needed to be pulled back after '99. It was getting a bit out of control and 9/11 changed everything and brought everything into proportion.

Colin Montgomerie: Things had been getting worse and worse over the years between the teams and crowds and it took 9/11 to change things. We had a three-year break after '99 because of 9/11. And it's been a better competition since for it. It needed something to calm things down. It took tragedy to do it. 9/11 brought the world together against terrorism and changed the Ryder Cup from an us-and-them event to a united world event.

Hal Sutton: Those planes going into the Twin Towers put things into perspective for everybody that this was just a competition and life goes on. The intensity was different afterwards.

When the teams gathered at the Belfry twelve months later, captains Sam Torrance and Curtis Strange made moving opening speeches. 'Not a day goes by when we don't remember just why we're playing these matches in the year 2002,' said Strange. 'There are some who have said that the excitement has lessened for the players and fans because of the postponement. We'll show, and all of you will show, how wrong they really are.'

The horrors of 9/11 had helped put into focus just how unnecessarily divisive things had become at Brookline. With the world plunged into chaos, the escalating rowdiness over a golf match was put into sharp context.

'I pledge that I and the team will maintain at all times the traditions of the Ryder Cup and of the game which we all serve,' said Torrance, before turning to his counterpart. 'Curtis, have a great week boys. May the best team win.' This was the spirit in which the 2002 Ryder Cup got underway.

Colin Montgomerie: 2002's Ryder Cup was intense, as it should be, but it was played in a different way. It was a calmer atmosphere. It was intense, but 9/11 was still very much in people's minds. It was a pity that it took that to calm it down, but it did.

Curtis Strange and Sam Torrance did a good job to say, 'Look, this is a game of golf and there are more important things in life.' At Brookline, there was nothing more important than America winning. But that was wrong, very wrong. So it was a good thing in 2002 that it was much calmer.

Sam Torrance: I was actually delighted it was going to be played the next year. Every other Ryder Cup captain in history has had three or four weeks after the team has been announced to prepare. I had over a year. And I made the most of it. I used that time to try to put the Ryder Cup in perspective after the terrible events of 9/11. And also after the way the match had got out of hand in 1999.

Despite home advantage, Europe were once again cast as the underdogs as a number of their players had dropped their form during the season, while the American team was filled with Major champions. The captains had previously announced that they would stick with the players that they had selected in 2001 and while this token was befitting of the spirit of the 2002 match, there appeared little doubt that the European team looked as if it would be hampered by out-of-form players.

Sergio García: I think keeping the two teams for 2002 as they were originally selected for 2001 was the right thing to do. Those players deserved to play in the Ryder Cup whatever anyone says.

Tiger Woods: I think it was the right decision. You have to understand that, going on 2002 form, we probably didn't have the two best teams we could have assembled, but then again who cares? After September 11, things were put into perspective real quick.

Sam Torrance: I had two picks, my highest ranked player who hadn't qualified was Sergio García, and I had to pick him. So it left me with one choice. And it came down to José María Olazábal or Jesper Parnevik. No one has ever given more to the Ryder Cup than Olazábal, it means the world to him. At the time his iron play was fine, his short play was great, but his driving was horrific. I couldn't pick him. But to tell him was awful.

I was behind the last green at the last counting event, the one where he failed to gather the points necessary to qualify automatically. I approached him and told him to his face. It was awful, a really, really horrible thing to do. It's far and away the worst part of the job. The other side of the coin, though, was that it was a nice call to Parnevik.

Paul McGinley: Some players in very good form in 2001 weren't playing well in 2002. I was one of them. Fifth in the Order of Merit in 2001, thirty-fifth a year later. I was really worried about how I'd play in the Ryder Cup.

A week before, with most of the European and US teams playing in a WCG event at Mount Juliet in Ireland, Sam took myself, Lee Westwood and Phillip Price to the Belfry for a practise round. I'd travelled with Sam and his driver.

On the way back he opened a bottle of pink champagne, produced two glasses, and said, 'OK Paul, this is how I see your involvement next week. You won't play the first morning, instead you'll go out in the afternoon foursomes with Pádraig [Harrington] and you'll play foursomes with Pádraig again the next morning.'

I was thrilled. I knew I would play three times, two foursomes and the singles.

David Feherty was a real help to me as a young Ryder Cup rookie. We talked quite a bit before the week and he gave me a gold-plated four-leaf clover ball marker that had been given to him by a member of his family and he'd used it in the Ryder Cup. Now, he wanted me to use it in my first Ryder Cup. So I said thanks and used it all week.

Sam Torrance: I will never forget the letter Seve wrote to the team and me in 2002 when I was captain. 'Dear Sam,' he wrote. 'I know the US team think they are the last Coca-Cola in the desert, but you have a better team, a better captain, so go and get them.'

As captain, it's so important to keep things light in the first part of the week. People have asked me ever since what speeches I made in the dressing room. I certainly didn't dip into the history books to check out a relevant quote from Lincoln or Churchill. What you have are situation speeches. Say you're going into the singles and you're three behind, someone is going to get up and say something that will move people. But that wouldn't be for the beginning of the week. In those early moments it's almost more about bringing players down, getting chilled out, having fun. The last thing you want to instil is pressure.

I knew I had managed to get things right when something happened just before the formal dinner on the Thursday. The wife had run me a bath, there was a glass of champagne by the side, perfect. I'd just got my arse in the water, when the phone goes. It was Pierre Fulke. 'I've got a problem', he says. 'I need to see you'. So I tell him to come to my room. I've barely put the phone down and there's a knock. I wrap a towel round me and open the door and he's standing there in his suit, shirt open. He's ashen. 'I've got a real problem only you can solve', he says. Then he brings his tie from behind his back and says: 'I can't do my tie'. The wee shite. But that's exactly what I wanted. Brilliant. Talk about taking the mickey. I knew from then on we'd be OK. Relax with the captain, take the mickey, that's the way to build a team.

You know, I never once looked at the US pairings in practise. I didn't care who was playing with whom and didn't care about what order they were playing in. I was determined to do it my way, right or wrong – it took all that second-guessing out of the equation.

In many ways it was relief that I didn't have to play, to deal with the pressure. It was just awesome to be there and not be playing. After I sank the winning putt in 1985, if you had something surpass that in my career, I thought it would have to be winning a Major. I never got close to winning a Major, but the captaincy just overshadowed it by a million miles, it was incredible. It was as good as it gets. I enjoyed the job, getting people motivated. It was just fantastic, just the greatest week of my life in golf – no question. From start to finish I revelled in it.

There was a year's cancellation, but there wasn't half-an-hour that I didn't think about my team, the clothes and the course. I also practised my speeches as that wasn't my vocation. Speaking was never something I enjoyed at all, much more of a heckler. I mean Woosie [Ian Woosnam] and I sat together for eight Ryder Cups and each time at the opening ceremony when the captain went up, we were nudging each other and giggling and saying 'Heck, we'll never do that.' But we both did it and we both did it very well. I wanted my players to look up to me and be proud of me being up there, not thinking 'God, I hope he can do this.' That's why I worked so hard.

Strange's team was made up of Paul Azinger, Mark Calcavecchia, David Duval, Jim Furyk, Scott Hoch, Davis Love III, Phil Mickelson, Hal Sutton and Tiger Woods alongside rookies Stewart Cink, David Toms and Scott Verplank.

Torrance's team, meanwhile, consisted of experienced stalwarts Bernhard Langer and Colin Montgomerie, solid deputies Darren Clarke and Lee Westwood and saw the return of Sergio García and Jesper Parnevik who had combined so well at Brookline, plus four fresh faces in the Swedish pair Niclas Fasth and Pierre Fulke, Irishman Paul McGinley and Wales' Phillip Price.

Yet in spite of this apparent disparity between the teams, the first two days proved there was little, if anything, between them. The biggest result of the Friday morning fourballs saw Clarke and Bjørn defeat Azinger and world number one Woods one-up in the opening match, leading the European charge as García and Westwood defeated Duval and Love 4&3, and Montgomerie and Langer defeated Hoch and Furyk 4&3, before Mickelson and Toms pulled back a point for the US in defeating Harrington and Fasth one-up.

Sam Torrance: The guys were really up for it and the way they performed was incredible. It was the best start we'd made to a Ryder Cup for over thirty years. I was so proud of the way Darren and Bjørn led from the front. But it wasn't just that one match. There were four matches, and we won three of them. It was just a great start. We also were up in three of the afternoon fourballs, but ended up losing two of them and halving one. So we ended the day just one point ahead.

The afternoon foursomes were more evenly poised as Sutton and Verplank defeated Clarke and Bjørn 2&1 before García and Westwood once again denied Woods (this time in partnership with Calcavecchia) to win 2&1. Montgomerie and Langer halved with Mickelson and Toms before Cink and Furyk clinched an important 3&2 victory against the Irish duo of Harrington and McGinley.

Bernhard Langer: I told Sam that I didn't think I could play all four matches in the pairs without being too exhausted for the singles. So we agreed I should play three. Sam decided to play everyone before the singles, which I thought was the right approach. It was good that Sam told everyone at the beginning of the week that they would play at least once in the foursomes or fourballs, otherwise players can get anxious about whether or not they will play. He asked us all for our preferences in partners, which again was a great thing to do. Of course we all knew that at the end of the day it was his decision.

One of the players who had received a lot of criticism in the press over his poor form coming into the Ryder Cup was Lee Westwood. I was personally delighted to see him (and Sergio) record two wins. Again there had been a lot of nonsense in the papers about the USA starting with a five-point lead as no one would beat Tiger. And Tiger lost both games on the Friday.

Lee Westwood: I was struggling with my game in 2002 and, lacking confidence, I approached the match with some trepidation. Sam came up to me early in the week with a question. 'Would you mind playing with Sergio García?' he asked. Just those words were enough to raise my level of confidence. Would I mind playing with Sergio García? Are you kidding me? One hundred per cent I wanted to play with him.

Sam Torrance: Collectively, we had twelve great players, but there was one pairing that came to me late on the Thursday. They hadn't even played together; they hadn't even played in the same fourball in the practise matches. It was Lee Westwood and Sergio García. I don't know where it came from. They were the best team, fantastic all week. They just fed off each other in the most brilliant way.

The US momentum continued in the first match of the foursomes the following morning as Mickelson and Toms defeated Fulke and Price 2&1 to draw the overall score level, before Westwood and García teamed up to defeat Cink and Furyk 2&1 and Montgomerie and Langer won one-up against Verplank and Hoch. The US squared the session when Woods finally earned a point for his side when he combined with Love to defeat Clarke and Bjørn 4&3.

Phillip Price: I knew before the week started that Sam was planning to sit me out on the Friday. He said, 'You are not going to play the first day, you are going to play the Saturday morning with Fulke.' So we knew the week before what I was going to be doing, which was good as I could focus my practise around that. I was never ready to play Friday. He said 'This is what you are going to do, you are going to play foursomes'. It was a bit of a shame, because we played very well, but they played even better. I think we were one up after eleven and we had about a seven-footer to go two-up after twelve but that lipped out and we just had a run of holes where we had couple of poor shots, they had a couple of good ones and the match was over. It was a very quick turnaround from looking in a good position.

Curtis Strange: I had some pairings that had been done for a year. I thought David Toms's and Phil Mickelson's personalities meshed well. I always liked Tiger and Calc and Tiger and Zinger, because I thought Calc was a wonderful best-ball player and Azinger was a great alternate shot player. But I switched that at the last minute. We were all in a little meeting one night and I said, 'Okay, Calc, playing with Tiger Woods, best ball or alternate shot?' He said, 'Alternate shot.' Both Calc and Zinger said they were comfortable in the opposite of how I'd paired them. Tiger said it didn't matter to him. Tiger and Calc lost in the afternoon foursomes [2&1, to Sergio García and Lee Westwood]. In the morning, Azinger and Tiger played really well in the fourballs and lost. Their match against Darren Clarke and Thomas Bjørn had nineteen birdies. We were one-down on the last hole, and Azinger stuck a four-iron in there to three feet. The Europeans both hit it to twenty or twenty-five feet, and Bjørn made it. All you can do is applaud. But if I could take something back, I wouldn't have switched Calc and Zinger.

Calcavecchia and Duval punched back with their one-up victory over Fasth and Parnevik in the opening afternoon fourball before Harrington and Montgomerie overcame Mickelson and Toms 2&1, and Love and Woods beat García and Westwood on the last green, before Clarke and McGinley halved with Hoch and Furyk to leave the teams level at eight points apiece going into the Sunday singles.

Lee Westwood: As I say, I wasn't in any kind of form that year, but playing with Sergio really helped. I didn't feel there wasn't so much pressure on me when I was playing fourballs with him and I putted really well that week which can hide a lot of things. Holing a few thirty- or forty-footers can mask quite a few faults elsewhere.

Our first match pitted us against David Duval and Davis Love III. We won that 4&3. We took out Tiger Woods and Mark Calcavecchia by 2&1 on the Friday afternoon. We saw off the combination of Stewart Cink and Jim Furyk in the Saturday morning foursomes by the same margin. That left only the Woods/Love pairing standing in the way of us completing a perfect four out of four record. Sadly, we lost the final two holes for a last-green defeat in a match we should have won.

Colin Montgomerie: When Pádraig and I beat Mickelson and Toms I don't think I'd ever played better up to that point in my career. And it had to be so because we were playing the second and sixth-ranked players in the world. There was so much pressure on us to secure a point and it was a magnificent sense of achievement when we did.

Pádraig Harrington: It's not a pleasant feeling these matches. It's like riding a roller coaster or bungee jumping. As it's happening, you're thinking, 'Why am I doing this?' When it's finished you're thinking, 'Oh, that was great.'

Curtis Strange: Everybody on our team was guaranteed one match before the singles. I don't believe in hiding anybody. You make the team, you play. I thought it was important that everybody got in the first day, and then it would be easier to sit someone out the second day. And you're so fired up at the opening ceremony to get started – then you have to wait a day? Get in the matches!

I put Davis Love with Tiger on the second day because I wanted to get Tiger on the scoreboard. One, it was important for Tiger to get a win, to get the press and everybody else off his ass. Two, it was important for the team to have Tiger win.

Paul McGinley: I played pretty well in the foursomes with Pádraig, but we lost 3&2 to Jim Furyk and Stewart Cink. Pádraig didn't think he was playing well enough and pulled out of the next session and I ended up playing the Saturday afternoon fourball with Darren Clarke against Scott Hoch and Davis Love. We were one down on the eighteenth and if we had lost they would have had a one-point lead going into the singles the next day. I hit a good shot onto the fairway, longer than Hoch or Love, but Darren hit into the rough by a bunker. I was naturally going to wait for him to lay up but then Sam appeared and tapped me on the backside, then got me into a headlock and said, 'Paul, I want you to play first, before Darren, put them under pressure.'

I hit a great shot to the green and made par, while they three-putted and we halved the match.

When I got back to the team room, the music was on, the place was buzzing. Sam came up to me, 'Paul, you showed a lot of balls out there. You will play number twelve tomorrow because I know if we need a point in the last match, you're the guy who will get it.' I felt ten feet tall. I went to my room, showered, came back down and saw the pairings. I wasn't at twelve, but hidden at number nine.

Completely deflated, I thought Sam was playing games with me. 'Sam, can I have a word?' He grabbed me by the ears, his moustache about three inches from my nose and looked into my eyes. 'Paul, in the history of the Ryder Cup, the winning point has never come from the player at twelve. It's always come from eight to ten and that's why I've switched you to number nine.' Then I felt twenty feet tall.

Sam Torrance: I had a relatively simple plan for the singles. I just thought that whoever was playing better should go out first and whoever was playing the worst should go out last. I could never envisage a scenario when it wasn't right. If we were behind then we could get back into it. If we were ahead then we could go further ahead.

Colin Montgomerie: I was just honoured that Sam had put me in a position of strength and number one. Sam had this plan of attack that he would fill his top end with strength. Some people thought it was a great strategy, some people thought it was crazy.

Strange, meanwhile, saved his big guns, particularly Love, Mickelson and Woods for last. The tactics adopted by each captain meant that the contest would either be over quickly as Europe stormed to an early victory, or the US would roar back into contention at the tail of the order to claim the cup.

Paul McGinley: One captain got it wrong, and one captain got it right.

Raymond Floyd: It's so unfair how much the buck stops with the captain. Yeah they pick the pairings and the order for the singles, but it's the players who play. The captain can only stand and watch, he can't play the shots. I think too much blame gets heaped on the shoulders of the captains who lose.

Paul Azinger: The captains have been getting criticised since the post-Tony Jacklin era. When Jacklin beat Jack Nicklaus in 1987, did Nicklaus get lambasted? Never. But ask Jacklin's replacement, Bernard Gallacher. He got hammered when he lost twice. Lanny Wadkins got pummelled in '95. Tom Kite in '97 was unbelievably thorough, yet he was criticised, as was Mark James '99. It was even worse for Nick Faldo in 2008 and for Tom Watson in 2014 and

Paul Azinger and Tiger Woods.

pretty bad of Davis Love in 2012. Every captain who loses now gets ripped.

Europe went on to capture four-and-a-half of the first six points. Montgomerie had schooled Hoch 5&4 in the opening match before Toms had pulled back a point by defeating García on the eighteenth hole. Clarke had halved with Duval before Langer defeated Sutton 4&3, Harrington beat Calcavecchia 5&4 and Bjørn had seen off Cink 2&1.

Colin Montgomerie: If you ask me who my best captain was, it was Sam Torrance. Our team wasn't as strong as theirs, we had four rookies on the team, and America were the holders. Sam's a gambler, a risk-taker and all credit to him for gambling and risk-taking as he did. We were 8–8 going into the singles and we needed momentum and he decided to put all his eggs in one basket and put all his strength at the top of the order. At that point in time I was still number one in Europe, so I went number one. Who's the second best in the team? García. He went number two. Followed by Westwood, Bjørn, Clarke, Harrington. That was our top six. And the rookies were left at the end. McGinley, Fasth, Fulke and Price were left at the end, so if it went belly-up at the start . . . we were absolutely fucked. And he said we needed four out of those six points to start us off and get momentum and we actually got four-and-a-half out of six. I was left to lead off for the first time and it was nice to see Sam on the first tee, a Scot from Ayrshire, from Largs, and I was from Troon. A small world and we were there on the first tee together. And I drew Scott Hoch again. And this guy was tough. I knew he was tough. He was one of those difficult opponents that were not going to give you anything, you had to earn it. Mickelson or Woods would give you the odd hole, but this guy didn't. He made pars. So to beat him, you had to make birdies.

I'll never forget the first tee. He went first, being the guest. And then I was announced on the first tee. And I took a practise swing and Ivor [Robson, first tee announcer] had to do it again. 'I've never had to do it twice,' he said. But the noise was extraordinary. So he announced me again and I backed off it to give the crowd a chance to have another roar. And then I hit a three-wood 308 yards; I'll never forget it. It was just pure adrenalin. I was so pumped up. I normally hit my three-wood about 260 yards. This thing went 48 yards further than it should have done, which is silly. I got to my second shot and of course I had no idea how far it was going to go after that first one. I was about 108 yards to the pin and Hoch hit a good second shot to about ten yards of the hole. But I was frightened to hit mine because I had no idea how far it might go. So I hit a sand wedge but tried to pull back on it a bit and I ended up hitting it about 30 yards short. And I was just thinking, 'Oh shit. I have no idea how far I'm going to hit the bloody thing!' I was having to try and second-guess my body because I'd obviously calmed down by then and I didn't have the same adrenalin pumping through me as I did on the first tee.

I got my putter out; it was a right-to-left putt with about a foot break on it. And everyone was watching because García hadn't teed off yet and I was thinking, 'God, I could make a complete arse of this.' So you have to revert to all your psychological training to focus on this particular putt, your visionary stuff, looking at flags, looking at the colours to try and get yourself composed, the breathing techniques, the centring techniques that you've learned. And I hit this putt and hit it far too hard, a good yard of pace too hard. Anyway, it started tracking about ten yards out and I said, 'Oh my God, it's got a chance here.' And it started tracking in right-to-left and it just hit the right-hand side of the hole and dived it. And the noise! By this time the stands are all full all over the course and the Ryder Cup has improved by this stage to now include huge TV screens all over the place, so everyone out there could see it. And they just went crazy when that putt went in. And that was us ahead. We were one up in the first singles. I've never witnessed a scene like that, it was amazing, the whole place had just erupted. And I continued on like that and played as well as I could at the time and he didn't really have a chance. And when I holed my putt on the fourteenth hole, all credit to him he said, 'Well played. I never ever want to play you again.'

Sam Torrance: Monty was king of the castle. I'd never seen him like that in any event before. He'd always been a great team man but that week he was incredible. The same can be said of Bernhard Langer. He had so much experience and it made it a very easy job to be captain.

Curtis Strange: Seve was their leader for a long time and then, in 2002, it became Colin. Every team needs a leader, not only for their play but also for the way they handle themselves. He led by example and the others took their cue from him. He certainly did not disappoint that week.

Although this had been a positive start for Europe, when Westwood lost to Verplank 2&1 in the sixth match all of Europe's best players were now in the clubhouse. With America trailing by just two points and with five matches left on the course, a US comeback looked on the cards as Strange's big guns began to prowl the Belfry. All that stood in their way were the hopelessly outranked Fasth, McGinley, Fulke, Price and Parnevik, who had to take on Paul Azinger, Furyk, Love, Mickelson and Woods respectively. It looked for all the world as if Brookline might be repeated. But the lesser lights stood firm. Fasth, Fulke and Parnevik would all halve their matches; and the key encounters would come down to Price and McGinley.

Nobody gave the Welshman Price much of a chance against Mickelson. But his captain did.

Phillip Price: When the Ryder Cup was delayed by a year I thought it might actually be good for me. I hadn't played very well at the end of the qualifying and I thought, 'Give me another year and my game will be in great shape.' But it actually made it worse. I struggled the whole year – probably worrying about the Ryder Cup and trying to prove that I was playing well enough to keep hold of my position, but it just made me play worse. The pressure was building.

I think there were probably quite a few guys in that sort of position, where you wouldn't normally make the team. If you are not playing well, you're not going to make it. It was the same for both sides, but it was probably inevitable you were going to have players off form, which you wouldn't normally get. I think there were maybe four guys in our team who had dropped in form quite a lot.

Sam knew I was fretting a little bit about it so he spoke to me beforehand and said, 'When you get there, you'll be fine.' He explained that I'd be playing with Pierre Fulke, so I knew what to expect. He was just always positive and very encouraging and that helped me a lot. But you know, Pierre and I only played once and we lost, so by the time it came to the singles the nerves were still jangling.

I looked at the draw and I was up against Phil Mickelson. I thought, 'Oh dear.' I had expected to go out in the middle, a little bit under cover.

I think what happened in the foursomes, losing despite playing well, helped me for the singles, because it made me double my determination, thinking, 'I could have got that one.' All we needed to do was seal the deal – and I thought I could do it, because I didn't think Mickelson was playing that great and I didn't think the course was overly suited to him, so I felt quite good about my chances. I didn't really mind who I was playing, but I was more concerned that I was going out in eleventh spot and I was thinking, 'Hang on, the Ryder Cup is coming down to me.'

Sam came up to me on the putting green and said: 'I need something from you today, I need a point.' The hairs on the back of my neck stood up and I knew that despite being the underdog, if I gave everything I had something would happen – and it did. Sam was brilliant like that. He made everyone feel really important. There were a couple of us who weren't playing very well and I actually didn't feel particularly wanted beforehand but when I got there to the Belfry everybody felt very important – and Sam made me feel like that, made me feel like I had to step up.

I was pretty excited and nervous at the same time. I knew the course well and it was one that suited my game. I was fresh while Mickelson had played every session, and so I felt I was in with a good chance.

Price was a rookie, ranked just inside the world's top one hundred and twenty. Mickelson was a veteran of three Ryder Cups and the world number two. This was surely a guaranteed point for the US. But after seven holes the match was going anywhere other than along the predicted lines, with Price leading one up after five. At the sixth, Mickelson drove straight down the fairway while Price was lucky to avoid hitting the lake on the left-hand side. Mickelson then swept his approach to within five feet of the hole. With the ball well above his feet, Price scooped a wonder shot onto the green that skidded inside Mickelson's ball. What a moment it would prove to be as Mickelson then rolled his putt beyond the cup and Price held his nerve to hole.

Phillip Price: My goal with my approach was really just to get it to where I could have a putt of some sort; you know, fifteen to eighteen feet from the pin would have been a pretty good shot from where I was. But I just hit it perfectly and it ended up two or three feet from the hole and I was then able to drain it.

Sam Torrance: Phillip Price played magnificently against Mickelson. Some of the shots he hit on that last day were some of the best shots hit by anyone all week. On the sixth hole, Mickelson had hit a great second to about two feet. Philip had one foot in a hazard, the ball about two feet above him, and hit an incredible shot to three feet. He holed it, and Mickelson missed. A huge swing around there.

Price was now two ahead, and he just kept on rolling, winning the eighth to go three up. Mickelson pulled back a hole at the ninth but Price regained it on the tenth.

Curtis Strange: Sunday is tough because you're so spread out and you feel like you're missing somebody all the time. Eventually things settled down to where everything was coming to the end, so I went back to try to get Davis in. Davis didn't birdie seventeen, the par-five, so now we were doomed [he was all square with Pierre Fulke]. Mickelson was still three down. He was three down after eight holes. I'd ridden up to him and said, 'You all right?' He said, 'I'm OK. I'm OK.' I said, 'Well, I hope so.' But what are you going to say? I mean, they're big boys.

Sam Torrance: At one point we had a lead in seven of the first eight matches, but I made a stupid mistake. I thought we'd won it on the eighteenth when Niclas Fasth was about twenty-five feet away and putting, and Azinger was in the bunker. We needed only a half on the hole for a point and that would win us the cup. And we all know what happened.

Curtis Strange: I was on the seventeenth fairway trying to get Davis through, and I heard this enormous roar. But there was something strange about it – it wasn't one of their roars. It wasn't a prolonged roar. And then over the radio came this screaming, and it was [vice-captain] Mike Hulbert trying to tell me that Zinger had holed a bunker shot on eighteen for a half with Niclas Fasth. But he was screaming. It was great, but I had to tell them all, 'Settle down.'

Jimmy Roberts: A lot of these players can hole bunker shots, but you think of the circumstances, and you just shake your head and think, 'Oh, man, Azinger . . .' A lot of players love playing in the Ryder Cup, but Zinger really loved it. I do really think some people are born to do certain things. Azinger was born to play in the Ryder Cup. It's in his DNA.

Price and Mickelson were now on the sixteenth, with the Welshman two up having just lost the fifteenth. Both men found the green, but Price had a much more daunting position, some twenty-five feet from the pin, downhill. Mickelson, meanwhile, was about five feet closer in.

Phillip Price: I remember standing there and thinking that I'd have been quite happy two-putting from where I was. I just wanted to roll it down and get it as close as I could. So I gave it a nice firm stroke and it began to roll down, and it was tracking a nice line, but I didn't really think much about it. But it kept going and kept holding its line . . . and it went in. It startled me, to be

Phillip Price celebrates as his winning putt drops.

honest. The hair on the back of my neck went up when the crowd began to go crazy, the adrenaline was going . . . for ten seconds or so, it was the most exhilarating feeling I'd ever had. All of a sudden I started to get a little carried away. Looking back, I should probably have kept my composure a little more. I lost control, I suppose.

It was a fantastic day, the momentum was with us from the first game. I think that made it a lot easier for us four rookies at the end, because the atmosphere we were going out in was a good one. I think that really made a difference.

Europe's fate was now in the hands of Irishman McGinley as he faced off against Furyk.

Paul McGinley: Jesper Parnevik gave me a tremendous piece of advice at the start of the week. He said that there is a huge amount of emotion that comes from the crowd and you can either fight that emotion and fight the nerves that come with it – and it can take away from your performance; or you can ride that emotion and take your game to a different level. And that's what I tried to do all week.

Jim and I had a real good battle in that one and we came to the eighteenth all square. My approach shot wasn't brilliant and I was standing there looking at it when Sam came up and said, 'If you get up and down, we're going to win the Ryder Cup.' And I sort of smiled at him putting all this pressure on me. 'This is exactly why I put you at nine,' he said. 'Do it for me.'

I didn't have a great lie on my approach, so it was really just a question of giving myself a position from which I could putt, you know, giving myself a ten or fifteen foot putt and see what happens from there. So I hit it pretty smoothly and that's exactly what I gave myself.

Furyk's approach had left him in the greenside bunker but he produced an exquisite escape shot that lofted high out of the sand and then rolled towards the pin. The crowd noise rose and rose as it approached the hole, only for the ball to slide a foot-and-a-half past.

Paul McGinley: As I walked by looking at my chip, I noticed that Jim had a perfect lie in the bunker so I knew he was going to get up and down. It was only later that night when I watched on TV that I realised Jim's bunker shot actually hit the hole. I hit a really good chip from a bad lie to about ten feet. It was a pretty straightforward putt, except my caddie, JP Fitzgerald, and I agreed that it was breaking two balls left. I hit a perfect putt. It bisected the hole. I looked up, and it was two feet from the hole, right on track and with perfect speed. It went straight into the back of the hole. It was a wonderful feeling. It was a feeling I wish everybody could experience. It was like an explosion. I don't know how I came up with the expression, but at the time I likened it to opening a bottle of champagne. You shake the bottle, and it's ready to explode. When you take off the cork, there's a massive relief. I put my hands in the air and then looked at the team as they ran towards me and I could see Sergio jumping up and down and that's why I started doing that stupid dance and jumping up and down. It was a win for everybody. That's the nice feeling that you have – that you've made so many people happy.

Phillip Price: I managed to get myself there for the occasion, running! It was great to be part of the scenes at the end. It was an incredible couple of hours, to be honest, just having won. I sprinted from the sixteenth to the eighteenth, managed to get there and enjoyed that sort of lost moment with everybody.

Paul McGinley: I wound up in the lake. I was doing an interview and Darren Clarke threw me in the water. Somebody later wrote that I dived in, but it was a muddy lake. I wasn't going in there on my own. When I headed into the water all I could think of was Feherty's ball marker . . . I was trying to get my hand in my pocket to make sure his ball marker was going to be secure. When I saw him later that night, he asked if it was at the bottom of the lake – it was a great moment being able to hand it back, having worked its magic again.

Colin Montgomerie: There were four rookies on that team and not one of them lost in the singles – that's why we won. It wasn't anything to do with us.

In the closing ceremony, Strange spoke eloquently again. 'We were committed to an event that we could walk away from and shake hands, drink beer and say well done. I think we have both won in that category.'

Despite the criticism he endured in the wake of the loss, Strange took understandable satisfaction in having worked so well with Torrance to restore the sense of sportsmanship and goodwill in a contest that had been so tarnished at Brookline.

Curtis Strange: I learned a great deal over the three years I was captain, and part of it is, like it or not, is that everybody is entitled to their opinion. That really helped me after I came home and read some of the negative press. Deep down in my heart I know it was the greatest week of my life, and I'm not going to let a few armchair quarterbacks ruin that for me.

We got beat. The score on Sunday was twenty-eight-under for the Europeans to eight-under for us. The facts ruin the stories a lot of times, so the facts never get in there. People liked to say it was to do with how I chose the order, but it came down to the European players playing better golf on the day.

Those who questioned my first three guys, insulted those players. I will defend all twelve of my players until the day I die. They insulted David Duval, David Toms especially and Scott Hoch by saying I didn't have good players up front. They were world-class players.

It was disappointing to lose but that certainly didn't spoil the occasion for me. I felt sorry for my players but you have to perform and we didn't. We didn't get the job done and that was that. The European team played the better golf so what more can I say?

Jimmy Roberts: Just as Seve didn't win the Ryder Cup at Valderrama, Curtis didn't lose it at the Belfry. I certainly didn't see him scoring any bogeys. Really, Phil Mickelson should have beaten Phillip Price. Had he done that, then Tiger would have had to have beaten Jesper Parnevik, and Tiger seldom loses when he has to win. So if they both had won, then the matches would have been tied and the USA would have retained the Ryder Cup. Curtis took way too much heat.

Paul McGinley leaps in the air in celebration.

Stewart Cink: It's tiny margins, but that makes it more important for every player to take care of the little stuff, to play their own game and to not let the environment overtake them. That happened to me a little bit in my first Ryder Cup, I let the environment overwhelm me a little bit and that probably cost me a few holes during the matches. But it's not always easy.

Colin Montgomerie: The running order for the singles came out and we realised they had put their top three guys – Love, Mickelson and Woods – in the last three slots. And it ended up with Woods playing Parnevik at the end and it didn't matter. It's like leaving your best penalty taker in a football penalty shoot-out until number five or six. Get him in there, get your goal, guarantee your point. And unfortunately for Strange he left his best until last – by which time it was all over. And that changed the whole system of the Ryder Cup singles thereafter because no one left their strength at the end, every captain saw what happened and learnt a lesson from it. No matter where they are, you get your best players out in the top six and try and get your points on the board early to give your team momentum. That's all it is. We had momentum, we carried it through. So all credit to Sam. He had a weaker team, but we won – because of him. He was the best captain I played under, he was great.

Sam Torrance: My fondest memories from golf are from the Ryder Cup. The captaincy was quite extraordinary. The best week of my life in golf.

Lee Westwood: Sunday night saw one of the biggest parties in Ryder Cup history. The huge bar at the Belfry was packed to capacity. Somehow, it fell to me to act as MC, introducing each player in turn and leading the singing. Who could forget Phillip Price tugging at my trousers and shouting in that distinctive South Wales accent of his, 'Tell them who I beat, tell them who I beat!'

Phillip Price: I think I've had that said to me every single week since that Ryder Cup. Not one tournament would go by without somebody walking past, saying, 'Tell 'em who I beat'. It was kind of my catchphrase, I think. I reckon every single week that I've played a Tour event, somebody will have said that to me, every single week since 2002. That is a lot of weeks.

Paul McGinley: It was the best moment of my golfing career, but I was a little uncomfortable with what happened, to be honest; a bit uncomfortable that everybody was making me out to be the hero when I knew how lucky I was. I felt like the guy in the ad for the National Lottery when the big finger comes out of the sky and points down. I didn't want that to be my epitaph; I didn't want that one putt to define my career. I knew I could do better than that and it became a huge motivation for me to make the team in Oakland Hills. The desire to get rid of that tag as 'the man who holed the winning putt' was huge.

Curtis Strange: There's certainly more to a Ryder Cup than winning or losing, and in the aftermath of 9/11 this was especially the case because it became bigger than just a 'win' or 'loss'. People got it. They knew the matches were played with such etiquette, respect and sportsmanship. And after what happened in Boston, those ends were really a goal of ours. The matches were wonderfully played, and we had a wonderful week. And on that – win, lose or draw – nothing will ever change my mind.

Sam Torrance with the Ryder Cup. *Getty Images*

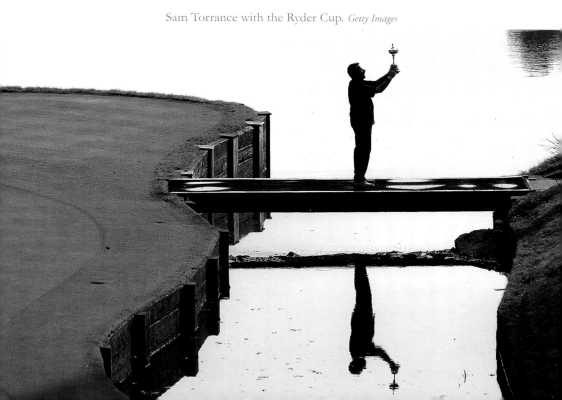

THIRTY-FIVE

2004

Oakland Hills Country Club. Bloomfield Township, Michigan
(USA 9½, EUR 18½)

As the home team and with five Major winners among their number, the US were the bookies' favourites as the teams converged on Oakland Hills Country Club in Detroit, Michigan. There was no doubt that the core of their team was stellar, with world number one Tiger Woods and world number two Phil Mickelson joined by Stewart Cink, Jim Furyk, Jay Haas, Davis Love III, David Toms and rookies Chad Campbell, Fred Funk, Chris DiMarco, Kenny Perry and Chris Riley.

Europe also had some seasoned campaigners in their ranks in Colin Montgomerie, Pádraig Harrington, Darren Clarke, Sergio García, Paul McGinley, Miguel Ángel Jiménez and Lee Westwood, and matched their hosts with five rookies in Paul Casey, Luke Donald, David Howell, Thomas Levet and Ian Poulter.

While the teams had a similar-looking balance of experience and fresh blood to them, their captains were completely contrasting characters: Hal Sutton, the larger-than-life Texan versus Bernhard Langer, the thoughtful and composed German. The question, therefore, was which leadership style would triumph – the passionate fire of Sutton or the cool calculation of Langer?

Bernhard Langer: I played under four captains: Jacklin, Gallacher, Ballesteros and Torrance; they all did a great job and all did it slightly differently. I tried to pick out all that I thought positive from what they did and incorporate it into my captaincy. I definitely learned that you want to play every player before Sunday. You don't want to have anybody sitting out all week and throw them in the deep end without having played before. That was a bit of a dilemma as I had such a strong team and so many strong pairings, but I had to break them up to get the other guys in.

Then I sent little cards asking them to give me one or two names of players they would prefer to play with and one or two they would not want to. All their answers were confidential, but they were a great help in getting me to think only of the pairings that would be acceptable to all concerned, not waste time considering partnerships that wouldn't have worked anyway.

I did a few other things: I researched colours, what they mean to us as human beings. It is a proven fact that some colours are more aggressive than other colours and some colours make you feel better in than others. Little things like that.

I think personal conversations are very important, more so almost than team meetings. I talked individually to all the guys most days. It was particularly important to speak to all those who were not going to be playing in one of the foursomes or fourballs; important to reassure them it was nothing to do with them not playing well. In the stress of that competition it is important to reassure them that you still think they are great players,

Opposite: European team captain Bernhard Langer (*right*) talks to team leader Colin Montgomerie (*left*) during the Friday afternoon foursomes. *Getty Images*

wouldn't be there if they weren't, but that, with four having to sit out each series the first two days, they couldn't be part of it that time.

Colin Montgomerie: Langer brought an ambassadorial, diplomatic approach to the captaincy. He was more of an ambassador than a team captain. There was nothing going to happen under Langer's watch that was remotely controversial. He had a great team, we were on a bit of a roll, he didn't do much, to be honest – he didn't have to, the team did it for him.

Thomas Levet: We knew it was going to be a tough week – and I think by expecting a really hard week it made it actually easier, because everyone was playing very well coming into the tournament. We showed it in the BMW International Open a few weeks before, virtually the entire team was in the top twenty-five there, and then we showed up with that form and took it into the Ryder Cup. It was a very strong team that Bernhard had at his disposal.

I had won the Barclays Scottish Open at Loch Lomond that summer. I knew I had qualified right after the Open, because I finished in a tie for fifth at Royal Troon the week after winning the Scottish. It put me in the team with no problems. I was leading the numbers for qualifiers and it was not possible for the tenth guy to overtake me at the time, so it was a nice feeling. I could prepare as much as I could for that Ryder Cup. It was a special moment in my career; it will always be special. Once you have played in it, you really want to come back and try to play in it again. I've not had that chance yet. I didn't play that well after 2004. I got very sick in 2006 [with severe vertigo] so I couldn't perform, but it's absolutely a fabulous competition. There are no words to describe the Ryder Cup. It's enormous, it's noisy, it's passionate, it's a lot of adjectives.

When picking his pairs for the opening morning's fourballs, Sutton opted for shock and awe tactics by assembling the 'dream team' of Woods and Mickelson to take on Harrington and Europe's talisman Montgomerie. Sutton wanted to make a statement of intent in that first match, to get the crowd pumped and his team on a roll with an emphatic win.

Colin Montgomerie: We weren't given a chance. I was up to about thirtieth in the world at the time, Harrington was about sixteenth. And Woods and Mickelson were one and two. The draw came out and Europe's pairing was announced first. 'Harrington and Montgomerie . . .' So we stood up on the stage, and we'd been told to keep standing there until the American pairing was announced. 'Against . . .' and then Hal Sutton announced, 'Tiger Woods and Phil Mickelson.'

Well, fucking hell . . .

I looked at Harrington and I just said, 'Shit, we've drawn a good one here, son . . .'

Ian Poulter: I didn't play the first day, so I went up to watch on the sidelines. I remember watching Phil Mickelson and Tiger Woods teeing off on the first and that was when the pressure of playing in the Ryder Cup hit me. I stood there and saw Tiger hit it fifty yards right of the fairway and then Mickelson hit it fifty yards left. You had the number one and number two in the world and they couldn't even get it to within fifty yards of the fairway. That settled me down a treat. I was there, I saw them – they were shaking. Mind you, had

Tiger Woods and Phil Mickelson were an uneasy partnership.

they striped it down the middle, it might have been a different story.

Tiger Woods: There was certainly a lot of excitement at the first tee. I was just trying to put the ball in play with the right to left wind; it was howling off the left and that's all I was really worried about. None of us hit the fairway, so it was a tough tee shot.

Colin Montgomerie: I said, 'Look, I'll take the first shot, Pádraig, don't you worry.' And I managed to push it in the right-hand bunker, which was reasonable under the pressure.

Pádraig Harrington: I remember feeling great on the first tee. That was my third Ryder Cup start and I went from not being able to see the ball at Brookline because I was so nervous, to not bad nerves-wise at the Belfry, to pretty OK at Oakland Hills. The only worry I had was putting the ball on the actual tee, after that, everything else was pretty solid. Because we knew for a while that Colin and I would be up against Tiger and Phil we knew what was expected of us, so I think that helped us, and I also think the build-up we had that week helped us going into the match. We definitely prepared properly and I think it showed the way we started. It was a perfect start.

Colin Montgomerie: It was interesting playing against Woods and Mickelson, they weren't together. I'll tell you what happened at the first tee and you'll understand more.

Harrington hit it into the left-hand rough. Woods came in and blocked it right of the bunker, Mickelson sliced it the other way, being left-handed, so they were opposite sides of the fairway.

There was about a metre of rough cut away from the tee down so that you could walk to the fairway without getting your feet wet from the dew in the grass. We all walked down the middle together and then separated; they started off on completely different sides, one was right, one was left and they weren't talking. And I said to Pádraig, 'Just stay in this, they're not comfortable here at all.' And I birdied the first hole, Pádraig birdied the second and we dovetailed brilliantly – every birdie we made we didn't make it together, we made it on top of each other. And I think we were eight or nine-under after seventeen and they were seven-under. Everything went right for us. We beat them 2&1. It was a hell of a game.

To beat Woods in America, first game out, with his number two in the world, Mickelson, was fantastic, something else, I loved it. Langer said, and he was right, that it was worth more than a point for us. But more importantly, it was worth more than a point *off* them. Everyone in the crowd, everyone in the team, had a tick against the American column for that game – and it went against them. It was a risk from Hal Sutton; if they'd won, fine; but if they'd lost, oh God. And that's what happened, they lost. And the whole Ryder Cup swung around in our favour from then on. There's no question. The team room after that one, my God . . .

Tiger Woods: Phil and I played well. We just didn't make enough birdies. I mean, jeez, they made eight birdies in fourteen holes and birdied six out of the first eight holes. That is awfully impressive. But we were right there. We were only one down. I thought we could, if we could get it to even somehow that might turn the momentum. We never got it to even.

Colin Montgomerie: The team room feeling was that 'we're going to win this'. The Americans were deflated by the failure of the Tiger/Phil combination. It turned there. It was all eggs in one basket stuff. It was a big risk, because it meant more for them to lose than it would have meant if they had won. And they didn't really get on, Woods and Mickelson didn't get on. Mickelson played his practise rounds separately; there were eleven players playing practise rounds on the south course where we were playing, but Mickelson was on his own on the north course, which I would never have allowed as a captain. If you don't want to play with your team, you can go home, we'll get someone else in who wants to be here.

Harrington was very thoughtful, very deep in his thoughts. And he said, 'You know, whatever we do here, we can't out-drive them, we can't hit better iron shots, we can't putt better than them, we can't out-think them, but I'll tell you what we can do, we can beat them.' And it was pure passion and pride that got us through it. Because individually they were better than us, but it was one of those times where on any given day anyone can beat anyone, you know? And it happened with us. And everyone got a lift from it, everyone got a boost.

By the time Montgomerie and Harrington put Woods and Mickelson to the sword, Jiménez and Clarke had already secured Europe's first point by dismantling Love and Campbell 5&4.

Riley and Cink were third out against McGinley and Donald and they battled each other to a standstill to halve the match and get the Americans on the board. It would be the only movement in their favour that morning, however, as García and Westwood combined well to defeat Toms and Furyk 4&3.

The afternoon session was almost as successful for Europe as they kept their foot firmly on the throttle. The US pulled back a point in the first of the afternoon foursomes as DiMarco and

Haas defeated Jiménez and Levet 3&2, but after that it was one-way traffic as Montgomerie and Harrington beat Love and Funk, Clarke and Westwood defeated the so-called dream team of Woods and Mickelson one-up, and García and Donald saw off Perry and Cink 2&1. Shock and awe it had indeed been – but from the Europeans not the home team, who held a 6½–1½ lead when play finally ended on Friday.

Darren Clarke: We had a great morning and were three points up after the first session, a huge achievement and impetus-builder. That lead was extended to five by the end of an afternoon which pitted myself and my old sparring partner Lee Westwood against Tiger Woods and Phil Mickelson. Hal Sutton had said at the pairings announcement that Tiger with Phil was something the world of golf wanted, he wanted and they wanted. That comment caused quite a bit of debate, particularly when they lost their morning fourball to Monty and Pádraig.

Colin Montgomerie: When Clarke and Westwood went out in the afternoon and beat them as well, the US had suffered a double-whammy, and it was gone. Gone. But it could so easily have been the other way around. A lot of it rests on one match, a point or half a point – so often that's all that's in it, and in 2004 that was the one match. We started well and got momentum and we never let it go.

Darren Clarke: I don't think that in those days Tiger and Phil actually saw eye to eye. There was an intense rivalry between them, which was healthy for the game, but they just weren't pals. Things have changed somewhat since, but they weren't close then and yet were paired together. As a result, there was always a chance of something going wrong with the team ethic and it not working out.

Tiger Woods: I thought we gelled as a team. We just didn't make enough putts.

Darren Clarke: For the life of me, I have no idea why the Americans in the recent history have often failed to gel as a team as well as we have. Tiger's indifferent record in the tournament was strange because he was far and away the best player in the world. You would think, too, when they come from a land where, at college level, everything is team, team, team, they would embrace the team spirit even more than we do. I honestly don't know why they don't. They are all fantastic players as individuals.

Hal Sutton: One thing that I wouldn't have changed was the pairing of Tiger and Phil, despite what people have said since. At some point, we had to find out if they were compatible to play. If anything else, we proved that that wasn't a good pairing. It wasn't a total loss. I can tell you that if I hadn't done that, every captain that came along would have been wondering, 'Should we do that or should we not do that?'

Phil likes to play with guys who he enjoys being around, obviously, but more than that, it's whose game he's going to trust. He's playing with a player who is real consistent, it allows him to be free to be who he is, which is a guy that can make a lot happen in a hurry.

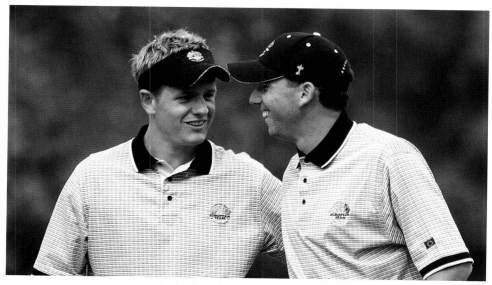

Luke Donald and Sergio García.

Phil Mickelson: Well, we got off to a good start [in the afternoon] and had a good lead and let it slip a little bit. And we had a tough match. We fought hard. I didn't play particularly well, but made some good putts. And I let it slide on eighteen with a poor tee shot after we pulled even and it basically cost us the match. So it was a very disappointing day for me. I played and fought hard but was coming up short and not playing the way I would like to.

Hal Sutton: Phil and Tiger ran into a buzzsaw early, got behind, although they didn't play badly to begin with. And then I saw a lot of frustration on both of their faces after that. You know, I said it in the opening ceremonies, I felt like the world wanted to see them together, I wanted to see them together, I think they wanted to see each other together and we gave it a good shot.

You know, I didn't see any downside risk to that. I thought when they got beat in the morning, they'd be on fire in the afternoon, and they started out on fire. Who would have thought they wouldn't hold on to that lead?

Bernhard Langer: It was huge, psychologically, for us to claim two points in the two matches against Phil and Tiger. What we got for the two wins was two points, but it was probably worth three or four. You know, it was huge psychologically, a huge blow to the Americans and a huge help for the Europeans. I was just thrilled it turned out that way for us.

Hal Sutton: I thought there was no bad way to pair our twelve guys. But obviously the pairings we sent out didn't create any charisma.

Tiger Woods: I basically missed some putts, hit a couple of bad shots and basically put us in a very difficult position to try and win the match. I just didn't have it – it was just not a good time to have that happen.

Bernhard Langer: We all know they are great players, all twenty-four, and it does come down to who makes the putts. You would rather have a ten-foot uphill putt than a twenty-foot downhill putt with a huge break. Bottom line is, the players can all hit good tee shots and hit the green most of the time but whoever makes the putts, wins most of the time. Hal and I said that early in the week when we had press conferences: the team who putted better would most likely be the winner.

I think some pairings just came naturally. You know, I have known these guys, many of them for years and years and others for a shorter time. I knew their strengths and parts of their game which might not be quite as strong, and I just knew that whoever I put up there would do well together. Pairings like Clarke and Westwood had proven over and over and over that they were just great together whether you play them in foursomes or fourballs, it didn't matter. They like each other's company and when you go out in a Ryder Cup you have memories that come back from past Ryder Cups. They had won far more matches or points than they had lost and that just gave them an up. It just gave them confidence. They just knew they were going to do well together. Then I looked at Sergio García and Luke Donald and they were just great friends. They, again, liked each other out on the golf course, they liked being together.

I was extremely surprised that Jiménez and Levet didn't win their foursomes match. I just thought that was a no-brainer. I think they might have struggled a bit because Jiménez had to play a different golf ball. He wasn't used to it, and I think that might have cost him a couple of holes. But maybe the putts just didn't drop or whatever. But I thought that was a banker. I could have put anybody against those two and I would have thought they would bring me points.

Anyway, I knew I had very strong foursome pairings and I knew there was some other guys who might not be foursome-type players. But out of the twelve, I knew there were at least ten or eleven that could have played foursomes very easily.

Colin Montgomerie: There was a lot of Irish support out there for us for that Ryder Cup, supporting Harrington. It was fantastic to see the reaction to him winning – and he was thrilled. He was just delighted. I went out in the afternoon and won again with him against Love and Fred Funk. We were just on such a high, we couldn't lose again after beating Woods and Mickelson. It was fantastic.

On Saturday morning, Sutton and his team knew they had to come out swinging in the morning fourball or risk facing an insurmountable scoreline. The US captain paired Haas and DiMarco against García and Westwood, finally abandoned the 'dream team' concept to pair Woods with Riley against Clarke and Poulter, pitched Furyk and Campbell against Casey and Howell and sent out Cink and Love against Montgomerie and Harrington.

And his players seemed to be responding to their captain's call-to-arms as they pulled ahead in all four matches. Crucially, however, García and Westwood were able to wrest back the American initiative to halve their match with Haas and DiMarco, and while Woods finally earned a point alongside Riley as they defeated Clarke and Poulter 4&3, and the Montgomerie/Harrington partnership finally stuttered as they lost 3&2 to Cink and Love, the duo of Casey and Howell battled manfully to overturn Furyk and Campbell and win one-up.

The Europeans once again dominated the afternoon foursomes. Clarke and Westwood combined effectively to defeat Haas and DiMarco 5&4 before Mickelson and Toms secured the only American point of the afternoon with their 4&3 victory over Jiménez and Levet. García and Donald showed some real grit to defeat Furyk and Funk on the eighteenth before the Irish duo Harrington and McGinley saw off Love and Woods 4&3.

At the end of play the score stood at 11–5 and Europe only needed 3 points from the Sunday singles to retain the cup.

Bernhard Langer: I told the guys not to go in there with the mentality that we were six points ahead. They were to look at it like it was a fresh start, a fresh match. We had won three out of the four series of fourballs and foursomes, but I wanted them to go out and win the singles – I wanted them to go out there like we were level and beat them at the singles as well.

Darren Clarke: This was where the balance of youth and experience in the European team came into play. I was among those who had reason to remember the bitter lesson of Brookline. Having been there before, myself and the other old hands ensured that the rookies were made aware of what could happen if we let our guard down.

Brookline was always there, not as something that worried us, but as a valuable lesson, painfully learned, and I could imagine the concern of European fans when a lot of red went on the scoreboard early in the afternoon. I don't know about the other guys, but I can assure you that I wasn't unduly bothered. I just looked down through our playing order, noting the terrific strength we had in depth. And everybody was playing well.

Colin Montgomerie: Brookline was obviously in the back of the mind, but Langer had plan B, C, D, E to deal with things going wrong as they had at Brookline, but he never had to use them. We had a fortunate incident that happened in the practise rounds. The Americans were told that because Tiger was in the team and because of the security issues surrounding that, that America were asked not to sign autographs on the course during practise rounds. So we got wind of this and thought, 'Right, great opportunity. Let's get this crowd on our side. We will sign everything. Get the babies out at the crowd, everything.' And we got the crowd on our side. It was a case of that thirteenth man was taken away from America and given to us. They weren't booing their team, but they definitely weren't as passionate for their own team as they could have been.

Paul McGinley: You know where you read that if you took an average player and put Jack Nicklaus's head on his shoulders, how good a player that guy would become? Being with Bernhard was a little like that. He gave us advice about course management and club selection and pin positions all the way round.

Pádraig Harrington: On all the par-threes, Bernhard came up to me, told me the club to play, the place to hit it and why I should hit it there. And while it wasn't like he was telling you to do it, you were definitely aware that he was advising you.

Bernhard Langer: It just helps the players to have a second opinion from someone they respect. When they're a little in doubt, if you tell them to take that club and hit it there, they will react 'that's what I was going to do anyway, but now I know for sure.' That kind of thing.

Paul McGinley: There's one little story from Detroit that just shows you the value of keeping your eyes and ears open. On the Saturday afternoon, myself and Pádraig Harrington played against Tiger and Davis Love in the foursomes. As you can imagine, in America when Tiger was in the middle of his top spell when he was the best player in the world by far, it was a massive challenge. But when we played it felt like the whole of Ireland was there watching us. We came back from two-down after the first three holes and beat them 4&3 and the Irish contingent in the crowd were going mad.

It was a great win for the team and afterwards in the car Pádraig said to me, 'We should make the most of that Irish support tomorrow by putting you and me one after the other in the singles. That way we'll keep all the Irish fans together around the same part of the course all day.'

So we went to our captain Bernhard with it and he said 'good idea' and put us out eleventh and twelfth in the order. That way the Irish crowd would centre on our two matches and it was very noisy and pro-European. That just shows you the value of keeping your mind and your ears open [as a captain] and never closing anybody's opinion off.

Colin Montgomerie: We had a discussion on the Sunday about the singles order. We were that far ahead that we knew we were going to win. But Langer very much kept it in order. And was there a point where number six was going to be the match that was going to finally do it? Eleven up, we needed three-and-a-half points to win.

Woods for the first time went out number one. That got rid of him.

Tiger Woods: My job was to go out there and get it started early with some red on the board, and I was able to do that. It was important for me to never show blue on the board. I had to show red early and then show it the entire time. That was a lot of pressure. I just treated it like the last round of a Major championship with Paul [Casey] and I tied going into the final round. That was my mindset, just go out there and play real solid, real steady and not give him any openings. I was lucky that Paul made a mistake on the first hole, and from there on, it was red on the board the entire time. I never really gave him an opening to get back in the match.

We felt like if we could get it started early and win the first four or five matches, you never knew what could happen, because that's exactly what we did at Brookline. When I was playing out there on the front, into the front nine, we were up in the first five matches and we were looking really good.

Woods defeated Casey 3&2 to give Sutton and his teammates the start they needed to stay in the match. Could a comeback similar to Brookline be on the cards?

Sergio García: Going out second I knew how important it was to get the first point for our team after Tiger won against Paul Casey. Phil [Mickelson] is a big player to come up against but I felt like I'd been playing well all week and felt confident that I could beat him. I didn't get off to the best of starts. I made a weak bogey on one to halve the hole, and Phil made a great putt to win the hole. I got two down early, but I fought back and I really felt like I hit a lot of quality shots and made some nice putts when I had to. I think I came out probably wanting it too much. You know, I was a bit nervous at the beginning and it showed up in a couple of shots. But I hit a great tee shot on the ninth and I had a huge putt there to win the hole. And then I just got on a great run, winning nine, ten, eleven. I missed a short putt on twelve for birdie and then won thirteen. And I just made a great four on the last, on sixteen, to win.

Colin Montgomerie: Sergio was magnificent. To be the youngest on the team and to have that effervescent personality that he does added a great deal to our team, and we all knew we could rely on him. Even when he went two-down, early on, we knew that that game wasn't over and he proved it yet again.

Phil Mickelson: I was in the first cut of rough on sixteen and as firm as the greens were, I didn't feel I could fly it over the water and get it stopped, but I was two down and I needed to make birdie. I was trying to hit a low, running hook that caught the left side of the green that ran over the hill up by the hole, giving me about a fifteen-footer.

It was probably about seven yards short of where I needed it, and it caught the slope and took it in the water and I made bogey and lost. I felt like I needed to take a little bit of a risk there trying to get it close.

Europe needed just two-and-a-half more points for victory. Clarke and Love were out third and they matched one another evenly around the course to halve their match on the eighteenth and leave Europe with a target of two points from the remaining nine matches.

Darren Clarke: I'll tell you a story about playing Davis. I got lucky going down the sixteenth and seventeenth and got a couple of birdies to bring the match level; we got to eighteen and I drove down the middle and Davis pulled his into the left-hand rough. And he was taking a stance and if he had moved his right foot six inches back he would have been standing on a sprinkler head and under the rules would have been afforded relief to drop his ball on the edge of the fairway and then hit it up to the green. He didn't take a drop. He played the ball as it lay because in his mind it wouldn't have been fair and the right thing to do – and that says everything about him and the spirit that that Ryder Cup was played in.

Davis Love III: And he then gave me a very long putt on the green and said, 'Let's call it a half,' and we went and had a cigar on the side of the green.

With the pressure ever mounting on the home team, succour was provided to the American cause in match number four when Furyk pummelled Howell in a comprehensive 6&4 victory. The next two matches out saw Perry take on Westwood and Toms tackle Montgomerie.

Colin Montgomerie: It's funny, at breakfast, Lee Westwood and I were talking about the line-up and we could see that it would probably come down to match number five or number six being the one that would give us the winning point.

I could see on the board that Darren Clarke had halved with Davis Love and Jim Furyk had beaten David Howell. Lee then beat Kenny Perry to take us within half a point to retain the cup and I knew that it was then on me to win the whole thing. Not that it mattered to me on a personal level, I just wanted to do it for the team – and I knew that there were still six guys out there after me who could settle it if I failed to get the full point.

I was up against David Toms – a very, very difficult opponent, someone like Scott Hoch who didn't give you anything; he made pars, was a good putter. And so I had to win the holes.

David Toms: It was a tough match, we kind of went back and forth. He got up on me early, I came back throughout the round and played really well. And I think thirteen was probably the key hole in our match because I had just gone back to even with two birdies and I hit it in really close and he made birdie before me and I missed. So he went one up. And then he birdied sixteen.

Colin Montgomerie: One up playing the last, I had two putts from the back edge. I hit the first to four feet, which was a very missable length. Clarke had just missed it before me to win his match; and there I was again in much the same position, but with the opportunity to not only win my match but to win the cup outright for Europe. And I was able to take it, which was great and it was a wonderful moment to be the one to have that winning putt.

David Toms: It was tough. He missed a putt on fifteen and other than that the whole day it seemed like he made every one he had to make. It was what the Ryder Cup is all about.

Colin Montgomerie and Bernhard Langer celebrate on the eighteenth.

Both of us had a chance to win and I just wished that the whole match had been a little bit closer so that it would have been even more intense going in during the final stages of the singles. But it was fun.

Colin Montgomerie: To be honest, I really felt like that putt was for Langer because I'd been one of his captain's picks, and he had become a very close friend. So that felt great to do. And it was wonderful to be able to then sit back and watch the other guys come in playing some wonderful golf. But it was a thrashing. A humiliation for America. They must have gone away from that thinking, 'Shit, what do we do? They really are ahead of us now.'

Bernhard Langer: I think it was very fitting for Colin to be given the chance to hole the most important putt that wins the cup – and when he made it, it was just fantastic. You couldn't have written a better script. I just told him, 'I'm so proud of you, you did it again. You deserve every minute of this.'

In the end it was a win of epic proportions, an 18½–9½ rout that set a record for margin of victory for a European team, and the largest by either side since 1981.

Colin Montgomerie: The Faldo, Woosnam, Langer, Seve era had gone and yet this new breed was coming through – it was Poulter's first Ryder Cup, Casey, García, Harrington, these guys were coming through and they were bloody good. Westwood was at his peak. I was hanging on. Harrington was coming into his peak, just about to win his Majors, so it was a real good team. We had strength at the top, we had strength in the middle, and we had strength at the bottom, which we proved all week.

Paul McGinley: When word came up to me that Monty had won it, I was delighted. It was almost his destiny to do it. No one was more deserving of holing a winning putt in the Ryder Cup than Monty. His contribution to the Ryder Cup down the years and again that week was phenomenal.

Paul Casey: For Monty of all people to hole the putt after all he had been through with abuse from the crowds and so on down the years, it was just perfect and we knew he wouldn't miss.

Colin Montgomerie: Yeah, I don't want to go into the past and the trouble I had with some crowds in the US. Oakland Hills was fantastic and there were no problems at all and it wasn't just me who was received warmly, all of our team were. I think we made a huge effort to make that happen – from the first day we arrived, Bernhard's decision to allow us to sign autographs and be open with the crowd worked in all our favour and not just mine. I think everybody was treated well by all the fans in Detroit and Michigan and in the end it all worked well for us.

Davis Love III: We were criticised a bit afterwards for not engaging with the crowd like the Europeans did. But listen, it's a heck of a lot more fun when you're winning and our fans were great. If we made a birdie they cheered for it. If we hit a fairway they cheered for it. Ultimately we didn't make enough birdies to give them something to cheer about but they were very supportive of us.

Bernhard Langer: We had beaten one of the strongest American teams ever assembled – it was a wonderful achievement for everybody involved. We had so much fun as a team and I was so proud of the guys. We were down early but came back strong and they showed they had a lot of heart.

Phil Mickelson: We are under constant ridicule and scrutiny over our play. And not coming together as a team and all that stuff that gets levelled at the team when we lose, we know within the team that none of that's true. We wanted so badly to win this event that when we arrived on the first tee we didn't play as though we had everything to gain and nothing to lose, we felt the opposite almost.

Hal Sutton: We just got outplayed. I made mistakes and I admitted it, I took full responsibility for the loss.

Davis Love III: You take twelve of the best players in the world and you put them out there and they have got to play. You could do all kind of pairings, all kind of formats, but if Tiger Woods and Davis Love and Phil Mickelson don't lead the team, it's hard for the next three or four guys to do it and it's hard for the rookies.

I got put out there with two guys who hadn't played in Ryder Cups before and I didn't carry them. If you're going to point blame at anybody, you should point it at the guys that are on the golf course, not at the captain.

Hal said he'd never been second-guessed so much in his life. Well, if we'd have won, he wouldn't have been second-guessed. If we'd have won our first two matches the first morning, Hal would have looked like a genius. And that's what I said about Tom Kite after we lost at Valderrama in 1997. We putted terrible for Tom Kite. We had, what, three Major winners for the year on the team at Valderrama? And we all putted bad. It wasn't Tom Kite's fault – and 2004 wasn't Hal's.

Colin Montgomerie: We have been very fortunate over the years to have had such great captains and I've played for a number of them. What Bernhard brought to the job was extreme professionalism. There wasn't the passion of some of his predecessors, just magnificent efficiency. He was immaculate in everything he did, totally prepared; there was never a moment when you worried something might go wrong.

Bernhard Langer: We were up the whole night drinking and dancing. I don't think any of the players, captains or vice-captains got any sleep that night. We truly had seven wonderful days, so many good experiences, terrific moments with each of the players, I can't imagine it getting any better than that.

THIRTY-SIX

2006

The K Club, Straffan. Co. Kildare, Ireland

(EUR 18½, USA 9½)

Ireland played hosts to the Ryder Cup for the first time in 2006 at the K Club in County Kildare.

The visiting team was captained by Tom Lehman and featured household names Chad Campbell, Chris DiMarco, Jim Furyk, Phil Mickelson, David Toms and Tiger Woods with rookies JJ Henry, Zach Johnson, Vaughn Taylor and Brett Wetterich and wildcard picks Stewart Cink and Scott Verplank.

European captain Ian Woosnam's wildcard picks were Lee Westwood (much to the chagrin of the overlooked Thomas Bjørn) and Darren Clarke, whose wife Heather had tragically died just three weeks before after a two-year battle with cancer. Clarke declared that Heather would have wanted him to compete and vowed to repay Woosnam's faith in him. Alongside these two experienced campaigners there was a very familiar feel to the rest of the team with Paul Casey, Luke Donald, Sergio García, Pádraig Harrington, David Howell, Paul McGinley, Colin Montgomerie and José María Olazábal all returning alongside first-timers Robert Karlsson and Henrik Stenson. With Clarke at the epicentre of the team, the thirty-sixth Ryder Cup looked certain to be an emotional affair.

Darren Clarke: A few days before Heather passed away she said to me, 'If Woosie calls you, you have to play.' But when the call came through I had to take a few days to think about it. I was obviously going through a lot of turmoil at the time and my first thought was for my two young boys and whether they could handle me going away to play for that week. And I also had to think about whether I could contribute to the team because I didn't want to go there and just get a load of sympathy; I wanted to go there and be a proper part of the team and contribute to our effort. So there was a lot to think about; but I eventually decided, yes, I could do this.

Tom Lehman: The Ryder Cup is everything golf should be. It's pride, it's passion, it's emotion, it's nationalism. It's competition in its purest form. I've been on winning Ryder Cup sides and I've been on losing Ryder Cup sides. Let me tell you, it's much more fun when you win. Much more fun.

Tiger Woods: I've been under different captains with different philosophies and personalities, I think Tom is probably right in the middle. He's not as fiery as Hal Sutton but certainly not as conservative as Tom Kite, though they were both competitive and wanted to win just as much as we all did. He was one of the spearheads at Valderrama and one of the leaders in the locker room at Brookline, so he had all the experience necessary to be a great captain.

Opposite: In the most emotionally-charged first shot in Ryder Cup history, Darren Clarke rises to the occasion to strip his drive down the middle of the fairway. *Getty Images*

Tom Lehman: We had four rookies in the US team that year in Zach Johnson, JJ Henry, Vaughn Taylor and Brett Wetterich, and Chad Campbell and Chris DiMarco had only played in one Ryder Cup before. But I wasn't too worried about that beforehand. Nick Faldo was a rookie in the Ryder Cup once upon a time. So was Seve Ballesteros. So was Jack Nicklaus. Everyone has to start somewhere.

I love being part of a team and I have always had a huge passion for the Ryder Cup. While my career may not have been as wonderful as other guys, I go back to five key career goals that I set for myself and not many guys can say they were number one in the world [in 1997], or PGA Player of the Year or won the Vardon Trophy.

Sometimes you can never dream big enough and captaining the Ryder Cup team was an honour beyond my wildest dreams. I consider the Ryder Cup to be the ultimate golfing experience, even greater than winning the Open. I'm not sure we fully understand how important it is to the European players. I know it's important to us, that the guys are happy to be part of the team and that they get very nervous and uptight, which I think is a problem. My thing from the beginning was this: the goal should not be to be on the Ryder Cup team; the goal should be to be on the winning Ryder Cup team.

Colin Montgomerie: If there was a team I was on that was the best, quality-wise, it was 2006. Our rookies were Stenson, Karlsson, the picks were Clarke and Westwood and we had just a fabulous, fabulous team in 2006. It was the best team I played on.

It was in Ireland and very emotional because Darren Clarke lost his wife a month beforehand. Darren was picked ahead of Thomas Bjørn and being Irish in Ireland, the first time the Ryder Cup had been played there, it was a very emotional time, but at the same time, it was a team that just couldn't lose. The Irish fans were phenomenal, the whole country just stopped for the Ryder Cup.

Darren Clarke: Being part of that team did a lot for me, especially seeing how much people cared for me and cared for Heather. There are too many memories for me to list, but my teammates and the American players were wonderful to me.

I tried to get myself into good shape when I finally arrived and it paid off. Woosie had been really supportive of me and he was a great captain. 2006 was my fifth Ryder Cup and the first time I had been picked. It was good to know that Woosie held me in high enough regard to give me one of the two places that were available to the captain.

The minute we got to the K Club the atmosphere was fantastic. There was instant camaraderie. I hadn't seen a few of the guys and their partners since Heather passed away and they all had hugs and kind words for me. Meeting my teammates and just getting into the style of things was quite settling, but I would not have been there at all had I not thought I could carry it off, on the course particularly, but also off it. Nevertheless, it was nice to feel the genuine warmth and kindness of everybody around me.

Tom Lehman: Having Darren there meant a great deal, to him personally and to his teammates, as well as to the US team and all the fans. I think having him part of it made that Ryder Cup significantly better. When it comes right down to it, we're all human beings, and whether or not we were playing in the Ryder Cup, you saw a man who had had a tragedy like he'd had to go through and you had an incredible amount of empathy for him.

Darren Clarke: Tiger had lost his father and Chris DiMarco his mum, so the Ryder Cup was not life and death. There were more important things than trying to win, but we were all professionals and wanted to win for our teams. As friendly as we were with the Americans, we would want to kick their butts as much they would want to redden ours.

Tiger Woods: Darren being there was an inspiration in itself and his play that week was remarkable.

Having performed so well as a duo at Oakland Hills, Woosnam once again paired Montgomerie and Harrington to lead the Europeans into battle. Lehman countered by sending out Woods and Furyk to meet them head on. Where the chemistry between the 'dream team' of world number one Woods and world number two Mickelson had failed so spectacularly in Detroit, Lehman decided to keep them apart in Ireland and instead looked for an almost as compelling combination of the world number one and world number three working in tandem. With a potentially epic opening fourball about to kick-start the 2006 Ryder Cup, the atmosphere as the players arrived at the first tee was electric.

Colin Montgomerie: That walk onto the first tee is something I will never forget. It made the hairs stand up on the back of my neck. It even got to Ivor [Robson, the starter] who announced, 'Welcome to the foursomes,' instead of fourballs. He was so nervous he said the wrong thing.

Tom Lehman: I hate that 'Olé, olé, olé' song because the Europeans sing it when they are winning, but I have to admit that without it, the Ryder Cup wouldn't be the same.

Colin Montgomerie: I was paired with Pádraig Harrington in the first match against Woods and Furyk. We knew they would be an incredibly tough pair to beat but we also knew what an impact we had had two years earlier when we had won the opening match against their top pairing. The crowd throughout that encounter were absolutely incredible, the atmosphere was very, very intense.

Ian Woosnam: I wanted us to get off to a fast start and so I picked Monty and Pádraig to go out first and lead from the front. There was a great moment when the matches started with the crowd going wild, but then everything seemed to go in a bit of a blur after that.

Colin Montgomerie: It wasn't a brilliant start for us as we lost the first hole. We got things back to all square on the fifth, went one up on the seventh, but were then pulled back again on the eighth. They then got into their groove and pushed ahead to go three up at one point and Pádraig and I had to work very hard to reign them back in. We won the fourteenth and sixteenth but just couldn't pull back that last point.

We wanted to lead off and give the team a good start, but disappointingly they just edged it at the end for that one-up victory.

First blood to the US, and what an important point it was for the team after the humiliation at Europe's hands two years earlier. Had a line been drawn in the sand?

If Woosnam had hoped to get the board moving in the second match, which pitched Casey and Karlsson against Cink and Henry, he was only partly satisfied when the match was halved. Europe at least had something to their name, even if Casey and Karlsson had let a three up lead slip between the eleventh and fourteenth, and had even been one-down after the fifteenth before making matters even at the sixteenth and holding on for the draw.

The third match saw García and Olazábal take on Toms and Wetterich. The Spanish duo won the first hole and held the advantage for the rest of the match, never once conceding the lead, on their way to a comfortable 3&2 victory that registered the first full European point. Their enthusiasm for the event was all in plain evidence as García milked the applause on the first tee and then rode the wave of exuberance for the next sixteen holes. His energy was infectious and would provide a focal point around which the rest of his team could gather.

One of the biggest questions for Woosnam coming into the Ryder Cup was whether Clarke would be able to deal with the deep emotion of the event so soon after losing his wife. He could either try to protect the Northern Irishman from the public glare or let him go out and embrace it. The Welshman decided that to deal with it head on was the best way forward and he threw Clarke into the mix in the last of the morning fourballs, pairing him with his old friend Westwood against Mickelson and DiMarco.

Darren Clarke: I knew that the first hole I played would be the toughest thing I'd ever faced on a golf course. I wasn't wrong. When we walked onto the tee the roar was unbelievable. It was a wall of sound. I just looked up at everybody and nobody and said, 'Thank you.'

Phil Mickelson and Chris DiMarco came on to the tee thirty seconds later and they both gave me hugs and said, 'Darren, it's fantastic you're here.' It was above and beyond what they had to say and do. If I can have two guys like Phil and Chris giving me a hug on the first tee, that's what the Ryder Cup is all about.

I stood over the ball and the noise of the crowd was just beating through me. To be honest, I actually have no idea how I hit the ball. I think it actually helped that I had watched Tiger shank his first shot into the water earlier that morning. That made things a lot easier – if the number one player in the world hooks his ball a hundred yards into the water, what was the worst that could happen to me?

Having Lee Westwood there with me made it an awful lot easier; it wasn't easy, but to have a friend like that by your side made a huge difference. But at the same time he wasn't that helpful because while I was standing there, terrified because I had no idea if I was going to be able to hit the ball, whether I might top it or shank it or whatever, that soft twat was standing there crying beside me!

But I knew I had to stand up and be counted. I had to get through it. That was my focus. Somehow I managed to flush it straight down the middle. Then I nearly holed the approach. I had a fifteen-foot putt and I knew, I just knew, that I was going to hole it. I'm sure that Heather was with me that entire week. She was looking over me on the first tee, on the first green. I'm convinced she was there – just watching out for me. I sunk the putt.

Lee Westwood: What Darren had been through was tragic and it was always going to be an emotional time for him. That first tee was so tough. Me, Phil Mickelson, Chris DiMarco, the caddies, Ivor Robson – we were all in tears. Then Darren steps up, hits a driver down the middle, knocks the approach to fifteen feet and holes it for a birdie. Amazing. We won the match one-up.

With a one-point lead at lunchtime, Woosnam sent out Harrington and McGinley as his first pairing in the foursomes, while Lehman countered with a combination of Campbell and Johnson. They were followed onto the course by Howell and Stenson who took on Cink and Toms before Westwood and Montgomerie faced Mickelson and DiMarco. In as closely poised a set of matches as you can imagine, all three were halved.

Colin Montgomerie: Darren was supposed to play with Lee Westwood in the afternoon of the first day, and I was supposed to be rested. But Darren finished his morning match with Westwood in a very emotional state and couldn't play that afternoon. I was finishing lunch when I got the message, 'Monty, you're on.' Darren was just too emotional to play. I went out with Westwood in the afternoon and managed to get a good half; it was for Darren. It was all for Darren.

Ian Woosnam: Our big concern with Darren, and why we rested him for the afternoon sessions, was because it was emotionally draining, obviously, and very tiring. It was tough for him but he did a great job.

In the final match of the day, García and Donald paired up to take on Woods and Furyk and the young Spaniard was once again in wonderful form as he continued where he had left off in the fourballs. In a repeat of the morning session, the Europeans took the initative at the first hole to go one up. They played brilliantly to only be drawn back to all square on four holes and were never once in arrears. The most outstanding piece of play came on the sixteenth when García was presented with a difficult lie on woodchip and with a shot across the water; he lofted his shot to perfection and landed the ball fifteen feet from the hole, which Donald then coolly sank for birdie. They would ultimately secure a two-hole victory.

Colin Montgomerie: Each of the first three foursomes were halved, so all attention then turned to Donald and García, who made a brilliant fist of winning at the last against Woods and Furyk. Europe had lost only one match all day (Pádraig's and mine) and the 5–3 scoreline made for a happy team room that evening.

The first of the Saturday fourballs continued the trend of close matches as Casey and Karlsson battled to a half with Cink and Henry. The Americans looked as if they might have won the match on the sixteenth when Henry eagled the par-five to go one up, but Casey kept his cool on the eighteenth to sink a fifteen-foot putt for birdie which drew things level.

García and Olazábal teamed up once again to face DiMarco and Mickelson in the second match of the morning and continued their rich vein of form with a 3&2 win. Clarke and Westwood then beat Furyk and Woods 3&2 with the world number one looking completely out of sorts throughout the round.

Darren Clarke: The next day had a similar pattern to the first – I played in the morning with Lee against Tiger and Furyk and had the afternoon off.

When you see Tiger across the tee, it's not intimidating, just thrilling. If you can't get up for playing the game against the best, you might as well retire. On the Saturday, as it turned out, he had a really, really off one, and we weren't complaining. Lee and I played really well. You never want to beat the best player in the world on one of his off days, but when it comes to the Ryder Cup, you take whatever you can.

Tiger Woods: There is often a perception that the Ryder Cup doesn't mean as much to the US players as it does to the Europeans. That's not the case at all. Not at all. It's just that we haven't tended to play as well as they have. We certainly haven't putted as well. Any match play event comes down to putting. Our team putted great at the Presidents Cup in 2005, for example, and we won. It's as simple as that.

Verplank and Johnson secured America's only full point of the morning session in the final fourball, beating Stenson and Harrington 2&1 to take the score to 7½–4½ at lunch.

García and Donald led the way for the Europeans in the afternoon, taking on Mickelson and Toms in the opening foursome and dovetailing brilliantly once more in a 2&1 victory.

Colin Montgomerie: Lee and I teamed up in the afternoon as we had the day before, and we halved the second match out, this time against Chad Campbell and Vaughn Taylor. I hadn't played in the morning fourballs but it did not bother me in the least. I didn't feel like it was a case of being 'dropped'; it was more to do with our team being the strongest Europe had ever assembled. Woosie had so many options. Four of us had to miss the morning session and I just happened to be one of them.

Lee had a twenty-footer on the last to win and to this day I don't know how Lee's putt missed. It was incredibly close and it meant we took a half instead of the full point, which was unfortunate. We should have beaten them, but it had been a great game against two of the soundest of our opponents. They might not have been household names but they were very, very decent players.

The third match out saw Casey and Howell take on Cink and Johnson and the Europeans won comfortably 5&4, thanks in part to a sensational hole-in-one from Casey at the fourteenth.

Ian Woosnam: As a captain your job is to just try and get the best out of each of your players and offer some advice. Like I remember saying to Paul Casey at the fourteenth, 'Just try and get past the hole a little bit on your drive because that gives you an easier putt and everyone else has been coming up short.' So he did that – and he drained it for a hole-in-one. Paul was so pumped up all that week, he was tremendous. And the crowd just went berserk when that happened, and the energy transferred through the whole team.

Paul Casey: David Howell and I had played some wonderful golf that day, but we were pretty lucky in some respects because Zach Johnson wasn't putting as well as he normally putted, and that just led to a situation that we were dormie walking onto that hole. It was damp and pretty cool and we knew that we wanted to close the match off at that next hole. I chose a four-iron, aimed a little bit right and just absolutely laced this thing. I was just trying to get it near the flag so that we could hopefully halve the hole in threes and be done with the match. And when the ball set off to the right of the flag, turning over, I remember thinking, 'That's a good-looking shot . . .' I'm not tall enough to see the bottom of the flag, and the reaction from the crowd kind of said it all because they erupted when it hit the green; the fact it released and trickled in at the speed it did was almost like slow motion and so there was a brief lull from the crowd followed by a huge roar, so I knew it had gone in. It was just a moment of pure shock followed by pandemonium on the tee.

It was a bit of a weird feeling because the other guys didn't even get to hit and so I was a bit sheepish and apologetic when I turned around and shook hands to thank them for the game.

Zach Johnson: Scott Verplank and I were paired for the last fourball match of the day against Henrik Stenson and Pádraig Harrington. It was a horrible cold, wet, windy day and the rest of the team were struggling, so Scott and I knew we had to try and pull a point out of the bag so that we had some hope to cling to that night.

Scott Verplank: Our team that year didn't have a whole lot of confidence but Zach and I did. He's a pretty good example of your mind being stronger than your body. That was the best Zach had ever played in his life to that point. He just believed he was going to do great things, with nobody else understanding why he would think that. I played pretty well but he made seven birdies and we won 2&1. He was unbelievable.

I guess we're kindred spirits. When we see each other now, we give this goofy little fist pump to the heart that we did in Ireland. But we look each other in the eye when we do it, and it's like, 'Yeah, that's who we are.'

Darren Clarke: At one stage it looked like we were going to win all four foursomes, but it didn't quite work out that way. We'd still won the series, which made it four out of four – all four series had been won 2½–1½ – and we needed only another four-and-a-half points to win the cup for the fifth time in six matches.

Woosie chose Monty to lead us out in the singles. We all wanted him out there as our number one and just as in 2002 at the Belfry, he made sure there were blue numbers on the scoreboard early on and even though we weren't meant to be looking at the boards, you could tell from the cheers around the course that we were ahead in the early games.

In 2004 he and Pádraig gave us the perfect start when they beat Tiger and Phil Mickelson in the top match on Friday morning, and Monty went on to hole the winning putt on the Sunday. In 2006 he holed a great putt on the eighteenth green on Friday night to help us extend our lead, and then defeated David Toms for the second match running in the singles.

Colin Montgomerie: I wasn't to know it at the time, but it was to be my last Ryder Cup match as a player. I'm glad it finished off the way it did. I've never had a walk like I did at the end of my singles match. The walk I had from sixteen to seventeen was the best walk I've ever had in golf. I managed to halve the sixteenth hole to remain two-up; two-up with two to play meant I couldn't lose and it was a record I was very proud of – I played eight times in singles and never lost a singles match.

I was never really interested in the personal aspect of the Ryder Cup, it was always for the team, but that was a walk of personal pride from sixteen to seventeen. It was a long walk around the river Liffey, about 300 yards. To stand on that seventeenth tee and be able to hit it anywhere and for it not to matter was wonderful. I was certain that we were going to win the Ryder Cup and I knew I wasn't going to lose.

Toms birdied seventeen and I managed to birdie the last, and he did as well, but I managed to get that birdie on eighteen and finished with a victory.

Sergio García was second in the order against Stewart Cink, but the Spaniard was unable to continue his previously irresistible form and fell to a convincing 4&3 defeat.

Stewart Cink: It was a great match-up for me. Not only a great match, but a great match-up for me, because I really wanted to be in the role of having to do something to help the team out, and I was the second match off. I don't remember exactly how many points we trailed by, but we needed to have a serious run. The first couple of matches were so important, and for me to be right there against their best performer of the week was something I relished, and to perform well myself and win that match was great, so good for my confidence. I just wish it would have done the team better in the end. Just our hole was too deep.

Darren Clarke: Paul Casey then played Jim Furyk; Paul knew he was facing one of the strongest players in the US side, and one who had never lost a singles before. Paul got ahead early on but Jim never backed off and played brilliantly on the inward nine, including an eagle at the sixteenth, to take the match to the penultimate hole. The pair shared eight birdies and an eagle on eight holes on the back nine. Throughout, Jim looked grimly determined, stony-faced and was clearly never going to give up, but Paul hung in there and managed to win 2&1. We only needed another two-and-a-half points at that stage.

Karlsson was out next and he had the tough task of taking on Woods, who was determined to make amends for his poor form from the day before. Although Karlsson went one up with a birdie on the first, Woods reeled him back in on the second and then moved ahead on the fourth. There was a moment on the seventh when Karlsson might have questioned whether the omens were going to fall in his favour when Woods lost his nine-iron into the lake, but it was a false promise as the world number one moved comfortably through the gears to secure a 3&2 victory.

Tiger Woods: I lost my nine-iron into the lake at the seventh green. The ball was muddy so I handed it to Stevie [Williams, his caddie] and he was going to rinse it in the lake and the nine-iron as well. He was dipping the towel in the water and slipped on a rock. It was either him or the nine-iron going into the water and he chose the nine-iron!

Donald and Campbell were playing just behind Karlsson and Woods and the Englishman played some lovely golf en route to a 2&1 victory, finally turning up the heat on his opponent when he won the eleventh, twelfth and thirteenth to go three up having halved the previous ten holes. Campbell fought back by winning the fifteenth and sixteenth but a bogey on the seventeenth put paid to any thoughts of a consolatory half.

At eighth in the order, the hero of 2002, McGinley, faced off with Henry and although the Irishman started strongly to move two-up after three the American rookie fought hard to bring the match all square on the thirteenth, which is how the score remained as they halved the final five holes.

Clarke, the hero of the week, was out next against Johnson. Unsurprisingly, his was a match that every spectator was desperate to watch.

Zach Johnson: When I saw that I was going to be up against Darren Clarke in the singles, I expected it to be loud, but it was like an 80,000-people stadium amassed around one tee box. It was pretty remarkable. Frankly, it was like that on every tee box for him.

As the scoreboard started to show blue after blue after blue, the result seemed no longer in question, but rather which of the Europeans it would be to sink the winning putt.

Darren Clarke: It was all a bit of a blur and I remember wondering if it might come down to me to win the cup – but Henrik and Luke were also in good positions and it could have been either of them.

I hit a good drive down sixteen, but neither of us could reach, so both had to lay up. I hit it onto the green – a twenty-five-foot downhill, fast and left to right. Zach hit a good shot, but it spun back and he had an uphill chip, closer than mine.

As we walked round past the big stand, everybody in it was standing up, roaring and shouting. I was trying to keep my head in check, but I was struggling.

I hit my putt and, although it was a very fast one, I left it about two feet short. I started to

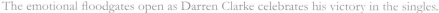
The emotional floodgates open as Darren Clarke celebrates his victory in the singles.

wonder how I was going to get it into the hole. My mind had gone. Everything was coming into my head. I had a two-footer to win my game, possibly the Ryder Cup in Ireland, my first ever singles win, and my wife's not there. I honestly didn't think I could hit the putt.

It was then that one of the most magnanimous gestures in Ryder Cup history occurred. I'm not sure if Zach realised my predicament but he was not going to put me through any more turmoil. He walked round, picked up my marker and the match was over. It was an unbelievable gesture to do that in his first Ryder Cup. I will never forget that.

Zach gave me a hug, and when I turned to Billy [Foster, his caddie], I just couldn't hold it back any more. Everything came flooding out. I was a mess. I had done what I had to do. The whole week had been a success, in Ireland, and Heather wasn't there. I couldn't hang on any more, the floodgates opened.

Ian Woosnam: At the beginning of the week if someone had asked me if I believed in destiny, I'd have said no. But when I stood on that sixteenth green seeing Darren finishing off his match it changed my mind; that week was destiny for Darren and for Heather. That was why we dedicated the win to her. And what a Ryder Cup he had – three matches and three wins. Incredible.

As it transpired, it was not Clarke who sank the winning putt as, just moments before, Donald had secured his victory over Campbell and Stenson defeated Taylor 4&3.

Ian Woosnam: There have been a few debates as to who won it, but we'll put it down to Stenson. At the end of the day, it's a team effort and it was just fortunate that it came down to Henrik. He's going to remember that moment for the rest of his life.

As the rest of the matches came down the home straight, the momentum remained very much with the Europeans. Howell defeated Wetterich 5&4, Olazábal defeated Mickelson 2&1 and Westwood won two-up against DiMarco. Verplank, playing in the final match against Harrington secured a consolation point for the US with a 4&3 victory that included America's first ever hole-in-one, but it wasn't enough to save his team from another heavy defeat at the hands of the Europeans. The final score of Europe 18½, USA 9½ mirrored that from Oakland Hills two years previously.

Tom Lehman: Our team came ready, but maybe we weren't quite ready enough. Our problem, I believe, is that deep down inside, the American players believe more in individual achievements. There's a part of us that believe we've always had the stronger team, man against man. Therefore, if you lose, it doesn't change that Tiger Woods is still the best player in the world. I've talked to some guys who have said, 'Yeah, maybe there's some truth to that mindset.' That attitude needs to be changed. Who cares what we're ranked? We need to want to win as badly as they do. It's as simple as that.

Colin Montgomerie: He's a lovely guy Tom Lehman and I think he did a great job. There are two guys who I think did a great job and lost and they were Tom Kite in '97 and Lehman in 2006. And that's why I feel for the captains because you can do a great job, but there is no grey in the Ryder Cup. You win or you lose – and if you lose you are opened up to everything and if you win, you're bulletproof. If you lose everything comes out – your relationship difficulties with the players, your relationship with the press, everything is picked apart. Look what happened to poor Tom Watson in 2014. No one now remembers that he won the thing as captain in 1993. He is remembered as a losing captain who was doddery and out-of-touch, which is grossly unfair on the man, especially one of his stature. But that's the way the Ryder Cup is. It can be brutal.

We had a great team, and a bit like Seve's, it was all set up for us; Ireland was as passionate a time as we've ever had and we weren't going to lose. Woosie just had to direct traffic, really. I'm not dismissing his role, but he had the best team that I played in – and he did a good job in directing traffic, because you still have to direct it, and he was super.

Afterwards, with the party having moved into the team room, there was a knock on the door. It was the US team who had come to congratulate us on our victory. It was a fabulous thing for them to do and not a common occurrence at a Ryder Cup. In 2010, Corey Pavin and his vice-captains made an appearance and had a drink with us, but I would not have expected the rest of his players to have done so.

But 2006 was different because of what Darren had been going through. That's why the Americans, to a man, all came down to support him.

Throughout the entire match, the Americans had been superb. From Tom Lehman and Tiger Woods down, each of them had rallied around Darren, helping whenever possible to make him feel comfortable. Golf is a close community and for one of its members to lose his wife in the way Darren had lost Heather had a huge impact on everyone.

All credit to each and every one of that visiting side; they were gentlemen. The integrity of the Ryder Cup was fully restored.

Graeme McDowell: I didn't make the team at the K Club, and I was dearly disappointed but I did a bit of commentary for RTE and some radio work for the BBC and I managed to get into the party on the Sunday night after the boys had won and, as you can imagine, that was one hell of a piss-up. David Howell fell off a piece of furniture that night – I think it was a €100,000 antique table that he was dancing on top of and he fell off.

Peter Baker: There were hundreds of thousands of pounds of antiques knocking around the K Club. And just before it really kicked off, I remember some of the staff taking the antique tables out and putting them away safely, just in case. And then we just got absolutely hammered.

Colin Montgomerie: The 2004 team of Langer's was building up to that team of Woosnam's, it was the best we'd had. Stenson and Casey were at the top of their game; I was back to number one in Europe; García, Olazábal, it was extraordinary. And the scenes at the sixteenth at the end were just wonderful and something I will always remember. The mud of Ireland. The rain. It was a fantastic Ryder Cup, it really was.

THIRTY-SEVEN

2008
Valhalla Golf Club, Louisville, Kentucky
(USA 16½, EUR 11½)

By 2008 America had lost five of the preceding six matches and so the task to arrest this trend was handed to captain Paul Azinger. Azinger was thorough and conscientious in his preparation. He made Olin Browne and former captains Raymond Floyd and Dave Stockton his assistants and drew on their experiences at the helm in 1989 and 1991 respectively. His team had class and experience in Chad Campbell, Stewart Cink, Jim Furyk, Justin Leonard, Phil Mickelson and Kenny Perry but many in the US feared that the team was also a little raw as it contained no less than six rookies in Ben Curtis, JB Holmes, Anthony Kim, Hunter Mahan, Steve Stricker and Boo Weekley. It was also the first time since 1997 that the US would play a Ryder Cup without Tiger Woods among its ranks, the world number one opting to undergo reconstructive surgery on the anterior cruciate ligament of his left knee, meaning that he would miss the tail end of the 2008 season.

Stewart Cink: I had no worries about how many rookies we had that year. I think being a first time Ryder Cupper in 2008 is maybe quite a bit different than it was in the '80s or the '70s because there are so many big tournaments around the world and it's such a world stage; golf is scrutinised more than ever before, and the Ryder Cup is just another event in which you have to really perform well. So they are tested. It's hard to think of them as 'rookies' in quite the same way. The six guys that were on our team had never played in the Ryder Cup before but they had a lot of experience in other ways.

Anthony Kim, for example, was hard to consider a rookie the way he'd played that year. He was immense and took that form and confidence right the way through the Ryder Cup.

Paul Azinger: I think it's interesting to analyse the psychological approach that both teams take to the Ryder Cup. For us it's in our mind. We want to win and we think about it. But for the European players it's like it's in their blood. It's in their hearts and it's different, there's a different emotion – and that's one of the great challenges for us: can the mind beat the heart. That was the challenge that I had to overcome.

The European captain bidding to make it four straight wins in a row for the first time was Nick Faldo, holder of Europe's all-time Ryder Cup points record.

Faldo, ever the main man, opted to have just one vice-captain in José María Olazábal (Paul McGinley had been announced as a vice-captain in May 2007 but had resigned in September 2007). Utterly single-minded as a player, Faldo had to work hard to change his mannerism to perform the role of captain effectively. He was faced with some difficult decisions to make when it came to his captain's picks, but managed to negotiate these without some of the public

Opposite: Young US rookie Anthony Kim came to the fore to become the stand-out player at the 2008 Ryder Cup. *Getty Images*

fallout that had befallen previous incumbents. In the event he opted to select Ian Poulter and Paul Casey over the more experienced Darren Clarke and the European talisman of recent years, Colin Montgomerie. It was a bold move and a gamble that he staked his captaincy on.

Alongside Poulter and Casey, the European team was made up of Sergio García, Pádraig Harrington, Miguel Ángel Jiménez, Robert Karlsson, Henrik Stenson and Lee Westwood alongside rookies Søren Hansen, Graeme McDowell, Justin Rose and Oliver Wilson.

Paul Azinger: I remember when I saw the final team that Nick picked. I called my wife and I said, 'We're going out to eat and we're going to order the nicest bottle of wine and celebrate,' and she said, 'How come?'

I said, 'Because Nick Faldo didn't pick Darren Clarke.' To this day, I think it was Faldo's greatest error.

Colin Montgomerie: I wasn't selected in 2008, so there is a limit to what I can say about what went on with the European team, but I can speak from my experience of partnering Nick Faldo over the years and playing against him. Nick was number one, the big dog during his playing career. A really focused guy, an incredible golfer, but I think those attributes that made him so successful when he played may have counted against him when he was captain. That mindset doesn't transfer easily over to a team. Communication might have been a problem as well because it's not one of Faldo's strengths – and I think he would admit that too. The management of a team . . . it's about managing the team to be prepared on the first tee, that's all you can do as a captain, as a manager, or as a coach – you prepare your team and then you let them go. And really there is very little more. But the preparation was vital, you have to prepare yourself to win. If you don't prepare to win, you've already prepared to fail. If Faldo is honest with himself, I'm not sure he could say that he did everything he could to prepare his team to win.

Faldo, so meticulous as a player, did indeed seem unprepared for his stint as Europe's captain. When he played, he would avoid cutting his fingernails during the week of a golf tournament in case his grip was affected. But when he was put in charge of Europe he made long rambling speeches that he made up on the spot, got the names of his team wrong, inexplicably introduced members of his family and then, during the closing ceremony, he made a weak joke that everyone should bring umbrellas to Wales for the 2010 staging because it always rains there (the joke, albeit a poor one, would actually turn out to be prophetic).

Graeme McDowell: That opening ceremony stuff wasn't great, but I don't care what everyone in the press said, Faldo was well prepared. He had done his homework and he really gave us some good stuff to work with as well. Should he come in for criticism? No, not at all.

Nick Faldo: I obviously came into the whole thing with a bit of a reputation for being aloof, but I don't know what else I could have done to address that issue. On the first day I stood up in the team room and said, 'If anyone sees me looking through them, they have my permission to kick my backside.'

I thought I had broken down that barrier of what I am supposed to be like. I just didn't want to walk beside them, and ask them, 'Do you want this, do you want that?' I didn't want to be overbearing or interfering as a captain.

Paul Azinger: Being the captain is, I think, the greatest honour you can bestow on a player. But we'd only won three times in twenty-five years, we'd lost five of the previous six matches and the last two by record margins in '04 and '06.

I looked at the Europeans as a bonded group and my whole assessment was 'How are they so bonded?' Well, they're bonded by nationality. The Spaniards love each other and would do nothing to let each other down. The Irishmen are the same and the Englishmen and then there are crossovers . . . Darren Clarke and Lee Westwood are best friends and there's a bond there that's unique. I think it gives Europe an advantage over America. We're not the Texans, the Floridians and the Californians – we're the United States. We're not as close, we're spread out and we're not bonded in the same way if you get that?

What Europe had naturally, we had to create. My philosophy was to take a militaristic approach, this Navy SEALs concept of taking a large group and breaking it into small groups and the press ended up calling them 'pods'. And so we had three four-man pods, and I told these guys in their little four-man groups that they should be sold-out for each other, that I would never take them out of their four-man group unless there was injury or an illness, that there was no short-cut to success, that they couldn't hope for it and they couldn't wish for it, it was all about preparation. And they did it, they bonded in their group. I didn't just put them together based on their like games; I put them together on their like personalities. I felt that like personalities in a pressure situation would bond better. So that's how I did it – that was hard for me, but I was convinced it was the right thing to do. I let three guys pick the fourth guy to fill out their pod. And I let the players decide who would play alternate shot and best-ball. These guys were invested; they had full-blown ownership of what they were doing.

Justin Rose: We'd heard a bit about Paul Azinger's pod system, but it's not really your job as a player to concentrate on what the other team are doing. You are so focused on your own job. Azinger turned out to be a really good captain, he really whipped up the crowd and they went for a different strategy in changing the atmosphere. I think it was maybe the first Ryder Cup where they were the underdogs and they tapped into that really well and got fired up throughout the team.

While so many rookies in the US team might have been perceived as a weakness, Azinger turned it into a strength. None of those players were blighted by the failed attempts to regain the cup since 1999; he just told them to go out and enjoy the competition, to play each shot as it came, to feed off the crowd and not to think about the result – just stay in the moment. It was a potent approach.

Paul Azinger: You know, I wanted to do this kind of drumline thing the night before the matches started and get the crowd pumped up. And then all of a sudden the city embraced this concept and created this huge pep rally. Fifteen thousand people showed up and there was this big stage with a marching band and cheerleaders, it was fantastic. It made me feel like a rock star.

I think this outside the box approach to team-building got the players engaged and intrigued in what we were doing. Instead of dreading the event because of past failings on this massive stage they started looking forward to the tournament in a way they hadn't before. Guys like Mickelson, Furyk and Cink started to get engaged by the idea that they were going to do something unique. I don't think it was a case of becoming uninterested. It just became an event that was sucking the life out of them because they kept getting beat.

Nick Faldo: Paul was very canny in the build-up to Valhalla. He kept saying that I was the one who was known for his attention to detail while he just liked to go with the flow, yet he changed the points system, changed the number of picks he had, changed the foursomes to fourballs. He played the game that I was big on preparation and yet he was changing things and monitoring everything.

I would have been happy to be captain on either side of the Atlantic. The only difference is that the home captain can set up the golf course how he wants . . . and I think it was a bit unsporting of Paul Azinger to cut down branches at the sixteenth, I think it was so that JB Holmes, who was a huge hitter, could thread his drive up there.

Paul Azinger: I wanted to change the format back to the way it had been in '99 with alternate shots played in the opening games. I felt like the Americans had an edge in alternate shot. And I think playing fourballs first is partly responsible for why Europe had got off to a hot start every year since '99.

It wasn't up to me how the guys played when they were out there. It was up to me to recognise the winning edge at that level is razor-thin. If I could do anything, it was to create the environment to get the proper side of that edge. Vegas has a one or one-and-a-half per cent edge in blackjack, and they kick butt in blackjack. I just wanted to get that one per cent edge. I didn't feel the burden to motivate anybody. I knew it was up to the players. All I could do was control the controllables.

The European campaign got off to an inauspicious start when Faldo inadvertently showed his proposed opening-day pairings to watching photographers when he walked around the course holding a piece of paper with the pairings clearly scrawled for the watching telescopic lenses. The episode was subsequently branded 'sandwich-gate' after Faldo claimed the names were sandwich requests for his players.

As the curtain rose on day one at Valhalla, 40,000 fans poured onto the course in rousing full voice.

Paul Azinger: I remember standing at the first tee on the first morning and realising, 'I have now given up control.' I felt like I'd been driving a car for two years and was now taking my hands off the steering wheel, looking to the side and pushing the pedal to the floor. I didn't know if we were going to hit a wall or have smooth sailing or what was going to happen.

Boo Weekley: It was by far the greatest golf moment and tournament and surroundings that I've ever had a part of. We're so used to playing golf by ourselves, playing against everybody week on week. Then you get to the Ryder Cup, you look over and you've got your buddies, the guys you competed against the week before last, and now here y'all are like teammates, trying to talk things out, listening to some of the veterans there and what they felt when they were there the first time. It was an experience.

Paul Azinger: It is amazing that on the biggest stage, in the most pressure-packed arena in the game, we see the greatest drama and the greatest highlight reel you can imagine. You hear broadcasters saying, 'nerves-this' or 'nerves-that', but I don't think that unless you have the great nerves you don't see greatness. The nerves are what cause a great performance, not what cause a poor performance.

Boo Weekley: I didn't usually pay much attention to golfing history but the Ryder Cup was unreal and I really got into it. That week was unbelievable. I honestly didn't know what the Ryder Cup was like before then but the feeling you get when the crowds shout your name . . . It ain't nothing like shooting a deer, it's a whole lot more.

The opening match saw Harrington and Karlsson pitched against Mickelson and the young tyro Kim. While the crowds were wild with anticipation of the match-up the pairings battled themselves to a standstill to ultimately share the spoils at the end of the round.

Stenson and Casey were two-up after two in the second match against Leonard and captain's pick Mahan, but after hitting a wondrous approach at the fourteenth, the US pair won the next three holes in a row and went on to win the match 3&2 and secure the first full point of the day.

Cink and Campbell were out third against the English duo of Rose and Poulter.

Justin Rose: You hear about the first tee shot for years, struggling to get the ball on the tee peg and all that kind of stuff. Ian and I played foursomes and the way the course was set up I would hit the first tee shot. And that was great, I was relishing the challenge.

One thing Nick did with us was walk down to the first tee as a team to really soak it up and to prepare ourselves for that opening shot as it is so different to anything we usually experience. And I got it in the fairway which, for a rookie and your first shot, you will always take. That settled me down and we got off to a great start and the nerves settled. We got three up against Stewart Cink and Chad Campbell but then lost on the last which was really tough to take.

The final match of the session saw Perry and Furyk face off against Westwood and García. Faldo would have felt justified in expecting two of his leading players to come back with the spoils, but honours were ultimately shared as they halved the match to take the teams into lunch with the US leading 3–1.

Nick Faldo: Would I have done things differently? Sure, every day you live you could do things differently. But things happened there I didn't expect. Little things, like coming in after the morning session two points down, and the whole atmosphere in the team room was down, long faces everywhere. I said, 'Hang on, let's change this, let's put some music on.' But you need foresight. I didn't have foresight.

After Mickelson and Kim had ironed out the kinks from their morning match together to defeat Harrington and McDowell two-up in the first match of the Friday fourballs, Europe finally secured their first full point of the day when Poulter and Rose combined to beat the rookie pairing of Stricker and the 2003 Open champion, Curtis, 4&2, while Westwood and Hansen secured a half against Holmes and Weekley.

Justin Rose: Nick had already put out the pairings out for the afternoon thinking we were going to win so we really had to pick ourselves up and we bounced straight back and beat Steve Stricker and Ben Curtis, which was awesome.

The US took home a point from the other match however, as Leonard and Mahan combined brilliantly to defeat García and Jiménez 4&3 to give the Americans a 5½–2½ lead at the end of day one.

Faldo make the bold decision to drop Westwood and García from the second day's foursomes. Westwood made it perfectly clear that he was annoyed at being 'rested', the reason being partly attributed to blisters on his feet, saying: 'I would play in the Ryder Cup with my arm hanging off.' It was the first time that the Englishman had been dropped during his Ryder Cup career.

For all the criticism surrounding the European captain's decision-making going into the session, there was no doubt that he was vindicated as his side reduced their first-day deficit from three points to two. Poulter and Rose demolished Cink and Campbell 4&3, Stenson and Wilson beat Mickelson and Kim 2&1, while Jiménez and McDowell halved with Leonard and Mahan.

Oliver Wilson: I was really disappointed that I only played once before the singles. I'd played well enough to qualify for the team without having to rely on a pick or anything like that. I'd earned the right to be there. I mean, fair enough, I'm the first to admit that I would probably have come down near the bottom of the pecking order in terms of the players on that team. But, that being said, I felt like I was playing well and my game is suited to foursomes, so much so that I genuinely thought I would play in them. I think everybody on the team thought that, too. We all knew each other's games and I would have thought Nick would have known everybody's strengths and weaknesses but I don't feel like he knew mine at all. So, it was a disappointment not to play on the first day. You get all up for it and you're in the middle of this thing you've wanted to play in for years and then, just like that, you're not involved, it becomes a big anti-climax and the Ryder Cup doesn't feel as good as you thought it was going to.

I played with Henrik the next day and I knew we'd be a good combination. After six holes, though, with Phil and AK having built up a big early lead, I remember thinking, 'Hmmm, this isn't going to plan,' but we did what we needed to do in match play and that's keep on applying the pressure. Against those two, you can either get blown away or win; that's just the way they play. They're very gung-ho and go at everything, so we fancied that they'd give us a few holes and we managed to get right back in it and, of course, win when I drained that putt on seventeen. So, yeah, it was a massive high but was followed again by another little bit of a low to find out that I wasn't playing in the afternoon. Actually, I found out on the fifteenth hole that I wasn't in because I overheard another of the caddies talking to Fanny [Sunesson, Stenson's caddie] about the afternoon pairings and my name wasn't mentioned.

It was a bit of a downer but I just had to get on with it. But I guess it does kind of explain why my reaction to holing the winning putt on the seventeenth was quite excitable, shall we say!

It was a robust response and the only real blot on the European copybook came in the final match which saw Furyk and Perry beat Harrington and Karlsson 3&1.

Europe continued their form in the afternoon as Poulter and McDowell beat Perry and Furyk one-up. McDowell played some beautiful golf during the encounter and combined well with Poulter to move one up with two to play. Poulter looked to have sealed the match with a birdie at seventeen, but Furyk showed real skill in matching him. As they came to the last, Poulter was determined not to be thwarted once again and drained a wonderful putt for birdie to claim the point for his team.

Ian Poulter: Sinking that putt on the last was a very special moment. What a day. G-Mac [Graeme McDowell] played awesome. To play as well as I played, it was brilliant. I was so proud to be in the team as one of Nick's picks, but I really felt that I had to do something special to pay him back.

Graeme McDowell: I woke up the next morning and my arm was sore. I couldn't work out why and then I remembered. We were high-fiving each other so hard because Poulter gets so charged up. No one can strut around like Poults. It's great.

Elsewhere, Weekley and Holmes clocked another red point by beating Westwood and Hansen 2&1, while Stenson and Karlsson halved with Mickelson and Mahan and Curtis and Stricker halved with García and Casey – although the Europeans were unlucky not to claim a full point from this tie. Stricker holed a twelve-foot putt on the eighteenth green to steal a half point that gave his side a crucial two-point advantage going into the singles.

Paul Azinger: Steve's putt was the decisive moment of the entire weekend.

Raymond Floyd: How close would it have been had Stricker not made the putt at the eighteenth on the second day? People don't realise that there are little movements during the play that can change everything. A half point loss or win. Maybe a half that turns into a win. It is huge.

Paul Casey: They played really well and never gave us anything. We would have wanted a full point, but we did well to get a half from a fantastic match.

Paul Azinger: We could have lost or won 3–1 in the afternoon but Steve Stricker's putt was amazing and JB Holmes and Boo Weekley coming through was incredible.

Going into the singles, the captains decided to go with completely divergent strategies. Faldo decided to back load his singles line-up, hoping for a strong finish – something which many felt was a gamble given that it ran the risk of ceding the early momentum on Sunday to the American team who had placed their strongest men at the top of the order.

Paul Azinger: There was a little bit of discussion among the team about putting Kim, Mahan and Leonard at the top. I had this in my mind of how I wanted to do it and got a little bit of confirmation. They were three guys who were very aggressive, the kind I wanted to go first. We were doing well at that stage but I wanted to seal the deal.

We sent the guys out in the order of their pods, with the aggressive guys all at the top, with AK out first and then that pod anchored by Phil Mickelson. Then we sent out Jim Furyk's pod, with Jim anchoring that group. We were all happy that we were going to attack things right from the top.

Kim was the youngest player on either side but showed no signs of nerves despite the huge excitement from the galleries that surrounded his match as he comfortably beat an out of sorts García 5&4 to extend USA's lead to 10–7.

Paul Azinger: Seve was the greatest at getting the crowd going. You need someone like that. In other Europe teams it was usually the Spaniards who caught the crowd's imagination, the more passionate personality types. It was Darren Clarke in '06 in Ireland. There's always someone who can get everybody behind you, and I think it's essential for your team to be successful. You can't force it though, it happens naturally. But there's always someone. Boo Weekley, JB Holmes and Kenny Perry, especially Holmes and Perry being from Kentucky all made a big difference, but for us the key player was Anthony Kim, he was the lightning rod for the crowd that year. His energy and enthusiasm, his killer instinct, it all converged into him becoming our team leader.

Anthony Kim: It's a tremendous honour whenever you get to play for your country. I played team sports growing up. I played soccer, basketball, football, and I felt like that was more my element than just being out there by myself. My ADD kicks in when I'm on my own and I start talking to my caddie about stupid things just because I'm bored. And I felt a real sense of pride and patriotism when I was out there. You're not just playing for yourself and your family and your friends, but for your country. It was an incredible week.

Paul Azinger: AK had said all week that he wanted to play Sergio. After splitting the first fairway, AK hit his second shot to two feet. Then Sergio hit his second shot three feet from the hole. As they walked onto the green, Sergio looked at AK and said, 'Good, good?' AK smiled and responded, 'No, let's putt them.' He didn't say, 'I've seen you putt,' out loud, but the message was clear. AK was taking no prisoners. Sergio made his three-footer and gave AK his two-footer to halve the hole in birdies, but the tone of the match had been set.

Phil Mickelson: The AK of 2008 was so impressive. He had guts. He wasn't afraid of anyone or anything. He had every shot, and he just kept coming, making birdie after birdie.

Sergio García: I'd played with AK a couple of times before and I knew what he was capable of. There were a couple of misses on seven that were huge, and after that I had a short miss on eleven that put the dagger in. It was a hard day – he played awesome and it's hard when you get in that sort of situation. I felt like I couldn't get anything going at all.

Paul Azinger: AK put the first point on the board for us when he closed out Sergio with an eight-foot putt for par on the fourteenth. He was so caught up in the moment that he didn't realise he'd won. He marched off the green and headed towards the fifteenth tee as Sergio and assistant captain José María Olazábal laughed at him. Once he realised what he'd done, AK charged back and gave Sergio a handshake and a hug.

Mahan was out second against Casey and they enjoyed a high-quality tussle as they made their way around the course. Mahan drained a huge forty-foot putt at the seventeenth to win the hole.

Paul Azinger: When that putt went in, the whole place went crazy. It was the first time I audibly just screamed full-bore, as loud as I could scream. I couldn't believe it. I was high-fiving with the crowd, the whole deal. I will never forget that moment.

Hunter Mahan: Yeah that was pretty amazing. It was thirty-five, forty feet up and over a mound and I thought when I hit it that it had a pretty decent beat on it, but you don't expect to hole those ones. But it held its line and the noise began to build in the crowd and then it luckily hit the back of the hole and went in. It was a great moment, really awesome.

Mahan was one up but, perhaps too pumped with adrenaline following his monster putt on seventeen, was unfortunate to find water with his drive at the eighteenth and Casey was able to keep his cool to claim a half for his team.

Europe needed to force their way back into things to keep their hopes alive and did much better than many had predicted in the opening exchanges, managing to sneak a one-point advantage over the opening four singles matches as Karlsson beat Leonard 5&3 and Rose overcame world number two Mickelson 3&2. But then the tide started to turn as Perry struck back for the home side with a 3&2 victory over Stenson.

Out sixth were Wilson and Weekley.

Hunter Mahan yells in delight as he holes his long putt at the seventeenth.

Already a crowd favourite, the alligator-wrestling Weekley had the galleries roaring as he smashed a drive off the first tee and then proceeded to gallop down the fairway with his driver between his legs like a hobby horse in tribute to Adam Sandler doing the 'bull dance' in the hit comedy Happy Gilmore.

Paul Azinger: We're all *Happy Gilmore* fans over here, it's like a cult following watching that movie. Boo Weekley put that club between his legs and hopped off the first tee. It was one of the funniest things I've ever seen.

Boo Weekley: I think it may have been the last day of the practise rounds, when an idea came to me. Me and my wife just got through having dinner and we came down and were grabbing some waters out of the little old room that was on our floor. There were two officers – a lady officer and another man sitting in there. I was talking and there happened to be *Happy Gilmore* running across the screen on the TV and they got to laughing. I turned to Karen and I said, 'Baby, I'm going to do that. I'm going to do that off one of the tee boxes.'

And the officers were like, 'Yeah right! Whatever. You ain't going to do that.' And I said, 'I'm going to do it. I don't know what day I'm going to do it, but I'm going to do it.'

When I got out there I was pumped, excited and ready for it to get over with, to tell you the truth. Win, lose or draw, it was one of those moments – I won't ever forget it. I went up there and I took my practise swing and it hit me right then. As I took my second practise swing, I always take two, there was a tree out there about two hundred yards. I said, 'If I can just start it over that tree, I'm going to ride this club out of here.' And that's exactly what happened.

Paul Azinger: There was just this incredible energy in the team and Boo summed that up in that moment. And then he went on to play an incredible round right after. The guys were just playing the most ridiculously good golf. Birdies were flying in everywhere.

Weekley was simply irresistible as he stormed to the turn in twenty-nine en route to overwhelming Wilson 4&2.

Europe needed to grasp every point they could, but when Holmes thundered a huge drive on the seventeenth and then swept his approach to within three feet of the pin, Hansen needed to do something miraculous to take the match down the eighteenth. The Dane almost managed it with a wonderful chip from twenty feet, but it rimmed the hole and swung a foot-and-a-half beyond. This left Holmes with a straightforward putt to claim a 2&1 victory that put the US to within touching distance of reclaiming the Ryder Cup.

Paul Azinger: It's unbelievable to see how far JB can hit a ball. When he hit his tee shot at the seventeenth, I heard whoops from the gallery behind the tee. For a second I thought I must have missed the ball, because I hadn't seen it come down. Then I realised that was because it hadn't come down yet. When the ball finally landed, I fell out of the cart laughing. 'Who can hit it that far?' I asked. JB had just driven it 400 yards! It was not only the longest tee shot of the week but maybe the longest in Ryder Cup history. He had a half sand wedge second shot from seventy-eight yards on a 478-yard hole.

Hansen was well behind JB off the tee. He hit what looked like a great approach, but it flew over the flag and ran off the back of the green, leaving him with an incredibly difficult shot.

JB's approach wasn't easy, even though it was short. He had to finesse a wedge over a large bunker, the kind of touch shot that is especially tough under pressure. And this was pressure. We weren't sure if this match would decide the Ryder Cup, but it was looking like it might.

JB took a couple of practise swings, stared down the flag, and hit one of the most deft short approach shots I've ever seen. The ball flew a couple of feet over the bunker and stopped within two feet of the hole. As JB was pumping his fist in the air for the fans, it was only appropriate that Johnny Miller called it 'the best shot of his career.' Hansen made us all catch our breath when his chip for birdie lipped out. Then JB made his putt for the match.

The US now needed just half a point for victory. Behind Holmes and Hansen, Jiménez and Furyk arrived on the seventeenth with the Spaniard one-down. Both drove onto the fairway and then landed their balls on the green with decent approach shots. Furyk was twenty-five feet from the hole and putted to within tap-in range. Jiménez was faced with a twenty-foot putt that would take the match to the eighteenth. He took his time over his shot as the crowd buzzed with anticipation. He stroked it evenly but as the ball slid past the hole, Jiménez knew it was all over and conceded the match – and with it the Ryder Cup as America had at last reached the golden tally of fourteen-and-a-half points.

Jim Furyk: The dream is to knock in a twenty-footer and fist pump with the crowd going bananas; mine was a two-foot concession. But I'll take it.

Paul Azinger: It was at the end of Furyk's match that it just hit me. This was a team and we became a family. I didn't cry, but I get a lump in my throat thinking back to it all.

Faldo still had some of his best players out on the course and although McDowell beat Cink 2&1 and Poulter saw off the challenge of Stricker 3&2, it was too little too late.

Stewart Cink: The Ryder Cup had already been decided before me and Graeme finished. We were fighting it out, he was maybe one or two-up and with about three holes to play our match stopped being relevant because we had already won. We were the ninth game out in the singles order.

The final two matches saw Curtis defeat Westwood 2&1 and Campbell beat Harrington 2&1 for an overall score of 16½–11½ – the biggest margin of victory for the US since 1981.

Astonishingly, the American rookies had accounted for thirteen of the fourteen-and-a-half points the US needed to reclaim the cup. The European 'big three' of García, Westwood and Harrington, however, had failed to live up to their billing and it had cost their team dearly.

Nick Faldo: The bottom line is we went there and played and were outplayed and got beaten. It was about professional golfers competing. But the way everyone remembers it, it was all my fault.

Boo Weekley rides his driver down the fairway like Happy Gilmore.

When Sergio says to me after the first day, 'I'm fucked, I don't want to play any more,' that's a belter for a captain. 'Um, you're one of my main guys and you don't want to play? Terrific, great, thanks.' How do you deal with that one?

Sergio García: 2008 was a great year for me on the Tour but unfortunately that Ryder Cup wasn't my best. The week before, I got sick and I was on antibiotics and stuff, so I wasn't feeling like my energy levels were that great.

Nick Faldo: Then I had Harrington exhausted and Westwood, who was in a different place. They were my top three players and gave me one-and-a-half points. It's pretty tough to do anything with that. That's the fact, but as a captain you get walloped with other stuff. Westwood, Harrington and García were my bankers and they only gave me half a point each; if they had managed to get me even a couple of points each that would have made a huge, huge difference. Sure, America played well and did their thing, they were at home, our gallery was seriously out-numbered – it was like 40,000 of their fans to our 1,000 – and that has a big effect.

As a golfer you go there to compete and all that matters is playing the match, so it's hard work for a captain when you get all sorts of things blamed on you afterwards.

But then I did pick Poulter, which I also got slaughtered for when I named him. And he went on to win four points out of five, which was then the best return for any wild card. Hey, my claim to fame. The only decent thing I did all week.

Ian Poulter: People say the US were a better team in 2008 without Tiger Woods but what happened was that their rookies really stepped up to the plate and they all delivered points. That's why they won.

Obviously, I'd rather have won the Ryder Cup in 2008 but I guess you could say it was good for the future of the Ryder Cup for America to win as they'd taken two big defeats in 2004 and 2006.

Hunter Mahan: I was so proud of everybody. We had six rookies on our team so I think we were definitely underdogs, but we just went out and played. I mean, we were not afraid of anything, scared of anything, and we just went out and played golf because we knew we were good enough to win it. We just had to go play.

In the aftermath, Faldo's captaincy was heavily slated, but there can be no denying that his decision to choose Poulter as one of his two captain's picks was an inspired one as the Englishman ended up as the top points scorer on either team. His other pick, Casey, played solidly and did extremely well to scramble a half point in the singles during his seismic clash with Mahan. But would the experience of Darren Clarke or Colin Montgomerie have made a difference? We will never know.

Lee Westwood: A captain can't have a significant effect on you winning a Ryder Cup but they can have a significant effect on you losing it.

Stewart Cink: The players teed it up, but that victory was a hundred per cent Zinger. He brought a very systematic approach. How we practised, who we played matches with, it wasn't willy-nilly like at times in the past. The most stressful part of Ryder Cup week is always the uncertainty, but his system went a long way to putting everyone at ease.

I liked the fact that Zinger had a plan. I don't know if that plan is the plan, because when you do win it is easy to say that that must be right. But he had a plan. He really invested in players, and gave us a lot of decision-making power. It felt like we were all captains and it felt great. I thought that week he did a job well done.

I've won one Ryder Cup and lost four, so 2008 is certainly the highlight of my Ryder Cup career. But if you are an American on the Ryder Cup team in the last fifteen years then you haven't won many, so I guess that doesn't really separate me apart too much. I think the highlight was certainly winning as a team, that was fun. The memories that I have, the relationships with other players and some of their wives, too, and the captains, they just don't ever go away.

Faldo was hammered as the source of Europe's collapse, but the players rallied around him in the press conference afterwards. 'We hold the golf clubs and we hit the shots, not the captain,' said Lee Westwood. 'If you want to talk about me being rested Saturday morning and Sergio being rested, that's the session we won, so Nick was right to do that.' It was a wonderful moment of solidarity, and even if the European players themselves might look back with dark memories from Valhalla, it was to their credit and to the spirit of the Ryder Cup that they didn't leap on the bandwagon to excuse their faults by solely blaming their captain for the defeat.

As with any Ryder Cup, it was the players who lost, not the captain; or, indeed, it was the American players who won the Ryder Cup. The post-mortem annihilation of Faldo's captaincy was, in many ways, due to the wave of success that Europe had been riding in the Ryder Cup. Suddenly, against the odds, they had lost and someone had to be blamed. But, as Colin Montgomerie noted during our interview in 2015, no team can go on winning indefinitely; there will always be times when it goes wrong, when momentum swings the other way. Who would have guessed before the tournament began that García, Harrington and Westwood would fail to win a match between them? Who would have known that the US would hole so many putts and make so many birdies, that rookies Holmes, Kim, Mahan and Weekley would play so well? Azinger was lauded to the heavens for his captaincy, but the role of the captain in Ryder Cups is always grossly overstated. They can only prepare their teams as best they can, pick the pairings and the singles order and soothe and massage egos in the team room. After that, it is all about the players and the buck should stop there. But it rarely does.

Nick Faldo: You win as a captain and you're an absolute hero. You lose and you're useless. That's how it works in the Ryder Cup. There were twenty-four guys giving their all and we came up short. The shot-making and putting were unbelievable – we were talking fractions. In that particular week they just did us and we had to congratulate them for it. The difference between a win, a loss or a half . . . you are talking maybe a chip or a putt. You can't point fingers.

José María Olazábal: I got pretty upset during the final press conference and some of the questions that were aimed at Nick. Nick fought hard for different issues and he got hammered because of his picks, but nobody mentioned that one of his picks, Ian Poulter, did very well and he has been one of our important players ever since. You know, it's my character; if I feel that something is not intended in the right way, or in a fair way, I will jump at it.

Nick Faldo: For all the criticism I've taken, I loved being in the team room. We all got on great. What I hate is that people make an assumption about what it was like in the team room and behind the scenes – and they were never there. That group of guys, we got on great. We had a debrief at the end, which we'd never done before, and all the guys sat around and we chatted and each guy talked about his experiences of the week and what I took from it was that, despite the result, everyone had a pretty good time; we didn't win because they beat us, or whatever happened, but the most important thing is that if each player knows he gave a hundred per cent, that's all you can do.

Justin Rose: From my perspective being a young English guy who had looked up to Nick he was a great captain. He gave me my opportunity to play lots of games, he communicated with me throughout the week, asking how I was feeling and playing, which is exactly what you want. There was a really comfortable relationship with the players.

From the result point of view and some of the pairings, in hindsight, maybe everything wasn't perfect. It is very difficult to keep everybody happy but for some of the older guys on the team they maybe felt like he could have done things differently. But for guys like myself and Ian Poulter we felt that it was a great week.

Lee Westwood: A lot of what I said in Valhalla during and after the Ryder Cup didn't come out quite as I intended and finished up sounding like sour grapes. But America absolutely deserved their victory, Paul Azinger's captaincy was excellent and the vast majority of the watching public who witnessed a titanic struggle between two very good sides were great.

I regret that I singled out a small minority of the crowd who had a go at me and my family during competition days because far and away the greater majority were impeccably behaved and got right behind their team . . . as did the excellent European supporters.

My comments about the hecklers and Paul's geeing up the crowd before the event were in no way intended to be an excuse or the words of an ungracious loser because the American team performed brilliantly and fully deserved to win.

Paul turned out to be a very good captain and both his ideas and tactics were spot on. I may not have been too thrilled with one or two things that happened in Valhalla, but I am taking absolutely nothing away from America's win. When you're beaten by a better side, you just have to admit it.

Nick Faldo: It was a tough experience and very tough for me to deal with afterwards. I wanted to leave with a win. I wanted to have that feeling because you know you only get one chance and I am a winner. Sure it left a scar. There's still a small one there, even now.

Graeme McDowell: 2008 was my first experience of it as a player at Valhalla and we lost, but it was one of the greatest weeks of my life. It was amazing and we had one of the best piss-ups you can imagine on the Sunday night. It had been an epic Ryder Cup and afterwards everyone was together, the US guys were up in our team room, we were all drinking and having an amazing time – it was just one of the greatest nights out I've ever had in my life.

My whole experience as a rookie Ryder Cup player was great. I felt like I'd had a decent week and played well personally and although we lost I think I almost enjoyed the week more than I enjoyed Celtic Manor two years later. Yeah we won then and it was great being part of the winning team – but the piss-up wasn't as good.

I don't know what it is, but the Ryder Cup is a special tournament, you know. You bond so much with the eleven guys in your team and the team room atmosphere is very special. Golf is such a selfish game, such an individual sport. When you're out there and all you care about is yourself and trying to do as well as you can; you know, you've got your team, your coach, your caddie, your agent, your family – and within that bubble you try to do the best you can. But for that one week every two years, you just play for each other. And there's nothing quite like that; for me it's always hit the spot.

THIRTY-EIGHT

2010

Celtic Manor Resort. Newport, Wales
(EUR 14½, USA 13½)

When the European Tournament Committee met in Dubai in early 2009 to choose the 2010 captain, several names were in contention, but Colin Montgomerie was considered by almost everyone in the room to be the man most likely to help regain the trophy lost in Kentucky a few months earlier – and thus was chosen. It was perhaps strange that, with the 2010 tournament being held at Celtic Manor in Wales, that the committee hadn't held out on the appointment of Ian Woosnam in 2006 until this moment, but they had decided in their wisdom to go for the Welshman in Ireland and a Scotsman in Wales (just as they would select an Irishman in Scotland in 2014).

Colin Montgomerie: It was a very different experience to find myself managing the team in 2010 while still being a current player on the Tour. You have to take your playing skills and park them away at the side somewhere, then pick them up on your way out. You have to change your mindset and become a manager, become someone that the other players rely on. The key to that is to earn and keep their respect – that's the number one priority. They've got to respect you and I was fortunate that I had that. Once we had the respect and I could feel the confidence that the team had in me, then we were on our way.

Corey Pavin was appointed by the US PGA to take the reins at the head of America's defence of the cup. Pavin, so synonymous with the '91 Ryder Cup and the War by the Shore when he had sported a camouflage cap in honour of American troops in the first Gulf War, had mellowed significantly in the intervening years and brought a more cool and calculating style to the captaincy than the wild passion of his predecessor, Paul Azinger.

The eight players to qualify for Pavin's team on points were Jim Furyk, Dustin Johnson, Matt Kuchar, Hunter Mahan, Phil Mickelson, Jeff Overton, Steve Stricker and Bubba Watson. Tiger Woods, who was still the number one player in the world according to the rankings, did not qualify for the US team on points and was reliant on Pavin selecting him as one of his captain's picks. The others to get the nod were Stewart Cink, Rickie Fowler and Zach Johnson.

Monty's men bidding to swiftly regain the cup at the Twenty Ten Course were the experienced hands of Luke Donald, Pádraig Harrington, Miguel Ángel Jiménez, Graeme McDowell, Ian Poulter and Lee Westwood alongside six rookies in Ross Fisher, Martin Kaymer, Rory McIlroy, Peter Hanson and brothers Edoardo and Francesco Molinari.

Pádraig Harrington: I think one thing you will always find about Monty, if you walked into a players' lounge anywhere in the world, and Monty is sitting at a table, that table will always be full. He attracts people in that sense in that he's always good company and he's always got something to say and he's got an opinion. His personality didn't need to change at all for when he was captain. He had the ability to build up somebody's confidence or say a kind word to somebody, but he also had the ability to make the tough decisions that needed to be made.

With a nod both to the Desert Storm caps of '91 and the Navy SEAL pods of '08, Pavin invited Air Force major, Dan Rooney, an F-16 fighter pilot, in to talk to the team. Patriotic fervour and ownership of their destiny was once again the order of the day for Team USA. 'I want these guys to be accountable to each other and have each other's backs, that's what happens in the military,' explained Pavin at the time.

Tiger Woods: A lot of my dad's friends were part of the Special Forces, or the Special Forces community. I grew up in that type of culture, that's what I saw, that's what I lived with. These guys had gone through the wringer and back. I saw that work ethic up front, wide-eyed, as a little punk kid. They kept me in line, trust me, they definitely kept me in line. They were always trying to get in my head. I got needled every single day, a constant needling, a constant badgering. It was to toughen me up – I knew that was what they were trying to do. They were trying to get in my head; eventually I learned how to get in their heads with my game. It all came back around.

The whole mentality I developed was to just beat everyone. That's why I played from a very young age. I've always been a person that likes to compete. I tried other team sports. I played baseball; I even ran track and cross-country in high school. But I just didn't find the same love as I did in golf. I kept coming back to golf. Some events were five holes when I was a little kid, some were eighteen, and eventually they became seventy-two-hole events. But my mentality was always the same – it was to beat everyone in that event.

Montgomerie, meanwhile, wanted to stoke the passionate flames that had so often been at the heart of Europe's finest Ryder Cup performances, often making emotional references to the ailing Seve Ballesteros who was at home in Santander enduring the final stages of his terminal battle with cancer.

Colin Montgomerie: I arranged for Seve to speak to the team from his home in Santander. He was too ill to travel to Wales for the Ryder Cup, but I wanted him to speak to the players if he could manage it. Every one of my team learned what the Ryder Cup meant to Seve, and they will all tell you it was one of the highlights of the week. He spoke for about ten minutes and it was very motivational, very passionate and also very sad to hear him, to hear the way he was. It was a real inspiration, especially for the rookies in the team, to speak to Seve and have Seve speak to them. He fired up the team and from that moment on we all wanted to win it for him.

Rory McIlroy: Seve brought so much passion and joy to the game of golf. He *was* European golf. He was the man. It definitely inspired me. I'd called the Ryder Cup a bit of an exhibition in the build-up but after that phone call I remember just sitting there and thinking, 'This is a big deal this thing.' And he wouldn't get off the phone, you know, it was just incredible. Monty was like, 'OK, thanks, Seve,' and he would say, 'No, no, let me finish, I have more I want to say.' He was amazing – and I know he inspired everyone else in that room. I thought we had an incredible captain and a great team, but that phone call was definitely in everyone's thoughts throughout the week.

Martin Kaymer: To listen to Seve and to [Welsh rugby legend] Gareth Edwards' speech, was very, very important. If you really listen, and if you try to get as much out of it for yourself as possible, these things can make a big difference to your psychology. These guys are not just athletes, they are legends. It was a great pleasure to hear them speak, to be able to talk to them and to listen to their thoughts. I loved it.

Peter Alliss: Seve created a great passion and people loved him. There's a great difference between admiration and love – and the world of golf loved Seve.

Montgomerie understood that players win Ryder Cups and captains lose them and took a little something from each of the captains he had played under during his long and illustrious career in the event. He built them up like Seve, took risks like Torrance and played the statesman like Langer.

Graeme McDowell: With the backroom staff of Thomas Bjørn, Darren Clarke, Paul McGinley and Sergio García, we had a great bunch of guys that week. I talked about not having the X factor in the team room in Valhalla, but I really felt we had that in Wales. The guys were excited and up for it, and we wanted to win the Ryder Cup back desperately.

Pavin, meanwhile, took a leaf out of Tom Watson's book, under whom he had played in 1993 at the Belfry, keeping an emotional distance from his players and treating them as adults rather than seeking to mollycoddle them. 'A good piece of advice that Tom gave me,' said Pavin, 'was to just let them go out and play.'

Bubba Watson: We didn't really bounce ideas off each other as a team. I never asked Tiger Woods about the Ryder Cup. Tiger's game is different than mine. Jim Furyk's is different than mine, Phil Mickelson's, well, his is pretty close to mine – we both miss fairways a lot of the time.

After the controversy surrounding Nick Faldo's opening and closing speeches at Valhalla, Montgomerie was not about to repeat the error. 'I think the players put great stock in their captain's opening speech,' he said at the time, 'and I've always thought it really does set the tone for the match. Sam Torrance's speech at the Belfry was the perfect example of a great opening gambit and we as players left the stage feeling like we were heading to the first tee with a one-shot advantage.'

It was his counterpart, however, who raised eyebrows during the opening ceremony when he overlooked Stewart Cink when reading out his team.

A great deal of effort went into preparing the course at Celtic Manor, which was just as well because it was hit with rainstorms similar to those that had lashed down on Valderrama in 1997. Whereas the Spanish course had been able to endure the heavy downpours, however, the

Twenty Ten Course had a few more struggles and continued heavy rain meant that play had to be suspended twice.

Colin Montgomerie: There's a so-called 'home-course advantage'. A lot of captains over the years have made changes to the golf course to set it up in favour of their players, but in 2010 I didn't play around with the golf course at all. I felt that it was already set up in a very, very fair manner to allow the best team to win. I don't think it was right to set the course up in any other way than to what it's been designed for; Celtic Manor is a great, great golf course and it was in super condition despite the weather we had that week.

Graeme McDowell: The course was really, really well set up. If you missed fairways at Celtic Manor, you were going to be punished. If you did miss them, you deserved to miss them kind of thing. The course had some length to it and the driving was a premium. You had to drive the ball in the fairway, preferably long; I know that works everywhere, but it certainly worked there, for sure.

Colin Montgomerie: Rory McIlroy had made a few throwaway comments in the build-up about wanting to play against Tiger and the press leapt on it. I wanted to avoid them playing each other if I could. Our whole approach was about the team, not about individuals.

Rory was twenty years old at the time and he thought of the Ryder Cup as an exhibition; Majors were what he wanted to win. OK, fine, you can say that. It was a shame that nowadays with the social media world things like that get bandied around so easily. I didn't do very much to convert him to the Ryder Cup, I just let him go out with his pal Graeme McDowell; I said to Graeme, 'Get him out there, get him playing, and he'll realise very quickly, even in the practise rounds, that this is no exhibition.' Because you don't know what it's like until you actually witness it. And I'm so glad that afterwards he said it was the best experience he'd ever had in golf. And I'm sure 2012 and 2014 were as special for him as well.

I think Rory was a bit upset about the comments made in the press about the Tiger situation and was feeling a little bit disjointed from the rest of the group, so we decided to get a bunch of big curly wigs and we wore them around the team room and in the practise rounds to help him feel part of the team again. It worked well, he loved it.

But the Tiger Woods thing was still something of an issue because he wanted to play Tiger Woods and he made it quite clear to the press that he wanted Tiger – in the pairings, in the singles, whatever. I went into the press conference just after Rory had come out, and they said, 'Do you know that McIlroy wants to play Woods?' And I said, 'Oh, does he? Well, with all due respect to Rory, I will do my utmost to keep them apart. I know what happens when people want Tiger Woods. Tiger gets angry; he licks his lips and he loves it.' So it was lucky that in the foursomes, fourballs and singles we were able to keep them apart.

Corey Pavin: Tiger was aware of Rory's comment and if they had played against each other it would have been entertaining, but trying to arrange that between Colin and myself isn't what the spirit of the Ryder Cup is about. It was more important for me to send my guys out in the order I want to send them out in. People have said things like that to Tiger in the past and maybe regretted it, but as far as Tiger was concerned, all he wanted to do was to win.

No exhibition match – Rory McIlroy yells in delight as he experiences
the adrenaline rush of his debut Ryder Cup.

Because of the impact of the rain on the course, only the four fourball matches were played on
Friday.

Westwood and Kaymer got Europe off to the best possible start when they took out Mickelson
and Johnson, winning 3&2 in the opening match, but things gradually worsened for the home
team thereafter as McDowell and McIlroy halved their match with Cink and Kuchar before
Woods and Stricker defeated Poulter and Fisher two-up, and Watson and Overton dovetailed
brilliantly to defeat Donald and Harrington 3&2.

Colin Montgomerie: When I was looking at how the pairings would go, I was very
comfortable with who I picked – although not all of them worked out to be quite as
successful over the first couple of days as I had hoped. The pairing of Rory with Graeme
McDowell seemed like an obvious one. They were both from Northern Ireland and were
great friends. I had high hopes for the two of them and was slightly surprised when, after
the second session, they had done no better than to halve one and lose the other.

Graeme McDowell: Rory and I had a great time playing together in 2010. Partnerships
are all about chemistry, knowing each other's games, knowing how to interact with one
another on the golf course. Having a good friendship is another factor. If we needed
lifting, we could do it. If we needed calming down, we could do that too.

Rory was off the charts in the opening fourballs. We both struggled a little bit to begin
with – with it being Rory's first experience of the atmosphere, it was very hard to get any
kind of rhythm going but then later he was unbelievable.

Rory McIlroy: I played OK that first day. I hit some nice shots but it was so difficult the
first few holes; it was made a lot trickier because the fairway was so wet and if you mishit
it slightly, it could make you look very silly.

I thought we did really well to come back from two-down and grab a half. We could have sneaked a win at the last but I think we probably would have taken a half on the twelfth tee.

It was great to play with G-Mac. At the start of the week, there was no one else I really wanted to play with. It was great to get three games with him. Even the match we halved and the match we lost, the first couple of games, we both played very, very well. To play with one of your best friends in the Ryder Cup is very, very special.

Jeff Overton: It was a dream come true to represent the US in a Ryder Cup and it's the most incredible experience when you go to the tee box for the first time and all the fans are there going crazy supporting both sides. It was an incredible honour to play in something like that, but the pressure is huge. You don't realise how huge it is going to be until you step out there. It was great to start things off with a win and Bubba and I played really well together; we enjoyed it a lot. To beat a couple of top players like Luke Donald and Pádraig Harrington 3&2 was such a positive start for us; we were pumped.

With play being truncated on the Friday (the Donald/Harrington versus Watson/Overton fourball match wasn't completed until Saturday morning because of poor light, let alone the planned foursome session even getting underway), the organisers had to try and cram as many matches as they could into day two as the weather calmed on Saturday to allow a full day's play. This saw all twenty-four players out on the course in six matches with both foursome and fourball matches played in the same session at the same time. Session two, therefore, contained six foursome matches; session three, which was played over both Saturday and Sunday contained two foursome and four fourball matches; and session four, the singles, were moved to a Monday for the first time.

Colin Montgomerie: My intention had always been to pace the team, giving each man at least one session off, but the weather put paid to that idea. With rain delays forcing the Friday fourballs to carry over into Saturday morning, it was clear there was no way we would be able to follow the traditional format of five sessions – two on Friday, two on Saturday and the singles on the Sunday.

Equally, though, no one wanted to cut the number of matches to squeeze them into the time available. Corey Pavin and I discussed the options with the Tour officials from both camps and we decided on what I thought was an excellent plan. Instead of the five sessions, we would have four; meaning that in sessions two, three and four (the singles) all the players would be out simultaneously. That suited me just fine.

After the Friday fourballs and the first of the foursomes, the US were dominating proceedings. Woods and Stricker paired brilliantly to beat Jiménez and Hanson 4&3, before Zach Johnson and Mahan defeated the Molinari brothers two-up. The only minor pause in the American momentum came in the third match where Westwood and Kaymer were able to claim a half with Furyk and Fowler.

Montgomerie realised that he needed to rally his troops and get the crowd pumping in order to effectively counter the American onslaught. And a response was exactly what his team gave him.

Colin Montgomerie: There was not enough passion on the golf course, we didn't have the passion. At lunchtime it was not looking so good, it was stale. I can't repeat exactly what I told the players but the Americans were silencing the crowd. We had to get the crowd back on our side.

Play began in the third session late on Saturday afternoon. When darkness finally halted play at 18:50, Europe was leading all six matches.

Colin Montgomerie: To go to bed on the Saturday with six blues on the board was incredible. That had never happened before. It was the best session of golf I'd ever seen played by any European team. But Saturday night was tough. Although we had all that blue on the board, two matches hadn't finished yet and so we were down, we were 6–4 down. We were favourites, we were playing at home, we hadn't lost at home for seventeen years and we didn't want to start now. We knew the Americans were better now than we thought they were; I wouldn't say we had underestimated them, but it was damned near that. And we had to get that passion back, we had to get the crowd back – and the only way to get that crowd back on our side was to give them something. It was up to us. We couldn't blame the crowd for being quiet because we weren't producing the goods for them.

Once again the storm clouds drew in over the Usk Valley and the start of Sunday's play was delayed until 13:20.

Pádraig Harrington: Yeah, we were in a difficult situation going out on the Sunday. Even though we had all blue on the board, we hadn't yet secured those points. It was very important that we converted them. Lee Westwood posted a notice on the doorway as we walked out warning us to expect the US to start fast and that we were going to have to be equally up for it.

Zach Johnson holed a putt straight off the bat to win the hole against Rory and G-Mac on the eighth and I'm sure we were all kind of thinking: here it comes. But no more than thirty seconds later, there was a cheer from the tenth green as Lee holed his putt. So we knew there was a response there.

Colin Montgomerie: I wish I could say it was because of my team talks or whatever, but it wasn't. The reason we won was that we all pulled together; we hadn't been playing for each other the way I had anticipated we would – I didn't feel that Westwood was holing putts for Kaymer, who wasn't holing putts for Donald, who wasn't holing them for Poulter . . . it wasn't quite knitting together – and that was what was said. And I allowed them to air their views as well – it was very important that we were working together, that I wasn't some kind of dictator, it was very much a democracy within our locker room; I wanted that team unity back again which I didn't feel was happening that first day or two.

We were living in a financially difficult time and I had been told by my bosses that a home win was very, very important economically for European golf. Sponsorship for the European Tour was hanging in the balance and it was crucial to its survival that we brought the cup home. So I said, 'Come on lads, this is for you but it's for others as well

– it's for the whole European Tour. If we don't do this, it will affect the whole Tour for, at the very least, the next two years, unless we can sort this out.' I needed them to know that it was important for them to perform for themselves but also for the rest of the European Tour and all those concerned with that.

Europe roared back into the contest. Westwood and Donald led the charge as they demolished Woods and Stricker 6&5. The scoreline represented Woods' biggest Ryder Cup defeat and made it 7-1 to Westwood in their matches stretching back to 1997 over six editions.

McDowell and McIlroy then found their groove as they dismantled Zach Johnson and Mahan 3&1.

It would prove to be an astonishing day for the Europeans as they picked three-and-a-half of a possible four points in the afternoon fourballs.

Colin Montgomerie: Mentally I played every shot for the guys, but I didn't interfere. There was only one time that I was involved and that was when Harrington missed a putt on seventeen on the Sunday afternoon fourball and he knew the Molinaris were playing behind him. 'Where's Monty?' he asked. 'Get him here; get him to tell Molinari to hit it further left than he thinks. Because I've just had this putt and it breaks more than I thought it would.' So I got my buggy and raced round to seventeen, ran on the green, which wasn't like me, and said to Molinari, 'Harrington's just had this putt, it breaks more than you think it does. So whatever you think it is, add a couple more inches to it and hit it firmer because that's going to help you.' And I'm so glad that he still missed it low anyway, because it did break more than he had thought, thank God, because if he had left it high he'd have thought I was a bloody idiot. So that was really the only time I got involved on the playing surface because I really didn't want to do it. And I learnt that from Seve because I didn't want to be a nuisance to the players.

Edoardo Molinari: Before we started I thought that, obviously, Francesco and I would be a great partnership. But I also thought that any of the other ten guys on the team would be a good partner. Francesco and I get along very well with each other but ever since we were starting to play golf, when we were ten, eleven years old, there has been a little bit of competition and rivalry between each other. But I think it's done very well for us, because when you see your brother playing better, you want to improve and you want to catch him. I think that's one of the reasons why we made it to the Ryder Cup team, both of us.

Colin Montgomerie: Francesco is quieter than Edoardo, perhaps because he is the younger of the two, and that is one of the reasons I felt it was so important that I keep him and his brother together all week, even putting them out one after the other in the singles. Edoardo could act as both a playing partner and a friend to Francesco, which I thought was vital.

One of my highlights of the week came when Francesco and Edoardo secured their half point against Cink and Kuchar. Francesco's putting had not been at its best but when he had to hole a clutch four-footer on the last to win the hole, halve the match and complete a fabulous five-and-a-half out of six points for the session, he didn't buckle. That putt ensured that every member of the team contributed, which was critical and meant a lot to me personally.

Pádraig Harrington: It was very important for the team that we were starting to respond and we countered well. To get five-and-a-half points out of the available six was phenomenal and gave us a crucial lead going into the singles. It was a serious momentum swing in our favour.

Colin Montgomerie: America were three points down going into the singles, so they needed points early and I knew they would want to get their top guys out first. So I knew Tiger would be nearer the top than not. I wanted to put my top guys out there too to counteract the American position. There was no point giving America momentum by putting a bunch of rookies out and leaving my strength to the end. We needed to counteract good with good because we were doing OK so didn't want to surrender the initiative. So I gave the honour of going out number one to Lee Westwood, because he was my number one player, with the most experience. I then put Rory out second, then Donald, Kaymer and Poulter. I had a strong top five. And I risked it, hoping like hell that America wouldn't put Woods number two – and they didn't, they put him eighth. Scoreable but not number one or two and I was so happy to see that. His record isn't great in the Ryder Cup fourballs or foursomes but in the singles he's only lost once against Rocca. A lot of his games haven't counted because he's been out number twelve, but his record is still good. There's an aura about him – I'm glad I never faced him in the singles.

Graeme McDowell: I remember sitting there on Sunday night when the singles draw came out. We were sitting in the team room and Monty was reading out the line-up. We got to number seven, eight, nine in the order and my name still hadn't come out and I was like, 'Okaaaay'. Then we got to the final two and Pádraig was at eleven and I was at twelve. I remember feeling disappointed by that because I figured that it would come down to the guys playing in sixth, seventh, eighth spot to win the thing for us, and my game would be fairly worthless by the time I played. But then again, maybe it could all come down to me. Who knew?

I was thinking all of this over and I think I had a fairly blank look on my face and Thomas Bjørn said to me, 'G-Mac, you OK?' I was like, 'Yeah, I think I'm OK.' I hadn't played in the anchor place before so I went and asked Ollie and Monty, 'How do I do this, how do I play number twelve?'

Colin Montgomerie: Graeme was riding high coming into the Ryder Cup, having followed a win in the Wales Open at Celtic Manor by capturing the US Open at Pebble Beach. It was an amazing crescendo in terms of achievements and it was fantastic from my point of view that the Ryder Cup came so soon after these twin performances. For me, Graeme's greatest strength lies in his confidence and it was gloriously and palpably intact.

Initially, Graeme was not very happy about being in the anchor slot. I took him to one side to discuss it. 'Graeme, I understand what you are saying, but just look at this American team for a second. They have surprised us all week. They are bloody good.

Woods isn't going to fall down. Mickelson isn't going to fall down. Do you really think this team is going to roll over and accept defeat? You know they aren't. This competition is far from over and I need you at number twelve if things go wrong elsewhere.'

Although Steve Stricker beat Lee Westwood at the seventeenth hole in the opening match, for much of the first few hours the Europeans seemed in control of the singles and were steadily progressing towards an emphatic victory.

Lee Westwood: We wanted to get off to a quick start again and I was the first out at the top of the order, but Steve Stricker was just too good for me. I got off to a nice start but he was strong from the back nine, he was about five or six-under. Incredible. The onus was on the American side to come out and be aggressive and attack because they were three points behind; but at the same time, three points was not that much, not that big of a lead as it appears – especially as they only needed to get to fourteen points to retain the cup, while we had to go out and push to get the points to win it back.

Colin Montgomerie: I put Rory McIlroy out second. He is all about talent. In my view he is the second most talented golfing individual ever to come out of Europe behind Seve. He brought a glorious rush of youthful enthusiasm to the locker room. I had watched him playing in the Vivendi Trophy (the rebranded Seve Trophy) with Graeme McDowell in 2009 when the two annihilated Søren Kjeldsen and Álvaro Quirós in the fourballs before putting paid to Henrik Stenson and Peter Hanson in the greensomes. It was impressive stuff. So I sent Rory out second against Stewart Cink and he played very well to halve that match.

Luke Donald: I went out third against Jim Furyk at a time when every point was absolutely crucial. We hadn't had the start we had wanted and I knew that Jim was going to be a really tough opponent. He's a very similar player to me. He grinds it out. He put some pressure on me at the end, but it was a hell of a relief to get a point on the board for us.

Colin Montgomerie: It was all still very nip and tuck. Dustin Johnson beat Martin Kaymer 6&4 and then Ian Poulter does what Ian Poulter tends to do in a Ryder Cup and went out and delivered a terrific point against Matt Kuchar.

José María Olazábal: On the Monday I was in the locker room waiting for the players to come out and was giving them encouragement. I looked at Ian Poulter's face and I said, 'OK, I don't have to say anything, you're ready.' He looked at me and said, 'Yes, and I can guarantee you a point.' That's Poulter at the Ryder Cup.

Colin Montgomerie: You would pick Ian Poulter if he was anywhere in the top fifty in Europe. He is our 'Mr Ryder Cup'. I rated every member of my team, without question, and I stand by Luke Donald being the most valuable player in terms of golf. But when it came to heart, passion and pride in representing Europe, Ian Poulter led the field; he was the public face of the whole competition.

Ian Poulter: I was interviewed on live TV before my singles match with Matt Kuchar and I said that I would 'deliver my point.' Tiger Woods was apparently watching in the US team room and he ran off and told Kuchar what I'd said. Some people were offended by the guarantee, sure. But in my mind, Tiger went in there and tried to fire his guy up. That's what the Ryder Cup is all about – passion. And whatever you feel you have to do to whip up the fire, you just have to do it. I didn't mean to be disrespectful although I suppose it's hard not to sound disrespectful when you say you're definitely going to beat someone. But I said it for a reason. I'm not sure I could have wanted to win any more, but by saying that, it put even more pressure on me to win. I would have been slated if I hadn't won after that comment. I also wanted to show my team how confident I was. I felt very good at the time. It came off. It was fine.

Colin Montgomerie: It was going great the first two hours, I was quite relaxed. The board was going all blue, the cheers were going up, the Europeans were holing putts. And the next hour-and-a-half was pretty poor to be honest because the Americans fought back very, very well. Tiger found his game and he beat Francesco Molinari 4&3. I'm only glad now that we put a lot of strength in the bottom. Pádraig Harrington was put at number eleven for a reason and Graeme McDowell was put at number twelve for a reason.

Corey Pavin: Jeff Overton beat Ross Fisher 3&2 and then Europe got another point on the board when Miguel Ángel Jiménez beat Bubba 4&3. The eighth match out in the order was Tiger against Francesco Molinari.

Tiger had had a target on his back for a long time as world number one and people have always got up for their matches against him. It's hard for him to win in the Ryder Cup because everybody raises their game to try and beat him. That's probably why, on paper, he has underperformed in the Ryder Cup, but in 2010 he delivered a point in the first session fourball with Steve Stricker and then they did it again in the second session foursomes. They struggled against Donald and Westwood in the third session foursomes and lost, but then he came right back out again in the singles to beat Molinari 4&3. He was fantastic, classic Tiger. We were really on the move by that stage and were right back in it. I really thought that we might do it.

Mickelson bounced back from a disappointing first three to beat Hanson 4&2 to take the score to 13–12 in Europe's favour; but the US were closing in fast.

Colin Montgomerie: We had six rookies in that team and suddenly if half your team hasn't played in a singles Ryder Cup match before it is a very different scenario. And it was interesting that not one of those six rookies won a point.

Fowler had gone out just ahead of Mickelson in the order and he played some of the most outstanding golf of the tournament as he fought back from being four-down against Edoardo Molinari. With four holes to play he was still three-down but then made three spectacular birdies, the best being the fifteen-foot putt to secure a half on the eighteenth.

A few minutes later, Zach Johnson beat Harrington 3&2 and the overall score was now thirteen-and-a-half points each.

Corey Pavin: It was back and forth, back and forth, a red win, a blue win, a red. Tiger beat Francesco Molinari and then Rickie Fowler halved with Edoardo Molinari. Rickie was amazing, I think he birdied fifteen, sixteen, seventeen, eighteen. The putt on eighteen was incredible. From a twenty-one-year-old, to be three down with three to play and to earn a half point for his team, it was amazing.

And then Phil Mickelson beat Peter Hanson and Zach Johnson beat Pádraig Harrington and all we needed to retain the Ryder Cup was a half point from Hunter Mahan's match with Graeme McDowell.

Comparisons to Brookline were floating ominously around the Welsh valleys. The rookies were crumbling, Phil Mickelson had won his first Ryder Cup singles since 1999 and Tiger had prowled imperiously. Could an unlikely US comeback once again be on the cards?

Graeme McDowell: I remember walking onto the fifteenth tee box and thinking, 'I don't know if I can do this.' The nerves were just so intense. I turned to my caddie and said, 'Is a half enough?' I was two up with four to play. 'Yeah,' he said, 'A half is enough. You're fine.' And I said to him, 'I'm not fine. I'll tell you what, if you're so calm why don't you play the rest of the way and I'll carry the bag?' Honestly I had that conversation with him.

And I remember on the sixteenth fairway a big roar went up because Rickie Fowler had just holed a putt on Eddie Molinari on the last green, and I could tell it was a USA cheer not a European one. And Monty has got the earpiece in and is jumping around and he's freaking out.

Colin Montgomerie: I'd heard that Rickie Fowler had holed another amazing putt on the eighteenth to get a tie with Edoardo Molinari. And I said to Graeme McDowell, 'Those cheers at the eighteenth, would you like to know the situation?' He nodded, so I said, 'You have to win this game.' And both he and his caddie looked back at me and nodded again. 'OK, we're on.'

Hunter Mahan: When you're told you're going out twelfth, you realise that it could be a match nobody knows about or the biggest match of your life. As it happened, it became a big match. I think probably around ten, Graeme and I started to think that it could come down to us. Rickie, I don't know how he did it, but getting it all squared was huge. It gave me a chance.

Graeme McDowell: I can safely say that I've never felt that nervous on a golf course in my life before. You know, we kind of said in the locker room that we weren't going to check out the leaderboards as we were going round, to just focus on our individual matches, the guys playing down the order were not going to focus on what was going on out there. But the screens by every green were quite big, and it was kind of tough to not notice.

I looked up at the scoreboard on the tenth green and I realised that things were really, really tight and that chances were that the last matches were going to come into play. I mean, obviously I hoped that I wasn't going to be needed. At that point, I got extremely nervous, and coming down the stretch, I'd never felt nerves like it in my life. It was a different level completely to Pebble Beach. I was so nervous at that point that it actually refocused my mind a little bit. It took away all the doubt, all the question marks that I'd had in my head, and I hit a decent little six-iron in to about fifteen feet.

Colin Montgomerie: It was as pressure-packed as any fifteen-footer can have been in the game's history – and he holed it for the birdie which took him back to two ahead.

Graeme McDowell: It was the best putt I'd hit in my life. It was fast, I just had to get it along and thankfully it caught an edge. The US Open win felt like a back nine with my dad back at Portrush compared to that.

Colin Montgomerie: I don't like to get involved in people's matches and come onto tees like other captains have done in the past, but I felt it was necessary to come onto the seventeenth to just say to Graeme, 'Are you OK, mate? That was wonderful, but focus, focus on this next shot here.' As they always say, the most important shot in golf is the next one you play. The next shot he had to play had to be the most important shot of his life.

I've played for twenty years in the Ryder Cup and along with that captaincy it had become my life. And it all came down to someone else. That's the hardest part about being a captain – your fate is entirely in someone else's hands.

José María Olazábal: G-Mac is a gutsy player. He plays with a lot of heart and those are elements that are crucial and essential to playing well in the Ryder Cup. He was one of

The European team. *Getty Images*

our main men in the team; a very gutsy player, and I think the Ryder Cup brings out the best in him. He loves it. Even if he didn't strike the ball as well as he sometimes could, he would always fight until the very end – fight for every shot, for every inch.

You know, when he was last in that singles matches on Monday at Celtic Manor, he was a little down on himself on Sunday night. But as the match progressed that Monday, what he did was outstanding. He became a real leader in the team and carried that forward in subsequent Ryder Cups.

Paul McGinley: As a vice-captain I was obviously part of the discussion about where we were going to put guys in the singles order. And we deliberately put Graeme and Pádraig at eleven and twelve because they were street fighters. If it came down to them, then we felt they had the grit to win it.

I remember Graeme coming off the tenth green and he stared up at the scoreboard for a good twenty seconds or so – which is a long time to look at the board. Then he turned to me with a smile and said, 'I think it's going to come down to me.' And I just shrugged and said, 'Maybe, yeah, maybe,' knowing full well that it probably would come down to him. But that was interesting because he knew from the tenth that it was looking likely that he would be the decisive match. That's the attitude of a champion and was exactly why we'd picked him there.

Graeme McDowell: Coming down the final hole, I was thinking about my teammates, I was thinking about Monty and the fans and I was also thinking about Seve. It was crazy. I had never felt so nervous in my life. I was trying to do it for eleven teammates, for all the fans, for the caddies, for Europe and for Monty – and we were all trying to win it for Seve.

I barely remember the events that happened in the next ten minutes. The elation of holing that putt and storming onto the next tee box, managing to get club on ball with a five-iron to get to the edge of the seventeenth green.

Colin Montgomerie: Poor Hunter came up short from the tee and then fluffed his chip. Graeme held his nerve and putted to within five feet of the hole and happily accepted his opponent's proffered hand when the American's par putt failed to find the hole. Europe had won the Ryder Cup, with the result a nail-biting 14½ points to 13½.

Hunter Mahan: It was a tough match. I hit it unbelievably at times, I just couldn't make a putt. Graeme played extremely solid. Sixteen was a perfect hole, he just drove it down the middle. I didn't know what he hit in there but he made a great putt.

We had a tough session on the Sunday where we only got half a point and that was really tough to come back from. They played well top to bottom.

That's what the Ryder Cup gives you, it gives you moments like that. It brings stuff out of you that you don't know you had, from an emotional sense, from a golf sense, and that's what's personal about it. You know, I don't think people give us credit as a team for how much we actually care about it. It's not fun to lose; it's not fun to watch them parade around and get a victory in their home place. But it is also great – it is one of the best events in the world because it's different to what you usually do as a golfer and what you're playing for.

Luke Donald: Hats off to the Americans, they pushed us all the way. You know, Graeme's birdie on sixteen was pretty special. You don't like to see what happened to Hunter on seventeen, but you'll take it any way you can, and we got fourteen-and-a-half points. It wasn't easy, but it was an amazing feeling.

Graeme McDowell: I remember just getting engulfed on the green and the next three or four minutes was just hugging and shouting. I remember Poulter being there and we were just shouting at each other, going crazy.

Jim Furyk: It's an emotional experience, the Ryder Cup. I've never been as happy as after winning the Ryder Cup and I've never cried after losing in anything else. Obviously I had a match that went to eighteen, and I know we needed that half point. So lots of us are looking at each other thinking, 'God, one half point, and we get to take the cup back home. One full point and we win the Ryder Cup.' Everyone could probably beat themselves up over and over again for that half point. What we had to remember is we win as a team and we lose as a team. It doesn't ride on one person, it falls on all of us.

Rory McIlroy: To regain the Ryder Cup and bring it back to European soil, to do it for European golf and for Seve and for everyone else involved, it was one of the best weeks of my life.

Hunter Mahan: Winning is great, and it comes and it goes and there's always the next tournament and there's the next Ryder Cup. But for some reason losing, it lingers. It hangs with you for some reason. Even though maybe it shouldn't, it does and it bites at you a little bit. 2010 is some time ago now, but it feels like just yesterday. I remember walking off that green and all of the fans were rushing onto Graeme and having a big party and I felt like I was walking by myself for 600 yards back to the clubhouse. It's a very lonely feeling.

Phil Mickelson: We came within half a point. But we could look anywhere throughout those 28 points for that half a point. I look at the three matches that I played in, and had many opportunities to try to get that clinching point. We just fell a little bit shy. We put a lot of heart and energy into that event. We really believed all week we were going to win. We not just talked about it, but we really believed that we were going to prevail.

Colin Montgomerie: I have twelve pictures up in my house of the team and I treasure them. I'll always have a bond with all twelve. I don't see Ross Fisher much but when I do, he says, 'Hello, Mr Captain.' Martin Kaymer, it was his first Ryder Cup, whenever I see him it's, 'Hello, Mr Captain'. We had a certain something between us and it will always be there.

I wanted to leave – win, lose or draw – thinking and knowing that I'd given one hundred per cent to the cause. That was my goal at the start of the campaign – I wanted to lead a team of winners, which I did. I wanted to lead a team that badly wanted to play in this Ryder Cup. Passion. That's what I wanted – to lead a team of passionate players. To win the Ryder Cup for the European Tour and not for themselves. And every one of them played that way.

THIRTY-NINE

2012
Medinah Country Club. Medinah, Illinois
(EUR 14½, USA 13½)

The Medinah Country Club just outside Chicago played host to the thirty-ninth Ryder Cup and two stalwarts from either side were named as captains, with Davis Love III charged with leading America's challenge to recapture the cup from José María Olazábal's European team.

José María Olazábal: It was such a great honour to be a Ryder Cup captain and I was really proud to be chosen, but at the same time the responsibility was huge, which you realise as time goes by after you have been named captain. From the moment you are elected as Ryder Cup captain, you have to be really careful about the things you do and say, you have to be really close to the players and it takes a lot of your time. It's a huge responsibility.

Davis Love III: Ryder Cup golf really is about bringing people together. I played on my first team in 1993, and my wife, Robin, remembers when a Ryder Cup team was much smaller than it is today, with fewer assistants and fewer PGA officials. In 2012 she had the inspired idea to have one giant table in the team room for our first night so that the entire team – the players, assistants, officials and wives – would all be in the same place, doing the same thing.

To me, a big part of the captain's job is to help people have a dream week. A bigger part of the captain's job is to put on a TV show that will make people want to take up this great game. The biggest part of the captain's job is to win. One thing I know – that we all know – is that Ryder Cup golf is not life and death. We all know what true heartache is.

Justin Rose: It was a devastating loss to all of us when Seve died in 2011. And when the Ryder Cup came around again a year later, all you could do was to think of Seve. I think with José María being named as our captain, we had a link to Seve. It was fantastic that José was the captain. You knew that if Seve had been around, he would have been a big part of that team. So it was nice that he was still a big part of that team.

José María Olazábal: There's no secret, everyone knows how special my relationship was with Seve. He took me under his wing in '87 at Muirfield Village and we were very close throughout our careers. We spent a lot of time together, we practised together; I have some wonderful memories.

Seve always said that winning the Open at St Andrews and making that putt to beat Tom Watson was his sweetest moment. We came up with the idea that it would be nice to have Seve's silhouette on our kit, so that every time somebody grabbed a club or something from the bag, they would see it. I thought it was important to have Seve's memory and presence there during the week. It was one way that Seve could be with us every step of the way. He meant a lot to me and the team and I wanted something to make him present for each player. His image certainly ensured he was alongside us throughout the week.

Davis Love III: I remember what Tom Watson said about the Ryder Cup – it's an adventure. It's not just a three-day golf match. You build relationships that you don't build anywhere else; friendships, respect for your competitors that you don't gain in a regular tournament. José María Olazábal also said that there will be moments that happen out there that only happen in a Ryder Cup, in that kind of pressure, and he was right. Going into that week I knew that the guys were going to have moments out there that would change their careers and that they would remember for the rest of their lives.

I made my picks based on pairings. I wanted them to be clear before they got there who they would be playing with in the practise rounds and in the matches. I didn't want there to be any lobbying about playing with certain guys come Monday night of Ryder Cup week.

That came from the success Paul Azinger had at Valhalla in 2008 and from what Fred Couples did as captain in the Presidents Cup. The more I think about it, the more I realise that being a Ryder Cup captain is like being a football coach. In football, you need to have your players ready before the game. It's the same thing with the Ryder Cup.

Webb Simpson: I'd played the Presidents Cup before so I had a little taste of what it might be like – but it was totally different. Every emotional feeling I had times ten; every nervous moment times ten. I remember on the Tuesday going out for the first practise round at 8:30 in the morning and the chants are going up from the fans on each side and I was like, 'What? It's Tuesday morning, it's a practice round, what's going on? These people think this thing is serious!' We went over to the putting green right before the first tee and there were tens of thousands of people around it. I'd never really been nervous before for a practice round but I was then and I remember thinking, 'Right, this is what the Ryder Cup is all about.'

Davis Love III: I struggled for two years to come up with a way to get an advantage with the way the course was set up at Medinah. We had twenty-four of the best players in the world and they were all pretty good at adapting to conditions, but the one thing I'd never liked was rough. I'd been lucky enough to have a little bit of an influence on two golf tournaments – the McGladrey Classic that I host in Georgia and the 2012 Ryder Cup – and neither one of them had a lot of rough. I just don't like rough. The fans want to see a little excitement. They want to see birdies. Valhalla was exciting. There were a lot of birdies. We wanted to let these unbelievable athletes freewheel it a little bit and play. You know, you're not going to trick them by all of a sudden having deep grass. But we had a long-hitting, freewheeling, fun-to-watch team and I figured the way Medinah was set up would play to our strengths.

The teams were incredibly evenly matched for quality. The eight qualifiers for Love's team were Keegan Bradley, Jason Dufner, Zach Johnson, Matt Kuchar, Phil Mickelson, Webb Simpson, Bubba Watson and Tiger Woods while his captain's picks were Jim Furyk, Dustin Johnson, Brandt Snedeker and Steve Stricker.

Olazábal's team was made up of qualifiers Luke Donald, Sergio García, Peter Hanson,

Martin Kaymer, Paul Lawrie, Graeme McDowell, Rory McIlroy, Francesco Molinari, Justin Rose and Lee Westwood. He selected Nicolas Colsaerts and Ian Poulter as his picks.

Paul Lawrie: I made it pretty obvious that playing in the Ryder Cup again was my biggest goal for 2012. I think when I did Ryder Cup commentary at Celtic Manor in 2010, I kind of realised that, man, I should be out there playing in this and not talking about it. We set about a programme and put it in place, to get back in the gym, work a bit harder and get a bit more focused, get some swing thoughts out of my head that were bugging me and get back to just thinking rhythm. You set out your stall early on. I made it known that I wanted to play in the team again, which kind of added a wee bit of pressure I suppose, but the Ryder Cup is so big it's in everyone's thoughts. You put yourself on the line . . . and I made the team, thirteen years after last playing at Brookline. It was just a phenomenal feeling to know that you are actually part of a twelve-man team to represent Europe, especially when you go away from home. It's a huge tournament and it's a huge honour.

The opening morning foursome saw McIlroy and McDowell take on Furyk and Snedeker.

Graeme McDowell: I was actually feeling very calm and very cool on the first morning until I stepped over the ball. I couldn't ignore the silence. The silence was deafening, and it made my mind go blank. It was very strange – and I didn't put a very nice swing on it after that.

Davis Love III: The difference between winning a Major and winning the Ryder Cup? To capture the feeling of the last nine holes or the last few holes of a Major – that nervousness. Friday morning, the first tee shot of the Ryder Cup is like your last shot into the last hole of a Major championship. You're nervous already, and I think it's that little bit of a difference of you're trying to win a Major championship, you don't have a fear of losing it. In the Ryder Cup, there's always that in the back of your mind: 'what if we lose this match, what if we lose this Ryder Cup?' That kind of pressure, you don't really feel in a Major.

Graeme McDowell: It was a great game to start the 2012 Ryder Cup and Rory and I played against two really great competitors in Jim Furyk and Brandt Snedeker. Jim was particularly magnificent. My job was fairly easy – I had the best player in the world beside me.

Jim Furyk: There was a bit of a hoo-ha on the second when Rory's drive landed behind a sprinkler. I looked over to see what was happening. I saw that Graeme was going to get relief and to probably drop the ball into the fringe so they'd be putting rather than chipping. When I looked to see where the ball was, I believed it was a good four inches – I'm probably being conservative – four to five inches ahead of that sprinkler head.

They were going to gain a big advantage by being able to drop that ball. He had a sticky lie and a very delicate chip and to be able to putt that ball would have been a huge advantage and I really didn't feel in any situation, whether it be match play or medal play, that it could be deemed a drop.

It created some tension for the rest of the round. As I told Graeme and Rory, 'I don't blame you for trying, for asking.' Trying is a bad word; I don't blame them for asking. Graeme said, 'I thought it was about a fifty-fifty and you're entitled to your opinion.'

I just disagreed with the official and to have the head referee come out and look at it, he didn't really waste a lot of time. He pretty much immediately said that Graeme needed to play the ball as it lies. I wasn't trying to incite any tension or bother anyone, but it's my job for my teammates and for my team to kind of protect ourselves and the rules.

Graeme McDowell: It was a great game of golf. It really personified the Ryder Cup. We played great to be three up and two very gutsy players came back at us with a few birdies and we were playing the last two holes all square and having to hit some quality shots down the stretch. We did well to win one-up. It's a great feeling to get your team's first point on the board; you need to start building some momentum – that's why we were picked to go out first, so it was great to be able to deliver on that.

Mickelson and Bradley were out second against Donald and García and the American fans suddenly realised that they had a potent team within a team unveiling before their eyes as the old hand Mickelson guided his exuberant young partner around the course; they complemented each other's game superbly and demolished the European pair 4&3.

The US momentum kept going in the third match as Dufner and Zach Johnson rode the wave to play some outstanding golf on their way to a 3&2 victory over Westwood and Molinari. With Westwood's impressive Ryder Cup record, the importance of claiming his scalp early in the tournament was a real fillip for Love's team.

The final match saw Stricker renew his partnership with Woods to take on the cool excellence of Rose and the beating heart of the European team, Poulter.

Ian Poulter: When I was sitting on the stage during the opening ceremony and they announced that Justin [Rose] and I would be playing Tiger [Woods] and [Steve] Stricker in the Friday morning foursomes, I had a bit of a wry smile. Tiger had been two of my three defeats at that point in the Ryder Cup, but Justin and I were pretty pumped to get out there and get a point on the board for Europe. It was all blue early, but they turned it around, and we only managed to secure that point right at the end.

Timing is everything. You know, sometimes if you can hole that birdie putt to win a hole, whether it be a long one and they've got a short one or vice versa, it still means a lot. It's momentum.

For example, I hit a poor second shot on the sixteenth, Tiger hit a great second shot and gave Stricker a chance to win that hole to get it to one down with two to play, which would have been key for them to try and do that. And he missed that putt. That's the wonder of match play. Whether sometimes it's to halve the hole or to win the hole, putts of that length just mean so much.

I don't really know why I tend to play so well in the Ryder Cup. I just love the event more than any other event in the world. I get very excited to play. I get very proud to pull the shirt on and have that crest on my chest. I want to give it my all. I just love it. I was transfixed in '93 watching my first Ryder Cup, and things haven't changed since then.

I wanted to play golf for a living but it was all a bit speculative. But in 1993, I was there when Nick Faldo had his hole-in-one in his singles match against Paul Azinger. That Ryder Cup changed my opinion on golf. It gave me the drive to be the best player I could be. That's where I set myself the goals, so to come from being outside those ropes to playing in so many Ryder Cups is more than a dream come true. But for that year at the Belfry, I might not have chased down any of my golf dreams.

The Ryder Cup is unique. That rivalry between the teams is so intense. It's not that we don't like each other. We are all good friends, both sides of the pond, but there's something about the Ryder Cup that kind of intrigues me. How can you be great mates with somebody, but, boy, you want to kill them in the Ryder Cup?

Sergio García: It's totally different to anything else in golf. When you play in the Ryder Cup and you see and hear the crowd and the energy they bring to the event, it's second to none.

Steve Stricker: I like to compete and I like to win – doesn't matter who it is. But when it comes down to playing Ian Poulter in the Ryder Cup, I don't want to lose to him. When he yells and screams his eyes bug out. That's why you want to beat him. He's a big time competitor. You can tell he's working hard at it and wanting to beat you. And when you come across a guy who really wants to beat you, you really want to beat him. And so I was pumped up going into the match and I was excited to play alongside Tiger.

Davis Love III: Tiger was trying to do it all by himself when he first broke into the team. He was the dominant player in the game and he was trying to give performances that reflected that. When you're that good it takes time to learn that you have to be part of the team rather than be the team, that you have to win points with the help of your partners.

Tiger Woods: I'm certainly responsible for often not playing my best in the Ryder Cup. I often didn't earn the points that I was put out there for. I believe I was out there, what, in five sessions each time [before 2012], and I didn't go 5–0 on our side. So I certainly am a part of that and that's part of being a team. I needed to go get my points for my team, and I didn't do that.

Graeme McDowell: I think it's very difficult to be critical of Tiger in the Ryder Cup. It's a huge game for an underdog to play a Tiger Woods, and they get up for it. They are not expected to win. When expectation levels drop, a player's game tends to improve. A guy who plays Tiger Woods, or a player of that calibre, doesn't expect to win so he lets it all go and he plays out of his skin and gets the upset.

Davis Love III: Match play is just so different. Tiger can play great and his partner not play well, or the other team can play extremely well. There's probably a lot of times where it's just a matter of who you're up against. The other thing is that somebody has to play in Tiger's bubble as his partner. You have to be a special guy to be able to handle that.

It would prove to be another epic battle, one of many that would be fought over the three days at Medinah. In this instance, it was the European pair that emerged triumphant, edging ahead to take the point for their team by winning 2&1.

José María Olazábal: The foursomes is the one format that we've struggled with as a team over the years. I'm not sure why. So I was really content after the first session. Two out of four was a really good, solid start.

Ian Poulter: Obviously you'd love it to be 3–1 or 2½–1½, but on their turf to get two matches each was good. It gets your foot in the door.

José María Olazábal: It wasn't easy to rest guys like Poulter and Donald when they were playing well, but I had told the team on Thursday that I wanted them all to play on that first day so I had to sit down some guys.

It was an understandable decision from the European captain, but not one that was mirrored by his opponent. Love sent the double act of Mickelson and Bradley back into the fray to face McIlroy and McDowell as well as sending out Woods and Stricker to face Westwood and Colsaerts. Love then threw in some new blood, with Watson and Simpson teaming up to play Lawrie and Hanson in the opening tie and then sending out Dustin Johnson and Kuchar to face Rose and Kaymer.

From the outset, it was all the home team. In the opening fourball, Watson came to the tee to rapturous applause and soon got the crowd pumping, conducting them to chant his name and then the war cry of 'USA, USA, USA!' as he swaggered around brandishing his luminous pink driver before settling in to make his shot. It had been a moment that had set the tone for the Americans as they swept through the first three fourballs.

Webb Simpson: I asked Bubba for some advice about how to deal with things because he'd done it before in Wales in 2010. And he said, 'Once you get through that first tee shot you kind of sync in to what it's normally like on a day-to-day tournament.' And I remember that first tee shot, Bubba and I were playing Paul Lawrie and Peter Hanson, and whenever Bubba and I were playing together I hit first. So I hit first and then I looked over to him teeing up and then he looks up at me and Teddy [Scott, Watson's caddie] and he gives him this weird look and Teddy nods back. And I was like, 'What is this, some kind of weird Ryder Cup lingo?' And then Bubba stands up and starts waving his hands up towards the crowd, and they start to cheer and are getting louder and louder – and he won't hit until they're as loud as they can go. And then he just ripped it down the middle, it went 350 yards. We had President George Bush on the tee, Michael Jordan was there, and it was a moment I'll never forget. I was like, 'This is as good as it gets in golf. The US Open was cool, but nothing like this.'

José María Olazábal: I think the reaction to Bubba on the tee caught everyone by surprise. It was the first time any of us had seen a reaction like that on the first tee. I have to say, it was amazing. But that's Bubba.

Paul Lawrie: I played nicely in the afternoon fourballs, even though Peter and I got beaten. I was under par on my own ball. But the American boys, I mean they were ten-under for fourteen holes, seven-under for nine, it was a Ryder Cup record.

The second match saw Mickelson and Bradley take on the Northern Irish pair, McIlroy and McDowell.

Keegan Bradley: I went to Brookline in '99 with my dad. We went Friday and Sunday. I was on my dad's shoulders when Justin [Leonard] made that putt. I was on the eighteenth green but I could see through the trees and I remember seeing all the red shirts running by. Then when the tournament was over, my dad told me to run out to the green with everybody and just meet them back in the same spot. So I took off running and I was running around the green, and that's when I fell in love with the Ryder Cup. The passion that I saw, I had never seen before in golf. And that was something that I promised myself I was going to work towards.

Just before Medinah, Phil [Mickelson] came to me and he said, 'We're going to play in the Ryder Cup and we're going to win.' I'll never forget him saying that to me. It gives me goosebumps even thinking about it. We just matched up well as a pairing. In alternate shot, I knew Phil could get up-and-down from anywhere. So if I hit a bad shot, he could wedge it or chip it and do whatever he does, and it just didn't matter where I hit it. He was going to get it up-and-down. That reassurance in each other's play is huge, it helps you to relax and get in the zone.

We were at the seventeenth in the afternoon fourballs and McIlroy and McDowell were threatening to come back into the match – and I hit my tee shot into the greenside bunker. Then Phil stepped up and hit his to just a few feet of the pin. It was the best shot I'd seen in my entire life. Afterwards, we were running down the fairway, we had our arms around each other, we were screaming; it was like a Patriots game out there.

Phil Mickelson: The way Keegan drives the golf ball off the tee, it just wears down your opponent, watching him hit the ball so long and straight. And the way he putts, it is just off the charts. It was a real pleasure playing alongside him.

It was one of the most emotional days playing a Ryder Cup that we'll ever have. It was one of the biggest highs that we'll ever have. I felt young, and it felt great. I had energy all day. I just felt terrific. I'd say to him, 'Hey, I need a little pep talk,' and he'd just give me something that would get me boosted right up, and I'd end up hitting a good shot.

Davis Love III: Keegan's a great player and he played well. He has that intense look in his eyes that the great players have. I was asking Phil, you know, 'How are you going to handle Keegan? Are you going to help him with his putts or not help him?'

Phil said, 'As long as he gives them that little sideways look, you've got to let him do what he wants to do.'

My son and I were sitting on the side of one green, and Keegan turned his head like that and I said, 'You know, he's going to make this one,' and right in it went. He's a competitor and he's confident in his game and he loves to be there. He loves walking out on that first tee.

Phil Mickelson: I think Keegan and I gelled as well as any American pairing ever has in this competition. The European side has had some great teammates with Seve and Ollie and some others, but to be able to share that experience with Keegan and to partake in his great play and experience the Ryder Cup together was really awesome. We had so much fun. The crowd provided so much energy, and brought our best golf out.

With the final fourball match pitching Woods and Stricker against Westwood and the rookie Colsaerts, it looked almost certain that America were going to make it a clean sweep in the afternoon.

José María Olazábal: Nicolas Colsaerts in the fourballs was extraordinary. Without a doubt. You don't see a rookie coming into a Ryder Cup and playing so well against a strong US pair like that; it doesn't happen.

Nicolas Colsaerts: When you are put under the gun in a match play situation, your focus gets more intense. That's why I like match play. I don't feel nervous about getting into a game and playing some guys in the Ryder Cup. I wouldn't really care who. Whoever you are drawn against and whoever you play with, it doesn't matter. Lee and I went in against Tiger Woods and Steve Stricker on the Friday afternoon fourball and Europe were having a tough time, but I was pretty relaxed and just focused on playing the best I could.

It's funny looking back – it didn't really strike me that much playing Stricker and Woods. When I saw the draw, I thought it was fine. I couldn't really ask for any better, I mean you are going out against Woods and if you get beaten, you get beaten. You have nothing to lose. I didn't want to play any of the guys that were on a hot streak like Keegan [Bradley] or [Jason] Dufner, so I was actually quite alright going out in that type of group. I asked to play with Lee because I knew he was a bit of a boss and I thought I would make my contribution here and there, but I actually turned out to be the big horse in the game.

When you stand on the first tee as a rookie your hands are shaking, your knees are shaking and you feel like you're only going to be able to hit the ball fifty yards – at best. It's like the hundred metres final at the Olympics. The stress and the intensity is there and people say you need to embrace it, but let me tell you, it's pretty difficult. The ball was just a little white blurry spot. I remember telling myself, 'You wanted to be here. Time to show why. There's no backing out now.' I basically closed my eyes and gave muscle-memory a chance to kick in. All of us dream to play in a Ryder Cup because it has such a different meaning and such a different vibe to the kind of golf tournaments that we usually play in.

Woods and Stricker had been trailing two-down on the fifteenth but had reduced the deficit by winning the sixteenth. Colsaerts' putt on the seventeenth maintained their advantage and when both sides parred the eighteenth, the European pair were one-up victors.

Nicolas Colsaerts: I would never have dreamed that I would play as well as I did. When you look back at pictures or footage from the match, you can see that I was just totally in the zone. I made eight birdies and an eagle up against Tiger and Stricker, and I had a great partner in Westwood.

Nicolas Colsaerts fist pumps after his extraordinary debut Ryder Cup round.

Playing at Medinah brought something out of me that doesn't come out very often. It's something very special, especially when you make shots like that down the stretch when you know how much it means and when you see the result at the end of that day. It's indescribable. Seeing how it makes people feel, the looks on their faces, and you feel that energy inside of you when you pull it off . . . not a lot of people get to live those moments and I was fortunate enough to experience them.

José María Olazábal: He made eight birdies and an eagle and the way everything unfolded down the last few holes . . . he made a twenty-foot putt at seventeen and then looked at the crowds, puffed his chest out and said, 'Come on, bring it on.' That was amazing. It was the best record in any Ryder Cup for a rookie. What else can you say?

Lee Westwood: Nicolas was just sensational on the Friday afternoon. I had the best seat in the house and then he brought me in to read a putt on fifteen and I panicked. I wondered why he was even asking me because everything he looked at went in. I mean, why ruin it now?

Nicolas Colsaerts: On the eighteenth, when somebody like Tiger Woods looks at you and says, 'Great playing you, man,' you understand you have done something pretty good. I was so focused. It felt wonderful to be able to produce and deliver on such a big stage with a lot of eyes on you and this unbelievable atmosphere. I also felt very comfortable going out there with Lee.

It was a lot of fun. I've never had so much fun on a golf course. I'd dreamt about times like that. It was the best round I'd ever played. In the circumstances, the eleven other guys I was playing with, a vital point, the last game of the day, first day of a Ryder Cup, then yes, that had to be my best round ever.

Tiger Woods: I really hit it well in the afternoon but we ran into a guy who just made everything. I don't know what Nicolas shot. He was like seven-under through ten. I quit counting after that. It was one of the greatest putting rounds I've ever seen.

Lee Westwood: You never know how people are going to react in their first round at a Ryder Cup. I think Nicolas took to it quite nicely. I don't know what he did Friday morning to set him off but whatever it was, it worked brilliantly.

The score at the end of day one was 5–3 in America's favour.

Graeme McDowell: That point that Lee and Nicolas got was huge. We had really struggled that first day and we got the hair dryer treatment from Ollie on the Friday night.

Rory McIlroy: We got a roasting from him. It was real Sir Alex Ferguson stuff.

Paul Lawrie: The captain was certainly upset on Friday night. He didn't think we had played well enough, made enough birdies, or were into it enough as you need to be for a Ryder Cup. He was really angry, I've never seen him like that before. You can put your arm around people or you can shout at them, and he decided to shout at us.

José María Olazábal: Yeah, I was really hard on them. To be honest, it wasn't my intention for it to come out like that. Some players must have been a little shocked but it wasn't badly intended.

We were behind straight away and at that level it is very hard to get level and then overtake your opponent. I don't try to hide anything, I try to show my feelings and be honest, while also being fair at the same time.

It was a bad moment that evening, I'm not going to hide that. I thought in the fourballs that we were going to do well and it didn't work out that way. But we had another two days to play and a lot of points still on the table, and that's what I told them. We had to step it up. We knew it wasn't going to be easy, so we just had to be ready for the next morning.

In the opening match of the Saturday foursomes, Watson was once again paired with Simpson and, having seen his performance on the opening tee the previous afternoon, his opposition for the session, Rose and Poulter, knew exactly what to expect.

José María Olazábal: I was really impressed with Ian. He knew what Bubba was going to do when he got to the tee, so Ian got in there first.

Poulter got the European fans going just as Watson had done with the home support the previous afternoon. He stood back from the tee and encouraged them to chant. Soon the deafening bawls of, 'Olé, olé, olé, olé!' were echoing across the course.

José María Olazábal: It was just one of those special moments at the Ryder Cup. Ian just transforms himself during that week. But his performance at that first tee said a lot. 'I'm ready for it, are you?'

Ian Poulter: I knew I had to get the crowd pumped up and on my side before we started. I knew Bubba was going to get the crowd going when he came to the tee, so I had to get in there first. It was a psychological tactic. I got the crowd pumping before I hit my first shot and I had to do it – he was going to do it. He had all their backing so I needed our backing. I said to the boys the night before, 'Don't worry, I'll have my two minutes tomorrow.' And it worked. It was great and it got the ball rolling.

Justin Rose: The crowd makes the intensity. It's red versus blue and two sets of fans, home and away; it's less the individuals out on the golf course. Personal friendships are put aside for the week. The Ryder Cup transcends golf and attracts sports fans, not just golf fans. There are different types of behaviour out there. The players have to go and play each other the following week, so there is respect inside the ropes. But emotions run way higher because the crowds charge the emotions so much. The players in recent years have done a great job keeping sportsmanship first and foremost because the lines outside the ropes do get a bit blurry at times.

It was a signal of intent and the European pair delivered on it, playing some magnificent and often gritty golf to win the encounter one-up.

Justin Rose: It was a good point for us. We didn't actually play our best stuff but to win that point was massive. It was a difficult game psychologically. Bubba is Bubba. He was pretty special on the Friday and Ian and I talked about it on the Friday night. We knew he was going to get the crowd to cheer as he was hitting so why not stand there and enjoy the fun of what it was? My heart rate went from, I would say, one hundred to one hundred and eighty pretty quickly; it was a great buzz for sure.

Bubba Watson: We just kept missing putts that morning. We could never get any momentum going our way. They were holing putts, they were playing great golf, and they just beat us. But that can be the problem with foursomes, it can be hard to get a rhythm playing every other shot.

That, however, was as good as it got for the visitors as the home team exploded back into life in the other three matches. Bradley and Mickelson played magnificently once more in a 7&6 evisceration of Westwood and Donald; Dufner and Zach Johnson beat Colsaerts and García 2&1; and then Furyk and Snedeker defeated McIlroy and McDowell one-up to take the overall score to 8–4.

Brandt Snedeker: I got the monkey off my back on the Saturday. Losing to McIlroy and McDowell on the Friday was hard to take, to give away that half a point on eighteen the way I drove it, but when you've got a player like Jim [Furyk], you're never out of it. Jim played great coming down the stretch on Friday and he played great again on Saturday for us to beat McIlroy and McDowell. I can't tell you how much pressure there was on those shots coming down the stretch and he just flagged it right every time.

Rory McIlroy: We made a couple of birdies coming in but it just wasn't enough. We got behind early again and then we tried our hardest to get back into the match but we just couldn't get there.

José María Olazábal: The matches weren't going well. It was a real worry. But you have a time frame when you have to put your pairings in for the afternoon and that happens before the morning matches are all finished. Your frame of mind is in a different process. You're not thinking so much about what is going on as what to do in the afternoon. For me, it was a very difficult moment. At that time you're thinking, 'OK, we're behind, we're going to lose some more points this morning.' So my original plan to have everyone out there again had to be thrown away. And those are the tough decisions you have to make. I had to go to Peter Hanson and Martin Kaymer and say, 'Listen, you're not going to play this afternoon.'

You just have to talk to them, look them straight in the eye and say, 'Listen, I know you're an important part of this team and the time will come when you're going to have to prove that.'

As the morning games are finishing, the afternoon games are teeing off, so you have no time to really talk to the guys in the locker room, you have to be out there on the course. So all I could do was to say, 'Look, if we are going to have even the smallest chance tomorrow, we need to do well this afternoon.'

But improvement was not forthcoming, not immediately anyway. The US were keeping their foot on the Europeans' throats as first Dustin Johnson and Kuchar beat Colsaerts and Lawrie one-up and Watson and Simpson made amends for their morning loss by comfortably beating Rose and Molinari 5&4 for the Americans' fifth consecutive win. Europe were facing oblivion.

Nicolas Colsaerts: I played the Saturday morning with Sergio and then fourballs with Paul in the afternoon. Both those defeats were a tough pill to swallow because it helped the US to get to a four-point advantage. It was a pretty close contest and it was maybe just the holing of a putt here or there that gave them that advantage coming into Sunday.

Webb Simpson: You don't realise how bad you want to win until you're on the team. We're on a tour that has $350 million in prize money every year and you'd think you'd be more excited about that, than an event where you don't get paid anything, but it's not about that it's about your teammates and your country and you want to win for them so, so bad.

Davis Love III: After three sessions we had a considerable four-point lead, with the team of Keegan Bradley and Phil Mickelson winning three times. Fred Couples, one of my four assistants, said to me, 'Man, that Keegan Bradley is on fire. Ride him all the way to the house.' In other words, he wanted me to play the Bradley–Mickelson team again on Saturday afternoon in session four. I know a lot of fans and commentators were thinking the same thing. But Phil told me he was tired after three matches and wanted to rest for

Phil Mickelson and Keegan Bradley. *Getty Images*

the Sunday singles. There was no reason to play Keegan with a partner with whom he had not practised. There was no reason to mess with the order.

Paul Lawrie: We were all surprised when Davis Love sat out Mickelson and Bradley from the afternoon fourballs. When you've got a partnership like that – the two of them were on fire – I just don't get how you sit them out. The captain's job is unbelievably tough, it's impossible to get it right every step of the way, but we were like, man, he's sitting out his two best players.

Phil Mickelson: As far as playing Keegan and I again on the Saturday afternoon, Keegan and I knew going into Saturday morning that we were not playing in the afternoon and we said on the first tee, 'We are going to put everything we have into this one match because we are not playing in the afternoon.'

And when we got to the tenth hole, I saw Davis there and I went to him and I said, 'Listen, I know you are going to get pressure to put us out again this afternoon because we are playing so well but you are seeing our best and you cannot put us on in the afternoon because emotionally and mentally we are not prepared for it.'

I told him we had other guys that were dying to get out there and that we had put everything into our morning match and that we wouldn't have anything later so we had to stick to our plan. So you cannot put any of the blame for that on Davis. If anything, it was me because I went to him on the tenth and said that to him.

Paul Lawrie: Nicolas Colsaerts and I played solidly against Dustin Johnson and Matt Kuchar, but we just couldn't get the win, losing by a single hole. How we lost that game is just incredible; the feeling in your gut is just horrible, when you know you should have won and you've actually lost. When you play on your own and you shoot 80 you're disappointed, but it's not a big issue, you get on with it. When you are there with eleven other people, a captain and vice-captains, it's a horrible feeling letting your team down.

The final two matches of the day pitted García and Donald against Woods and Stricker, and McIlroy and Poulter against Dufner and Zach Johnson. If the home side continued winning, the Ryder Cup returning to American shores was all but a foregone conclusion.

José María Olazábal: There's very little for a captain to do at that stage. You just have to bite your nails and hope that your players will do it for you.

Sergio García: Luke and I knew how important it was to the team to get some blue on the board. I was struggling a little bit that week. I didn't feel very comfortable, but I putted well, I hit some good birdies and then he took over. The way Luke held the match together on the back nine was amazing.

Luke Donald: We knew it was going to be a tough match that afternoon. You never give up against Tiger and Stricker. They are a formidable pairing and they played great on the back nine. They birdied all the tough holes like twelve and thirteen, Tiger hit an unbelievable shot there and again on sixteen. The holes where you thought par may have been good enough for a half, you needed birdie.

I felt really calm all day. I don't know why but I just did. They were making birdies all the time and I knew we had to do the same. We had to hold them off. We hung in there and we were able to match birdies on seventeen, which was key for us, and we just held on there right at the last. That was big. It gave us a lift that we needed. We were still going to be in it on Sunday.

García and Donald's one-up victory gave Europe their first point of the afternoon, but if they were to stand any real chance the next day, they desperately needed another.

Ian Poulter: It was a surprise to be paired with Rory, to be honest, I wasn't expecting it. I'd played a lot of golf with Rory down the years but I'd never partnered him before. But I thought it was going to be exciting, going out there with the world number one.

We went down early and we weren't holing putts. That was difficult because you find yourself having to try to get something going. But it took forever. We were getting royally beaten at that stage and I remember talking as we went up eight and nine and saying, 'We have to hole something, whether it's a chip, a long putt, something to give us a spark.'

We both recognised during the round that I was flat, he was flat, there was no energy in the side at all and it was because we were being beaten so badly. It's really hard to get your adrenaline back up when things aren't looking good.

It took all the way until thirteen to get that. Rory got a great iron approach and then drained a fifteen foot putt and it was just enough to get us going and start to turn that match around.

We'd been two-down on the thirteenth and Rory's birdie reduced it to one. After the thirteenth, my putter warmed up nicely then it just went crazy. It was tough out there with the crowds; we were in Chicago, they'd had a few drinks and they weren't making it easy for us. I'll be honest, it was pretty brutal.

I went crazy when I holed a twelve-footer at the sixteenth. That's me being me, I guess. The Ryder Cup is like nothing else; you can't do that in any other situation. I've seen it over the years with Seve and Ollie and Faldo and all the guys. You know that's why the Ryder Cup is so special, because you can hole a putt at the right time and it can mean so much, all your emotions just come out.

Davis Love III: Poulter's eyes looked like they would pop out of his head if he got any more excited. He got under our skin, but there's nothing wrong with that. That's Ryder Cup golf. Seve was the same way. Poulter got five birdies on those last five holes. We couldn't stop him.

Ian Poulter: The pressure was immense. You can't help but see 20,000 people in the grandstand. I had all that in my peripheral vision and I was thinking, 'I cannot wait to hole this putt, to fist pump, to go straight to my team and just give them all the energy that I have possibly got because we've still got the chance to win.'

I was stunned, overwhelmed by how much of the attention focused on me afterwards. When you're involved with the team, you are part of the team and don't want to take anything away from them. But I suppose what happened on that Saturday night was a big turning point and that's why there was so much interest in me. That and the way I responded, I guess.

Sergio García: Ian's 'Mr Ryder Cup', he thrives on it. He's the one player you really want in your team. He will give everything for his team and he somehow always manages to play at an even higher level when it comes to the event.

Rory McIlroy: Ian just gets that look in his eye, especially when he makes one of those big putts, and he's fist pumping, and he'll look right through you. It's just great to see the enthusiasm and the passion that he has. The Ryder Cup brings the best out of Ian and if it wasn't for him we wouldn't have even had a chance.

José María Olazábal: I think the Ryder Cup should build a statue to him. That's Poulter. That's why we say he's such a special character for the Ryder Cup. He thrives in it. He loves to be in the spotlight. He loves to be in the kind of situations that he found himself in coming down the back nine. And what he did was just outstanding.

What many people don't realise is that his back was to us when he made that putt on eighteen. And when he made it, instead of just celebrating, he turned around and looked at the team. And that is when everything changed.

Ian Poulter: The trick is to feel that pumped up, but to keep your focus. For me, getting to that state of intensity actually helps me perform. I don't know why. I went through the photos of the high points in my career while working on my autobiography and what I noticed was that on the pictures where I'd won individual events, or even been doing well at the Majors, the faces I pulled weren't anything like that guy in the Ryder Cup pictures. My expressions are totally different in the Ryder Cup photos, but it's exactly the same expression in the snaps of 2004, 2008, 2010, 2012 and 2014. And it's not just when I've been playing, but when I've been in a buggy watching my teammates holing a putt or something. The same expression. That just shows me there is something about that event which gets to me like nothing else. Yeah, I knew the feelings were different. But seeing the way my face changed amazed me.

For 103 weeks of the cycle as a pro golfer, it's not just about winning or losing. Face it, pros lose for the majority of their careers. Even the greats have more weeks when they don't win than when they do win. So if you finish second, or third, or whatever, you have 'lost' but you've had a good week. That's the way golf is. There's a lot of grey. But in the Ryder Cup it's black and white. When the game starts on Friday, you know that come Sunday evening you're either going to have won or lost. There's nothing in between, not even a draw because the team who keep the cup has essentially won. That's exhilarating and unique. Everything has to go on the line, because it's all or nothing. And that's why the passion pours out.

Zach Johnson: They birdied the last six holes and Poulter birdied the last five holes by himself. It wasn't like we gave it to them, either. We had opportunities. We missed a couple of putts but made some putts, too. That was just a buzzsaw at the end. There's nothing you can do, just tip your hat and shake his hand. But we were pleased to be up 10–6 at that point.

José María Olazábal: To be totally honest, I thought early in the afternoon session, when we were losing three and tying in one, that it was pretty much over. But the boys did fantastically to come back and fight all the way. We managed to win the last two and we actually had a good chance of tying the third. I think that was crucial. I always thought that they were vital – they gave us hope, not just by winning them but the way it happened, especially with Ian. Birdying the final five holes, and knowing that they were a must because the US team had shorter birdie putts that were pretty much conceded, knowing that, on top of all the pressure that goes around it, it was just amazing. I've never seen anything like it in the Ryder Cup before.

Paul Lawrie: I'm not sure any other player on either team would have holed all five putts. The shortest one was about twelve feet. Man, Ian just loves it. I was sitting with [one of the European vice-captains] Darren Clarke on the last green, when he was over his putt. I said to Darren, 'What do you think?' And he said, 'Not only will he hole it, but he'll take ten minutes to hole it!' It's just a great line and Darren was right, he was pacing and strutting about! Ian just feels as though he was born for moments like that.

José María Olazábal: I didn't believe that it was over. That's what I learned from Seve, and that's what I tried to pass to the players. It's not over until it's over.

Justin Rose: I did a lot of thinking on the Saturday night. I took my clubs back to the hotel.

I went back to my room and hit a few putts on the carpet. I thought, 'If I'm going to win my game tomorrow, I need to do something different.' For five minutes on the carpet, I clicked onto something about my grip pressure that allowed the putter to swing a little bit more freely. Just those little things; you never know when they're going to pay off.

Luke Donald: Spirits were low midway through Saturday afternoon, but when we came and won those last two matches, we really had a pep in our step. I think we just talked about it, that we still had a great chance, that we had an opportunity to make history. That Seve was watching down on us. And we hoped some of Seve's magic could rub off on the boys coming home.

Ian Poulter: The team spirit in that room on Saturday night was special. I spoke to a few guys. We were four points behind but there was something in that team room that just sparked the whole thing. There was a glimmer of hope, something made us think we had a chance. No one really made a speech. We discussed certain things about the golf course, decisions to make on certain holes, the par fives and other bits.

We had the pin locations, we discussed certain holes that could be key during the round. But, honestly, the team was pumped. We were really, really up. We were four points behind but it was as if we were just going out to play all square. We were ready. Did we honestly think we could win eight-and-a-half points? Yes, we did.

Paul Lawrie: We talked about the draw on Saturday night and José went through it. 'I need you all to know, I'm looking at that and I'm telling you, this is possible, this is possible,' he said. All of a sudden the whole team room was up for it. He was good at that, the motivational stuff and his speeches. I've never cried so much in my life. All of us were crying just about every meeting. Unbelievable, you've no idea the stuff he was coming away with. One of the meetings, the night before the gala dinner, he went through each individual player and told a story about playing with that player and what that player meant to him. We were all just blubbing. At team meetings he was just phenomenal.

The pressure was incredible. We were sitting in the team meeting on Saturday night and José said the first five guys must win or we've no chance. I was fifth. So you say, 'Right, I've just got to beat my guy, take him down.'

Sergio García: Some of us were in this position in '99, although on the other side, and you know, we knew what happened there. When you're in that position with the 10–4 lead, you're expected to win it, so the pressure goes on the team in the lead to close it all out. So we knew if we got going early, as they did in '99, we could put the American team in a situation where the pressure was on. Obviously everything was going their way throughout the whole week. You know, they were making the putts, they were getting the good breaks here and there. We were just wanting to change that a little bit and see if we could do the same thing they did to us in '99 and see how they reacted to that.

José María Olazábal: Seve's favourite colour was blue and I wanted our team to play in that, but as the home team the US had first pick and their colours are obviously blue and red. I spoke to Davis and explained what I wanted to do and why and I think it's a real measure of the man that he understood and agreed to let us go out there in blue and white.

Davis Love III: We loved our Sunday line-up. I say 'we' because the team functioned as a group. I was a players' manager. I listened to my assistants, the caddies, the wives and most particularly the players. We reached a consensus on every big decision we made, from the four players I hand-picked for the team to our Sunday order. Tiger said, 'Put Strick and me at the end. I don't think it will come to us, but if it does, we'll be ready.' Tiger had won three times that year. He's the greatest match play golfer ever. He's the greatest golfer ever. Hearing those words from him was enough for me.

Luke Donald: It was a big honour for me that Ollie had enough trust in me to go out and get that first point for Europe. It means a lot to go out first and lead the team, and I did what I had to do. But I felt a lot of responsibility. I think Ollie expected a lot from me. He rested me on the Friday afternoon for a reason: to be strong for the end of Saturday and for Sunday, and I managed to deliver two points.

I had to go out there and get up early against Bubba and put some blue on the board to inspire the others. Standing on that first tee, it's as nervous as you feel in golf, I think. You are not just playing for yourself, you are playing for your teammates. The atmosphere and the vibe, it makes you nervous, but in a good way. I killed that tee shot down the first and I knew I was off and running. It was a fun match.

Bubba pushed me really hard but luckily I was able to get a good lead on him. I had my chance on fourteen to kill the match and misread the putt. Bubba pulled off an incredible chip in on sixteen to keep the match going.

There was a real worry in the back of my mind that he might push me all the way, and I began to worry that it might go to eighteen – and I don't know what I would have done if it had got to eighteen having been four up on fourteen. The nerves were starting to build and Bubba was putting some serious pressure on me. He made some great birdies and the chip in on sixteen was unexpected but in the Ryder Cup, you've got to expect that.

The strategy was to get out and get some blue on the board early. Step one was me and luckily I managed to get the job done.

Webb Simpson: I was pleased when I drew Ian Poulter for the singles and that we would be going out second. I'd been playing well all week, and I knew he had been playing well, so I wanted to play him – but I found the course tough to play. I was hitting some pretty good shots, but just couldn't quite make any putts. It was unfortunate to bogey seventeen like I did. Seventeen was a tricky hole, and I felt pretty good over it, it was just a tough hole. The last thing you want to do is balloon one and leave it in the water, so I hit it hard but it kind of got away from me. It was unfortunate to end it the way I did, but you know what, it was an incredible week. Ian had a great week and hats off to him. He's a great match play player, a great player in general. I have a ton of respect for him.

Ian Poulter: I just had to take seventeen on. The Ryder Cup is not for the faint of heart. Sometimes you just have to buckle up and hit a shot. You know, it came off on seventeen and I hit a pretty good shot on the last.

I didn't have my best golf early on and I made a few mistakes and Webb is a solid player, a gutsy player, and he was always going to be in the hole. But the plan was to bring home blue points early and I was able to play my part in that. We were getting ourselves back into it.

José María Olazábal: Rory was due out third and we were all getting ready on the Sunday morning when all of a sudden we realised Rory was not there and started to look for him.

Rory McIlroy: I'd been in my hotel room relaxing and then I noticed I'd had a few calls from the guys. I was like, 'Why are they ringing me? I've got two hours before my tee-time.' I had been watching TV and it said that I had a 12:25 pm tee-off time – but it was Eastern Time – one hour ahead of Chicago.

I started to get ready and there was a knock on the door. It was some of the European Tour people who said 'You've got half an hour before your tee time.' I started to panic and they said, look, we've got everything organised,' and told me that there was a state trooper outside who would drive me straight to the course.

It would have been bad enough missing my tee-time playing for myself but letting down all my teammates and the whole of Europe? I've never been so worried in my whole life. I didn't know if I was going to make it. I haven't even considered what would have happened if everything had gone pear-shaped that Sunday morning in Medinah. It would have been huge. Imagine if it had come down to a point, that point. It would have been fine if it was just me that I was going to let down. But it wouldn't have been. It would have been the eleven other guys on the team and the captain and the vice-captains and all those fans. So no I don't dare to think about what would have happened. It was scary, it really was.

José María Olazábal: Everyone was asking 'Where's Rory?' He was teeing off in bloody twenty-five minutes. Once we got hold of him on the phone and he was updating us on where he was on the road, telling us that he was in a police car and going really fast, we knew by 11:05 a.m. that he was going to make it.

Rory McIlroy: We were already in a bad enough position. It was 10–6 and the last thing the team needed was me to have to forfeit. I calmed as soon as I got to the course. If I warm up for forty minutes, it's a long time for me anyway. I only warmed up for twenty-five minutes before I won the PGA in 2012. So getting there late was probably a really good thing. I didn't have to think about it too much. I was lucky the state trooper was there and once I knew I was going to make it, I told myself: 'Let's try and keep it together for the first six holes, try to keep it tight, keep it all square or even to one-down'.

There was a lot of positivity in the team room on Saturday night, especially the way we finished. Winning those two points in the last two games was crucial and we focused on carrying that momentum into Sunday. When I got the match-up with Keegan, I liked it. I liked the idea of playing one of their strongest players and going out there and putting a point on the board early for the team, although it wasn't the pre-round preparation that I'd envisioned! As it turned out, I was two-up after six, and then I was like, 'Well, this is

Justin Rose celebrates holing his huge putt on the seventeenth. *Getty Images*

actually OK.' It ended up that it was the best golf I'd played the whole week. I shot a 65 or 66. It all worked out.

Justin Rose: I was at number four in the singles, up against Phil Mickelson so I knew I had to play my top game to beat him. I have always enjoyed playing with Phil and he is always an exciting player to watch. We all behave a bit differently at a Ryder Cup and there is a bit more eye-to-eye contact than at a PGA Tour event; you're not walking down the fairway asking how the family are. He is the perfect gentleman, that always strikes me about him and he was a gracious loser that day. We played together in a PGA Tour event about a year later and my caddie and I were trying to pull his leg a bit asking how he got on in the singles. And he truly couldn't remember who he played so we were thinking that we really must have left a big impression on him! But that's one of Phil's biggest strengths that he can let go of things that happen on the course, even if they don't go his way.

The Ryder Cup is as big as it gets, and to make three putts like I did on the last three greens, it felt like a lot of hard work paying off. I wouldn't say I've made three bigger putts back-to-back in my career ever.

Having an eight-foot putt to halve the hole on sixteen, to dig myself out of that game was incredible. I felt like we needed that point, as well, to have any chance. On the seventeenth, Phil was looking confident like he was going to make his chip. Then he missed and I buried a forty-foot putt – that was one of the best feelings of my life.

And then the eighteenth. Well, then I knew how Ian Poulter feels. I had a glance down and looked at my left sleeve where we had the silhouette of Seve. That's the kind of stuff he would have pulled out of the bag.

Those putts on sixteen, seventeen and eighteen were the three biggest putts I'd ever made back-to-back in my career under pressure. When I was standing over the putt on the eighteenth, I was shaking a little bit and I said to myself, 'Rosey, this is what the whole week could come down to for you. If you miss it, you might feel disappointed, but if you make this putt, it's going to be a good week for you.' And I just did what I had to do.

Phil Mickelson: I felt like I had control. I had a chance to go two-up on sixteen, and Justin made a good twelve-footer on top of me to halve it, and he then made that forty-footer to win the hole on seventeen; and then on the last hole he made a great birdie. He played some great golf. I thought I played pretty good and shot a decently low round. But the last three holes, he played phenomenally.

Paul Lawrie: When Justin Rose turned his match it was then that I thought we had a chance. For him to hole putts on sixteen, seventeen and eighteen to win against Mickelson when he was one down was just huge.

I remember Lee Westwood summed it up well: 'Once it starts going wrong, and once one or two start faltering, it just goes down the whole team.' You couldn't fail to look at the boards. It just snowballed down to everyone.

Davis Love III: We had a couple of matches that got flipped by guys making incredible putts. I mean, I was behind the sixteenth green, I came to watch Phil play sixteen, seventeen and eighteen, and when Phil made that putt at sixteen, I thought he had just done something spectacular for the Ryder Cup.

And then right on top of him Rose hits those putts, boom, boom, boom, and all of a sudden Phil got beat. I don't think he lost, he just got beat by a guy that finished well. Things like that kept happening to us. You know, Phil played great. As I said, Tiger played great. A lot of guys played great and just got beat by a guy that played a little bit better.

Paul Lawrie: There is not a golfer or sportsman in the world that does not go through poor spells and questions if they can do what they are supposed to be good at again. In golf things can change so quickly. It's amazing how in January you can be hitting it like a dog and missing every cut and then in February, March you have one good week and you are off. This game can be a torture like that. You hit a poor shot and you have to wait before you can put it right. You might hit two in a row, make a double and you are thinking, 'Man, I just can't do this anymore.' That's how it is.

I had a few years when things were hard, but two things changed for me. Doing Ryder Cup commentary at Celtic Manor in Wales had a huge impact. Sitting there talking about something you think you should be playing in was very motivating. I had not been to a Ryder Cup since playing in '99, just watched on television. The whole thing was massive. I was thinking, 'I want to be part of that again. I think I'm capable if I just knuckle down.'

Around about the same time, my eldest son beat me. It sounds a bit silly, and I was proud of him, but I was thinking that I should not be getting beaten by a fifteen-year-old kid. So I did what I had to do to start climbing the rankings again. A lot of hard work, basically.

So I had that all in mind when I went out against Brandt Snedeker. I had been there in '99 and experienced the pain of losing and I wanted to make amends, to set the record straight again. It was great to be able to come out and get a blue point on the board and be a real part of it all.

When I holed my twelve-footer for par at the third I knew I would beat him. It's amazing how you get those feelings. Then I chipped in at four, eagled five and just played some lovely golf. I was six-under after fifteen holes. I played unbelievable tee to green on the Sunday. You will never ever feel more pressure than I felt in the Sunday morning singles. If you can stand up and handle that you can do anything.

Nicolas Colsaerts: I was out after Paul and I had a very close match against Dustin Johnson. He and I pretty much played the same. He gave me two holes and then I gave him two. Then when you go down with six, seven holes to go, you can't be giving away two holes to your opponent. And then he made a birdie on sixteen and I just couldn't follow. I remember seeing that I was the first game that was red on the board. I was devastated. I kind of lost it a little bit on the last couple of holes. I couldn't handle it. When you realise that you are the first game to lose . . . I remember bawling at the back of the sixteenth green; I was interviewed by the BBC and I answered a question and then started bawling like a twelve-year-old. I had seen all the blue and I felt like I had let everybody down, knowing that I was playing well, the match was still in my grasp and I didn't deliver and lost 3&2. I lost three holes in succession, fourteen, fifteen and sixteen and it was game over. It just went past so quickly but it was a great experience. It gets you through the guts and it's very, very special.

Zach Johnson: There was a lot of blue on the board by the time I stepped out to play Graeme McDowell. But that wasn't very surprising, to be honest. Good teams rise up. We rose up in 2010 early on, and the European team rose up in 2012 early on.

It was very tough. I mean, early on I felt great, one foot in front of the other and I just got going in a good rhythm, hitting solid shots that put some pressure on him. I didn't have to make putts to win holes, which was nice. But the putt on sixteen, I hadn't made a putt all day – frankly, I didn't make many putts that week – but I knew that with Europe making a comeback I had to get the halve at least. To win it was great to get another point back on the board for us and with Dustin [Johnson] winning as well [against Nicolas Colsaerts], I hoped it would help stem the tide and get us back in control. I was playing a very formidable foe in Graeme, who has an amazing Ryder Cup record, and was a good friend more than anything – he and Kenny, his caddie. It was hard; those two guys are as classy as it comes, so I felt very fortunate to come out with the win.

Sergio García: I had a really tough match against Jim Furyk. And it was probably a little bit tougher for myself because I wasn't feeling a hundred per cent with my game that week, but somehow I managed to hit enough good shots. I think there were a couple of key moments. I was able to halve on eleven and then won thirteen with a great up and down; I think the sixteenth hole was probably heartbreaking for him, because he hit a great putt. I managed to get a great up and down from the front bunker to win the hole and go two-up with two to go and he lipped out.

Seventeen is a tough hole with the pressure. He pulled it left and I hit a decent shot to the middle of the green, and he didn't manage to get up and down.

Jim Furyk: I think the wind was a little confusing for the players at times. At seventeen I was a little bit in between clubs. I didn't want to go long there so I took the lesser of the two, tried to give it a little bit more, and in doing so, you know, hit the ball a little too hard. It rode the wind, got in that back left bunker. I hit a great bunker shot but it caught the collar and shot to the right and left myself, what, about a twelve-footer straight uphill that I misread.

Davis Love III: Jim walked by me after losing the seventeenth hole, the Ryder Cup on the line. I wanted to say something, but what could I say? He walked by me with that fierce game face of his on, and frustratingly I found myself saying nothing. But the fact is, in golf it's better to err on the side of saying too little than too much. And I'm sure there were times I said too much.

Jim Furyk: At eighteen I hung my drive a touch to the right. I was actually surprised it was in the bunker. I hit a very good second shot and was a little surprised to see it go as long as it did. I hit my first putt exactly how I wanted; I thought I hit it within three or four feet, but it just kept trickling out; and I hit my second putt pretty much exactly where I wanted to, and it never took the break. I hit it what I thought was right edge or outside, and it stayed there the whole time and caught a piece of the hole.

Sergio García: It was huge to get that point for the team and to take us right to the brink of retaining the cup. We knew it was very difficult to be able to put ourselves in front of a very good team, but we believed we could do it. We absolutely believed.

Luke Donald: I watched Sergio come in against Furyk and when he won, a little unexpectedly, turning over a couple of holes at the end, then I sort of started doing the math and thought, well actually, we might have a chance here . . .

Lee Westwood: It was such a nerve-wracking day. I was nervous over that one-footer at the end [he won 3&2]; I tell you what, that's pressure. I don't blame Matt Kuchar for not giving it to me. I was shaking like a leaf. It is the ultimate pressure in golf. You're playing for a lot of pride, and it was so nice to roll it in and win.

I felt like I let my teammates down over the first two days, I didn't play well. But thankfully I played really well in the singles. The whole thing was just immense.

Steve Stricker: You know, I had a pretty good idea that my match against Martin Kaymer was going to be important pretty early in the round, maybe even at the turn. When I went past the board at the tenth tee, I saw a lot of blue and I started doing the math – and I figured that it was going to come down to Tiger or me in the last two groups.

Martin Kaymer: Saturday was very difficult for me. I wanted to prove I could do better than I'd done on Friday because on Friday I didn't play good golf. And I didn't get the chance to play on Saturday which was fair enough. It was José María's decision, and I had to respect that, but I definitely wanted to show him that I could win a match at Medinah.

I texted Bernhard Langer on the Friday evening and asked if we could meet on Saturday. I wanted to talk to him about the Ryder Cup because I felt like my attitude . . . I would say I was not as inspired as I should have been. We talked a little bit about a bunch of stuff, and he has been a fantastic role model for me, and he's always there if I need him. And that is very rare to have someone like him that you can ask whenever you need to.

I got to sixteen and José María told me, 'We need your point. And I don't really care how you do it; just deliver.' But I like those instructions; very straightforward. That's the way we Germans are.

I was only six when Europe lost at Kiawah Island but I know it was talked about a lot afterwards. When I went behind my putt [on eighteen] I saw a footprint and for half a second Bernhard crossed my mind. But I thought, 'OK, it's not going to happen again, it's not going to happen again.' And to be honest with you, I didn't really think about missing. There was only one choice you have; you have to make it. If you stick to the facts of the putt it was the easiest one you could have, uphill, inside right. We have that putt a million times so I just thought, 'Step up, make it.'

Steve Stricker: I knew it was going to be important and we just . . . I didn't get it done. I had a couple of opportunities but just let a couple putts slip by, a couple shots here and there.

It was pretty disappointing, but still a great experience. We really came together as a team and we had so much fun. And to see everybody get together after it was all said and done, and still be a team, be united as a team, I thought was pretty cool to see.

Yeah, disappointing, but still, I love all those guys. We all played very well all week and just came out on the short end.

Martin Kaymer: It felt a little strange being called the hero. It was such a fine line between being the hero or the biggest idiot. I was very surprised how many people came up to congratulate me. I made the last putt but at the end of the day I only got one point while other guys inspired the team a lot more than me. What Ian Poulter did on Saturday is difficult to put into words. I think he at least deserves more credit than anyone else on the team.

I was inspired talking to Bernhard but I got even more inspired by Poulter. I told Ian that I thought about him on the sixteenth on Sunday afternoon. When I had to make a par putt on sixteen, I thought, 'Come on, if he can do it, you can do it, too, so show him that he inspired you.' Ian should be part of the Ryder Cup forever.

And you know, when I stood over that final putt on the eighteenth, I was not that nervous. I was so very controlled because I knew exactly what I had to do. But if you ask me now how that putt went and how it rolled, I have no idea. I can't remember. When it went in, I was just very happy, and that is something that I will remember probably for the rest of my life and hopefully I can talk about it when I have some grandchildren one day.

It's a feeling that I'd never had before. The Major wins [PGA 2010 and US Open 2014] were just for myself, but I could see the guys behind me, my brother was there and my father was there, Sergio ran onto the green. Now I knew how it really feels to win the Ryder Cup.

José María Olazábal: The rollercoaster of emotions that I had to go through that week was unbelievable. You all know how much the Ryder Cup has meant to me in my career, and on top of that I had Seve's memory present all week. It was a huge relief in a way, and a huge satisfaction. That's why when Martin made that putt I looked up in the skies

Martin Kaymer celebrates his putt which retained Europe the Ryder Cup.

and gave a thought to Seve. That was it. I didn't completely express my emotions at that moment, because I was trying to hold on.

Ian Poulter: It was one of the most incredible experiences I'm probably ever going to have in my golfing career. I just don't know how you can possibly top that. There were so many factors – Justin's putts, Sergio's chip in. It was the most amazing team rally you could ever see; the best sporting comeback of all time. That's what makes me proud. Not what I did individually.

Tiger Woods: Despite all that had been going on, I had just kept focused on my point. But I was two-down through three, so I didn't really pay a lot of attention to the boards. Just because I had to get my own game, my own match back to where it was all square, if not put a red on the board. And I didn't really start paying much attention until I got to seventeen and everything started coming together and it looked like Europe had a really good chance of retaining the cup.

I went one up at seventeen, and I asked Joey [LaCava, his caddie] what was going on down eighteen; because my responsibility was to be able to get my point. And then he said that Europe had a chance to win on that hole, or retain the cup.

Then after that all went down, my putt was useless. It was inconsequential. So I hit it too quick, and gave him [Francesco Molinari] his putt, and it was already over.

It's the second time that's happened to me, losing the Ryder Cup while still being on the fairway. It happened at the Belfry [in 2002] on seventeen playing Jesper [Parnevik] and our match was inconsequential and it was the same thing here – our match suddenly became inconsequential, the cup was already over before we finished.

Francesco Molinari: I went out against Tiger two years previously, I played good golf and I just got crushed. So the plan was to go out, do the same, play my golf, and I played well. I had a couple of chances on the last three holes to go one-up. But then, you know, to get the half, obviously seeing Martin holing the putt on the eighteenth was a huge relief, and getting the overall win was even better.

Davis Love III: We were all kind of stunned. We suddenly knew what the '99 Ryder Cup must have felt like for Europe. It was a little bit shocking. We were playing so well, everybody on our team was playing so well, we just figured it didn't matter how we sent them out there. But we put who we thought was our hot players up front and we put who we thought was our steady players in the back that would get us points. We all thought it would come down to Jason Dufner, and he played very, very well [beating Peter Hanson two-up]. We just got a couple of matches flipped there in the middle that cost us. But that's golf. In the end we didn't play well enough. We could have laid them out there in about any order and played like that. It wouldn't have really mattered. The guys had a great week, had a lot of fun, and they played well. They played a lot of good golf, and so did the other side. It was a tough defeat to take but ultimately the team understood, that's just golf sometimes.

Nicolas Colsaerts: You ride such a big emotional wave when you play in a Ryder Cup and when you win it, when you've dreamed about playing in it for so long . . . I kind of felt a little depressed after it was all over. It had been such a high, such a major thing to be part of.

Davis Love III: We came to Chicago as a team and left as an even more united one. We'll be bonded for life by what we did at Medinah. Being captain of those players was the greatest honour of my golfing life.

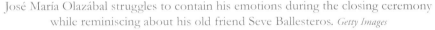

José María Olazábal struggles to contain his emotions during the closing ceremony while reminiscing about his old friend Seve Ballesteros. *Getty Images*

Webb Simpson: The hardest part for me was seeing Davis and how much he wanted it for us – and then how he took a lot of the criticism for Sunday. A lot of people fail to recognise that the captain's greatest challenge is Friday and Saturday because he's pairing guys together and sorting the order and having to sit some guys down; but Sunday everybody plays and the order, in my opinion, doesn't really matter. Typically you might send some hot player out first and some veterans at the end, which is what he did. And it was so hard to see how much he was hurting afterwards because we'd wanted to do it for him. Even guys like Tiger Woods and Phil Mickelson sitting there, you could see they wanted to win it for Davis more than anything.

José María Olazábal: Seve was never beaten. You learn from what you see, and I did that from the way Seve played and the way he acted on the golf course. He broke down barriers. He took the concept of golf to a new audience and he opened a lot of doors for European players when he went to the States and won the Masters that first time. We started to believe, as young players, that we could follow in his footsteps. The way he played golf had not been seen before. In his prime, he played from places you weren't supposed to play from, yet ended up making a birdie or saving par with some huge shot. Seve taught me one thing above all else. Never give in, never quit, anything is possible in this game.

I remember hugging Ian and just being unable to speak for four minutes or so. It was just so emotional the whole thing. One of the best moments of my life, if not the best.

Paul Lawrie: You put everything into what you're doing. I think everyone gets a bit emotional as they get older. I've been blubbing away at celebratory dinners since 2012 and I was watching it one night in early November 2012 at home. I had a bit of jet lag after playing in China and I watched the whole singles programme again from start to finish. I was sitting there on my own, with the cover around me, crying!

José María Olazábal: Oh I was nervous speaking afterwards at the closing ceremony. I don't feel comfortable speaking like that. You know you are talking to a huge audience – not just the people there but those who are watching on TV. You don't want to make any mistakes. But it went pretty much as I had hoped. I had a couple of moments where I was struggling a little bit, trying to control the emotions. The only thing I forgot to say, although there is a limit to how much you can say, was to mention [the late] Payne Stewart and one or two other players, especially some Spaniards who helped me in the early stages of my career – Santiago Luna, José María Cañizares, José Rivero and Manuel Piñero.

The start of the week was a tough one. Nothing went our way, but the guys kept on believing, and I'm sure that not just the silhouette, but the phone call Seve made at Celtic Manor in 2010 and all the images of Seve around the clubhouse, the locker room and things like that, kept that spirit alive. So it wasn't just me. The guys did it also for him. I said at the time that all men die, but not all men truly live, and those players made me feel alive again that week.

That one was for Seve.

FORTY

2014
Gleneagles Hotel. Perthshire, Scotland
(EUR 16½, USA 11½)

Paul McGinley was named as captain for the European defence at Gleneagles, becoming the first Irishman to hold the position. Having played in three Ryder Cups as a player, McGinley had also served as a vice-captain in 2010 at Celtic Manor and in 2012 at Medinah and had taken charge of the Great Britain and Ireland team in the 2009 and 2011 Seve Trophy matches. During those non-playing stints he had shown an impressive array of organisational skills which he would develop to breathtaking lengths as he prepared for Gleneagles. From his unveiling in Abu Dhabi in January 2012 through to the last week of September 2014, McGinley's meticulous preparation set a new standard for every European captain to follow him into the role. He had fastidiously stored up years of accumulated knowledge in dozens of notebooks and he was relentless in his pursuit of pushing Europe's winning formula of recent years to new heights. His approach was forensic in its thoroughness; but at the end of the day, he knew that he could only provide the platform and it was, as always, up to the players to deliver out on the course.

Paul McGinley: We had had a great purple patch in Ryder Cups and I wanted to continue that. I didn't see my job as coming in and saying, 'Right, I am a maverick, watch this.' What I saw was bringing a lot of experience to the job. I'd ridden shotgun – as a player or vice-captain – on five of the previous seven Ryder Cups, all five of which we won. To me, my job as captain was to identify the template of success, take that template, move it forward. I wasn't looking to change the world.

Pádraig Harrington: The greatest thing about McGinley is that he's the most unorganised person ever. If he didn't have his wife Ally and the kids to organise him he wouldn't function. Then, when it came to the Ryder Cup, he did a phenomenal job. I can't tell you how much he impressed me, because I knew him as the messer; I knew him as a disorganised person; I knew him as the person who is always late. And he was the complete opposite in his captaincy. Paul set the bar very high for anyone who wants to follow him. Every other captain I played for used instinct and emotion and fly-by-wire: 'Yeah, that looks like a great partnership, off you go.' McGinley did his research and used cold, hard facts. He really was phenomenal.

Graeme McDowell: Paul left no stone unturned. No disrespect to any other captain, but he was the best I've played under and I'm sure he is the most meticulous ever. To me, he proved once and for all that the emphasis should be on leadership qualities, not on golfing credentials. Nothing was left to chance, he thought of everything. Even the fish he had swimming around in the team room were yellow and blue.

Opposite: Henrik Stenson of Europe tees off on the first hole of the PGA Centenary during the Friday morning fourballs. *Getty Images*

Paul McGinley: Well, everything in that room was blue and gold, from the carpet to the wallpapers to the images on the wall to the fish inside. I wasn't interested in the breed, so long as they were fish and they swam. It was the colours I was interested in. Everything had to be right.

Graeme McDowell: His playing credentials didn't necessarily make him a first-choice Ryder Cup captain (that's a whole other debate), but his leadership, meticulous attention to detail and way with words helped him command huge respect in the team room.

Paul McGinley: There's certainly a strong sense of bonding and I think one of the reasons for Europe's success is we all have that feeling. For example, I haven't seen Pierre Fulke on tour since 2002 but if he walked into the same room as me today I would immediately have that sense of bonding with him. Immediately we would go back to 2002 and there would be a smile and a connection straight away. That's how powerful the bond is with the guys with whom you have shared these great moments.

Then it becomes even deeper with the guys you've been in regular touch with through the team over the years. Guys like Sergio García, for example. Then watching someone like Rory coming into the Ryder Cup fold, having been a little bit sceptical at first but then getting involved and understanding what it's all about. Watching him become passionate about the legacy of the Ryder Cup and the history that was there before in terms of Olazábal and Seve and all the great players who preceded him – that's what makes it so special. That sense of having each other's backs. The passion involved makes it unique, not even the Majors stir that kind of passion.

When Ted Bishop, president of the US PGA, scoured his list of potential candidates for the captaincy at Gleneagles, his thoughts were drawn to the last US team to win on European soil. That honour had belonged to Tom Watson's class of 1993 at the Belfry. If anyone might know how to staunch Europe's dominant run of seven victories in the previous nine Ryder Cups, surely Watson, a man much beloved on both sides of the Atlantic (and particularly in Scotland where the 2014 matches would be held), was the man to do it.

It was a romantic story. Of the five Open Championship titles that Watson had won, four of them had been achieved in Scotland – and indeed he had almost worked his magic again at the 2009 Open at Turnberry, only to be denied at the last by Stewart Cink. But for all of Cink's brilliance that year, there had been no doubt that Watson had been the people's champion. So it was that Bishop felt he had an ace up his sleeve when he appointed the veteran as captain of the 2014 US team, who would be sixty-five when battle commenced at Gleneagles in Scotland. Watson was a proven winner as a player and a captain and if any American was to pull the heartstrings of the Scottish crowd, it would be Watson. The US PGA also like their Ryder Cup captain to be a Major champion. He ticked every box.

Tom Watson: I was out on the pheasant field at David Feherty's IED Pheasant Hunt up in South Dakota in November 2011, and I get this call. 'Hi, this is Ted Bishop from the PGA, and I'd like to talk to you about the Ryder Cup.' I said, 'Well, Ted, I'm just a little bit busy right now, can I call you back?' and put the phone down. When I called him back, I said, 'I sure hope this is the call I've been waiting for for almost twenty years and that I'm going to be asked to be the Ryder Cup captain again.'

Things changed a lot in those twenty years. There's a lot more to do these days as the captain. Throughout the year building up to the Ryder Cup itself, I think the biggest pleasure that I had was getting to know some players that I would never have had the chance to get to know before. It was fun to be able to go out and play a few more of what I call the 'kids' tournaments' and to have a chance to play with some of the kids and get to know them.

You create lifelong bonds at the Ryder Cup. I remember all the Ryder Cups that I had. In fact, the best memory I think I remember in the Ryder Cup was in '77 watching the American flag go up, and realising that I was on a team of Americans playing for my country. That was unique.

Tom Lehman: It is one thing to play for a captain like Paul Azinger, Corey Pavin, Davis Love or me, and it's another to play for Nicklaus or Watson. Tom is the toughest competitor I know.

Paul McGinley: I've had two sporting heroes in my life. Trevor Brooking, who played for my football team West Ham, and Tom Watson. As a kid at school, I wrote a quotation from Watson into my textbook. 'What makes success? Desire, dedication, determination and a little bit of talent.'

The second Major I played in the US was the PGA at the Athletic Club in Atlanta, 2001. First morning I woke at 5:00 am, rang my caddie, JP Fitzgerald, and we were walking to the first tee an hour later. That tee was behind a hedge, but one player was already there: Tom with his caddie Bruce Edwards.

As a student at the University of San Diego, I'd stalked Tom during his practise rounds when he played at Torrey Pines. This was like a love affair. He'd always intrigued me. The brisk walk, the ability under pressure, the sense of destiny. Now I had one of those, 'Should I stay or should I go' moments.

I walked up to him, stretched out my hand, 'Tom, I'm Paul McGinley from Ireland, would you mind if I joined you?' He looked at me and the moment seemed to last for a long time. Then he said, 'Irishmen are always welcome in my company'. We chatted the whole way round, became friends and have been ever since.

For Tom to be US captain for 2014 . . . well, what a thrill to go up against your hero. If this was Hollywood and I was writing the script, Tom Watson would have been US captain. Tom Watson stands for everything that is good about golf.

In the months that preceded the final selection of the US team, Watson found himself facing several issues that had to be negotiated. The first surrounded the fitness of Tiger Woods. In the weeks before he announced his team, Watson was hounded at every turn with questions about Woods and whether the former world number one would be a wildcard pick, even though his fitness was in question. Watson skilfully parried every question but there was no doubt that he was caught between Scylla and Charybdis. As the world's most famous golfer, Woods would have been nearly impossible to ignore as a captain's pick (he had not collected enough points to be an automatic qualifier for the team). But his Ryder Cup record was a pretty woeful 13–17–3, going 4–8–1 in foursomes, 5–8–0 in fourballs and 4–1–2 in singles out of thirty-three matches played. Furthermore, the only time that America had won the Ryder Cup since Brookline had been in 2008 – when Woods hadn't played. Many pundits opined that his absence had helped galvanise Paul Azinger's team at Valhalla as no player had been overshadowed or intimidated by his stardom. In the event, the decision was taken out of Watson's hands as Woods declared himself unavailable through injury; following back surgery earlier in the year, he had decided that rest and recuperation was what his battered body needed.

Two other selection choices were also discounted in August when Dustin Johnson announced that he was stepping away from golf to tend to 'personal issues' for an indefinite period of time and Jason Dufner declared himself unfit with a neck injury.

With these three players out of contention, it was a surprise that Watson's final team selection omitted the in-form Chris Kirk and Billy Horschel – although in fairness to Watson, he had been forced to name his team before Horschel walked off with a bumper $11.4m payday at the FedEx Cup. Despite this, however, there was no doubt that the US team still packed plenty of punch. Of the twelve players looking to atone for that extraordinary final day collapse at Medinah two years earlier, nine had previous Ryder Cup experience: Keegan Bradley, Rickie Fowler, Jim Furyk, Zach Johnson, Matt Kuchar, Hunter Mahan, Phil Mickelson, Webb Simpson and Bubba Watson, while Patrick Reed, Jordan Spieth and Jimmy Walker would be experiencing the competition for the first time.

Tom Watson: I can tell you that all the players that I talked to, every one of them without a doubt had one thing to say about the Ryder Cup: they wanted a chance to make amends for what happened at Medinah. The Europeans played great in the last round in 2012, and that was a hard, hard loss for the American players, and it stuck with a lot of them. Keegan Bradley was my first captain's pick and I learned from speaking to him that he still had a bag of clothes at home that had sat unopened since 2012. He was the epitome of somebody who wanted to get on the team to make amends for Medinah. There are a lot of great pluses about Keegan, but the most important thing he brought to the team was his unbridled passion to play in the Ryder Cup.

Keegan Bradley: Getting the call from Tom to say I had made the team was like nothing I'd ever experienced before. It was so emotional. I had invested so much time in making the team and I wasn't sure if I was going to get that call or not. I was up in Boston, and I was walking up eighteen and the entire crowd basically started chanting 'Ryder Cup', which was very special for me personally. It's my hometown. So I got done playing and was in the parking lot with my girlfriend, Jillian, and I was pretty down thinking there was a good chance I wasn't going to be on the team. Then the captain called me and told me I was on the team and I just hugged Jillian, and months and years of emotion came out. I made no secret of how important the team is to me, and how bad I wanted to go back and win the Ryder Cup.

We play all year for all this money and all this fame and all these amazing trophies but the Ryder Cup has such a force to it. To be part of that team and be in the team room and have a captain like Tom Watson, it's something that can't be put into words. Especially after what happened in Chicago; we had a big majority of the guys on the team that were there and experienced Medinah, and to think that I wouldn't have a chance or a little say so in what happened in Scotland would have been really, really tough. The Ryder Cup just has this pull. It's amazing; it can make you do some crazy things. But it's an amazing event.

McGinley's team also had a familiar feel to it with only three rookies – Welshman Jamie Donaldson, Frenchman Victor Dubuisson who qualified on points and Scotsman Stephen Gallacher who was a captain's pick – and who brought with him not only local experience but also family pedigree being the nephew of Ryder Cup legend, Bernard Gallacher. McGinley's other two picks were Ian Poulter and Lee Westwood and the rest of the team were just as synonymous with the European cause: Thomas Bjørn, Sergio García, Martin Kaymer, Graeme McDowell, Rory McIlroy, Justin Rose and Henrik Stenson.

Paul McGinley: I've always been a team player. I've been very fortunate that I'd had great experiences when I'd been in Ryder Cups in the past, nothing but positive experiences. In light of that, having to make the call to Luke Donald to tell him he wasn't in the team was a very, very difficult conversation for a number of reasons, personal more than anything else. I was his partner in his first ever Ryder Cup match in 2004 and in every Ryder Cup he'd been involved in, I was involved in it with him. I played twice with Luke on the team in 2004 and 2006, and obviously vice-captained him in 2010 and 2012. I forged a very strong relationship with him.

When we spoke about 2014 he said, 'You know, Paul, I publicly backed you to be the captain. Even though you've not picked me, I still believe you'll be a great captain.' His last few words were, 'Go Europe.' I think that said a lot about Luke. His record in the Ryder Cup was absolutely outstanding and it was a very, very difficult call for me to make, but one I had to do in the interests of the European team because Stephen Gallacher had undoubtedly earned his place. His performance in Italy the week before selection was huge.

Gallacher had shown consistent form throughout the year on the European Tour and competed well in the Italian Open when he went to within one stroke of automatic qualification for the team.

Stephen Gallacher: I wanted it badly, it was a lifetime ambition to emulate my uncle, Bernard, and play in the Ryder Cup. I knew what I had to do to qualify for the team, it was in my own hands. But it was nerve-wracking, purely because I wanted it so much.

I needed to finish second outright in Italy to qualify and I finished third. Hennie Otto shot twenty-under. I was close to missing the cut early on, but fought back. It's just one of those things. If you set your stall out and you want something badly, you kind of work your way to achieve it. That was my only focus, to win world ranking points to try and qualify automatically. To just miss out and then to get in with the pick was special.

Paul phoned me the night before the announcement, but when he said my name out live on TV, I still had to pinch myself. Yeah, it was something special.

McGinley felt unable to ignore such form and fighting spirit. And, of course, the enthusiasm of the Scottish crowd would only be enhanced by the presence of a man whose home was just thirty-five miles from Gleneagles – especially when the European captain knew that Watson would also be given a warm reception from the locals.

Tom Watson: You couldn't be anywhere but Scotland when you're in Scotland. It is a special place. Scotland is where the game of golf was invented and the history of the game is rich with wonderful stories about different players, different events, different contests. I remember as a boy reading stories about the older players from Allan Robertson to Old Tom Morris, the big matches they used to have. They played twelve or fifteen rounds for one match for £500 and that was an enormous amount of money. The game of golf evolved from that. There's a certain element in me that I feel like I'm part-Scottish that way. I love the game so much and the reason is reading the history when I was just a young boy.

I was very grateful for the opportunity to be captain in Scotland, a place that has been very special to me during my career. I remember when I won the Open at Carnoustie in 1975, a little girl came up to me in her bare feet on a cold rainy morning and gave me a good-luck charm; it was a piece of white heather, wrapped in aluminium foil. I kept it in my golf bag for well over a year. It helped my understanding of what golf is in Scotland. People embrace it, they respect it. They appreciate when you hit a good shot under difficult conditions and it just trickles off the green. They will give you a round of applause that acknowledges how tough it was. That is just part of the fabric of life there.

As the countdown to play began, McGinley brought in former Manchester United manager Sir Alex Ferguson to speak to the team at the start of the week to encourage his players to relish being the bookies' favourites to win the cup.

Graeme McDowell: McGinley was hungry for knowledge – everything from in-depth statistical analysis of players and Ryder Cup history, to picking the brains of great man-managers like Sir Alex Ferguson.

The team spent an hour listening to Ferguson on the Tuesday evening, hanging on his every word, United fans or not. We talked about complacency and how we would deal with being the favourites, a tag with which European Ryder Cup teams were not familiar. We talked about concentration, work ethic and respecting our opponents.

Rory McIlroy: It was an amazing thing when Sir Alex Ferguson came in to talk to us. I was just sitting there and looking up at him and I didn't take my eyes off him, I was in this trance just listening to everything that he was saying and I'm thinking, 'This is all the stuff that he's probably said to Manchester United teams over the years.'

He told us a couple of stories of past experiences in some big games and big matches, and about some of the players that he managed. It was a great evening. It was a really cool thing to be a part of and we got to ask some questions about different things and what he thought was the key element to being successful, and successful as a team.

Paul McGinley: We had pressure on us, but I referenced Rory McIlroy who was the number one player in the world at the time. He had pressure on him and he knew how to deal with situations when you're the favourite. Obviously one of the reasons why Alex

Ferguson was a guy that I asked a lot of questions of, was for that very reason. Most matches Manchester United played in under him, they were the favourites, and dealing with that tag was something he was used to and comfortable with. He gave me a couple of pointers in that direction and I said to the players, 'Let's embrace this situation.'

Over the years I always made a point of watching and listening and observing all the time. I've got at least half a dozen notebooks filled with things I've collected over the years. I started doing it when I was Seve Trophy captain in 2009 and kept other notebooks when I was Monty's vice-captain in 2010, Seve Trophy captain in 2011 and vice-captain again to José María at Medinah. There are always lessons to be learned and not just from captains and players. I took a lot of information from the press too. I did a lot of research before matches in terms of statistics on players and where they were at with form. So I had a profile on each player I could go to. Then as the matches evolved I'd assess little things that might explain why a pairing worked or didn't – or something the Americans did that was very clever.

So I'd evolved to the captaincy position by 2014. My view was that we'd been very successful in Europe, winning seven of the previous nine, and there was a template there, a reason why we were winning the Ryder Cup. There are a lot of things that go on behind the scenes that work year after year that we don't mess with. Meal times can be a challenge, for example, because you've got different cultures with different eating habits. Some guys want to eat at six or seven o'clock in the evening but then the Spaniards, like Jiménez, like to eat at nine or ten at night. So what we've always done is rather than forcing the guys to eat together as a team, we have a running buffet that goes from 5:00 pm to midnight. That way the guys can come and go whenever they want.

Ian Poulter: There's lots to digest about what Paul did very, very well. Tom Watson is way more accomplished as a player than Paul McGinley, so he knew he couldn't go up against his personal playing record. But what he could do was try and out-think him. By doing his homework, by being respectful, by being unbelievably clever in the way that he went around getting all of his statistics to make sure he had the right players on the course at the right time – he did all of that.

There was a moment of controversy on the eve of the matches when Nick Faldo, acting as a television pundit, claimed that Sergio García had had a 'bad attitude' in 2008 when he scored just a single point from four matches despite being considered one of the team's leading players. Faldo had taken a lot of flak in the aftermath of the 2008 defeat to Paul Azinger's team, but his players had all rallied round him. To many, Faldo's comment felt like a gross betrayal of that support. One of Europe's vice-captains, Sam Torrance, was equally vociferous in views on Faldo's slight.

Sam Torrance: To say that right in the middle of the Ryder Cup, what was the arsehole thinking about? The reaction in the team room was magnificent. The guys rallied round García like he was an injured goose. Really, it was pathetic from Faldo. I've no idea where he was coming from with that stuff. You can even quote me on that, I don't care. He's an arsehole. It was beyond belief that one of our greatest-ever players would come out with a comment like that. García's not a team player? Have a look in the mirror, pal. García's one of the best team players there is. He's an incredible kid, with the heart of a lion and he's incredible in the team room. Really, I've just no idea where those comments came from.

Sergio García: I'm an open man and I'm always willing to forgive and forget. I think it was an unfortunate comment – I don't know if Nick regrets it or not. I've moved on.

In glorious Perthshire conditions, the opening morning fourballs saw Rose and Stenson open the 2014 Ryder Cup against Watson and Simpson. Working in exquisite synergy the Europeans put the first blue on the board with a towering 5&4 victory.

Graeme McDowell: When it comes to fourballs and foursomes, pairing up players is an art form. The captain has to consider the dynamics of each player's game, the balls being used and the chemistry between the two. You have to consider if a player can handle the emotional energy of an Ian Poulter, for example, or perhaps they would prefer the relative calm of playing alongside a Martin Kaymer. You have twelve very different personalities, needs and, of course, games. Myself, Poults and Lee Westwood were handed the role of 'blooding' the rookies, which is hugely important, especially when the captain has the goal of introducing all the newcomers on that opening Friday.

Justin Rose: Going out first at the Ryder Cup is a big thing, there's no doubt about it. The captain puts you in that position to go and deliver and that's what me and the ice man [Stenson] were able to do against Bubba and Webb. We got off to a good start and we knew that was key.

Bubba Watson: It was disappointing to lose that opener. We played well. I hit the ball really good, I just didn't make any putts. If you go back to their round, I don't think they hit it better than us, but they obviously putted better than us. They made their key putts. If one wasn't making the birdie putt, the other one was. They worked together as a team. And me and Webb just never made a putt.

The second match out saw Bjørn and Kaymer take on Fowler and Walker.

Martin Kaymer: Thomas and I started off very well and we were three up after four holes. Then Jimmy holed a bunker shot on nine and chipped in on sixteen, which was a little surprising. But I guess in match play, those things happen. We were two-up, three to go. That's why it was a little bit frustrating that we only got half a point out of it. But we had enough chances. On seventeen I had to make a putt, and unfortunately I didn't. But a half point at that stage was better than none.

Rickie Fowler: Any time you can score a point, whether it's a point or half point, especially being three-down, is huge. It was a great comeback from us to secure that half point on the eighteenth green.

Tom Watson: A good match play player is someone who I think understands, first of all, you have to play the course, but your opponent is an element you have to deal with. I remember Sam Snead saying that there were certain things he would notice about an opponent when they got nervous that they didn't do normally. That's the element of a good match player, you assess your opponent. They all know how to get under each other's skin when they're on the golf course, needling them or doing something like that. That's part of match play. It's mano a mano. I love it. I love that element of the game. When I grew up, that's all I played is match play. It's an element that we don't see in professional golf except for the Ryder Cup, and maybe one or two other match play events over the entire year. It's something that I truly love.

The crowd around the first tee went wild as Gallacher and 'Mr Ryder Cup' Poulter arrived to play Spieth and Reed. This was the pairing McGinley had hoped would send the fans into fever pitch, carrying his pairing on a thundering wave of adulation to, hopefully, an irresistible victory. The decibel level was indeed impressive as the players navigated the course – but so too were the American rookies.

Stephen Gallacher: The hardest thing about the week building up to the matches is trying to conserve energy. You're there quite a long time before the Friday start. My uncle told me it would be a long week, early mornings and late nights, so you just have to try and conserve energy. Poults touched on it as well with me – get rest when you can and get your game plan and just be ready for the three days.

'These are the happiest days of your life' is the quote Paul put up from Bob Torrance in our team room and it's true. That was the last message we saw before hitting the course and it all meant something special to each of us. After an amazing week, it was an unbelievable reception on the first tee on the Friday. It was just euphoric, really. The first tee in a Ryder Cup is special, but when it's in your own country it takes it to another level. The reception that Poults and I got when we started out was just incredible.

Ian Poulter: Stevie's going to remember that walk to the first tee for a long time, and I'll remember it as well. It was a special moment. There was a sea of people out there. Gleneagles is a great golf course to have spectators around, everybody got a good view. The atmosphere was incredible. It was just a shame we couldn't deliver a point, but we were up against two guys who were just on fire.

Patrick Reed: I could barely breathe on the first tee. It's one of those things, you think you're nervous, and you think you've got the nerves out and you feel real confident, even if you have a great warm-up like we did. And you get to that first tee, and all of a sudden, you're stepping up and they call your name out and you put that peg in the ground; I was the first to hit – I didn't know if I could pull it back. I was like, 'Good thing the wind is howling off to the right, because I can hold onto it a little bit and hit this fly floater and know it was going to come back.' The good thing is I was able to put it in the fairway so Jordan could go and hit his long three-wood.

Jordan Spieth: That first tee was a really, really cool experience, one we won't forget: the cheers, the songs, everything. Captain Watson lightened the mood for us, too, and got up there and tried to pump the crowd up. They gave him a cheer and it was all in good spirit. Over in Scotland, most people would agree, they may be the most knowledgeable fans in golf. They are very respectful, but at the same time you could definitely feel the adrenaline and you could feel that they were trying to get their team off to the right start early. With both of us hitting the fairway before they even hit and getting it down there in a good position, we couldn't ask for much more off the first hole.

The Americans started as they meant to go on and as the four players worked their way around the course Spieth and Reed played magnificently on their way to an emphatic 5&4 victory.

Stephen Gallacher: There was a bit of criticism about the pairing as I was a rookie and Ian was a bit out of form coming into the week, but I wouldn't have changed it – it was just one of those things. There's been nobody better than Ian in recent years in the Ryder Cup. I was just honoured to play the first day, with the saltire on the jumper and having the home crowd behind us. It just never worked out. We came up against Jordan, soon to be world number one, and Patrick, who is a quality player too. In fourballs, you have got a limited time to gel. When one is out, one needs to be in, and we didn't really click. First day nerves maybe didn't really play well on us. We got off to a poor start, we missed a little putt early doors. It's just one of those things, you give it your best shot. You are playing against the best guys in the world so if you are not six and seven-under, you're going to get beat.

Jordan Spieth: Patrick and I made a great team that week, and we weren't sure how that was going to work, but the captain put his trust in us and we wanted to repay him for that. It was great to go out and play so well for him and the team.

Ian Poulter: The start Stevie and I made wasn't obviously what we were looking for. We were looking to get off to a fast start. That didn't happen, and we couldn't seem to get anything going. Putts weren't dropping when we had good looks, and we missed when we had outside chances and a few putts were left short. All in all it was a disappointing morning, but hats off to Jordan and Patrick, they played great. You know, when you're playing against guys who are just rolling putts in, then they're going to be hard to beat, and that's exactly what they did. I thought they ham-and-egged very well.

Fourth out saw a clash of the heavyweights. Tom Watson sent out Bradley and Mickelson to see if they could recreate the wonderful form they had shown as a pairing in Medinah to see off the potent pairing of García and McIlroy.

Tom Watson: García was an experienced campaigner; Rory McIlroy was the number one player in the world. Rory was someone that we desperately wanted to see on the losing end of a match. If you knock off the big dog that gives your team a boost. Phil and Keegan beating them on the first morning was huge for us.

Keegan Bradley: That was big. Rory and Sergio were a great team but Phil and I played really well coming down the stretch to win that match.

Phil Mickelson: It was tough conditions, we gave a few holes away and the match was very, very close. Keegan made an eagle on sixteen which was just huge because it gave us a big momentum boost coming down the stretch. It was a big point to get from McIlroy and García. [The US pair won one-up.]

With the score standing at 2½–1½ in the visitors' favour, McGinley needed his players to respond in the afternoon. The first of the foursomes saw the veteran Westwood team up with the rookie Donaldson to face Furyk and Kuchar.

Jamie Donaldson: Wow, the Ryder Cup – it's quite an experience. That first tee, it was just like a sudden death play-off in a Major.

It was quite a journey to make the team. I kind of lost my way after having an injury in 2004 and ended up losing my card at the end of 2006. As a result, I found myself on the Challenge Tour in 2007 and started off the year with a three-week swing in South America. It was a case of either pull the finger out and make some changes or find something else to do. It genuinely got to the point where I contemplated giving it up.

So I knuckled down and worked really hard and then I got my reward on 1 July 2012 at Royal Portrush in Northern Ireland. It was a long time coming. After all those years in the wilderness, not knowing what I was doing, it was brilliant to finally stand there as a European Tour winner. It was like winning the Open; it was incredible and it was the validation that the changes and decisions I'd made all those years before had been the right ones. So to make all those changes, to really improve my game and then to be out there on the first tee on the Friday afternoon in the Ryder Cup was just the most unbelievable feeling.

Lee Westwood: When you've played a few Ryder Cups, it's fun watching somebody who has made their debut play so well and take to it like a duck to water like Jamie did. I had no doubt he would. He plays well in the big events. He plays well under pressure. You don't tend to get much more pressure than a Ryder Cup, especially when you're making your debut, and a format like foursomes, where you don't get going immediately, it's so hard to build a game and get some momentum. We complemented each other well.

The crowds at Gleneagles were amazing. The atmosphere on the first tee was as good as anything I've ever experienced in the Ryder Cup, it was incredible.

Rose and Stenson teamed up once again, this time to face Mahan and Zach Johnson.

Zach Johnson: Hunter and I put the ball in the fairway for the most part, gave ourselves a lot of good opportunities but we just didn't capitalise on them. They made a lot of nice putts, long putts. That was really what took it.

They got off to a good start. We came back and played really well, but just kind of killed ourselves in the end and they came back strongly.

Having fought back from an early deficit to take the lead, the US pair suffered something of a collapse down the back nine, eventually surrendering to a 2&1 defeat.

Henrik Stenson: Yeah, it was a great day at the office. Justin and I played even better in the afternoon than in the morning. I had a quick session with my swing coach, Pete Cowen, on the range before going out in the afternoon, and I felt like I was hitting the ball better before I teed off in the foursome, and I certainly hit the ball better on the course in the afternoon. I think we made six birdies together, and we knew it was going to be a tough match against Zach and Hunter, the two players who don't give away anything for free, I guess up until the seventeenth. But we won fifteen, and we both halved with birdies on sixteen. I guess they felt forced to try to make something happen towards the last couple of holes and they three-putted and the match was over.

The third tie out saw Jimmy Walker team up with Fowler to take on McIlroy and García. It was all square at the sixth but then a wonderful putt from García moved Europe one hole ahead and many felt that might be the first move in a comfortable drive to victory. But the Americans hung in there and soon began to fight back with a string of birdies that saw them pull back and then overtake their opponents, moving them to two-up with two to play. McGinley needed his players to pull something out of the bag and they did just that, first with a stunning twenty-foot putt from McIlroy on the seventeenth and then, when it looked as if the Northern Irishman's efforts might be for naught as he sliced his drive on eighteen into the right-hand rough, García executed a spectacular five-wood approach which went between a tree and a hospitality pavilion to the back pin position on the raised green. Fowler was faced with a twelve-footer to halve the hole but he swung it two feet to the left and Europe had scrambled a crucial half point.

Rory McIlroy: That half point was pretty crucial at that stage. We needed it, we really did. We'd made life difficult for ourselves – I don't think either of us was playing from the fairways very much. But we were three-under for the last three holes. We just wanted to ask them a question and get them going and we were able to do that. And Sergio had the shot of the day at the last.

My putt on seventeen was one of those 'you knew what you needed to do' moments. There was actually a little piece of dirt in the line, and it was sort of embedded in the ground, so I couldn't move it. Sergio said it was easier to hit the hole than hit that. I stood up and it was going at quite a speed, and I was lucky to hit the hole.

Jimmy Walker: We were in control of the match and then Rory made that bomb on seventeen. We were in a good position on eighteen, but the putt just wouldn't get down. But, although it hurt, we were happy to take the half point.

Sergio García: I was very pleased with my shot on eighteen. That was a great feeling. After Rory's putt on seventeen, I felt like I needed to do something, find something in me, and obviously we got a little bit lucky, I'm not going to deny that. We got a nice lie on eighteen in the rough. But you still have to hit the shot and I was able to hit a really nice five-wood from 229, I think it was, into the wind off the left, which is always an uncomfortable wind. I was trying to make sure I gave my partner a chance; a chance to make three, try to win the hole, and get a massive half after how the team was doing in the afternoon. I felt like I owed him a lot.

Rory McIlroy: We owed each other a lot, I think.

The final match of the day saw McDowell guide the enigmatic young Frenchman, Dubuisson, around his first Ryder Cup match. But they had a hard pairing to face in the process, as Tom Watson pitched Mickelson and Bradley back into the breach against them.

Thomas Bjørn: I thought one of Paul's best moves was to put Graeme and Victor together. Graeme is great with people and really good at looking after younger players. I imagine that he was probably a bit disappointed not to play more, but he delivered a big point on the Sunday and he played a huge role in looking after Victor the way he did.

Victor Dubuisson: It was amazing playing with Graeme against Mickelson and Bradley. Playing with Graeme was important for me, for the whole week. He is someone I love, I love the player, I love the guy, and he helped me a lot. I was feeling a little nervous the night before and then, because we sat out the morning session, there was a long wait for us to play. I think we teed off at 2.35, you wake up at 8.00 and you think about the afternoon all morning. But the fact that I spent a lot of time with Graeme over the previous few days, it really helped me. When I was walking with him to the tee, he was next to me, and then the stress completely disappeared. I was only feeling positive and I was able to just play my game, which was all I wanted.

Graeme McDowell and Victor Dubuisson. *Getty Images*

Graeme McDowell: It was a long wait having to sit out and sort of watch the boys play. Victor and I were really fired up for our match in the afternoon, and I've got to say, one thing about my Ryder Cup experience is I always get great partners. I played with Rory McIlroy the last couple and Victor is without doubt the next superstar in Europe.

Gleneagles is one of the toughest foursome golf courses I've ever played. I hit my first iron shot on twelve and it was a six-iron and it was very difficult, I have to say. It was tough to stay in your rhythm, but I told Victor to go and enjoy himself and use the crowd. The crowd were phenomenal and I told him to use them any time he needed them. The way he played, he didn't need much advice. I just had to kind of wind him up and let him go.

Victor Dubuisson: Everybody says it, but the energy from the crowd was amazing. It's very different to playing Majors. You only get positive energy at the Ryder Cup. As Paul said in his speech at the opening ceremony, when you're about to hit a shot, you really want to hit it well to really please the crowd.

The European pair emerged as 3&2 winners.

Phil Mickelson: The afternoon stung a little bit. We needed that point. Keegan and I had a great morning, but I just didn't play well in the afternoon.

Tom Watson: The Friday started off looking pretty good, and then we didn't perform in the afternoon, and that was very disappointing. The big question that kept being asked was why I didn't play Jordan Spieth and Patrick Reed again in the afternoon. It was a decision that my vice-captains and I made. That was a decision that we felt very strongly for. When I told Patrick that he wasn't going to play in the afternoon, I said, 'How does that make you feel?' He said, 'Well, I'm all right with it.' Then he paused. 'Well, really, Captain, I'm not all right with it.' I said, 'That's the way I want you to be.'

Patrick Reed: You know, whenever you feel like you're playing really well – I felt like Jordan was hitting the ball really solid and making a lot of putts and I was hitting it well and I was putting extremely well – you want to keep playing. I felt like in alternate shot, him and I would have been great to go back out and carry the momentum of what we had just done in the morning. But at the end of the day, Captain Watson, he picked the pairings for a reason. He decided to put us in certain spots for a reason. I was over it when he told us we weren't going back out. We went and got some rest, hit some balls and then went out and cheered on our team.

Tom Watson: I wanted to rest them but I also wanted them fired up for when they next played. You can't play everybody.

Webb Simpson and Bubba, they had a bad day. They really did. We all have bad days. Phil and Keegan, they struggled that afternoon. They missed a lot of putts. But that's the game. There are ebbs and flows. We had a better flow in the morning and it all kind of ebbed in the afternoon – culminating with that putt that Rory McIlroy made at seventeen, which hit the back of the hole, popped up and went in.

I told them in the locker room, I said, 'It's 5–3. That's two matches. You win two matches, you're back to even; you win four, you're up by two.' That's the way the Ryder Cup works, that's the reality of it.

Rose and Stenson played together for the third consecutive time in the opening fourball on Saturday morning and played their most dominant golf yet as they reeled off ten birdies in succession to triumph 3&2 against Bubba Watson and Kuchar.

Justin Rose: Things weren't going brilliantly for us at one stage and Henrik and I were two-down to Bubba and Matt after six, but we levelled on the eighth and I really got into reading the greens well and just had that feeling of anticipation of what it was going to feel like to make putts. From the seventh we made ten birdies in a row which was incredible.

Henrik Stenson: Yeah, it was an amazing thing – all the more so because Bubba and Matt made nine birdies themselves and I think we posted a new Ryder Cup record in that match [twenty-one in total]. That's a highlight to put on the big screen with the grandkids one day.

Tom Watson would have been getting nervous as the Europeans moved to 6–3, but things started to turn around as his team dug in and showed their class throughout the remainder of the morning session. First Furyk and Mahan went out against Donaldson and Westwood and won 4&3. Reed and Spieth then continued their wonderful partnership by defeating Bjørn and Kaymer 5&3, before Walker and Fowler secured a half point against the talismanic pairing of McIlroy and Poulter.

Jim Furyk: Captain Tom asked for a little red on the board early on Saturday morning. He was tired of seeing blue, so it was nice for me and Hunter to get out there and get a good start by beating Donaldson and Westwood. It was great to then see the rookies [Reed and Spieth] also getting some red up there by taking out Bjørn and Kaymer. We thought that we were starting to exert some control on proceedings at that stage.

Graeme McDowell: The ebb and flow of momentum is spooky when watching the Ryder Cup on TV. One good thing happens for a team, followed by more from the same team.

With the score now standing at 6½–5½ in Europe's favour, all appeared to be rosy in the American camp as they steamed back into contention. But appearances can be deceptive.

Pádraig Harrington: The biggest flag we had that there were maybe problems in the US team room was Saturday morning when Phil Mickelson didn't play. We were shocked. I couldn't wait to see the team sheet in the afternoon to see if he was there. I thought: 'Can you leave Phil Mickelson out for a whole day? Can you leave Keegan Bradley out for a whole day?'

Tom Watson: Phil lobbied to play the afternoon foursomes. He texted me and said, 'Give us a chance.' I had to tell him no. The main reason I sat them down was that I played Phil for two rounds on the Friday and he was tired. I sat at the table with him. He was exhausted. And maybe that was the wrong choice for me playing him two rounds. But he wanted to play in the alternate shot on the Friday afternoon, and I had to give him his due. He said, 'I've got a good record in the alternate shot.'

Phil Mickelson: I didn't feel like I was out of gas as far as out of energy was concerned on Friday, but I stopped hitting good shots. I didn't play very well in the afternoon. I ended up not making putts that I normally would make and hitting some shots that I hadn't been hitting. I didn't play the best.

Keegan Bradley: The big excitement for me coming into Ryder Cup, as I've said before, was playing with Phil. We talked about it months and months beforehand. We were bummed when we were sat down for both sessions on Saturday. We understood that we were getting rested on Saturday morning, but we expected to play in the afternoon.

Tom Watson: When I went to the clubhouse on the Saturday lunchtime and talked to Phil and Keegan and Webb, and said they would be sitting down in the afternoon, I expected exactly what Phil said to me. He said, 'We can get it done, Captain. We want the chance.' I said, 'Well, I think the way this golf course sets up, the four teams I put out there gives us the best chance.' He lobbied again. I felt that we had the four best teams possible in the afternoon for alternate shot. And again, we can talk about decisions on teams all you want. It's the players that perform who are the people that you have to talk about; who performed the best. I have to give credit to the Europeans in the afternoons, they performed the best.

Pádraig Harrington: For me, personally, I thought the US lost a tremendous opportunity with Phil Mickelson; every player on that team looks up to, admires and would follow Phil Mickelson, and the biggest thing Tom Watson could have done was to recognise Phil as his ace and to use his influence in the team room. If he had let Phil loose in the team room, you wouldn't have been able to contain those guys, they would have played like Keegan Bradley in Medinah. But the captain didn't do that. If he had let Phil have the floor in the team room they could have been devastating.

It would prove to be a rampaging afternoon of golf from the home team as they secured three-and-a-half points from four. First Donaldson and Westwood dispatched Johnson and Kuchar 2&1 in the opening foursome and then García and McIlroy found their groove in a 3&2 victory over Furyk and Mahan.

Jamie Donaldson: It was a long, tough old day. The fourball was disappointing to lose to Furyk and Mahan, but in the afternoon foursomes Lee and I both played very well. I think we were four-under par for the round in foursomes, which is very good obviously. Lee said to me down the first, 'Right, come on, fairways and greens, let's keep it simple.' We had a bit of banter about that on the way round after we finished.

Stenson and Rose were expected to continue their fruitful partnership, but the Swede had a tight back after the morning round and withdrew from the afternoon session, but Rose continued his marvellous form alongside Kaymer to earn a half point against Spieth and Reed, finally denying the previously imperious US rookie pairing a full point.

Jordan Spieth: The afternoon foursome Patrick and I played against Justin and Martin was a great match. We were disappointed to concede the half after taking an early lead, but it was some contest.

Patrick Reed: After sitting out Friday afternoon we started out strong again on Saturday morning. It seemed like we had the most control and command of our golf ball, felt like we were making a lot of putts. The afternoon was just sloppy, on both sides. Justin and Martin said the same. It was one of those matches that we hoped we might be able to grind out and get the full point but unfortunately we weren't able to do that – but at least we were able to put some more points on the board with a half.

Justin Rose: We were two down by the time we got to the twelfth tee but then we started to click and got things back to all square at the sixteenth. I think our experience began to tell then because the pressure was immense. Patrick Reed missed a two-footer on the sixteenth but they recovered well to win seventeen and go one up. We caught a break on the eighteenth because they got a poor lie against the back of a greenside bunker and only managed to make par while we managed to birdie it for the half point.

Jordan Spieth: Patrick and I made a great team that week. I don't think many people expected much out of the two of us coming in, and I think we showed them that we're going to be a force to be reckoned with for many years in this tournament. We battled for a point and a half on the Saturday and we were upset about it. A few of the best players in the world didn't play a match that day, and they were itching to get out there in the singles. We really felt that we were still very much in it at that stage, even though we were trailing.

The last match of the paired sessions saw Dubuisson and McDowell in harness once again and they were utterly commanding in their 5&4 demolition of Walker and Fowler.

Graeme McDowell: One of McGinley's strokes of genius was the appointment of a fifth vice-captain. There was an assistant with each of the four games on Friday and Saturday morning and afternoon. The fifth was made available throughout both days to manage the practise requirements and expectations of the four players who sat out sessions. As I was one of the players who sat out Friday and Saturday morning, the level of communication coming in via the fifth vice-captain was huge. As a result, Lee Westwood, Jamie Donaldson and myself, along with Victor Dubuisson, came out all guns blazing on both afternoons. We contributed 3½–½ demolitions in the two foursome formats.

I have been very fortunate with my playing partners at Ryder Cups: Pádraig Harrington, Miguel Ángel Jiménez and Poulter in 2008, Rory McIlroy in 2010 and 2012. Pretty decent partners in crime. 2014 was no exception. I sensed early that McGinley had chosen my potential partner in Victor. This was long before the media got their teeth into whether or not Rory and I would play together because business was getting in the way of our friendship.

The truth of the matter was Rory and I did not have an overwhelmingly impressive record, and at best we might play foursomes together. The captain knew what he was doing. Victor and I hit it off beautifully and his play was stunning on Friday and Saturday, making my job as sidekick very easy indeed. We picked up two points from a possible two.

Tom Watson: Jimmy Walker played brilliant golf for us. My only regret as far as the pairings are concerned was that Jimmy got tired out on the Saturday afternoon. He went eighteen holes every round. I played him thirty-six the first day and thirty-six the second, and that was a mistake on my part.

That fourth match on the Saturday afternoon, I didn't know his physical condition. Then that third hole I saw him hit a shot and thought, 'Oh my God, I think he's lost his legs.'

Jimmy Walker: We kept trying to hit good shots, just missed a couple of putts that we needed to make to give ourselves more of a chance. They played solid. You've got to think you could catch them, but they didn't make any bogeys and we made a few. They hit the ball good, kept the ball in front of them, just didn't make any mistakes. We made a few, and so it was tough to come back.

Rickie Fowler: Obviously we wanted to get off to a better start, but unfortunately weren't able to do that. They got off to a good start. You take the both sides of that and there is instantly a gap between you. We tried to push them as far as we could, but they played great and made it difficult for us to make a comeback.

Alternate shot is tough. Like Jimmy said, we made a few mistakes, and they didn't really make any. It's tough to beat guys when they play that well.

While the contest was often exceedingly, agonisingly close in the fourballs, the US were ultimately blown out of the water in the two foursome sessions, where Europe clocked up a 7–1 scoreline. The US were still in the hunt come Sunday, but it was a big mountain for them to climb. Not that such mountains hadn't been climbed before, as witnessed in 1999 and 2012.

Justin Rose: It was a pretty special moment going back into the team room at the end of the day knowing we had just won the foursomes 7–1. Momentum was completely with us and it felt great – although we were all well aware that we had come back from a similar scoreline at Medinah, so we couldn't get ahead of ourselves.

Graeme McDowell: We took a 10–6 lead into Sunday – a complete reversal of how we stood in the previous Ryder Cup at Medinah. The big key was that we took a last ounce of momentum out of the Saturday with Justin Rose holing a clutch six-footer as he and Martin halved their match against Spieth and Reed.

Unlike two years earlier, when Europe gained huge belief despite being 10–6 behind, we had denied America any momentum. We took that with us to the team room thanks to Justin's putt. That night, though, the word 'complacency' was talked about at length. We readied ourselves for the storm that would potentially come the following day – and come it did.

After our performance on Friday afternoon, when Victor and I beat Mickelson and Bradley 3&2, we were disappointed not to get the nod for the fourball on Saturday morning. The captain took me to one side and, in true Sir Alex fashion, told me that leaving me on the bench was part of a bigger role he had for me on Sunday. He wanted me fresh and ready to lead the team off as number one in the singles matches. It was a huge honour and one that intimidated me slightly when he first told me. I saw myself as the more steady figure further down the order, maybe a number twelve kind of guy. The captain told me he wanted a battler and a fighter out there as number one, and that I was his man.

I was up against Jordan Spieth in the singles and for the first five or six holes, I felt like a guy who hadn't played enough golf. I'd played with Victor on Friday and Saturday afternoon and I literally hadn't hit any iron shots, it was really weird. And it's so late each evening when you get off the golf course you can't get any work done. So here comes Sunday and I feel under-prepped.

I was three-down; Justin Rose was four-down. There was a lot of USA red on the board. We were in a storm. We had talked about being in this position the night before. No matter how bad your situation was, just try to win the next hole. Get the crowd to make some European noise and send a signal to the rest of the team. Just try to prolong your match, and keep the US point off the board for as long as possible. I knuckled down.

It's not until the sixth that I hit a decent shot – but then I missed the putt. On seven, he hits two shots to ten feet and I'm thirty feet away and miss. So I'm watching this kid hit this ten-footer to win the hole thinking: 'If I go four-down here I'm really in the shit.' He misses it and the next two holes are key. He hits a decent shot into eight and I follow him. On nine, he hits a phenomenal chip shot up close and I follow him in close and that kind of gets me going. It's the first chink in his armour. He hits it to fifty feet on the tenth and lags it up to three feet. I hit this putt that couldn't miss but it misses, and then he misses and I'm like: 'Oh! I'm almost four-down two holes ago and now I'm back to two!' And I'm energised. He misses a twenty-five-footer on the next and he gets really angry with himself because I'm fifteen feet away and I think he knows, that I know, that I'm going to make it. And I make it. And he doesn't hit a shot for the next two holes. I'm thinking: 'This kid is gone!'

To be honest, I thought his temperament was a bit suspect; I'd played with him a few times and he had a tendency to be hot-headed and that came out when he missed on eleven. But he hasn't shown much of that since. His eight months after that day were fairly epic, and mine were fairly ordinary.

Thomas Bjørn: I think the way Graeme turned that match around was one of the major turning points in that Ryder Cup. After two, two-and-a-half hours of play, things weren't looking good for him, but he turned it around. Justin did the same. I think those two points made the overall victory look a little bit easier than it was; if those two games had gone against us it would have suddenly become very difficult for us to win it.

Following McDowell and Spieth onto the first tee were Reed and Stenson. The Texan had been in voluble form all weekend, goading the chants from the European galleries, fist pumping and cajoling his teammates along. Having played such a key role for the Americans alongside Spieth in the pairings, Reed would once again deliver in the singles.

Patrick Reed was in rumbustious form in the singles, doing all he could to take the fight to Europe. *Getty Images*

Patrick Reed: Just to be able to play for your country is something else – it was amazing. To be able to come out and perform the way Jordan and I did in the team matches and then individually to go out and get my point in the singles meant a lot to me, especially after only pulling in half a point on Saturday afternoon. I felt like a lot of that was because of me and on me, so I felt like I had to go out and contribute. It didn't change the result, but I felt like I did all I could.

I thought that my one role, when I made the team, was I could really fire up the team and get them going just because, you know, I'm a fiery kind of guy. I got the crowd fired up on both sides on Sunday and it was a lot of fun, the crowd loved it. They were heckling me all day, yet we were being respectful on both sides. It was a lot of fun.

McIlroy went out third and took Fowler to pieces. 'I was more up for this than I was for the final rounds of the two Majors I won this year,' he said. 'It just meant so much to be part of this team'.

Rory McIlroy: Paul wanted to play me up the order and I was very comfortable with that – I knew what was expected of me and I knew what I expected of myself, so I was very happy to go out third against Rickie Fowler. I was probably more up for the singles than I was the first two days. I was just so up for it, there was no option other than to win. I played my best golf of the week. I started so well, six-under through six holes; that built a comfortable lead that I was able to hang on to.

Somebody told me that it was the first time since 1977 that a player had won two Majors and been on a winning Ryder Cup team in the same season [when Jack Nicklaus achieved the feat]. Of course that makes me proud and being part of a great European side and a period of dominance is something I value very highly. I was not joking when

I said I felt more pressure on that first tee on Sunday than I did the final rounds of the Open and [US] PGA [Championship]. That's because I wasn't just playing for myself but for so many others, too.

Tom Watson: Rory McIlroy is a guy I like a lot. I like his manner. I like the way he plays. He reminds me of me, the way I played. He just picks it up, gets on with it. He's ready to go. He plays his shot and takes the consequences. Finds it and hits it again. Going into Gleneagles he was driving the ball better than anybody in the game. He had confidence in the driver and when you have confidence in the driver and you have the ability to hit the ball as far, the game is easy. He knew it and everybody else knew it.

Paul McGinley: I had experience of managing Rory already in the Seve Trophy, and, OK, he wasn't the player then that he was in 2014, he wasn't the world's number one player. But I really enjoyed working with him then and I used that experience in 2014. I like Rory; he is easy to be around, he is an open book, a sponge, he'll listen to everything you have to say. He mightn't agree with it, but he'll take it all in and he'll give you the opportunity to manage him. He won't walk around with his head in the air like 'I know it all'. That's very important to the whole team dynamic.

The fourth match pitched Rose against Mahan. Having started slowly, Rose battled back into contention with five consecutive birdies around the turn. Still one-down on the eighteenth, as he had been with Kaymer the day before, Rose again rescued the hole and gained a half point for Europe.

Rory McIlroy celebrates his comprehensive victory over Rickie Fowler. *Getty Images*

Justin Rose: It was a great match. I played well and Hunter was awesome, he really was. He was five-under through seven and threw it all at me, and I responded with birdies at seven, eight, nine, ten and eleven, and I was really proud to just get back into the match. He's a great friend of mine. We share the same full game and short game coach, so it was an honourable half, I would say.

Hunter Mahan: Justin was arguably the best player that week. He played great every match. I think I made seven or eight birdies in my singles match against him and still had to go to eighteen. He played great. You play a guy that's playing as good as you and it's a hell of a contest. It was a tough battle all day.

The fifth tie saw Mickelson take on Gallacher. The rookie Scotsman had yet to register on the scoreboard from his one outing and he was facing a considerable task to buck that trend as he took on America's most senior player.

Phil Mickelson: It was a great Ryder Cup in the sense that people in Scotland treated us very well. People there are so nice. I loved playing golf there, it was a real pleasure to be there and to play against the local hero Stephen Gallacher in the singles was great. It was one of the better matches in that until the seventeenth, until Stephen bogeyed the seventeenth, we didn't have a bogey. I thought we both played some really good golf. I was just fortunate to have a great break on fifteen. That was a shot that to get close was, I thought, impossible, and yet it got the perfect bounce and I was able to make birdie.

Birdies on fifteen and sixteen are what ultimately did it for me. The birdies that Stephen made on ten and eleven were extraordinary, and I had a hard time kind of stabilising the match then and was fortunate to keep it at even until I made those late birdies. It was a good point and although we were up against it at that stage I was hoping that we could still battle on to get the result.

Stephen Gallacher: Yeah, it was a good match. I felt I holed a good putt at twelve which kind of swung the momentum, maybe kept it level, but then when he birdied fifteen and sixteen, it was an uphill struggle for me.

It was tough not to be able to contribute anything to the score, but that whole week was just brilliant. The eleven other guys and Paul and all his vice-captains were exceptional. I'll remember it as long as I live, something I'll cherish forever.

Momentum continued to shift back and forth as Kaymer took on Bubba Watson and holed out with an astonishing chip on the sixteenth to secure another point for Europe with his 4&2 victory.

Bubba Watson: I played pretty well against Martin and I hit two goods shots off the first hole and made birdie, but he obviously backed it up with a birdie just before me. On two I hit a bad second shot and he pushed ahead. I didn't hit the shots I needed to hit. Obviously he hit the shots and made the putts. Then the chip in on the sixteenth to win, what a shot that was.

Martin Kaymer: Everybody talks about the momentum and with Phil beating Stevie I wanted to get some more blue on the board. I played very well against Bubba. I made a couple of mistakes coming in that was not good and I just wanted to finish the match before the par fives because I know he hits irons to greens. But to chip in like I did to win, it was a big rush. And the noise from the crowd was unbelievable. I got goosebumps on every hole – it was one of the best Ryder Cups I've played in.

Bubba Watson: Any time you make a Ryder Cup team, what a pleasure, what an honour; you feel blessed to represent your country and the game of golf. Hopefully I represented them well. I know I didn't win a point, but hopefully I represented the US the right way and everybody had fun.

If the fairytale story before Gleneagles had focused on Tom Watson, the narrative at its conclusion was all about an unheralded rookie from Wales. Donaldson, the thirty-eight-year-old journeyman, who had secured his place on the team thanks to a win at the Czech Open in August, had been playing on the second-tier Challenge Tour in 2007 and did not win his first European Tour title until 2012. McGinley carefully paired Donaldson with Westwood for the Friday foursomes and both Saturday sessions and they dovetailed wonderfully with each other, returning two crucial points for the team. Westwood, playing in his eighth Ryder Cup, said that it had given him as much pleasure to watch his partner take to the Ryder Cup experience 'like a duck to water' as it had to play well himself.

Coming to the fifteenth four up against Bradley, Donaldson had already secured the half point Europe needed to retain the Ryder Cup. As he stood over his ball, pitching wedge in hand, 146 yards from the cup, the crowds around the fairway and the green were swollen and tremoring with anticipation. He swung, the still air filled with a pure crack and as the ball sailed away he shouted, 'Be good!'

The ball hit the green, checked and spun to within two feet. Bradley looked to his captain for guidance. 'They've won it,' said Watson and Bradley duly nodded, removed his hat and offered his hand to Donaldson in congratulations as a deafening roar erupted in the Perthshire evening.

Donaldson was mobbed by his teammates, an eighth Ryder Cup triumph in the last ten meetings secured. And Poulter, García and Dubuisson were still out on the course, battling with Simpson, Furyk and Zach Johnson respectively. Poulter, who had struggled throughout the week yet still contributed as only he could, returned a half point; García fought back from a two-hole deficit to claim a point against the veteran Furyk; and Dubuisson capped another spectacular rookie appearance by halving with Johnson. As the champagne flowed and bear hug followed bear hug, McGinley and his team stared up at the scoreboard which registered the heaviest defeat for the US since 2006, 16½ to 11½.

Jamie Donaldson: After Martin got his point, Justin scraped in for a half and we were within half a point of retaining the cup. Everybody was building around my group, but I was trying not to spend too much time looking at the scoreboard and just tried to concentrate on my match against Keegan.

The crowds had been building from the eleventh. They were gathering every hole, then to suddenly come down the fifteenth, it looked like everybody that had been watching was on

Jamie Donaldson and Keegan Bradley shake hands at the conclusion of their match before the former is mobbed by his teammates. *Getty Images*

fifteen, so it was pretty obvious what was going on. It looked like it was coming down to my game. I didn't really pay too much attention to leaderboards and just didn't get carried away with myself. McGinley talked about complacency. That was the important thing. Focus on your game, win your point, and afterwards you get into discussions with everyone else about what else happened. You do your bit to try and win the match. It just so happened to come down to me, I had the opportunity and hit the right shot at the right time.

I hit a really good tee shot down fifteen and I had 146 yards to the hole which is a perfect wedge for me. Sometimes you can hit a really good tee shot and not have a good yardage and you've got to make something up. But it was a perfect number for a wedge with the wind being slightly down off the right and I just started it perfectly on the right edge of the green. All I had to do was get it on line and it was going to be good. To that extent, obviously you don't know. I just had to get it on line and make good contact and I did that, but for it to finish a foot from the hole was quite a bonus. It was the shot of my life. What a way to finish. It was an incredible week, just a total one-off. There is nothing else like it in golf. It was just amazing to be a part of it.

José María Olazábal: If you have to write a movie script, I would win it like we did at Medinah. But for your heart, for a lot of people's hearts, I'd rather do it like we did at Gleneagles.

Jamie Donaldson: There's a plaque with my name now on the fifteenth fairway of the PGA Centenary at Gleneagles, which is a bit mad. There are a few plaques in golf; I think there's a Seve one at Crans-sur-Sierre, an Arnold Palmer one at Royal Birkdale, Ben Hogan's two-iron plaque where Justin Rose won the US Open at Merion. It's mad to be in that company, for different reasons. I don't know how many Ryder Cup plaques there are out there, a couple at the Belfry, I think. It's very special to be in that kind of company.

Stephen Gallacher: I thought it was a perfect week. I don't think you would change anything. The course was immaculate, the weather was great. The demand for hospitality was the biggest ever. I spoke to a couple of the American vice-captains and they said, 'Why don't we just make it here every year?' because of the hotel and the grounds, and the infrastructure there. I thought it was tailor-made for what happened, you couldn't have asked for a better venue or a better week. Weather-wise, we got so lucky, not one drop of rain. I was up the week before and it was torrential.

Thomas Bjørn: It was a great week and a lot of credit had to go to Paul McGinley for his organisation and leadership. Paul was hands down the best captain I'd ever played under. He was unbelievable for the week. He was so prepared, he knew every player inside out. I think he would play down the Alex Ferguson factor a little bit, but when I look back at it you can see that there were a lot of things Paul drew from the conversations he'd had with Alex over the previous two years or so.

There was a plan he put in place and he stuck to it. He never got panicked, he never worried if what he was doing was the right thing, never doubted his plan, and he made all twelve players feel very comfortable.

There was just a feeling all week that we would win. We thought it would be close, but there was a feeling that we were all in a good place. Some guys played really well, some guys played maybe not as well as they would have wanted to, but we carried each other as a team and that allowed everybody to play well and get the points that we needed.

Paul McGinley: The guys did the work and I feel very lucky that I had twelve guys able to carry it out. It's six Ryder Cups I've been involved in and it's six wins. I didn't feel under pressure at any stage. We were prepared for the Americans coming at us on Sunday morning. We wanted wave after wave of attack, relentless, just like Manchester United used to play.

I had to make some tough calls. Luke Donald still eats away at me. Ian Poulter not playing in the second afternoon. That was a tough call. At the eleventh hour I went with Martin Kaymer and broke up that dynamic of Ian Poulter and Justin Rose – that was a big call. But the way Poulter accepted that decision – he was consoling me. That means more to me than Ian Poulter harping in Medinah. The acceptance of a big decision like that, putting his arm around me, saying 'You're the captain; you make the big calls.' What more can a captain ask for?

On Sunday night my phone was buzzing with messages every other second and I put off reading them until I had time to do it properly. But I was talking to Sergio at the bar and my phone buzzed and I looked down and saw that the message was from Luke. I don't want to break confidences but it was a long text which was very respectful to me, very respectful to the team and very regretful that he wasn't part of it. It meant a lot to me.

I had a lot of goals – I wanted the players to leave with a sense of bonding that will last a lifetime and I think we achieved that. I feel privileged to have been on this journey with Tom Watson, who has been a hero of mine. He's a competitor, there's no tougher competitor in golf than Tom Watson. I saw him on Monday morning. He was very disappointed, but he had that steely grin. He's a hard man but a very fair man and I have the greatest respect to be able to share that journey with a hero of mine.

Graeme McDowell: There is often too much emphasis put on decisions made by the winning captain at the Ryder Cup, and the inevitable criticism of the losing skipper. In this case, McGinley was class personified. He streamlined and sharpened a European winning template, which is no doubt on a roll.

Paul McGinley: Sam [Torrance] was on my shoulder and in my thoughts a lot during the week because of his dad [who passed away just a few weeks earlier]. Of course, Bob Torrance was there, his spirit was with me all week. I didn't want to say it to Sam on the first tee, but I thought it a number of times, should I say it to Sam: Bob would be proud. I could just see him standing behind, drinking it all in, being Scottish and being so proud of what was happening. I didn't want to do it, because I knew Sam would have cried, and I probably would have cried myself, too.

The whole experience of being captain was tremendous. But I said to the players, as much as I enjoyed being captain and it was a real honour and a real privilege to be the captain, nothing beats playing and they had to enjoy that and enjoy what they were going to face. There's nothing like the adrenaline of walking to that first tee with the home support bellowing at you. It's a great thrill, and I wanted the players to enjoy that and drink it in and enjoy every moment of it, because your career goes very fast. I'm now in the twilight of my career and I loved being captain. It was fantastic, but there's nothing beats playing and what those twelve guys enjoyed as players. There's nothing can compare to that.

Jamie Donaldson: Growing up, I just loved the whole Ryder Cup. I loved watching Seve and Olazábal, people like that, playing in it. Faldo, Woosnam, Langer, the people I watched as a kid, going up to my pal's house up the road and watching it in his father's front room. It's great to play in it, but it's weird, in a way. Even now, I was at the Honda Classic and there are pictures all down a corridor of all different Ryder Cup teams. I'm looking at all these Ryder Cup teams and thinking: 'Hang on, I've played in that!' It's a bit way out there, you know? Bizarre. It doesn't really sink in that, having watched them play in it for so many years, I've now played in it.

And it looks different watching it back. When you are there, you're soaking it in and it's an unbelievable event. But you are concentrating on going through your routine to let you win matches. You don't see it from the outside. So it's still a bit way out there that I hit the winning shot, that I had the privilege to be in the position to hit that shot.

From the scenes of joy and unity pouring from the euphoric European camp, things became much less edifying among Team USA. In the immediate aftermath of Europe's victory, Mickelson was asked by NBC what he thought had gone wrong. 'We had a great formula in '08,' he said, referring to the last US win at Valhalla. 'I don't know why we strayed. I don't know why we don't go back. What Zinger [Paul Azinger, the 2008 captain] did was great.' A couple of hours later at the post-match press conference he was asked to expand on this comment. Mickelson, visibly aching from another Ryder Cup defeat (and suggestions on the Saturday night from Watson that he wasn't fit enough to play thirty-six holes on two consecutive days, as well as the Sunday singles), did not hold back.

'There were two things that allowed us to play our best I think that Paul Azinger did,' he

said as he sat at a long table with his teammates and with his captain just a few seats away. 'One was he got everybody invested in the process – who they were going to play with, who the picks were going to be, who was going to be in their pod.

'And the other thing Paul did really well was he had a great game plan; how we were going to go about playing together; golf ball, format, what we were going to do, if so-and-so is playing well, if so-and-so is not playing well – we had a real game plan. We use that same process in the Presidents Cup and we do really well. Unfortunately, we have strayed from a winning formula for the last three Ryder Cups, and we need to consider maybe getting back to that formula that helped us play our best.'

Not only was the attack both scathing and undignified, it publicly revealed the schism that had formed within the team despite their efforts throughout the week to display a happy and united front. Mickelson flew home alone the next morning.

Graeme McDowell: The criticism of Tom Watson was perhaps a little unnecessary, especially by his own team. It left a sour taste for the US side travelling home. There's kind of an unwritten rule, you don't call your captain out at a Ryder Cup. Win, lose or draw, you just don't.

Pádraig Harrington: I met Phil that night and got the feeling he was thinking, 'Gee whiz! Why did I go down that road?' He stood behind what he had said, and there's no question he was being honest, but he had created a storm he didn't need to. Phil has the same failing I have, if you ask him a question he will answer it. And we like talking. He's too honest but that's who he is.

Watson, with his usual old world charm, took Mickelson's swipe on the chin. 'I had a different philosophy as far as being a captain of this team,' he countered. 'You know, it takes twelve players to win. It's not pods. It's twelve players. And I based my decisions on that. I did talk to the players, but my vice-captains were instrumental. Listen, the Europeans kicked our butt. The bottom line is they were better players.'

Perhaps Watson's age came into play (as did that of his vice-captains Andy North, sixty-four, and Raymond Floyd, seventy-two). He was the USA's oldest ever Ryder Cup captain, more than three times the age of rookie Jordan Spieth, and that distance seemed to manifest itself acutely throughout the week. But perhaps the biggest warning shot was fired before a club had even been swung when Watson admitted, startlingly, that he had not even attended a Ryder Cup since 1993. It was a tacit admission (although he did not recognise it as such) that he had no first-hand knowledge of how the tournament had evolved in the intervening twenty-one years and how meticulous the captain's preparation and execution of that preparation had to be in the modern Ryder Cup to ensure his team had the optimum platform for success.

Tom Watson: I take complete and full responsibility for my communication, and I regret that my words may have made the players feel that I didn't appreciate their commitment and dedication to winning the Ryder Cup. My intentions throughout my term as captain were both to inspire and to be honest. The guys gave everything. They played their hearts out. I was proud to get to know each and every one of them. I know they are all going to

McGinley's Marvels celebrate their victory. *Getty Images*

win tournaments, be on future Ryder Cup teams and have wonderful careers. The bottom line is this: I was their captain. In hindsight whatever mistakes were made were mine. And I take complete and full responsibility for them.

Phil and I had an open and candid conversation a few weeks after Gleneagles and it ended with a better understanding of each other's perspectives. Phil's heart and intentions for our team's success have always been in the right place. Phil is a great player, has great passion and I admire what he's done for golf.

But the press conference afterwards was a disappointment to me. Phil was very disappointed about not being able to play. What he said was kind of sour grapes. That's understandable, and we had just got waxed, the whole team, and the disappointment was just there. We let our hearts talk for us. I did everything I possibly could in my own mind with the help of my captains and the US PGA to do everything possible to have us win, and the other team was better. We had a chance to win it on the last day, and we had them tied or with all the matches on the board; we were up in the whole match, if the matches ended that way. We got off to the start that I asked them to do that previous night. We were in the right position there and just didn't carry on.

I look back at Gleneagles now and I think to myself, 'I made the best decisions I could at the time with the best information I had and that's all I can ask'. Our team was not up to the European team's standard – they were better than we were. They played better golf, although as I say, we had an opportunity on the Sunday morning if we'd managed to keep the positions we found ourselves in after making a great start.

Paul McGinley did a great job, there's no doubt, but it ultimately always comes down to the players. As a captain, you can do your job well when you have the players. I give credit to Paul for the way he prepared his team. He did a lot of things that you have to do to win it. You basically set the stage for your players and he did all the right things.

While Mickelson and Bradley lambasted their captain, world number one McIlroy had nothing but praise for Europe's leader: 'He has just been the most wonderful captain,' said McIlroy as the champagne corks were still popping. 'The speeches he gave, the videos he showed us, the people who came in to talk to us, the imagery in the team room. It all tied together and he was meticulous in his planning. He left no stone unturned.'

Sergio García: In the aftermath, a lot was made about the different captaincy styles of Paul McGinley and Tom Watson. Of all the captains I have played under, Paul's had the most modern style to it. He examined every detail and improved it. I remember talking to Thomas [Bjørn] and he said he strongly feels that Paul is the new wave of captains: a lot more modern, every detail, it was right there. Paul thought of everything. He was so methodical. Every single aspect he needed to touch on, he did. I've been fortunate to have a lot of great captains. Paul did things a little bit differently, but with great style.

Sam Torrance: When Alex Ferguson had come to speak to the players during the week, he told a story about the geese that fly 5,000 miles in two formations, the second lot in the slipstream of the first. One gets tired, two come down and look after him until he recovers, then they all catch up. On the Sunday night, we were on the first tee of the King's, doing the team photos, we looked up and two flocks of geese went past. It was such a moment.

Stephen Gallacher: Paul commissioned a painting to be done, with the geese and Fergie. We've all got that. It was Fergie's way of talking about teamwork, if one is down you all rally round. It was a great speech. There is a wonderful picture of us all laughing at the geese flying over – right at the last moment the geese went right over the tops of our heads. It was just something really special.

Paul McGinley: Sir Alex Ferguson came back into the team room on Sunday night and said it had felt like he was back in the boiler room at Man United and said to the players: 'Thank you for the pleasure.' It was great that he said something like that, that he felt that connection. All of the players were up there treating him as a friend, having a drink with him, pulling his leg. Alex also told us to be merry, have fun, but to be able to remember it. And then we went into the American team room, played them at table tennis and we got our arses kicked.

Rory McIlroy: My memories of Sunday night get a bit fuzzy about midnight. But I remember what happened on the golf course, that's the most important thing. These moments don't come around very often. We only have a chance to celebrate as part of a team once every two years, and that's something that's very special and something that we don't get to do as individual sports people. So any time you do have a chance to do that, I think it's important that you take advantage of it. So we all had a great time.

I slipped out of the European team room around 10:00 to join my friends and parents in the bar and then I got a text from Keegan Bradley about 10:30 inviting me to the US team room. So I texted him back and was like, 'Yeah, that sounds great,' and headed over there. When I got to their room I was met by these two security guys at the door and I said, 'I'm here to see the guys, I've been invited over.' They just looked down at me and one of them said, totally deadpan, 'Oh, I'm not sure they are letting anyone in at the minute.'

I said, 'What are you talking about? I've been invited over by one of their guys, I know them all really well.'

He just looked at me like I was a fan chancing my arm and then said, 'Let me go in and check.' So he disappeared inside and left me standing there. He was away for ages. Eventually he came back and said, 'No, they're not letting anyone in yet.'

And I was like, 'What? Really? Are you kidding me?'

'Yeah,' he said, standing in front of the door. 'Patrick Reed said.'

So I went, 'Fine,' and went back to the European team room, totally mystified, and was just starting to text Keegan when a couple of the US guys jumped out at me just outside the team room – they were killing themselves laughing and had obviously planned the whole thing. We had a good laugh about it and then the whole European team got together and piled into the US team room and had a good time with everyone. It was a great way to cap off what was obviously a great week. That's the kind of thing that makes the Ryder Cup special. It was the same when I chatted with Tom Watson out on the course. I just said to Tom that it had been great to spend a little bit of time with him and Hilary, his wife, that week – and that's what the Ryder Cup is all about. OK, it's obviously about the competitiveness and the rivalry but also about getting to know people a little bit better and spending time with people. And he just said to me, 'Great playing. We were outplayed and you guys deserve it.' It was a special moment.

Jamie Donaldson: It was just a great night. I celebrated mainly with family and friends because there were so many of us there. Everyone got in the hotel and just got hammered and obviously mixed with the team as well. Naturally, you have a lot to drink celebrating an unbelievable week. I like whisky, especially the single malts up there; thankfully I somehow managed to catch my flight in the morning!

The following day, McGinley came out in support of his embattled counterpart. Having already stated that one of the fondest memories he would take from Gleneagles was his walk with Watson down the fifteenth behind Bradley and Donaldson, he appeared at a press conference while Mickelson was halfway across the Atlantic and said, 'I'm sorry to hear that if that is the case [Mickelson's public criticism of Watson]. As a man, I have a huge respect for Tom Watson. He's been a great talent in this game and a great figurehead in this game for so many years. For me personally, as European captain, I will now be forever linked in the game's history books to my golfing hero Tom Watson.'

While the ties that bound the captains remained as strong and respectful as ever, the fall out from Gleneagles left a lot of work for the next US captain to overcome on the road to Hazeltine in 2016.

Graeme McDowell: There will be positive and negative connotations as to how the US respond to the defeat at Gleneagles. I think the negative being that maybe it takes too much emphasis off the European victory and a little bit more on the US failure. And I think the positive being their renewed effort to win the Ryder Cup, and that can only be very, very good for the tournament. It means that Hazeltine is going to be fairly epic.

BIBLIOGRAPHY

'1951 Ryder Cup at Pinehurst – In Skip Alexander's Hands' by Alex Podlogar, *Golf News, Pinehurst Heritage*, 27 September 2012

2014 Ryder Cup Official Magazine, The

An Evening with Peter Alliss, BBC documentary, 2015

An Open Book by Darren Clarke

Arnold Palmer: A Personal Journey, Arnold Palmer and Thomas Hauser

'Barnes missing golf like crazy since end of his colourful career', *The Scotsman*, 17 March 2004

'Battle of Brookline, The' golftoday.co.uk

'Bernard Gallacher is feeling the Ryder Cup fever' *Sunday Post*, 21 September 2014

'Bernard Gallacher's Ryder Cup memories', *The Times*, 30 September 2010

'Bernard Hunt knows something about playing in Ryder Cup matches' by Clive Agran, *World of Golf*

Bernhard Langer: My Autobiography, by Bernhard Langer

'Best Remember the Ryder Cup' by Mike O'Malley, *Golf Digest*, 17 September 2008

Better Golf by Percy Alliss

'Big Interview, The: Paul McGinley' by Paul Kimmage, *The Times*, 1 January 2006

'Big Interview, The: Seve Ballesteros' by Alasdair Reid, *The Times*, 14 December 2003

Billy Casper: The Big Three and Me by Billy Casper with James Parkinson and Lee Benson

Captain at Kiawah by Bernard Gallacher with Renton Laidlaw

'Caught in time: The Ryder Cup at Muirfield, 1973' by Paul Forsyth, *The Times*, 29 July 2007

'Centres of Attention' by Bill Fields, *Golf Digest*, 13 September 2010

Charles Whitcombe on Golf by Charles Whitcombe

Christy: From Rough to Fair Ways – The Christy O'Connor Jnr Autobiography by Christy O'Connor Jnr with Justin Doyle

Christy O'Connor: His Autobiography, by Christy O'Connor with John Redmond

Cracking the Code by Paul Azinger

Dai Rees on Golf by Dai Rees

'Darren Clarke relives walking onto the first tee at the 2006 Ryder Cup' Your Golf Travel, YouTube

David Feherty's Totally Subjective History of the Ryder Cup by David Feherty

'Dave Stockton Slams Bernard Gallacher 21 Years On' *Golf, by TourMiss*

'Demaret: A Great Showman' by Bill Fields, *Golf Digest*, 17 December, 2007

Education of a Golfer, The by Sam Snead

'Europe won the Ryder Cup for first time as a united continent 30 years ago... so what do the players remember of their win?' *Daily Mail*, 14 September 2015

'Graeme McDowell: Paul McGinley my standout Ryder Cup leader', BBC Sport, 1 October 2014

Faldo: In Search of Perfection, George Weidenfield and Nicolson Ltd, Orion, 1994

Faldo On: The 2008 Ryder Cup, Golfing World, YouTube

Faulkner Method, The by Max Faulkner and Louis T. Stanley

Feherty: Graeme McDowell, The Golf Channel

Feherty: Simpson's Ryder Cup experience, The Golf Channel

Feherty Live: Countdown to the Ryder Cup, The Golf Channel

'Fond memories for mighty Oosterhuis', *The Scotsman*, 17 September 2006

'Gael force helps push Paul McGinley to the Ryder Cup summit' by Owen Slot, *The Times*, 23 December 2013

Golf by Charles Whitcombe

Golf Anecdotes: From the Links of Scotland to Tiger Woods by Robert Summers

Golf: A New Approach by Lloyd Mangrum and Julian G Keller

Golf at the Gallop by George Duncan

Golf Illustrated, 1933

Golf Illustrated, 30 October 1967

Golfers on Golf

Golfing World: Gordon Brand Jnr. talks Ryder Cup

Golfing World: Sam Torrance Ryder Cup memories

Golf's No Mystery by RA Whitcombe

Golf World Big Interview: Thomas Bjørn, YouTube

Good Walk Spoiled, A: Days and Nights on the PGA Tour by John Feinstein

'Harry Bannerman, the economy-class Ryder Cup star' by John Huggan, *The Scotsman*, 16 February 2014

Heroes All by Darren Clarke

Hogan: The Man Who Played for Glory by George Gregston

'*Himself*': Christy O'Connor, compiled by Seamus Smith

History of the Ryder Cup, A, TV show, 22 September 2014

'Hogan's Heroes' *Golf Digest*, 8 September 2008

How I Played the Game by Byron Nelson

I Remember Ben Hogan by Mike Towle

Ian Poulter: The Biography of Britain's Golfing Hero, Gavin Newsham

'Ian Poulter preparing to unleash his alter ego at Gleneagles' by James Corrigan, *The Telegraph*, 19 September 2014

'I'm a Ryder for the James Gang: Torrance, Brown are Skipper's Right-Hand Men', *The Scottish Daily Record*, 1998

'I'm scarred by Valhalla: Faldo finally opens up about failure as Ryder Cup captain in 2008' by Derek Lawrenson, *Daily Mail*, 26 September 2012

Independent, The 26 September 2012

'Inside Golf's Greatest Comeback' by Tim Rosaforte and John Hawkins, *Golf Digest*, September 2001

Interview with Bernhard Langer, *The Irish Times*, 23 September 2014

Interview with Bernhard Langer, *The Telegraph*, 28 September 2012

Interview with Boo Weekley by Rex Hoggard, GolfChannel.com

Interview with Graeme McDowell by Paul Kimmage, *Irish Independent*, 26 April 2015

Interview with Ian Poulter by Jamie Corrigan, *Daily Telegraph*

Interview with John Cook, *Golf Digest*, 1999

Interview with Justin Rose, *National Club Golfer*, 17 September 2012

Interview with Nick Faldo, *The Independent*, 26 September 2012

Interview with Nick Faldo, *The Irish Times*, 23 September 2014

Interview with Nick Faldo, *The Telegraph*, 21 November 2012

Interview with Oliver Wilson, *Bunkered Magazine*, Issue 98

Interview with Pádraig Harrington, *Bunkered Magazine*, June 2000

Interview with Sam Torrance, *Golf Digest*, 11 June 2008

Interview with Tony Jacklin, *Bunkered Magazine*, Issue 99

Interview with Ted Ray, *Daily Express*, September 1927

Into the Bear Pit by Mark James

'It's Major Tom', *The Scotsman*, 4 July 2004

It's Only a Game: Words of Wisdom from a Lifetime in Golf by Jackie Burke Jnr with Guy Yocom

'I've got to beat my boyhood hero — you couldn't write the script' by David Walsh, *Sunday Times*, 4 May 2014

'One Final Parting Shot' by Martin Dempster, *The Scotsman*, 2 July 2015

Jack Nicklaus: My Story, by Jack Nicklaus with Ken Bowden

'Jamie Donaldson: I came close to giving up' by Michael McEwan, *Bunkered Magazine*, 27 August 2014

Jewel in the Glen: Gleneagles, Golf and the Ryder Cup by Ed Hodge

Johnny Revolta's Short Cuts to Better Golf by Johnny Revolta and Charles B Cleveland

Johnnie Walker Ryder Cup '87, Virgin/Optomen 1987

Johnnie Walker Ryder Cup '89, Virgin/Optomen 1989

'José María Olazábal leads tributes to Severiano Ballesteros' *The Times*, 7 May 2011

'José María Olazábal – Right where he belongs', *Golf Today*

'Ken Brown: Seve was our pilot: bold, generous, glamorous – and a great team man', *The Independent*, 8 May 2011

Knave of Clubs by Eric Brown

'Larry Nelson's 1979 Ryder Cup heroics against Seve Ballesteros should be an inspiration for US team at Gleneagles' by Mike Dickson, *Daily Mail*, 25 September 2014

'Little Big Man' *Golf Digest*, 29 September 2015

'Mark James interview' *Golf 360°*, 25 September 2014

'Major champion Paul Lawrie on Open victory and Ryder Cup joy' by Mark Townsend, *National Club Golfer*, 24 September 2015

'Moments that Made the Ryder Cup' by Lee Honeyball and Matthew O'Donnell, *The Observer*, 2 September 2001

'Meet the mentor' by David Walsh, *Sunday Times*, 14 September 2014

Miracle at Medinah: Europe's Amazing Ryder Cup Comeback, Oliver Holt

Miracle of Medinah, DVD, 2012

Monty: The Autobiography by Colin Montgomerie

My Partner Ben Hogan by Jimmy Demaret

'My Shot: Peter Oosterhuis' *Golf Digest*, 31 August 2015

Neil Coles on Golf by Neil Coles

'Nicolas Colsaerts on being a Ryder Cup rookie', YouTube

'Nick Faldo left in lurch' by David Walsh, *The Sunday Times*, 28 September 2008

'Nick Faldo on his greatest Ryder Cup moment, why there will never be another Seve and the Tiger vs. Jack debate' Golf.com

'Olazábal reflects on career', *Golfing World*

Out of the Bag by Eric Brown

'Pádraig Harrington: I'd love to be Ryder Cup captain one day' by Paul Kimmage, *Irish Independent*

'Paul Azinger Interview, The', Joe.ie

'Payne Stewart, in their words' by Erik Brady and Steve DiMeglio, *USA Today Sports*

'Rickie Fowler comes of age at Ryder Cup 2014 to encapsulate USA's gutsy, underdog spirit' by James Corrigan, *The Telegraph*, 23 September 2014

'Rory McIlroy can still barely consider the possible consequences of his narrow escape at Medinah', by James Corrigan, *The Telegraph*, 21 September 2014

Ryder Cup 2006 by Dermot Gilleece

Ryder Cup, The: A History 1927–2014 by Peter Pugh and Henry Lord

'Ryder Cup 2014: Sam Torrance says the hardest day is already over for Europe's captain Paul McGinley', by Jim White, *The Telegraph*, 6 September 2014

Ryder Cup, The: An Illustrated History by Dale Concannon www.rydercup.com

Ryder Cup, The: Golf's Greatest Event, by Bob Bubka and Tom Clavin

'Ryder Cup, The: My Way', *Golf Digest*, 3 September 2008

'Ryder Cup live: Seve is our inspiration, says Montgomerie', *The Times*, 29 September, 2010

Ryder Cup Revealed: Tales of the Unexpected by Ross Biddiscombe

'Ryder Cup: The art of captaincy – "They play, you've got to pray"' by Rob Hodgetts, BBC Sport at Gleneagles, 23 September 2014

Sam Torrance: Out of Bounds, by Sam Torrance

'Sam Torrance tears into Faldo', by Michael McEwan, *Bunkered Magazine*, 16 December 2014

Samuel Ryder: the Man Behind the Ryder Cup by Peter Fry

Seve: The Autobiography, Yellow Jersey 2008

Seve: Golf's Flawed Genius by Robert Green

'Seve's Story – interview with Nick Faldo' YouTube

Seve the Legend documentary, YouTube

Sir Walter and Mr Jones by Stephen R Lowe

Sir Walter: Walter Hagen and the Invention of Professional Golf by Tom Clavin

Snake in the Sandtrap, The by Lee Trevino and Sam Blair

Super Mex: An Autobiography by Lee Trevino and Sam Blair

'Sporting Rivalries (The Ryder Cup)' on Sky Sports HD4, Tuesday 22 July 2014

Sports Illustrated, 23 September 1985

Sports Illustrated, 19 June 1989

Sports Illustrated, 07 October 1991

Sports Illustrated, 04 October 1993

Sports Illustrated, 18 September 1995

Sports Illustrated, 02 October 1995

Sports Illustrated, 30 October 1995

Sports Illustrated, 06 October 1997

Sports Illustrated, 04 October 1999

Sports Illustrated, 25 November 2002

Tales from Pinehurst: Stories from the Mecca of American Golf

Taylor on Golf: Impressions, Comments by John Henry Taylor

Thanks for the Game: The Best of Golf with Henry Cotton by Henry Cotton

Them and Us: An Oral History of the Ryder Cup, by Robin McMillan

'Tiger Woods: moulded by Special Forces' by Joseph Brady *Bunkered Magazine*, 29 July 2014

Thirty Years of Championship Golf by Gene Sarazen

'Three Ryder Cup Heroes re-live their most memorable moments in Metro Golf, indoor golf lounge & bar' YouTube

'Tony Jacklin Interview – Captain Fantastic', *Golf Today*

Tony Jacklin: My Autobiography by Tony Jacklin

Tom Watson, *The Golf Paper*, June 2015

'Tom Watson takes 'full responsibility' for United States Ryder Cup defeat', *The Times*, 4 October 2014

Touching Greatness: Memorable Encounters with Golfing Legends by Dermot Gilleece

Trevino on US Ryder Cup, YouTube

Two Tribes by Gary Newsham

'US Turns Its Focus to Playing Like a Team' by Damon Hack, *The New York Times*, 18 September 2006

'US Wins Ryder Cup for 1st Time Since 1999' Associated Press, YouTube

Victory: The Story of the 1995 Ryder Cup by Dermot Gilleece, Jock Howard, Graham Spiers, Alex Spink

Walter Hagen Story, The, Heinemann, 1957

War by the Shore, The: The Incomparable Drama of the 1991 Ryder Cup by Curt Sampson

Way to Golf, The by Harry Weetman

'When Ollie Met Seve' by John Huggan, *Golf Digest* October 2012

www.ASAPtexts.com

Zinger by Paul Azinger